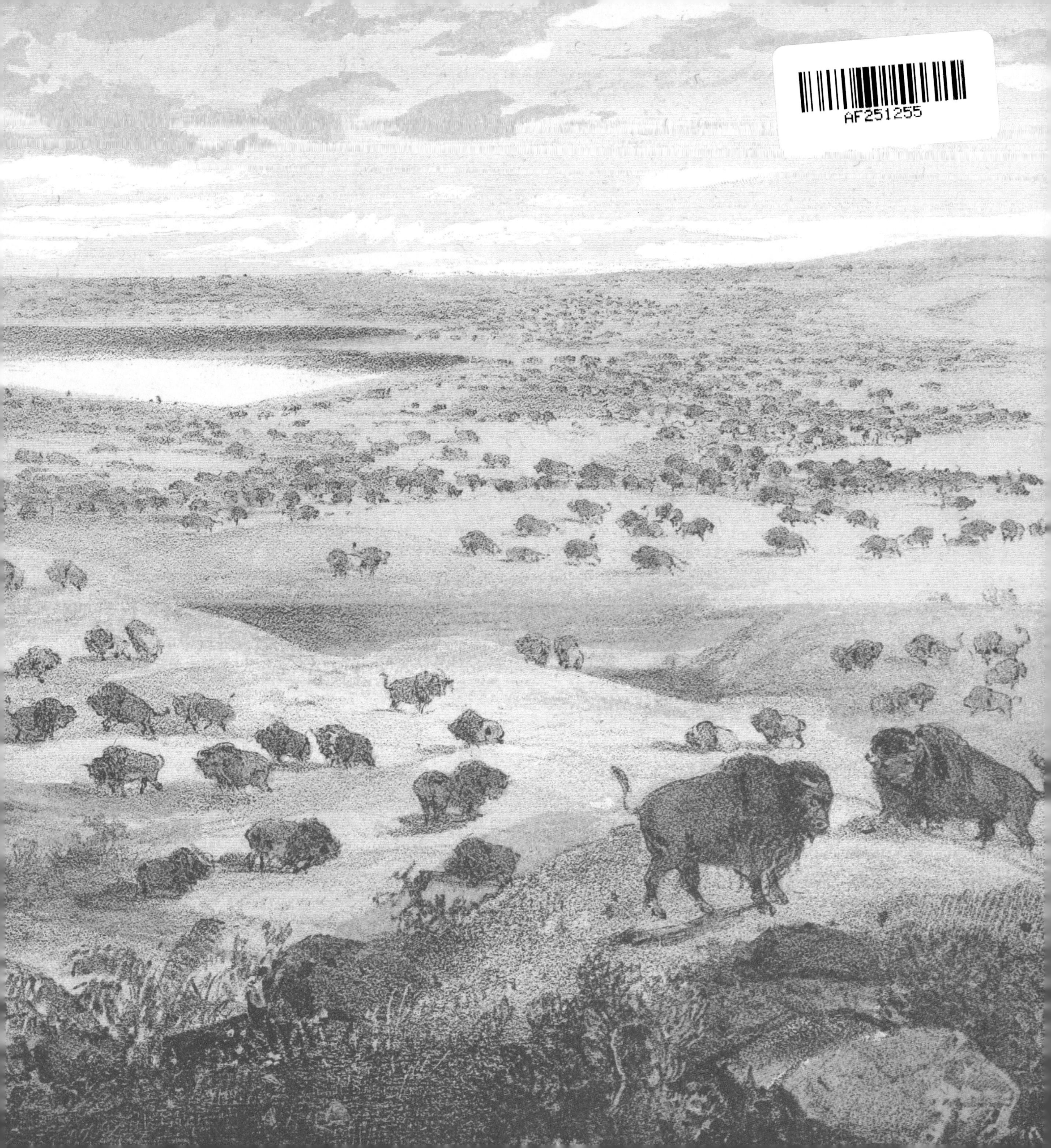

The
American
West
in Bronze

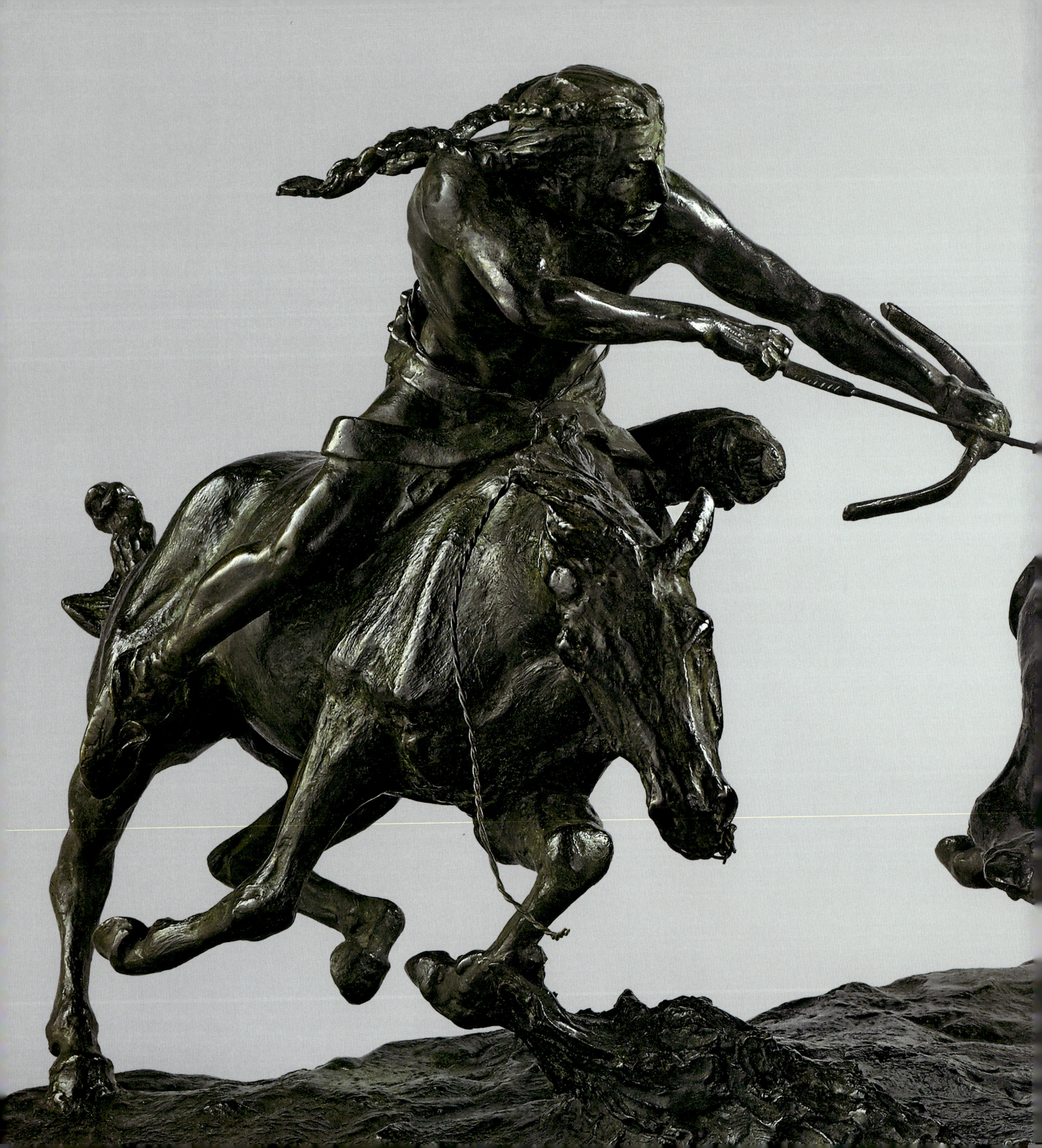

The American West in Bronze
1850–1925

Thayer Tolles

Thomas Brent Smith

With contributions by Carol Clark, Brian W. Dippie, Peter H. Hassrick,
Karen Lemmey, and Jessica Murphy

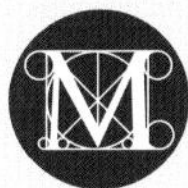

The Metropolitan Museum of Art, New York

Distributed by Yale University Press, New Haven and London

This catalogue is published in conjunction with "The American West in Bronze, 1850–1925," on view at The Metropolitan Museum of Art, New York, from December 18, 2013, through April 13, 2014; at the Denver Art Museum from May 9 through August 31, 2014; and at the Nanjing Museum, China, from September 29, 2014, through January 18, 2015.

The exhibition is made possible by The Peter Jay Sharp Foundation, the Henry Luce Foundation, the Terra Foundation for American Art, and the Enterprise Holdings Endowment.

It was organized by The Metropolitan Museum of Art, New York, in collaboration with the Denver Art Museum.

This publication is made possible by the William Cullen Bryant Fellows of the American Wing.

Published by The Metropolitan Museum of Art, New York
Mark Polizzotti, Publisher and Editor in Chief
Gwen Roginsky, Associate Publisher and General Manager of Publications
Peter Antony, Chief Production Manager
Michael Sittenfeld, Managing Editor
Robert Weisberg, Senior Project Manager

Edited by Nancy Grubb
Designed by Steven Schoenfelder
Production by Christopher Zichello
Bibliography by Penny Jones
Image acquisitions and permissions by Jane S. Tai and Ling Hu

Typeset in Arno
Printed on 150 gsm Magno Matt Classic
Separations by Professional Graphics, Inc., Rockford, Illinois
Printed and bound by Die Keure, Brugge, Belgium

Jacket illustrations: front, Alexander Phimister Proctor, detail of *Buckaroo*, 1914 (cast 1915 or after). Cat. 43; back, Paul Manship, detail of *Indian Hunter and His Dog*, 1926. Cat. 34

Endpapers: John Mix Stanley (American, 1814–1872). Detail of *Herd of Bison near Lake Jessie*, 1853–55. Plate 10 in *Reports of Explorations and Surveys, to Ascertain the Most Practicable and Economical Route for a Railroad from the Mississippi River to the Pacific Ocean, Made Under the Direction of the Secretary of War* (Washington, 1855–60), vol. 12, bk. 1, p. 59. The New York Public Library, Astor, Lenox and Tilden Foundations

Frontispiece: Charles M. Russell, detail of *Buffalo Hunt*, 1905 (cast 1905). Cat. 59
Page vi: Hermon Atkins MacNeil, detail of *The Sun Vow*, 1899 (cast ca. 1906 or after). Cat. 29
Page xvi: Solon Hannibal Borglum, detail of *Lassoing Wild Horses*, 1898 (cast ca. 1900–1902). Cat. 5

The Metropolitan Museum of Art endeavors to respect copyright in a manner consistent with its nonprofit educational mission. If you believe any material has been included in this publication improperly, please contact the Editorial Department. Photographs of works in the Metropolitan Museum's collection are by Bruce Schwarz, The Photograph Studio, The Metropolitan Museum of Art, unless otherwise noted. Additional photography credits appear on page 192.

The Metropolitan Museum of Art
1000 Fifth Avenue
New York, New York 10028
metmuseum.org

Distributed by
Yale University Press, New Haven and London
yalebooks.com/art
yalebooks.co.uk

Cataloging-in-Publication Data is available from the Library of Congress.
ISBN 978-1-58839-505-4 (The Metropolitan Museum of Art)
ISBN 978-0-300-19743-3 (Yale University Press)

Contents

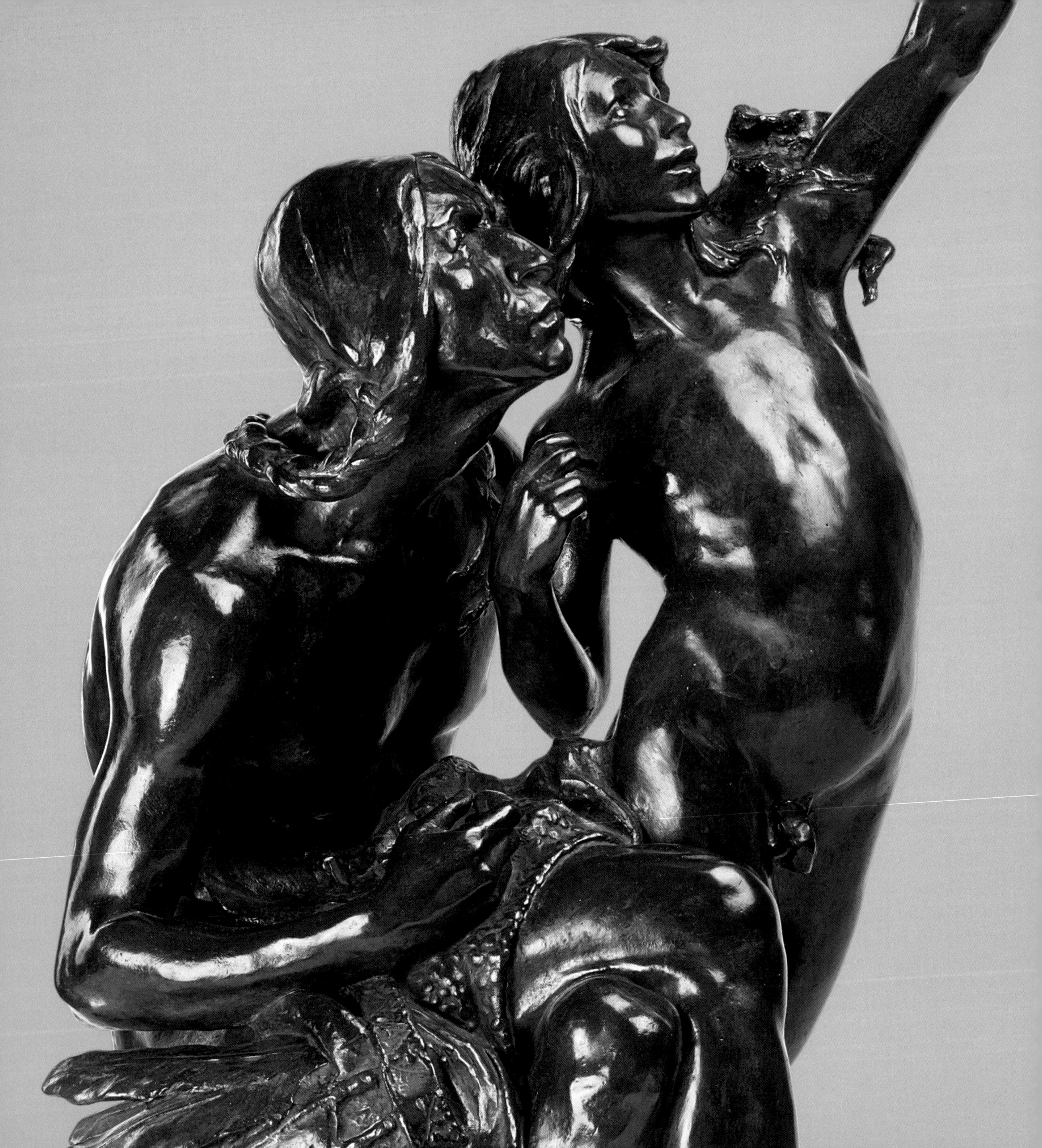

Director's Foreword

The American West—imagined or real, past or present—is an ever-shifting, endlessly fascinating place. Our visions of the American West are often mediated through words and images—literature and the popular press, paintings and photographs, and of course film and television. Sculpture, too, and particularly the bronze statuette, has played a significant role in creating a perception of place and of time, often fixed in the Old West.

Frederic Remington, Charles M. Russell, and scores of other sculptors produced bronze statuettes of American Indians, cowboys, wildlife, and settlers that were eagerly collected across the country and around the world, and still are today. The development of the American fine-arts bronze-casting industry around 1850 enabled three-dimensional expression of complex issues of the era—Euro-American settlement, American Indian relocation, and the wanton destruction of bison and other wildlife—in statuettes of outstanding quality and technical sophistication. Remarkably, "The American West in Bronze, 1850–1925" is the first exhibition to examine the impact of this medium.

The Metropolitan Museum of Art has choice holdings of sculptures with western themes, some of which were commissioned by the museum directly from their makers—the likes of Remington, Solon Hannibal Borglum, and Alexander Phimister Proctor, each of whom is amply represented in this exhibition. "The American West in Bronze" follows the opening of the redesigned American Wing in 2012 with the Museum's first gallery devoted to art depicting the American West. We thank Thayer Tolles, Marica F. Vilcek Curator of American Paintings and Sculpture, for enthusiastically building on the momentum of that project with this groundbreaking exhibition. We have enjoyed our collaboration with the Denver Art Museum, long a leader in western art programming, which serves as the second venue for "The American West in Bronze," under the able stewardship of the exhibition's co-curator, Thomas Brent Smith, Director of the Petrie Institute of Western American Art. This accompanying publication is the result of the co-curators' vision, with additional essays by Carol Clark, Brian W. Dippie, and Peter H. Hassrick, all preeminent scholars of western American art, and with contributions by research associates Karen Lemmey and Jessica Murphy.

We offer sincere gratitude to all of our lenders as well as to our generous donors. Leading supporters of exhibition initiatives The Peter Jay Sharp Foundation, the Henry Luce Foundation, the Terra Foundation for American Art, and the Enterprise Holdings Endowment have our deep appreciation for their substantial funding of this project. We also thank the Chapman Family Trust for its continued support of the Museum's programming and, as always, salute all our dedicated supporters of The American Wing. In particular, we thank the William Cullen Bryant Fellows, who have underwritten expenses for this book and have ensured the Metropolitan's enduring commitment to bringing American art publications of the highest quality to its public.

Thomas P. Campbell
Director, The Metropolitan Museum of Art

Lenders to the Exhibition

American Museum of Natural History, New York

American Museum of Western Art—The Anschutz Collection, Denver

Amon Carter Museum of American Art, Fort Worth, Texas

The Art Institute of Chicago

Autry National Center of the American West, Los Angeles

Birmingham Museum of Art, Alabama

Brooklyn Museum

Buffalo Bill Center of the West, Cody, Wyoming

Corcoran Gallery of Art, Washington, D.C.

Denver Art Museum

Detroit Institute of Arts

Fine Arts Museums of San Francisco

Gilcrease Museum, Tulsa, Oklahoma

Hood Museum of Art, Dartmouth College, Hanover, New Hampshire

Los Angeles County Museum of Art

The Metropolitan Museum of Art, New York

The Museum of Fine Arts, Houston

National Cowboy & Western Heritage Museum, Oklahoma City

Oregon Historical Society, Portland

Sagamore Hill National Historic Site, Oyster Bay, New York

Saint Louis Art Museum

Santa Barbara Museum of Art, California

Smithsonian American Art Museum, Washington, D.C.

Woolaroc Museum, Bartlesville, Oklahoma

Charles and Barbara Griffith

John Russell Kaufman, William Tyler Kaufman, and Meredith Anne Kaufman

Pete and Lindsey Leavell

Gerald and Kathleen Peters

The Petrie Collection

Private collection (3)

Private collection, courtesy Gerald Peters Gallery, New York (2)

The Rees-Jones Collection

Daniel and Mathew Wolf

Preface and Acknowledgments

"The American West in Bronze, 1850–1925" is the first full-scale exhibition to explore the aesthetic and cultural impulses behind the creation of statuettes with American western themes, which have been so popular with audiences then and now. Both the exhibition and this accompanying catalogue offer a fresh look at the multifaceted roles played by these sculptors in creating three-dimensional interpretations of western life, whether based on historical fact, mythologized fiction, or most often, something in-between. Examples by such archetypal representatives of the West as Frederic Remington and Charles M. Russell are complemented by the work of sculptors such as James Earle Fraser and Paul Manship, who contributed to the popularity of the American bronze statuette even though their western subjects were less frequent.

Although the twenty-eight artists in the exhibition are bound together by their use of bronze, they are distinguished by diverse life experiences and artistic approaches. Alexander Phimister Proctor and Gutzon Borglum, for example, grew up in the West, and that firsthand experience informed their work, even after the artists had moved to cosmopolitan centers, notably New York and Paris. Other sculptors, including Theodore Baur and Haig Patigian, brought a foreign-born perspective to their subjects. Some resided in the West their entire lives—notably Russell, who settled in Montana—punctuated only by brief travels east or abroad. Others, such as Edward Kemeys and Charles Schreyvogel, were transitory explorers and frontline recorders of the western experience. Still others rarely traveled west of the Mississippi River—Frederick William MacMonnies, for example, spent most of his career in France.

Despite such dissimilarities, these sculptors collectively glorified an Old West of cowboys and Indians, wildlife and settlers, in marked contrast to the gritty realities of industrialization and immigration then altering East Coast cities and pushing inexorably westward. Remington no doubt spoke for many of his colleagues in 1907: "My West passed utterly out of existence so long ago as if to make it merely a dream. It put on its hat, took up its blankets and marched off the board; the curtain came down and a new act was in progress."[1] The opening essay in this catalogue, "Western Dreams and Buckskin Fantasies," by Brian W. Dippie, addresses the responses of artists within the context of these transformative decades.

Many of these sculptors were rigorously trained at academies in New York and Paris, and they applied sophisticated French-inspired techniques to depicting human and animal subjects in statuettes that were celebrated at home and abroad as authentically "American." Those several who were self-taught similarly achieved a naturalistic treatment of form and a lively play of light and shadow in their bronze representations of life in the West. One writer assessing the state of American sculpture for the *Craftsman* in 1908 spoke about "the inspiration of the great new-old West" on these artists: "They reveal the frankness of a land still edged with pioneer habitation; the vast, clean, empty spaces of the prairie have touched the spirit of these bronze sculptors; tradition has not pressed upon them and so their expression is spontaneous, audacious."[2] Indeed, the confluence of thematic, technical, and aesthetic innovations resulted in bronze sculptures that mediated between eastern and western, old and new, cosmopolitan and roughhewn.

The widespread appreciation of the bronze statuette had been anticipated by the popularity of other art forms reproduced in multiples. Photographs, lithographs, and other types of illustrations, especially those circulated by the ever-expanding popular press, familiarized Americans with majestic scenery, Native peoples, and western wildlife. Editions of small bronze sculptures, beginning with the midcentury work of Henry Kirke Brown and John Quincy Adams Ward, were logical extensions of these visions. In addition, the presence of monumental sculptures with western themes at the world's fairs, which attracted audiences of millions, branded the West in popular consciousness. Artists shrewdly capitalized on widespread familiarity with their large-scale sculptures on temporary view at these fairs, or permanently installed in parks and squares coast to coast, by issuing editions of these works in reduced scale.

These bronze statuettes offered the vicarious experience of distant adventure on the western frontier to eager collectors who installed the sculptures in their parlors, libraries, and gardens. On the one hand, this market generally reflected the artistic taste of a wealthy, urban, male constituency; on the other, it confirmed and extended the unprecedented popularity of statuettes during the so-called American Age of Bronze, spanning the decades from 1890 to 1930. From the genteel mother-and-child subjects of Bessie Potter Vonnoh and dance groups by Harriet Whitney Frishmuth to western statuettes by Frederic Remington and Cyrus Edwin Dallin, American sculptors (and often their estates) catered to this evolution in taste by issuing their bronzes in large editions. Some sculptures quickly became icons of the West. *The Broncho Buster* (cats. 50, 51), a cowboy resolutely taming a wild horse, was Remington's first and most popular sculpture, with more than 275 authorized statuettes produced. Likewise, Dallin's *Appeal to the Great Spirit* (cats. 17, 18), an American Indian on his horse making a postbellum plea for peace, was issued as a statuette in three different sizes, with a total of more than four hundred authorized casts.

This robust demand for small bronzes was complemented and enabled by several factors, especially the professionalization of American art bronze foundries beginning in the 1850s. While some sculptors cast western bronzes in Paris and Rome (especially while based there), most relied on American foundries. The development of foundries in this country paralleled a call for American subjects modeled in a realist style, a reaction against the prevalent idealizing, Neoclassical aesthetic, carried out by expatriate sculptors and rendered in Italian white marble. Less expensive and more democratic than marble, bronze was also particularly well suited to the complex compositions, textural variety, physical action, and narrative detail of these western works. Early on, foundries even shared facilities with munitions makers, as Henry Kirke Brown did after moving his casting business from his own nascent Brooklyn foundry to Ames Manufacturing Company in Chicopee, Massachusetts, in about 1850. The spread of sand-casting foundries—first in the Northeast, from Washington, D.C., to Rhode Island, and later west to Chicago and beyond—liberated bronze sculptors, so that casting abroad became an alternative rather than a necessity. The American casting industry was further transformed by the importation of the lost-wax technology in the mid-1890s. Perfected by Roman Bronze Works in New York around 1900, this technique enabled sculptors to make changes to their models in the wax, encouraging experimentation and individualization. Certain artists—Remington, for instance—developed symbiotic relationships with particular foundries, while others, like Proctor, frequently moved their models in pursuit of lower estimates or better facilities. Some, following in Brown's footsteps, even established their own foundries, as Arthur Putnam did in San Francisco.

By the turn of the twentieth century, sculptors had become savvy about exhibiting and marketing their work in commercial venues, with an eye to individual and institutional sales. For instance, after relocating from Paris, Solon Hannibal Borglum displayed thirty-two works to a New York audience at Frederick Keppel & Co. in spring 1903. Even Russell, the consummate Westerner, sold his bronzes in New York through Macbeth Gallery as well as showing his work widely on his home turf. Showrooms in New York emporia such as Tiffany & Co. and Gorham, which were affiliated with leading foundries, catered to a range of sculptural tastes. Proctor had several comprehensive one-artist exhibitions of sculptures, paintings, and watercolors, including one in 1913 at Gorham's gallery. Individual dealers also sought out and represented sculptors. Theodore B. Starr led the way, representing Borglum, Russell, and Henry Merwin Shrady, among others, displaying their statuettes in his Fifth Avenue gallery and often fronting the money and arranging for the casting of their bronzes, then paying the artists royalties on sales.

Museums began acquiring small bronzes with western themes in the early twentieth century. Kemeys placed forty-seven works at the United States National Museum (now at the Smithsonian American Art Museum) in Washington, D.C., in 1906. The Brooklyn Museum was given ten of Proctor's bronzes in 1912–14 by his hunting companion George D. Pratt (fig. 85), and Ralph Harman Booth purchased a group of bronzes by Borglum to donate to the Detroit Institute of Arts in 1916 (cats. 8, 9). The most systematic collecting program was undertaken by The Metropolitan Museum of Art, which acquired numerous American western bronzes through the auspices of trustee and sculptor Daniel Chester French, including works by Edwin Willard Deming (cat. 19), Remington (cat. 56), and Olin Levi Warner (cat. 77), most of them cast specifically for the Museum.

This exhibition and catalogue cover the period 1850 to 1925 (with several later exceptions) and center on four specific themes: the American Indian, wildlife, the cowboy, and the settler. "Indians on the Mantel and in the Park," by Carol Clark, presents a range of sculptures—both small scale and monumental—that convey the changes experienced by the Indian nations. The documentary impulse to record individual American Indians had begun in the 1820s with painted portraits and extended to bronzes by the 1870s. However, the majority of sculptural representations of American Indians are records of their ways of life, from day-to-day activities such as hunting to sacred ceremonial rituals. The nostalgia and regret projected in many of these groups are symptomatic of the complicated response by Euro-American artists to the so-called march of progress. "Preserved in Bronze: The West's Vanishing Wildlife," by Thayer Tolles, is devoted to representations of animals, particularly the disappearing indigenous species brought to near extinction during the closing of the frontier. These sculptures—whether based on trips out West to study animals in their natural habitats or just observed at the local zoo—served as powerful reminders of the Old West, emphasizing emotional resonance as well as physical accuracy. Artists sometimes portrayed the playful side of wildlife, but more often they focused on elemental struggles between rival animals, allowing audiences to imagine, from a safe distance, the violent drama of these conflicts.

While the American Indian and animals were favored subjects throughout the chronological span of this exhibition, the cowboy was not portrayed in sculptural form until the 1890s, and the settler not regularly until the turn of the twentieth century. The rough-and-tumble vision of the American West is addressed in "Cowboys in Bronze," by Peter H. Hassrick. The rugged and manly cowboy was a familiar stereotype, a colorful American hero popularized through illustrations, artworks, literature, and traveling performances at home and abroad, notably Buffalo Bill's Wild West. These statuettes celebrate a frontier where cowboys tested their honor and proved their manhood in forbidding lands and under challenging circumstances. Finally, "Settling the West: Fearless Men and Strong Women," by Thomas Brent Smith, examines the perseverance of trailblazing soldiers, mountain men, and pioneers confronting the land, wildlife, and American Indians. Sculptors recorded the march of Euro-Americans across American plains and peaks, memorializing adventures both real and imagined.

With great pleasure, we offer thanks to the many people who contributed to the realization of this exhibition and catalogue. The project originated in several study trips to institutional and private collections in 2008–9 by a group of collectors and scholars of American sculpture, several of whom have contributed to this publication. As we traveled around the country, the enthusiastic response to our close examination of these bronze sculptures motivated us to explore the topic further. For moving the project from conception to implementation, we owe enormous credit to Peter H. Hassrick, Director Emeritus and Senior Scholar, Buffalo Bill Center of the West, Cody, Wyoming, and Director Emeritus, Petrie Institute of Western American Art, Denver Art Museum, and to Rick Stewart, former Director and Chief Curator, Amon Carter Museum of American Art, Fort Worth, Texas. At The Metropolitan Museum of Art, Thomas P. Campbell, Director and Chief Executive Officer, wholeheartedly endorsed the resulting exhibition project and, along with Carrie Rebora Barratt, Associate Director for Collections and Administration, has offered valuable support and wise counsel. Jennifer Russell, Associate Director for Exhibitions, negotiated a range of issues with good judgment, ably aided by Martha Deese, Senior Administrator for Exhibitions and International Affairs, with her meticulous attention to detail. Emily Kernan Rafferty, President, has been a steadfast advocate for the exhibition from the outset. Nina McN. Diefenbach, Vice President for Development and Membership, and her colleagues, especially Christine S. Begley, Lesley Cannady, and Sarah Higby, capably coordinated fund-raising for the exhibition, including contributions from The Peter Jay Sharp Foundation, the Henry Luce Foundation, the Terra Foundation for American Art, the Enterprise Holdings Endowment, and the Chapman Family Trust, and for the accompanying catalogue, from the William Cullen Bryant Fellows of the American Wing.

We are deeply grateful to the institutions and individuals that lent to the exhibition, not only for sharing their objects but also for generously assisting us with myriad inquiries. Special thanks are due to the following individuals, as well as their colleagues: Ellen V. Futter and Jannelle Riley, American Museum of Natural History, New York; Philip Anschutz, Sarah Anschutz Hunt, and Darlene Dueck, American Museum of Western Art—The Anschutz Collection, Denver; Andrew J. Walker, Margaret C. Conrads, Jonathan Frembling, and Rebecca Lawton, Amon Carter Museum of American Art, Fort Worth, Texas; Douglas Druick, Judith A. Barter, and Denise Mahoney, The Art

Institute of Chicago; Jonathan Spaulding and Amy Scott, Autry National Center of the American West, Los Angeles; Gail Andrews and Graham Boettcher, Birmingham Museum of Art, Alabama; Arnold L. Lehman and Teresa A. Carbone, Brooklyn Museum; Bruce Eldredge and Mindy Besaw, Buffalo Bill Center of the West, Cody, Wyoming; Fred Bollerer and Sarah Cash, Corcoran Gallery of Art, Washington, D.C.; Graham W. J. Beal, Kenneth Myers, and Jane Dini, Detroit Institute of Arts; Colin Bailey and Timothy A. Burgard, Fine Arts Museums of San Francisco; Duane H. King, Malinda Blank, Ann Boulton, and Carole Klein, Gilcrease Museum, Tulsa, Oklahoma; Michael R. Taylor and Barbara MacAdam, Hood Museum of Art, Dartmouth College, Hanover, New Hampshire; Michael Govan and Ilene Susan Fort, Los Angeles County Museum of Art; Gary Tinterow and Emily Ballew Neff, The Museum of Fine Arts, Houston; Chuck Schroeder, the late Anne Morand, and Melissa Owens, National Cowboy & Western Heritage Museum, Oklahoma City; George Vogt and Nicole Yasuhara, Oregon Historical Society, Portland; Thomas Ross and Amy Verone, Sagamore Hill National Historic Site, Oyster Bay, New York; Brent R. Benjamin and Janeen Turk, Saint Louis Art Museum; Larry J. Feinberg and Eik Kahng, Santa Barbara Museum of Art, California; Elizabeth Broun and William H. Truettner, Smithsonian American Art Museum, Washington, D.C.; and Kenneth Meek and Linda Stone, Woolaroc Museum, Bartlesville, Oklahoma. Furthermore, we are indebted to the private collectors who temporarily parted with their sculptures so that they might be enjoyed by visitors to New York and Denver: Charles and Barbara Griffith; John Russell Kaufman, William Tyler Kaufman, and Meredith Anne Kaufman; Pete and Lindsey Leavell; Gerald and Kathleen Peters; Tom and Jane Petrie of The Petrie Collection; Trevor and Jan Rees-Jones of The Rees-Jones Collection, and their associates Sally King and Murfy Stewart; Daniel and Mathew Wolf; and five anonymous lenders, two of whom were represented by Gerald Peters Gallery, New York.

Other individuals provided assistance with loans, advised on research questions, or offered valued professional advice. We are pleased to thank: Kiara Vigil, Amherst College, Massachusetts; Michael Frost, J. N. Bartfield Galleries, New York; Kevin Stoehr, Boston University; Megan Emery, Cincinnati Art Museum; Janis Conner, Joel Rosenkranz, and Mark Ostrander, Conner•Rosenkranz, New York; Laura Foster, Frederic Remington Art Museum, Ogdensburg, New York; Alice Levi Duncan, Ana Archuleta, and Alexandra Polemis, Gerald Peters Gallery, New York; Cameron Shay, James Graham and Sons, New York; Susan Anderson, Harvard University Art Museums, Cambridge, Massachusetts; Adam Harris, National Museum of Wildlife Art, Jackson Hole, Wyoming; Dennis Montagna, National Park Service, Philadelphia; Ayesha Saletore, Natural History Museum of Los Angeles County; Gaylord Torrence, Nelson-Atkins Museum of Art, Kansas City, Missouri; Byron Price, University of Oklahoma, Norman; Martha A. Sandweiss, Princeton University, New Jersey; Sarah E. Boehme, Stark Museum of Art, Orange, Texas; Patrick Thomas and Madeleine Thompson, Wildlife Conservation Society, New York; Laura Proctor Ames; Mike Bozzini; Judith Burngen; Phimister Proctor Church; Roberto C. Ferrari; Jeffrey Gibson; George Gurney; Mauro Orpianesi; Bruce Parkhurst; Michaela Potter; Michael Reed; Rebecca Reynolds; Henry Roath; Richard and Sheila Schwartz; Lewis I. Sharp; Joan Carpenter Troccoli; and Ron Tyler.

At the Metropolitan Museum, planning and implementation of the exhibition were adeptly carried out by staff in many departments: Kirstie M. Howard and Lee White Galvis managed preparation of contracts with the input of Sharon H. Cott, Senior Vice President, Secretary, and General Counsel. Meryl Cohen expertly organized registration, with the advice of Aileen Chuk,

Chief Registrar, and Nina S. Maruca. Willa Cox oversaw the arrival and unpacking of loans with Gerald Lunney and other hardworking Storeroom One colleagues. Conservator Linda Borsch, with guidance from Lawrence Becker, Sherman Fairchild Conservator in Charge, Objects Conservation, deserves tremendous credit for her attentive care of bronzes from the Metropolitan Museum's collections as well as those on loan. Research scientists Federico Carò and Mark Wypyski offered useful technical insights that often guided the treatment of objects. Great credit is due to Linda Sylling, Manager for Special Exhibitions and Gallery Installations, for coordinating all aspects of the installation, with the assistance of Patricia A. Gilkison. The creative talents of Michael Lapthorn, Senior Exhibition Designer, and Norie Morimoto, Graphic Designer, have resulted in an elegant, approachable installation. Taylor Miller supervised gallery construction, with input from colleagues in the machine, paint, plexi, and rigging shops. The installation's final appearance owes much to the hard work of Pamela T. Barr, who oversaw the editing of labels, and to Clint Ross Coller and Richard Lichte, Lighting Design Managers, who are masters of lighting bronze sculpture. Frederick J. Sager and other skilled conservation preparators ensured that the sculptures were installed both beautifully and safely. The high professional standards and steadfast dedication of American Wing technicians Sean Farrell, Dennis Kaiser, Chad Lemke, and Mary Beth Orr are apparent in this installation. In The American Wing, curatorial colleagues offered day-to-day encouragement and useful perspectives, led by Morrison H. Heckscher, Lawrence A. Fleischman Chairman of The American Wing. Elaine Bradson and Catherine Mackay deftly managed the innumerable details of loan record-keeping, with the assistance of Kelly Mulrow, Leela Outcalt, and Lauren A. Ritz. The research associates for the exhibition, first Karen Lemmey and then Jessica Murphy, were indefatigable on all fronts, not only handling research and photography requests with scrupulous attention to detail but also managing any and all projects, small or large, that were placed in their capable hands. Interns and fellows Caitlin Beach, Margot Bernstein, Renée Brown, Emily Burns, Caroline Culp, and Shannon Vittoria deserve thanks for their wide-ranging contributions.

The staff of the Thomas J. Watson Library, led by Kenneth Soehner, Arthur K. Watson Chief Librarian, and of the Archives, with James Moske, provided necessary support as we researched and confirmed information for the publication. The uniformly high quality of photography is due to Barbara J. Bridgers, General Manager for Imaging and Photography, with the particular assistance of Einar J. Brendalen. Bruce J. Schwarz photographed nearly all of the sculptures in the Metropolitan and Denver collections with his customary enthusiasm and unwavering high standards. In the Editorial Department, Ling Hu and Jane S. Tai diligently managed acquisition of images from outside the museum. Special thanks are owed to Sheena Wagstaff, Leonard A. Lauder Chairman of Modern and Contemporary Art, and Cynthia Iavarone in the Department of Modern and Contemporary Art for facilitating loans to the exhibition, as well as Maxwell K. Hearn, Douglas Dillon Chairman, and Zhixin Jason Sun, in the Department of Asian Art, for offering guidance on potential venues. We are grateful to those colleagues who ensured the success of our mandate that this exhibition should reach the broadest possible audience. Harold Holzer, Senior Vice President for External Affairs, and Donna Williams, Chief Audience Development Officer, offered useful insights, while Elyse Topalian, Vice President for Communications, and her staff, notably senior press officer Egle Žygas, got the word out with efficiency and effectiveness. The exhibition's presence extended to the Metropolitan's website, and around the world, through the good efforts of the Digital Media Department, particularly Staci Hou, Paco Link, Christopher A. Noey, Robin Schwalb, and Eileen M. Willis. We are indebted to able colleagues in the Education Department who planned and implemented a fresh, stimulating range of public programs designed to appeal to all ages and interests. Particular thanks are owed to Molly Kysar, Joseph Loh, Jennifer Mock, Alice W. Schwarz, Jacqueline Terrassa, and Limor Tomer.

We are truly grateful to our talented colleagues in the Metropolitan's Editorial Department, who transformed words and illustrations into this lasting record of the exhibition. Mark Polizzotti, Publisher and Editor in Chief, offered consistently enthusiastic endorsement of this project. Michael Sittenfeld, Managing Editor, and Gwen Roginsky, Associate Publisher and General Manager, coordinated administrative details for the publication, fielding our many inquiries and providing astute guidance. Nancy Grubb edited this volume with extraordinary good sense and proficiency, fine-tuning prose with particularly discerning insight into the subject. Penny Jones confirmed our bibliographic references, ensuring their consistency and accuracy. The design by Steven Schoenfelder reflects his creative eye as well as his ability to balance the written word with a clean, appealing layout. Peter Antony, Chief Production Manager, and his colleagues Douglas Malicki and Christopher Zichello skillfully shepherded this volume through the production stages.

At the Denver Art Museum, the exhibition was expertly managed by the staff of the Petrie Institute of Western American Art: Nicole A. Parks, Curatorial Assistant; Karen Brooks, Department Assistant; and Mary Willis, Staff Aide. Lori Iliff, Director of Exhibition and Collection Services and Registrar, adeptly brought the presentation to Denver with the able support of Laura Paulick Moody, Associate Registrar; Jill Desmond, Associate Director of Exhibition and Collection Services; Kara Kudzma, Exhibitions Project Manager; and Jeff Wells, Manager, Photographic Services. The installation was coordinated by John Lupe, Manager of Installations, with Mitchell Broadbent, Preparator; David Griesheimer, Exhibitions Coordinator; and Kevin Hester, Installation Associate. The exhibition design was conceived by Tom Fricker, Fricker Studio, and the graphic design by Amy Schell. Steve Osborne, Exhibition Technician and Mount Maker, and Gina Laurin, Senior Objects Conservator, helped ensure that every object appears at its best. Fund-raising was skillfully managed by Arpie Chucovich, Director of Development, with Chiara Robinson, Associate Director of Development, Foundation and Government Support. Thanks are owed as well to Nancy Blomberg, Chief Curator and Curator of Native Arts; Molly Medakovich, Master Teacher for Western American Art; and Ashley Pritchard, Communications and Media Relations Manager. We are particularly grateful to Christoph Heinrich, Frederick and Jan Mayer Director, for his ongoing enthusiasm and support, along with Curtis Woitte, Deputy Director, Chief Financial Officer; and Andrea Kalivas Fulton, Deputy Director, Chief Marketing Officer.

We are pleased to acknowledge these varied contributions of our lenders, sponsors, and colleagues, whose generosity has resulted in this groundbreaking project. We hope that this exhibition and catalogue will encourage and sustain interest, from first-time museum visitors to historians and specialists, both in the art of the American West and in bronze sculpture generally.

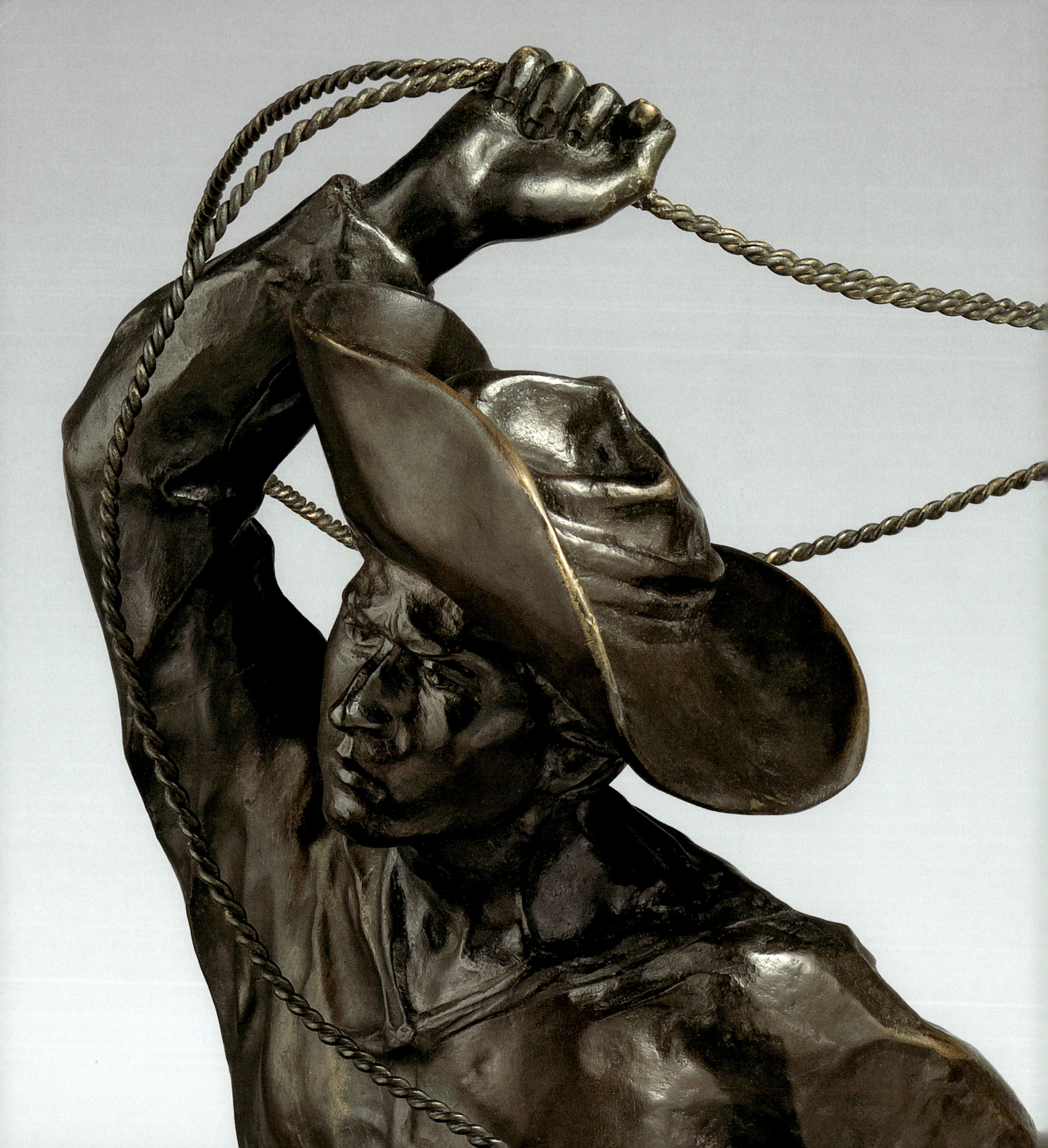

The American West in Bronze

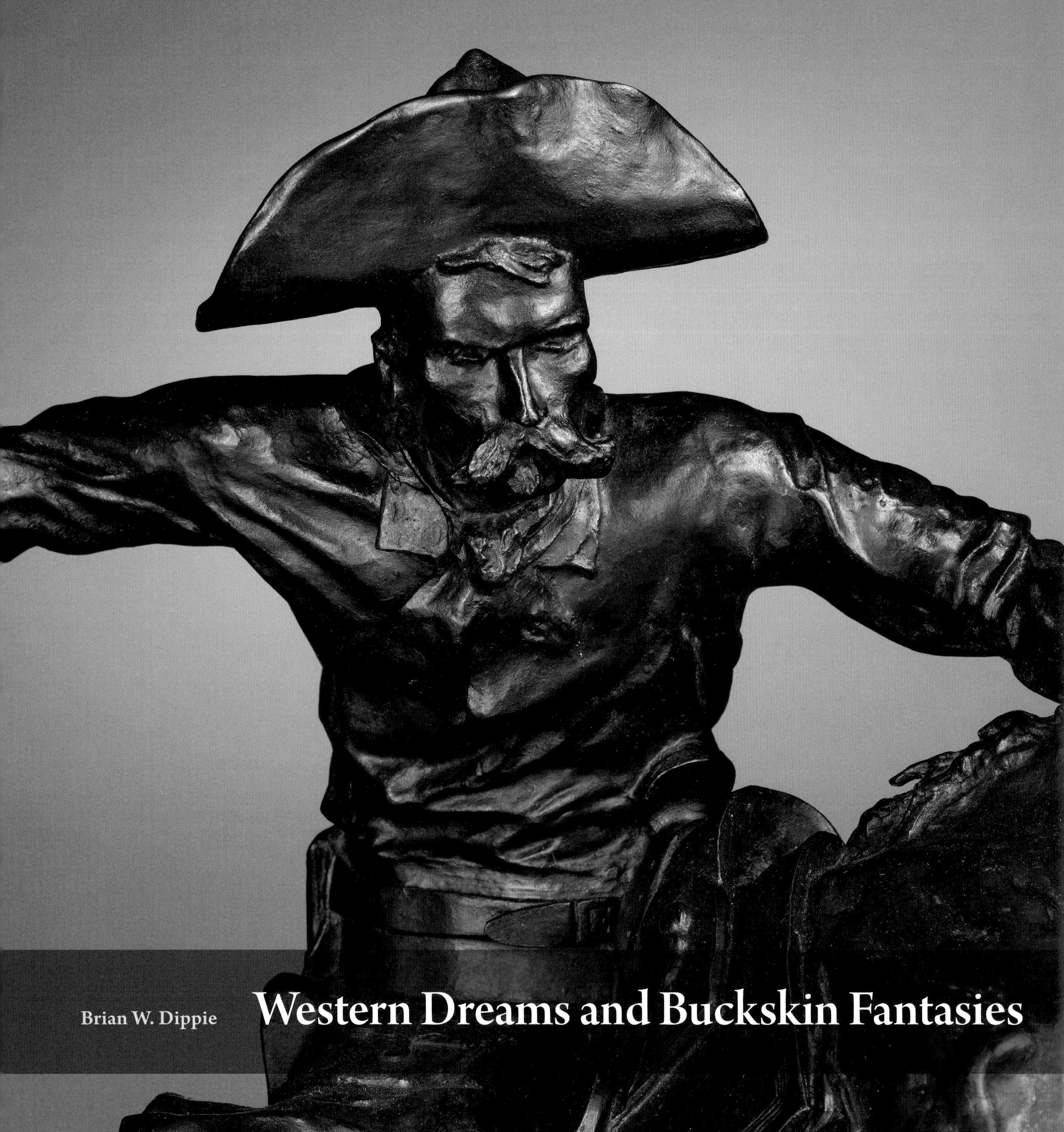

Brian W. Dippie
Western Dreams and Buckskin Fantasies

We are leaving on our great expedition after tomorrow. I am overjoyed at the prospect of realizing all I have hoped for on this trip: visiting the Indians, seeing them in their meetings and assemblies, watching them dance, joining them in buffalo hunts, killing bears with a carbine. I am about to die of excitement. Today I bought a carbine and a complete leather outfit embroidered Indian fashion.

Count Albert-Alexandre de Pourtalès to his mother,
Saint Louis, September 14, 1832

Over a century ago — basking in the adulation that had been his since his troop of volunteer cavalrymen known as the Rough Riders helped bring the Spanish-American War in Cuba to a victorious close — President Theodore Roosevelt stood in front of the Alamo and invoked the heroic legend of its defenders. It was April 7, 1905, the occasion a reunion of the Rough Riders in the city where the regiment had been organized. Though together only four months, they had played a key role in advancing their lieutenant colonel's political ambitions. Two months after the regiment was mustered out on September 13, 1898, Roosevelt had been elected governor of New York. In 1901 he entered the office of vice-president of the United States, and that September, following William McKinley's assassination, became the nation's youngest president, at the age of forty-two. He was swept back into office in 1904 and was still riding the wave of public enthusiasm when he spoke at the Alamo. His generation, he explained, had grown up in awe of their fathers' generation, the men who had fought the Civil War. Yet Roosevelt could not suppress his pride in his own generation's showing in Cuba:

I cannot say how much it meant to me to be able to take part in raising that regiment under the shadow of the Alamo. . . . Since I have been a boy and first studied the history of this country my veins have thrilled and tingled as I read of the mighty deeds of Houston, of Bowie, of Crockett, of Travis, of the men who were victorious at the fight at San Jacinto, of the even more glorious men who fell in the fight of the Alamo. . . .

I remember so well seven years ago when we were raising this regiment, riding in here one day to see the Alamo, and going away feeling that come what would I was going to try to handle myself so that there should no disgrace come to the memory of the Americans who died there.[1]

Today Roosevelt is usually associated with a later western mythology — the cowboy as the last frontiersman. After all, he had gone to Dakota Territory in 1883 to hunt buffalo and had acquired a ranch of his own, which he actively managed over the next nine years. He wrote about his experiences in 1888 in one of the popular monthlies, *Century Magazine*, and was instrumental in defining cowboys as a heroic type. "They are," he said, "as hardy and self-reliant as any men who ever breathed. . . . Their appearance is striking . . . , and picturesque too, with their jingling spurs, the big revolver stuck in their belts, and bright silk handkerchiefs knotted loosely round their necks."[2] They were literally picturesque, since Roosevelt's words were illustrated by a rising star of western art, Frederic Remington. The first essay in their collaboration appeared in the February issue of *Century*; the last, titled "Frontier Types," in the October issue summed up what author and artist had found

Fig. 1. Frederic Remington, detail of *The Broncho Buster*, 1895 (cast by 1898). Cat. 50

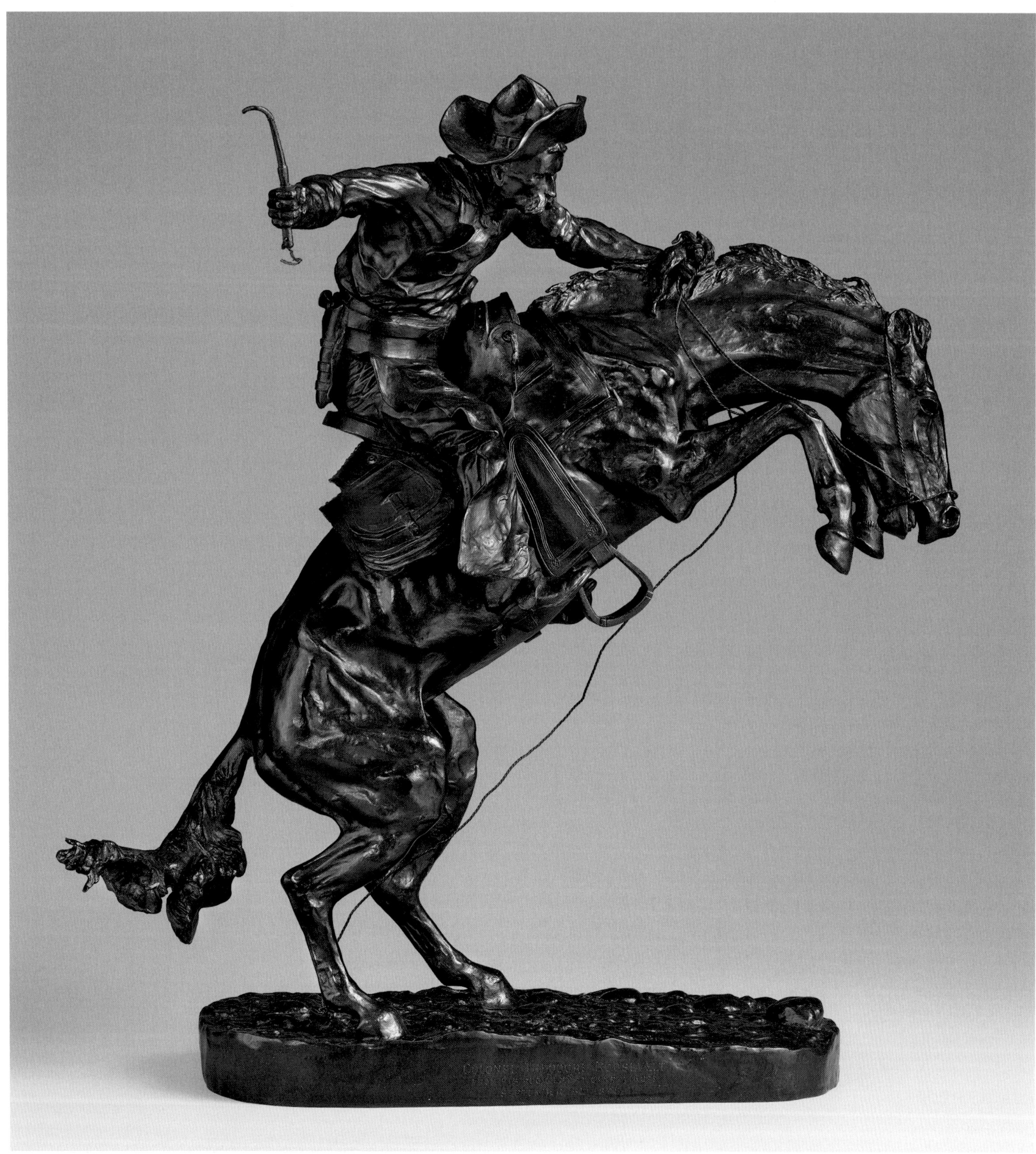

Fig. 2. Frederic Remington. *The Broncho Buster*, 1895 (cast by 1898). Cat. 50

in the West: the *real* American, by which they meant the Anglo-Saxon who, astride a fiery bronc or faced with hostile Indians, harsh conditions, and wild animals, demonstrated the mastery that had built a nation out of wilderness. Roosevelt located the cowboy in a frontier lineage. "The rough-rider of the plains, the hero of rope and revolver," he wrote earlier in the series, "is first cousin to the backwoodsman of the southern Alleghanies, the man of the ax and the rifle."[3] The cowboy personified the rude virtues that had made America a world power by the end of the nineteenth century and that, properly cultivated, would assure its dominance in the twentieth.

In mustering out, the Rough Riders had presented their lieutenant colonel with an enduring memento of their service together: a cast of Remington's bronze *The Broncho Buster*, modeled in 1895 (figs. 1, 2). It was Remington's first sculpture, and the first sculpture ever to portray a cowboy in classic attire — chaps, vest, broad-brimmed hat — on a bucking horse. Appropriately, before 1898 ended, Remington helped crystallize Roosevelt's fame with a painting that shows him on horseback, urging on his men at San Juan Hill (*The Charge of the Rough Riders*, 1898; Frederic Remington Art Museum, Ogdensburg, New York). But in his four-volume history *The Winning of the West* (1889–96) — dedicated to the historian Francis Parkman, "to whom Americans who feel a pride in the pioneer history of their country are so greatly indebted" — Roosevelt never got as far as the Alamo, let alone the cowboy. He had meant to. He wrote to the conservationist Madison Grant in 1894 that "the next volumes I hope will be the Texan struggle and the Mexican War."[4] And to Remington he wrote, in 1897, "If I am able to get on with the next volumes, I shall try to give some account of what the plains were to the first plainsman, and what these plainsmen did, just as I did with the backwoodsman." That is, he

would complete the frontier lineage in a grand "last Epic of the Western Wilderness, before it ceased being a wilderness."[5]

It was a simple epic, really, a nation's creation myth. The story of America was the story of civilization's triumphant advance across a continent, as transplanted Europeans transformed a wilderness, displaced a native race, and were themselves transformed into Americans. The West loomed large in the epic as fact — the land to the west of settled areas yet to be occupied — and as idea. Out there, after overcoming every obstacle that lay between the seeker and the goal, was eternal happiness in a mythic home for heroes. "The West of the imagination," as William H. Goetzmann called it, was everything an American idea should be.[6] Deeply rooted in European culture, it was nevertheless unburdened by the past. It was all hope and yearning, enticing and elusive. The West was a process, not a place, and thus unattainable. It retreated before the seeker like a phantom, the artist George Catlin observed in 1833, flying "before us as we travel, . . . our way . . . continually gilded, before us, as we approach the setting sun."[7] The landscape painter Albert Bierstadt gave the phantom visual form in *Emigrants Crossing the Plains* (fig. 3) — a prosaic title for an allegorical masterpiece showing a wagon train dissolving in a molten sun while passing, in the distance, a cluster of tipis representing the Indians that progress is leaving behind. For most nineteenth-century Americans, the real West where ordinary people lived out their lives may not have mattered much; but as an idea, the West was charged with meaning.

The lure of the West was irresistible to the restless seeker eager to exchange workaday routine in town or city or on a quiet farm for the vast, open world of the buffalo's domain. The restless and the romantic saw in that domain a world closer to the Maker's hand. There were, of

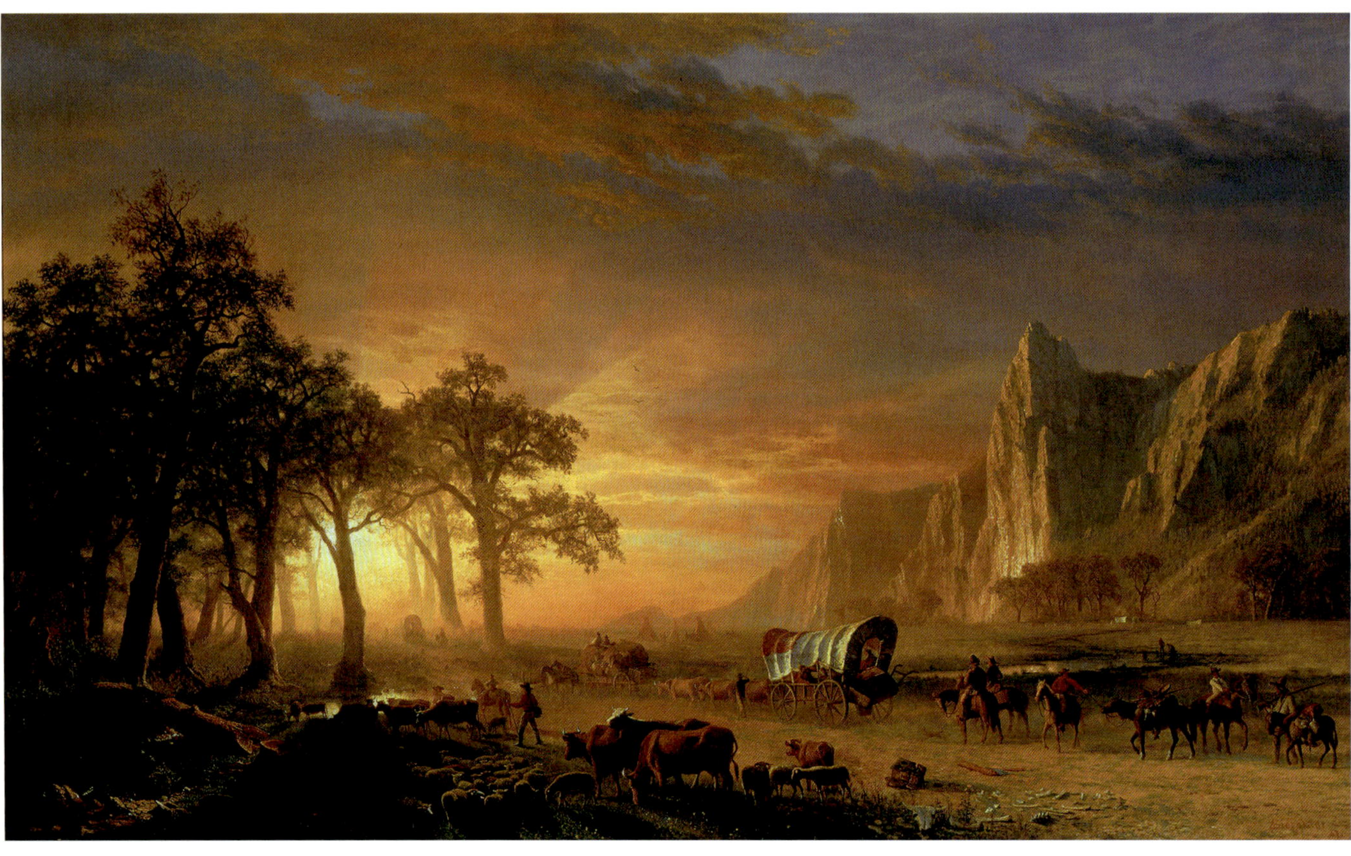

course, serpents in Eden: brackish water, or no water at all; boredom beneath the blazing sun and misery under drenching rain; Indians to fret about and fear; and, of course, the mosquito, which the writer Matt Field, traveling on the Santa Fe Trail in 1839, addressed in clever doggerel:

Our blood to them I think is Brandy
They suck it in like sugar candy
And they are quick as they are thick,
You may kill a hundred at a lick.
But who the Devil wants to kill
When 'tis our own blood that we spill![8]

Even the wildly enthusiastic Count de Pourtalès, embarking on his western excursion in 1832, had to acknowledge the plague of mosquitoes. They had eaten him "almost entirely," he wrote to his mother from Saint Louis, but "I am assured that there will not be any in the prairies."[9] Westward ho, then, to the land of the buffalo, where Field studied "Moonlight upon the great prairies" from under his "musquito bar."[10]

Such realities, a constant in explorers' reports and travelers' journals, did not cure "prairie fever."[11] Close up, the great western rivers were a disappointment. Field observed that the Arkansas "is a murky flood / With a constant ripple of eddying mud," while a tourist in the 1880s described the Missouri as "simply a vast mud-puddle in motion."[12] Even Catlin, ever the romantic enraptured with the river that carried him to Indian country in 1832, admitted that the Missouri was "turbid and opaque," with the color of "a cup of chocolate."[13] But distance lent enchantment. Field waxed poetic again:

We looked from a hill on the Arkansaw
Winding away on its Journey far
Reality never usurped so well
The fairy creations of fancy's spell.
Beautiful Islands all bright and green,
Glass-like water flowing silent between.
Groves of brush-wood and timber tall
And a carpet of silk more lovely than all.[14]

That, too, was Catlin's perspective on the Missouri, in prose and in paintings like *View in the Grand Detour* (fig. 4), which shows a green world occupied by red men and buffalo, with a river running through it that was no less than a magic carpet transporting him to "fairy land."[15]

Dreamland. Fairy land. Such is the West in western art, where painters put on a light show while capturing the distinctive features of that magical land "out there." Matt Field—whose knack for verse of the sort he wrote on the Santa Fe Trail helped secure him a job with the New Orleans *Daily Picayune*—made a second western excursion in 1843, this one along the Oregon Trail to a mountain man rendezvous. He reported it in letters showing a gift for prose as well. One striking description of an evening camp at Chimney Rock is a Bierstadt painting in words: "A heavy storm was gathering across the sky, and all was black above us, while the level beams of the descending sun shot from an opening in the western horizon, kindling up the bluffs into burnished silver, and no sunset exhibition ever produced a more superb and sublime effect."[16] Sunsets belonged in western art, along with the Indians and buffalo that, according to the explorer John C. Frémont, "make the poetry and life of the prairie."[17] Two German-born American artists, both trained in Düsseldorf in the 1850s, agreed. After following in Catlin's footsteps on trips upriver from Saint Louis to Fort Union and beyond in 1858 and 1859, Carl Wimar painted *Indian Encampment on the Big Bend of the Missouri River* (fig. 5).[18] Albert Bierstadt accompanied a government expedition to the Wind River Range in 1859, the first of several western excursions on which he gathered firsthand impressions that he later incorporated in huge "great pictures" like *Emigrants Crossing the Plains* and more modest

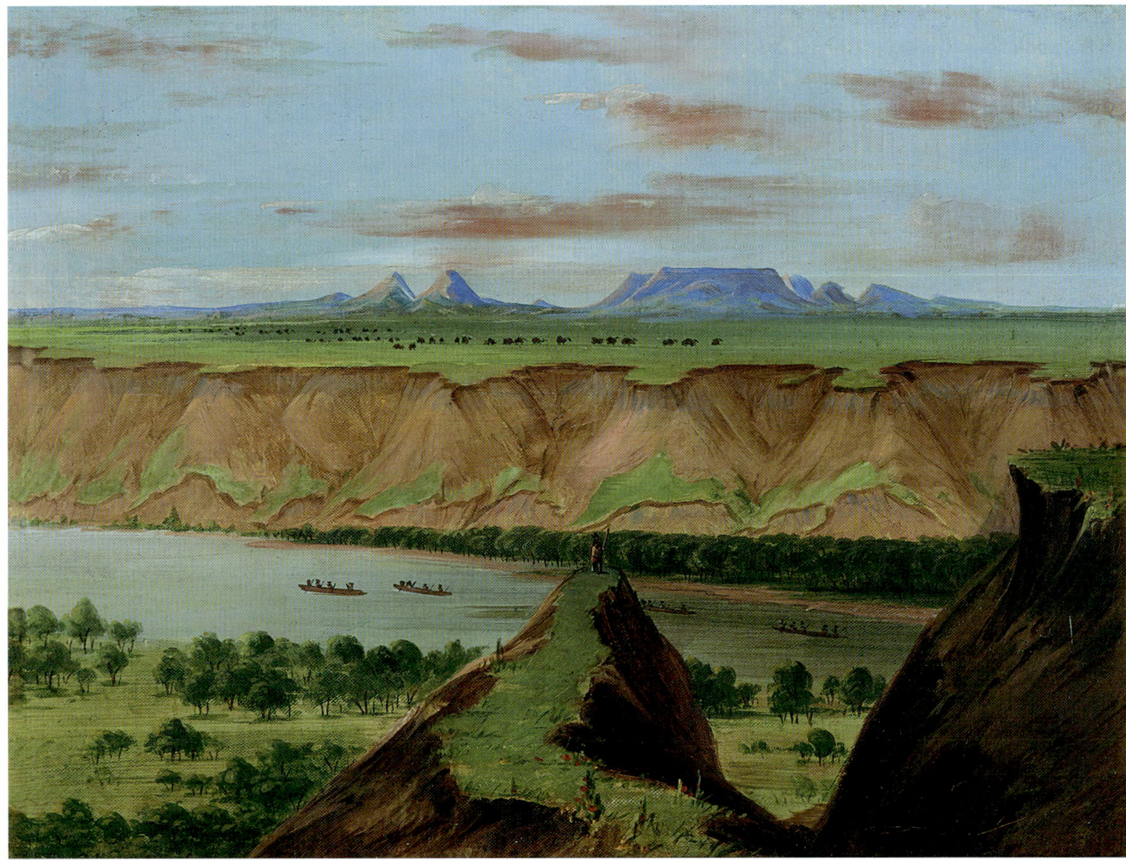

Fig. 4. George Catlin (American, 1796–1872). *View in the Grand Detour*, 1852. Oil on canvas, 13¾ × 17 in. (34.9 × 43.2 cm). Gilcrease Museum, Tulsa, Oklahoma

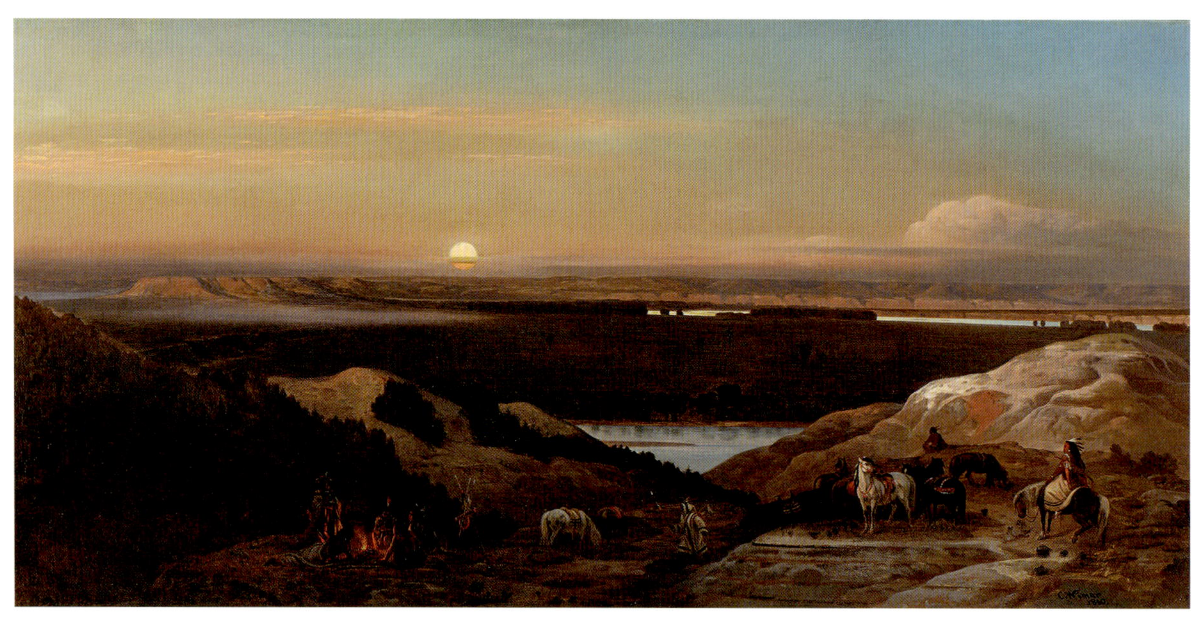

Fig. 5. Carl Wimar (American, born Germany, 1828–1862). *Indian Encampment on the Big Bend of the Missouri River*, 1860. Oil on canvas, 25 × 49 in. (63.5 × 124.5 cm). Gilcrease Museum, Tulsa, Oklahoma

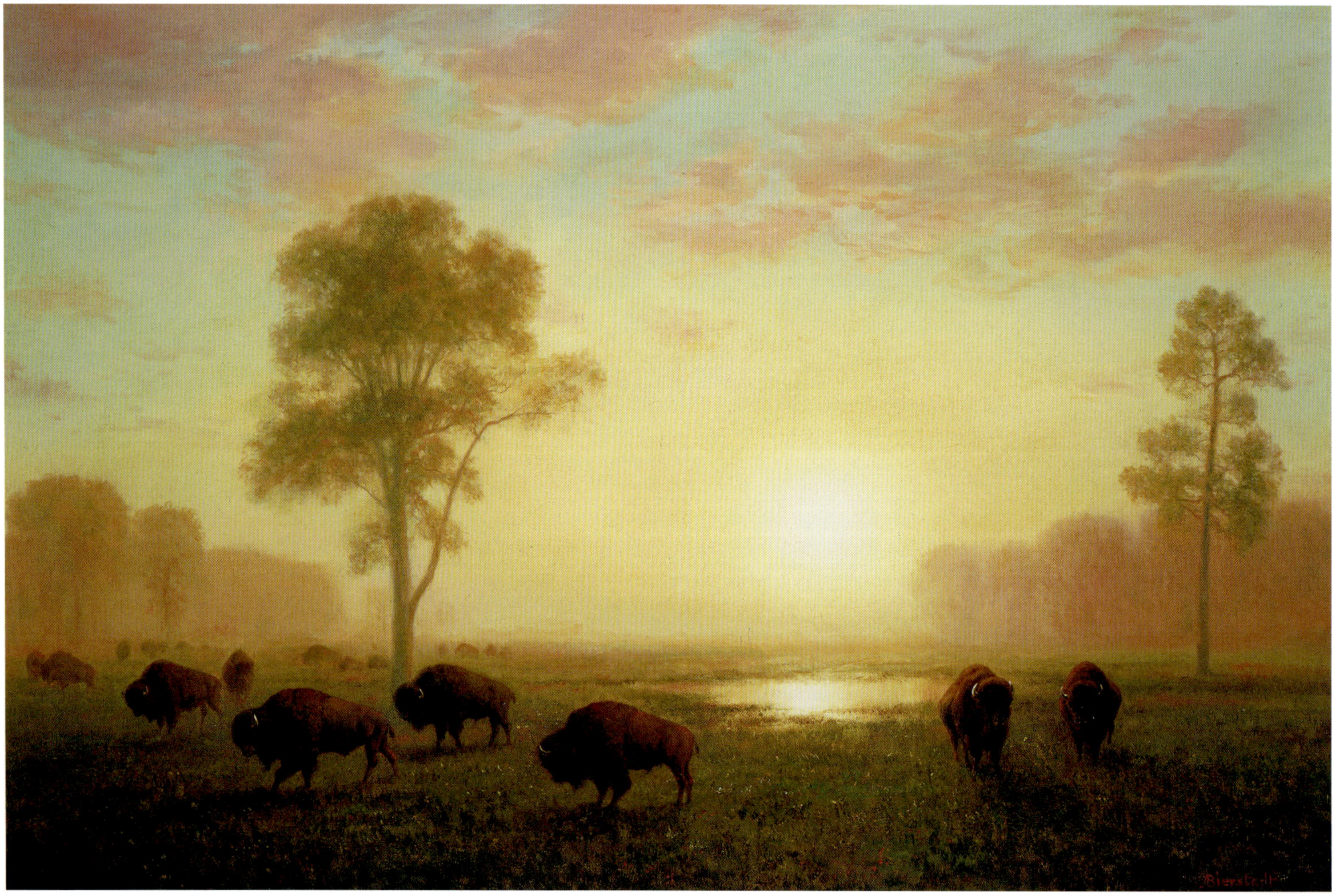

Fig. 6. Albert Bierstadt (American, born Germany, 1830–1902). *Sunset on the Plains*, n.d. Oil on canvas, 23 × 33 in. (58.4 × 83.8 cm). Autry National Center of the American West, Los Angeles

concoctions like *Sunset on the Plains* (fig. 6), with its herd of buffalo in lieu of a westbound wagon train.[19]

Sunsets were fraught symbols, complicated by the logic of beginnings and endings. They meant the dawn of a new day for the pioneer heading west, but yesterday for the Indian swept aside by advancing civilization. *Boone's First View of Kentucky* (fig. 7), by William Tylee Ranney, has a late-light glow that conveys the double meaning of pioneering, as escape from and advance of civilization; understood either way, it entails a celebration, albeit one potentially tinged with regret. Ranney's scene could as readily be set in early morning light, as in *The Trappers* (fig. 8), as he proved when he repainted *Boone's First View of Kentucky* (1849; American Museum of Western Art—The Anschutz Collection, Denver) using a "fresher" palette and, according to a modern assessment, "converting a dreamy, self-absorptive calm to one of cheerful, national ordination."[20] Such manipulation of light was unavailable when the artist turned to Indian themes, where the setting sun had a single meaning. John Mix Stanley carried the entrenched convention of the "vanishing American" to its logical conclusion in *Last of Their Race* (fig. 9) by showing a party of Indians huddled on the Pacific shore, out of land, out of hope, the sun setting before them.

In nineteenth-century art, lighting was the province of the painter. Sculpture was a figurative medium in which an overarching theme like the "vanishing American" might be implicit in the details of a composition or explicitly stated in an elaborate allegory. Adolph Alexander Weinman's *Destiny of the Red Man* (fig. 10) hardly required a vulture looming over its group of Indian men, women, and children to make its point, but a vulture there is, atop a totem pole, signifying the Indians' march to extinction. Disconsolate Indians brooding on their fate became a common motif in American art and letters, in response to tastemakers

in the first half of the nineteenth century who encouraged a national culture grounded in distinctive homegrown subject matter. American Indians obviously filled the bill, and the anticipation of their certain demise enhanced their

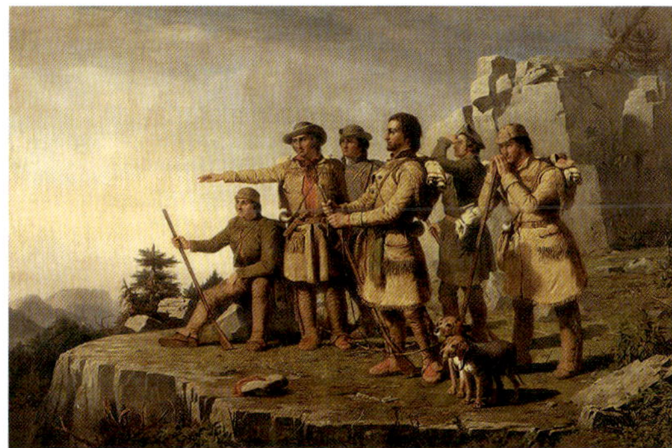

Fig. 7. William Tylee Ranney (American, 1813–1857). *Boone's First View of Kentucky*, 1849. Oil on canvas, 41¾ × 59⅝ in. (106 × 151.4 cm). Gilcrease Museum, Tulsa, Oklahoma

Fig. 8. William Tylee Ranney (American, 1813–1857). *The Trappers*, 1856. Oil on canvas, 23½ × 36 in. (59.7 × 91.4 cm). Autry National Center of the American West, Los Angeles

Fig. 9. John Mix Stanley (American, 1814–1872). *Last of Their Race*, 1857. Oil on canvas, 43 × 60 in. (109.2 × 152.4 cm). Buffalo Bill Center of the West, Cody, Wyoming

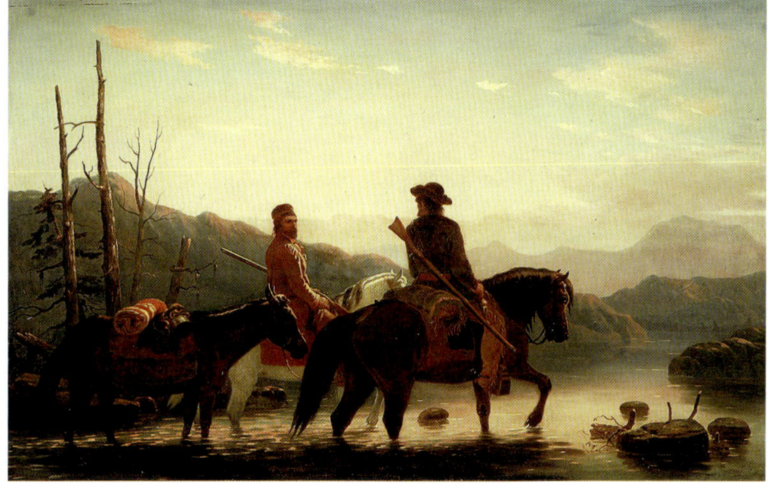

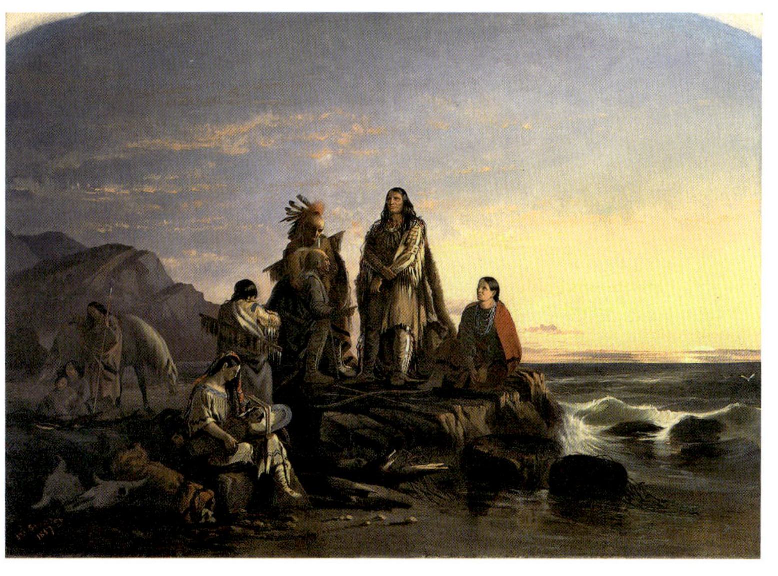

romantic appeal. Even so committed a champion of the winning of the West as Frederic Remington would have his go at the theme in *The Last of His Race* (1908; Yale University Art Gallery, New Haven), showing a gorgeously costumed Plains Indian on a bluff staring into space—the void, presumably. Its message resides in the cultural understanding that the Indian's world—indeed, the whole world of western art—was transitory.[21]

"Civilization has a destroying as well as a creating power," Francis Parkman observed at midcentury. "It is exterminating the buffalo and the Indian."[22] Buffalo skulls like those tucked into the corner of Stanley's *Last of Their Race* and at the rear of Weinman's *Destiny of the Red Man* offered artists a symbolic shorthand for

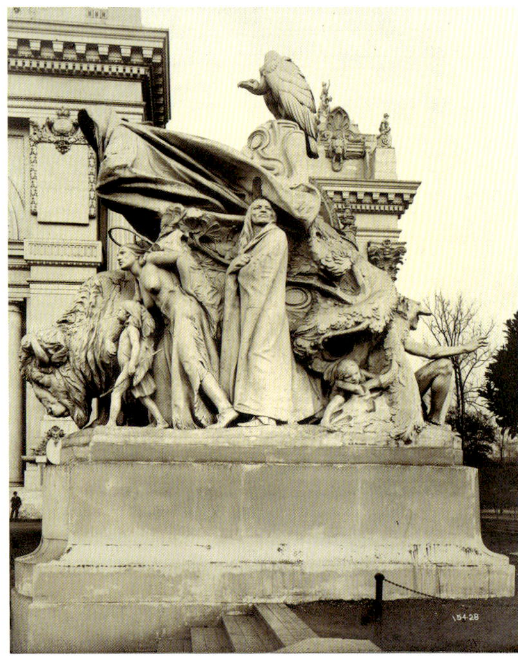

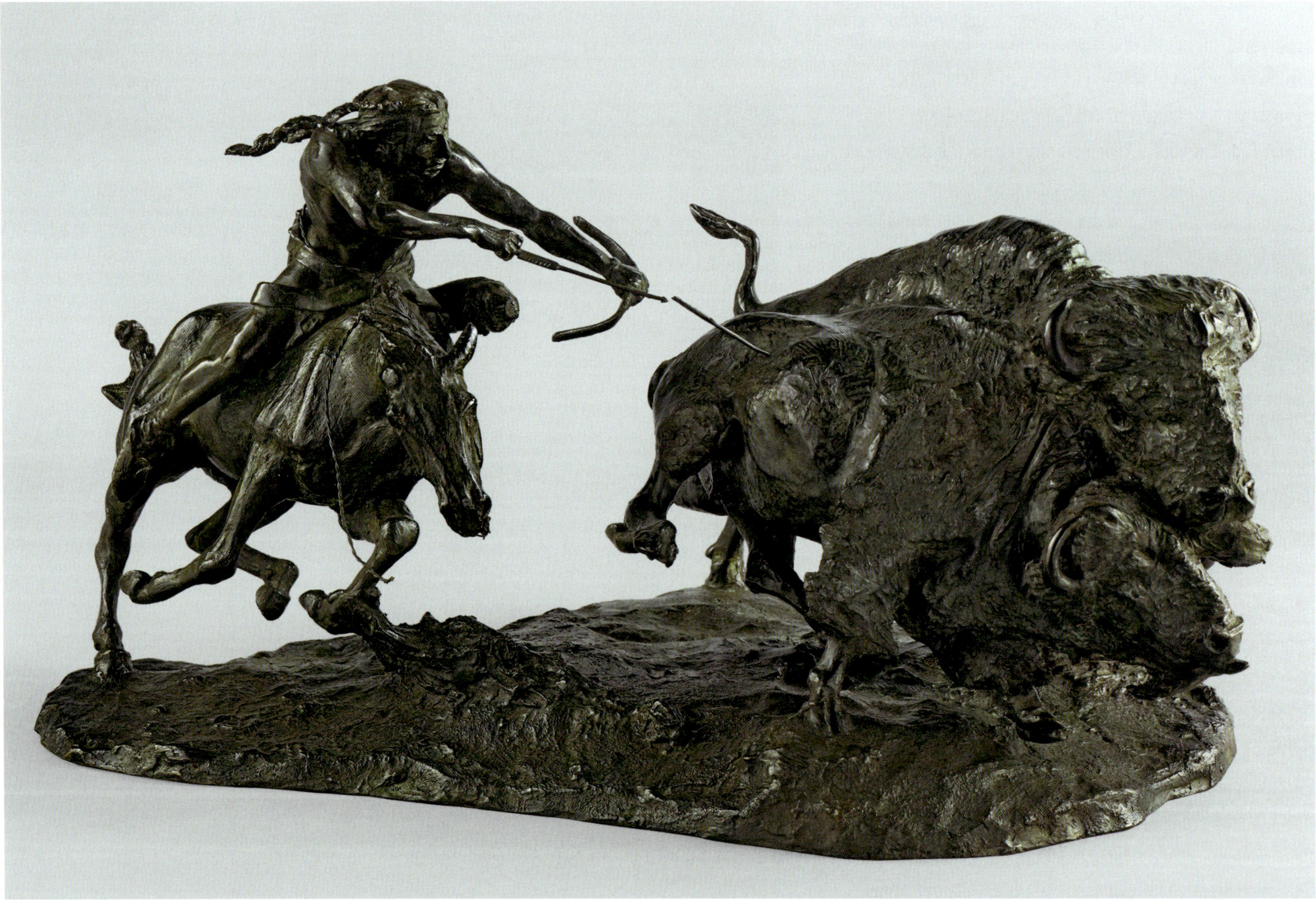

Fig. 10. Adolph Alexander Weinman. *Destiny of the Red Man*, Louisiana Purchase Exposition, Saint Louis, 1904

Fig. 11. Charles M. Russell. *Buffalo Hunt*, 1905 (cast 1905). Cat. 59

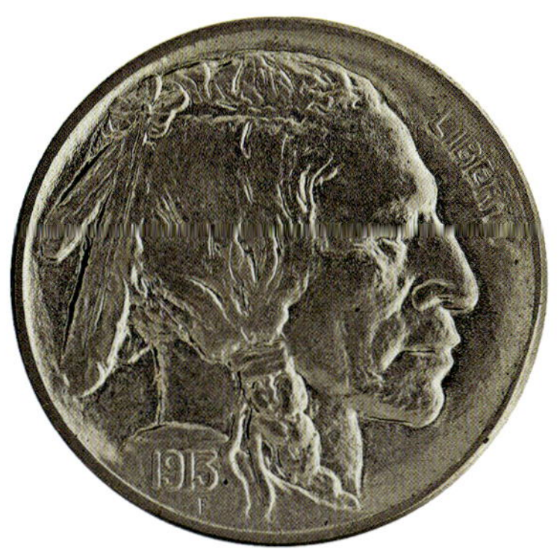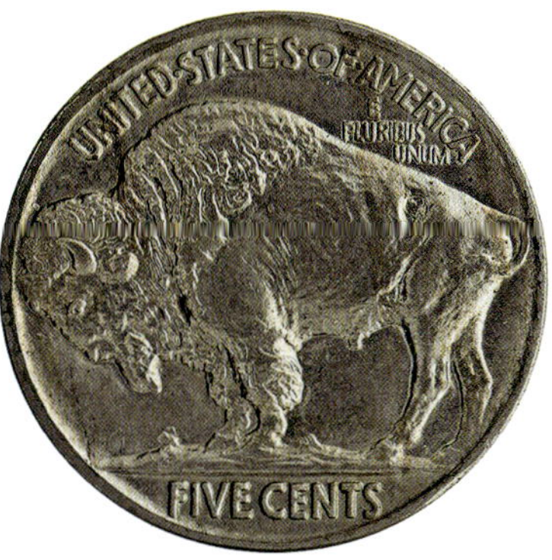

Fig. 12. James Earle Fraser. Buffalo nickel, 1913. American Numismatic Society, New York

Fig. 13. James Earle Fraser. *End of the Trail*, Panama-Pacific International Exposition, San Francisco, 1915

transformative change in the West (see also fig. 89). An outline of a buffalo skull became the personal insignia of Charles M. Russell, who titled two exhibitions of his paintings and bronzes "The West That Has Passed." Few overland travelers in the nineteenth century seemed able to resist the urge to chase after bison, and almost no western artist failed to depict the buffalo hunt in all its rambling appeal (fig. 11; see also figs. 35, 63). But by the 1880s the vast herds of bison once synonymous with the plains and prairies had shrunk to a pitiful remnant, leaving only bones as a reproach for what was no more. When the American government chose to commemorate the vanished West, a buffalo and a buffalo-hunting Plains Indian became two sides of the same coin: a nickel first minted in 1913 and designed by James Earle Fraser (fig. 12). Fraser had earlier sculpted another American icon, an equestrian statue of an Indian warrior slumped on his exhausted horse, the buffalo robe around his waist tossed by the wind as he contemplated the end of the trail (fig. 61). Fraser hoped that a bronze cast of his group, originally modeled in 1894 and enlarged for display at the 1915 Panama-Pacific International Exposition in San Francisco (fig. 13), would be permanently placed in that city's Lincoln Park, where nature (outrivaling John Mix Stanley) would paint sunset skies over the Pacific to complete the symbolism.

Indians and buffalo aside, western sculpture was populated with frontier types clad in the rough-and-ready apparel demanded by a raw environment. Costume made the man—as well as allegorical points—in sculpture. Emigrants on their way to the promised land had been given a homespun appearance ever since they were shown as families moving through a paradisial setting in the popular Currier & Ives print created by Fanny F. Palmer in 1866, *The*

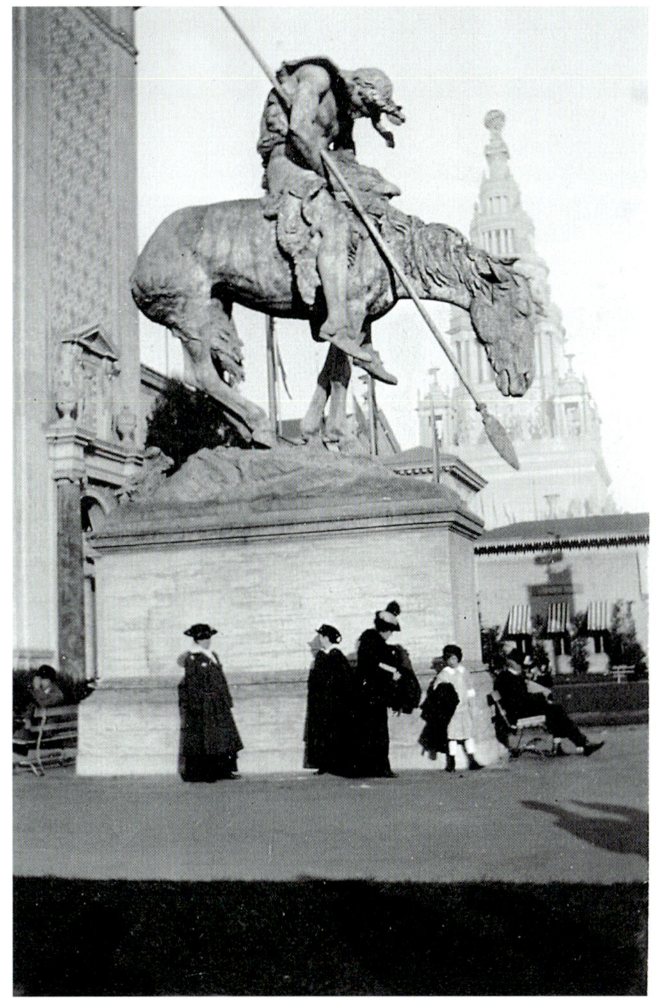

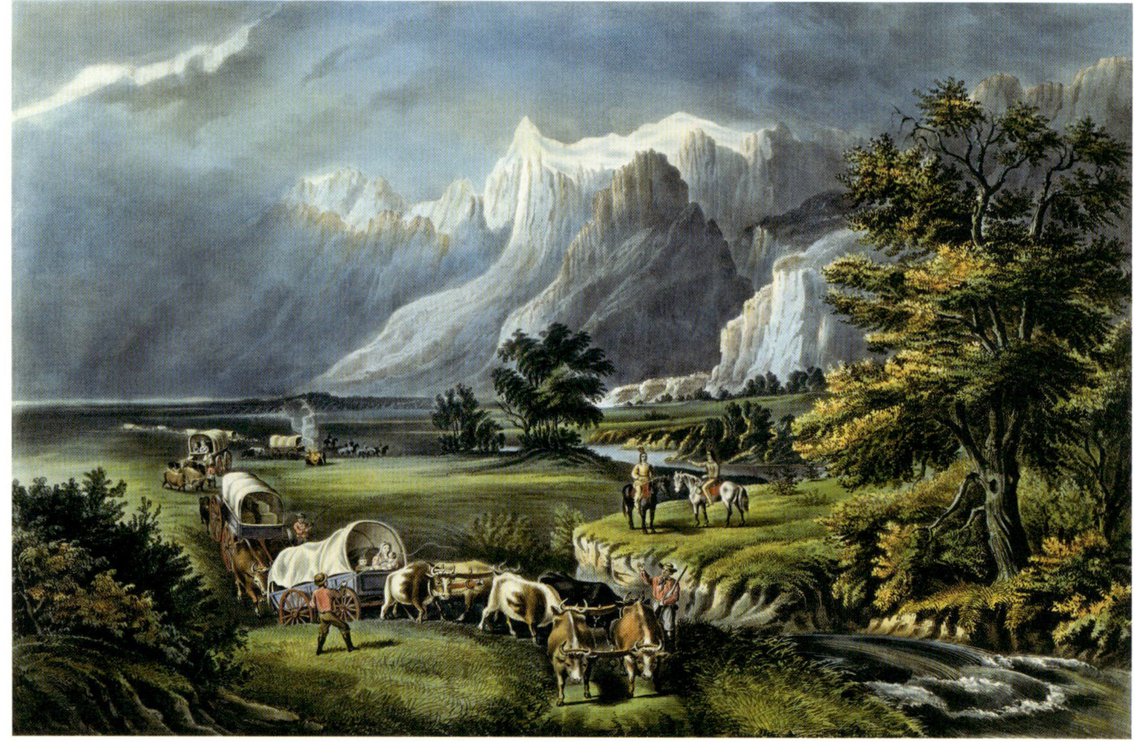

Fig. 14. Currier & Ives (Fanny F. Palmer, del.). *The Rocky Mountains. Emigrants Crossing the Plains*, 1866. Hand-colored print, image: 17½ × 25¾ in. (44.5 × 65.4 cm), sheet: 22¾ × 30⅝ in. (57.8 × 77.8 cm). Amon Carter Museum of American Art, Fort Worth, Texas

Fig. 15. Alexander Phimister Proctor. *Pioneer Mother*, 1925–27 (dedicated 1927). Penn Valley Park, Kansas City, Missouri

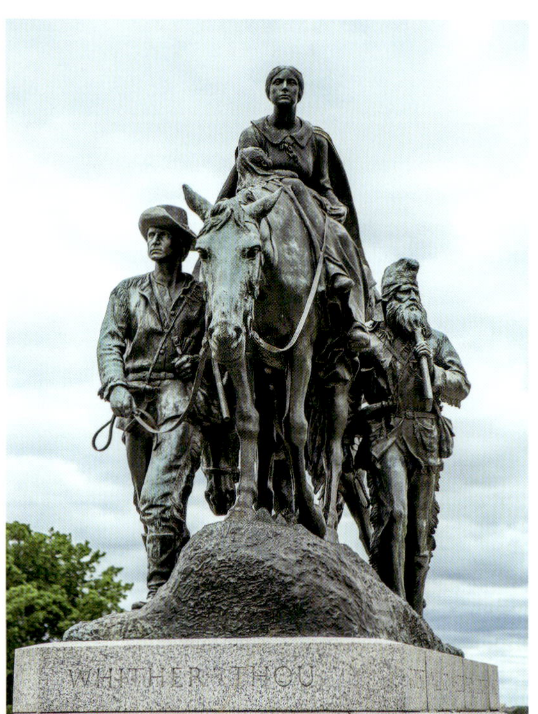

Rocky Mountains. Emigrants Crossing the Plains (fig. 14). Two Indians look on at the passing wagon train, witnesses to their own passing but powerless to change what they see. They are spectators left behind by progress, serving the same symbolic function as the tipis in Bierstadt's *Emigrants Crossing the Plains*. Families figured prominently in emigrant imagery, anticipating the flurry of early twentieth-century monuments to pioneer women (see figs. 164, 170). With infants in arm and children in hand, women represented "the hope for the future of the West," as sculptor Alexander Phimister Proctor said of his monumental group *Pioneer Mother*, unveiled in Kansas City, Missouri, in 1927 (fig. 15).[23] His ambitious sculpture portrays a mother with her baby mounted on a horse, a pack horse trailing, and a man walking on either side. One, presumably the guide, is a grizzled plains veteran, all beard and buckskins; the other, the young father, strides purposefully toward tomorrow.

Proctor's grizzled plainsman owes a debt to Remington's version of the old-time trapper. As a prolific illustrator through the 1890s, Remington specialized in western types. He conceived of trappers, for example, as hairy primitives decked out in buckskin outfits. Wakeman Bryarly, a Maryland physician bound for California in 1849, met a trapper named Rogers who could have served as Remington's prototype. Rogers relished telling of an emigrant he once tried to hail—perhaps a young husband too—who glanced at the approaching rider in his buckskins with long hair billowing behind and promptly fled, sure he was about to be scalped. "He evidently took him for an Indian," Bryarly concluded, anticipating a famous 1890 Remington pen sketch of two bearish mountain men conversing, one commenting to the other, "I took ye for an injin."[24] They epitomized what Remington called "men with the bark on"—roughhewn, plainspoken types—and he titled a 1901 portfolio of drawings of his western types *A Bunch of Buckskins*.[25]

Remington had identified the costume that artists would most often seize upon to represent the spirit of pioneering. The *Pioneer Monument* unveiled in Denver a decade later is topped by an equestrian figure in full buckskin costume meant to represent Christopher "Kit" Carson leading the way west (fig. 16). The sculptor, Frederick William MacMonnies, originally intended to put a Plains Indian in the place of honor on his fountain monument but was dissuaded by public protest. And so Carson, the pathfinder, literally supplanted an Indian—an outcome appropriate for a monument honoring pioneers in 1911. MacMonnies did not neglect to include a pioneer mother at the base of his monument, but it is Kit Carson who carries the day.

Sixteen years later, with his *Pioneer Mother*, Proctor wanted to qualify such heroic triumphalism. His pioneer family are trail-worn travelers, as tired as their horses but still resolute. Their weariness might resemble that of Fraser's slumping Indian, but for them the end of the trail was full of hope. As a clergyman put it at midcentury: "Tears, blows, privations, hardships, toil and blood, did these . . . [pioneers] pay down as the ransom for this goodly

heritage. The land is ours in virtue of the price."[26] (Indian rights did not figure into their calculations.) Proctor's group acknowledges that civilization's advance came at a steep cost. Individuals wore out. Some did not make it. But even higher a cost was what Parkman meant in saying that civilization has a destroying as well as a creating power. Winning the West spelled

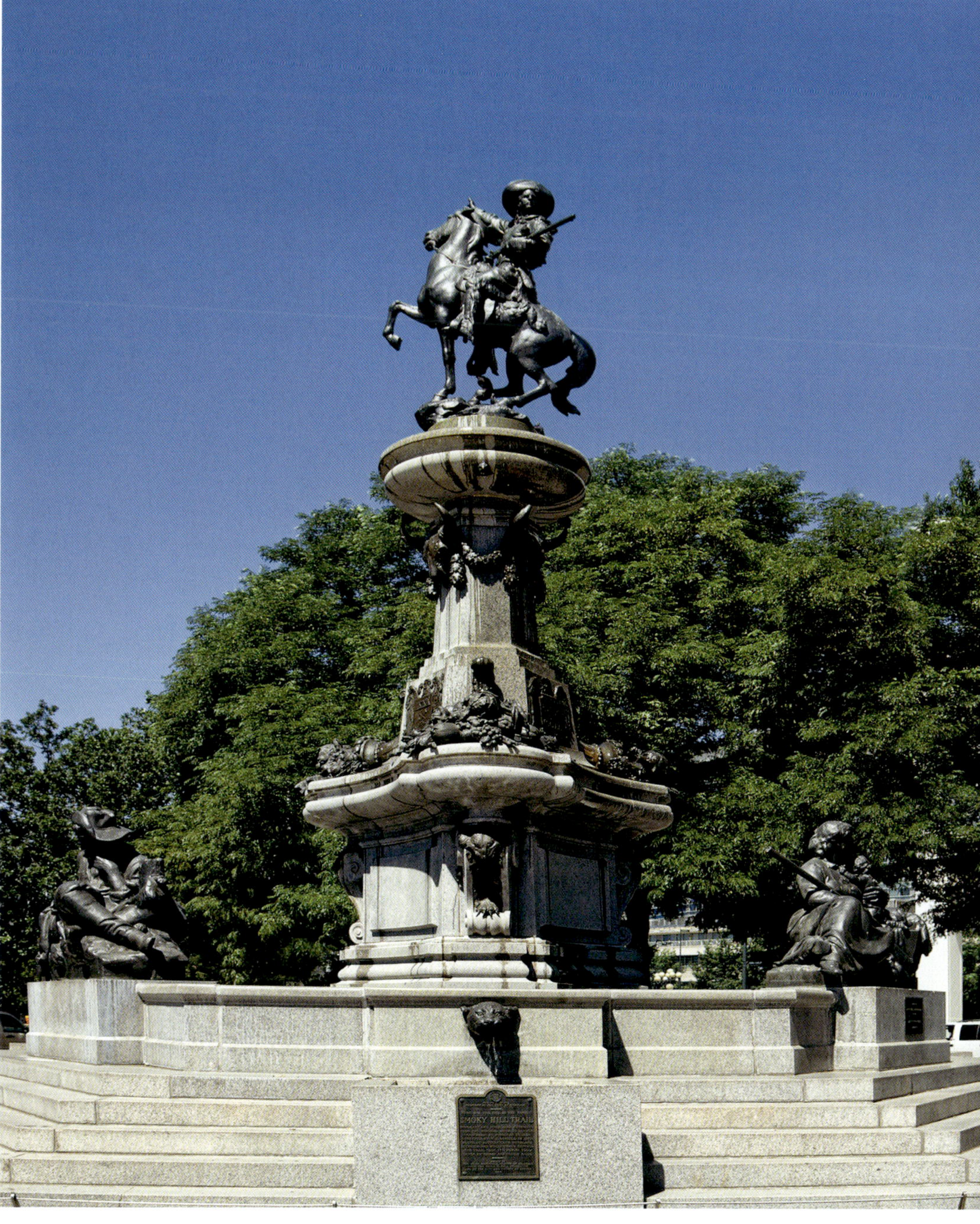

Fig. 16. Frederick William MacMonnies. *Pioneer Monument*, 1907–11 (dedicated 1911). Broadway and Colfax, Denver

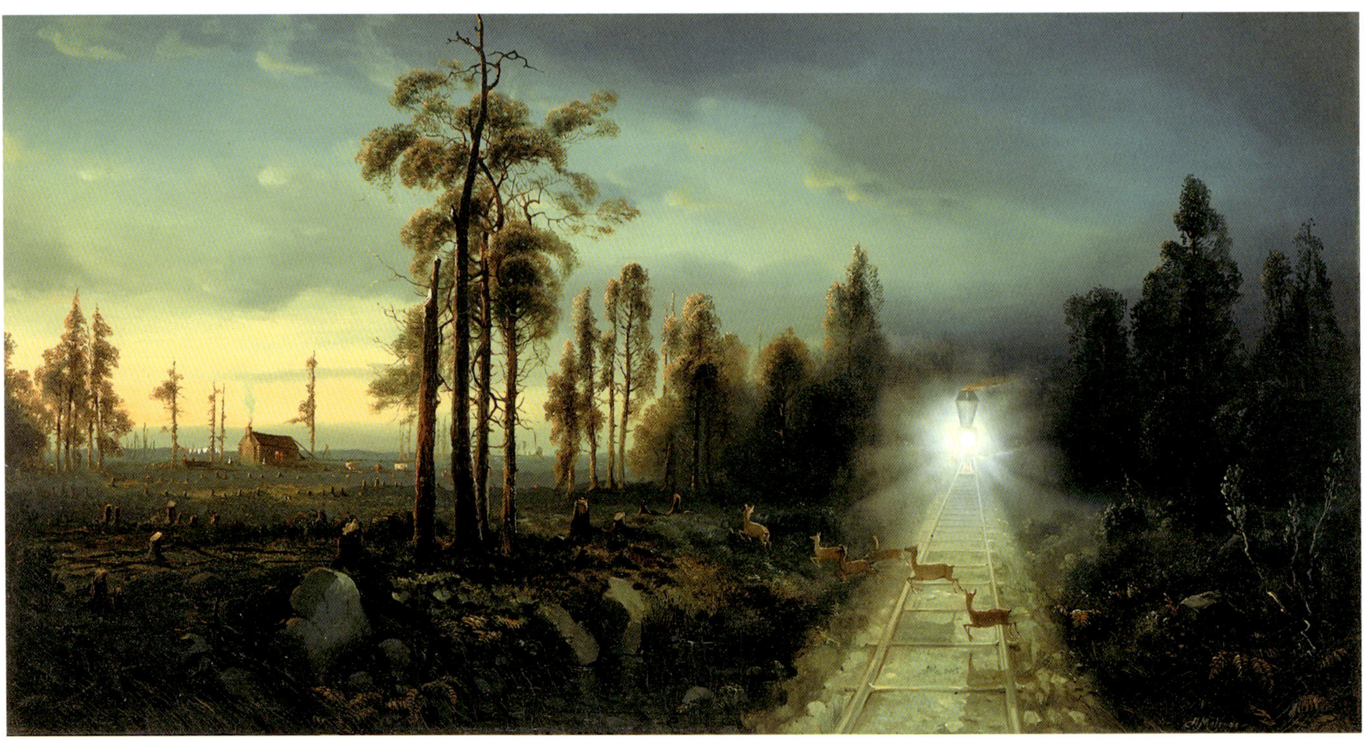

an end to the winning of the West. Buckskin memories would be all that was left. The sun had set on everyone.

What James Fenimore Cooper and Washington Irving had offered an earlier generation in their romances and narratives of frontier derring-do, journalists, travelers, hack writers, dime novelists, and press agents provided in the years after the Civil War. Travel accounts celebrated the completion of the first transcontinental railroad in 1869, recognizing that the Golden Spike signaled a beginning and an end. Andrew W. Melrose made the point visually in *Westward the Star of Empire Takes Its Way—Near Council Bluffs, Iowa* (fig. 17), an allegorical oil painting set in Iowa but with a transcontinental theme as a locomotive rushes directly at the viewer, its blinding headlight brighter than any star save that of empire, its tracks dividing the world left and right between a fledgling homestead cleared of forest cover and the still-uncultivated wilderness. Deer flee from its path, fulfilling

the symbolic role of wildlife in western art: to be imperiled by the headlong rush of progress. Had this painting been set on the plains, perhaps a startled bear (but more likely bison) would have substituted for the deer. A publicity booklet issued by the Great Northern Railway in 1898 commented, "It seems but yesterday that 'Beyond the Mississippi' was a dimly known region, lying off toward the sunset." Then the locomotive "entered the vast solitude and scattered population and prosperity in its wake. . . . The day of the buffalo and Indian is past—like a story ended."[27]

But the public still craved western stories with the boring parts left out. The frontier adventure might be over, but a fascination with frontier heroes thrived. In 1883 William F. "Buffalo Bill" Cody created a show-business phenomenon, Buffalo Bill's Wild West—an arena entertainment with buffalo and Indians and much else besides. It capitalized on Cody's autobiography, published in 1879, and on a mound of dime novels in which he featured as his fictional self, and it inspired a multitude of imitators. For a generation of Americans (and Europeans, after he began touring abroad in 1887), Buffalo Bill personified the ideal of the plainsman, the buckskin-clad hunter-hero of frontier days (fig. 18).[28]

Cody was born in 1846, "the year of decision" by historian Bernard De Voto's reckoning, in which the United States expanded its western borders to the Pacific Ocean.[29] The Oregon Treaty with Britain, the war with Mexico, the Mormon migration to Utah, and the ongoing conflicts with American Indians wherever white settlers ventured represented the expansionist energies at midcentury known as Manifest Destiny. America's final boundaries north and south still required refinement, but after 1846 the western boundary was not in doubt. There would be no "statue of the fabled god, Terminus" erected on the ridge of the Rocky Mountains, as the Missouri senator Thomas Hart Benton had proposed in 1825; the United States would be a transcontinental nation.[30] With the discovery of gold in 1848 and the flood of population into California, the West as a geographic entity gained a new prominence in public debate. The controversy over the expansion of slavery, exacerbated by adding so much new territory, became a pressing national issue. Civil war was imminent.

The West might remain a potent draw after the Civil War, but it was no longer an elusive phantom leading the dreamer on an open-ended chase. In 1876, the nation's centennial year, Herman Melville sounded its knell:

Columbus ended earth's romance:
No New World to mankind remains![31]

That sense of closure made all the more shocking the news received in the East on July 6, 1876, of the total annihilation by Sioux (as the Lakota were known historically) and Cheyenne Indians of George Armstrong Custer and five companies of the Seventh Cavalry on a distant western river with the unlikely name the Little Bighorn. It was as though the Old West had been reborn in blood and a "Century of Progress" erased with a stroke. Buffalo Bill, already an established theatrical performer playing himself, seized the moment to journey west, renewing his earlier service as army scout and Indian fighter. He killed the Cheyenne Yellow Hair in single-handed combat, thereby taking the "first scalp for Custer" and securing his own position in the pantheon of frontier heroes. Fourteen years later, by then a middle-aged international celebrity, Cody was expected by his public to respond to a new Indian crisis, dubbed the Ghost Dance War. Do something, Buffalo Bill, save the day—as he did in every performance of the Wild West. Cody's intervention with the Sioux, whom he knew as performers in his show, proved inconsequential and his mission to arrest Sitting Bull a failure, but the fact that he was involved at all reaffirmed his credentials as an authentic hero.[32]

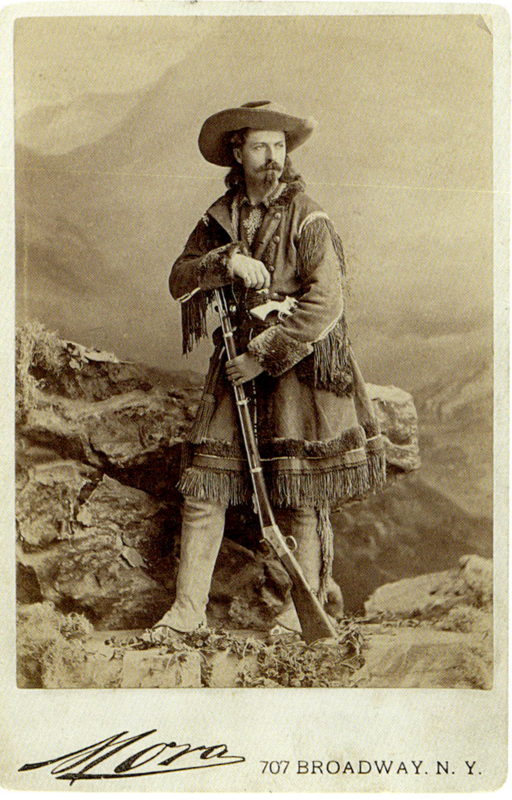

Fig. 18. *William F. "Buffalo Bill" Cody, New York*, ca. 1873–74. Photograph by Jose Maria Mora

Remington covered the war as a field correspondent for *Harper's Weekly*. As the acclaimed pictorial historian of the Indian-fighting army he, like Cody, had no choice. Both had to be on hand to witness the events leading to the tragic culmination at Wounded Knee on December 29, 1890. The Ghost Dance War proved to be the last act in the drama on which both had staked their careers: the winning of the West. Two years later Remington would be sketching Buffalo Bill's Wild West while it performed in London. What did he and Cody talk about? Now that the West was won, Remington fretted about his impending irrelevance. Cody touted his recent exploits, devoting pages in the program for his show to pictures of the Ghost Dancers and a stark scene of the Indian dead at Wounded Knee. The Wild West's publicist concluded that the "once happy empire" of the Sioux "has been (rightfully or wrongly) brought thoroughly and efficiently under the control of our civilisation."[33]

In 1893 Chicago hosted a spectacular World's Columbian Exposition to celebrate four hundred years of unstoppable progress since Columbus discovered the New World. Sculptors used the occasion to display their wares, several on western themes (see figs. 79, 111). The exposition also lured Buffalo Bill's Wild West back home from Europe for a hugely successful run outside the fairgrounds. The exposition's theme invited ruminations on the changes that had transformed America, and a historian attending a professional meeting held in conjunction with the fair seized the opportunity to reflect on what used to be. Frederick Jackson Turner's "The Significance of the Frontier in American History," at once a celebration and an elegy, could not have been better timed. Census data, Turner said, confirmed that "four centuries from the discovery of America, . . . the frontier has gone." The future loomed, but what did it hold for Americans shaped as a distinct people by their encounters with

successive frontiers as they moved across the continent, each furnishing "a new field of opportunity, a gate of escape from the bondage of the past; and freshness, and confidence, and scorn of older society?" Now "a great historic movement" was finished, and "the first period of American history" over.[34]

By the 1890s, with the old century pressed against the new, Turner's was merely one of the more eloquent voices sounding the theme of transformative change. The significance he found in America's history of frontiering was faithful to the precepts of environmental determinism and evolutionary progress, reinforcing notions of American exceptionalism. On each frontier, inherited culture had been diminished as pioneers first adapted to primitive conditions and then rebuilt their civilization in accordance with distinctively American traits. Something new had been forged on the cutting edge of western expansion, a national character marked by "coarseness and strength," "acuteness and inquisitiveness," a "practical, inventive turn of mind," a "masterful grasp of material things," a "restless, nervous energy," a "dominant individualism," and a "buoyancy and exuberance which comes with freedom"—all "traits of the frontier."[35]

What better to symbolize this process than the frontiersman, made instantly recognizable by his costume and thus ideal for the artist? He stood at a midpoint between wilderness and civilization, the former represented by the Indian, the latter by prosperous farms, brick buildings, and citizens in conventional attire. Such evidence of progress might satisfy the Westerner but would never satisfy the eastern taste for western romance. What was interesting about the West to those east of the Mississippi was what was different. Buffalo Bill bet his future on that proposition. When the Wild West set up in Chicago during the Columbian Exposition for what proved to be a record-breaking run, the show's publicist hit all the right notes. "As Columbus was the pilot across the seas to discover a new world," he wrote, "such heroes as Boone, Fremont, Crockett, Kit Carson, and last, but by no means least, Cody, were the guides to the New World of the mighty West, and their names will go down in history."[36] Buckskin heroes held the key to the frontier treasury; they were golden, and artists would be the principal beneficiaries.

When Theodore Roosevelt reached the end of his narrative trail in 1896, four volumes into *The Winning of the West*, he was only at the beginning of what Americans beguiled by Buffalo Bill and the final Indian Wars meant by that phrase: the winning of the *trans-Mississippi West*, inaugurated with the Louisiana Purchase and the explorations of Lewis and Clark and Zebulon Pike. But for Roosevelt, the tale had its genesis *east* of the Mississippi River, and its greatest heroes were the backwoodsmen of Daniel Boone's day. Backwoodsmen, mountain men, plainsmen—they were frontiersmen all, cut from the same piece of buckskin.

In the preface to *Our Pioneer Heroes and Their Daring Deeds* (1900), D. M. Kelsey defined "frontiering" as "the differing phases of the same long battle on the frontiers, from decade to decade, through centuries, as the Indian races were gradually pushed back by the march of the encroaching white race, till it enveloped them on all sides."[37] There was an understood progression here—a thread running through America's past that linked Boone to later heroes in one seamless narrative. Fat biographical compendiums like Kelsey's, stuffed full of buckskin-clad frontiersmen, enjoyed a popular vogue in the last quarter of the nineteenth century. Their titles were self-explanatory—*Western Wilds, and the Men Who Redeem Them* (ca. 1877), *Conquering the Wilderness* (1883)—and their cast of characters predictable. The title on the front board of J. W. Buel's *Heroes of the Plains* (1881) continued,

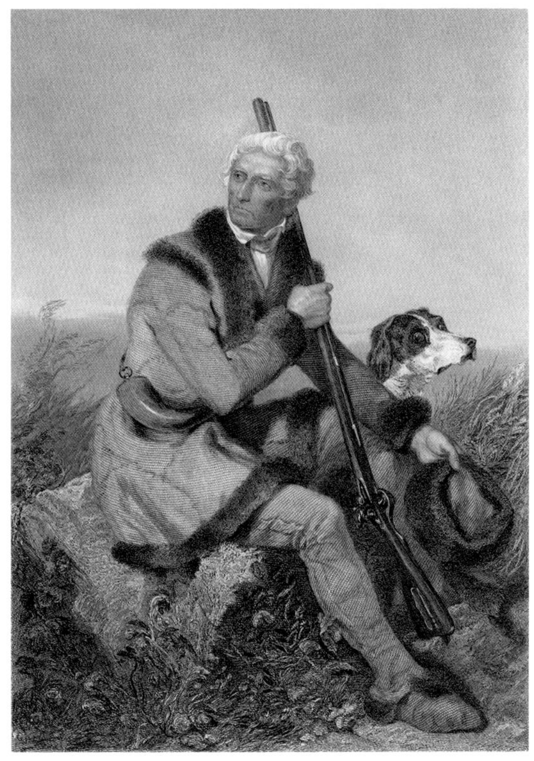

Fig. 19. *Daniel Boone, Seated in Hunting Outfit*. Engraving, ca. 1861, after a painting by Alonzo Chappel

"*or, Life and Wonderful Adventures of Wild Bill, Buffalo Bill and Exploits of Gen. Custer, Kit Carson, California Joe, Capt. Jack, Capt. D. L. Payne, &c., &c., &c.*" Etc., etc., etc., indeed. One could trace an even older buckskin lineage, but in American frontier mythology it conveniently began with Boone (d. 1820; fig. 19)—"his tall and manly form cased in buckskin, his face bronzed by wind, and sun, and storm; silent as an Indian, agile as a deer, tough as a panther"—and proceeded through figures like Davy Crockett (d. 1836; fig. 20), Kit Carson (d. 1868), and General Custer (d. 1876) to its apogee in Buffalo Bill and his "flamboyant fraternity."[38]

At the time the Rough Riders presented their lieutenant colonel with a cast of Remington's *Broncho Buster* (fig. 2), he considered it "the most appropriate gift the Regiment could possibly have given me."[39] But earlier, when he was a rancher in Dakota in the 1880s, Roosevelt had favored not the cowboy costume lovingly detailed in Remington's bronze but a fringed buckskin outfit that linked him to the tradition he most revered, that of the wilderness hunter (fig. 21). His suit, he wrote, "was the dress in which Daniel Boone was clad when he first passed through the trackless forests of the Alleghanies and penetrated into the heart of Kentucky . . . ; it was the dress worn by grim old Davy Crockett when he fell at the Alamo."[40] Small wonder that when Roosevelt got together with eastern friends in 1887 to form a club dedicated to promoting "manly sport with the rifle," they named it the Boone and Crockett Club.[41] At the Columbian Exposition the club

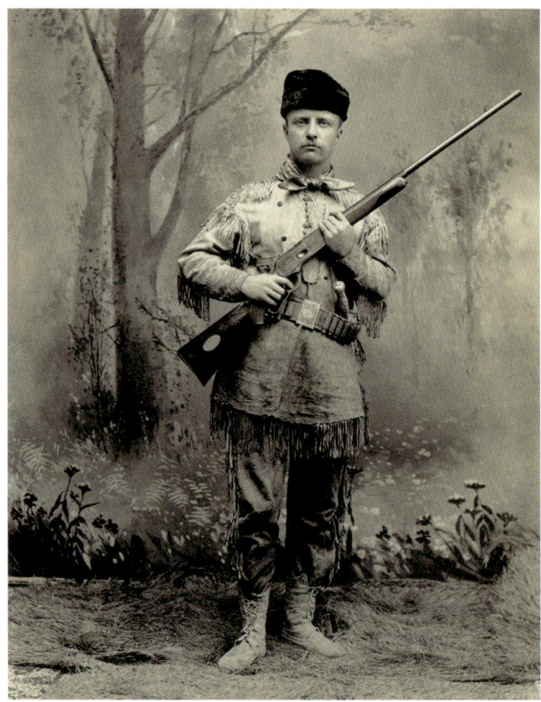

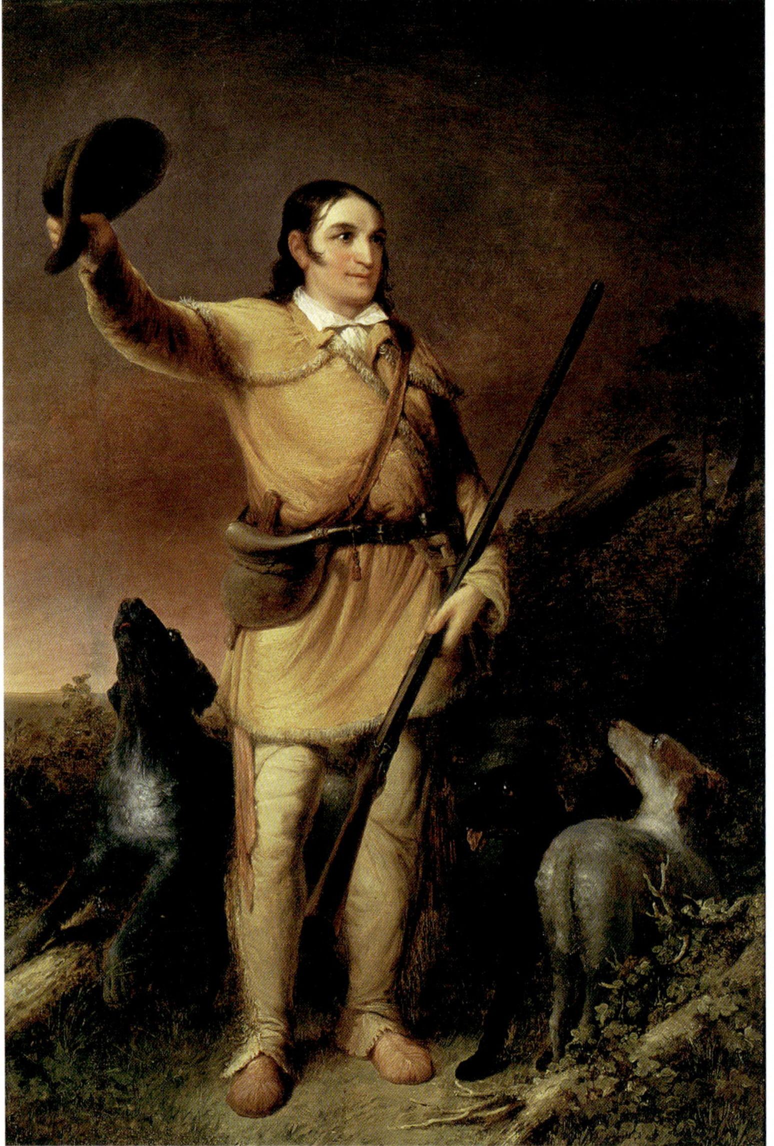

erected a log cabin on a wooded island in one of the fairground lagoons, meant to replicate the kind of rustic cabin occupied by early hunters and settlers on the frontier. In advance publicity, Roosevelt hinted it might contain Davy Crockett's own rifle.[42] For the future president, Boone and Crockett plus Kit Carson made a triumvirate "renowned in every quarter of the Union for their skill as game-hunters, Indian-fighters, and wilderness explorers. . . . They stand for all time as types of the pioneer settlers who won our land."[43]

The buckskin costume was a boon to painters and sculptors: its woodsmoke aura reeked of the Old West. For visual purposes, it distinguished eastern fops (Roosevelt as blue-blooded Harvard graduate) from western men (Roosevelt in his hunting outfit). And from western women, for that matter: when Martha Jane Canary, a character of dubious reputation who ordinarily wore a dress, assumed her full-blown frontier alter ego, Calamity Jane, she donned a buckskin suit (fig. 22) and, in some of her publicity pictures, clenched a knife

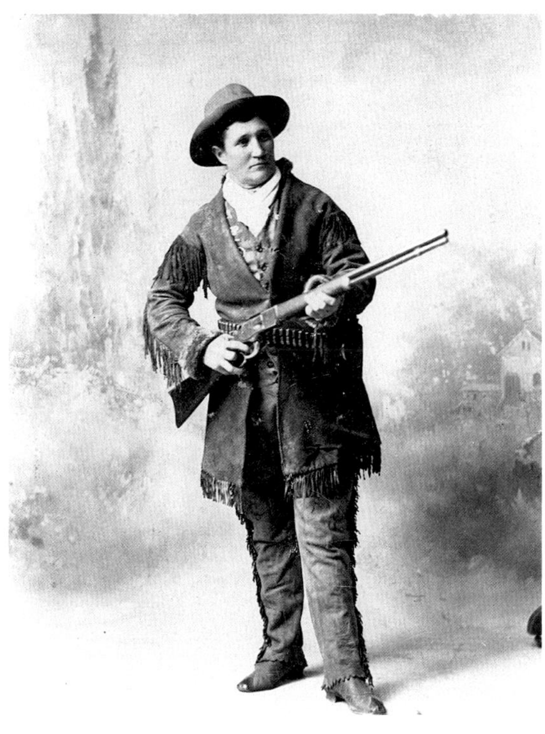

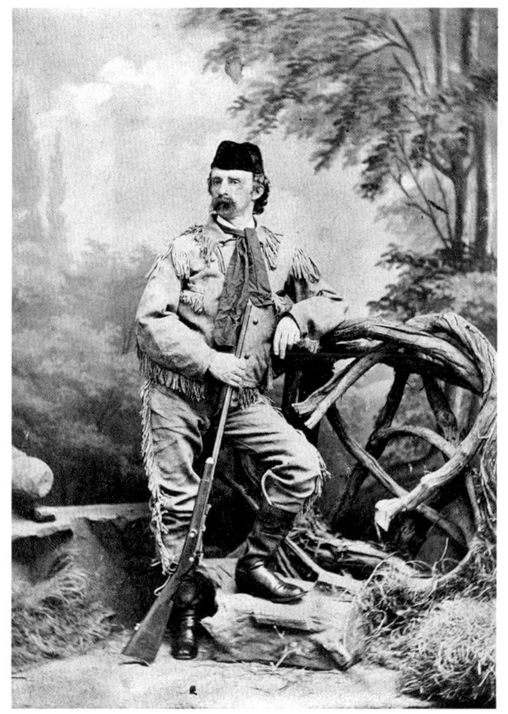

between her teeth.[44] (Remington's New York studio collection of western props included one of Calamity's buckskin outfits—jacket, trousers, and a beaded vest—though he included no women in his *Bunch of Buckskins* portfolio of 1901.)[45] Calamity Jane was kin to all the others who staked a claim to frontier celebrity by adopting buckskin costumes.

James Butler Hickok, who as Wild Bill gained lasting fame as a prince of pistoleers and, in romantic legend, as Calamity Jane's paramour, caught the eye of a different admirer in 1872:

"Wild Bill" was a strange character, just the one which a novelist might gloat over. He was a Plainsman in every sense of the word, . . . about six feet one in height, straight as the straightest of the warriors whose implacable foe he was; broad shoulders, well-formed chest and limbs, and a face strikingly handsome. . . . His hair . . . was worn in uncut ringlets falling carelessly over his powerfully formed shoulders. Add to this figure a costume blending the immaculate neatness of the dandy with the extravagant taste and style of the frontiersman, and you have Wild Bill, then as now the most famous scout of the Plains.[46]

The smitten admirer, none other than General Custer, acquired a leather outfit of his own in 1869 and wore it hunting bison with Buffalo Bill in 1872 (fig. 23). The Boy General of Civil War fame, through service on the plains, had transformed into the "cavalier in buckskin."[47]

Custer was dressed in full plainsman garb when he led the Seventh Cavalry on an expedition into Sioux country, the mysterious Black Hills, in 1874. As a romantic himself, he relished the opportunity to join the ranks of heroes of western exploration. Now he was one with Boone and Carson, whose biographers described them, respectively, as "the most renowned of American Pioneers" and "the most noted of . . . the pioneers of civilization in its advancement westward."[48] Such extravagant claims, like those Custer made on behalf of Wild Bill, aimed to establish a buckskin pecking order. Few contenders for top spot, however, could outrival the fame Custer won two years later by losing a battle with the original owners of the Black Hills. His

Fig. 22. *Martha Jane Canary (Calamity Jane)*, ca. 1895. Photograph by H. R. Locke

Fig. 23. *George Armstrong Custer in Hunting Outfit, Saint Louis*, 1872. Photograph by James A. Scholten

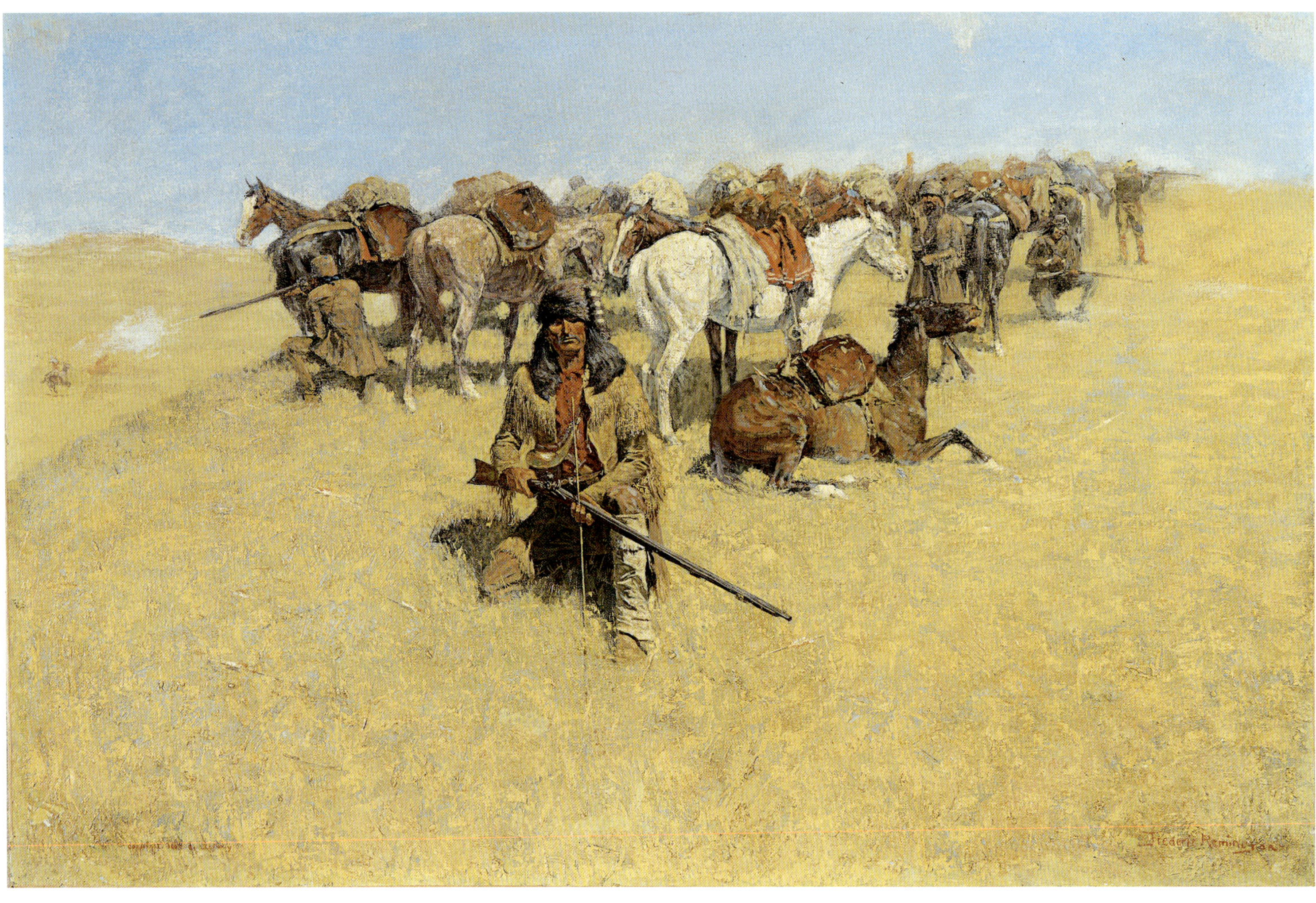

Fig. 24. Frederic Remington. *An Old-Time Plains Fight*, ca. 1904. Oil on canvas, 27 × 40 in. (68.6 × 101.6 cm). Frederic Remington Art Museum, Ogdensburg, New York

buckskin jacket was strapped on his horse in deference to the late June heat, but he went to his death in buckskin trousers.[49]

A rider in buckskins shading his eyes or gesturing into the distance was a generic frontier type, whether intended to represent Kit Carson, Buffalo Bill, or someone else. By the 1890s, artists were smoothly making the transition to another instantly identifiable western type, the cowboy, igniting a love affair with what Owen Wister, in his runaway best seller *The Virginian* (1902), called "a horseman of the plains." Remington showed how easy it was to move back and forth between buckskins and cowboy hats in his paintings of pioneers in either guise (or often army blue) making a desperate stand against circling Indians.

Although the reality of frontiering was that the Indians were, as Kelsey said, "pushed back by the march of the encroaching white race, till it enveloped them on all sides," in art, it was the Indians who did the enveloping. Depictions of desperate stands put the blame for violence on the victims of aggression, thereby assuaging the aggressor's guilt while advancing the master narrative of American progress.

The Progress of Civilization—a "great drama enacted by frontier heroes" that was staged in New York in 1888—featured as its concluding act "Custer's Last Rally" to honor the "myriads of our countrymen who from time to time have been willing to sacrifice home, friends, life and all, to battle in the defense of American rights and American civilization."[50] Remington's painting *An Old-Time Plains Fight*, of about 1904, reverted to buckskin days to make the same point (fig. 24). That the most prominent defender of American civilization in the painting appears to be a mixed-blood trapper adds a new wrinkle, but the motif is unchanged. The vanguard of civilization had advanced with unflinching courage in the face of overwhelming odds. Violence was woven into the epic advanced by Roosevelt in *The Winning of the West*, following on naturally from rugged individualism in an untamed land. As a mountain man told Matt Field in 1843, his credo was simple: *"I should like to see the man to make me do what I dont want to—that's all I live for!"*[51] When the cowboy rose to cultural prominence in fiction and eventually in film, a version of

that credo made Judge Colt the final arbiter when right met wrong in the shoot-outs that became a staple of Westerns (see fig. 144).

Nostalgia was in the air by the time the cowboy took center stage in the nation's frontier mythology. Charles M. Russell, who arrived in Montana in 1880 when he was sixteen and went on to fame as "the Cowboy Artist," left his boyhood home in Saint Louis with parental warnings in his head and buckskin fantasies in his heart. He had grown up on stories about Kit Carson and Buffalo Bill and about his family's links to the fur trade. For Russell, the West was still the land of romance and adventure. In the painting *When I Was a Kid* (fig. 25), he recalled with unabashed nostalgia the days he spent in the company of an experienced

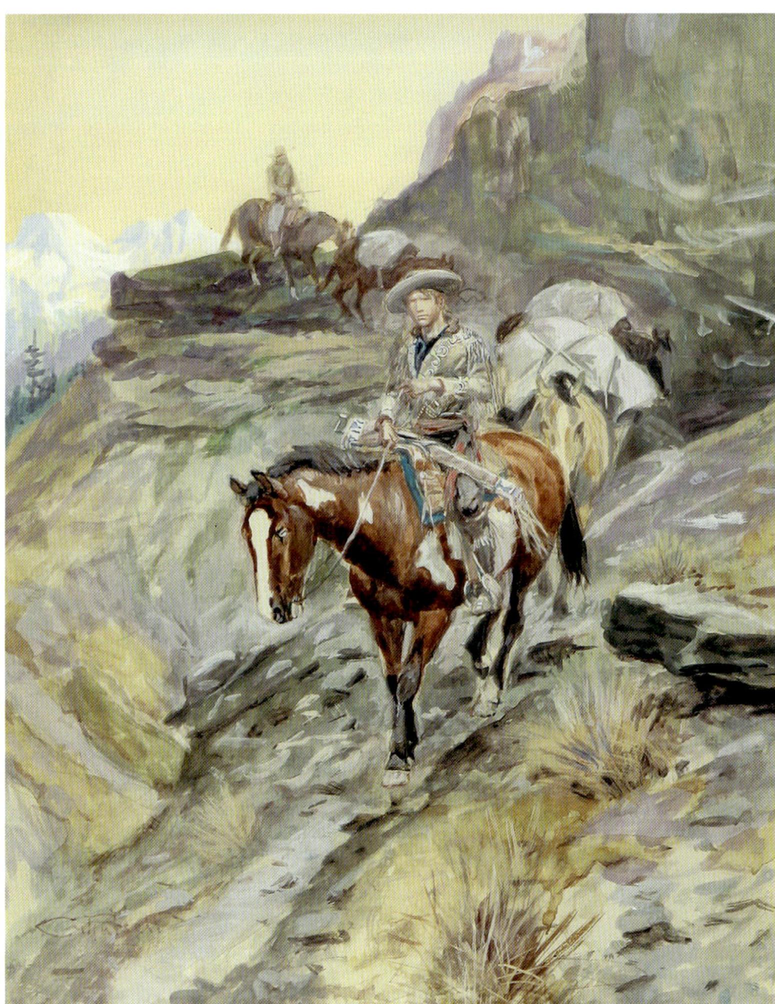

Fig. 25. Charles M. Russell. *When I Was a Kid*, 1905. Watercolor and gouache on paper, 14¼ × 11 in. (36.2 × 27.9 cm). C. M. Russell Museum, Great Falls, Montana

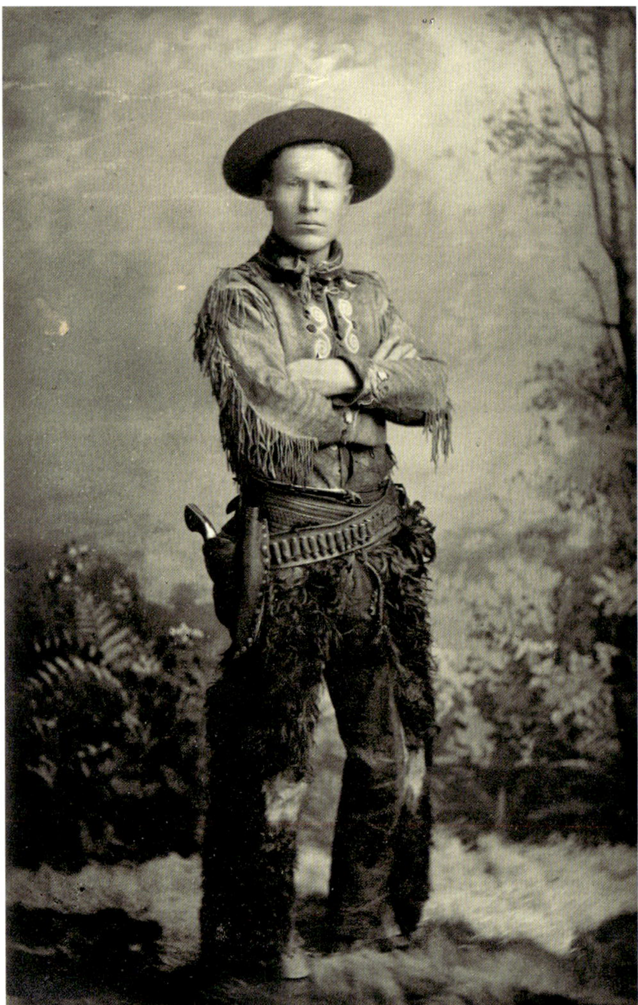

Fig. 26. *Charles M. Russell
("Kid Russell," aka "Buckskin Kid"),
Montana, ca. 1885*

Fig. 27. Charles M. Russell. *When
White Men Turn Red*, 1922. Oil on
canvas, 24 × 36¼ in. (61 × 92.1 cm).
Sid Richardson Museum, Fort
Worth, Texas

hunter in the Judith Basin, living out his boyhood dreams in "a hunter's paradise, bounded
by walls of mountains and containing miles of
grassy open spaces, more green and beautiful
than any man-made parks."[52] When he moved
on to cowboying, Russell kept the buckskin
jacket he had worn (fig. 26). The Buckskin
Kid, as he was known, never lost his longing
for an imagined past "when the land belonged
to God," and Indians and trappers rode across
an open country, unfenced and free, with the
world all before them. His late-life painting
When White Men Turn Red (fig. 27) aches with
yearning, not for an old-time plains fight but
for an old-time love affair with a way of life that
was no more.

George Bird Grinnell, a cofounder of the
Boone and Crockett Club, recalled years later an
incident on his first trip west in 1870, when he
met three beaver trappers encamped with their
Shoshone wives and children in buffalo-skin
lodges. Theirs was, he concluded, an ideal life:

All these men were dressed in the costume that pre-
vailed in the early days of plains travel. . . . Coats,
shirts, trousers, and moccasins were of soft tanned
buckskin, fringed along the seams, ornamented with
stained porcupine quills or with beads, and the coats
in some cases trimmed at cuffs and about the collar
with beaver fur. . . .

These men lived in just the fashion of the old-time
trappers of early western days. They possessed that
independence which all men seek. Theirs was everything that man needs—food, clothing, shelter, and

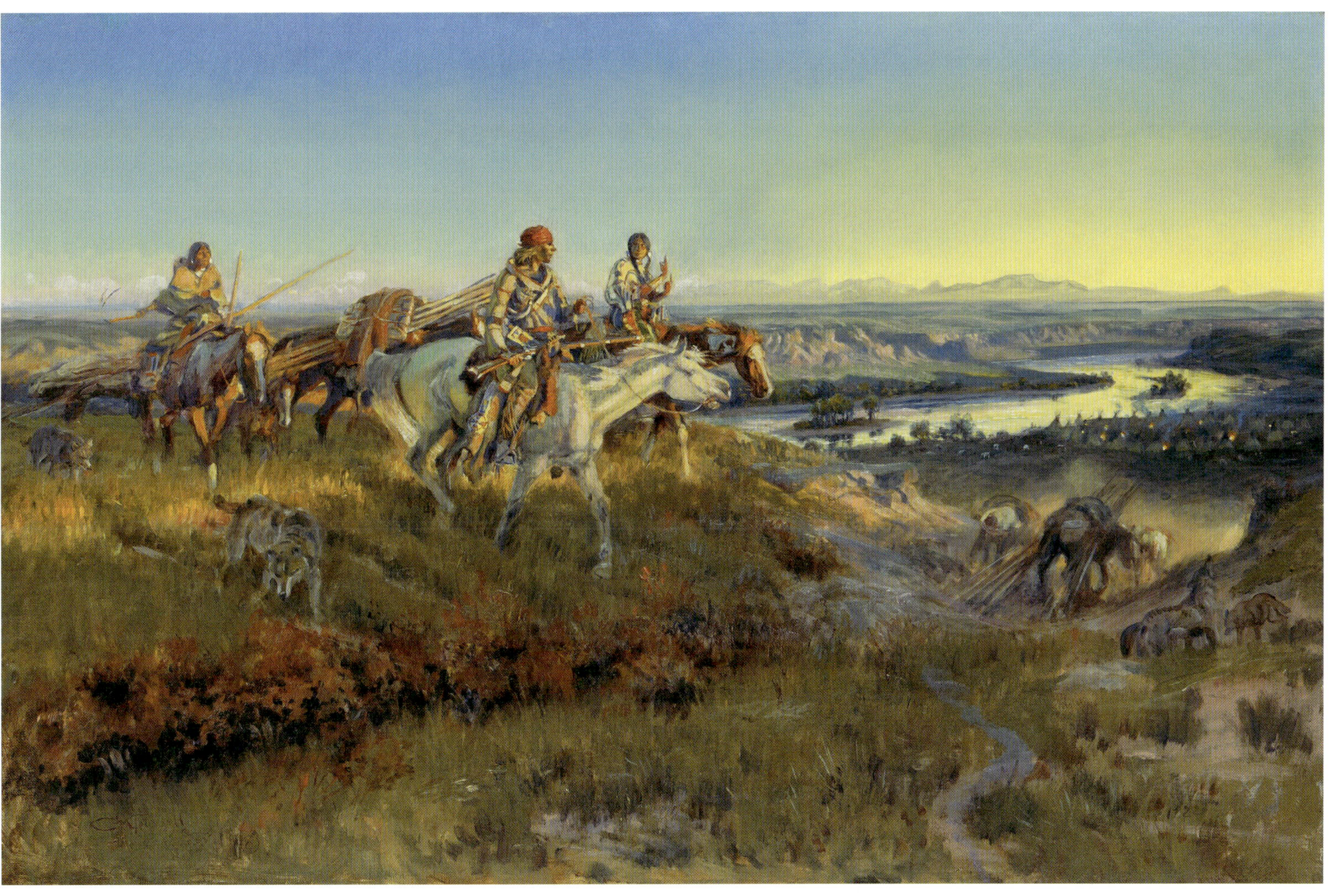

family. They were masters of their own lives. When they felt like it, they pulled down their lodges, packed their possessions on their animals, and moved away to another place which pleased them, and their home was there so long as they wished. . . . Their mode of life appealed strongly to a young man fond of the open, and while I was with them I could not imagine, nor can I imagine now, a more attractive—a happier—life than theirs.[53]

When White Men Turn Red captures these sentiments perfectly, giving visual form to the broad nostalgic streak in twentieth-century western art.

Helen Cody Wetmore titled an 1899 biography of her famous brother *Last of the Great Scouts*. It concluded with a fin-de-siècle flourish: "The story of frontier days is a tale that is told. The 'Wild West' has vanished like mist in the sun."[54] Cody's passing in 1917 brought an end to the day. Wetmore's biography was reprinted with a new afterword by Zane Grey, a "finishing touch to the story": "The sunset, the descending twilight, the sweet silence of the hills, the brightening star, the lonely darkness of the night—these things Buffalo Bill loved. And these he will have."[55] In death, the "Last of the Great Scouts" shared the same stage with the "Last of the Mohicans." Catlin's phantom had run out of room. Western dreams belonged to memory, and art that had once celebrated progress became a sustained elegy commemorating what used to be.

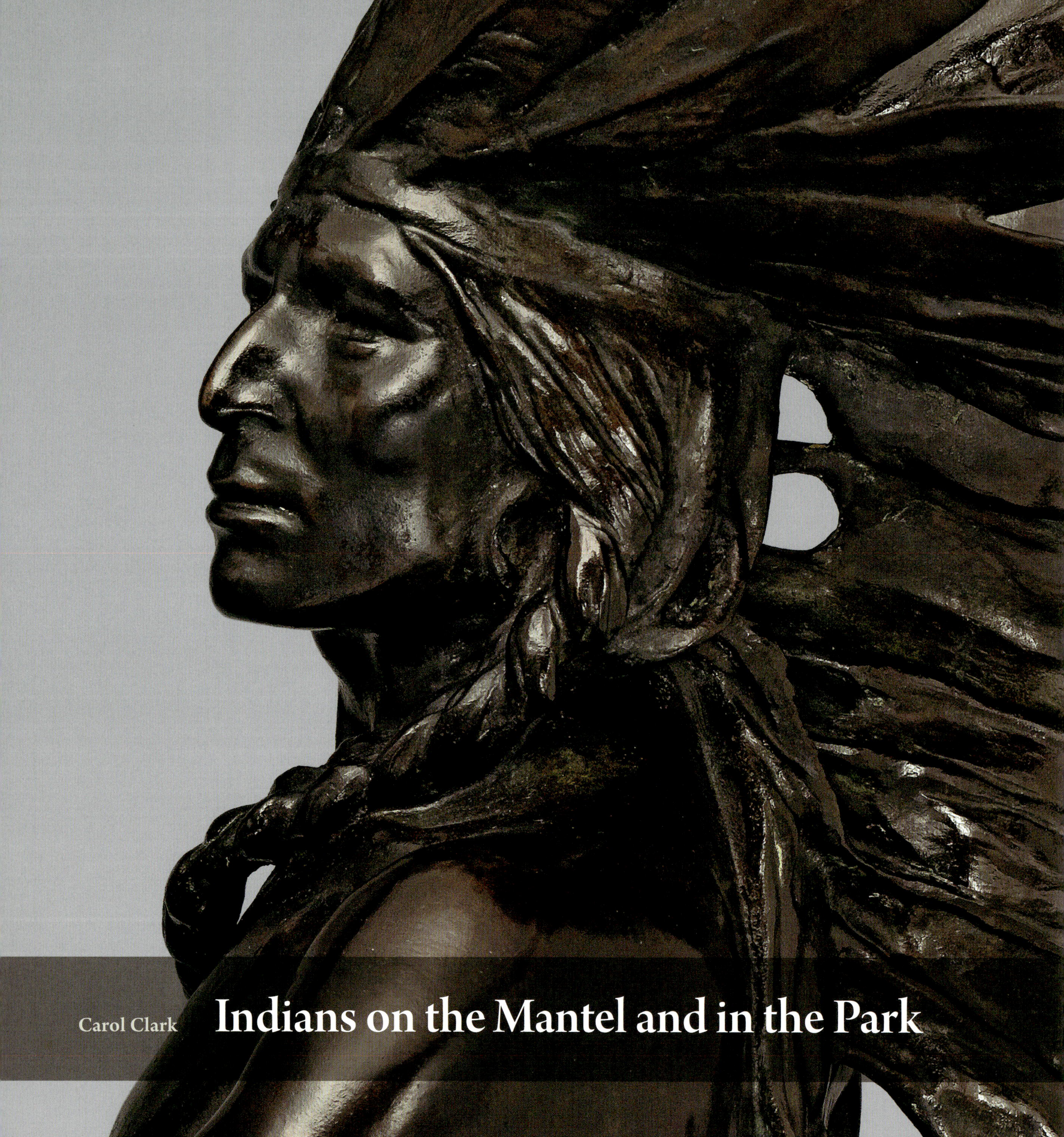

Carol Clark
Indians on the Mantel and in the Park

On a spring day in 1922, four men posed for a photograph in front of the Museum of Fine Arts, Boston (fig. 29). On horseback and dressed as traditional Plains Indians, the men look up at *Appeal to the Great Spirit*, Cyrus Edwin Dallin's lifesize statue of a mounted Indian. Nude but for a breechcloth, the bronze Indian wears a feather bonnet not unlike the head-dress of Chief Bald Eagle, the rider at far left, who along with the other "warriors" was likely in town to battle cowboys in a Wild West show being staged by the Dingling Brothers Circus.[1] The Indians' contract with the circus may have required this stop at the museum, where the sculpture had been installed a decade earlier. There, against the sight and sound of auto-mobiles and electric streetcars along Hunting-ton Avenue, was captured a scene that fixed Plains Indian horsemen, sculpted and live, as performers in a pageant of the American past.[2]

Telling "the history of the relations between white and red men" was Dallin's goal for his series of four monumental bronze sculp-tures of mounted Indians, first inspired by the Plains Indians he saw performing as "Show Indians" in 1889 at Buffalo Bill's Wild West in Paris.[3] The series ends with *Appeal to the Great Spirit*. Arms outstretched and head thrown back, Dallin's horseman turns his back on the world of the white man to entrust his future to an unseen spirit. A critic in 1909 dismissed Dallin's Indian as a member of a race soon to be "as extinct as the dodo or the mastodon."[4] Yet in 1922 there were Bald Eagle and his fellow performers, clustered around the bronze Indian at the museum's entrance. Later that year the photograph appeared in a brochure from P. P. Caproni and Brother, selling small plaster casts of *Appeal to the Great Spirit*. Touting the statu-ette as "suitable for educational institutions and homes,"[5] the brochure used the photograph to link Caproni's cast both to the civic authority of the museum that owned the monumental version and to the endorsement of "real" Show Indians. Sales of the statuettes underscore the popularity of Indian subjects in the first half of the twentieth century. Between 1916 and 1947 Gorham Co. Founders, which like Caproni sold reductions of the popular *Appeal to the Great Spirit*, cast about four hundred authorized bronze statuettes in three sizes (figs. 30, 214).[6]

"You haven't done a man. You've done a race," declared Augustus Saint-Gaudens of James Earle Fraser's *End of the Trail*.[7] "Doing a race" describes more than Fraser's 1918 statu-ette (fig. 61). The sculptures of Indian subjects that public and private patrons favored in the early twentieth century, as they had from the mid-nineteenth, usually depict representatives of a race set in an unspecified past, as Fraser had done. Indian men predominated among sculpted representations of Natives because, as William H. Truettner has argued, such images met "the need of elite white males to believe in the racial stock of ancient America, and to see that stock, in the form of heroic Plains Indi-ans, as a model for the present, regardless of the then-present condition of Plains Indians."[8] Sculptors who visited contemporary Indians on reservations, who met recently defeated warriors, or who watched Natives perform in Wild West shows chose to present Indian men in bronze not as they then lived but as first inhabitants of a land they were destined to

Fig. 28. Alexander Phimister Proctor, detail of *Indian Warrior*, 1898 (cast 1913 or after). Cat. 38

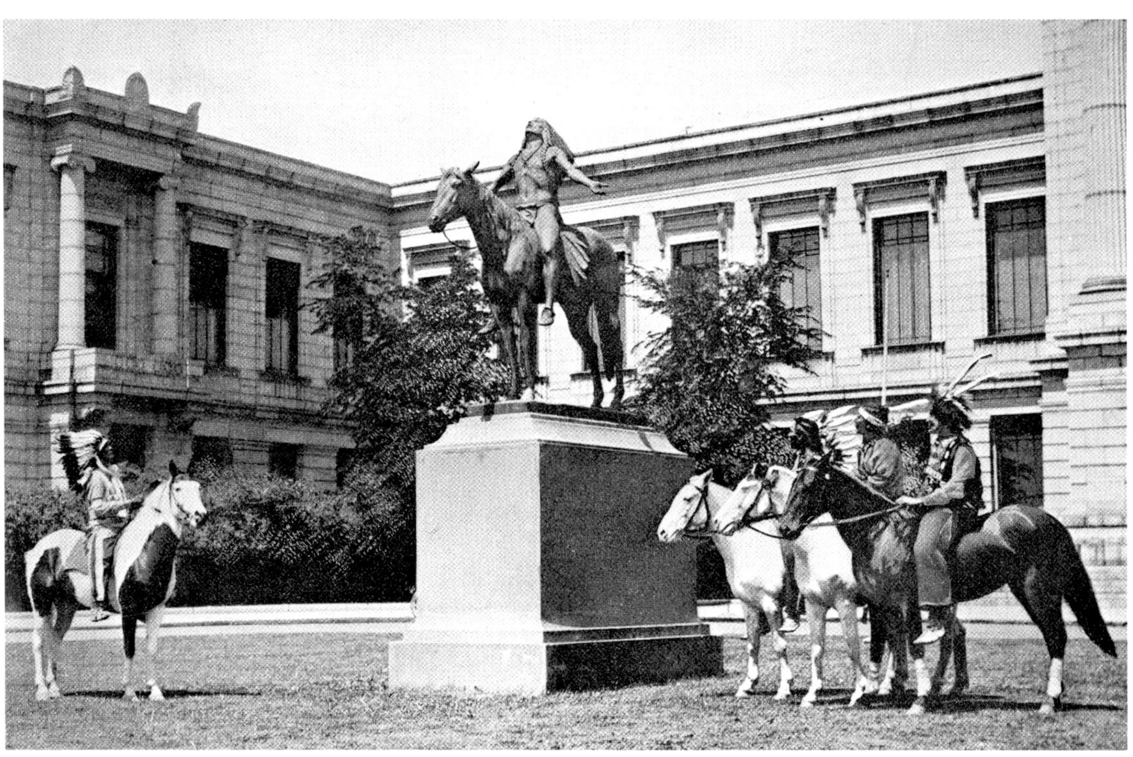

relinquish. Shown hunting, performing rituals, fighting, dying in battle, or otherwise surrendering to their fate, bronze Indians acquired a patina of nobility. By recovering the stories these sculptures projected within a web of contemporary white attitudes toward Indians and their histories, this essay explores the public and private possession of bronze Indians.[9]

The figure of an Indian was one of the first bronze sculptures to be cast in the United States. Seeking works of national subjects, the managers of the American Art-Union commissioned Henry Kirke Brown to create twenty statuettes of a figure "illustrative of Indian form and character"[10] for distribution to the organization's subscribers in 1849. Well suited to the project both philosophically and professionally, Brown believed that affordable editions of small bronzes would put sculpture within the reach of middle-class Americans, and he had already established a foundry in Brooklyn. In anticipation of the Art-Union commission, he spent the month of September 1848 on

Mackinac Island, studying Native people in Upper Michigan.[11]

Even though Brown believed that a successful sculpture of an Indian subject required firsthand observation, with *Choosing of the Arrow* (figs. 31, 32) he looked more to classical Italy than to Native America. This figure of a male youth in graceful contrapposto, reaching to draw an arrow from the quiver on his back, evokes ancient sculptures of Apollo, which Brown had seen during a four-year stay in Italy. It also affirms a well-established connection between North American Indians and classical sculpture, famously codified in Benjamin West's purported 1760 exclamation before the Apollo Belvedere (ca. 2nd century; Vatican Museums): "My God, how like it is to a young Mohawk warrior!"[12] While the pose of Brown's Indian aligns him with the god Apollo, his bow and arrow and his decorative topknot are Native as well as Apollonian.[13] The youthful hunter's ease, too, recalls the ancient world but also parallels the artist's admiration for "the freedom and independence of [Indians']

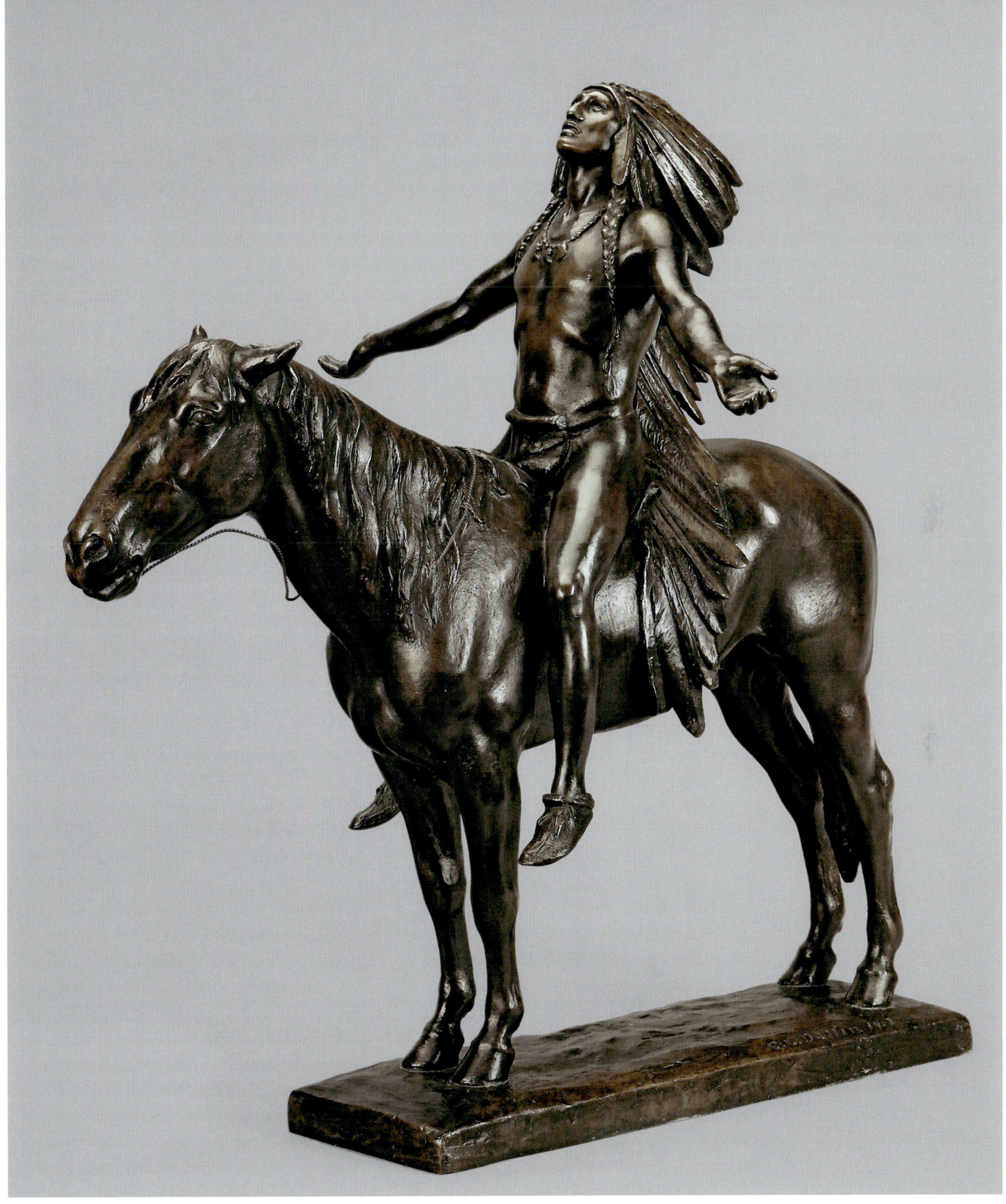

Fig. 30. Cyrus Edwin Dallin. *Appeal to the Great Spirit,* 1913 (cast ca. 1916). Cat. 18

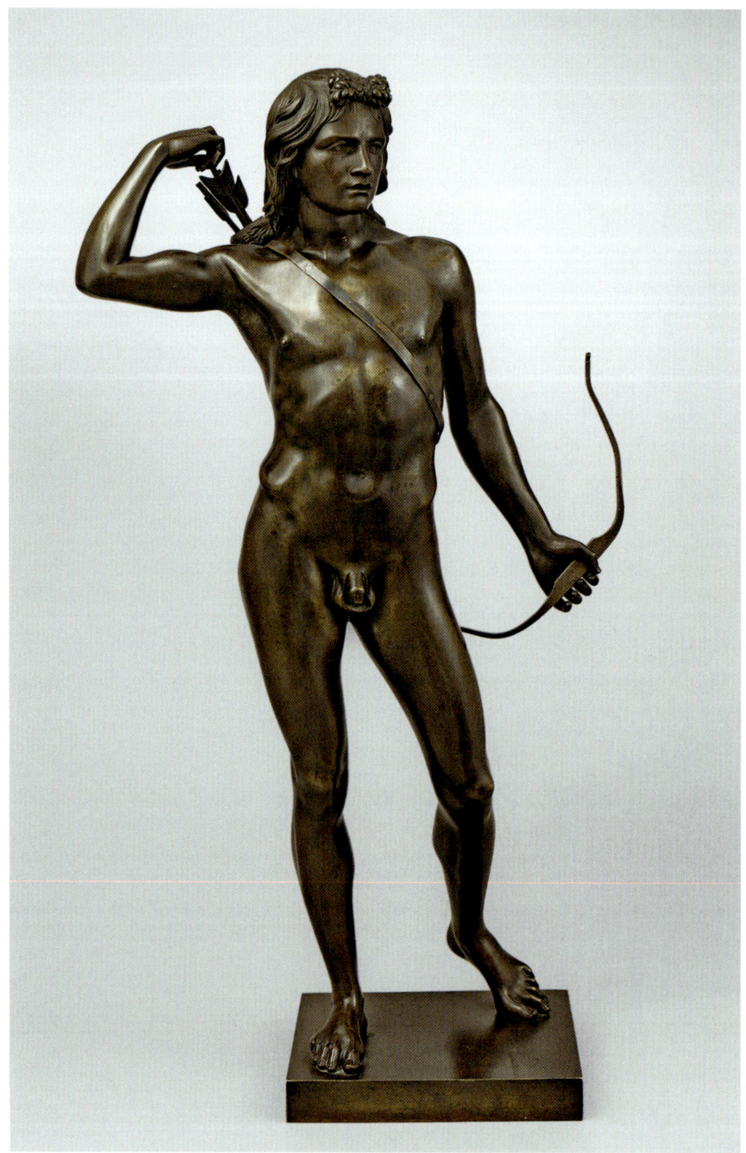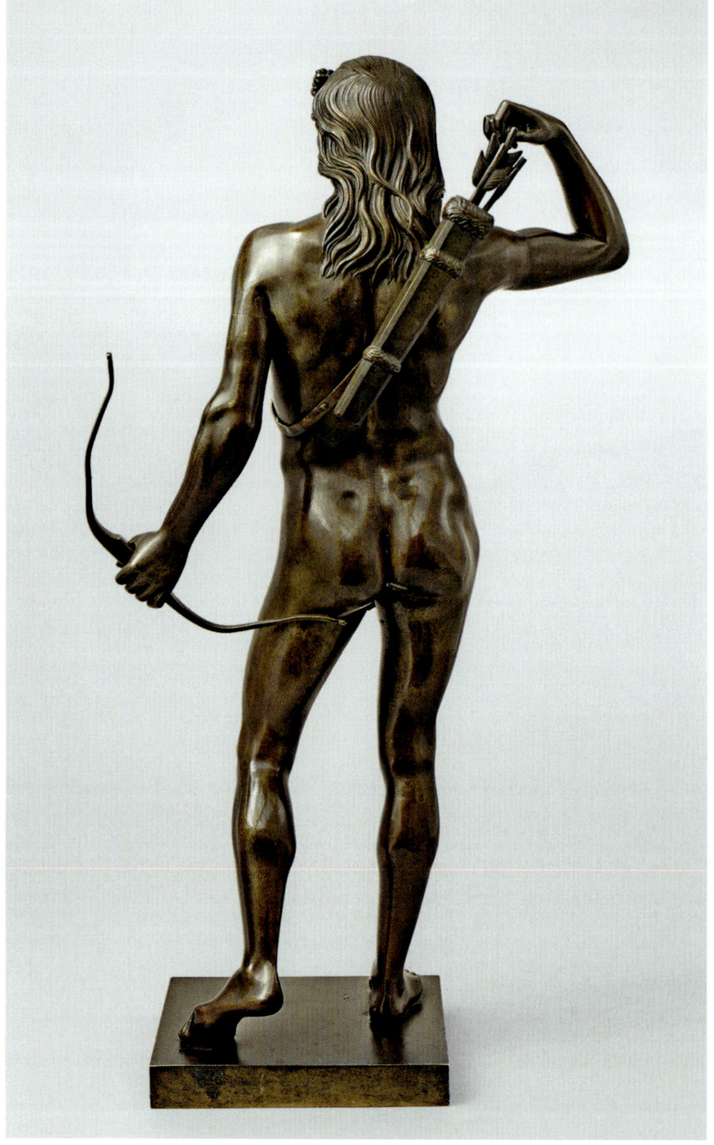

minds . . . closely allied to the freedom of nature." The ideal of freedom that Brown celebrated in his sculpture was not, however, the condition in which he found the Indians themselves. Those he met in Michigan, whom he regarded as "degraded" from their distinguished past,[14] had gathered there to collect payments from the United States government.

The artistic heritage and general popularity of *Choosing of the Arrow* did not shield it from controversy. A visitor to the Art-Union's New York galleries judged the statuette improper for women's eyes. In an open letter published in the *Providence Journal*, he mused that the "entirely nude" sculpture might "do well enough . . . in a gentleman's private library, or on the mantle piece of a bachelor; but imagine a beautiful young lady drawing such a thing as this."[15] The statuette might have discomfited viewers not only because the subject, a male nude, was rare in American art. The sculpture's striking naturalism, especially the color of the bronze, also summoned thoughts of the man's race. A writer for the *Home Journal* observed: "The bronze is so near to the natural copper of the skin, that there is nothing to modify the complete disgust with which its undisguised nakedness must be looked upon." The "movable tin-foil fig-leaf" that the Art-Union added to each cast at the time of distribution did little to satisfy the critics.[16]

No such qualms greeted *The Indian Hunter* (fig. 33), with a bison robe modestly wrapped around the figure's waist, when John Quincy Adams Ward exhibited it a decade later. Although the sculpture recalls sources from the antique—notably the Louvre's marble Borghese Gladiator (3rd–1st century B.C.), a reduced plaster cast of which Ward had in his studio—to contemporary viewers, the face of Ward's hunter was "subdued to no fancied requirement of the classic ideal."[17] The critic for the *New York Times* called the hunter a "wild 'varmint' of the woods, . . . himself

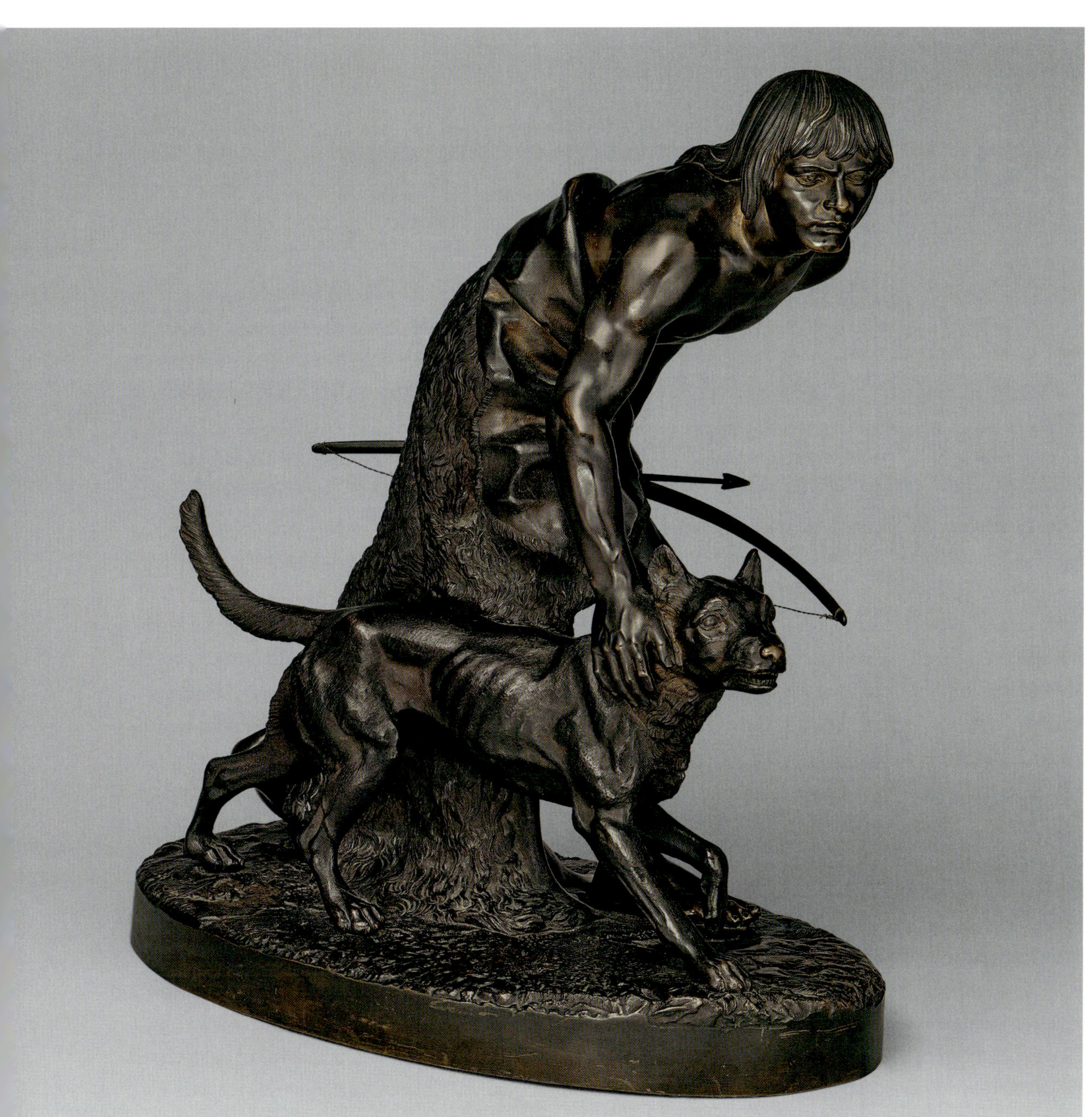

Fig. 33. John Quincy Adams Ward. *The Indian Hunter*, 1860. Cat. 75

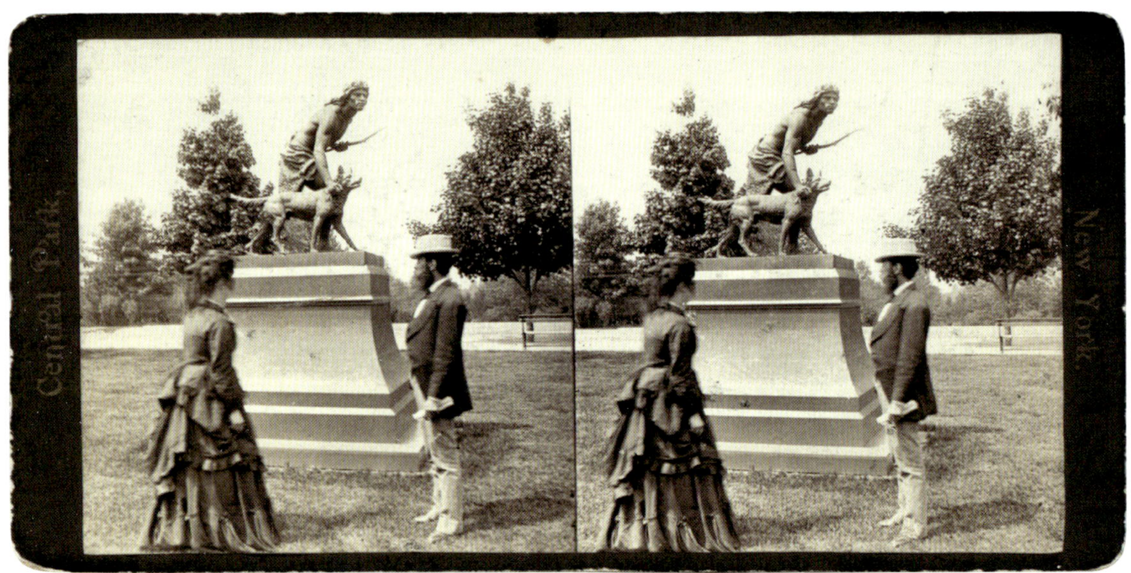

Fig. 34. John Quincy
Adams Ward. *The Indian
Hunter*, 1866 (dedicated
1869), Central Park,
New York. Stereograph,
ca. 1875

an animal fierce and instinctive as the dog by
his side."[18] The statuette's extraordinary surface treatment in the trailing fur robe and the
dog's curly ruff visually links man and beast.
Ward's construction of a pair who move in
concert—the man's body bent forward, right
arm reaching down to restrain the hungry animal—counters the elegant stance of Brown's
Choosing of the Arrow in favor of a tense narrative of hunting an unseen prey.

The *Indian Hunter* statuette, with leaves
scattered on its base, achieved its implied place
in nature when a monumental version was
dedicated on the Mall in Central Park in 1869
(fig. 34). Before undertaking that version, Ward
traveled to Dakota Territory in 1864 to study
Indians in the West, after which he transformed
the small pair into a tighter composition of a
more mature hunter with a fiercer dog; there is
greater determination on a face more phenotypically Native than that of the statuette. Recognizing that the "bison skin cannot stay where
it is if there is hard running to follow," one critic
would have been "glad to have had this statue"
of a man "whose daily work is done unclothed"
be "entirely undraped."[19] Would nudity have
been more suitable in the park than on the
mantel? And would an encounter with *The*

Indian Hunter be more authentic out of doors?
Despite the popularity of the domestic-scale
statuette, which Ward continued to cast until
his death in 1910, the sculptor and historian
Lorado Taft in 1903 judged the outdoor setting
of the lifesize sculpture to be superior because
in a museum "one might wonder whether this
is a real Indian." In the park he is "a sudden
apparition, low-bent among the foliage. His
copper glow, his preoccupation, his silence,
make the illusion complete. It is a glimpse of a
forgotten past."[20]

An Indian hunter was also Theodore
Baur's subject for a commission from the Meriden Britannia Company to model a statuette
for the Centennial Exhibition in Philadelphia in 1876 (fig. 35). But Baur's Indian, unlike
Ward's, engages his prey—a charging bison
bull—from the back of a terrified mount. Baur
had likely seen Indian ethnographic material at
the American Museum of Natural History in
New York and bison at the nearby Central Park
Menagerie;[21] he may also have known earlier
paintings and illustrations of the hunt, such as
those by George Catlin. Whatever knowledge
Baur brought to the commission, contemporary circumstances extended the sculpture's
reach to encompass the decimation of the

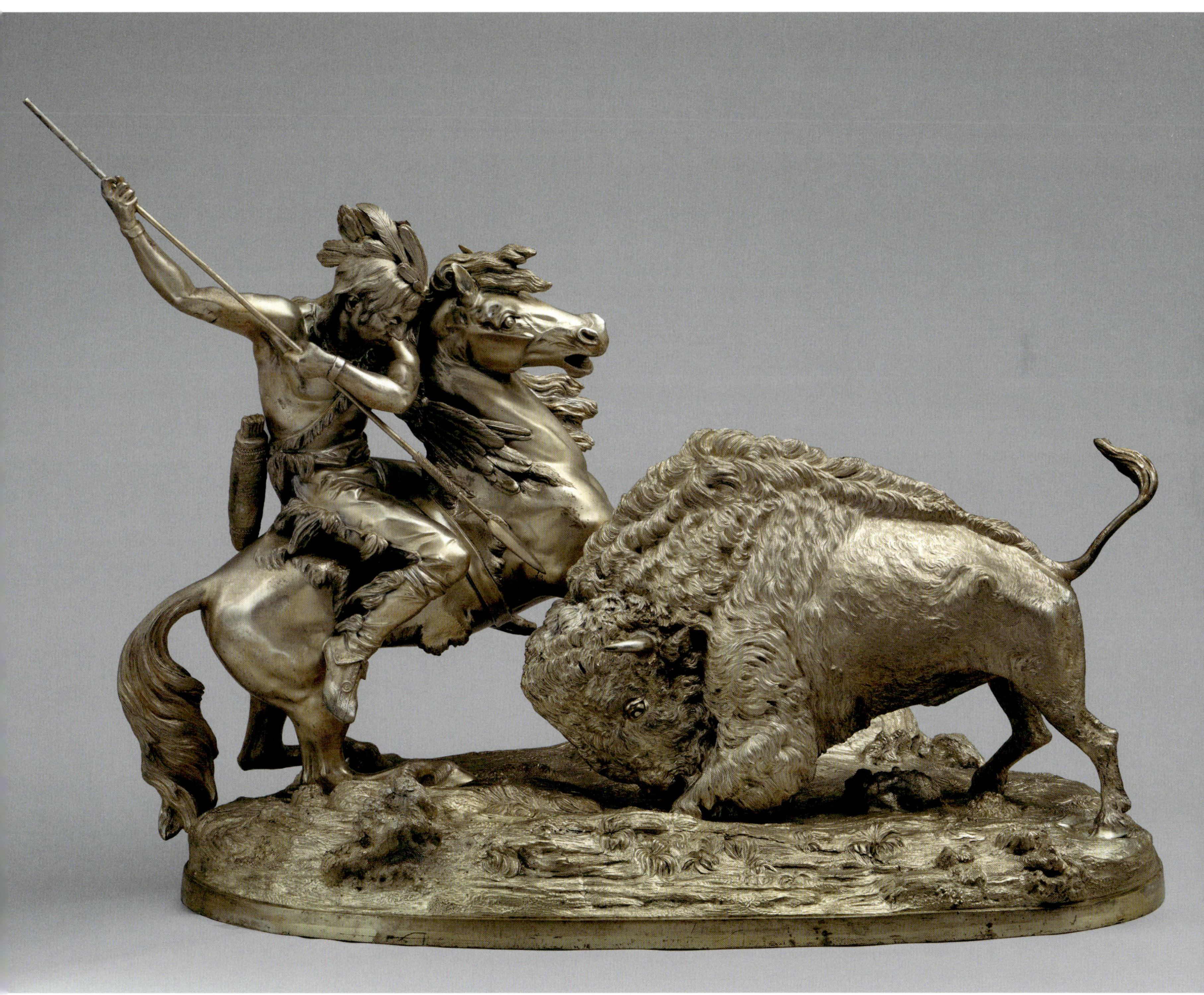

Fig. 35. Theodore Baur. *The Buffalo Hunt*, 1876 (cast ca. 1876–86). Cat. 2

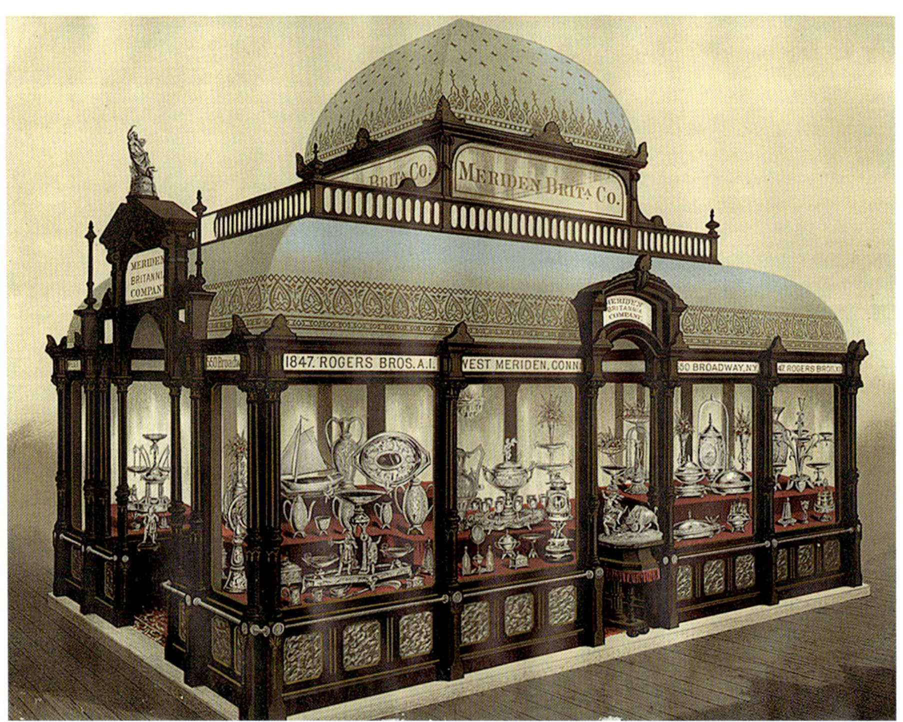

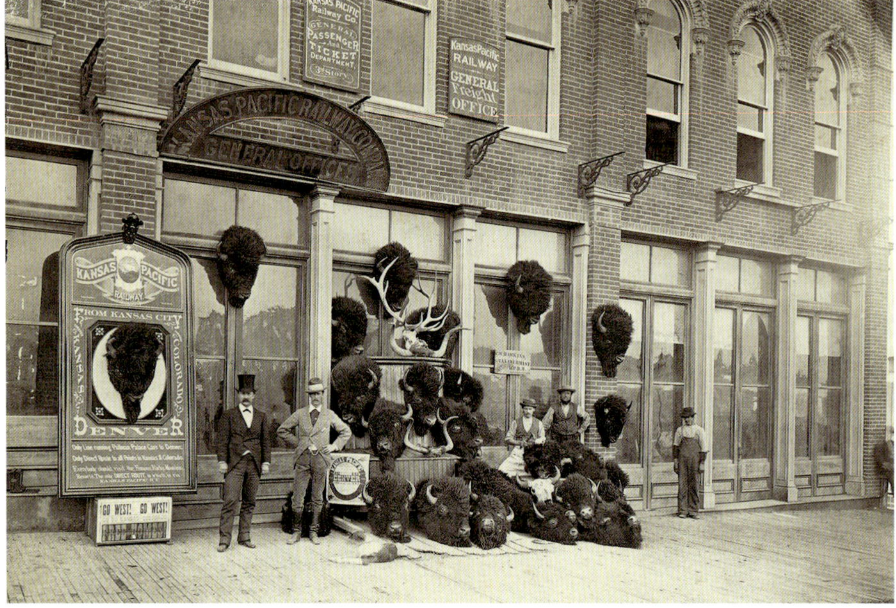

Fig. 36. Meriden Britannia Company display, including Theodore Baur's *Buffalo Hunt*, Centennial Exhibition, Philadelphia, 1876

Fig. 37. *On the Kansas Pacific Railway*, ca. 1869. Photograph by Robert Benecke

bison. A writer who noticed *The Buffalo Hunt* among other decorative wares at the Centennial (fig. 36) distinguished Baur's one-on-one hunt from the current practice, "when brutes are slaughtered by hundreds for mere sport."[22] Fairgoers, likely familiar with images of indiscriminately slaughtered bison (fig. 37), might have valued what they imagined was the hunt's more honorable history; as the centennial critic wrote, the "equality in such a contest . . . makes the group one of thrilling interest."[23]

Violent resistance is the theme of *The Last Arrow*, of 1879–80, created in Rome by the expatriate sculptor Randolph Rogers (fig. 38). Twisting on his rearing horse, one Indian has just released an arrow from his still-taut bow.

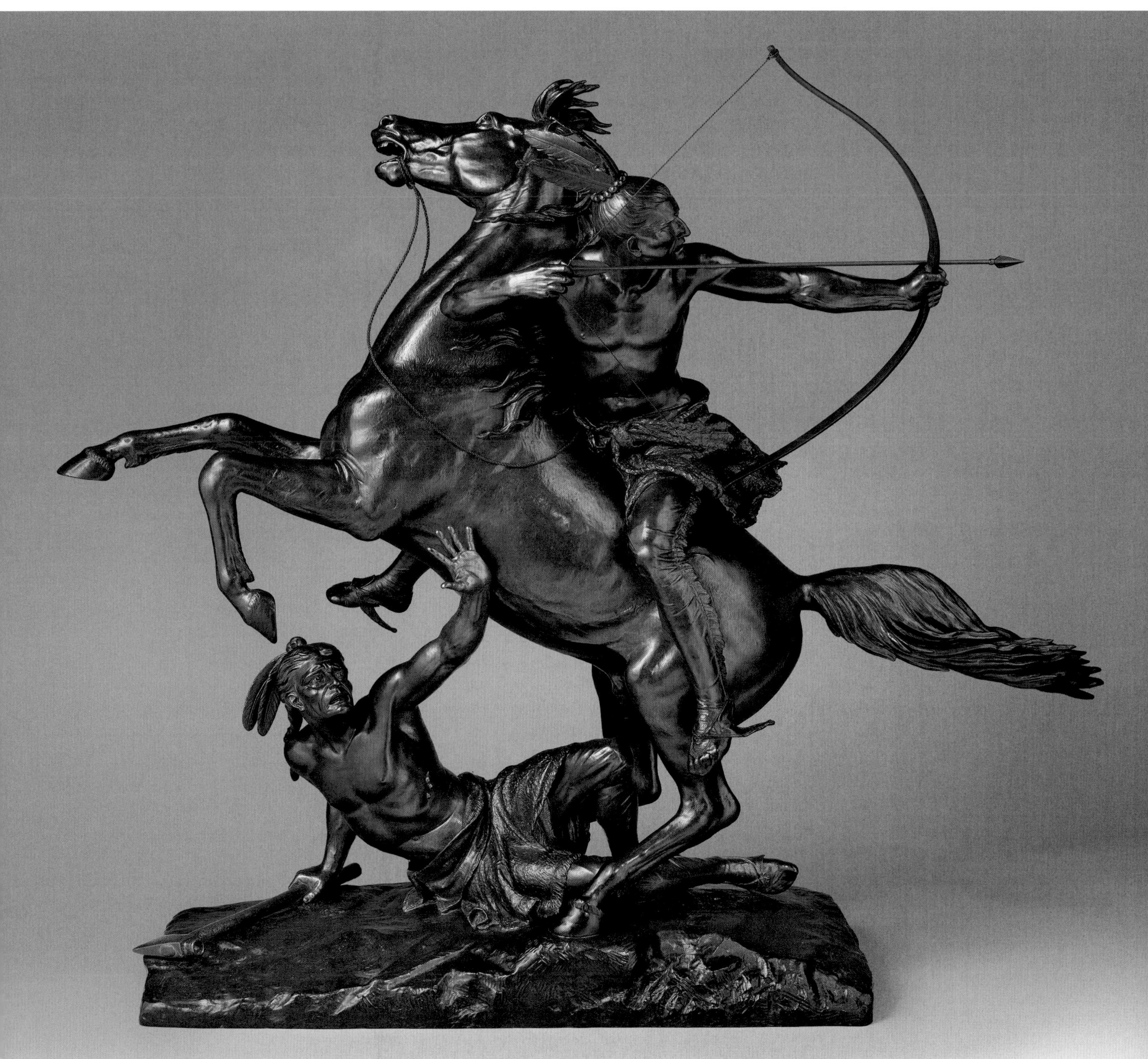

Fig. 38. Randolph Rogers. *The Last Arrow*, 1879–80 (cast 1880). Cat. 57

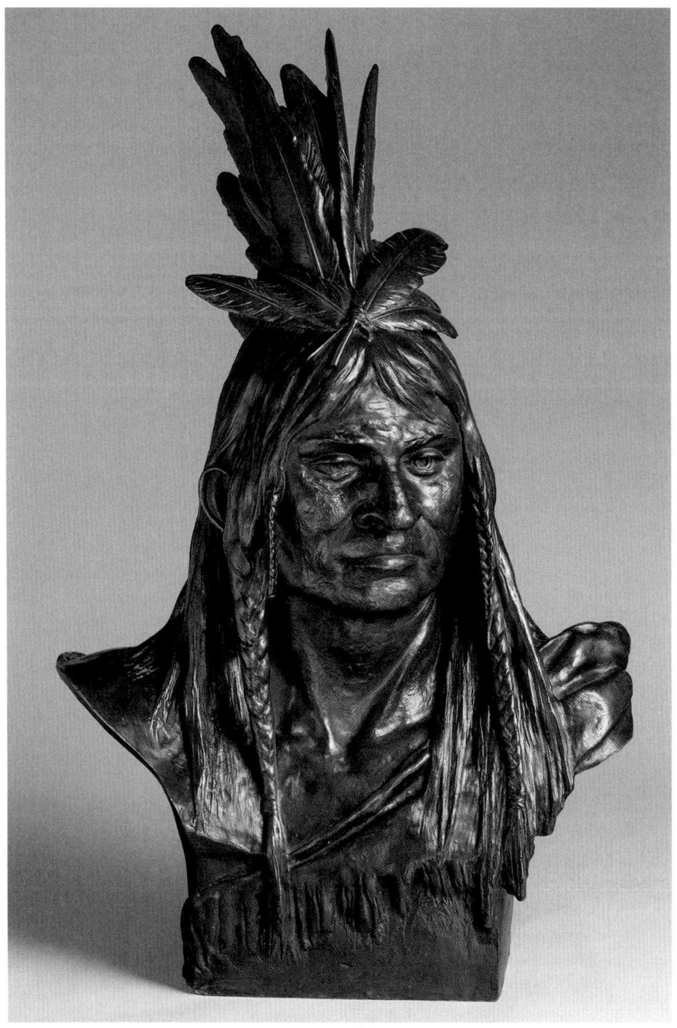

would have been valued by a collector of this imposing work.

"Full of character" was one way the critic Montague Marks described Theodore Baur's *Indian Chief* of 1885 (fig. 39). In this rare contemporary mention of the bust, Marks did not call attention to the tall feather headdress and long locks of braided hair that would have immediately identified the subject as an Indian to contemporary viewers. Instead, the critic focused on the man's phenotypically Native features — "high cheek bones, heavy jaw, dilated nostrils," to which he added "and cruel mouth." Marks's analysis points to an uneasiness about the portrayal that contemporary viewers might have shared. The "admirable" bust showed a man whose face was a "personification of brute courage, combined with savage cunning."[26]

Baur's bust, which may possibly have been modeled after Sitting Bull, is generic enough to have later carried the alternate title *Crazy Horse*.[27] No such confusion surrounds the identity of *Joseph, Chief of the Nez Percé Indians*, Olin Levi Warner's naturalistic relief from 1889 (fig. 40). That year Warner's patron Charles Erskine Scott Wood introduced him to Joseph in Portland, Oregon. The Nez Percé chief was

Fig. 39. Theodore Baur. *Indian Chief*, 1885. Cat. 3

Fig. 40. Olin Levi Warner. *Joseph, Chief of the Nez Percé Indians*, 1889 (cast 1906). Cat. 77

He protects his comrade who, unable to use the battle-ax in his hand, faces multiple dangers. Unlike the antique Dying Gaul (Roman copy after Greek original of ca. 230–220 B.C.; Capitoline Museum, Rome), which inspired Rogers,[24] the downed man here raises a hand against his enemy. Rogers's narrative could be read as a hopeless fight against white dominance, but close looking reveals another story. An early plaster cast for this work included an arrow through the fallen man's torso; the wound remains visible in the bronze.[25] Rogers's group, then, once told a tale of intertribal warfare. Whether *The Last Arrow* implies an Indian or a white foe, the narrative projects the end of the warriors' race. Yet in their last stand, Rogers's Indians display courage, a character trait that

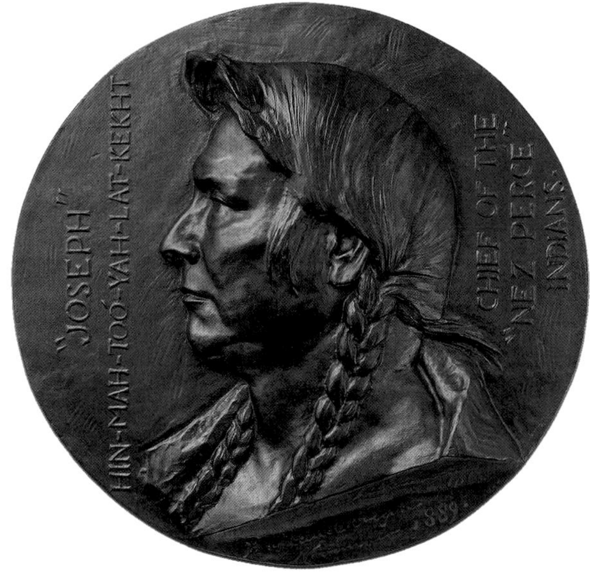

living nearby, on the Colville Reservation in Washington, having surrendered to the U.S. government in 1877 after a courageous attempt to retreat to Canada.[28] Warner's inscriptions on the medallion indicate Joseph's Native name, Hin·mah·toó·yah·lat·kekht; his Anglo name; and his French-imposed tribal affiliation. One contemporary writer described Joseph as a hybrid "possess[ing] many of the peculiarities of the savage," yet also "a very high type of Indian as regards brains and courage." "Were it not for the broad plaits of hair and absence of beard, . . ." this writer continued, "the face might be that of a European."[29] Courage, even to this sympathetic observer, was a white trait.

By the late nineteenth century, American sculptors were exhibiting works abroad with Indian subjects already familiar to British and European audiences from seeing Show Indians in performances from George Catlin's troupe in the 1840s to Buffalo Bill's Wild West beginning in 1887. In Paris to study at the Académie Julian, Gutzon Borglum exhibited his first sculpture, *Fallen Warrior (Death of the Chief)* (fig. 41), at the 1891 Champ-de-Mars Salon.[30] It shows the Indian's lifeless hand still clutching the hide

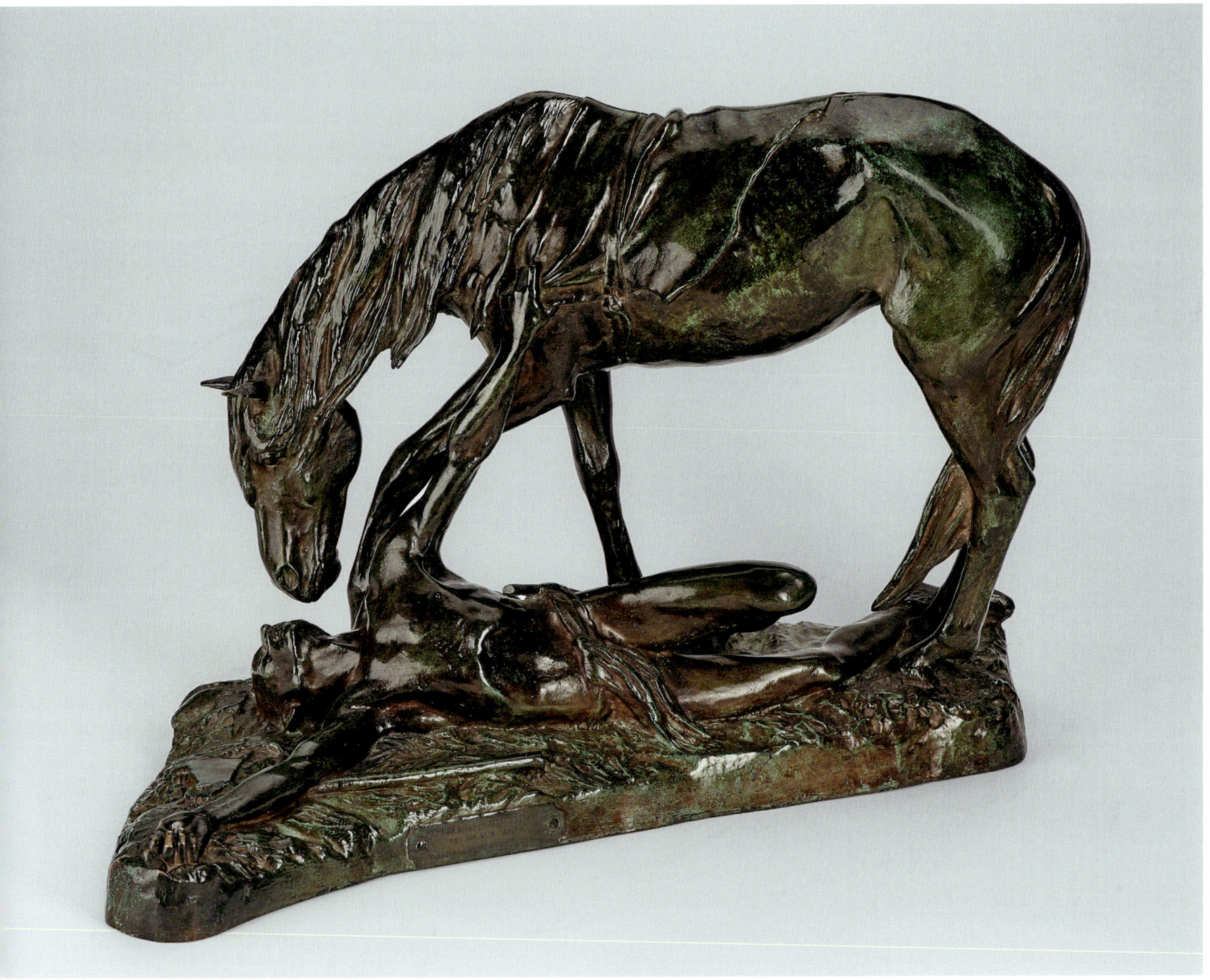

Fig. 41. Gutzon Borglum. *Fallen Warrior (Death of the Chief)*, ca. 1891. Cat. 4

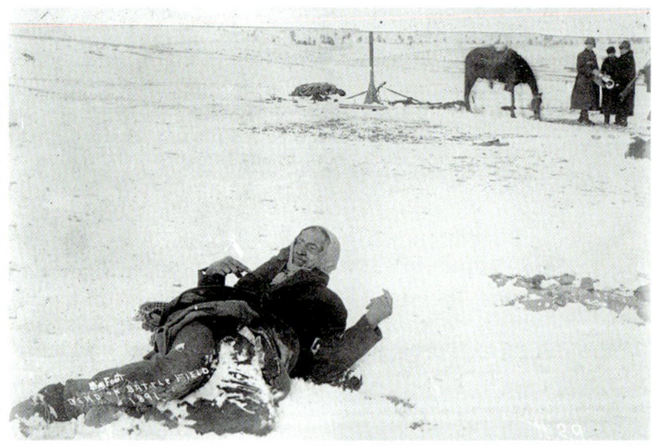

Fig. 42. *Big Foot, Dead in the Snow*, 1890. Photograph by Northwestern Photographic Company

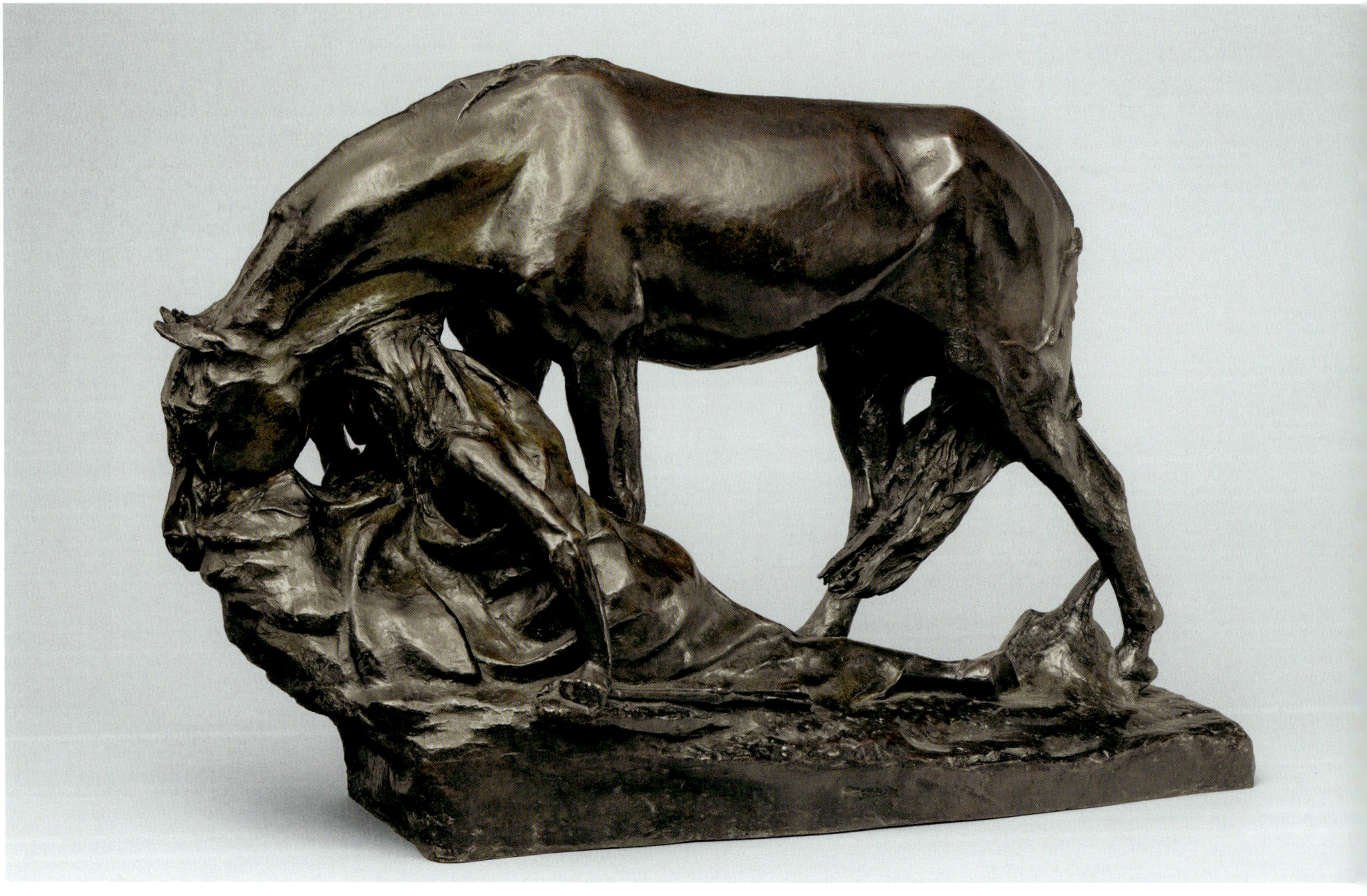

Fig. 43. Solon Hannibal Borglum. *On the Border of the White Man's Land*, 1899 (cast 1906–7). Cat. 6

blanket cinched to his skeletal horse, which bends its head in what seems to be anthropomorphic mourning. The now-useless battle-ax by his right arm reinforces his identity as a fallen warrior. Soon after the U.S. Army's massacre of the Sioux on the Pine Ridge Reservation near Wounded Knee Creek, South Dakota, on December 29, 1890, photographs of dead Indians spread quickly in the press and were widely marketed.[31] The conjunction of *Fallen Warrior* with contemporaneous images of the frozen body of the Miniconjous leader Big Foot, propped up for a photographer on a South Dakota field (fig. 42), brings the statuette into a visual culture of dead Indians at the conclusion of the Plains Wars, which had assured the nation's dominance over the land and over Indians on the Great Plains.

On the Crow Creek Reservation in South Dakota in the summer of 1899, Solon Hannibal Borglum, Gutzon's younger brother, began to model a subject new to him: the Indian. Shown in plaster at the American pavilion of the 1900 Exposition Universelle in Paris and later cast as

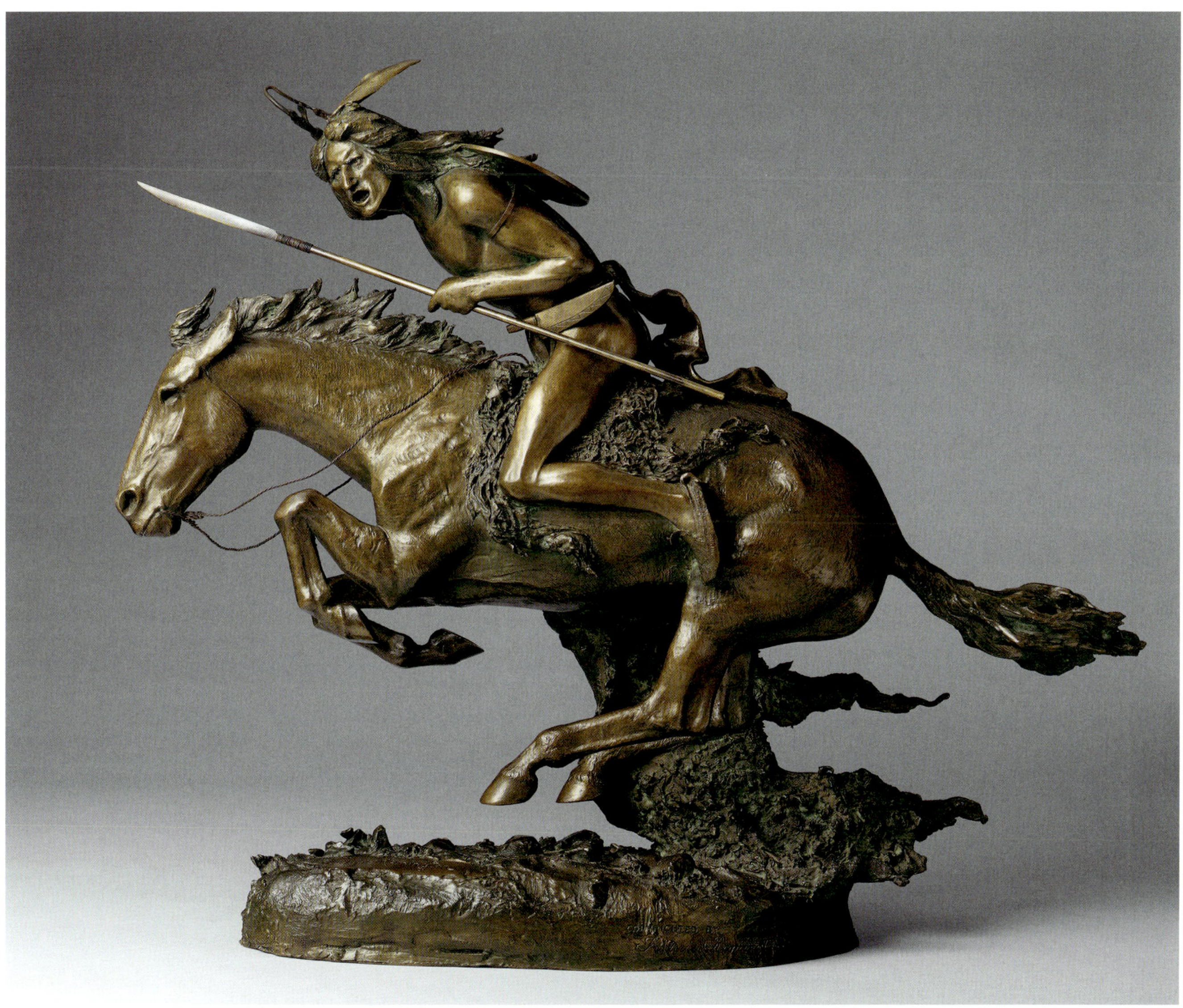

Fig. 44. Frederic Remington. *The Cheyenne*, 1901 (cast by 1903). Cat. 54

a statuette (fig. 43), *On the Border of the White Man's Land*, like Gutzon's *Fallen Warrior*, shows a man in close connection with a horse above him. In Solon's work, the horse bends its neck to conceal the prone Indian, who, raising his upper body on his left arm and grasping a rifle with his left hand, frees his right hand to part the horse's mane so he can peer into the distance. The sculpture implicates viewers in its narrative by transforming them from partners when standing behind the Indian to potential targets when in his gaze.

The narratives spun around *On the Border of the White Man's Land* are telling in their contradictions. The first, published in 1899, claims that the artist made it after "listening to the stories of [the] past and wilder life" of the Sioux he met at Crow Creek. According to this version, the subject is Black Eagle, who had scouted for George Armstrong Custer against neighboring "wild" Indians.[32] A second version, published in 1902, describes the Indian as "looking down at an emigrant train or paleface settlement."[33] In another, similar interpretation, the Indian "spies upon those whom he regards as his worst enemies, the white men."[34] In each of these narratives an underlying theme is stealth; one critic described

Fig. 45. "The Snake Dance of the Moqui Indians," *Harper's Weekly*, November 2, 1889

the man's barely visible face as "peculiarly an Indian one, crafty, observant and resolute."[35] The authors of all three narratives appear to have interviewed Borglum, so the sculptor may have been equally comfortable with having his work read as showing the Indian to be "good" (a former scout for Custer) or "bad" (a scout for fellow Indians who attacked white families moving west).

On the Border of the White Man's Land presents an Indian hidden from view at the turn of the twentieth century, in keeping with government policies and mainstream attitudes toward contemporary Indians.[36] In contrast, Frederic Remington's *Cheyenne* (fig. 44), made two years later, presents a historical image of a highly visible defiant warrior on a pony, a sculpture that Remington described as "burning the air."[37] His patrons admired the statuette's tour de force modeling, the extraordinary casting in which a draped bison robe supports the flying horse, and the patination and chasing that animate the tactile surface. The animal moves as swiftly and as confidently as its rider, who tilts forward at the waist, gripping his mount with muscular buttocks, thighs, and calves. Mouth open in a cry that distorts his face, one hand holding a lance, the other clenching a quirt, with a shield on his back and knife at his waist, the man exudes power. But against whom does he ride into battle—enemies from another tribe or soldiers of the U.S. Army? Whoever the foe, by the time Remington's sculpture was made in 1901, it presented a vision from the past.

The title *The Cheyenne* identified the subject as a member of a tribe that Remington had briefly visited, reported on, and even featured in a novel. In this way he claimed knowledge of his subject, yet his sculpted warrior bore little resemblance to the contemporary Cheyenne he had observed on the reservation in Indian Territory in 1888—horsemen who chased and shot cattle rationed to them by the

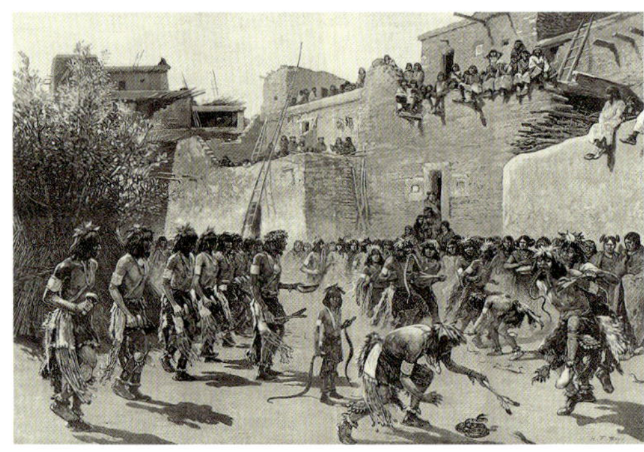

U.S. government.[38] The performance embodied in Remington's sculpture is closer to the skirmishes he watched being reenacted in Buffalo Bill's Wild West. The idea that Indian violence could be admired once it was comfortably in the past is expressed in a story Remington published in 1899 about an army clash with Sioux and Cheyenne in 1868: "There was a nobility of purpose about their resistance which commends itself now that it is passed."[39]

The illusion of speed—of "burning the air"—can also be seen in Hermon Atkins MacNeil's *Moqui Prayer for Rain* of 1895–96 (fig. 46). By 1895 ethnographers and tourists had published illustrated descriptions of the Snake Dance at the Hopi (or Moqui) pueblos in Arizona Territory (fig. 45). Hamlin Garland recounted in *Harper's Weekly* the experience that he and MacNeil shared in August 1895 when they witnessed the dramatic ceremony, which took place over several days. Hopi efforts to bring rain to the arid region included pleading with snakes they believed could carry their message to the gods. After bringing snakes up to the mesa and dancing with them in their mouths to communicate the need for rain, Hopi men of the Snake and Antelope fraternities concluded the ceremony by running down from the mesa.[40] In Rome a few months later, MacNeil isolated a single figure from those he had observed at the ritual's culmination. The result was a statuette of a lone runner returning snakes to their home on the plains.

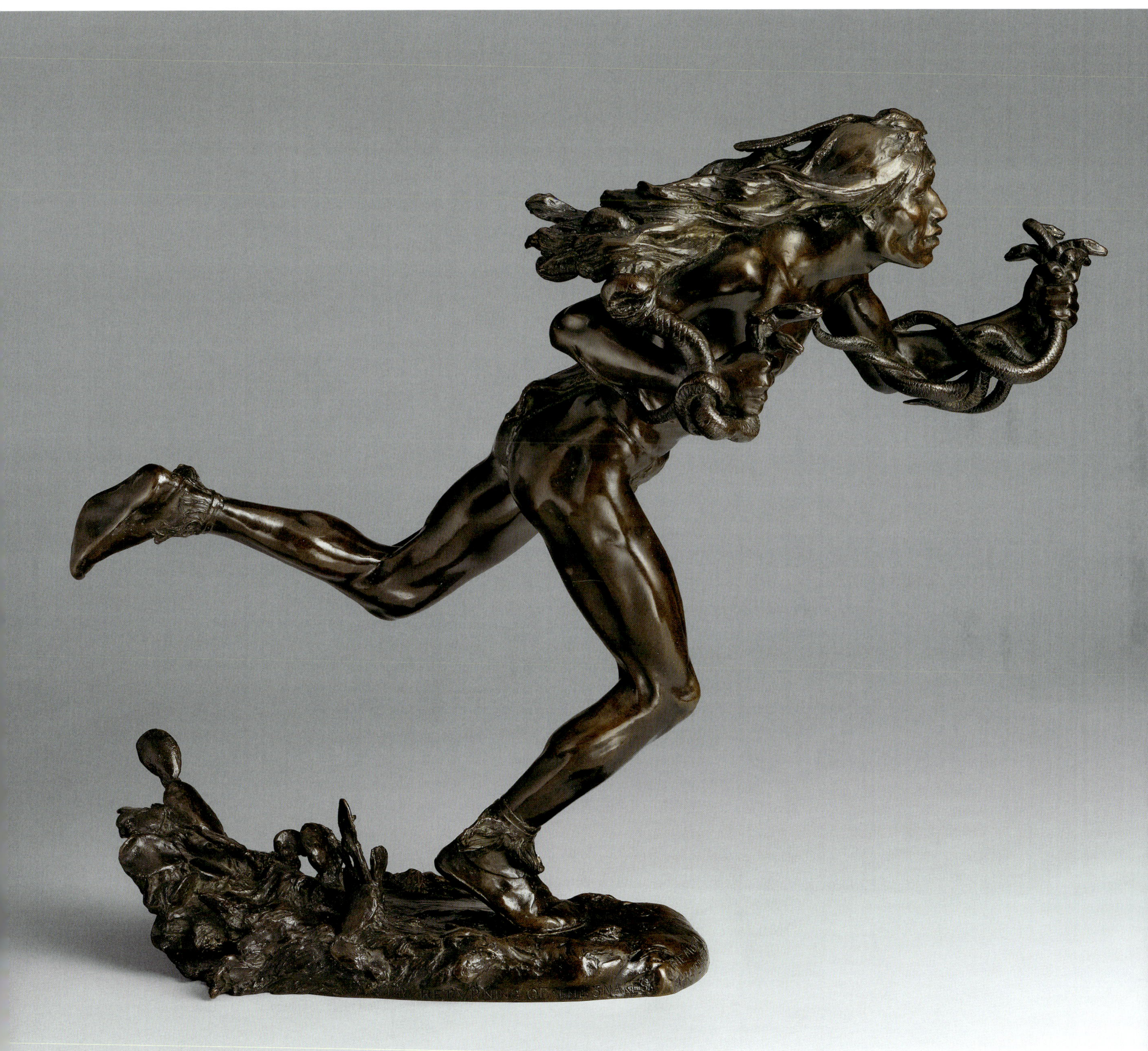

Fig. 46. Hermon Atkins MacNeil. *The Moqui Prayer for Rain*, 1895–96 (cast ca. 1897). Cat. 28

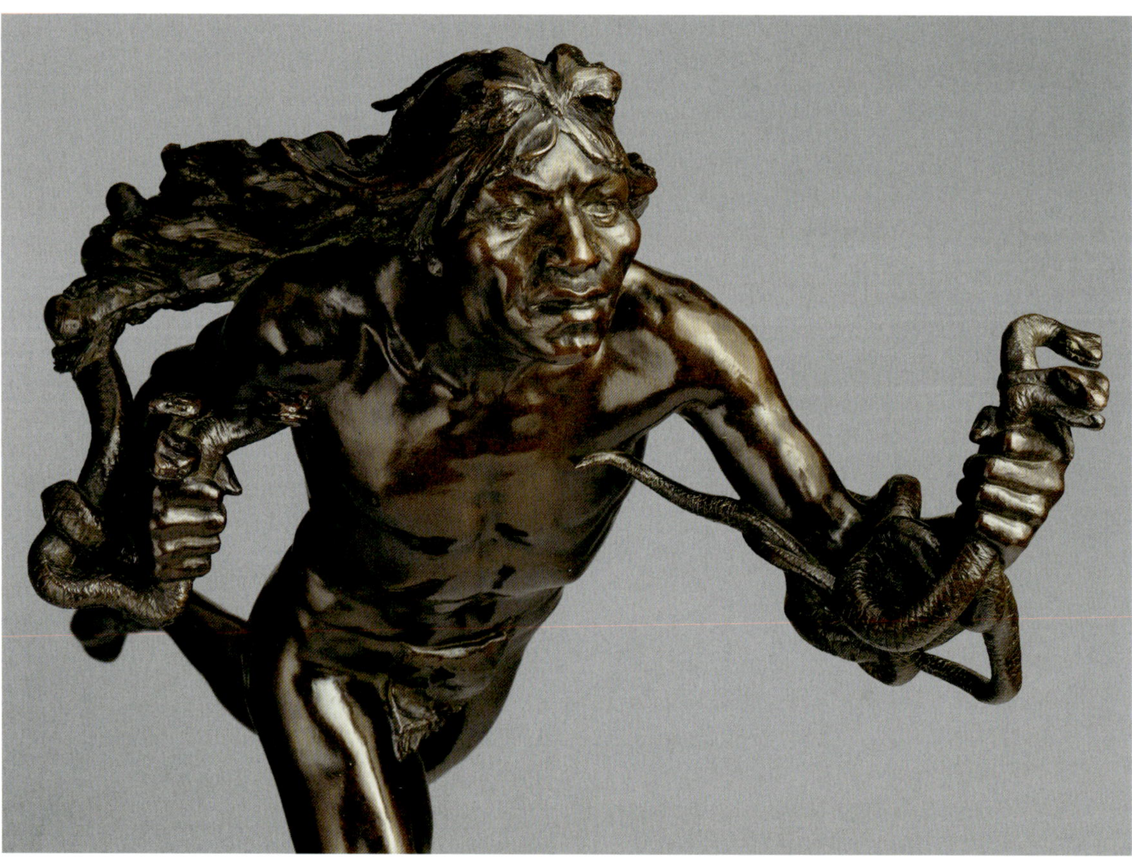

MacNeil's choice of subject was different from contemporary illustrators who emphasized in their captions the "weird" and "hideous" practice of men dancing with venomous snakes dangling from their mouths.[41] Instead, the snakes in *The Moqui Prayer for Rain* are subordinate to the drama of a runner captured midstride, supported only on the ball of one foot. A viewer's eye moves from admiring the silhouette of this dynamic figure to noticing the snakes that coil around his arms and into his thick hair, which is held aloft by the wind his running generates (fig. 47). MacNeil's combination of swift runner and exotic snake ceremony proved successful. The subject caught the attention of the artist's acquaintance Edward E. Ayer, a Chicago lumber magnate and voracious collector of Indian trade and ceremonial objects, who visited MacNeil's Rome studio in 1896 and underwrote the cost of casting the statuette at the Nelli foundry.[42]

In 1899 MacNeil chose another Indian ritual as his subject, but instead of the exotic drama of *The Moqui Prayer for Rain*, the ritual he chose—coming of age—was one his white audience could relate to their own lives. The lifesize bronze *The Sun Vow* (fig. 48) capped off his stay in Rome. Reworking his small model from 1894 called *The Vow of Vengeance* (fig. 49), MacNeil changed the theme from retribution to generational passage. He repositioned the feather bonnet, for example, from the old man's head to his lap, as if the elder were ready to transfer power to the successful young archer. The subject, as MacNeil described it, was a Sioux legend "picked up" during his 1895 summer in the West: if a young man demonstrated his skill to the chief by shooting an arrow so high that it momentarily disappeared into the sun's rays, he would become a warrior of his tribe.[43]

MacNeil later identified his subject as "the contrast of *closing* age + *opening* youth,"[44] and

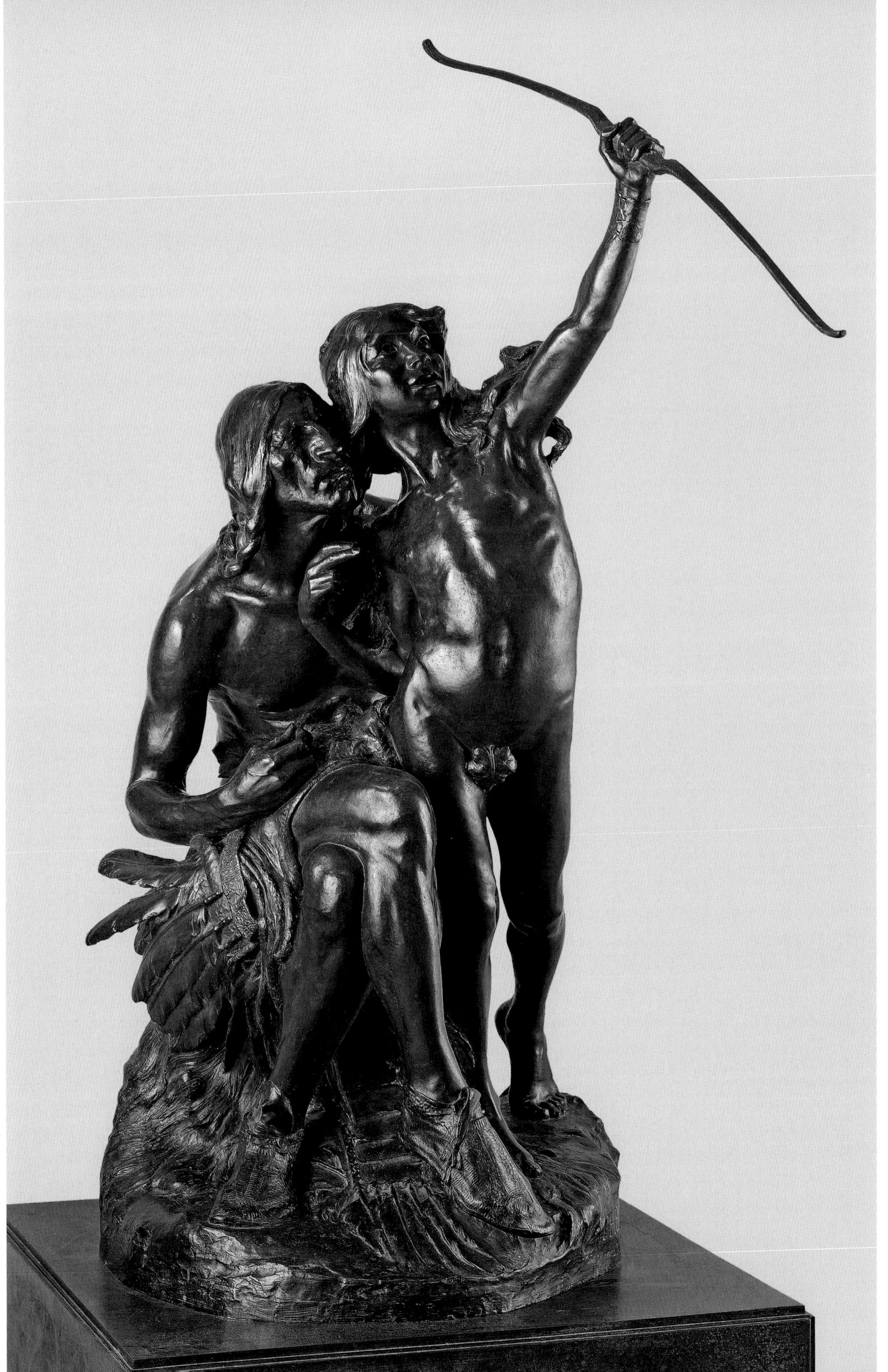

Fig. 48. Hermon Atkins MacNeil. *The Sun Vow*, 1899 (cast 1919). Bronze, 72 × 32½ × 54 in. (182.9 × 82.6 × 137.2 cm). The Metropolitan Museum of Art, Rogers Fund, 1919 (19.126)

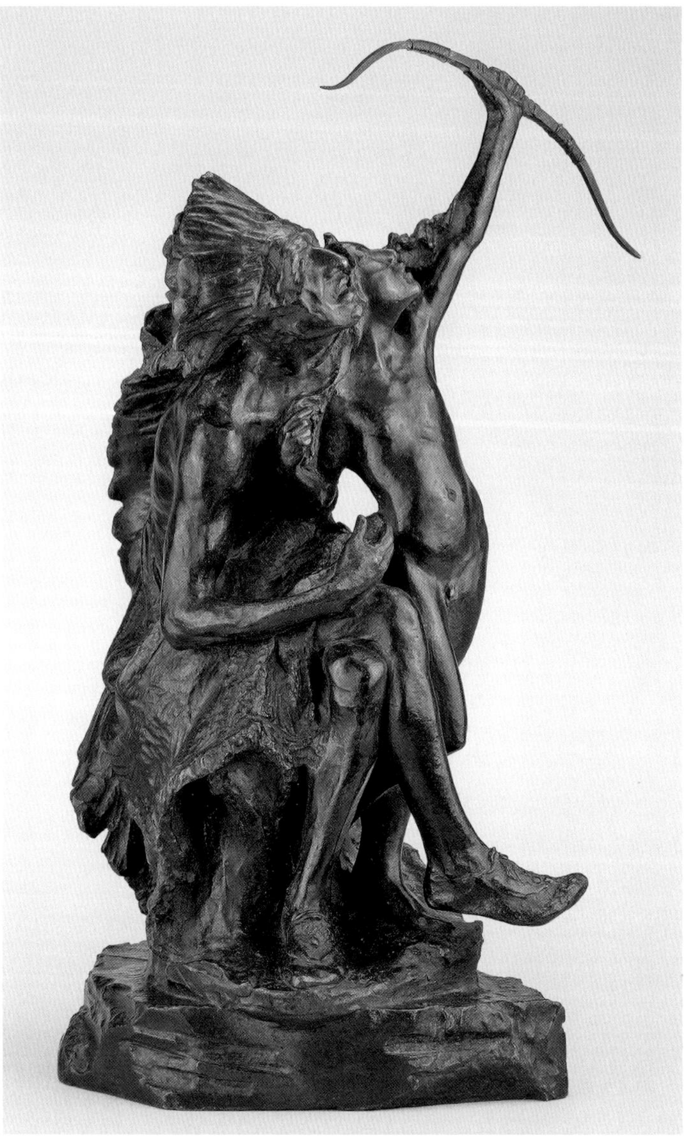

Fig. 49. Hermon Atkins MacNeil. *The Vow of Vengeance*, 1894. Bronze, 16¾ × 7⅜ × 8½ in. (42.6 × 18.7 × 21.6 cm). The Art Institute of Chicago, Restricted gift of Wesley M. Dixon, Jr.

people"—his white audience—MacNeil transformed the meaning of his sculpture from an Indian legend he admitted that he may have "invented"[46] into a more universal story. A contemporary critic admired *The Sun Vow*'s "essential idealism" of an "older man . . . teaching his grandson to aim high."[47] White patrons, in other words, shared values with Indians of the past, whose sculptural presence fit comfortably into family settings: the first cast of MacNeil's lifesize version graced the lawn of its owner's suburban home near Chicago, and the half-size reductions that MacNeil cast at Roman Bronze Works, in New York, beginning in 1906[48] likely found their place in bourgeois parlors (fig. 50).

The female figure was not favored by sculptors of bronze statuettes of Indian subjects at the turn of the twentieth century. Women's work, however, was the focus of Louis McClellan Potter's *Basket Weavers* of 1905 (fig. 51), one of a series he devoted to the Tlingit after a 1904 trip to Alaska. It was perhaps on this trip that Potter acquired a photograph (fig. 52) that appears to be an inspiration for *Basket Weavers*.[49] Shot and published about 1897 by Winter and Pond, whose Juneau shop advertised for sale "Alaska Views, Indian Curios, Totems, Carvings, Baskets," the photograph features three women holding baskets of spruce root and grasses.[50] The women sit behind their handiwork—baskets, beaded pouches, and other useful decorative objects—arrayed to catch the eye of a tourist, a collector, or a trader passing through their Sitka village. In transforming photographic inspiration into bronze statuette, Potter dressed his trio in simple robes rather than shirtwaists and skirts and did not show them displaying baskets for sale. At a time of intense ethnographic and commercial interest in Native basketry, of which women were prominent collectors, the sculpture emphasizes the ancient craft of basket making over contemporary basket selling.[51]

the composition reflects this: the older man in *The Sun Vow* folds his body forward, hunching to see the arrow from the youth's perspective; the young man, arching his back to extend the bow's string, appears to spring from his elder. It is a moment of hope for the future, but what kind of future and for whom? Andrew J. Walker has observed that the features of the youth, unlike the elder's, are "anglicized," which might signal the erosion of Indian culture by assimilation.[45] MacNeil wrote that he believed the subject of generational transition "is what (unconsciously) interests most people." By addressing the cultural concerns of "most

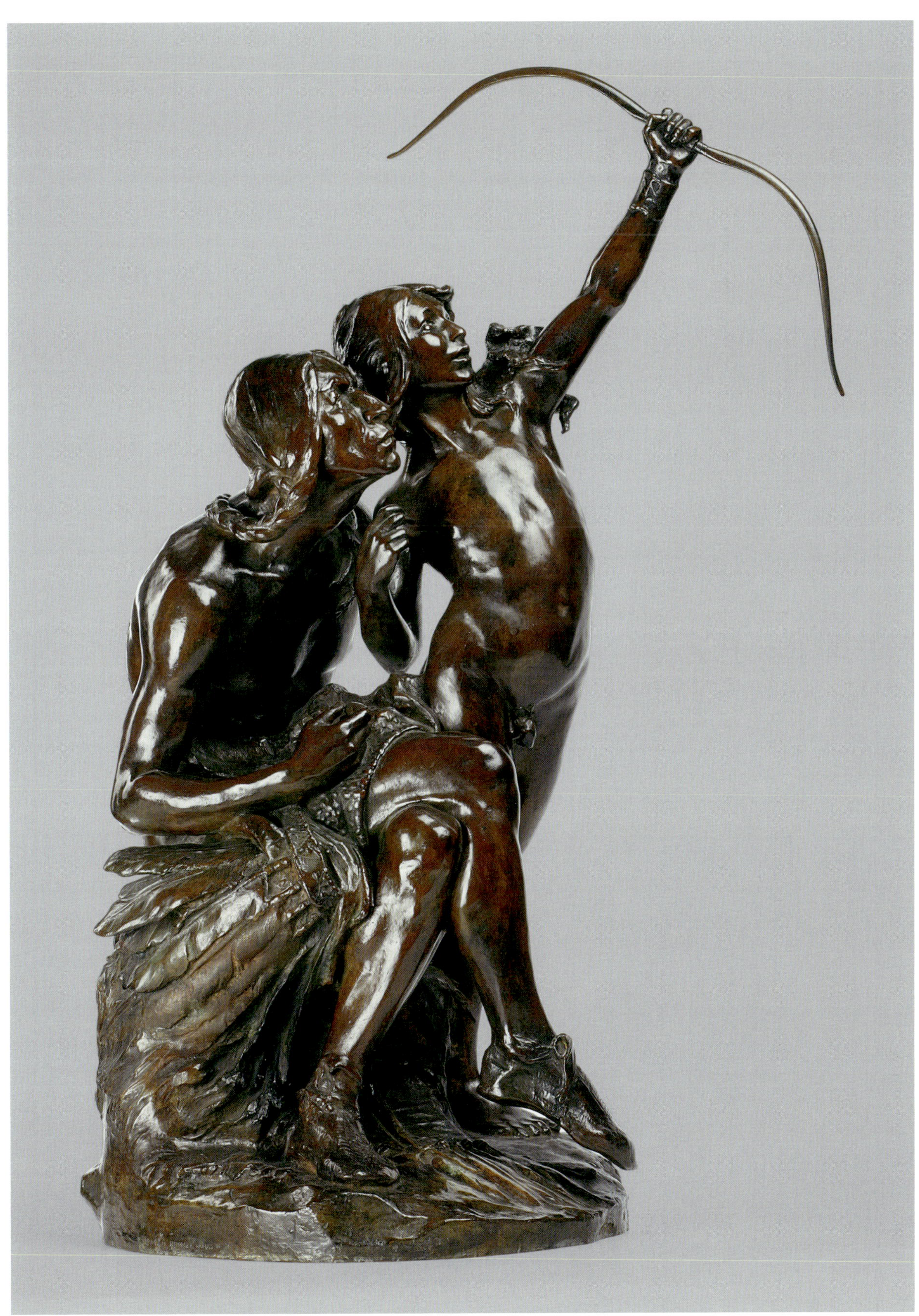

Fig. 50. Hermon Atkins
MacNeil. *The Sun Vow*, 1899
(cast ca. 1906 or after). Cat. 29

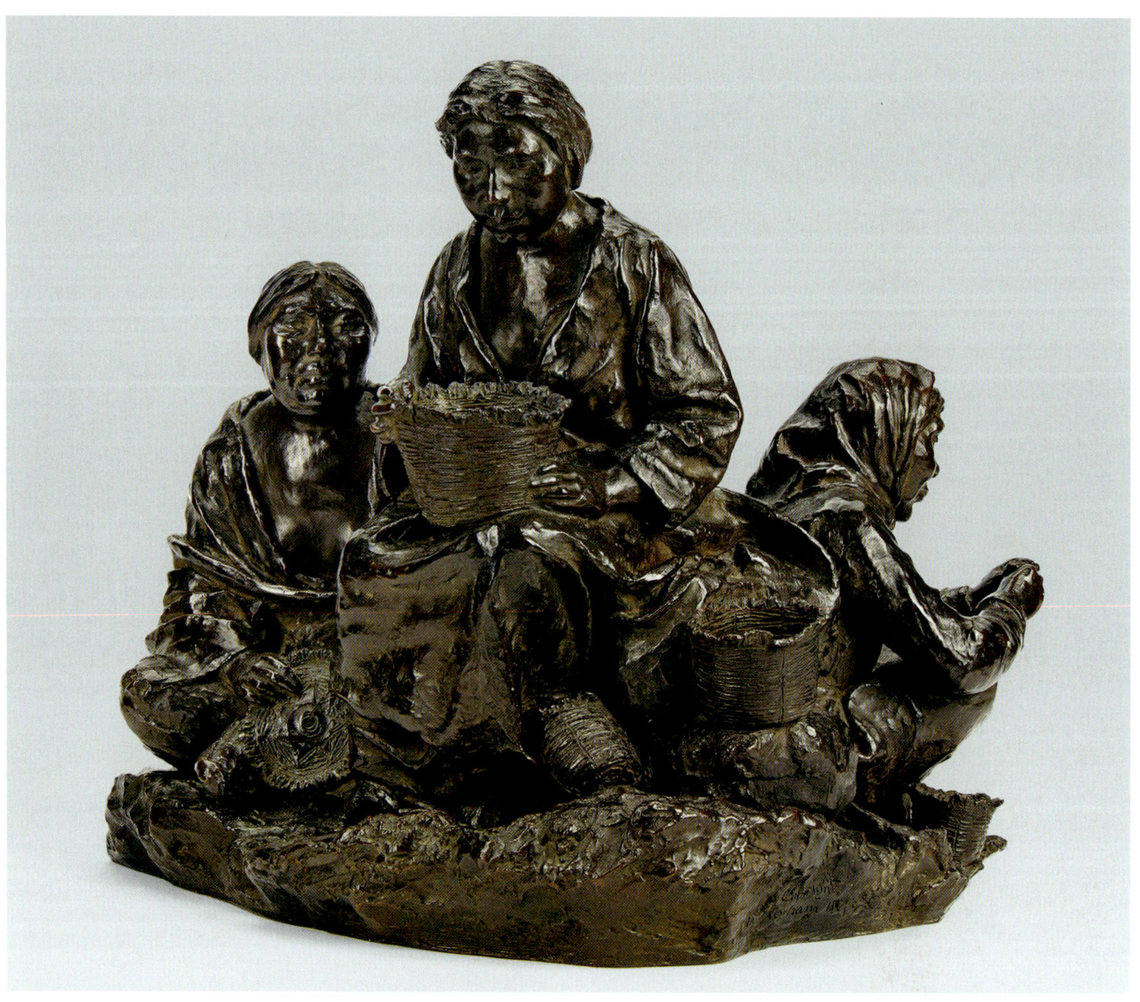

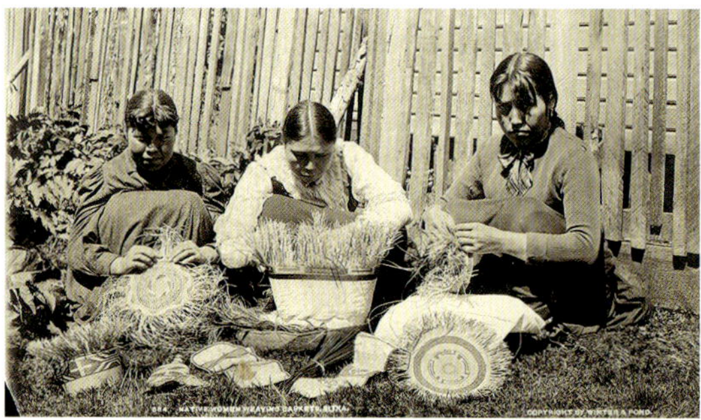

Potter's seated Tlingit women represent a view of Native life far from the erect male warrior—arms crossed at his swelling chest, chin upraised, and mouth turned down—that MacNeil created in 1903. *A Chief of the Mult-nomah Tribe* (fig. 53) is a reduced and modified version of one of the pair of Indians modeled by MacNeil for a lifesize monument, *Coming of the White Man* (fig. 54). Commissioned to create a public sculpture for Portland, Oregon, and in anticipation of the 1905 Lewis and Clark Exposition, MacNeil chose for his subject an imagined historical moment: two tribal members, looking east, see "the white man" for the first time. Even before the group was installed in Portland's City Park (now called Washington Park) in 1904, MacNeil had cast a small version of the chief. He added a feathered headdress, a bow, and a quiver of arrows not included in the monumental version, but more telling is what he eliminated. By extracting one figure from the pair, he deleted the emotions expressed by the wary medicine man, leaving only the chief's defiant resolve. MacNeil consulted Frederick W. Hodge, an anthropologist at the Smithsonian, for ethnographic information about the Multnomah tribe,[52] but the

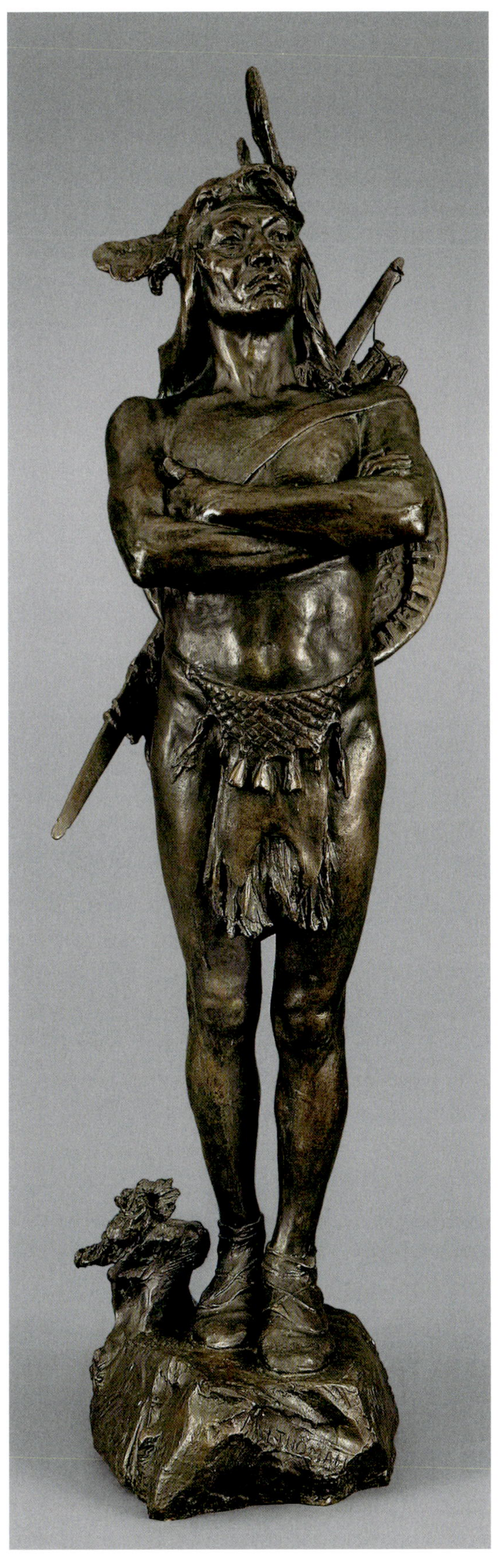

sculptor's contemporaries received the figure as a generic brave expressing "his attitude toward his own vanishing tribes, and his point of view toward the white race which has absorbed his country."[53]

Adolph Alexander Weinman, like MacNeil, relied on historical research to create a major Indian group. For his *Destiny of the Red Man* (fig. 10),[54] a monumental group commissioned for the Louisiana Purchase Exposition (Saint Louis, 1904), Weinman consulted George Catlin's and Francis Parkman's accounts of a western past. He expressed his point of view in the title, *Destiny of the Red Man*, much as Mac-Neil had signaled his larger meaning by titling his monument *Coming of the White Man*. Each monument assumed the Indian's disappearance. Yet, unlike MacNeil's, Weinman's models included a recognizable, living hero: Chief Blackbird, an Oglala veteran of the Great Sioux War of 1876, whom he met in 1903 in New York when Blackbird performed in Colonel Frederick T. Cummins's "Indian Congress and Life on the Plains."[55] *Chief Blackbird, the Ogalla Sioux* (fig. 55) is a bust portrait that Weinman

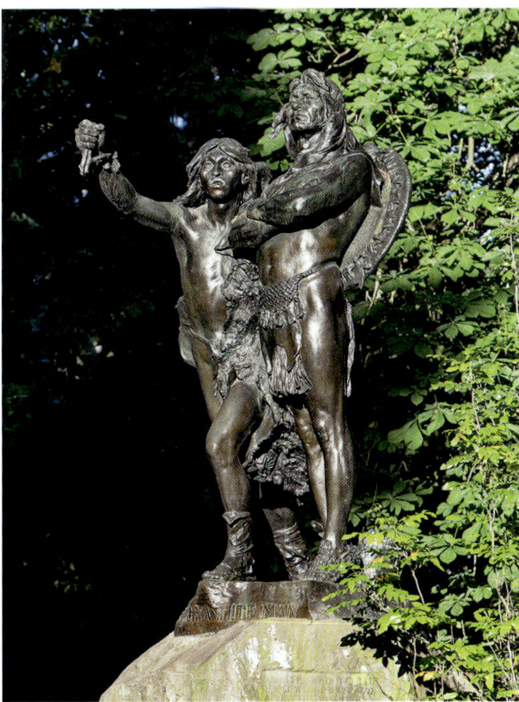

Fig. 53. Hermon Atkins MacNeil. *A Chief of the Multnomah Tribe*, 1903. Cat. 30

Fig. 54. Hermon Atkins MacNeil. *Coming of the White Man*, 1904. City Park (now Washington Park), Portland, Oregon

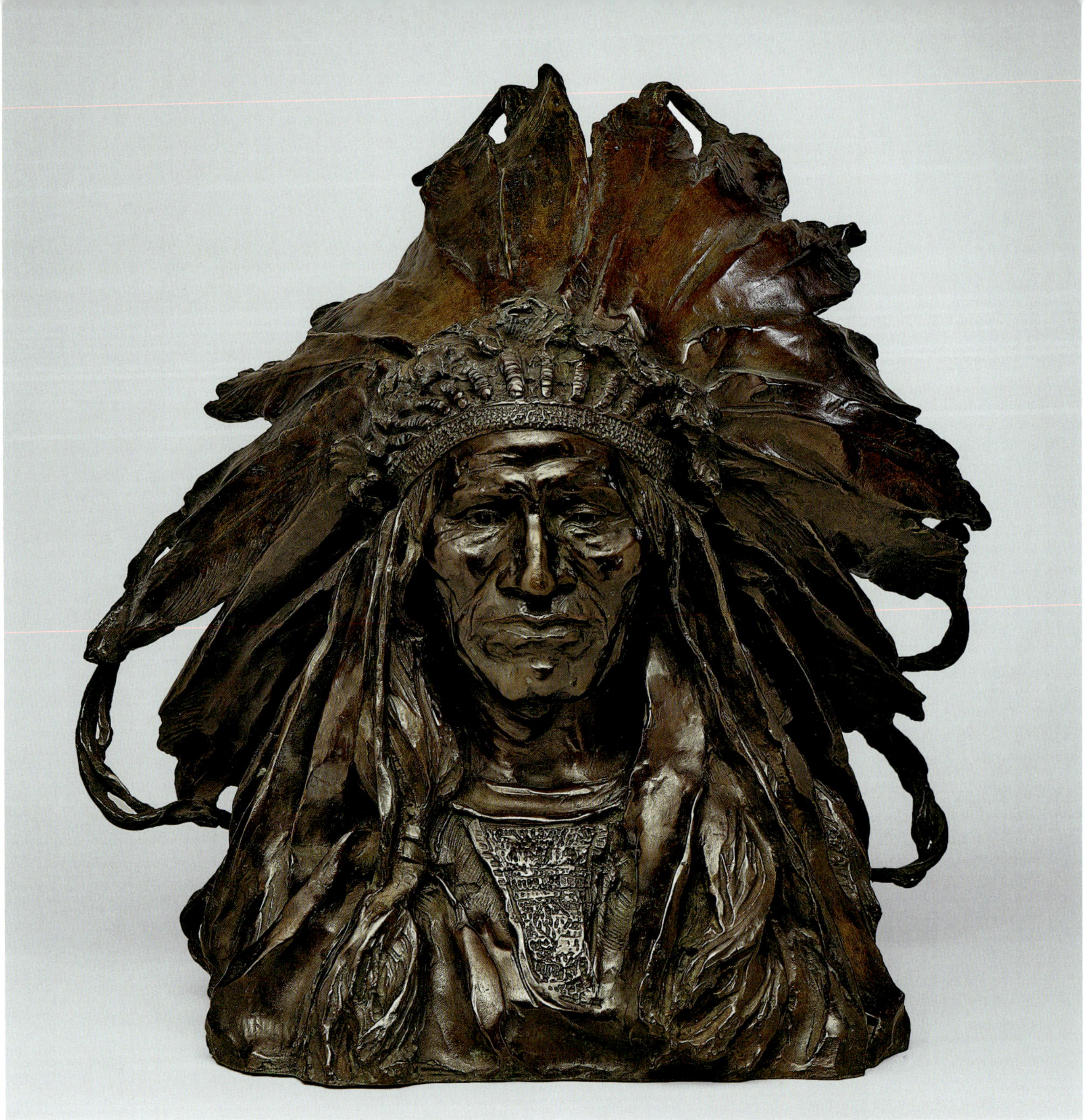

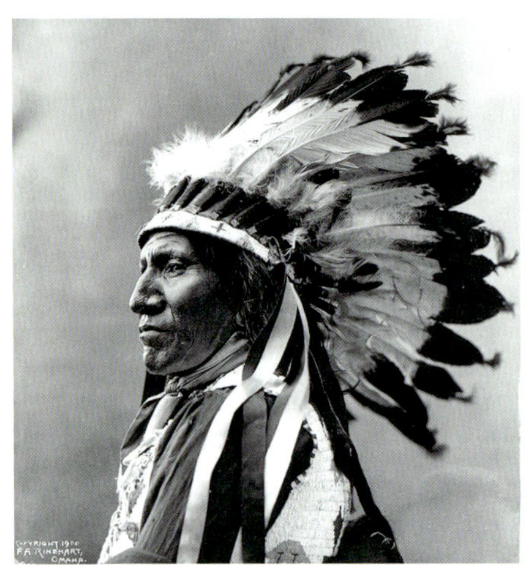

Fig. 55. Adolph Alexander Weinman. *Chief Blackbird, the Ogalla Sioux*, 1903. Cat. 79

Fig. 56. *Chief Black Bird*, 1900. Photograph by Frank A. Rinehart

derived from the figure standing at the left in *Destiny of the Red Man*. In the photographs published by the Omaha photographer Frank A. Rinehart in 1900 (fig. 56) and in the bronze, Blackbird wears the eagle-feather headdress and beaded-hide shirt that mark his status as a warrior.[56] The face that emerges through the feathers, ribbons, beaded hide, and long locks of hair is a fusion of artist's model, Wild West performer, and stoic warrior a quarter century after his defeat by a white army. Nonetheless, the bust conveyed a broader meaning. Weinman described *Destiny of the Red Man* as a symbol of "the passing of a heroic race . . . foreordained and inexorable."[57]

Alexander Phimister Proctor found inspiration elsewhere for his ambitious *Indian Warrior* of 1898 (fig. 57). He consulted North American sources from West to East—from men he met on Montana's Blackfoot Reservation in the summer of 1895 to a horse stabled in New York—to structure a group completed

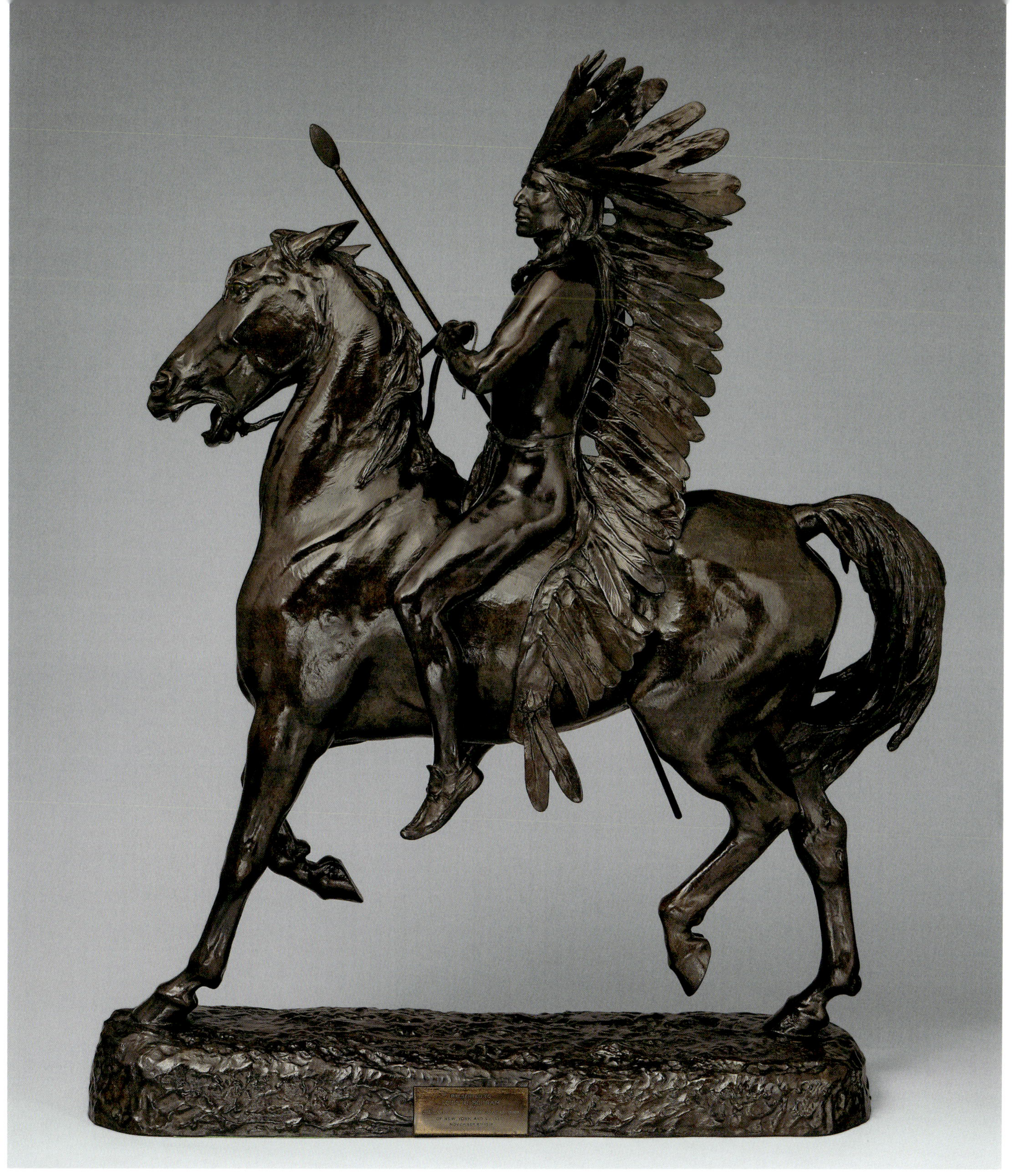

in Paris. Such specific sources, though, bow to the sculpture's evocation of a classically ideal equestrian ruler whose power courses from his haughty expression through a commanding posture to an equally spirited horse. Described as a "fine specimen of savage manhood" when on display in a Chicago home, this statuette soon found private buyers and museums from

Fig. 57. Alexander Phimister Proctor. *Indian Warrior*, 1898 (cast 1913 or after). Cat. 38

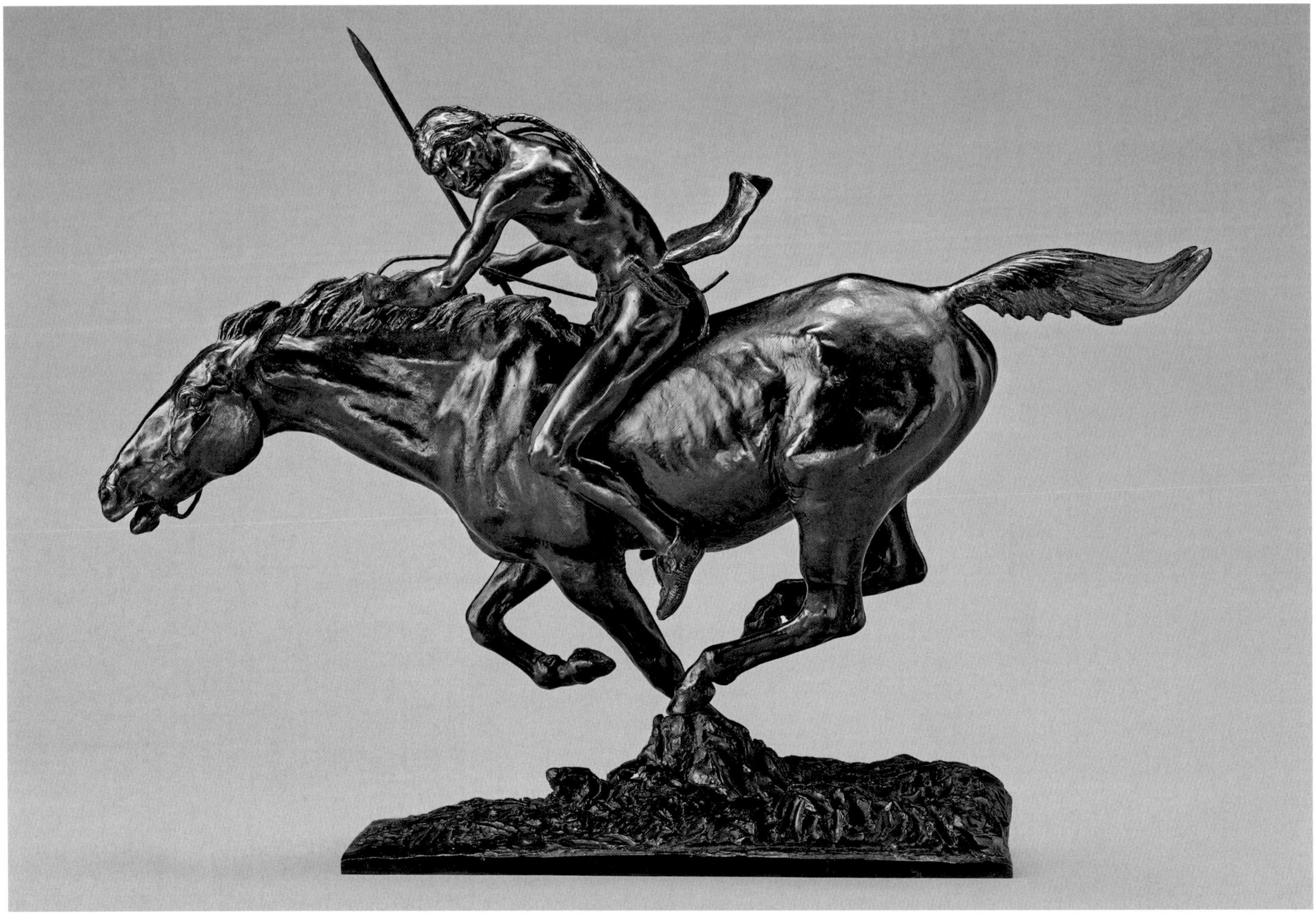

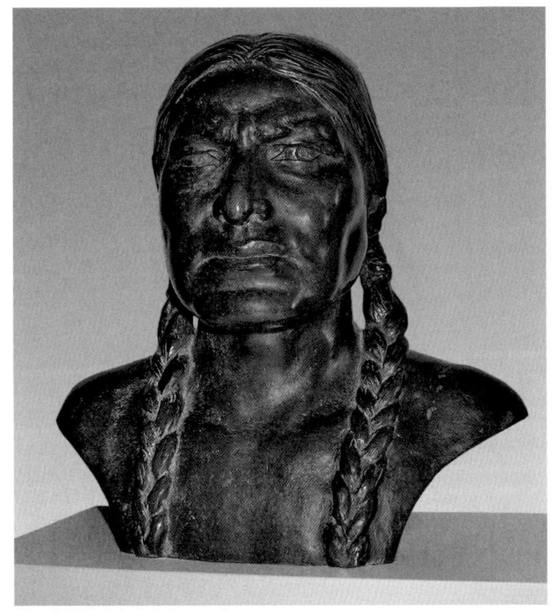

coast to coast and in Canada eager to add it to their collections.[58]

Why, then, when Proctor returned to an Indian subject in 1914 does it lack the commanding presence of his *Indian Warrior*? A visit to the Northern Cheyenne Reservation in Montana yielded a sculpture, *Pursued* (fig. 58), that abandons the classical monument in favor of a visceral image of a man in flight. Proctor may have been prompted to travel west in the summer of 1914 by reading about the Cheyenne Frontier Days rodeo in Wyoming, but he did not seek models among rodeo or other performers. Instead he chose a young cattle ranch hand, Robert Little Wolf (see fig. 59), who repeatedly galloped his horse downhill so the sculptor

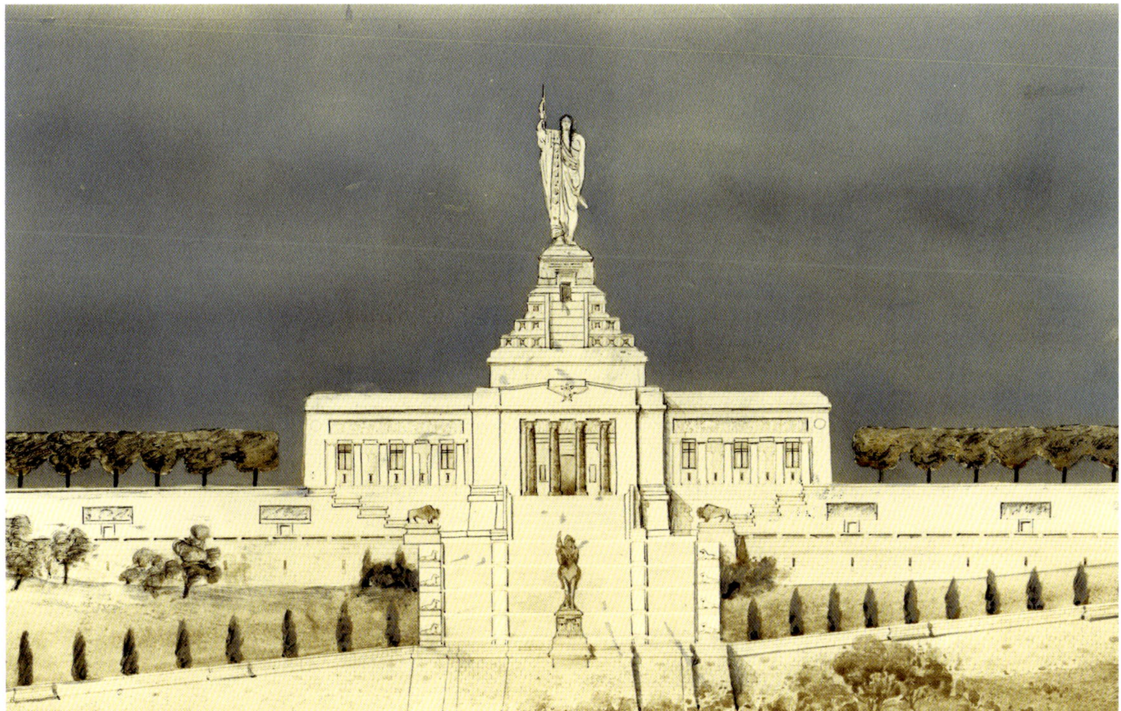

could observe them.[59] That modeling session yielded the form but not the content of *Pursued*: a man trying to outrun peril.

By this time, the battles of the Cheyenne were history. "Their wars have long been over," Proctor's friend the naturalist George Bird Grinnell wrote in his book *The Fighting Cheyennes* (1915).[60] As Indians were presumed to fade into history, white men like the impresario and author Joseph K. Dixon adopted idealized images of their past to serve as noble American ancestors in a country now swelling with immigrants. Dixon and his patron, Rodman Wanamaker, planned a National American Indian Memorial (fig. 60) at the entrance to New York Harbor, which was to include an ethnographic museum and two sculptures, one "a mammoth bronze figure of the North American Indian upon the highest hill-crest in the harbor as a witness of the passing race to all the nations of the world as they come to our shores."[61] Among the thousands in attendance at the 1913 ground-breaking ceremony was President William Howard Taft, along with representatives from a dozen Indian tribes in traditional regalia.[62]

James Earle Fraser's *End of the Trail* (fig. 61) expresses the Indian's place in history more viscerally than did the apparently unbowed equestrians envisioned for the unrealized memorial in New York Harbor. But the two projects told the same story: the Indian was forerunner in a white man's nation, appropriately cast into bronze as noble ancestors for public and private contemplation of history. The *End of the Trail* statuette had a long gestation. Late in his life Fraser identified the sources for it in his own experience and in old tales he had been told. He expressed sympathy for the Sioux who, chafing at their confinement on the Crow Creek Reservation, would "slip away at night and move into their old hunting ground" near his childhood home in Dakota Territory.[63] And, he said, he would often hear old trappers who were friends of his grandfather "speak about the Indians . . . and where they would end up." The trappers "all thought that would be in the Pacific Ocean.

Fig. 60. *Design for National American Indian Memorial*, ca. 1912–13. Photographic print with ink and gouache additions, 8 × 12⅜ in. (20.3 × 31.4 cm). Mathers Museum of World Cultures, Indiana University, Bloomington

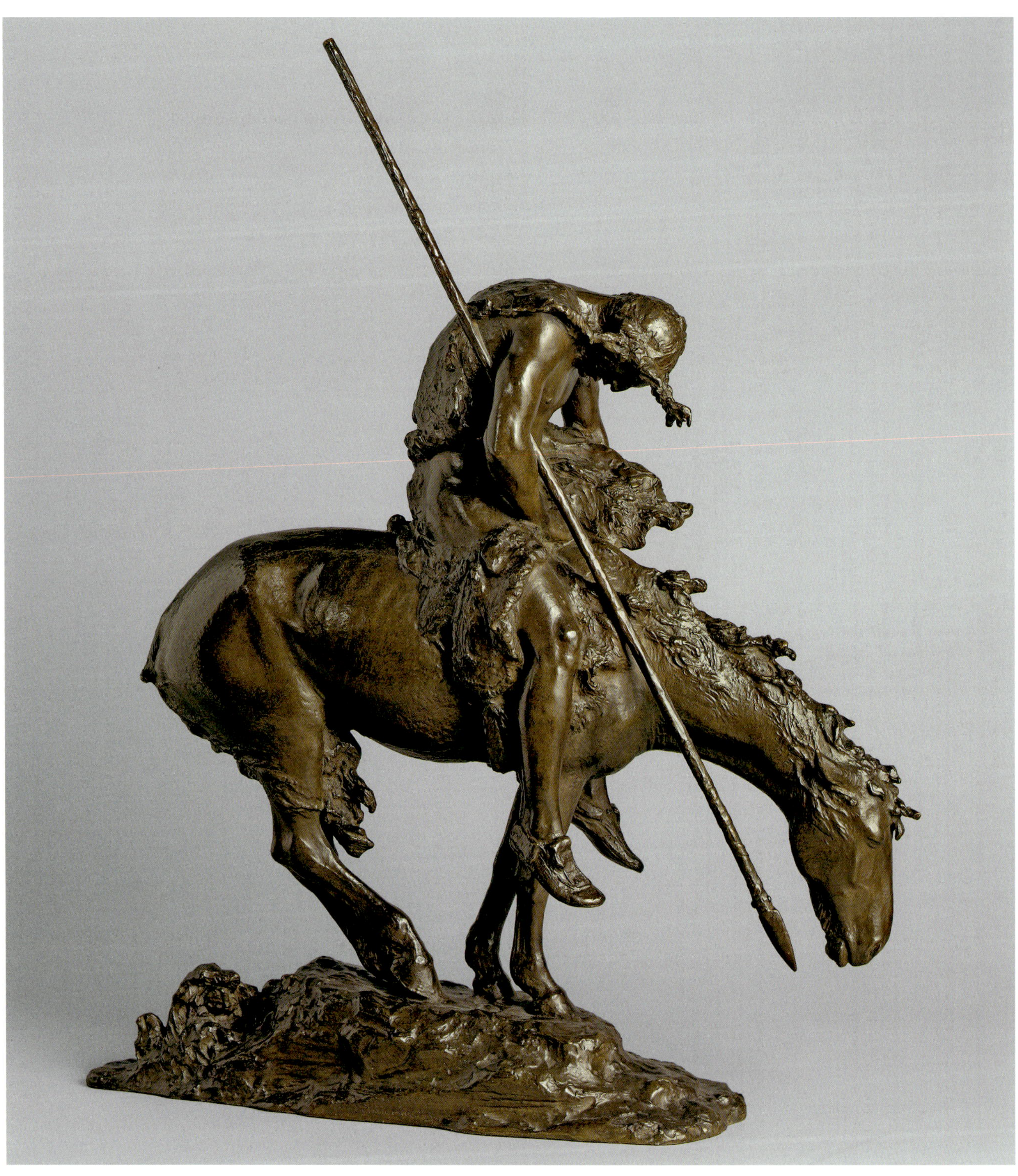

. . . Finally," he said, "after I had seen other sculptures, the idea occurred to me of making an Indian which represented his race *reaching the end of the trail*, at the edge of the Pacific."[64]

And so he did. First modeled in sketch form in 1894, the sculpture appeared in monumental form in 1915 at the Panama-Pacific International Exposition in San Francisco, where, installed in a corresponding place along the prominent Avenue of Palms (fig. 13), it echoed the theme of Solon Hannibal Borglum's equestrian group *The Pioneer* (fig. 62). In a recap of Manifest Destiny, "the pioneer," upright on a lively horse, triumphed at the expense of "the Indian." *The Pioneer* was presented as having absorbed the Indian's history by wearing the "symbols of Indian life, the teepee, the canoe, the star," on the "leather trappings of the horse."[65] But each group's time had passed. Borglum envisioned his aged pioneer "thinking over the old days," and Fraser's slumped figure, according to the fair's catalogue, was "a reminiscence of early American history and its traditions of courage and endurance, and the pathos of the Indian's decline."[66]

If, as this statement suggests, *End of the Trail* embodies "American" values like "courage and endurance," we might better understand the popularity of the monumental sculpture and of the statuettes Fraser cast in two different sizes beginning in 1918.[67] Some saw the work as an indictment of "the national stupidity that has greedily and cruelly destroyed a race of people possessing imagination, integrity, fidelity and nobility," as one critic wrote in 1920.[68] Others regarded the Indian's end as necessary to the white nation's progress. The sculpture allows for either judgment because what it conveys most forcefully is more fundamental. The official guide to the Panama-Pacific exposition, for example, proposed that "the work may be interpreted merely as a picture of physical exhaustion."[69] It is, even more, an embodiment of suffering: a muscular, well-formed man slumps in exhaustion on a horse that barely stands against the east wind driving what they represented into history.

The romance rather than the pathos of the West drove Charles M. Russell's devotion to themes from its history. Two bronzes depicting a bison hunt, which bracket his career in sculpture, embodied what, for whites, was the quintessential activity of Plains Indian life. Even though the subject engaged him more than any other, Russell never saw a bison hunt. His knowledge came instead from historical accounts, from the work of earlier artists, from conversations with Indians who remembered such hunts, and from his own participation in bison roundups in 1908 and 1909.[70]

Russell modeled, had cast in bronze, and offered for sale his first buffalo hunt sculpture in New York, traveling there in 1905 from his home in Montana to promote his work (fig. 11).[71] Unlike Theodore Baur's *Buffalo Hunt*

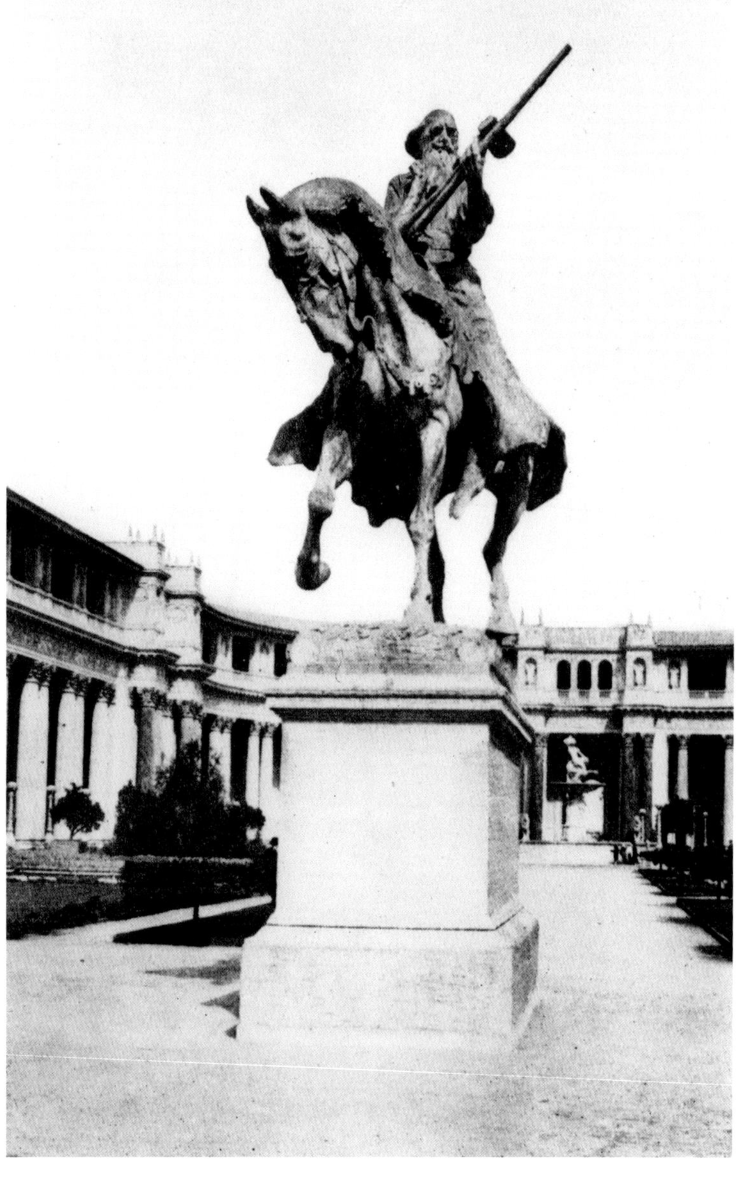

Fig. 62. Solon Hannibal Borglum. *The Pioneer*, Panama-Pacific International Exposition, San Francisco, 1915

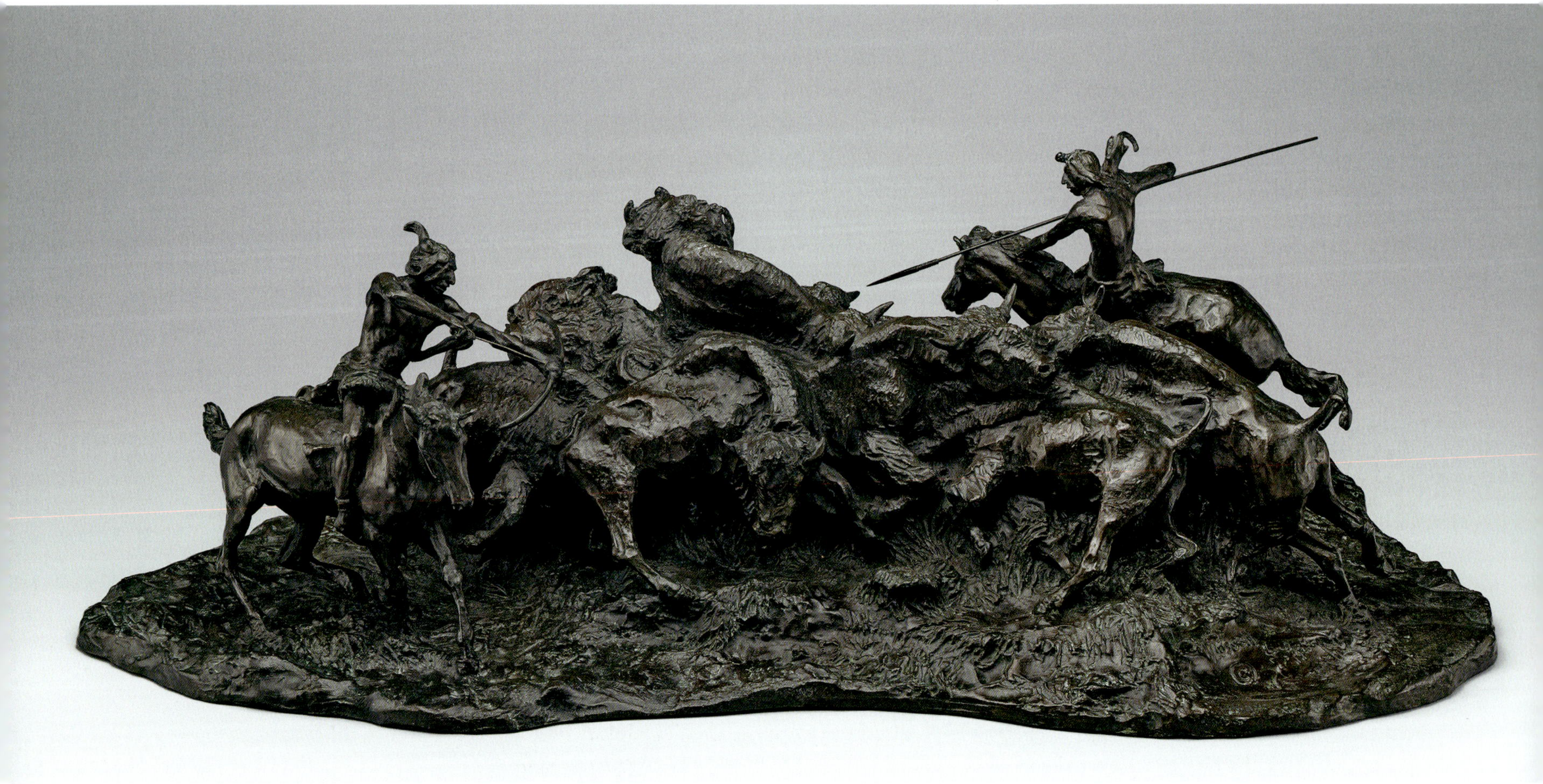

Fig. 63. Charles M. Russell. *Meat for Wild Men*, 1924 (cast 1924). Cat. 64

Fig. 64. Charles M. Russell. *Buffalo Hunt [No. 40]*, 1919. Cat. 62

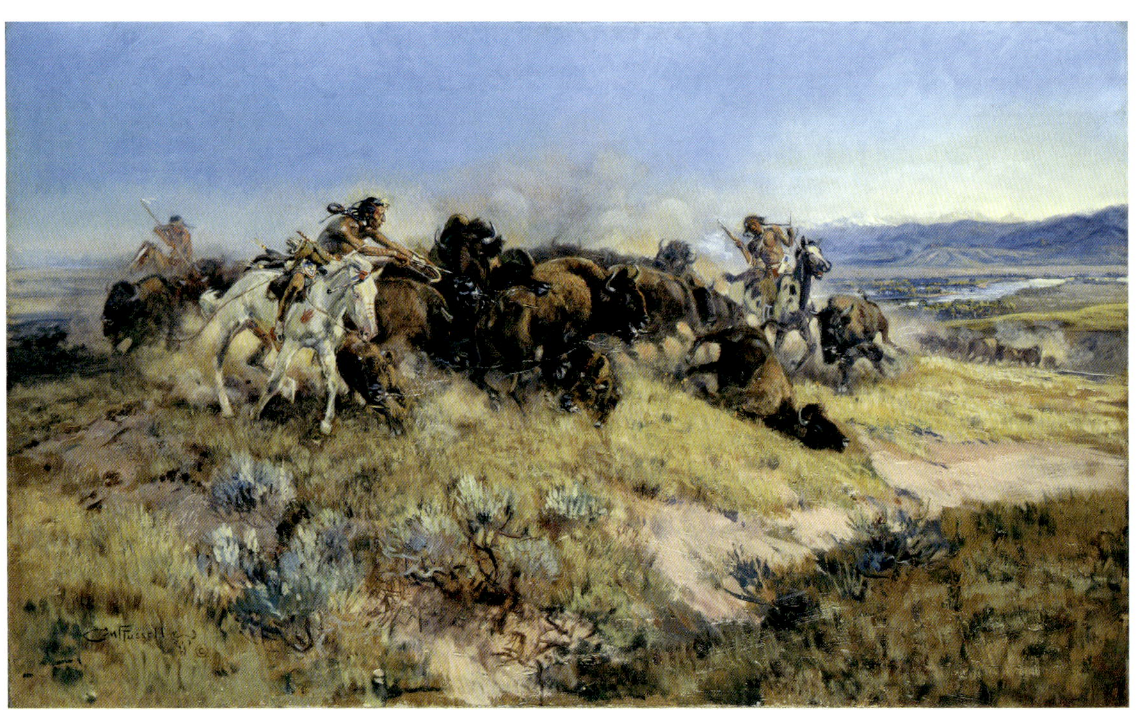

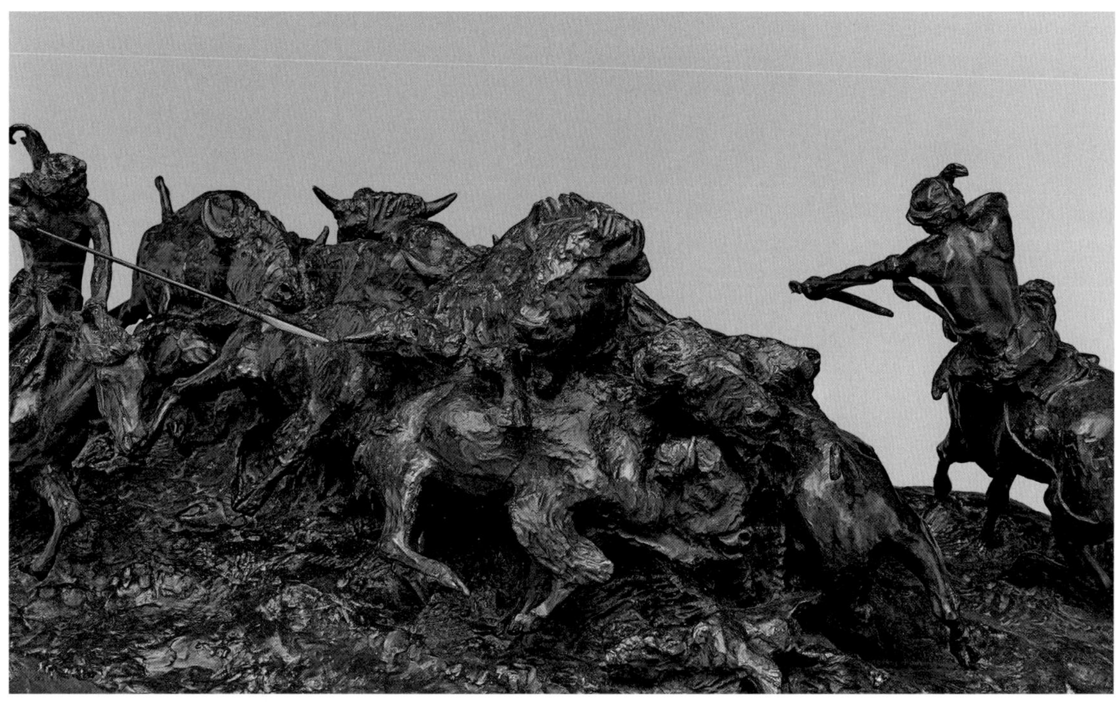

of 1876 (fig. 35), with its rearing horse and single dying bison decoratively contained on a base, Russell's exuberant *Buffalo Hunt* threatens to veer off its support: the bison lurch, the pony scrambles, the hunter strains to keep his seat. Perhaps striving for even greater verisimilitude, Russell packed even more action into his last sculpture on this theme. Commissioned in 1924 by a Wyoming oil man, *Meat for Wild Men* (fig. 63) features a type of hunt called a "surround," which Russell had also painted (see fig. 64, for example), likely based on what he had read about such hunts in Catlin's books. Two mounted hunters close in on a dozen frenzied bison they have chased into "a crowded and confused mass, hooking and climbing upon each other," as Catlin earlier described the practice.[72] Crushed animals pile up in Russell's sculpture, appearing to bellow in pain (fig. 65). His title distances his subject from sport hunting to recall that the bison had once been a source of sustenance essential to a now-vanished way of life.

With *Indian Hunter* and *Pronghorn Antelope* (figs. 66, 67), of 1914, Paul Manship infused

an American western subject with a past far more distant than the nineteenth century that Russell invoked in his buffalo hunts. Inspired by Archaic Greek sculpture he had seen on travels during a 1909–12 fellowship at the American Academy in Rome, Manship endowed his hunter with the power of ancient archers, like those on the pediments of the Temple of Aphaia at Aegina. Yet bourgeois domesticity also played a role: Manship created the statuettes specifically for pedestals at either end of the mantelpiece in his New York apartment. His archaistic style of broad forms articulated by crisp lines allied these sculptures with modernism.[73] Fully developed in the round yet designed to be seen in profile, *Indian Hunter* and *Pronghorn Antelope* enact a narrative to be read from left to right. The silhouetted figures are frozen at the moment the arrow (whose implied path charges the space between the pair) finds its mark in the beast's side.

At the time Manship made his sculpture, both the Indian and his prey would have been perceived as equally endangered. A species

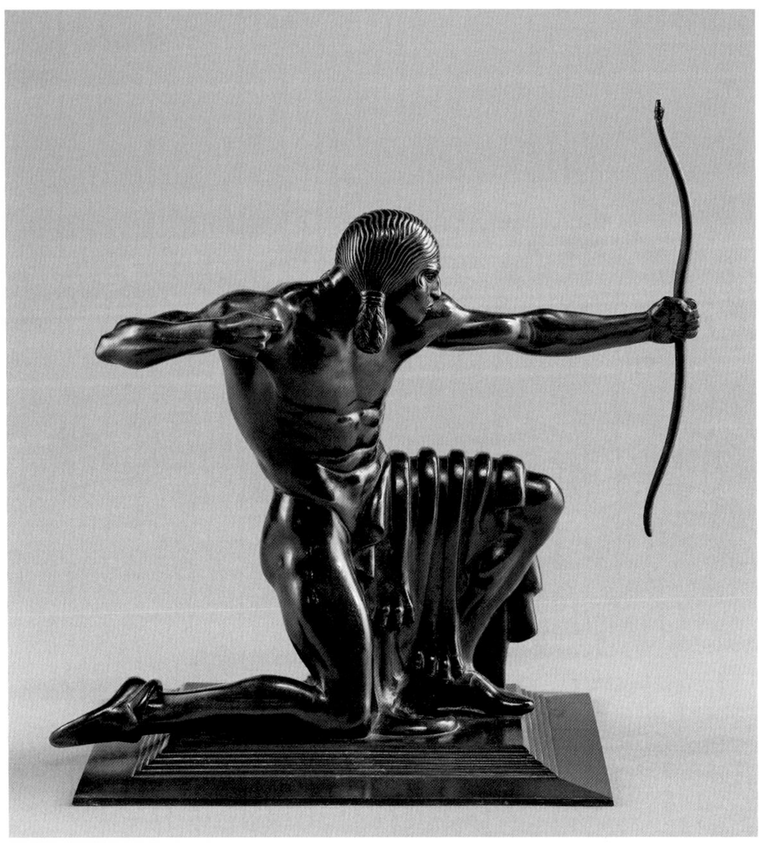

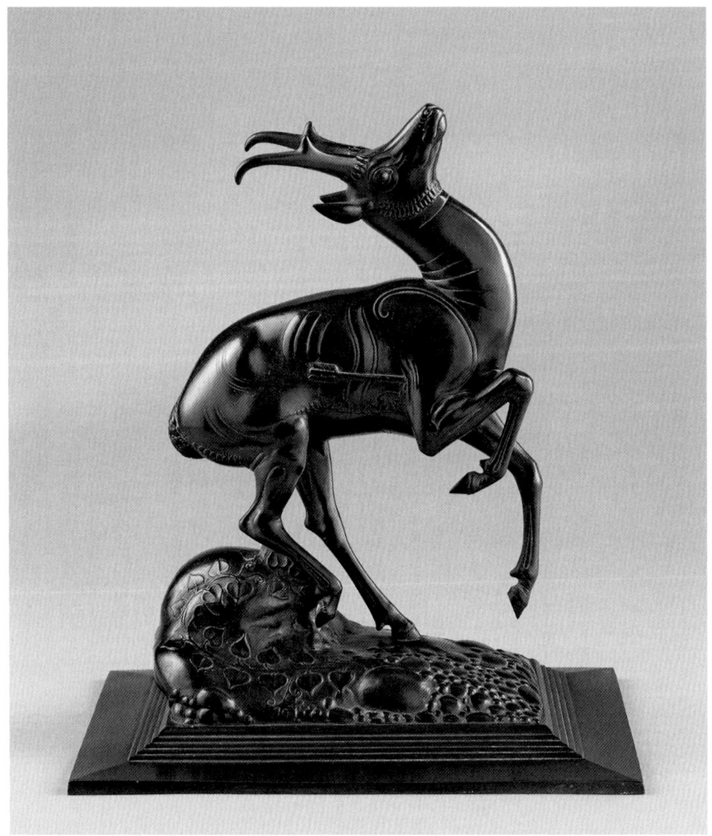

Fig. 66. Paul Manship. *Indian Hunter*, 1914 (cast 1915). Cat. 32

Fig. 67. Paul Manship. *Pronghorn Antelope*, 1914 (cast 1915). Cat. 33

Fig. 68. Paul Manship. *Indian Hunter and His Dog*, 1925–26. Cochran Park, Saint Paul, Minnesota, 1936

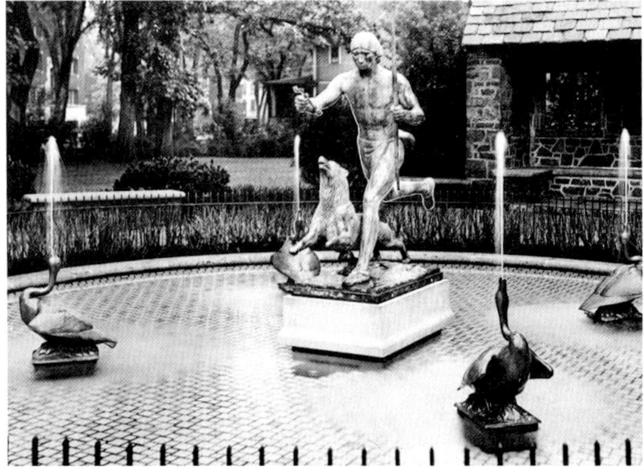

unique to North America, the pronghorn antelope was deemed in 1913 to be one of the first North American big-game animals at risk of becoming extinct and hence worthy of preservation in the New York Zoological Park in the Bronx.[74] *Indian Hunter* and *Pronghorn Antelope* entered the upper-class world of conservation and big-game hunting when George D. Pratt, who had hunted antelope in Canada with Alexander Phimister Proctor, purchased a pair of the statuettes.[75] In 1917 Pratt's brother Herbert, seeing the sculptures' potential as garden ornaments, commissioned monumental versions for the grounds of his summer estate in Glen Cove, New York. Installed sixty feet apart against trees that towered forty feet above them, the pair struck Manship as misplaced. "Here it was contrived to appear natural which, of course, it isn't," he is reported to have said. "The group was really a rather artificial mantel ornament."[76]

Manship had no such qualms about the setting for *Indian Hunter and His Dog*, a group commissioned in 1925 as a fountain centerpiece for a park in Saint Paul, Minnesota. Unlike Manship's brawny hunter of 1914, this slim youth carries a bow and arrows that are more attributes than weapons. The dog at his side, hind feet planted on the sculpture's base, leaps forward in synchrony with its human companion. These choreographed, buoyant

figures turned playful the following year, when
Manship added four bronze, water-spouting
Canada geese to the pool (fig. 68). Reduced
and cast for domestic display, the statuette
(fig. 69) retains a joyful air.

No specific ancient source inspired *Indian
Hunter and His Dog.* Yet, like Henry Kirke
Brown's Indian figure in *Choosing of the Arrow*
(fig. 31) seventy-five years before, Manship's
Native projects a world of perfectly graceful
bodies: the American Arcadia was populated
with imaginary Indians. But Arcadian ease was
just one ideal that sculptures of Indians carried
to their audiences. Almost nude and powerfully built, skilled with weaponry, allied with
animals, and (usually) male, bronze Indians
were appealingly proud, defiant, violent, and
valiant in defeat. Contemporary Indians did
sometimes serve as the sculptors' models, but
it was the historical Indian—soundly defeated,
gleaned from research, or experienced in popular entertainment—who emerged in bronze to
take a place in the modern world on the mantel
or in the park.

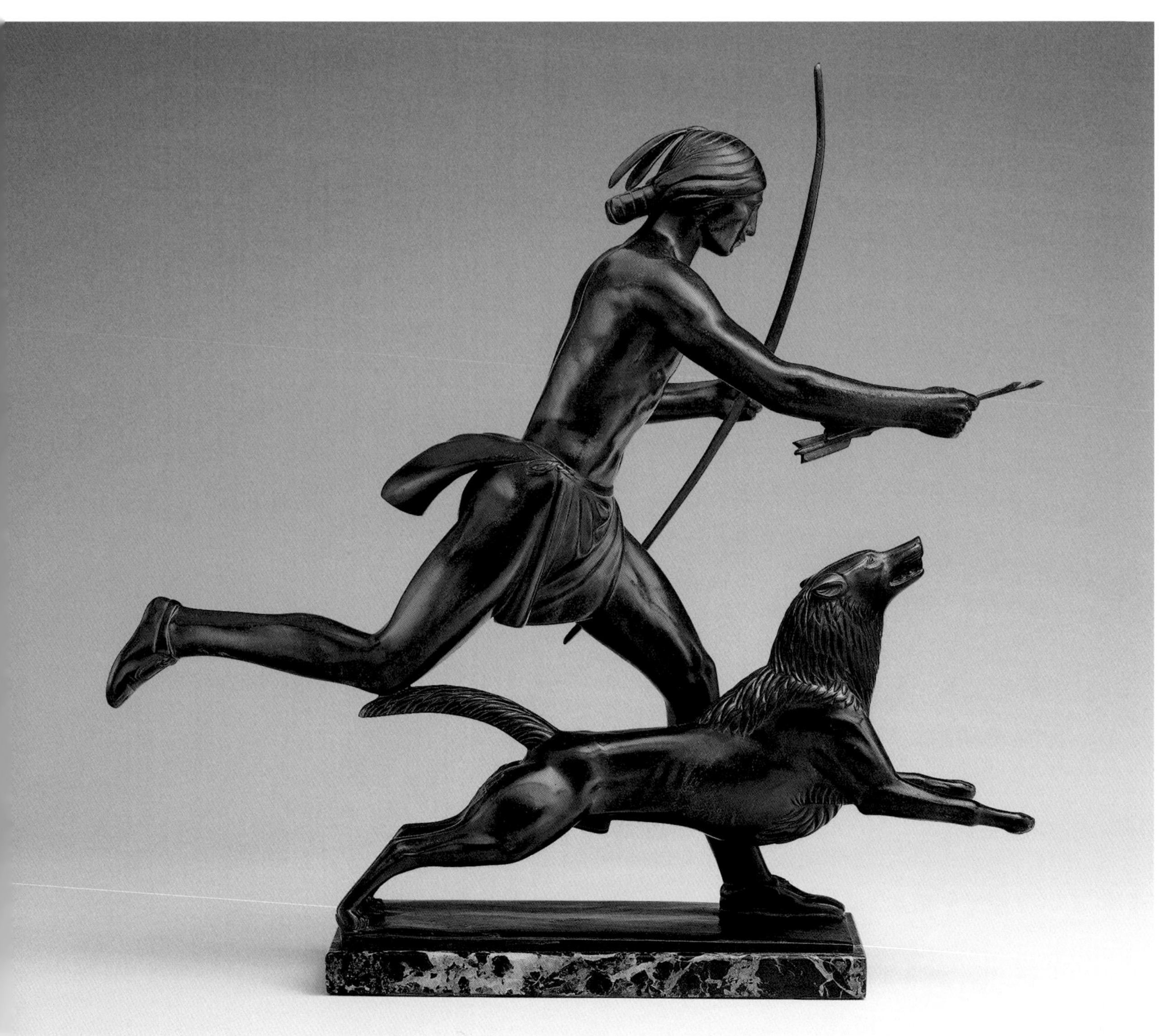

Fig. 69. Paul Manship.
*Indian Hunter and His
Dog,* 1926. Cat. 34

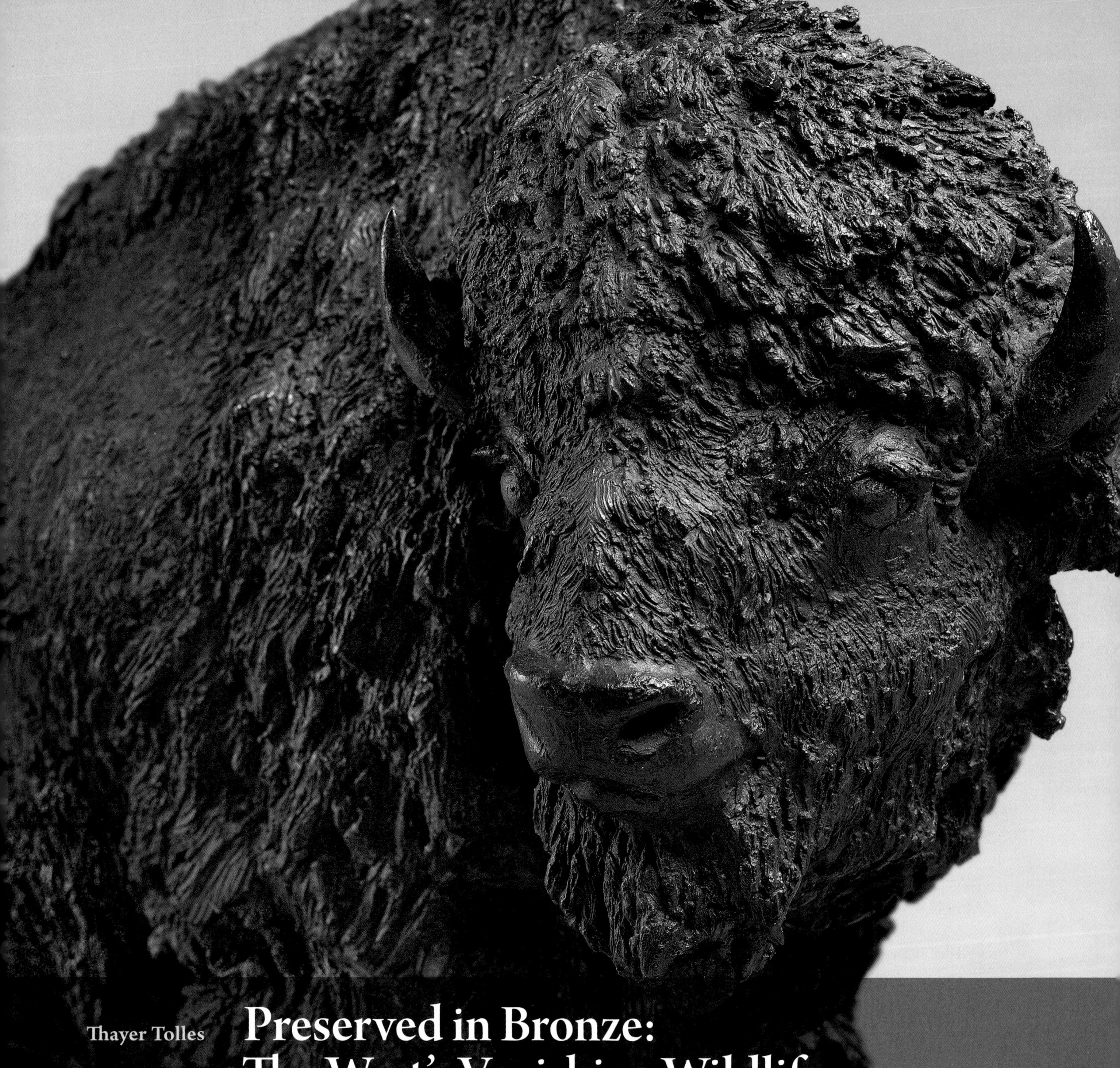

Preserved in Bronze:
The West's Vanishing Wildlife

In the years after the founding of the American nation, the animals inhabiting the vast swath of continent beyond the original states attracted increasing attention, subjects of the Linnaean impulse to preserve, catalogue, and illustrate. Charles Willson Peale put specimens of bison, panthers, and other North American mammals on view at his American Museum in Philadelphia in 1794, adding to its inventory until his death in 1827. In 1819–20 his son Titian Ramsay Peale joined Stephen H. Long's scientific expedition up the Platte River, producing 122 finished drawings of flora, fauna, and Native peoples. John James Audubon's *Viviparous Quadrupeds of North America* (1845–48), a three-volume compendium of 150 lithographs (fig. 71), was bolstered by his specimen-collecting trip along the Missouri River in 1843. Meanwhile, George Catlin and Alfred Jacob Miller portrayed animals as well as American Indians and the western landscape, and the well-established eastern animal specialists William Holbrook Beard and William Jacob Hays ventured west to expand their repertoires. By the mid-nineteenth century, with the professionalization of the popular press, sporting and wildlife imagery was being widely disseminated through prints—notably, those by Arthur Fitzwilliam Tait published by Currier & Ives.

At the same time, the animals themselves —live, taxidermied, and sculpted—became part of the everyday landscape. City dwellers began to visit zoological gardens: New York's Central Park Menagerie originated informally in 1859 and was chartered in 1864; the Philadelphia Zoo, founded in 1859, opened its doors in 1874 after a hiatus caused by the Civil War. The American Museum of Natural History was established in 1869 and was housed in the Arsenal, just steps from the Central Park Menagerie, before moving in 1877 to its present site on Central Park West. Within the park, Christophe Fratin's *Eagles and Prey* (1850; installed 1863) and Auguste-Nicolas Cain's *Tigress and Cubs* (1866; installed 1867) brought grand French animalier sculpture to American shores in all its romantic, if at times gory, naturalism, providing an alternative form of animal-based entertainment. John Quincy Adams Ward's *Indian Hunter*, a young man accompanied by what may be a crossbreed of dog and wolf, was dedicated in the park in 1869 (fig. 34), becoming the first sculpture by an American to be placed there, after making its debut at the Paris Exposition Universelle of 1867.

Even the earliest efforts of American sculptors of animals, in the 1850s–70s, reflected the general perception that it was their duty as artist-naturalists to record both the physical and the behavioral aspects of native fauna, whether in combat or at play, in motion or at rest, at a time when animals were increasingly subjected to human threats to their well-being. These sculptors became linked to a larger movement of consciousness-raising, conservation, and wildlife repopulation in the American West that gained traction in the 1870s and matured through the first several decades of the twentieth century. The resulting statuettes, eagerly collected by an urban (mainly East Coast) populace as authentically American art, were also valued as metaphors for the "vanishing West."

Fig. 70. Henry Merwin Shrady, detail of *Buffalo*, 1899 (cast ca. 1901). Cat. 72

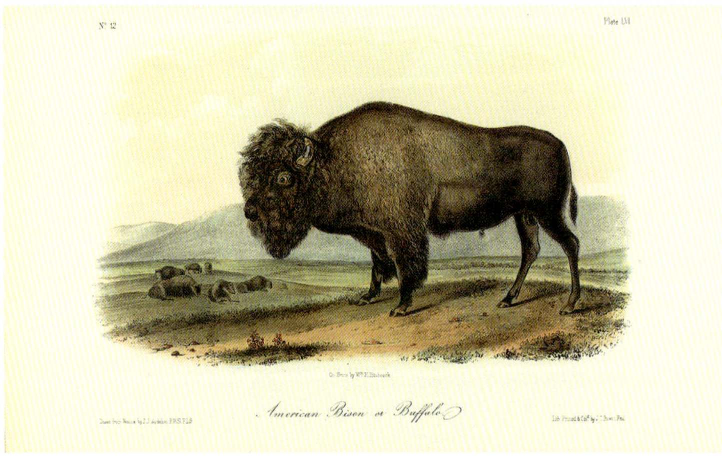

Fig. 71. *American Bison or Buffalo*, plate LVI, after drawing by John James Audubon, in John James Audubon and John Bachman, *The Viviparous Quadrupeds of North America*. Philadelphia, 1851. Hand-colored lithograph. The Metropolitan Museum of Art, Bequest of Emma Sheafer, 1974 (1974.661.3)

In 1886 Theodore Roosevelt, friend and patron to several American sculptors, offered observations based on his time in the Dakota Badlands:

To see the rapidity with which the larger kinds of game animals are being exterminated throughout the United States is really melancholy. Twenty-five years ago, or even fifteen years ago, the Western plains and mountains were in places fairly thronged with deer, elk, antelope, and buffalo; indeed there was then no other part of the world save South Africa where the number of individuals of large game animals was so large. All of this has now been changed, or else is being changed at a really remarkable rate of speed.[1]

Almost without exception, American sculptors echoed Roosevelt's lament in three-dimensional form, but their creative techniques and backgrounds varied widely. Some—Edward Kemeys and Edwin Willard Deming, for example—were hunters and explorers, tracking wildlife across western plains, mountains, and deserts, while others —Henry Merwin Shrady and Eli Harvey— preferred to observe animals in captivity, safely caged in urban zoos from Paris to New York. Alexander Phimister Proctor and James L. Clark approached their art through the lens of science, performing anatomical studies to produce the most accurate physical representations possible; still others—for instance, Arthur Putnam and Charles M. Russell—preferred to emphasize emotions, whether pathos,

triumph, or humor. Those, like Solon Hannibal Borglum, who were rigorously trained in East Coast and Paris academies and hence were more familiar with the distinguished lineage of animal sculpture since ancient times, took a different approach than autodidacts like Russell. Several, especially Kemeys, Proctor, and Clark, wrote eloquently about their perceptions of North American mammals. And some made a specialty of animal sculpture, while others pursued it only sporadically or as part of larger narratives (for instance, bison hunting or equestrian groups featuring American Indians or cowboys; see figs. 35, 63, and 116).

Into the latter camp fell Henry Kirke Brown, who led the transition from a foreign-based Neoclassical aesthetic in marble to a homegrown emphasis on realism in bronze. Having trained in Italy between 1842 and 1846, he returned to New York determined to encourage popular interest in sculpture as a democratic art form. Beginning in the late 1840s, Brown cast statuettes of superlative quality, the first American to do so—initially in his Brooklyn studio-foundry (see fig. 31) and later in collaboration with the Ames Manufacturing Company in Chicopee, Massachusetts. *Panther and Cubs* (fig. 72), probably cast at Ames, is a reduction after his lifesize group *Indian and Panther* (1849; unlocated), in which a muscular male figure towers over a snarling panther and her threatened cubs, raising a club to deal a death blow.[2] By not including the Indian in the statuette version, Brown set up an entirely different narrative for this first-known American wildlife bronze. The identity of the implied predator—whether human or animal—is unclear, and the emphasis shifts to the universality of the maternal instinct to protect her young. The device of the undetermined outcome is commonly employed in animal sculpture, allowing viewers to complete the drama for themselves. Brown's painstaking attention to detail is particularly evident in the minute

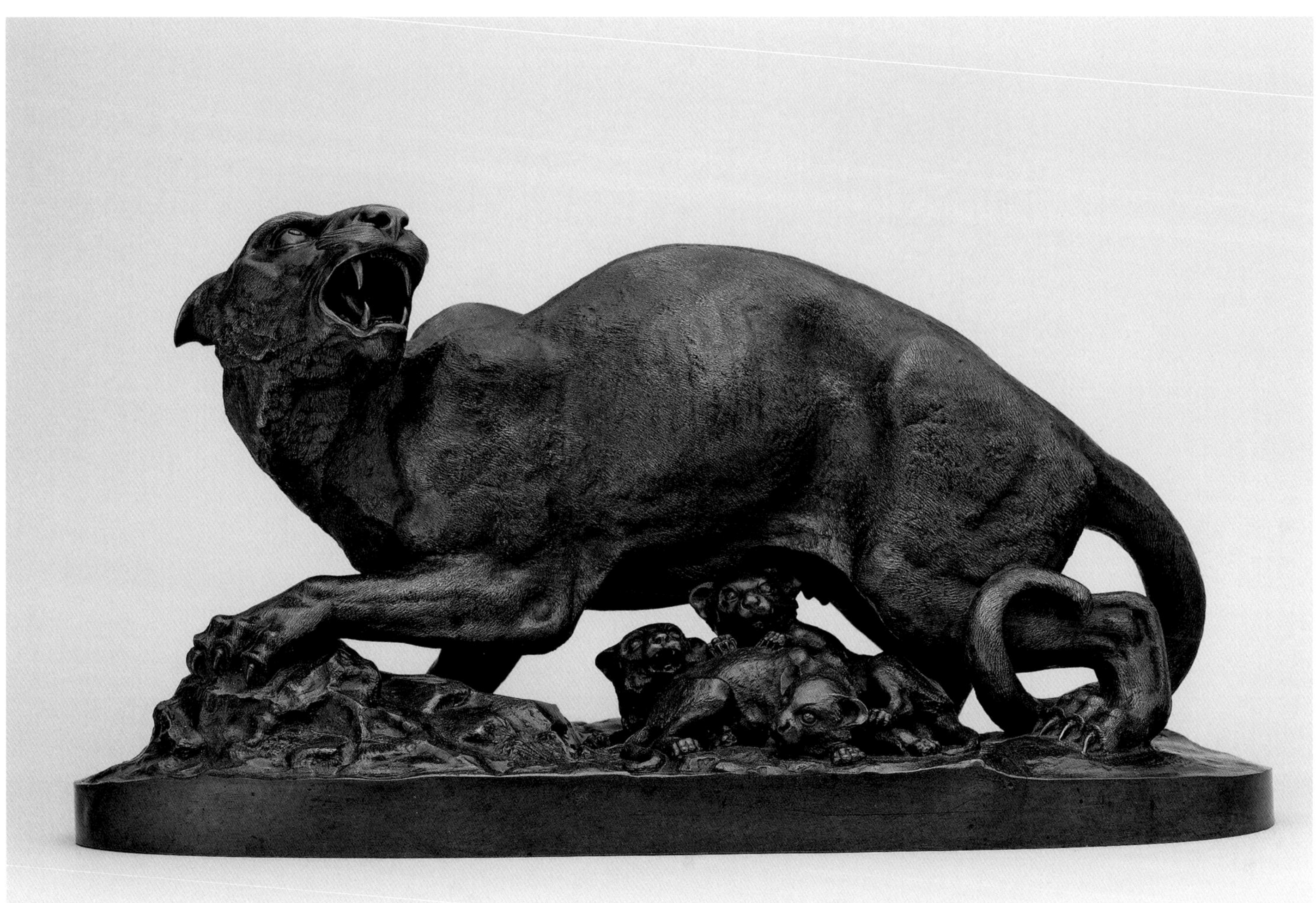

Fig. 72. Henry Kirke Brown. *Panther and Cubs*, ca. 1850–55. Cat. 12

strokes of the panthers' fur, the carefully articulated teeth and claws, and the swirling incisions denoting the pupils of the eyes.

America's first sculptor to specialize in animals was Edward Kemeys, who devoted his thirty-five-year career to producing a vast oeuvre that comprised principally wildlife subjects but also included American Indians. Self-taught, Kemeys was inspired to model the animals he observed in the Central Park Menagerie, beginning in 1868. In the early 1870s he focused on the wolf as predator, notably in the lifesize sculpture that launched his career, *Hudson Bay Wolves Quarreling over the Carcass of a Deer,* the first American public wildlife group, installed in Philadelphia's Fairmount Park in 1872 (now in the Philadelphia Zoo). With the earnings from this commission, Kemeys traveled as far west as Colorado and Wyoming in 1873, living among Indians and trappers and studying wildlife, alive and dead —a pattern he would repeat throughout his career. On that first extended trip, he participated in expeditions in which mounted hunters slaughtered bison. As he recalled, hunting and dissecting were integral to his artistic expression: "I met the mountain animals, I killed them, grizzlies, sheep, wolves. . . . I went to the heart's core of our American wilderness, and it yielded up its most carefully guarded secrets."[3]

That western sojourn reinforced Kemeys's dedication to animal sculpture, and in 1876 he displayed three groups in the Philadelphia Centennial Exhibition: *Coyote and Raven, Playing Possum,* and *Panther and Deer.* The exhibition

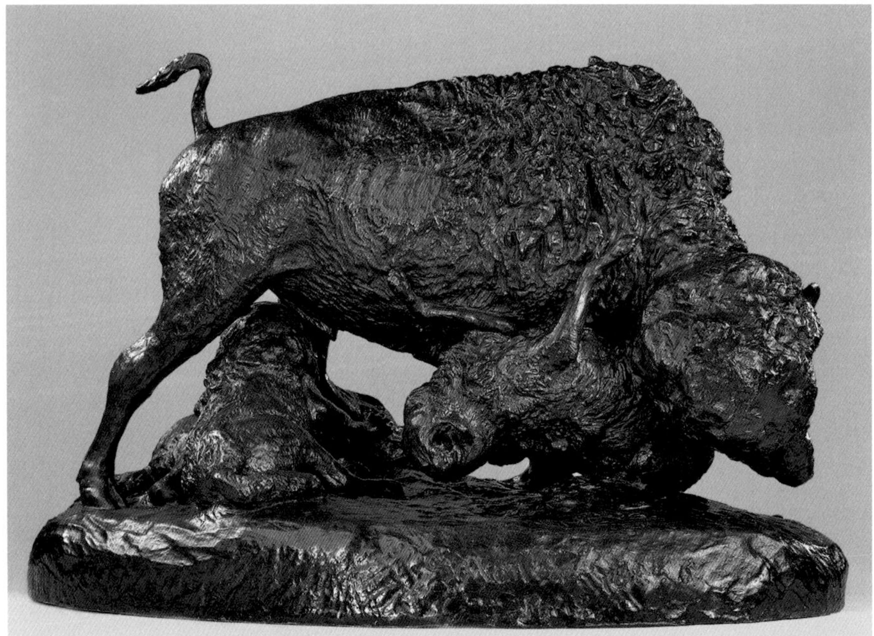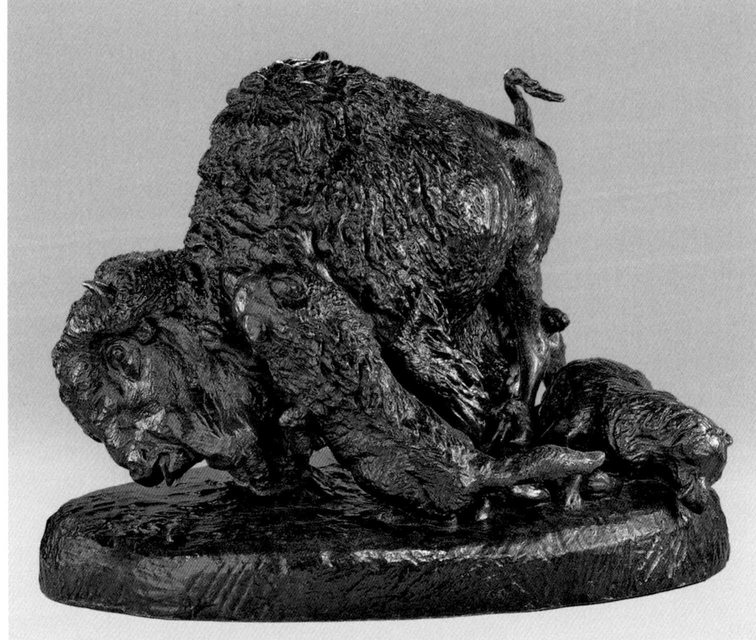

proved to be the swan song of the Neoclassical marble aesthetic favored by expatriates, but it signaled a new direction in American sculpture: naturalistic form cast in the responsive medium of bronze. In 1877 Kemeys traveled overseas, following the examples of George Catlin and Albert Bierstadt, who had promoted the mystique of the American West by exhibiting in London, as Kemeys did there with a one-man gallery show of plasters and bronzes that fall. Then, like hundreds of other ambitious American artists, he went on to the proving ground of Paris. His *Buffalo and Wolves*, modeled in 1876, was shown in plaster in the Salon of 1878,[4] where it announced to a cosmopolitan audience his signature style, in which narrative and projection of animal mood and expression took precedence over anatomical exactitude. It also presented two distinctly American animals—the once-ubiquitous bison and the wolf, long the most hated of North American predators, both subject to deliberate campaigns of extermination that peaked in the late nineteenth century.[5]

The bronze cast of *Buffalo and Wolves* (figs. 73, 74), proudly inscribed "Salon de 1878/ Paris," is rendered with Kemeys's trademark impressionistic texture, with broad toolmarks that convey spontaneity rather than precise musculature. The narrative of this deadly combat may have been inspired by Kemeys's 1873 western trip. He, like other travelers, may have observed hungry wolf packs surrounding a young or weak bison to isolate it from the herd. One contemporary witness described the moment of attack:

Suddenly they leaped forward, two to feint attack upon his head, the others to run swiftly to and fro behind him, getting ever closer to his heels, their purpose to hamstring him. He seemed to know their plan—perhaps he had been attacked by wolves before—he sought to protect his rear, and to do that tried to face all ways at once. . . . To run from them was impossible; the battle had to be fought there on the spot. He lunged now at this wolf, again at that one, wheeling all the time; in fact, he spun round and round like a huge, erratic top. We could hear his snorts of rage.[6]

As in this firsthand account, so it is in Kemeys's sculpture, where wolves surround the weighty beast. Even though the bison is clearly doomed, the outcome is not without cost to the victors, with two of the four wolves lying gravely wounded.

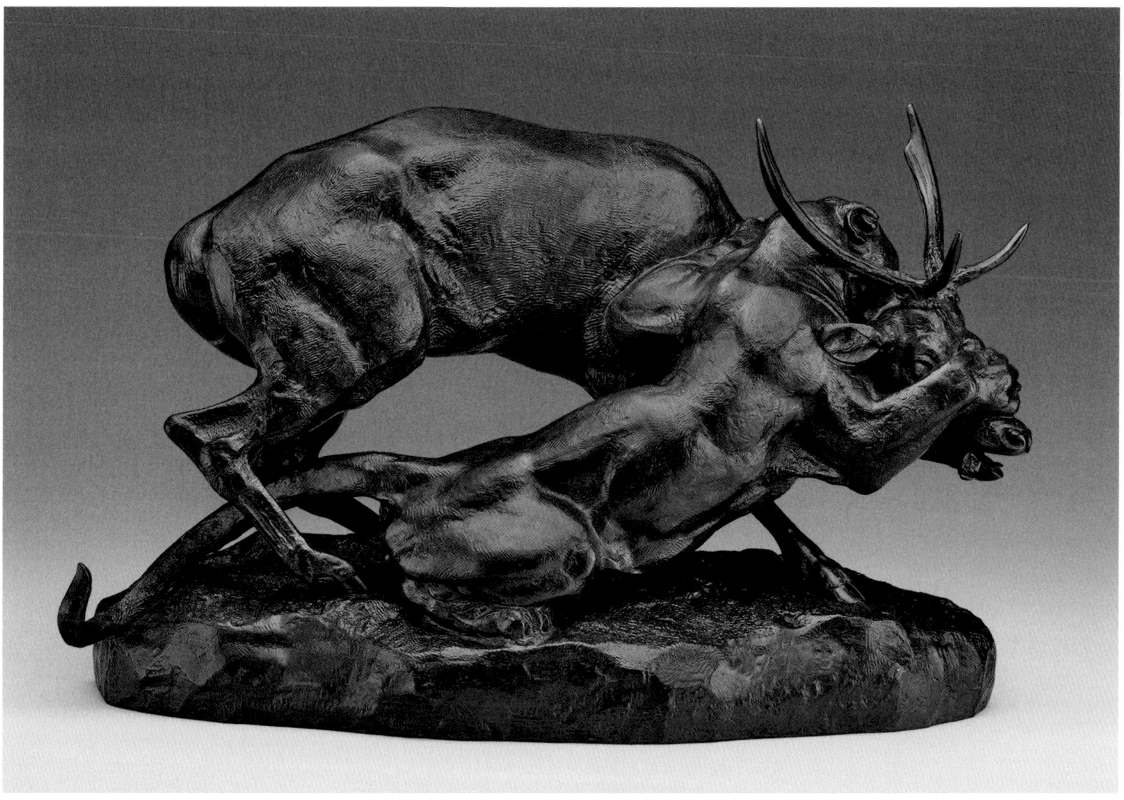

In Paris, Kemeys presumably encountered the works of the great French animaliers Auguste-Nicolas Cain and Emmanuel Fremiet, if not the sculptors themselves. He also visited the zoological gardens at the Jardin des Plantes (although throughout his career he swore off studying caged animals). Although Antoine-Louis Barye had died in 1875, he still loomed large, and Kemeys familiarized himself with Barye's animal groups in Paris, almost certainly both lifetime casts and the posthumous ones that flooded the market. From early in his career, Kemeys was referred to as the "American Barye," but the Frenchman's work (fig. 75) achieved far greater technical refinement. To resist Barye's spell was impossible for American animal sculptors in the late nineteenth century, and his fight-to-the-death groups served as inspiration for Kemeys and his compatriots.[7]

Following his return to New York in 1878, Kemeys established a national reputation as the sculptor par excellence of the North American mammal. *Still Hunt* (fig. 76), a crouching panther in bronze installed on a rocky outcropping in Central Park (East Drive and Seventy-Sixth Street), was unveiled in 1883, the funds for its casting and installation having been raised by public subscription. The title refers to the feline technique of stalking prey slowly and deliberately; passersby below are turned into potential victims as the predator, with ears erect and back arched, readies to pounce. Kemeys's output was vast, in part because he generated variations on successful themes. He adapted *Still Hunt* to statuette scale in bronze and in terracotta in the mid-1880s (bronze; Sagamore Hill National Historic Site, Oyster Bay, New York) and to high-relief format in 1894, applying his signature wolf's-head mark to the surface (figs. 77, 78).[8] In an affiliation that was novel for an American sculptor of his day, Kemeys went into partnership with the Chicago foundry Winslow Bros. to offer his statuettes and objets d'art through mail order.[9] The relief version of

Fig. 75. Antoine-Louis Barye (French, 1796–1875). *Panther Seizing a Stag*, before 1847. Bronze, 14⅛ × 21¾ × 10¼ in. (35.9 × 55.2 × 26 cm). The Metropolitan Museum of Art, Gift of M.A.S. de Reinis, 1981 (1981.241)

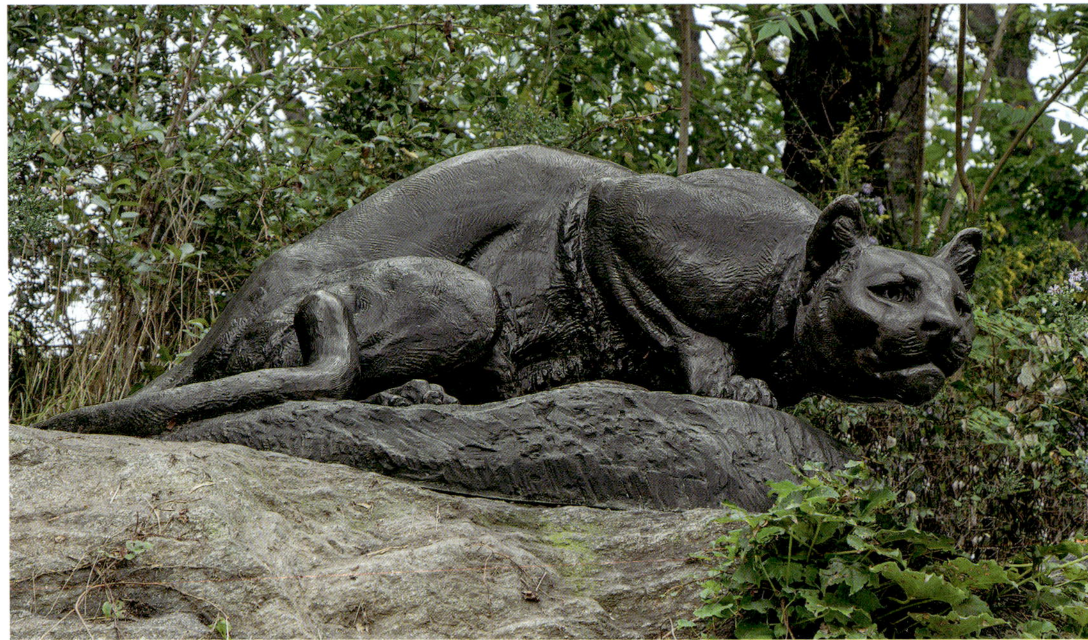

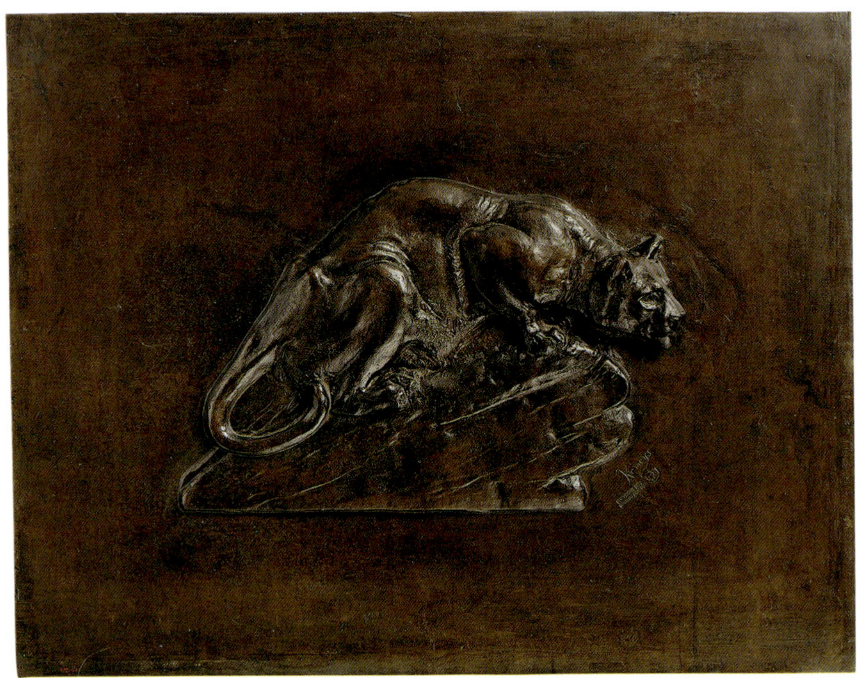

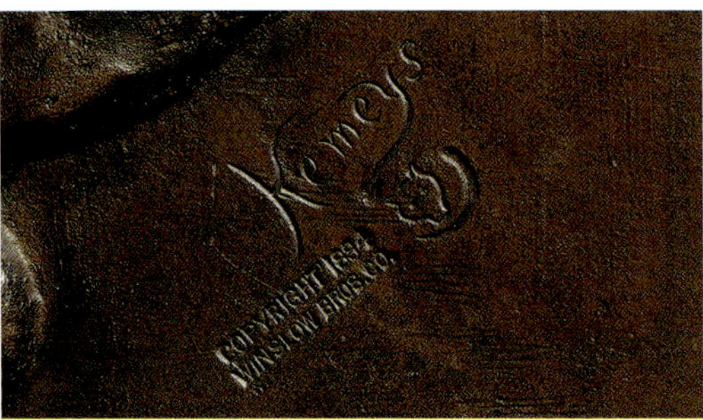

Still Hunt was one of four panels depicting large cats offered through Winslow; the others were *Feeding* (unlocated), *At Bay*, and *At Play* (both National Museum of Wildlife Art, Jackson Hole, Wyoming).[10]

Kemeys's work enjoyed increasing national prominence, and he promoted himself assiduously. He displayed his statuettes in a small gallery in his New York studio, which was decorated with hides, horns, and other relics from his western trips, and he exhibited at major urban venues. In June 1884, Julian Hawthorne, a close friend who had traveled with the sculptor abroad, published an article in the nationally circulated *Century Magazine* touting Kemeys's commitment to his western subjects:

He has done a service of incalculable value to his country, not only in vindicating American art, but in preserving to us, in a permanent and beautiful form, the vivid and veracious figures of a wild fauna which, in the inevitable progress of colonization and civilization, is destined within a few years to vanish altogether. The American bear and bison, the cimarron and the elk, the wolf and the 'coon—where will they be a generation hence? Nowhere, save in the possession of those persons who have to-day the opportunity and intelligence to decorate their rooms and parks with Mr. Kemeys's inimitable bronzes.[11]

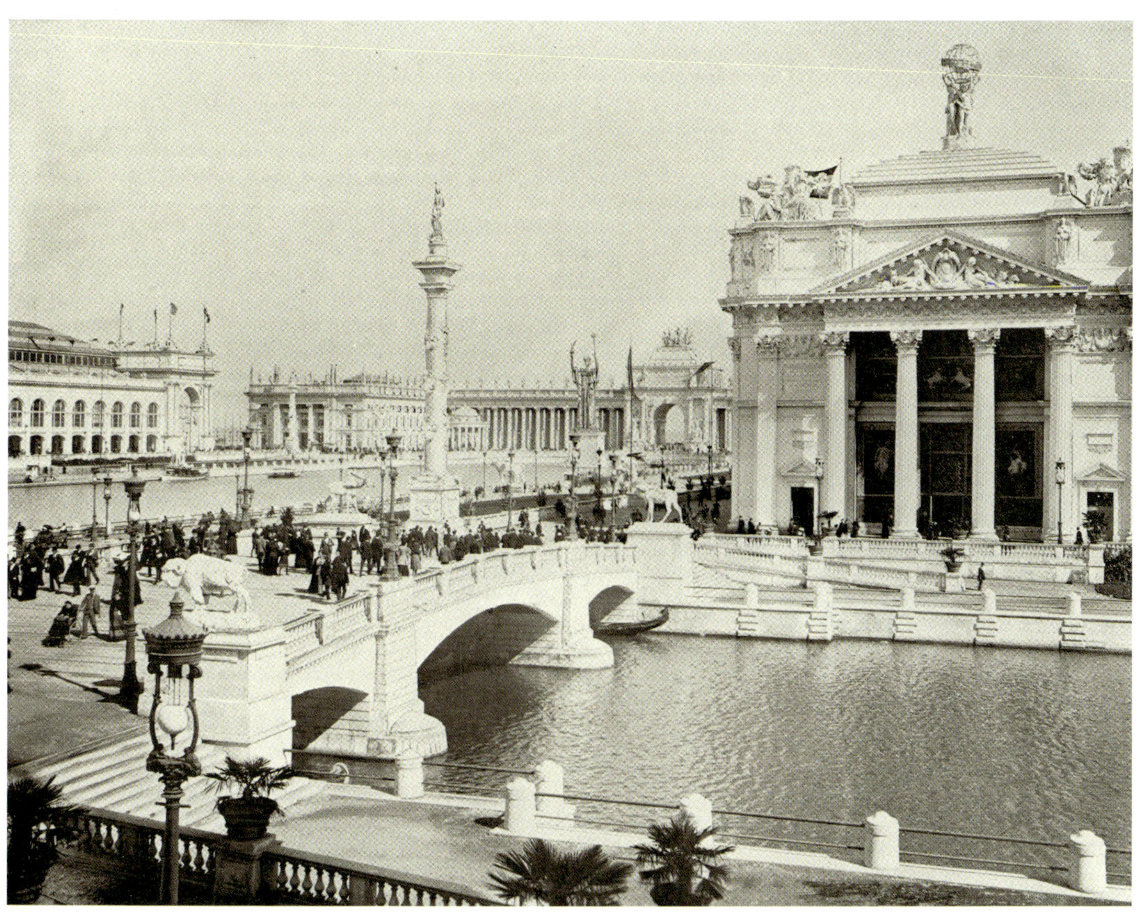

Kemeys engaged in his own self-promotion in a series of ten articles that loosely recounted his western travels. Titled "The Sunset Land: A Tale of Rocky Mountain Adventure," the writings were published between June 1886 and January 1887 in the newly founded *Outing: An Illustrated Monthly Magazine of Recreation*. Happily for Kemeys, his articles overlapped with Theodore Roosevelt's series "Ranch Life and Game Shooting in the West," in the March–August 1886 issues. Roosevelt would staunchly endorse Kemeys from then on, acquiring his bronzes for his personal collection and recommending him for public commissions.

In 1892 Kemeys relocated to Chicago, having earned a significant commission (along with the up-and-coming Alexander Phimister Proctor) for monumental animal sculptures to decorate the bridges over the lagoon and canals of the World's Columbian Exposition fairgrounds (fig. 79). With the assistance of his wife, the sculptor Laura Swing Kemeys (fig. 80), he produced twelve larger-than-life models, including six American panthers plus pairs of bison, bears, and lions. In addition to these outdoor works in the impermanent medium of staff (a mixture of plaster of Paris and fibrous materials such as

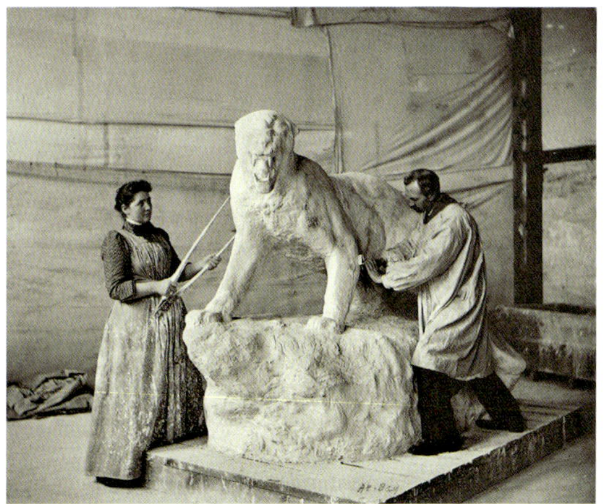

Fig. 79. *Looking Eastward from Canal and Bridge*, World's Columbian Exposition, Chicago, 1893, with bison by Edward Kemeys and moose by Alexander Phimister Proctor on the bridge between the Agriculture and Mechanical Arts Buildings

Fig. 80. *Edward Kemeys and Laura Swing Kemeys at Work in Their Studio*, ca. 1893. Photograph by C. D. Arnold

hemp and straw), he also displayed twelve sculptures in the Fine Arts Building, more than any other American. Included in this group, which earned a gold medal, were the large *Panther and Cubs* (ca. 1878; The Metropolitan Museum of Art, bronze, 1907) and the whimsical *Soul of Contentment* (fig. 81), an American black bear lolling on its back, scratching its haunch in an absurdly flexible pose.[12] Kemeys enjoyed modeling bears; though finding their gangly, lumbering forms particularly winsome, he resisted anthropomorphizing them, unlike other artists of the day.

Kemeys's work had been in the public eye long before 1893, but Proctor was only just establishing himself as an artist. He represented an entirely different type: raised in Colorado with rifle and sketchbook always close at hand, he moved to New York in 1885. There he began the academic training standard for an aspiring artist, enrolling in classes at the National Academy of Design and then at the Art Students League. From the outset, Proctor approached wildlife as a scientist-artist, undertaking anatomical dissections, sketching at the Central Park Menagerie, and studying specimens at the American Museum of Natural History.[13] Having trained first as a painter, he shifted to sculpture after seeing a comprehensive exhibition of Barye's works at the American Art Galleries in 1889–90.[14] Proctor's earliest statuette, *Fawn* (1887; R. W. Norton Art Gallery, Shreveport, Louisiana), was displayed at the Century Association, where the delicately modeled newborn caught the eye of Francis Davis Millet, later director of decorations for the Chicago world's fair.[15] In 1891 Millet commissioned Proctor to model six monumental groups, an assignment that eventually expanded to include pairs of elk, moose, jaguars, and polar bears (replicated to a total of thirty-five), as well as equestrian

Fig. 81. Edward Kemeys. *The Soul of Contentment (Black Bear)*, 1886 (cast ca. 1886–99). Cat. 24

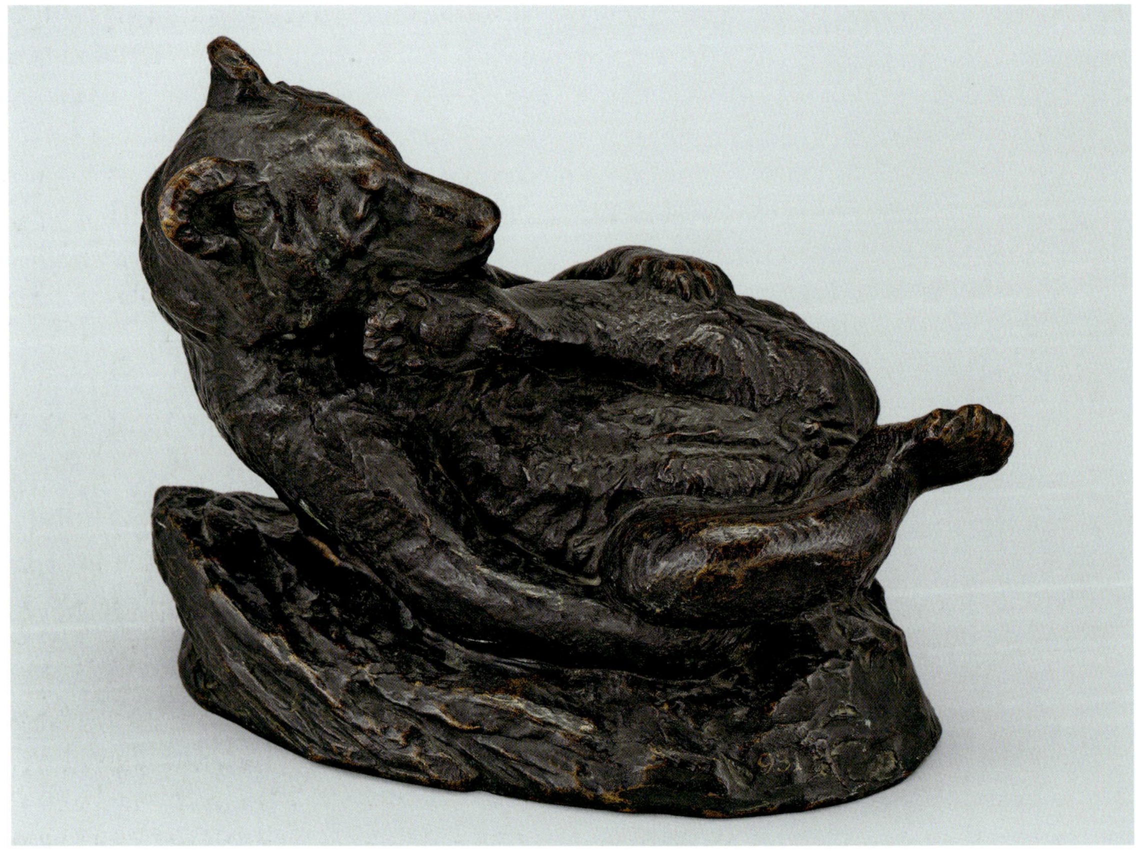

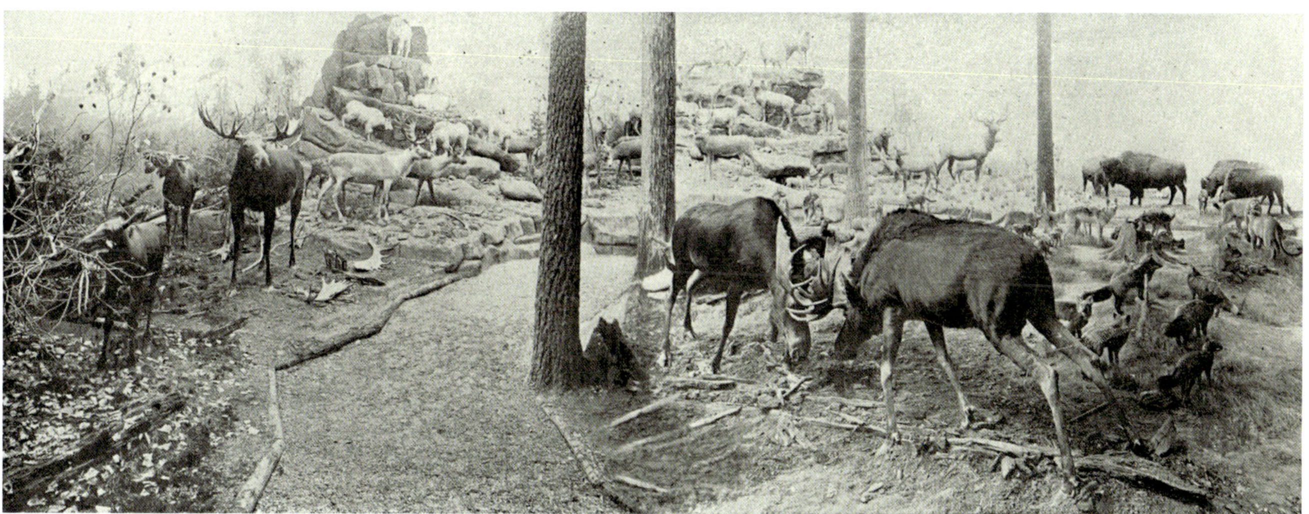

sculptures of an American Indian and a cowboy (see fig. 111). The animals—poised and static on their rectilinear pedestals (see fig. 79)—were based on sketches from his western experiences as well as trips to the zoo in nearby Lincoln Park.

As Kemeys's career developed during the 1870s and Proctor's launched in the 1880s, so too did the congruent movements of sporting and land and game conservation, which are interconnected with the American wildlife bronze and several of its more prominent sculptors. The founding in 1872 of Yellowstone National Park, which became a wildlife preserve,[16] was the opening salvo in the Conservation Movement, followed in 1890 by the establishment of Yosemite National Park. Several sporting journals commenced publication, and artists contributed articles and illustrations to them based on their own firsthand experience. These included *American Sportsman* (1871), *Forest and Stream* (1873), *Field and Stream* (1874), and *Outing* (1885), all of which became powerful organs for the Conservation Movement.[17] Not surprisingly, there was considerable overlap in the individuals (usually male, wealthy, and socially well-connected) who wrote for these publications, engaged in big-game hunting, joined sporting associations, and patronized sculptors of western themes.

This linkage was particularly manifest in the Boone and Crockett Club, spearheaded by George Bird Grinnell and Theodore Roosevelt in 1887. An influential invitation-only band of one hundred sportsmen, including artists Bierstadt and Proctor, this organization promoted an ethic of purposeful hunting of large mammals (as game trophies rather than for meat or hides) while also effectively advocating for the protection of threatened species and their wilderness environments.[18] Popular literature that focused on native fauna as protagonists reinforced public awareness, particularly bestselling writings such as Ernest Thompson Seton's *Wild Animals I Have Known* (1898) and Jack London's *Call of the Wild* (1903).[19]

The World's Columbian Exposition, which attracted some twenty-seven million visitors during its six-month run, was a highly visible stage for western sculpture (notably Kemeys's and Proctor's monumental outdoor groups) and a seminal moment for the growing awareness of America's native animals and the Conservation Movement. Of the several displays featuring taxidermied mammals, the Kansas Building's installation of over one hundred specimens was singled out "by artists and professional men from all over the world who have seen it" as "the finest group of mounted animals" (fig. 82).[20] Supervised by

Fig. 82. *"A Combat to the Death,"* Kansas Building, World's Columbian Exposition, Chicago, 1893

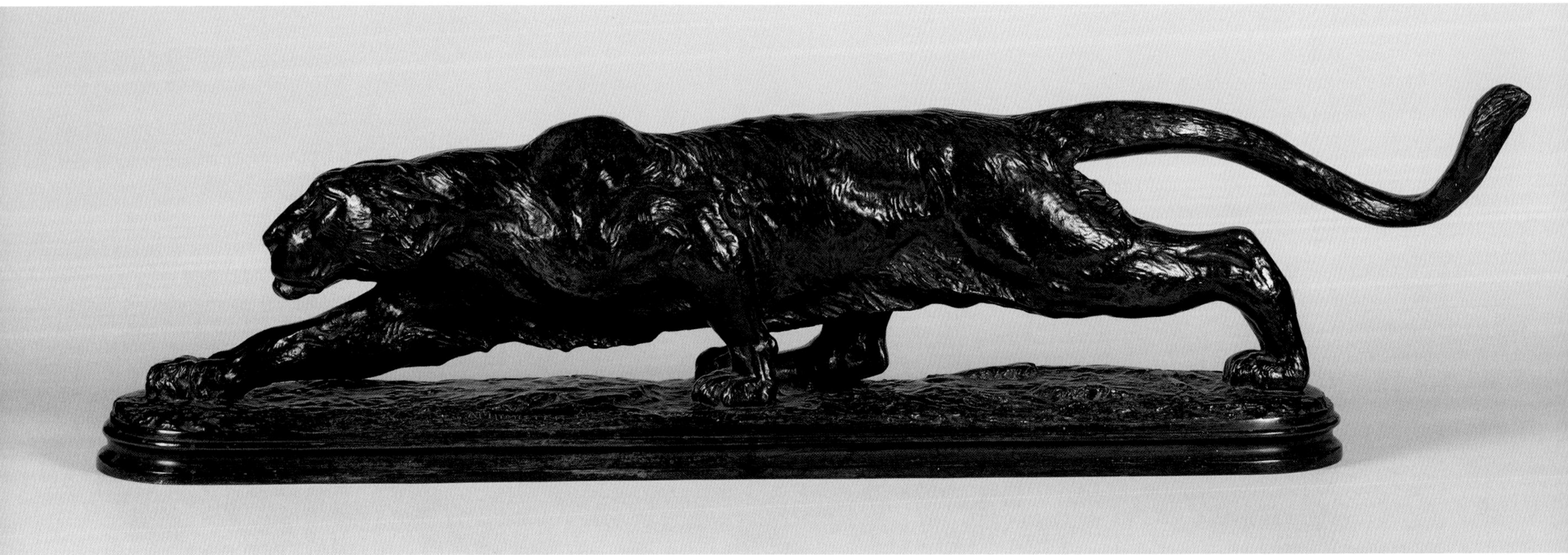

William T. Hornaday, who would become director of the New York Zoological Park in 1896, the exhibit displayed the animals in natural-habitat settings, an innovation at the time, with dramatic action poses that thrilled fairgoers. The Boone and Crockett Club's "hunter's cabin," a log cabin on the Wooded Island in the lagoon, was another popular destination, especially for its members, who used it as a clubhouse of sorts; Proctor was initiated into the club's ranks there, at its annual dinner.[21] With trophy heads, pelts, and hunting gear, the masculine space was set apart from the civilized and highly planned fairgrounds—a tangible metaphor for the interconnectedness of the frontier preservation movement and a select cultural authority.

In the years just following the World's Columbian Exposition, Chicago provided a consistent source of patronage for its home-town sculptors, corresponding with the peak of Kemeys's career. He worked in nearby Bryn Mawr in his studio, "Wolfden," and continued to make "pilgrimages to the wilderness,"[22] as he referred to the western trips during which he produced rough sketch models that became

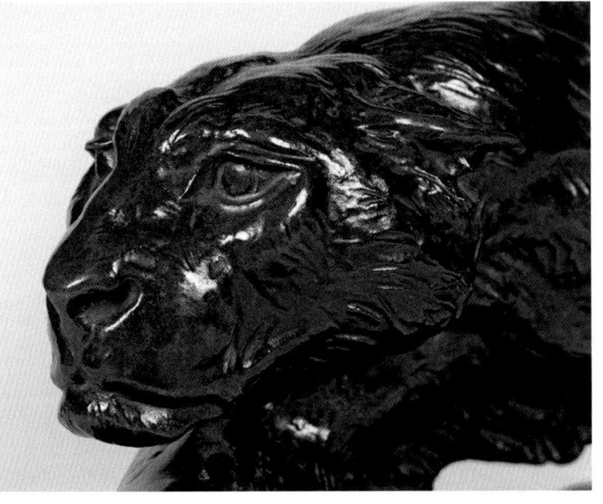

the basis for his small bronzes. Meanwhile, even though Proctor's success at the World's Columbian Exposition put his name in the spot-light, he aspired to more rigorous training. He went to Paris in 1893, where he trained at the Académie Julian, and later returned to study at the Académie Colarossi, having received a Rine-hart Scholarship in 1896 that funded three years' study abroad.

Stalking Panther (fig. 83) highlights the relation of Proctor's art to his principal self-identity as a sportsman-adventurer, which he had cultivated from a young age.[23] He began the statuette in New York, basing it on observations of panthers made during an 1887 trip to Colorado and at the Central Park Menagerie, as well as on dissection studies. After displaying the sculpture at the World's Columbian Exposition, he took the plaster model to Paris, where he refined it using a shaved cat for reference. For its freeze-frame motion, Proctor applied his method of "getting a picture of a whole action": "I found I could get an action picture by closing my eyes, opening them for a split second, and then shutting them again. I practiced this exercise until I arrived at the point where I could retain the picture long enough to do a rough sketch. It was in this manner that I made the sketches for my panther."[24] The muscular and skeletal structures of the low-slung animal are convincingly rendered, from its muzzle (fig. 84) to the tip of its sweeping tail.

Proctor, like Kemeys before him, set up an unresolved drama in *Stalking Panther*, allowing viewers to supply the outcome for themselves.

The statuette earned immediate plaudits. The Chicago sculptor and historian Lorado Taft wrote approvingly in 1898: "The striding panther is a powerful work, almost too thin and 'anatomical' for comfort—either ours or its own—but betraying everywhere the knowledge and research of its creator. By those who know, this study is counted almost as a masterpiece."[25] *Stalking Panther*, termed by Proctor his "first real bronze,"[26] was a career-long success, judging by a steady production of bronze casts in two sizes. One (Sagamore Hill National Historic Site, Oyster Bay, New York) was presented to President Theodore Roosevelt in 1909 by his so-called Tennis Cabinet—an unofficial group of advisers whose names were inscribed around the sculpture's base.[27]

Proctor took full advantage of his Parisian tenure, defining himself principally as an animal sculptor not only of western wildlife but also of dogs and horses, elephants and lions. He modeled several other small bronzes, some based on his Chicago groups (fig. 85),

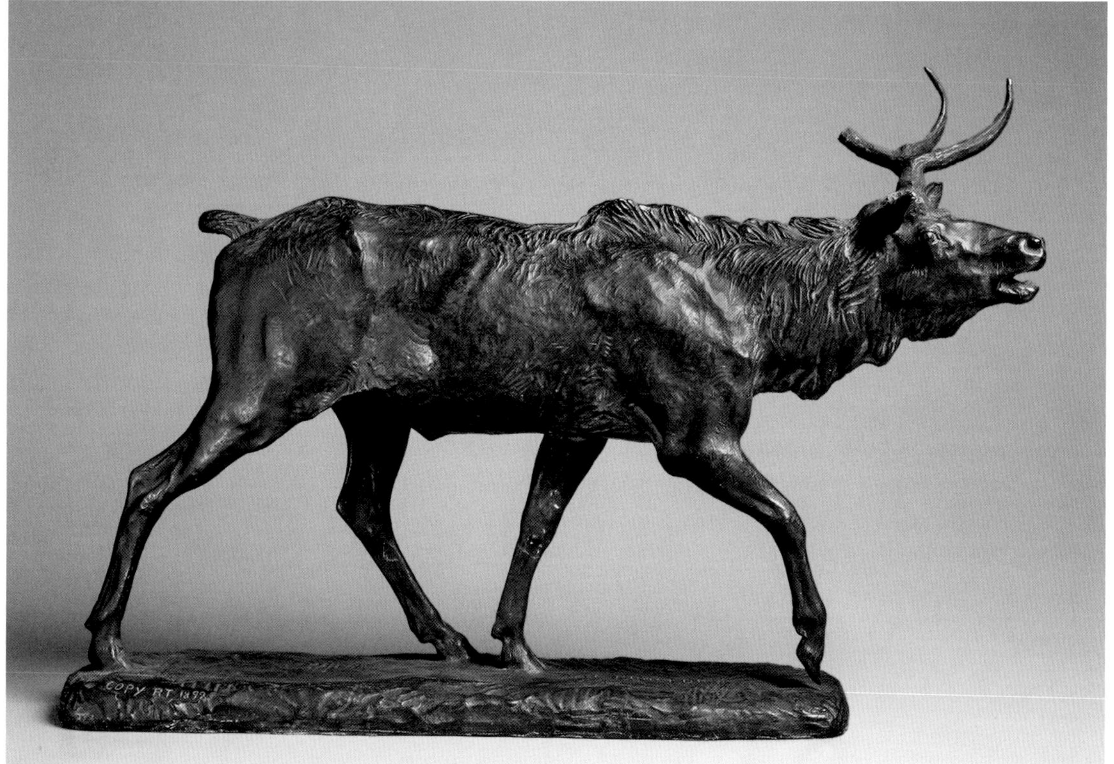

Fig. 85. Alexander Phimister Proctor. *Elk*, 1899. Bronze, 16½ × 20 × 7½ in. (41.9 × 50.8 × 19.1 cm). Brooklyn Museum, Gift of George D. Pratt

which were exhibited at the 1900 Exposition Universelle, along with his massive quadriga for the roof of the United States Pavilion, and earned him a gold medal. Proctor also launched a successful career as a monumental sculptor: for instance, his commission for colossal pumas on the gateposts at the south entrance to Prospect Park in Brooklyn (1896–97) was based on studies in the Ménagerie du Jardin des Plantes. When he returned from Paris in 1900 and settled in New York, he represented a sophisticated new type of American animal sculptor—one with modern academic training grounded in Beaux-Arts techniques coupled with rigorous study of his subjects' flesh and bone. With one foot in the cosmopolitan centers of Paris and New York, and the other in the American West of game hunting, Proctor —and the work he made—was defined by this composite of talent and experience, civilization and wilderness.

Solon Hannibal Borglum, like his friend Proctor, also grew up in the West and came of age artistically in Paris. Arriving there in 1897, Borglum trained at the Académie Julian and observed animals at the Jardin des Plantes; he also studied with Emmanuel Fremiet. In Paris, Borglum parlayed his "Sculptor of the Prairie" identity to great effect, delighting audiences with his interpretations of the American frontier based on personal experience. In addition to such cowboy groups as *Lassoing Wild Horses* (fig. 116), he was lauded for his naturalistic representations of horses, which benefited not only from his stint as a Nebraska ranch hand and his dissections as an art student in Cincinnati but also from time spent in one of Paris's largest stables. Although the horse is among the oldest of artistic subjects, Borglum looked at it afresh, emphasizing its essential role in the American West for hunting, ranching, fighting, trading, and transit. As he succinctly put it: "There is not a phase of Western history that has not been influenced by this animal. . . . [H]e was the sine qua non of the exploitation of the West."[28] Borglum's sympathetic portrayals of horses enduring the challenges of frontier life (with such titles as *The Round Up*, *The Lame Horse*, *Our Slave*, and *The Intelligent Bronco*)[29] were supplemented by poignant depictions of intense human-equine bonds, whether an Indian shielding himself behind his horse in *On the Border of the White Man's Land* (fig. 43) or a cowboy and his mount huddled together in *Blizzard* (fig. 119).

Borglum's *Bulls Fighting* (fig. 86) resonates with Old West versus New West symbolism. He began modeling the sculpture in

Fig. 86. Solon Hannibal Borglum. *Bulls Fighting*, 1899–1900 (cast 1906–7). Cat. 7

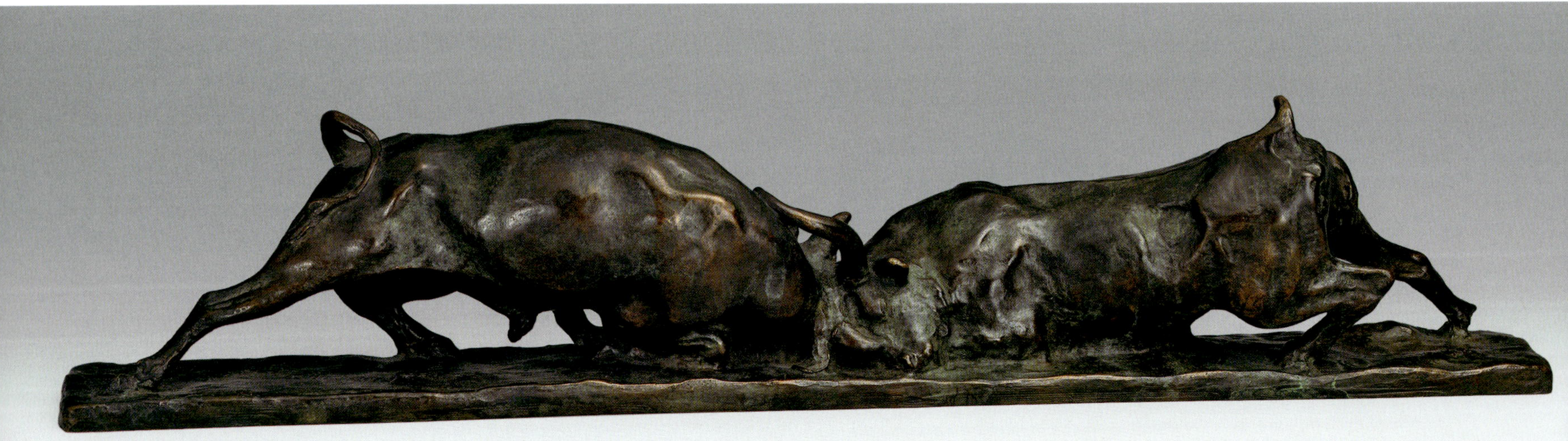

summer 1899 among the Sioux of the Crow Creek Agency in South Dakota and completed it in Paris, where he exhibited it at the Salon of 1900. The low horizontality of this small bronze emphasizes the intensity of the clash between the wild Texas longhorn and the stouter shorthorn. *Bulls Fighting* is emblematic of the transition from longhorn cattle as beef supply to domesticated steers, which yielded greater quantities of meat—a triumph of commercial breeding over natural selection. As Borglum explained in 1910: "Vast herds of cattle were driven from the Texas ranches to the Northern markets. These enormous bunches required many men to attend to them. In the

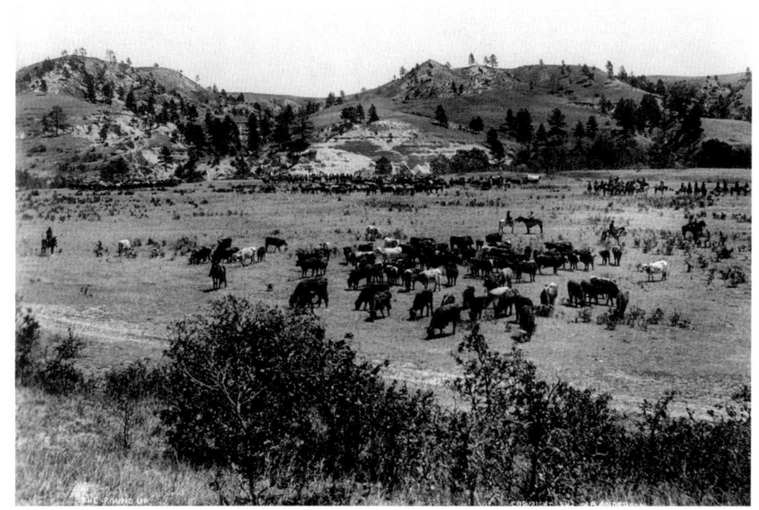

Fig. 87. *The Round Up*, ca. 1889. Photograph by W. A. Anderson

Fig. 88. *Last Remnants of the American Bison, Yellowstone National Park, U.S.A.*, ca. 1903. Photograph by American Stereoscopic Company

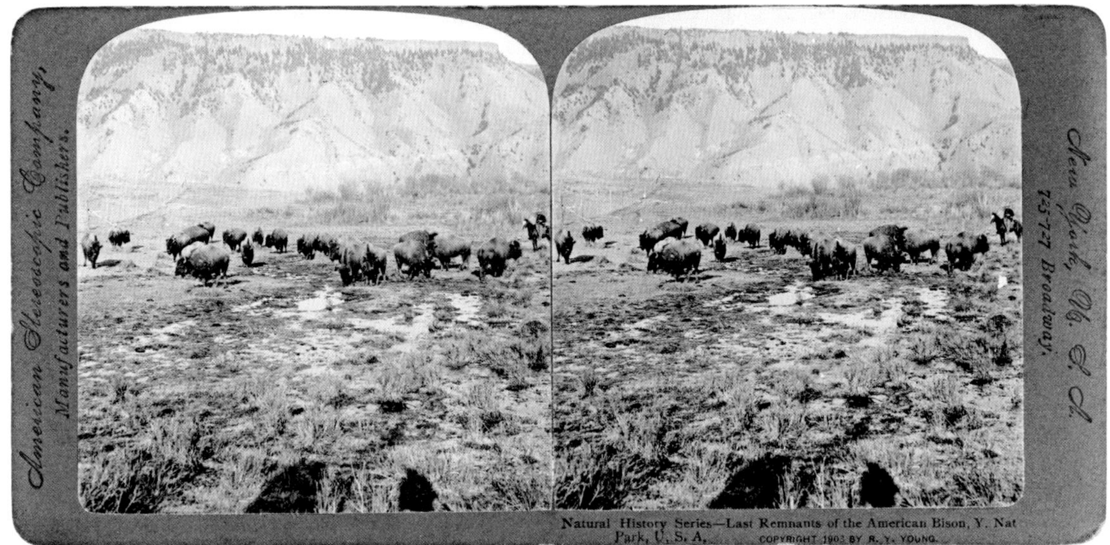

mixing of herds and brands fighting frequently occurred."[30] The ever-increasing masses of livestock driven to market along overgrazed cattle trails (fig. 87) inevitably displaced the longhorn on the open range, and by the 1920s the breed was all but extinct. Efforts to repopulate it were launched successfully in Kansas and Texas, no doubt partly out of nostalgia for the Old West.

Of course, of all the "vanishing" native animals, none attracted more attention than the North American bison (fig. 88). After government-sanctioned hunting reduced the number of bison from millions to mere hundreds by the early 1880s (see fig. 37), awareness of its plight inspired statuettes that focused on the breed as a metaphor for a bygone past and for the squandering of natural resources. Nearly every sculptor of western themes, whether an animal specialist or not, at some point modeled the bison. Perhaps the most remarkable in terms of its naturalism and quality of casting is Henry Merwin Shrady's *Buffalo* (figs. 70, 89), which was produced in two sizes (approximately fourteen and twenty-three inches high). This bronze exemplifies Shrady's command of animal anatomy, acquired in

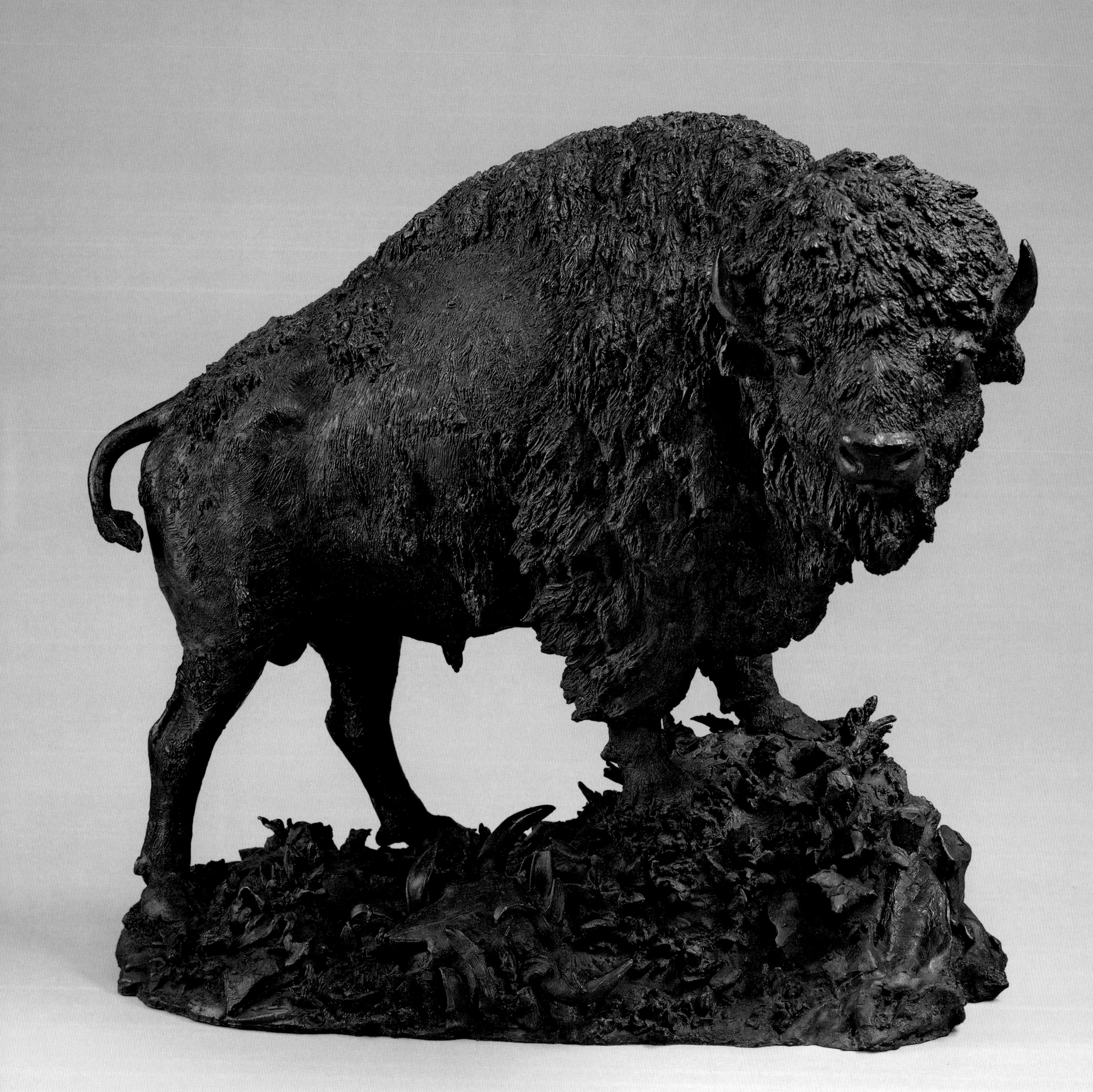

Fig. 89. Henry Merwin Shrady. *Buffalo*, 1899 (cast ca. 1901). Cat. 72

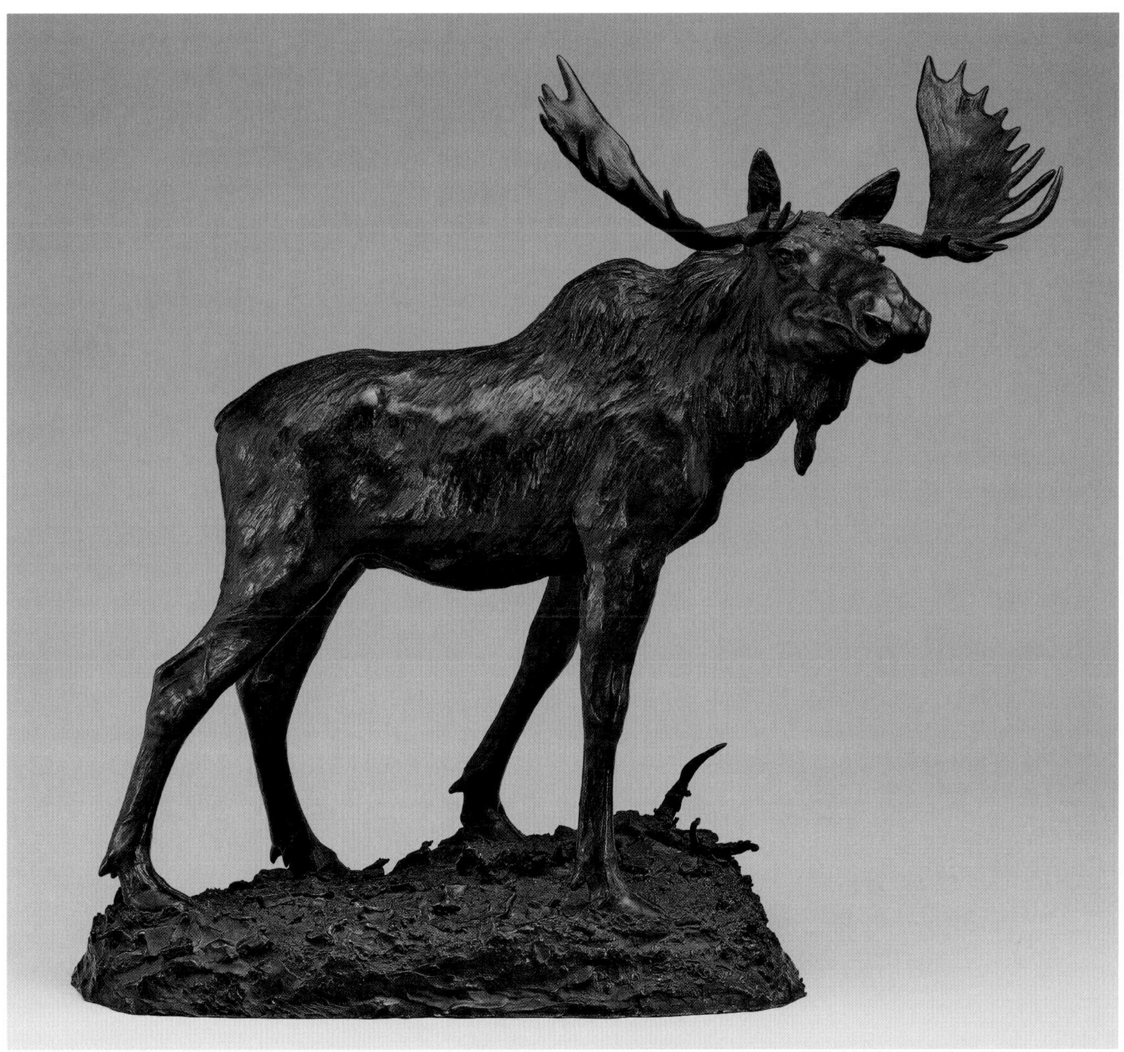

Fig. 90. Henry Merwin Shrady. *Bull Moose*, 1900. Cat. 73

biology studies at Columbia University as well as through his observation of animals at the New York Zoological Park (the Bronx Zoo). He convincingly recorded the bison's solid form, rendering its weighty coat as a textural tour de force. The skull on the rocky base is resonant with meaning, as Brian W. Dippie has observed: "The buffalo skull is to the western plains what the tree stump is to the eastern forest: a symbol of progress that leaves in its wake an uneasy sense of loss."[31]

Shrady's statuette appeared at an auspicious moment, concurrent with the importation of lost-wax casting to the United States around 1900. The Old World technique was promoted in particular by Riccardo Bertelli at his newly established Roman Bronze Works in New York, where Shrady, Frederic Remington, and others began to cast their bronzes. Remington was so impressed by Shrady's *Buffalo*, which had been cast there, that he purchased an example in 1908, calling it "bye [*sic*] and large the best buffalo I ever saw modeled and it has become one of the things that I had to own."[32] Unlike sand casting, the lost-wax process allowed for refinements to the wax model, which gave sculptors freedom to make changes, experiment, and lavish care on details, as Shrady did here.

Buffalo, along with *Bull Moose* (fig. 90), propelled the novice Shrady to notice. Both the stolid bison and the lanky moose were issued in sizable editions through the entrepreneurial New York jeweler and dealer Theodore B. Starr. He encouraged Shrady to model small bronzes for "their mutual benefit," purchasing the copyrights and paying the artist royalties on casts sold.[33] The sculptor Karl Bitter saw the bronzes at Starr's shop and, in his role as director of sculpture for the 1901 Pan-American Exposition in Buffalo, asked Shrady to re-create the animals at full size for the fairgrounds. Bitter opened his Weehawken, New Jersey, studio to Shrady during the six-week process of enlarging the moose to nine feet and the bison to eight. A total of eight casts produced in staff decorated bridges at the fair; paired together, the bison of the plains and the moose of the eastern and western forests were instantly recognizable to contemporary audiences as near-extinct types.[34] Just as Kemeys's and Proctor's sculptures had done in Chicago, Shrady's offered a powerful commentary on the price of progress—the vulnerability of native animals caused by Euro-American settlement of the West.

The emergence of a new generation of sculptors as well as the professionalization of American zoos highlighted a difference in approach between artists committed to studying and hunting wild animals in their native habitats and those artists who limited their observations to captive animals in zoos and specimens in natural history museums. Proctor did use zoos for supplementary studies, but he believed "that only one who has known the wild, free life of the mountains and forest as the beasts themselves know it can transmit this spirit to his clay . . . as a positive force."[35] Others—Shrady and Eli Harvey among them—would assemble their easels and modeling stands by the animal houses of East Coast zoos. The most influential, the Bronx Zoo, founded as the New York Zoological Society in 1895, was brought about by efforts of the Boone and Crockett Club, which "came forward almost in

a body—practically every New York member—with money and with time."[36] The zoo formally opened to the public in November 1899 with 843 animals, allotting many North American herds—including bison and caribou—enough acreage to roam in natural-habitat settings. Sculptors not only garnered inspiration from the zoo but also contributed to its appearance, providing freestanding and relief sculptures for the various animal houses. Proctor contributed most extensively—modeling decorations for the Reptile, Aquatic Bird, Antelope, Primate, and Elephant (south end) houses, while Charles R. Knight embellished the Zebra and Elephant (north end) houses, and Eli Harvey, the Lion House (which included an artists' studio).[37]

Harvey's extensive commission for the zoo (1901–3) occasioned his return in 1901 from twelve years in Paris, where he had studied with Fremiet at the Jardin des Plantes as well as in private menageries. Like Proctor, he modeled a range of wild creatures and carried out dissections, but his live studies were based exclusively on animals in captivity. Harvey's small bronzes of animals in various moods enjoyed great commercial success and were replicated in large editions, including *Jaguar Rampant* (1908; Newark Museum, New Jersey) and *Bull Elk* (fig. 91), which was derived from modeling sessions at the New York Zoological Park (fig. 92). In his autobiography, Harvey wrote entertainingly of the challenges of interacting with the male elk, one of the largest North American mammals, especially as rutting season approached: "I took more risks with this animal than with any other I ever modeled."[38] Working in a shed in close proximity to the agitated, pacing elk, the sculptor deemed the points on its impressive rack of antlers as "sharp as bayonets."[39] Harvey's expert rendering of the animal's skeletal structure and shaggy coat reflects his extensive Parisian training. *Bull Elk* was reproduced at both statuette and

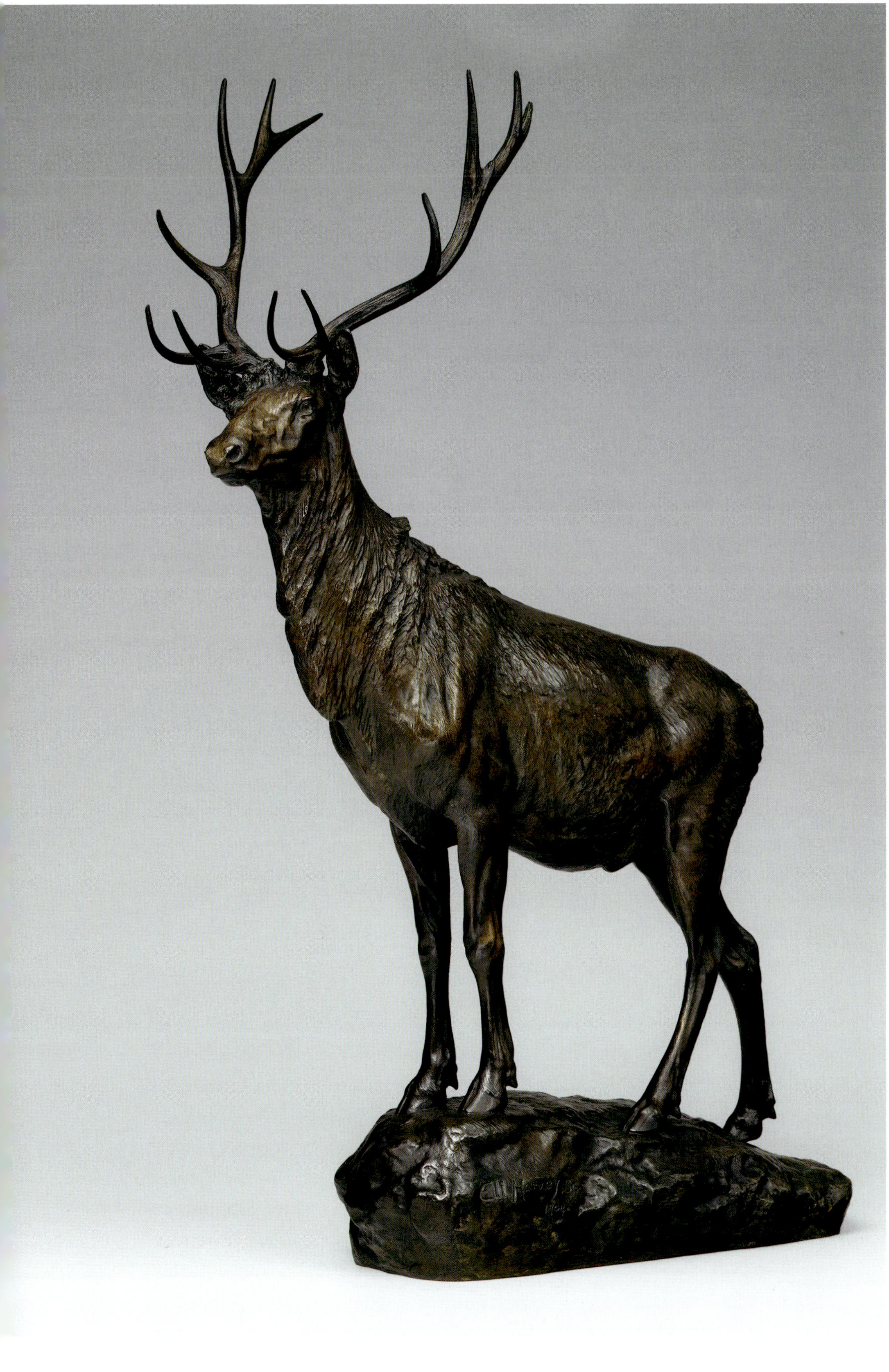

Fig. 91. Eli Harvey. *Bull Elk*, 1904
(cast probably 1905). Cat. 22

Fig. 92. *Eli Harvey Completing a
Life-Size Model of an Elk, New York
Zoological Park*, ca. 1904

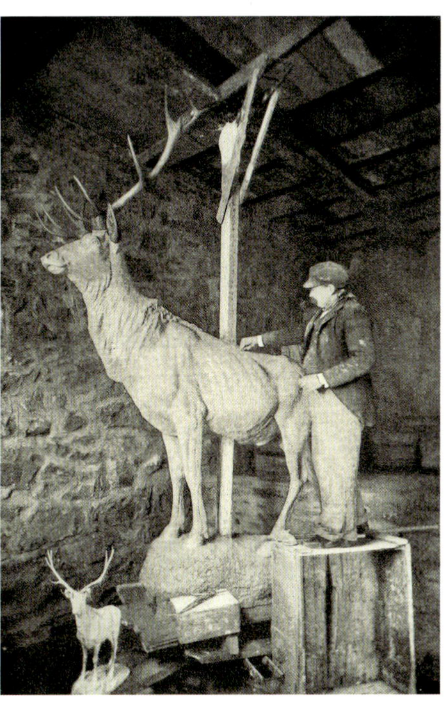

monumental scale, serving as the mascot for the Benevolent and Protective Order of Elks, with bronze casts placed at fraternal lodges across the United States.

As artists relied on zoos for inspiration, so too did they depend on natural history museums. Proctor, for instance, used the American Museum of Natural History in Manhattan as a research lab, studying its plaster casts and dissected animals. In 1902, after killing a bull moose in Canada said to be one of the largest ever recorded, he displayed the mounted specimen there.[40] Harvey, who had a one-artist exhibition of eighty-four works at the museum in 1914, recalled, "Before starting the model of any wild animal I informed myself on its behavior in its natural habitat by consulting authoritative books procured from the library of the Natural History Museum."[41] The artists most closely affiliated with the museum were those who were its employees: they joined in wildlife expeditions, taxidermied and mounted animals for preservation, and painted the backgrounds for the carefully researched habitat dioramas.

At the turn of the twentieth century, a new group of scientist-artists emerged, centered on Carl Akeley, naturalist and father of modern taxidermy, who worked at the Field Museum in Chicago from 1895 and at the American Museum of Natural History beginning in 1909. As with Kemeys and Proctor, their work was propelled by the belief that the greatest wildlife species—in North America as well as in Africa and Asia—were moving inexorably toward decline and possible extinction. As James L. Clark succinctly observed, "how easy it is to exterminate, and how utterly impossible it is to bring them back to life."[42] Akeley's circle of artists in New York, which included Clark and the sculptor Robert Henry Rockwell, traveled the globe in search of specimens and scientific information to share with the museum-going public. Their efforts focused on the preservation and the accurate mounting

and presentation of species, but they also created independent works of art.

Clark came to the American Museum of Natural History in 1902, fresh from studies at the Rhode Island School of Design. His role was as much sculptor-naturalist as taxidermist, since he modeled the forms of the animals upon which the skins were mounted (fig. 190). Clark worked with Akeley on the African Hall and, following Akeley's death in Africa in 1926, oversaw its completion. He also led the creation of many other displays, including those for the Hall of North American Mammals (opened 1942), which were based on some twenty-five museum trips to the West, beginning in 1907.[43] He wrote of his travels to Alberta to get his "toes in the ground," "hunt[ing] and stud[ying] the wild sheep, the mountain goat, moose, caribou, and bear. . . . As usual I spent most of my time studying my subjects through glasses, collecting them afterwards as specimens, and dissecting them to study their characteristic anatomical features. I made photographs, pencil sketches, and motion pictures and supplemented all with observation."[44]

Clark's expansive knowledge is reflected in his small bronzes, which he referred to as "my major hobby."[45] *Alaskan Kodiak Bear* (fig. 93) is representative of his statuettes in its faithful reproduction of form and its motionless pose upon a self-base. Given that Clark did not visit Alaska until years after the statuette was modeled, he probably based his bear on one observed during frequent trips to the Bronx Zoo. At the time, the zoo boasted sixteen North American bears, including two full-grown Kodiaks (fig. 94), "ponderous specimens" captured in Alaska in 1899.[46] In his *Trails of the Hunted*, Clark proclaimed the fierce Kodiak bear to be "very much more powerful than a lion, and . . . at least as dangerous . . . no gentle creature waiting in pleasant glades for some tourist to feed him peanuts."[47] Nevertheless, his compact statuette emphasizes

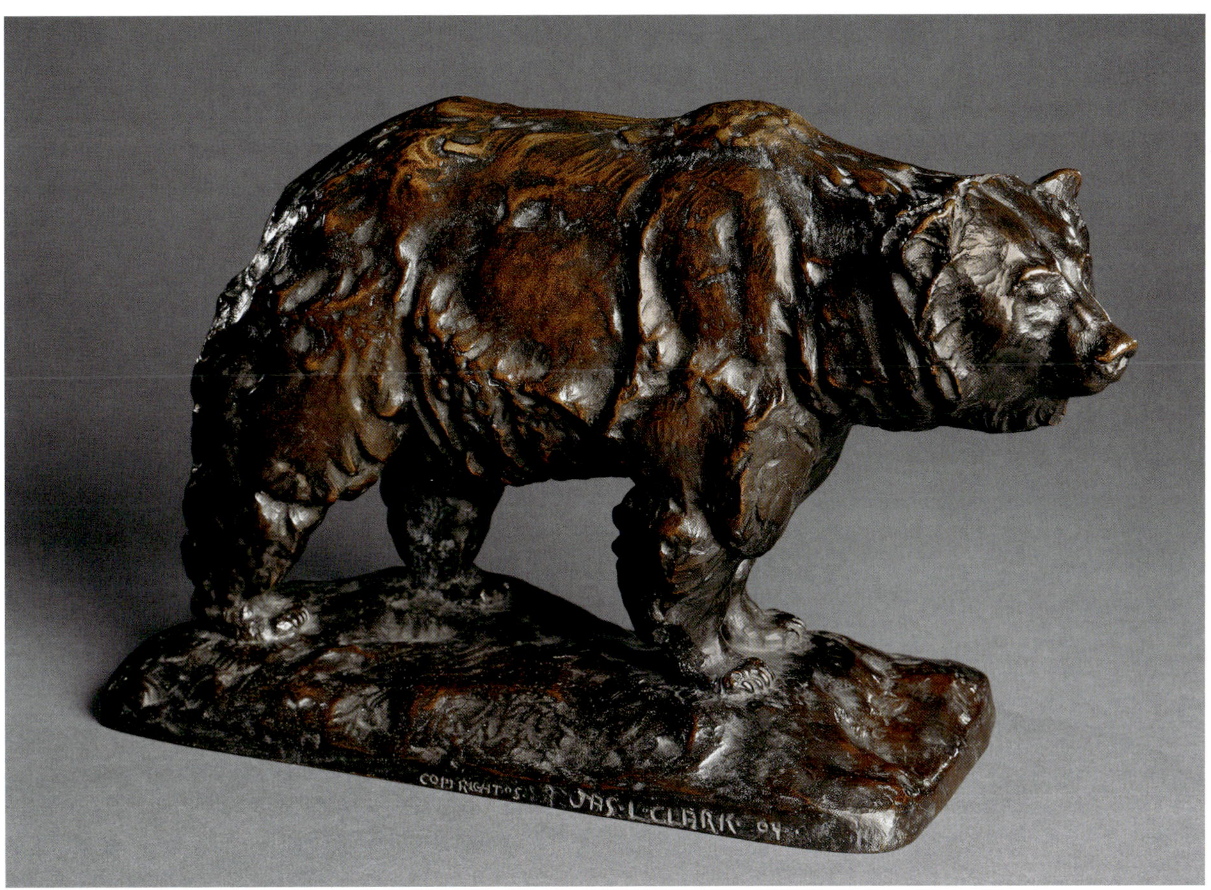

Fig. 93. James L. Clark. *Alaskan Kodiak Bear*, 1904. Cat. 14

documentary reportage over the fearsome predatory behavior that had come to be associated with this, the largest species of bear.

The bison remained at the forefront of public consciousness after the turn of the twentieth century, with preservation efforts by western ranchers motivated by potential profit (in part from selling the rights to sport hunters to shoot bison on their land) and by members of the wealthy and powerful East Coast establishment who saw the animals as emblematic of a purer, wilder America. In 1905 the American Bison Society was founded by Theodore Roosevelt and William T. Hornaday, director of the New York Zoological Park. This elite urban organization, which counted Remington among its members, led efforts to repopulate bison—including with animals from the zoo's own herd—on western preserves, in an attempt to perpetuate this "living icon of an

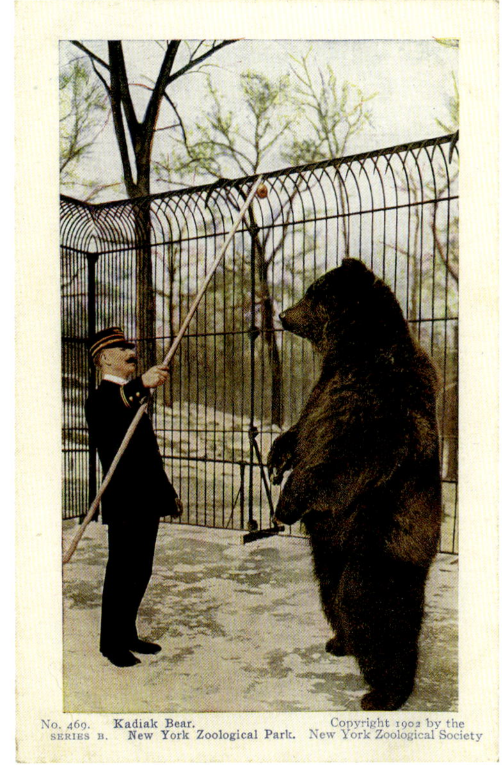

Fig. 94. New York Zoological Society, publisher, and American Colortype Co., printer. *Kodiak Bear. New York Zoological Park*, 1902. Colored-photograph postcard, 5½ × 3½ in. (14 × 9 cm). Wildlife Conservation Society Archives, New York

imagined heroic West."[48] Proctor's close affinity with this nexus of conservationists and sportsmen garnered public and private patronage for his work. At Roosevelt's behest, in 1909 he completed two bison heads for the limestone mantel in the White House State Dining Room to replace the lions the president rejected as inappropriate because they were not native animals.[49]

Proctor's most recognizable work, both at full scale and in reduction, is his *Buffalo*. In 1911 he received a commission from the city of Washington, D.C., to create four monumental bison for the stone pylons of the Q Street (Dumbarton) Bridge. That fall he traveled to Buffalo National Park (established 1907) near Wainwright, Alberta, where bison were being regenerated with relocated herds. There Proctor made preliminary sketches based on direct observation (fig. 95). The massive final bronzes (two different models, *Buffalo I* [fig. 96] and

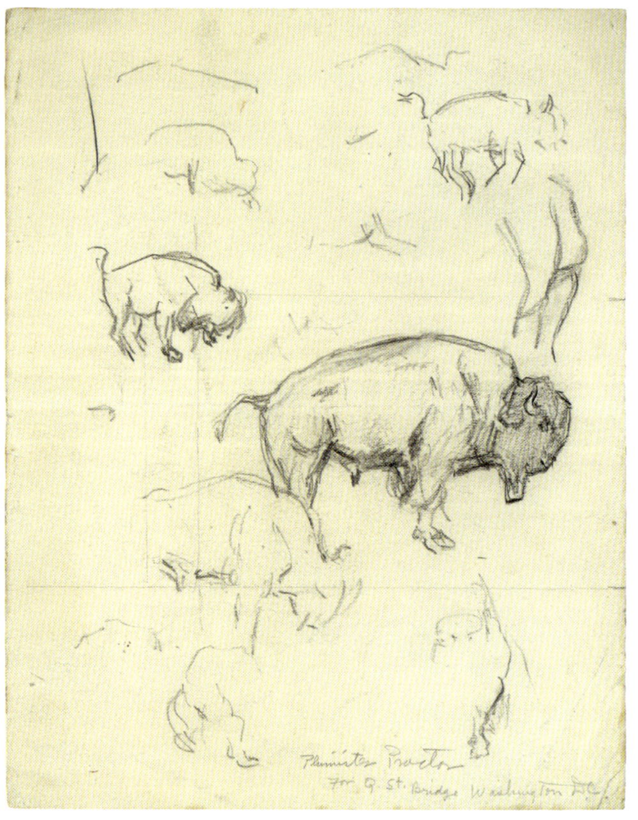

Fig. 95. Alexander Phimister Proctor. *"For Q Street Bridge Washington D.C.,"* ca. 1911. Graphite on paper, 11 × 8⅜ in. (27.9 × 21.3 cm). The Metropolitan Museum of Art, Gift of Gifford MacGregor Proctor, 1993 (1993.80)

Fig. 96. Alexander Phimister Proctor. *Buffalo I,* 1911–14. Q Street (Dumbarton) Bridge, Washington, D.C.

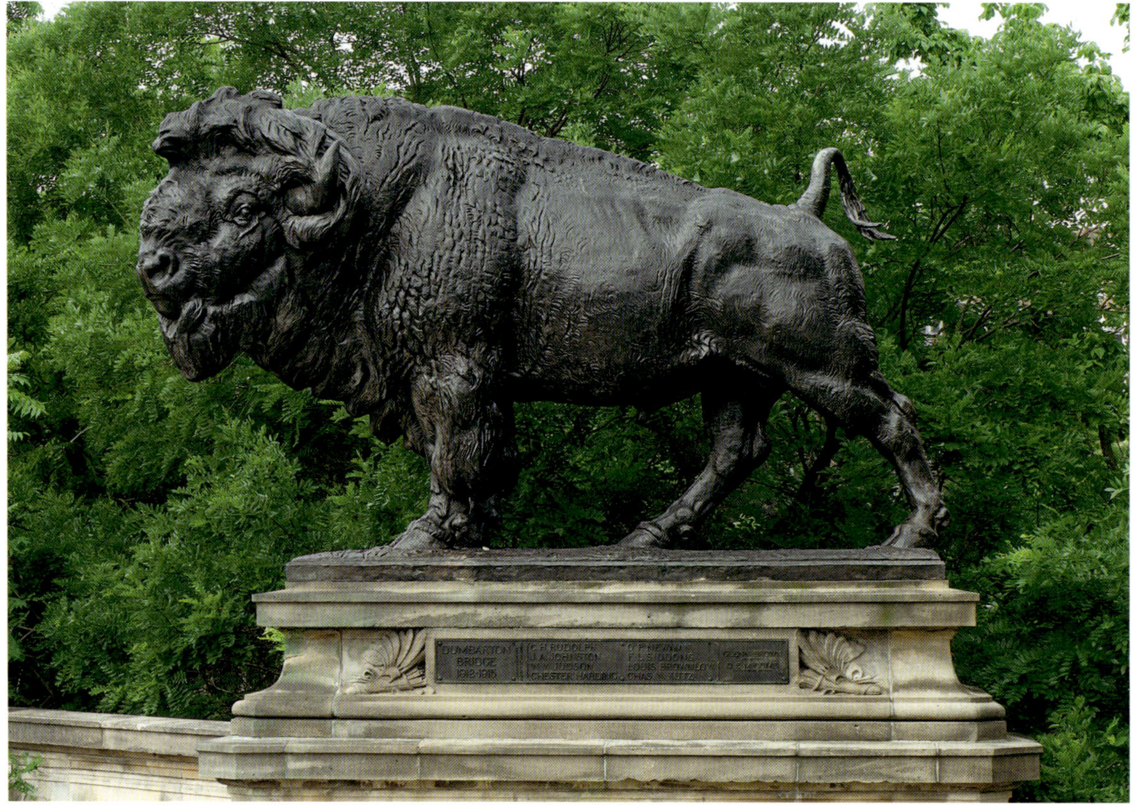

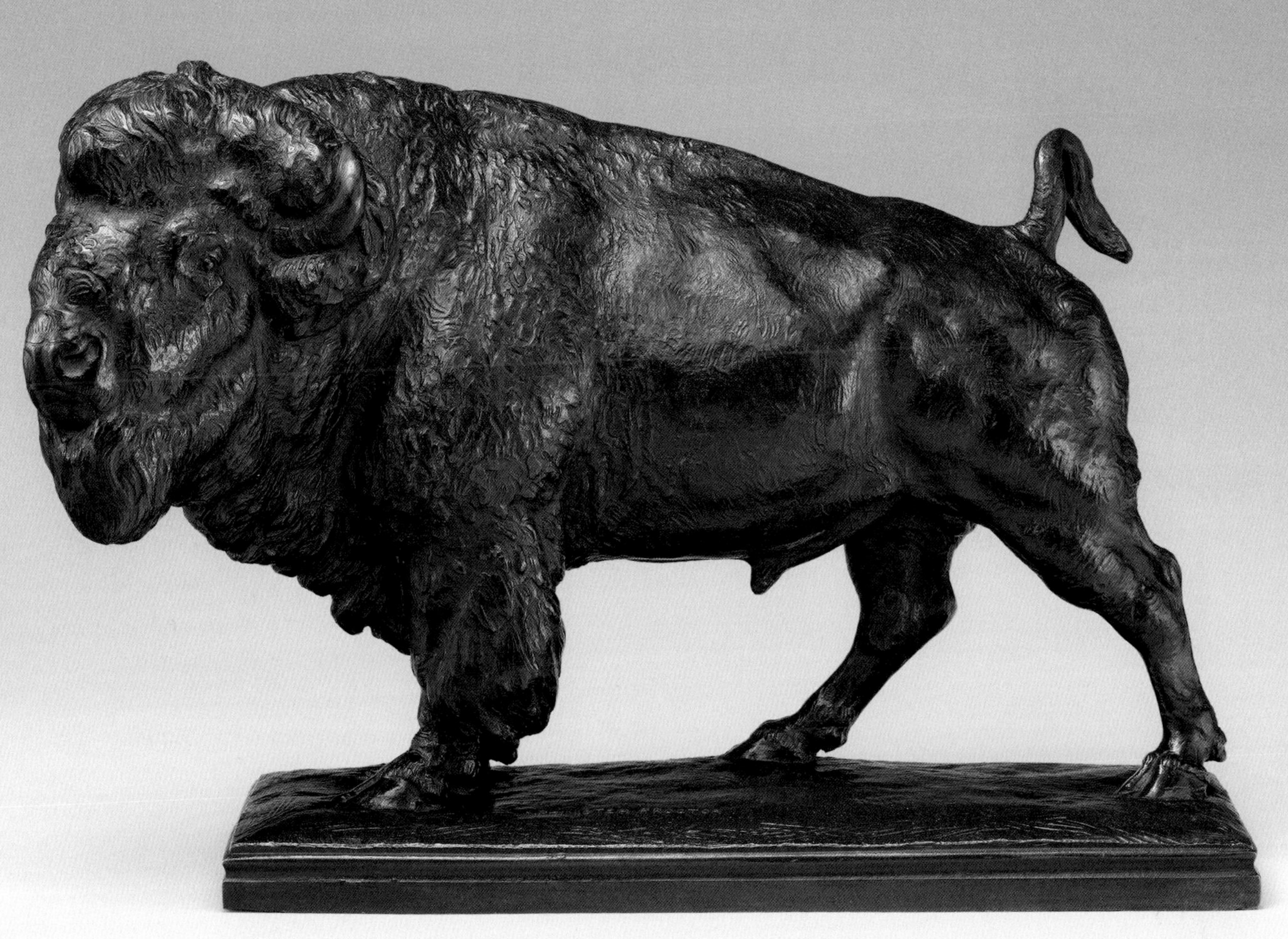

Buffalo II, each replicated twice) were—at eight feet tall and fourteen feet long—larger-than-life reincarnations from the Old West brought to the nation's capital. Unlike many of Proctor's sculptures in which narrative is implied by figural action, *Buffalo I* presents the woolly-maned beast in a stately pose commandingly grounded on its rectangular base. The only motion is the swish of its raised tail. Two years before the large sculptures were cast at the Henry-Bonnard Bronze Company, New York, in 1914, Proctor copyrighted and began to cast statuette versions of *Buffalo I* (fig. 97), savvy to the commercial potential of the emblematic animal. Nostalgia may account for the relatively large editions of these casts produced at both Gorham Co. Founders and Roman Bronze Works; witness the five that were given or bequeathed to American museums by Proctor's hunting companion George D. Pratt, who undertook a deliberate campaign to place them in public institutions.[50]

Although most of these wildlife sculptors passed through New York, whether as students or residents, others had only minimal contact with America's art capital. The San Francisco artist Arthur Putnam, of a slightly younger generation, followed a different path, although he did steadily consign bronzes with the prominent New York dealer William Macbeth. After

Fig. 97. Alexander Phimister Proctor. *Buffalo*, 1912 (cast 1913 or after). Cat. 41

training in San Francisco and working in a slaughterhouse, Putnam went to Chicago in 1897 to apprentice with Kemeys for a year. Putnam frequented the zoo in San Francisco, but unlike most sculptors, he preferred to model his wildlife subjects from memory rather than from life, believing that slavish attention to detail (such as textured fur) would dilute the emotional impact. "The damn thing disturbs me," he said, "by thrusting his individual peculiarities between my conception and the work I am doing."[51] Putnam was well established in San Francisco before going abroad in 1905—first to Rome, where he learned the casting techniques he would later employ in the foundry he established back in San Francisco with his brother-in-law, Frederick Storey. Once in Paris, Putnam certainly looked to the statuettes of Barye and his animalier colleagues. Not surprisingly, he was also attracted to the expressive, fluidly modeled bronzes of Auguste Rodin, who admired Putnam's work on exhibition in Paris.

The sculptures that predate Putnam's Paris sojourn—for instance, *Puma and Deer* (fig. 98) of 1902—already demonstrate an interest in Rodinesque activated surfaces and captured motion. They also find a source in Kemeys's vibrant groups, which favor behavioral narrative over anatomical specificity. Pumas (California mountain lions) were Putnam's preferred subject, a longtime fascination honed while tracking the animals near the family ranch in San Diego County. In *Puma and Deer*, the puma (by then nearly extinct) remains a dominant force in bronze, at least, if no longer in reality.[52] With its confusion of interlaced forms, the group evokes a range of responses, from awe at the puma's power to sympathy for the freshly felled deer hanging across its muscular back. The smooth surfaces and large masses of light and shade of Putnam's bronzes appealed to a modernist sensibility. Four of them were displayed at the International Exhibition of Modern Art (the Armory Show) in 1913, including a sculpture listed in the catalogue as *Deer and Puma*, which may well have been his 1902 group; he copyrighted it in 1912, as the inscription on this bronze attests.[53]

Like Putnam, Charles M. Russell was based in the West, principally in Great Falls, Montana, from where he developed an impressive patronage network. Nearly one-quarter of Russell's extensive oeuvre—paintings, watercolors, and sculptures—has wildlife as the principal focus. From a young age he created painted-wax animals and human figures for the amusement of himself and his friends, sometimes adding tree branches, hemp fibers, and other materials to simulate naturalistic outdoor settings. But Russell (like Remington) did not come to bronze sculpture until midcareer, successfully casting his first statuette, *Smoking Up* (fig. 126), in 1904 and completing some twenty animal groups over the next two decades, a significant portion of his forty-six models eventually cast in bronze. His wife, Nancy C. Russell, who shrewdly managed the artist's business affairs, encouraged him not only to produce small bronzes but, even more specifically, to focus on animal themes with widespread appeal, as already demonstrated by the commercial success of such specialists as Proctor, Harvey, and Frederick George Richard Roth.[54]

Russell's western adventures, particularly his time spent with mountain man Jake Hoover in the early 1880s and then as a night herder of cattle for eleven years, provided lifelong inspiration for his art. As with his Indian and cowboy works, Russell based his wildlife subjects on recollection and imagination rather than direct observation. Unlike Kemeys and Proctor, Russell was neither hunter nor anatomist in the traditional sense; he stalked game in the name of observation, as a self-professed "harmless hunter."[55] Nancy C. Russell recalled that "living with a trapper [Hoover], [Russell]

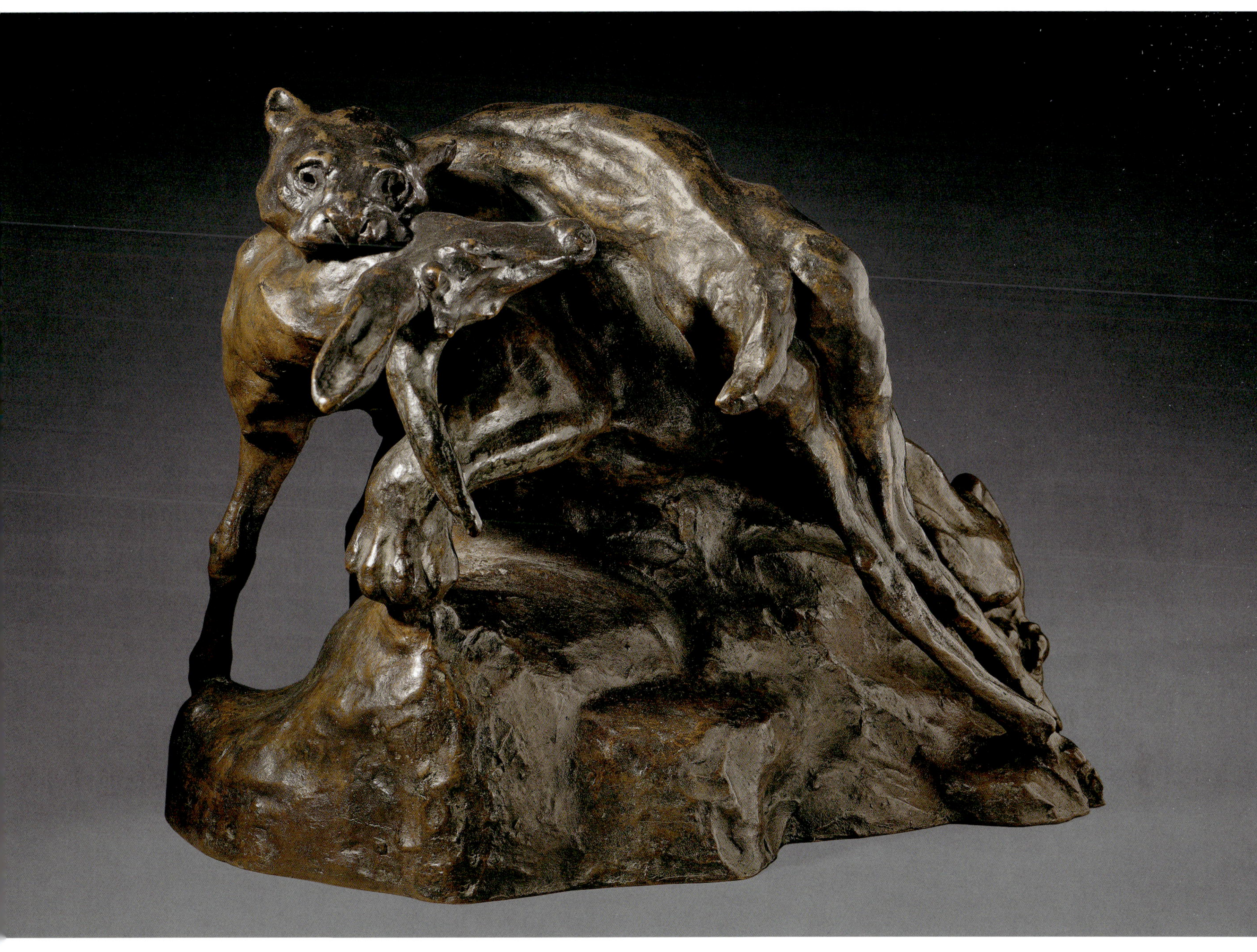

Fig. 98. Arthur Putnam. *Puma and Deer*, 1902 (copyright 1912). Cat. 47

got close to the wild hearts of animals. He never was a willful killer of wild game."[56] Russell shared other sculptors' appreciation of indigenous wildlife and concern for its preservation. He later described the South Fork of the Judith Basin of Montana Territory in the early 1880s: "These parks and the mountains behind them swarmed with deer, elk, mountain sheep and bear, besides beaver and other small fur-bearing animals. . . . Nature had surely done her best, and no king of the old times could have claimed a more beautiful and bountiful domain."[57]

Russell's bronzes focus on these endangered animals. With their self-bases modeled as rocks, trees, and earthy terrain, his animal

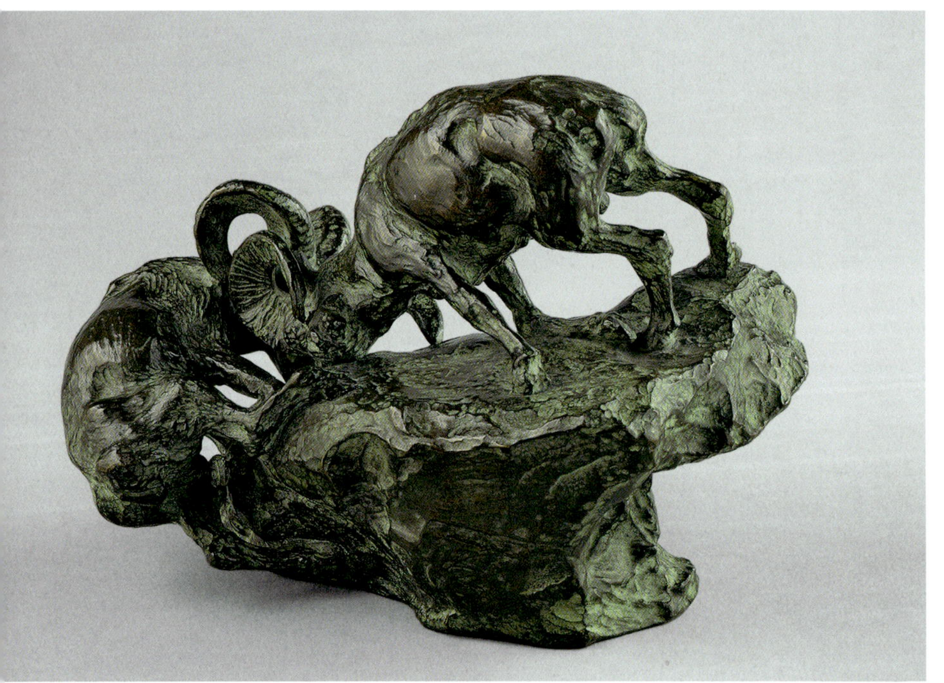
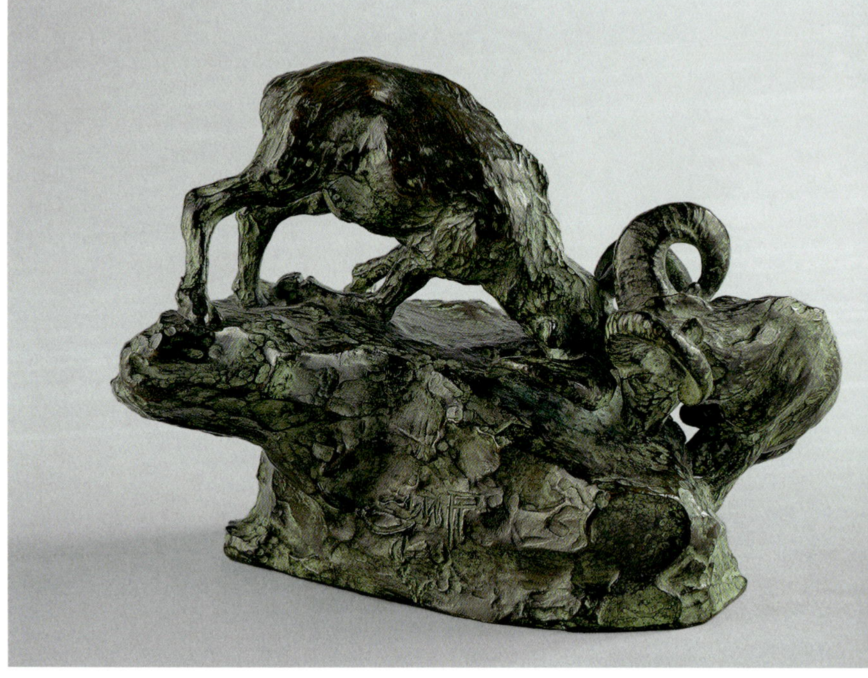

Figs. 99, 100. Charles M. Russell. *The Combat*, 1908 (cast ca. 1912). Cat. 60

statuettes are clearly situated in the open, natural West rather than in indeterminate locations such as zoos. *The Combat* (figs. 99, 100) depicts two mountain rams, heads lowered, curved horns locked, in an intraspecies battle recalling Borglum's *Bulls Fighting* (fig. 86). In this, his only depiction of wildlife conflict, Russell increased the tension by positioning one ram over the edge of the craggy base, suggesting how the struggle will end. He was well familiar with the overhunting of Rocky Mountain sheep, which had reduced their range to the most mountainous territory. *The Combat* alludes not only to that rugged habitat but also to the vulnerability of the sheep. Rick Stewart has suggested that Russell may have drawn on wildlife stories by Ernest Thompson Seton, whom he met in New York, in this case referencing Krag, a Rocky Mountain sheep featured in Seton's *Lives of the Hunted* (1901). Krag violently defeats his rival, sending him over a cliff, a fate also implied in *The Combat*.[58]

Bison are a recurring theme in Russell's art. In 1908 and 1909 he participated in the Pablo roundups, where he witnessed at close range bison being herded and readied for transport to Canada.[59] Although bison were saved from extinction over the next decade, being successfully regenerated on preserves in the United States and Canada, Russell preferred to portray them as enduring symbols of the Old West. For instance, in *The Buffalo Family* (1921; Amon Carter Museum of American Art, Fort Worth, Texas), he emphasizes their protective nature, with a stolid bull defensively standing guard over a recumbent cow that shelters their calf. Russell's most ambitious sculptural groups represent old-time buffalo hunts (figs. 11, 63) in complex multifigure statuettes with frenzied motion, again alluding to a purer Old West, before Euro-American settlement forever altered the lives of both American Indians and bison.

Russell's several depictions of wolves ran counter to prevailing attitudes that reviled these fearless hunters. As William T. Hornaday wrote in his widely circulated book *The American Natural History* (1904): "Of all the wild animals of North America, none are more despicable than wolves. There is no depth of

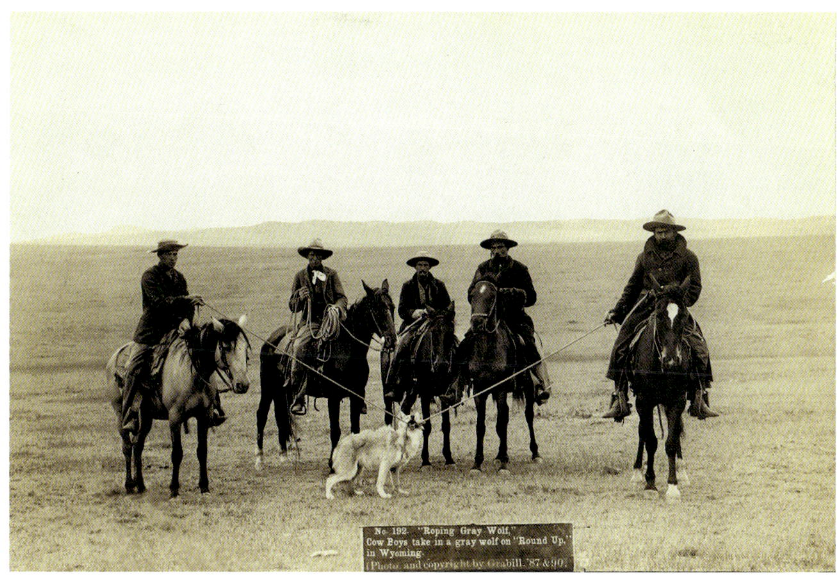

Fig. 101. *"Roping Gray Wolf,"
Cowboys Take In a Gray Wolf on
"Round Up," in Wyoming,* 1887

Fig. 102. Charles M. Russell.
An Enemy That Warns, 1921
(cast ca. 1922–28). Cat. 63

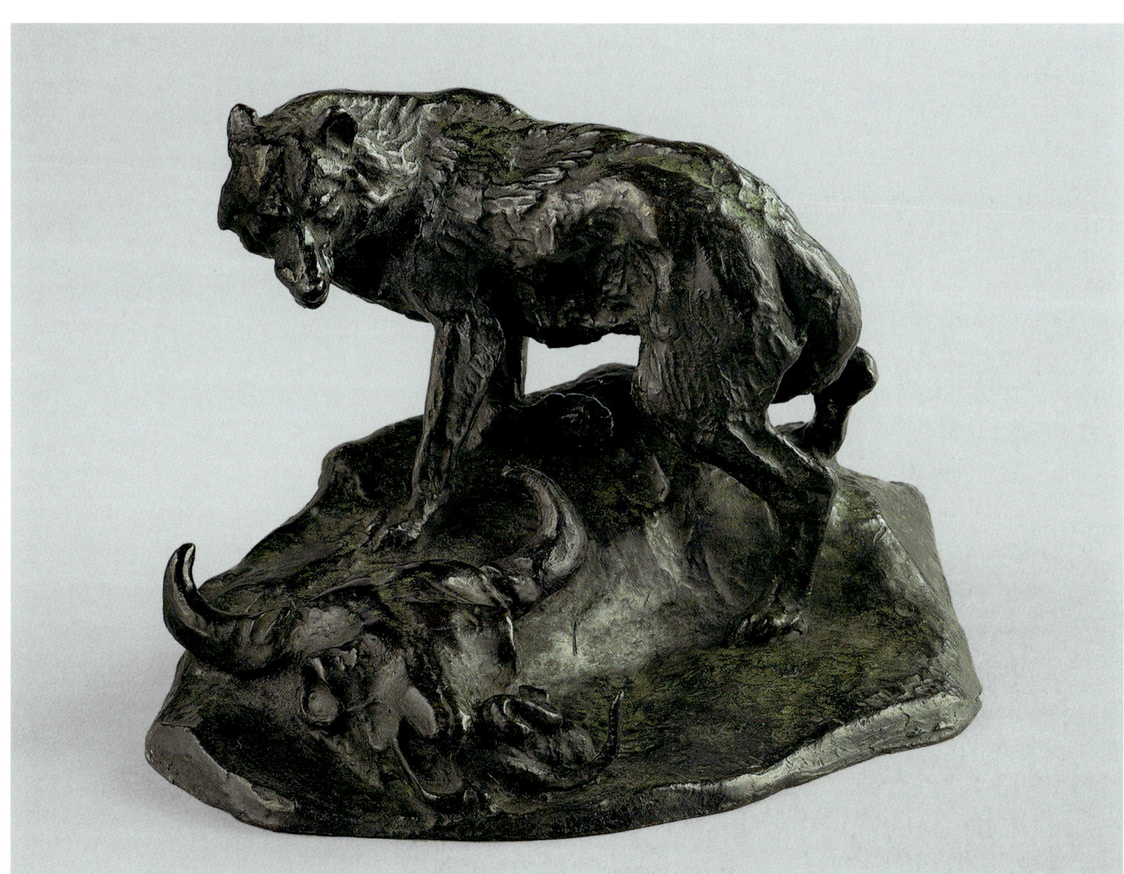

meanness, treachery, or cruelty to which they do not cheerfully descend."[60] Russell focused instead on their status as endangered creatures, rightful citizens in the life cycle of western fauna and hapless victims of an extermination campaign by ranchers and farmers to protect their livestock (fig. 101). His wolf groups are imbued with a cautionary symbolism. *An Enemy That Warns* (fig. 102) depicts a wolf recoiling from a bison skull where a rattlesnake has menacingly appeared. According to Nancy C. Russell's account: "The mice of the plains make their nests in the skulls of the buffalo. . . . This . . . wolf was about to turn over the skull in search of mice when a rattlesnake warned him by rattling that he was trespassing."[61] The sculptor's condensed narrative refers to the everyday perils of seeking sustenance, even for such a cunning predator. Like the wolf, the wild horse was perceived as a threat to cattle and domesticated horses, but Russell took a kinder view. In a late group, *The Range Father* (fig. 103), he once again turned the tables by depicting a wild horse chasing a wolf. The vigorous, animated handling of form that characterizes his bronzes accentuates the sense of swift pursuit, with the leaning, straining animals almost suspended in midair.

Russell's statuettes of animals projected many moods, from predatory to whimsical.

Bears, in particular, were a favorite subject. As Rick Stewart has observed, Russell's interest in depicting bears as anthropomorphized creatures may have resulted from his ongoing contact with American Indian culture, particularly nations such as the Blackfoot, who believed that bears were part human, given similarities in their physical traits and behavior.[62] He represented them as family members engaged in everyday activities, hunting for food and learning life lessons. In *The Lunch Hour* (1910; Amon Carter Museum of American Art, Fort Worth, Texas), a mother grizzly dislodges a rock so her cub can discover the grubs and plants underneath. *Mountain Mother* (fig. 104) depicts a grizzly bear and her two cubs navigating a fallen tree, its shape reminiscent of Russell's painted-wax sculptures with real branches incorporated. He stresses the

Fig. 103. Charles M. Russell. *The Range Father*, 1926 (cast ca. 1926–28). Cat. 67

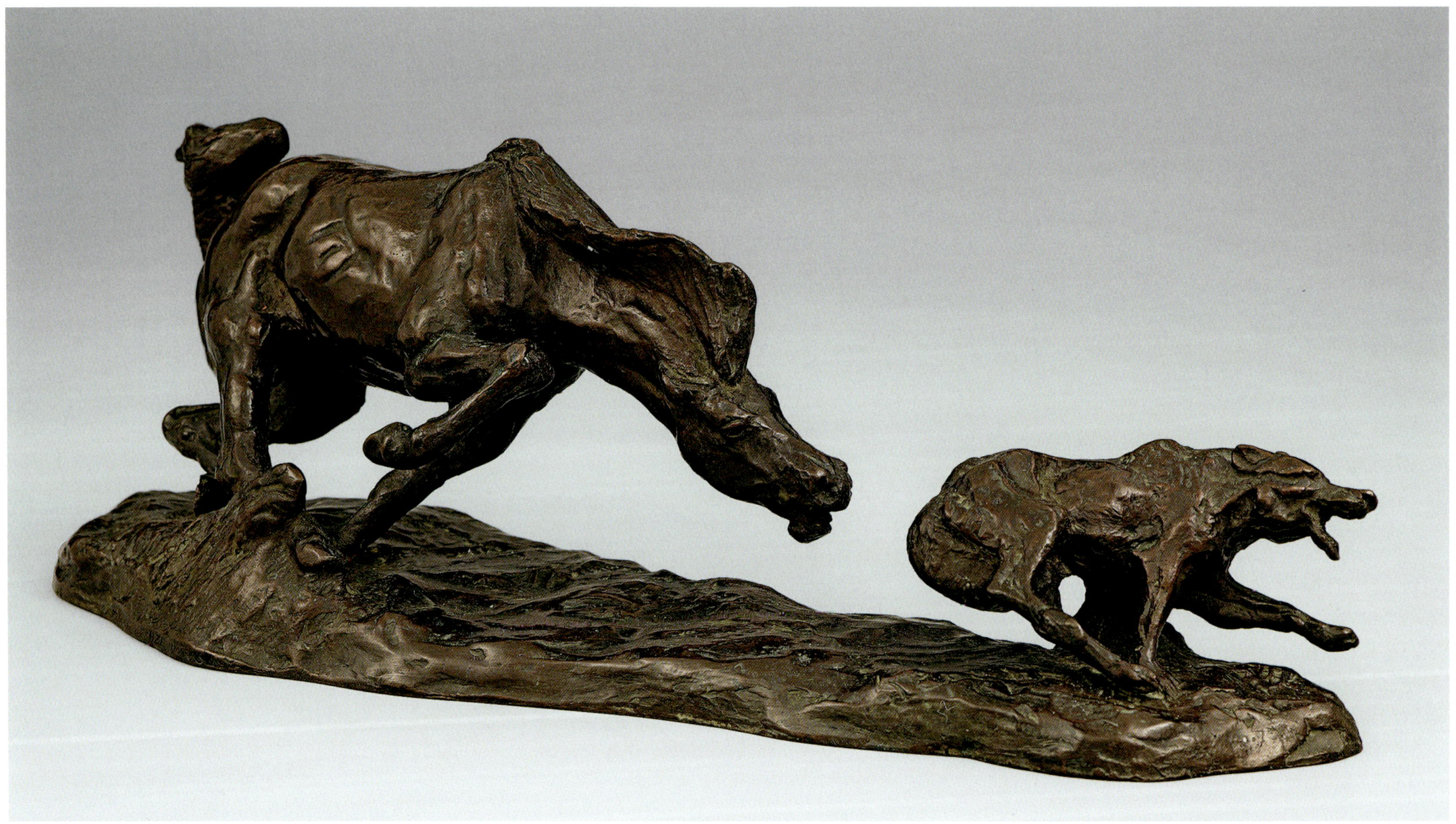

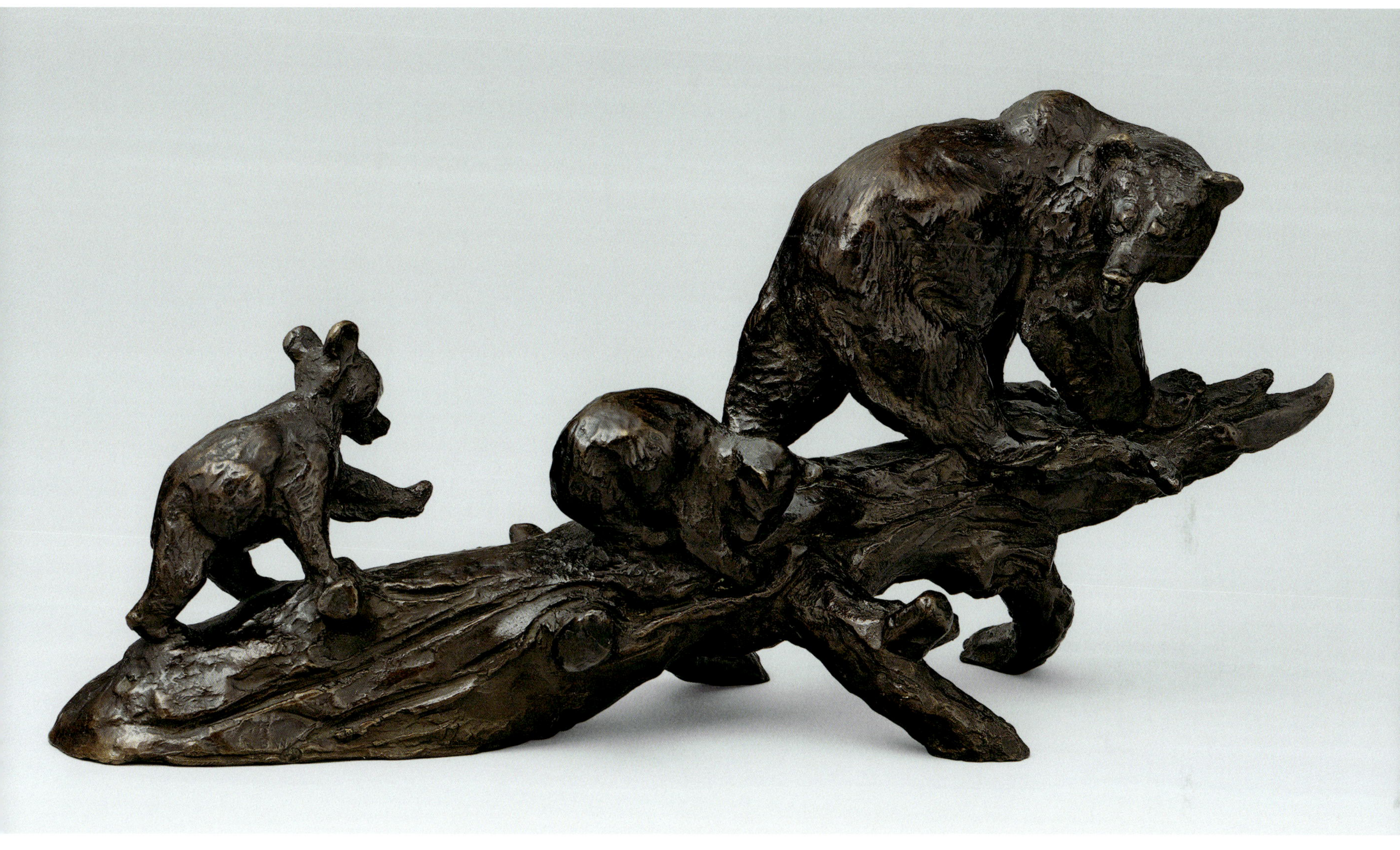

Fig. 104. Charles M. Russell. *Mountain Mother*, 1924 (cast ca. 1924–28). Cat. 66

bear's maternal instincts as she attentively looks back at her cubs, one curious and bumbling, the other purposeful.

Russell's life-span (1864–1926) coincided with the proliferation of American wildlife bronzes, both as private statuettes and as public monuments. The art critic Royal Cortissoz observed in 1909 that "this and no other is emphatically the age of the animal sculptor."[63] The appeal of the small sculptures was enhanced by a confluence of factors—the establishment of zoos and natural history museums, the founding of the national parks and the Conservation Movement, the rise of the fine-arts bronze industry, and not least, the increasingly sophisticated training and professionalism of American sculptors. While these artists brought different life experiences and aesthetic approaches to their representations of animals, collectively they produced an enduring menagerie that celebrates the distinctive appearance and lifeways of western wildlife.

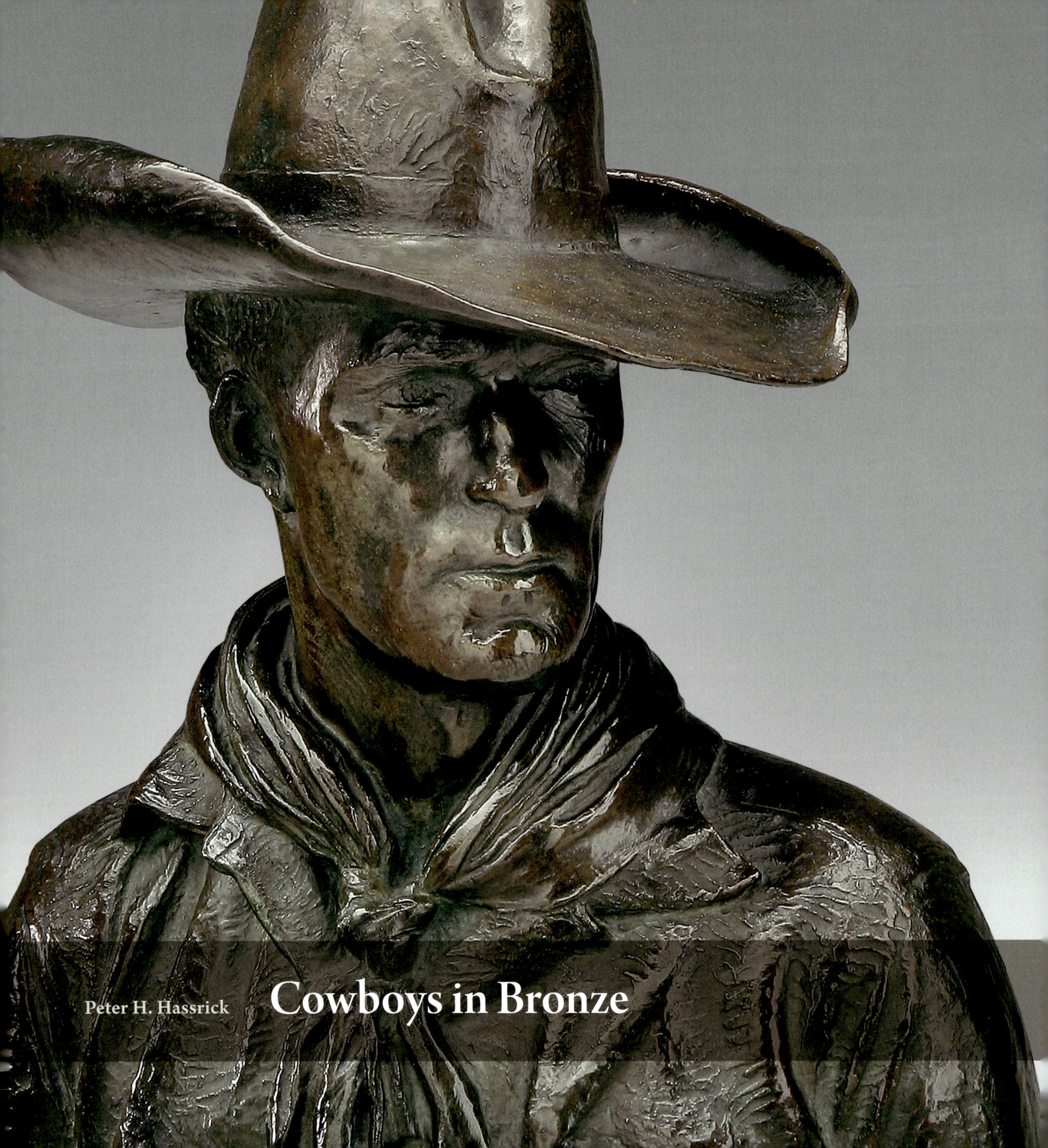

Peter H. Hassrick
Cowboys in Bronze

At the close of the Civil War, the nation began a concerted effort to explore the American West as a resource for rebuilding the cultural, economic, and political foundations of the United States. The summer of 1866 saw scores of journalists, artists, and travel writers scurrying west to the Rocky Mountains and beyond to assess the state of the land and report back to the East. Among the things they sought were symbols of national unity and regional heroes that might help rejuvenate the country's battered self-image. For many, the mountains themselves served as emblems of undiminished power and uniquely American grandeur. Others sought personifications of the national spirit that could salve the collective conscience. The satirist painter William Holbrook Beard, who traveled west that summer, was "disappointed in the Rocky Mountains somewhat," but hoped he might encounter "the real American type of Western Hunter," genuine "Western characters," in Colorado.[1] Presumably in pursuit of a contemporary replacement for the mountain man, who had been venerated as a national symbol by such artists of the previous generation as Charles Deas (see fig. 154) and William Tylee Ranney, Beard looked in vain.

Another such traveler, the landscapist Worthington Whittredge, embraced the "vastness and silence" of the prairies rather than the sublime peaks he beheld west of Denver.[2] He also sought genuine western personalities, but not until his group arrived in Santa Fe did he discover the exemplar of his quest. There he was introduced to Christopher "Kit" Carson, the revered scout and champion of the West. Carson embodied all the qualities of the epic western man—reticence, valor, honor, modesty—and had a life history that recalled Natty Bumppo, protagonist of James Fenimore Cooper's *Leatherstocking Tales*. "It was certain," wrote Whittredge, "that he had lived the greater part of his early life away from white people [civilization] and had come as near living a solitary life."[3] But Carson's moment in history had temporarily faded. The ascendance of a western scout to the position of national icon would have to wait until William F. "Buffalo Bill" Cody arrived on the scene over a decade later. In the meantime, it was the inanimate spires of the Rocky Mountains that rose in the public mind to represent the West and the promise of the nation's regeneration. This theme was subsequently explored and exploited by two of Whittredge's colleagues, Albert Bierstadt and Thomas Moran, with their grand canvases of nature's magnificence in places like Yellowstone National Park and the Yosemite Valley (see figs. 173, 177).

Just slightly after the flamboyant Buffalo Bill emerged in the mid-1870s as the archetypal western figure, another character surfaced who would typify the West and eventually captivate the nation—the American cowboy. Beard's traveling companion, the author and lecturer Bayard Taylor, had seen a few "Mexican vaqueros" with their horses in the frontier town of Lawrence, Kansas, in 1866, but thought little of it.[4] By 1867, though, cattle drives from Texas to Kansas railheads were initiated, and the wave of cows and cowboys would swell every year; by 1886 a total of between six and nine million cattle had reached Kansas for shipment to eastern markets.[5]

Fig. 105. Alexander Phimister Proctor, detail of *Slim*, 1914 (cast 1915 or after). Cat. 45

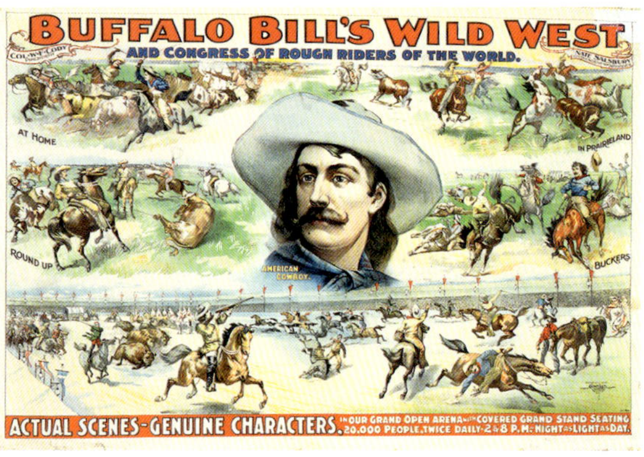

Fig. 106. *Buffalo Bill's Wild West and Congress of Rough Riders of the World*, 1896. Lithograph, 28¼ × 41¾ in. (71.8 × 106 cm). Buffalo Bill Center of the West, Cody, Wyoming

The cowboy began to appear on stage and in dime novels in the early 1880s. Nearly half the segments for Buffalo Bill's inaugural Wild West exposition of 1883 featured cowboy-related scenes.[6] In the show's program that year, Cody's publicists described the cowboy as misunderstood, not the "feckless fellow" of American imaginings but one so well-intentioned and stalwart that he merited the status of an American icon. The next year, a vaquero graced the cover of the show's program, and the cowboy

star Buck Taylor soon began appearing in Wild West posters (fig. 106).[7] Within a few more years, through spectacles like the fanfare of roping, horse breaking, and riding feats that were famously known as "Cowboy Fun," Buffalo Bill had shaped American—and European—perceptions of the cowboy. As the New York *World* reported in 1887, Cody had "encircled the earth with his Wild West" and spread "the fever."[8] Soon, a whole world of young men wanted to be cowboys.

Among them was a cadre of artists, many of whom actually preceded Cody in having such aspirations. The New Yorker Frederic Remington, fresh from Yale, had gone to Montana in 1881 to try life on a ranch (see fig. 107). His younger contemporary, Charles M. Russell from Saint Louis, had gotten there a year earlier. And Solon Hannibal Borglum of Nebraska began a five-year stint running his family's ranch in 1887. These were but three of the many artists who, in the course of their careers, would produce sculptural renditions of the cowboy, leaving an enduring

Fig. 107. Frederic Remington. *Self-Portrait on a Horse*, ca. 1890. Oil on canvas, 29¼ × 19⅜ in. (74.3 × 49.2 cm). Sid Richardson Museum, Fort Worth, Texas

Fig. 108. Detail of cowboy from the facade of the National Live Stock Bank, 1888. Terracotta relief. Chicago History Museum

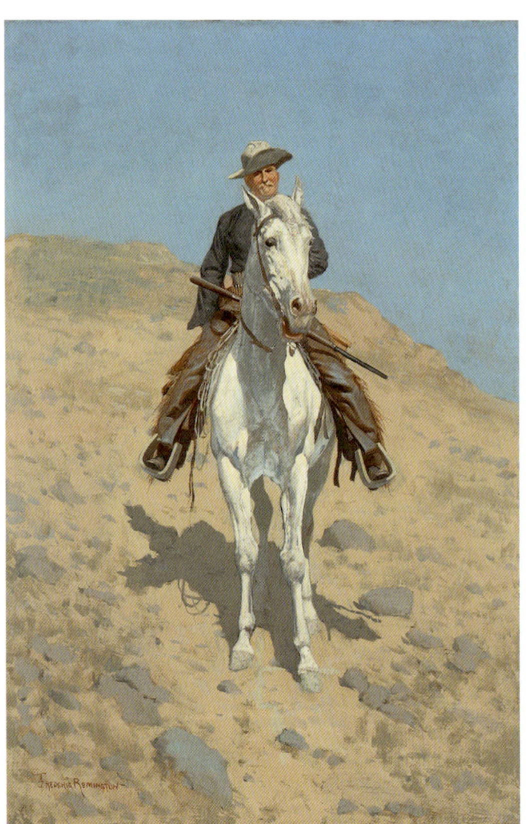

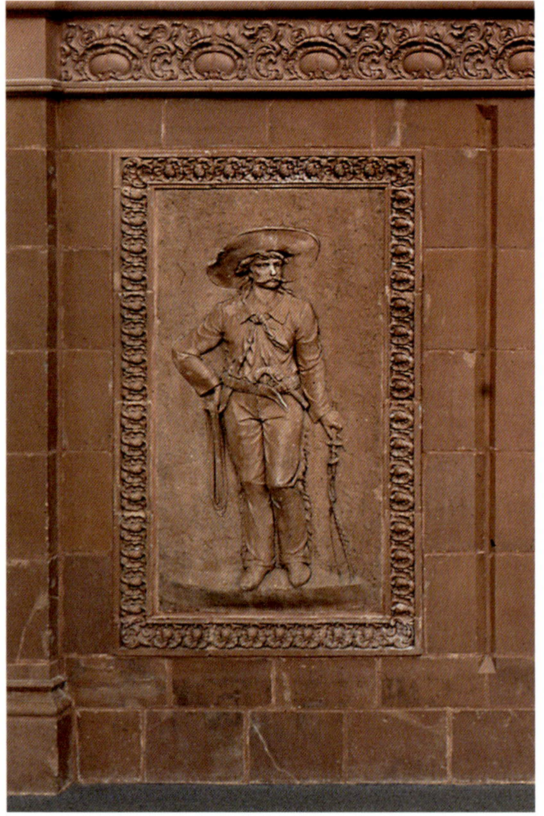

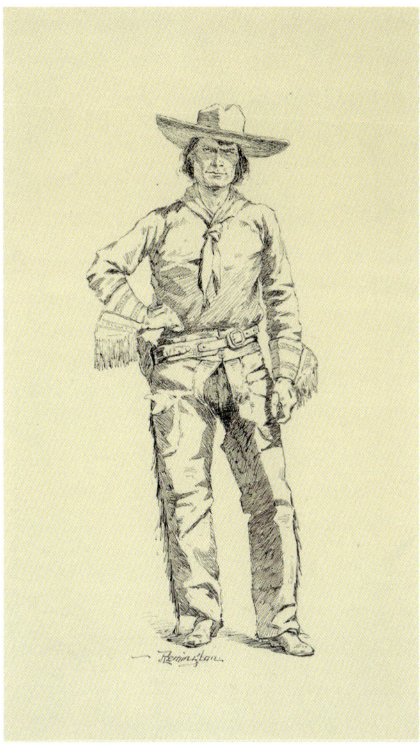

record in bronze of this omnipresent though ephemeral idol.

Chicago was the hub of the early cattle business, and cows were shipped there to be processed in the vast Union Stock Yards. Chicago was also, appropriately, the first city to celebrate the cowboy in public art. In 1888 the architectural firm Burnham and Root designed the National Live Stock Bank at the stockyards. They were asked to embellish the bank's facade with bas-reliefs related to the cattle business, and the cowboy was one of several terracotta figures to appear (fig. 108). It is not known who posed for the figure, but he was identified as "a Texan Cow Boy, with broad brimmed hat, buckskin suit and lariat in hand."[9] Perhaps a connection can be made with drawings by Remington (fig. 109) that began to appear in *Century Magazine* that year to illustrate a series of articles called "Ranch Life in the Far West," by Theodore Roosevelt, who had, in the midst of a nascent political career, purchased a ranch in the Dakota Badlands.[10]

Roosevelt presented cowboys quite sympathetically as quiet, faithful, pleasant-spoken, honest fellows who worked hard. In his evolutionary perspective on history, they were descendants of the old mountain men, leading "lives that are almost as full of hardship and adventure."[11] Remington tended to follow Roosevelt's lead, evincing a reverence for cowboy life that went back to his own experiences in Montana in 1881 and with Arizona cowboys in 1886, whom he remembered as "quiet, determined and very courteous and pleasant to talk to."[12] A similar respect can be seen in paintings by Remington's illustrator colleague Rufus Fairchild Zogbaum, who after visiting Montana in 1885 affectionately portrayed cowboys as romantic, pastoral horsemen of the plains, as in *Montana Cowboy* (fig. 110).[13]

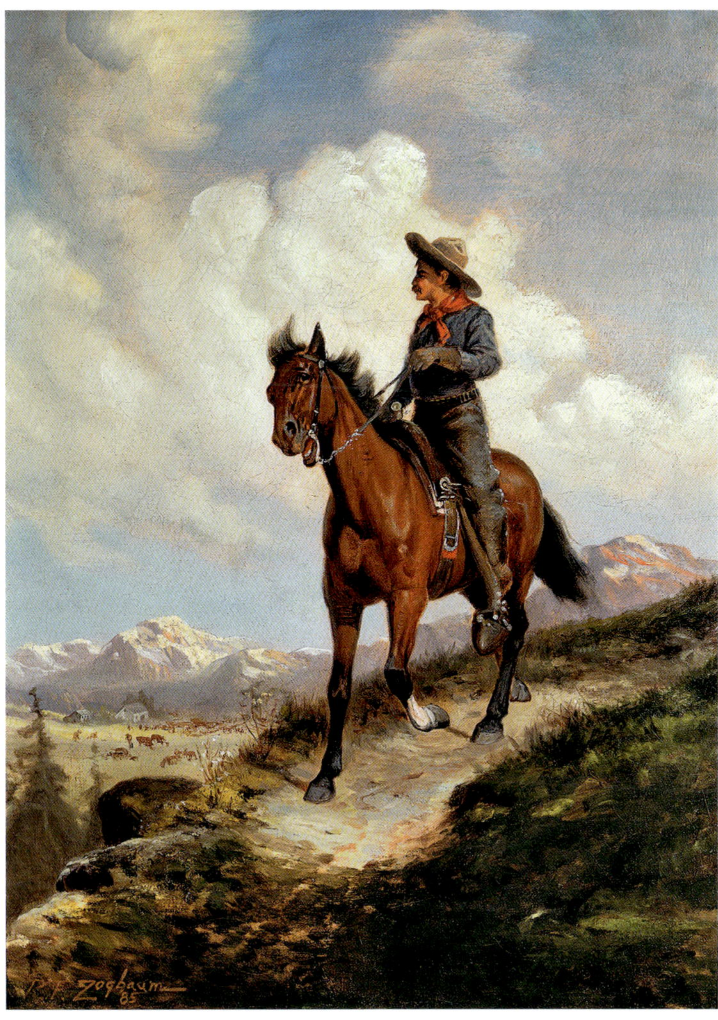

Fig. 109. Frederic Remington. *A Texan Cowboy*, 1888. Pen and ink on artist board, 15 × 8⅞ in. (38.1 × 22.5 cm). Museum of Art, Carnegie Institute, Pittsburgh

Fig. 110. Rufus Fairchild Zogbaum (American, 1849–1925). *Montana Cowboy*, 1885. Oil on canvas, 30 × 22 in. (76.2 × 55.9 cm). The Petrie Collection

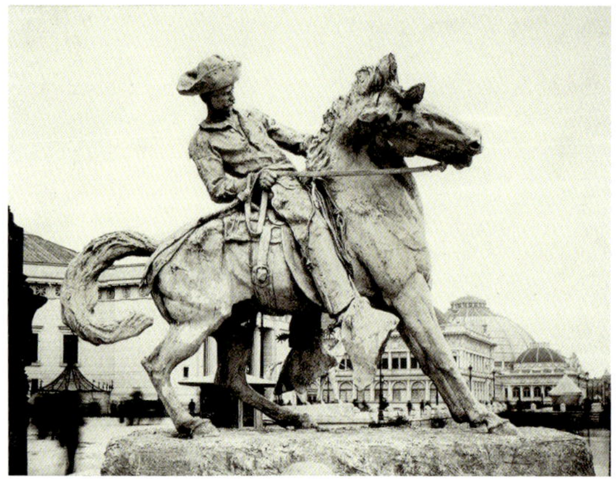

Fig. 111. Alexander Phimister Proctor. *Cowboy,* World's Columbian Exposition, Chicago, 1893

Fig. 112. Frederic Remington. *Mexican Vaqueros Breaking a Bronc',* 1893. Pen and India ink wash on paper, 26¼ × 38½ in. (66.7 × 97.8 cm). Museum of Fine Arts, Boston, Bequest of John T. Spaulding

If the terracotta at the National Live Stock Bank was the first sculpture of a cowboy, the second was made of staff (plaster and straw). Again the site was Chicago, but now it was 1893, at the grand World's Columbian Exposition. The Denver artist Alexander Phimister Proctor, who had studied painting and sculpture at the Art Students League in New York, produced thirty-five monumental sculptures of wild western animals for the fair's bridge abutments (see figs. 79, 179). He was then assigned to sculpt two heroic equestrian works, one a mounted

Indian and the other a cowboy (fig. 111). The latter was modeled after one of the cowboys in Buffalo Bill's Wild West, which was performing near the fair. The sculpture expressed a vigor and excitement that elevated it above the pastoral and into the realm of masculine adventure. Critics claimed that Proctor had succeeded "beyond their most sanguine expectations," and Augustus Saint-Gaudens, America's leading sculptor, offered his "unqualified praise."[14] Despite all this critical enthusiasm, Cody's cowboys complained about the pose of Proctor's horseman and, in fact, conspired to drag the massive sculpture into an adjacent lagoon. Buffalo Bill saved the day, diverting the prank and once again preserving the image of the cowboy for the world's enjoyment.[15] Proctor's plaster was later moved to Denver, where it was displayed for the next decade in the new City Park. The cowboy in sculpture had come west, and this one was so treasured in Colorado that, in the 1910s, citizens pressed to have it made permanent as a bronze. Nothing came of the idea directly, but the effort proved that

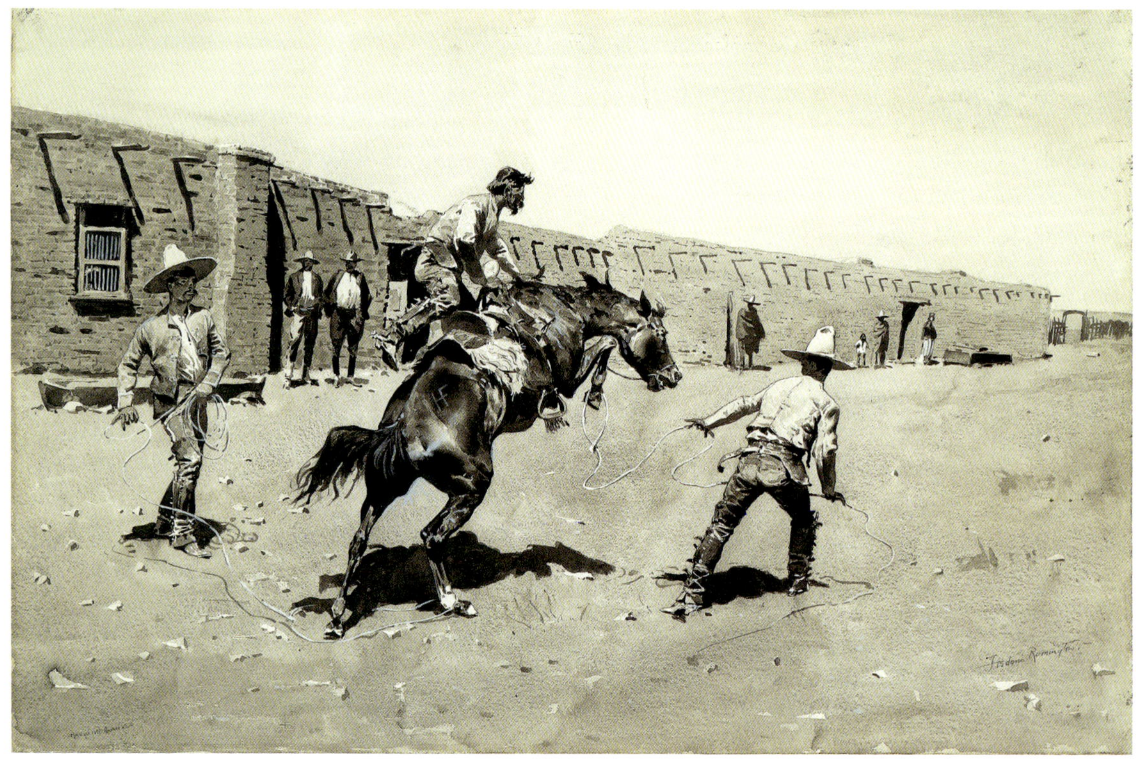

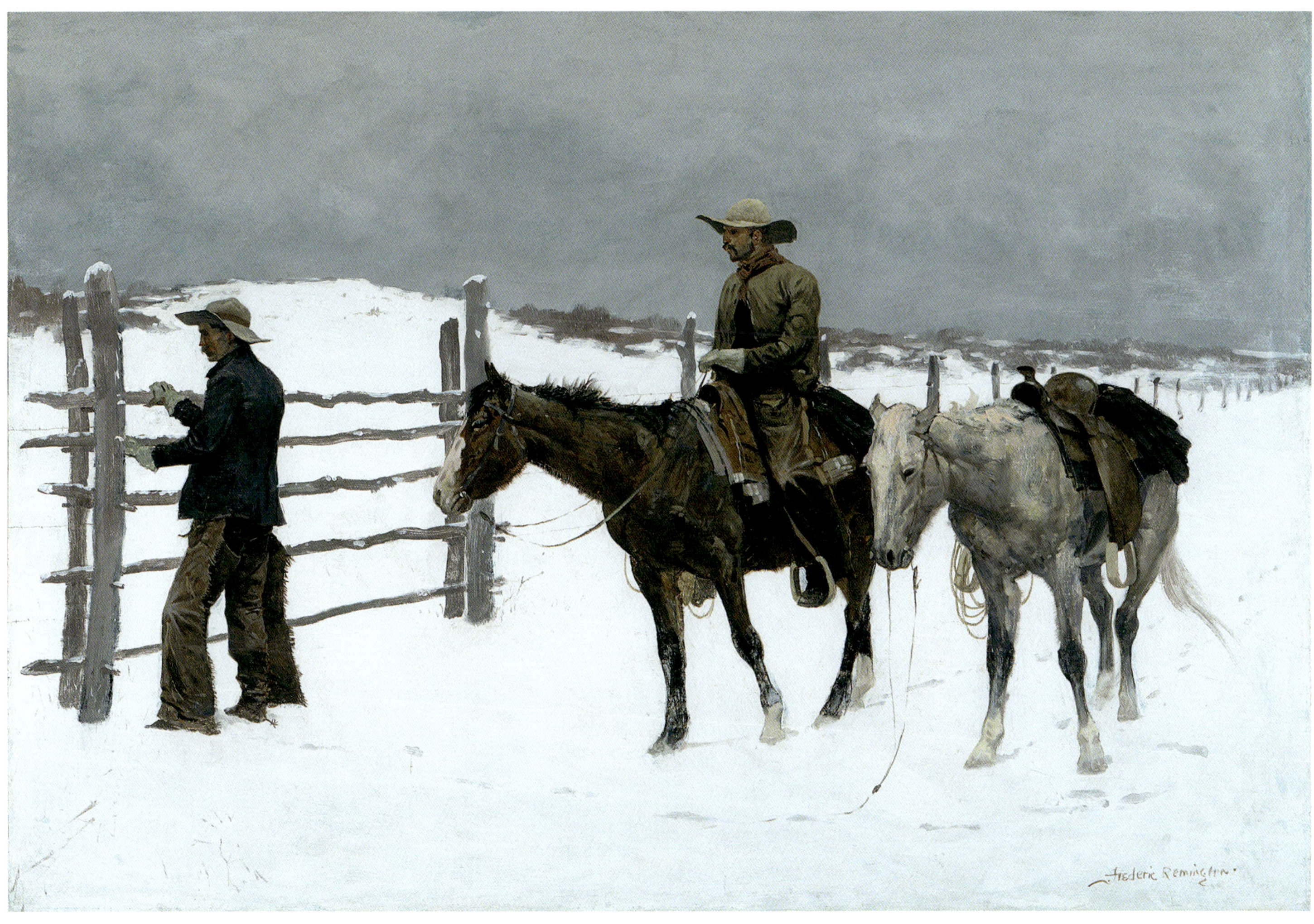

the cowboy would retain his heroic stature and public allure well into the new century.[16]

Remington visited the fair in 1893 and saw Proctor's cowboy there, following a fateful trip to the Babicora (called Bavicora by Remington) Ranch in northern Mexico, where he relished some of the last remnants of actual cowboy life. Remington had long contended that the original cowboy had come from the vaquero tradition, and by 1893, as the gradual demise of the open-range cowboy was becoming evident north of the border, the artist visited the ranch to record the Mexican counterpart in action (fig. 112). Remington and his friend the writer Owen Wister began working together that winter on a eulogy to the cowboy that would be titled "The Evolution of the Cow-Puncher." It was published in *Harper's Magazine* in 1895, just a month after another writer, William Trowbridge Larned, pronounced in *Lippincott's Monthly Magazine* that "the cowboy, like the buffalo, is fast becoming extinct."[17] Roosevelt had already suggested a historical paradox about the cowboy's role in the American experience in his "Frontier Types" article of 1888, writing, "Brave, hospitable, hardy, and adventurous, he is the grim pioneer of his race; he prepares the way for the civilization from before whose face he must disappear."[18]

One of the Remington illustrations in the Wister article, *The Fall of the Cowboy* (fig. 113), pictures two cowboys stopped before a gate in a barbed-wire fence. One has dismounted in submission to the cattle industry's lamentable

Fig. 113. Frederic Remington. *The Fall of the Cowboy*, 1895. Oil on canvas, 25 × 35 in. (63.5 × 88.9 cm). Amon Carter Museum of American Art, Fort Worth, Texas

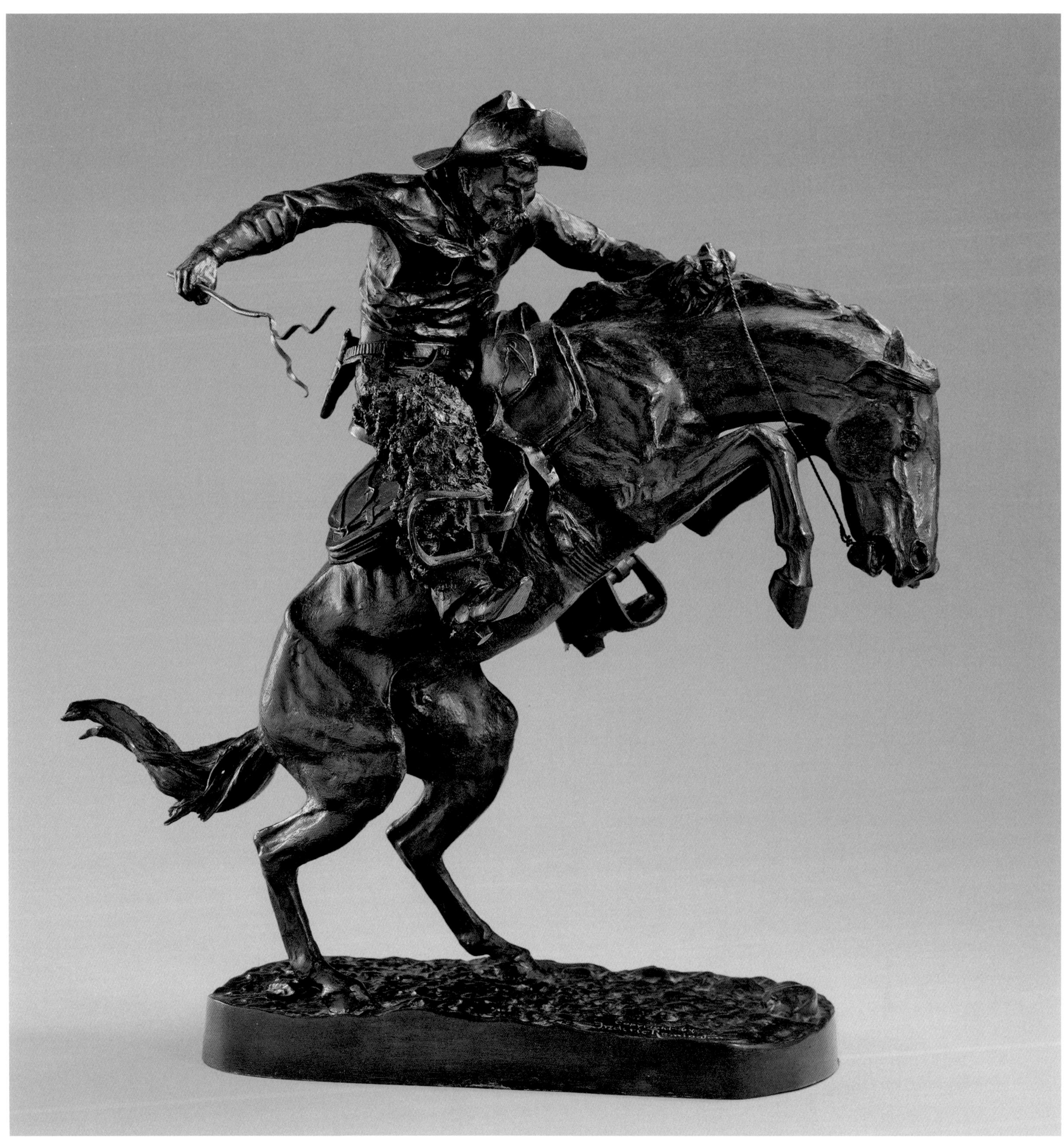

Fig. 114. Frederic Remington. *The Broncho Buster*, 1895 (cast 1906). Cat. 51

new closing of the open range. For observers of ranching at this time, an unhorsed cowboy was an emasculated figure; virility was associated with the cowboy exclusively as a mounted hero.[19] Remington's first bronze, *The Broncho Buster* (fig. 114; see also fig. 2), produced that same year, provided an emphatic counterbalance. In this contest between man and nature, man is positioned to win, with the cowboy virtually guaranteed to stay in the saddle. When the artist wrote to Wister about it that "I am to endure in bronze," he was implying that the cowboy would endure as well.[20] Like the "Cowboy Fun" segments of the Wild West exhibitions, *The Broncho Buster* was a national sensation (over 275 authorized casts were ultimately made). It garnered applause for its technical accomplishment, purely American flavor, and "extraordinary representation in bronze of wild and violent action."[21] Especially in the West, Remington was recognized as being important as "one of the few men who have taken up the unpromising subject of the American cowboy. . . . And out of a subject formerly devoid of interest and looked upon as beyond the range of sentiment, he has created a most fascinating being."[22] *The Broncho Buster*—because of its novelty, medium, commanding affirmation of survival, and transcendent popularity—ensured that at least the spirit of the cowboy would persevere.

Remington produced another seven bronzes of cowboys in his brief career, more than any other theme in his sculptural oeuvre. Each piece offers a somewhat different perspective of the cowboy. *Coming through the Rye* (fig. 123), for example, presents frolicking horsemen shooting up the town; *The Wicked Pony* (1898; Buffalo Bill Center of the West, Cody, Wyoming) pictures a fatal encounter between bronco and rider; and *The Norther* (figs. 120, 121) unites man and horse against the forces of nature. Only in *The Wicked Pony* does Remington extend the metaphor of the

cowboy's demise. Roosevelt, however, discussed not only the vanished hero but all he represented. In an 1898 article, "In Cowboy-Land," he portrayed the cowboy in even more profoundly fatalistic terms than Remington's painting *The Fall of the Cowboy*. These types, "who in certain stages of civilization do . . . good work, when the stages have passed, find themselves surrounded by conditions which . . . make their best qualities useless."[23] For Remington, the cowboy's "best qualities" would never become irrelevant, even long after his passing. To him, the cowboy was mythic hero, not hapless victim.

For all the celebrity showered on him in 1895, Remington would not hold the limelight unshared for long. In 1898 Solon Hannibal Borglum, a quiet ex-cowboy from Nebraska with a conspicuous talent for sculpture, rose to challenge Remington from a most unlikely quarter—Paris (fig. 115). At Christmastime that year, in the display window of Theodore B. Starr Company, a prominent Manhattan jeweler,

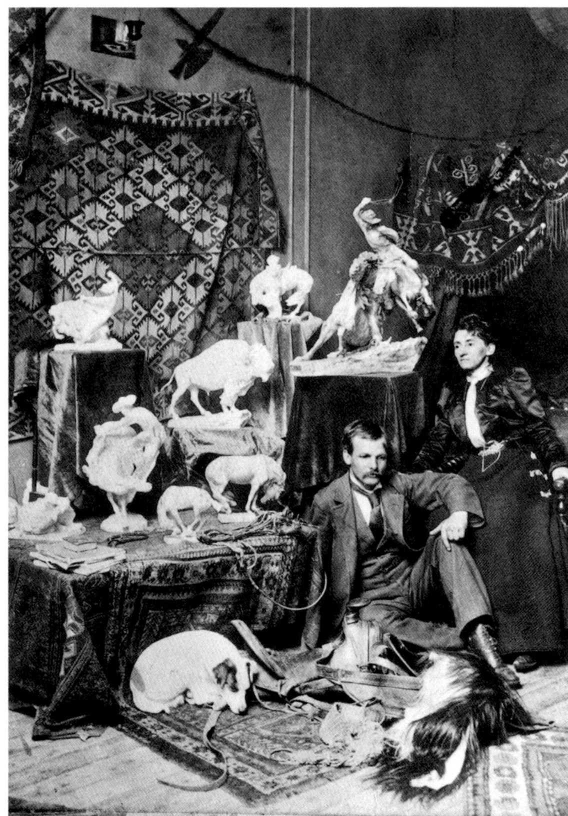

Fig 115. *Solon and Emma Borglum in the Artist's Paris Studio,* ca. 1899

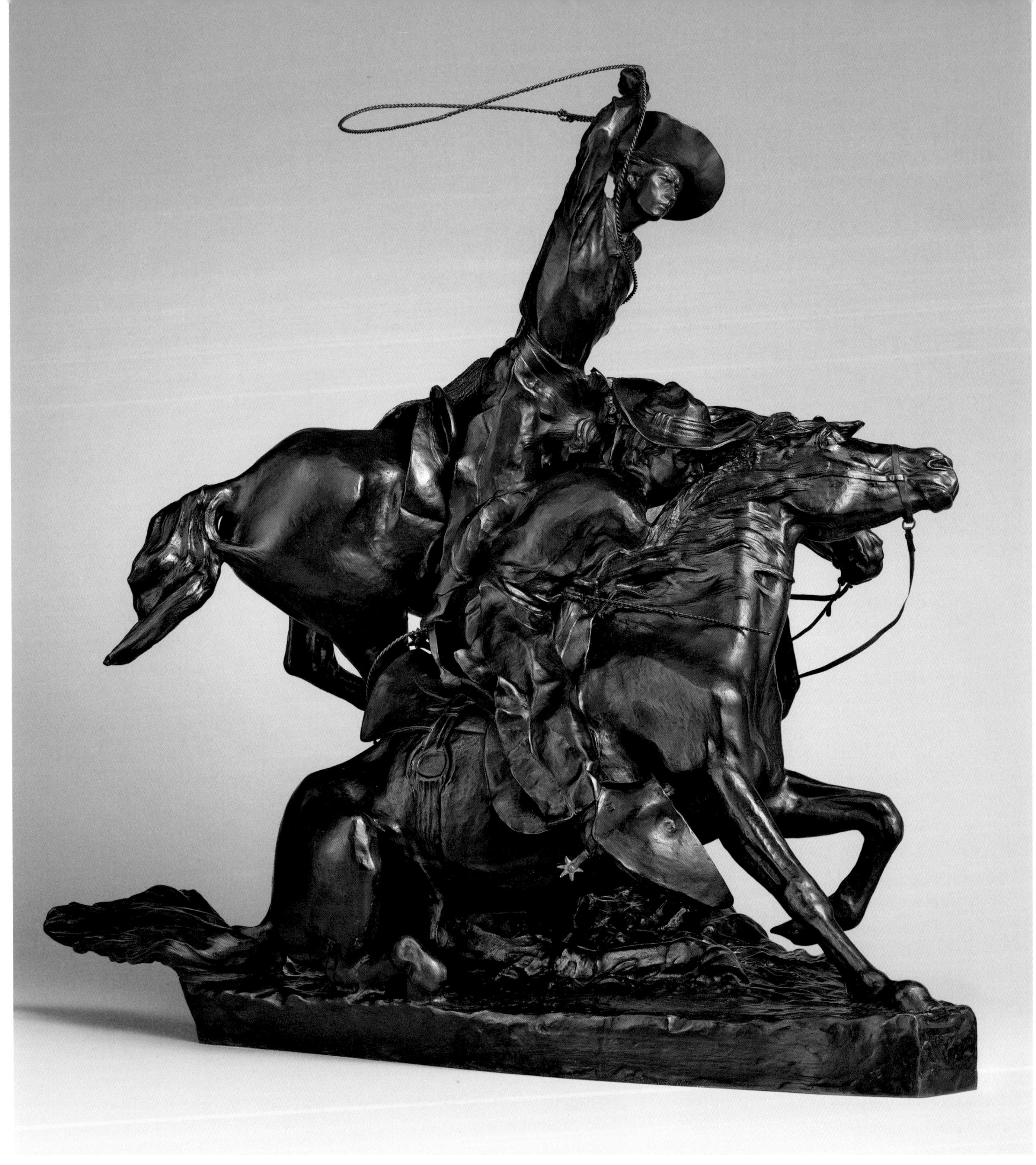

Fig. 116. Solon Hannibal Borglum. *Lassoing Wild Horses,* 1898 (cast ca. 1900–1902). Cat. 5

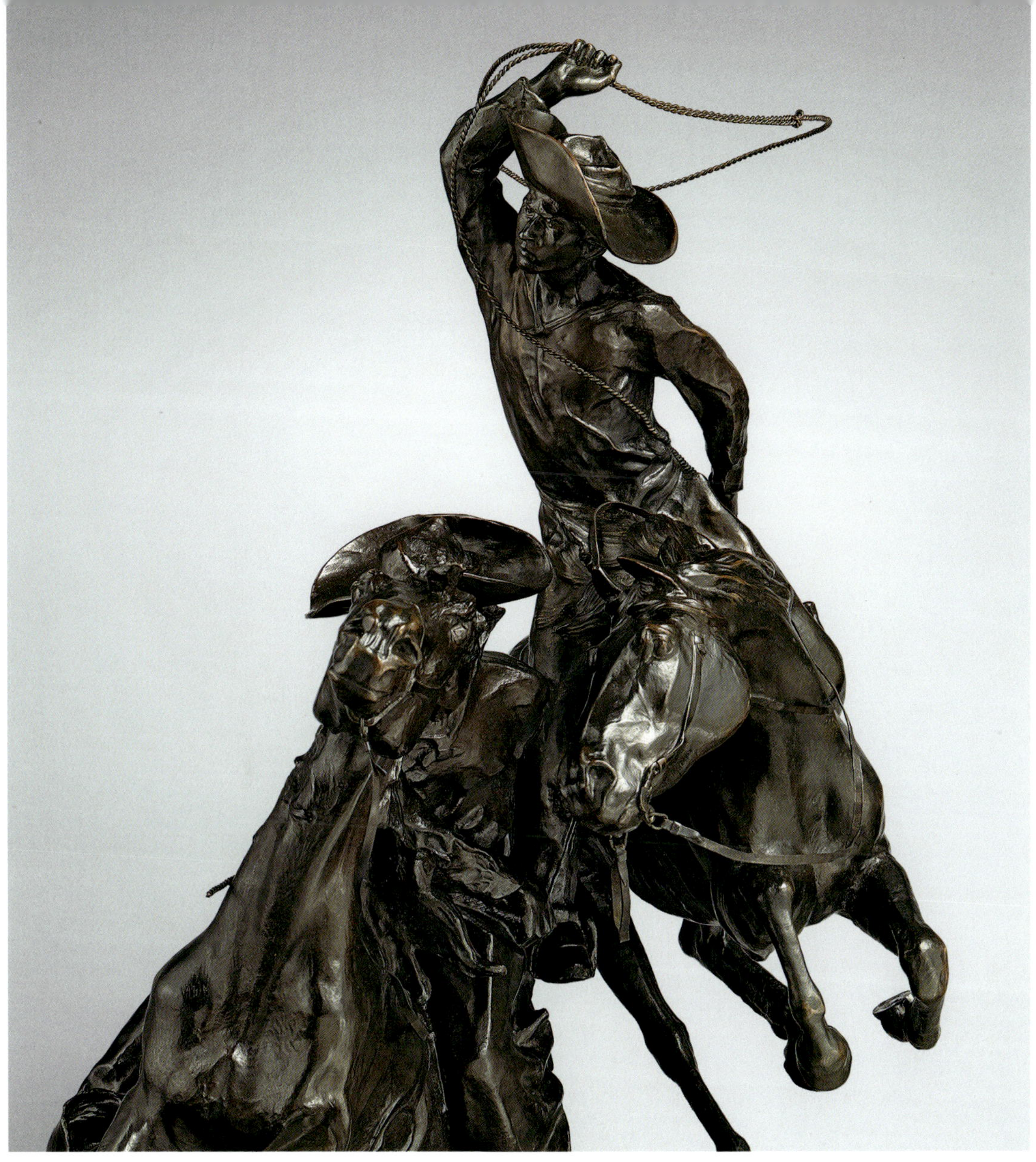

appeared five cowboy bronzes conceived in Borglum's Paris studio. The largest, most complex of the pieces was *Lassoing Wild Horses* (figs. 116, 117). Like Remington's *Broncho Buster*, it pictures a common cowboy activity (though catching horses rather than breaking them), but it stands about nine inches taller and is more explicitly three-dimensional. Borglum's is a walk-around sculpture, while Remington's sculptures are usually viewed most advantageously in profile. Some critics of Remington, in fact, complained that he had simply carried "certain of his illustrations over into another medium" and was quite unable to "conceive a theme sculpturally."[24]

Lassoing Wild Horses was Borglum's first major sculpture. It was begun in Ohio, where he first studied at the Art Academy of Cincinnati, and finished in Paris while he continued his education at the Académie Julian. When it was shown (thanks to his admirer Augustus Saint-Gaudens) as a centerpiece at the Paris Salon in 1898, the acclaim caused him to commit his life's career to sculpture.[25] The work focuses not on the wild horse that was being captured, as suggested in the tension of the rope that extends from the lead rider's right side, but on the concordance of the two cowboys. With this sculpture, Borglum rose to fame meteorically in the United States. He was

Fig. 117. Solon Hannibal Borglum, detail of *Lassoing Wild Horses*

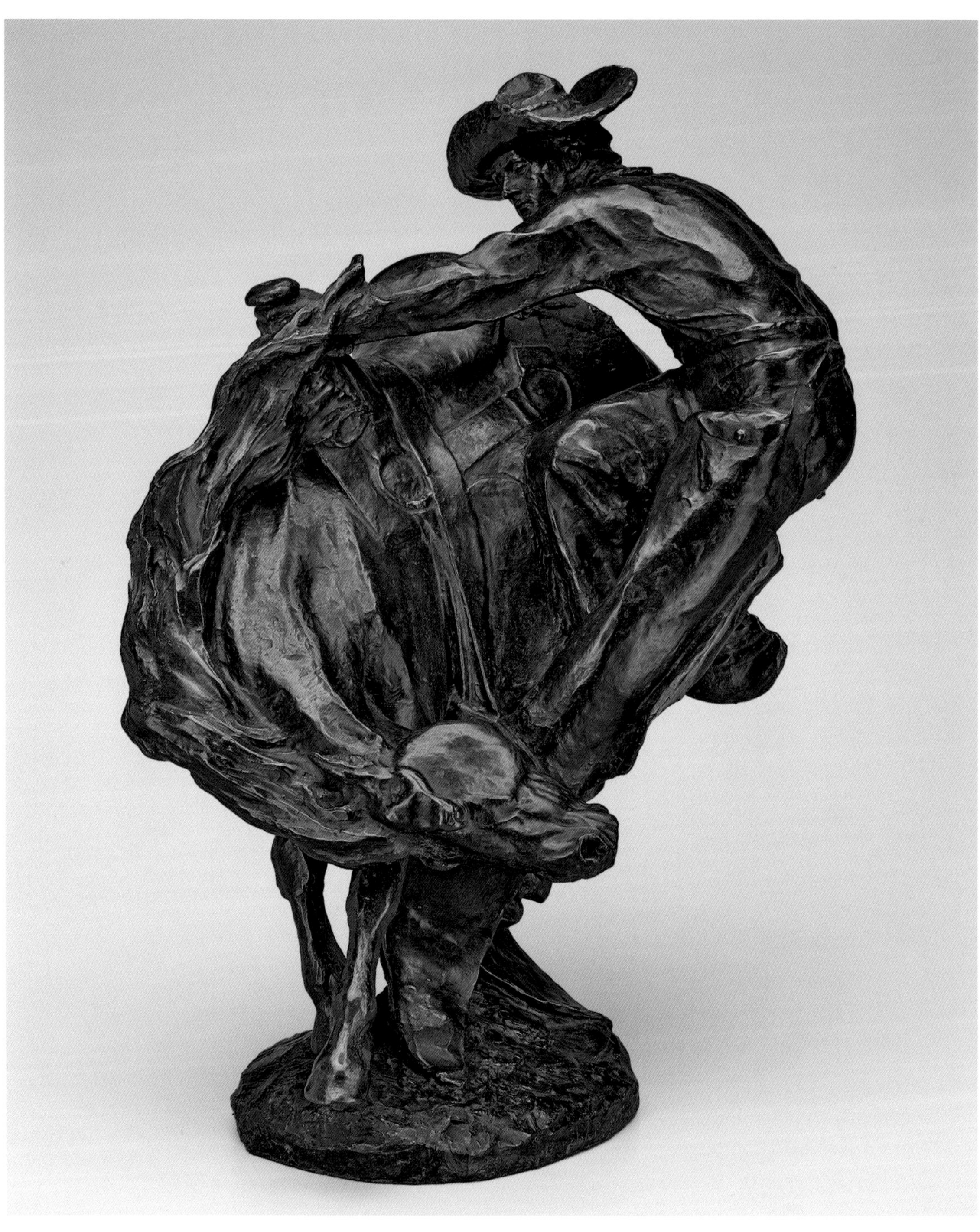

introduced as a prophet of the prairies and as "the first . . . to produce sculpture that was both truly western and truly art."[26]

Borglum's closest match to Remington's *Broncho Buster* is a bronze *Rough Rider* (fig. 118). Picturing a cowboy mounting a bucking horse, it emphasizes the connection between man and horse rather than man's domination. The circular composition underscores Borglum's empathy with the animal, suggesting a synergy between rider and horse. It is as if the man and horse have established a bond, assuring each other that they are meant to work together once the immediate ordeal is concluded. As a practicing cowboy, Borglum knew how important it was for the process of breaking a horse to produce not an "outlaw" but a working companion that would subsequently collaborate with as well as serve its rider.

One critic observed that Borglum's interpretation "differs" markedly from those that have "recently become conventional."[27] His brother, Gutzon, once wrote about Solon's work that one feels "the inner soul, which lingers through all the hardship . . . the poetry and grief" of each situation portrayed.[28] Another of his early cowboy bronzes, *Blizzard* (fig. 119), accentuates this point. Here a spiritual bond connects horse and cowboy in a moment of adversity, as they battle the forces of nature together. Solon's humanism in searching for

the soul of his characters, as well as his basic aesthetic, reveals his ties to the great French sculptor and pioneer of the modernist aesthetic, Auguste Rodin. Ilene Susan Fort has ventured that "the Impressionist surface treatment of Rodin's sculpture as well as the French modernist's use of humanistic themes served as an inspiration for Borglum."[29] Although not always affirming Rodin's influence, most of the critics in Borglum's day defined him as an Impressionist in bronze.[30] In many other works—such as *Night Hawking* (1898; R. W. Norton Art Gallery, Shreveport, Louisiana) and *Snowdrift* (1902; Allyson Miller, Baltimore)—he would choose situations in which snow and wind sweep over a figural group, blurring lines and details.[31]

Fig. 119. Solon Hannibal Borglum. *Blizzard*, 1900. Cat. 8

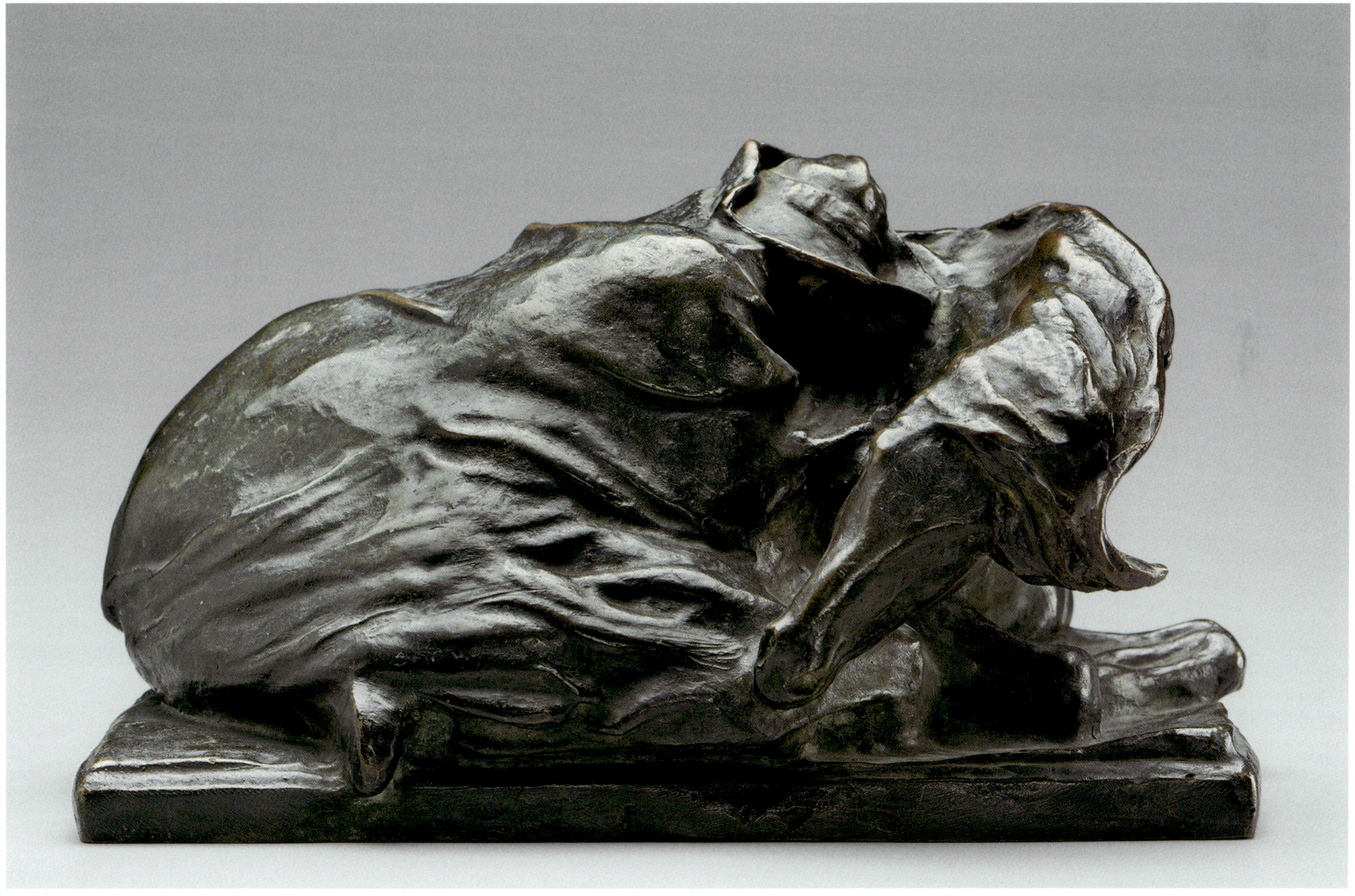

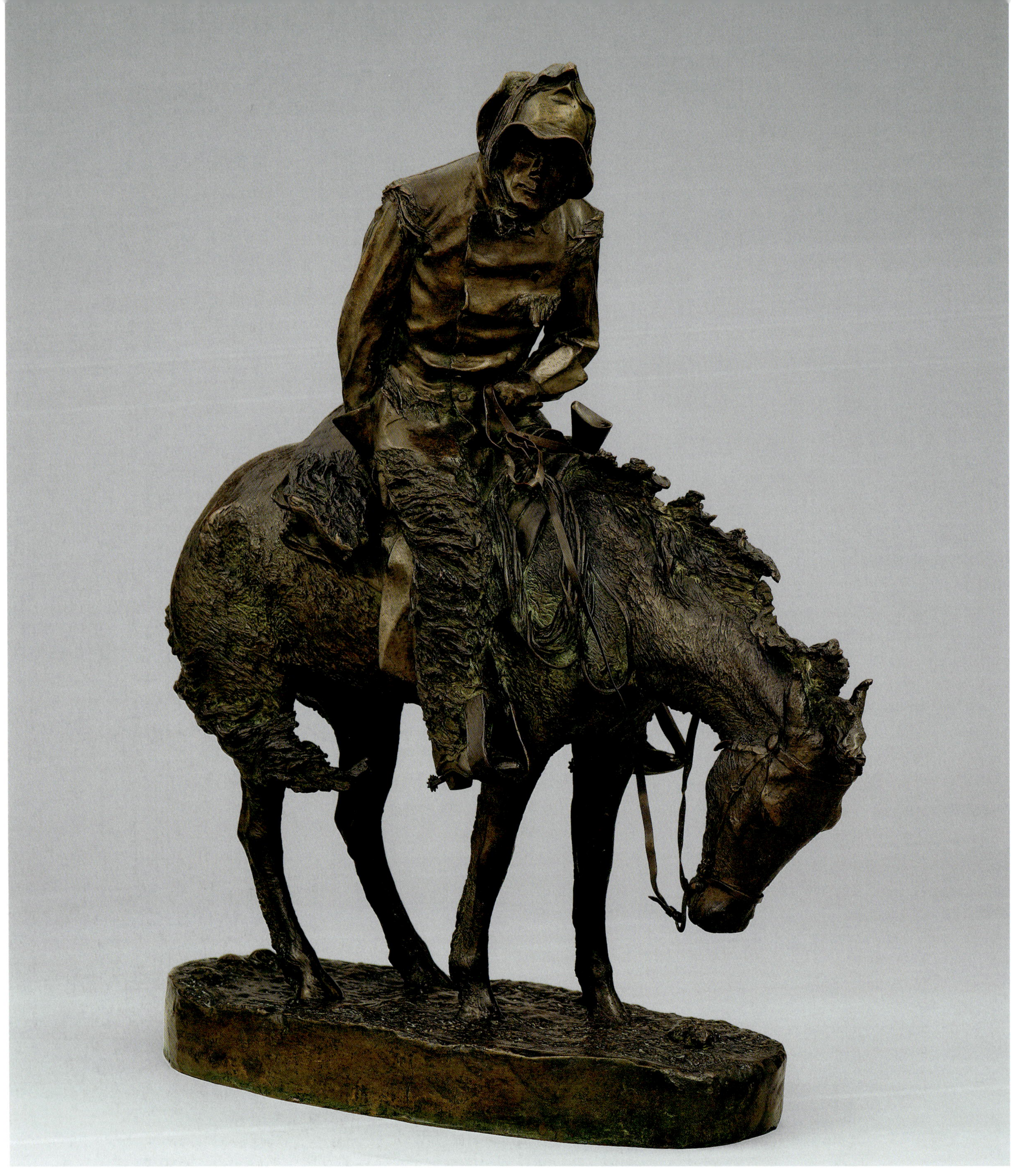

Fig. 120. Frederic Remington. *The Norther*, 1900. Cat. 53

Remington probably was aware of, or maybe even saw, both the Starr exhibition in 1898 and a review of Borglum's work in the *Art Collector* that same year. In 1900 Remington switched foundries in New York, from Henry-Bonnard Bronze Company to Roman Bronze Works, changing in the process from sand casting to the lost-wax technique, which allowed him far more freedom than the previous method. It is said that he also met Borglum and encouraged him to begin casting at Roman Bronze Works too.[32] It would not be surprising, then, if Remington picked up on the theme of the snowbound cowboy from Borglum's *Blizzard* when he produced his first bronze with Roman Bronze Works (figs. 120, 121). Remington had initially referred to this, his fifth bronze, as *The Blizzard* but changed his title to *The Norther*, perhaps in deference to Borglum.[33]

Remington's new sculpture was really not so much about physical, kinetic force as about the invigorated, textured surface that gives it a dazzling, impressionistic look. The rider's

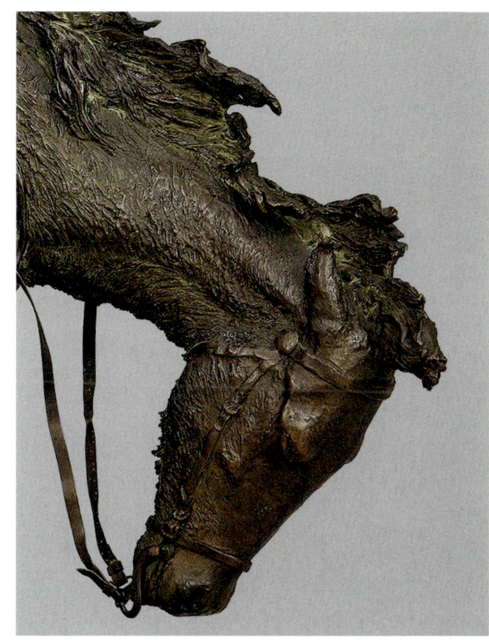

interiority is suggestive of Rodin's *The Thinker*.[34] The storm theme would consume Remington's creative thinking over several years; in about 1904 he revisited the topic in a painting and print, *Drifting before the Storm* (fig. 122).[35] While Borglum's treatment of the snowstorm

Fig. 121. Frederic Remington, detail of *The Norther*

Fig. 122. Frederic Remington. *Drifting before the Storm*, ca. 1904. Halftone color print from *Collier's Weekly*, 5 × 7½ in. (12.7 × 19.1 cm). Frederic Remington Art Museum, Ogdensburg, New York

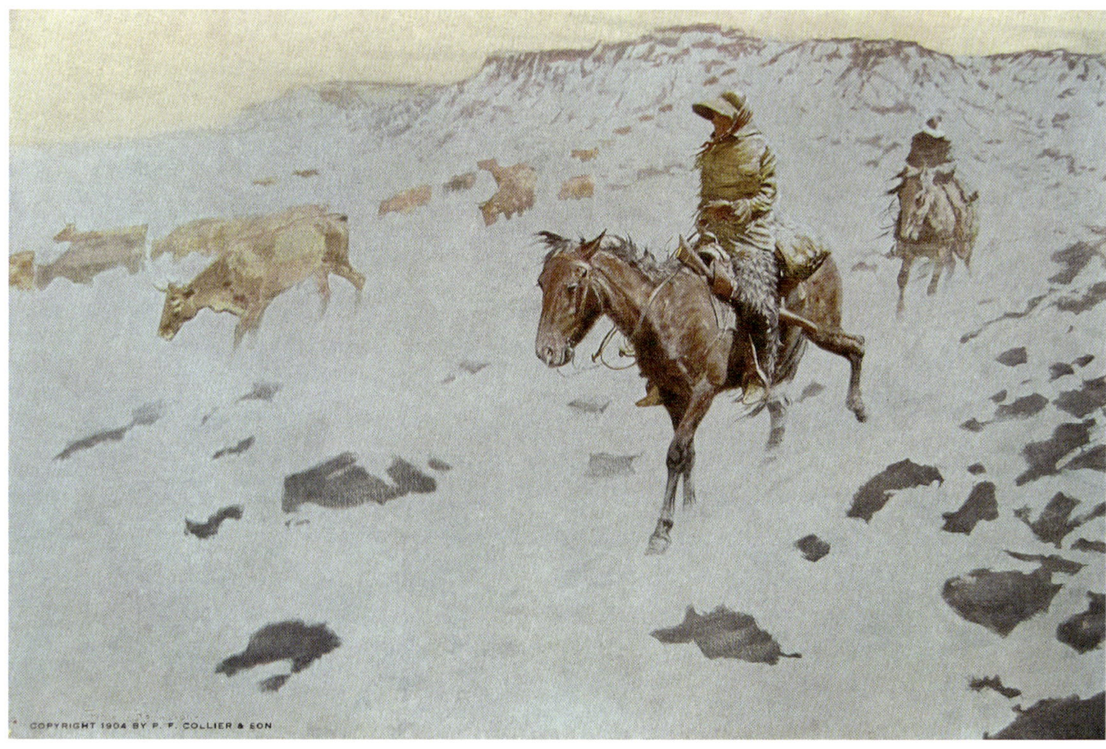

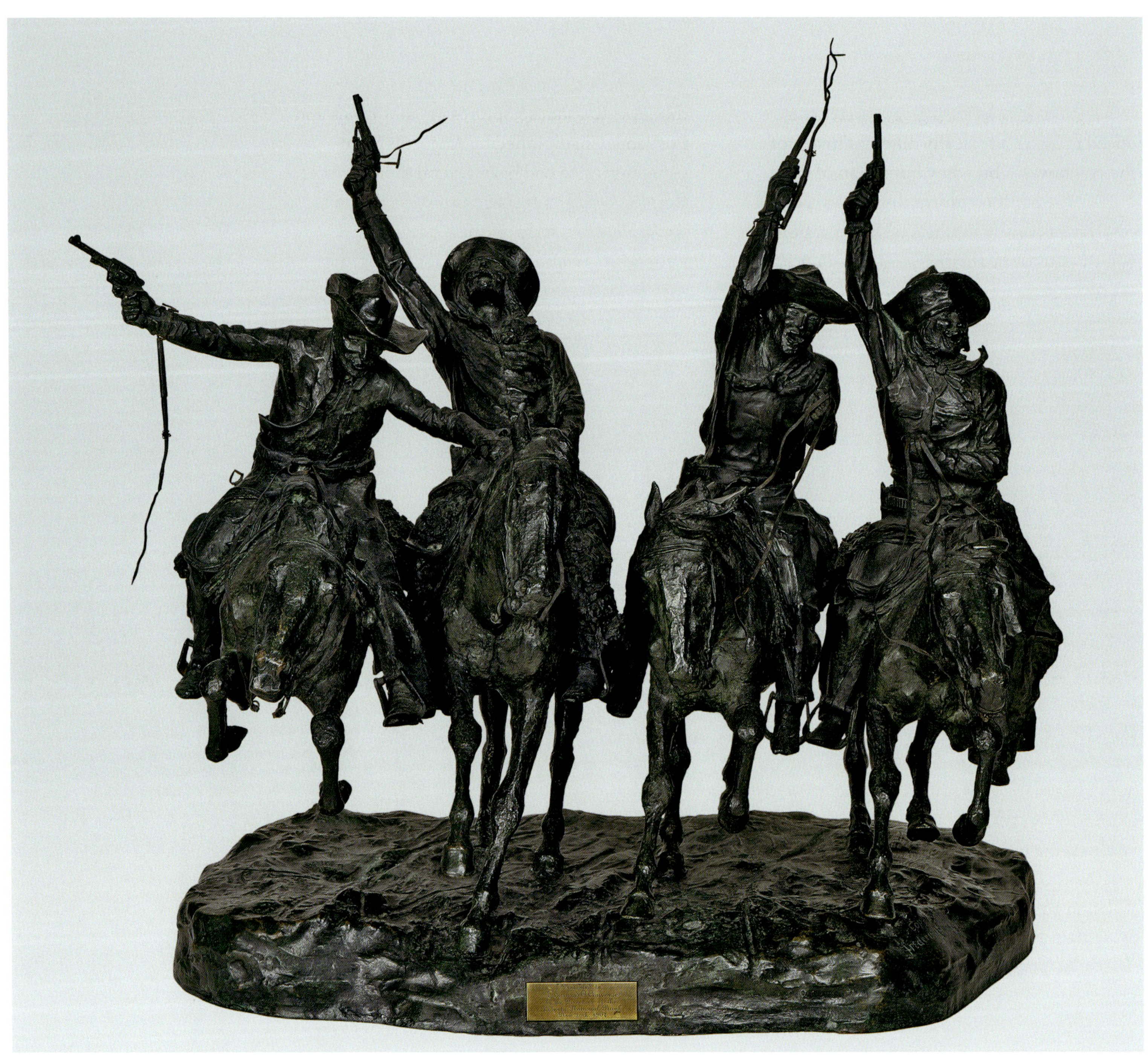

Fig. 123. Frederic Remington. *Coming through the Rye*, 1902 (cast 1907). Cat. 55

advocates union in adversity, Remington's appears to be more a metaphor for finality. As Wister wrote in *The Virginian* (1902), "The horseman with his pasturing thousands . . . will never come again."[36] Nonetheless, Remington could not leave the cowboy moribund. Within a few months of painting *Drifting before the Storm*, he created another variation on the theme, *Trailing Texas Cattle* (ca. 1904; Private collection, on loan to the Buffalo Bill Center of the West, Cody, Wyoming), in which the horseman with his pasturing thousands rides happily north through the balmy evening shadows.[37]

With his sculptures, Remington had breathed new life into the cowboy hero. In 1902 he copyrighted his raucous foursome *Coming through the Rye* (fig. 123), which introduced many to a radically different image of the cowboy—a brawling horseman of the plains. The composition and the theme of cowboys as rowdy hooligans had been born as an illustration, *The Dissolute Cow-Punchers* (fig. 124), for one of the early Roosevelt stories in 1888.[38] Roosevelt had referred to this as "mere horse-play . . . the cowboy's method of 'painting the town red,' as an interlude in his harsh, monotonous life."[39] Western towns, though, viewed such activity in quite another light. Livingston, Montana, for example, regarded a cowboy "shooting off his mouth and his revolver" as "an unmitigated nuisance, and an offender against the public peace."[40] In Arizona the problem had gotten so severe in the early 1880s that President Chester A. Arthur threatened to call out the cavalry.[41] Charlie Siringo, who in 1886 published one of the more credible memoirs of cowboy life, came to the defense, saying that the "wild and wooly" members of his fraternity were mostly imaginary because that was how "eastern people" had them "pictured."[42] Remington was certainly trying to please eastern audiences, and whether it was pure invention or reality-based in some way, *Coming through the Rye* presented a popular trope.

One of the most complex of the artist's sculptures, *Coming through the Rye* is a decided tour de force, with only six of the horses' sixteen hooves touching the ground. It was one of his first works ever sold to a museum (Corcoran Gallery of Art, Washington, D.C., in 1905), and it was later enlarged to heroic (if temporary) proportions in staff for the grounds of two world's fairs: the 1904 Louisiana Purchase Exposition in Saint Louis and the Lewis and Clark Exposition of 1905 in Portland, Oregon. Yet, like *The Broncho Buster,*

it was essentially one-sided—frontal rather than profile, but one-sided nonetheless.[43]

Solon Hannibal Borglum also exhibited monumental staff sculptures in Saint Louis and Portland. Championed by Augustus Saint-Gaudens (as he had been several times before), Borglum was granted a commission for four works, one being his ultimate paean to the puncher, *Cowboy at Rest* (fig. 125). Reminiscent of Zogbaum's early genre piece *Montana Cowboy* (fig. 110), it was Borglum's counter to

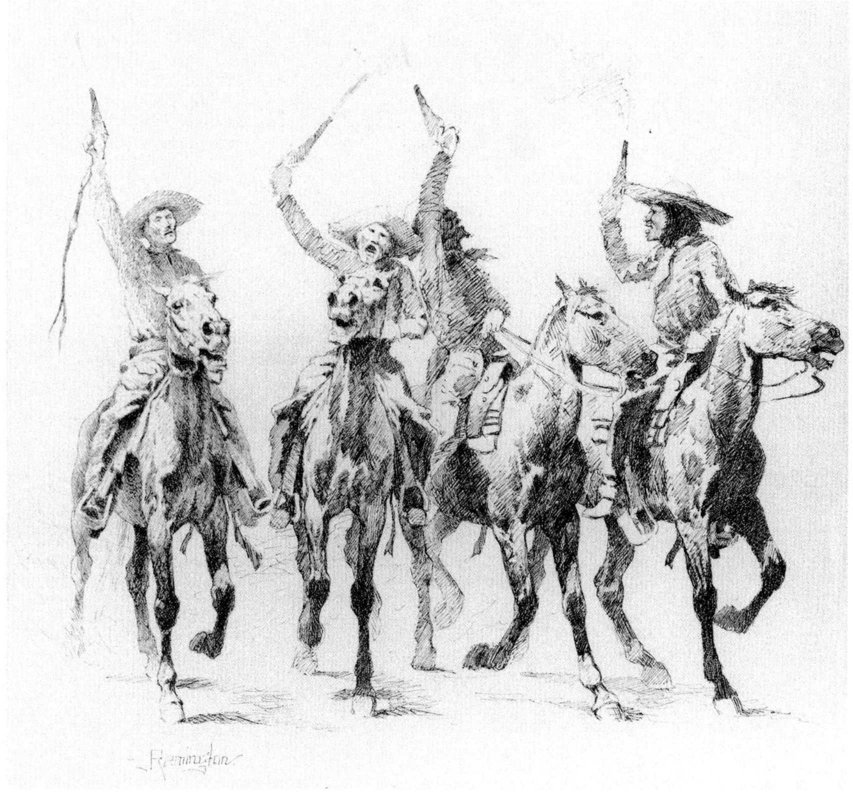

Remington's four horsemen on a spree. Contemplative, poetic, peaceful, and for the times, rather visionary, *Cowboy at Rest* prefigured Borglum's comment in 1910 that the cowboy was "the most misrepresented of all the western types." "The people of the East have been led by ignorant or careless writers, painters and sculptors," he continued, "to confuse him with the cattle 'rustler' or raider. He has been pictured as a desperado, going about 'shooting up' towns and leaving a trail of carnage behind."[44] The

Fig. 124. Frederic Remington. *The Dissolute Cow-Punchers,* 1888. Pen and ink on paper, 14 × 15 in. (35.6 × 38.1 cm). Private collection

work reflected Borglum's personal experience when, as a cowboy himself, he had dismounted on a ridge to "watch the wind mow paths in the bunch grass below."[45] Unlike Remington's painting *The Fall of the Cowboy* (fig. 113), in which a rider has dismounted in a servile accommodation to civilization, Borglum's reclining cowboy pays homage to nature and man united in the kind of bond that Ralph Waldo Emerson would have extolled as mutual reverence.[46] Yet, like Remington's *Broncho Buster*, Borglum's monument, perched on one of the highest points in the Saint Louis fairgrounds, was an unbridled expression of Manifest Destiny—no accident,

1904. Though born and raised in Saint Louis, Russell was living in Montana, where he had worked on various ranches for over a decade. As the open-range cattle business diminished in the early 1890s, Russell had given up his job as a wrangler and turned to practicing art professionally. He had already garnered the regional nickname of "the Cowboy Artist" for his paintings and illustrations of western life. His intent in 1903 was to submit half a dozen paintings to the fair's fine-art venues. In the process, he wandered the grounds and would have seen both Borglum's and Remington's monuments. From Saint Louis, Russell

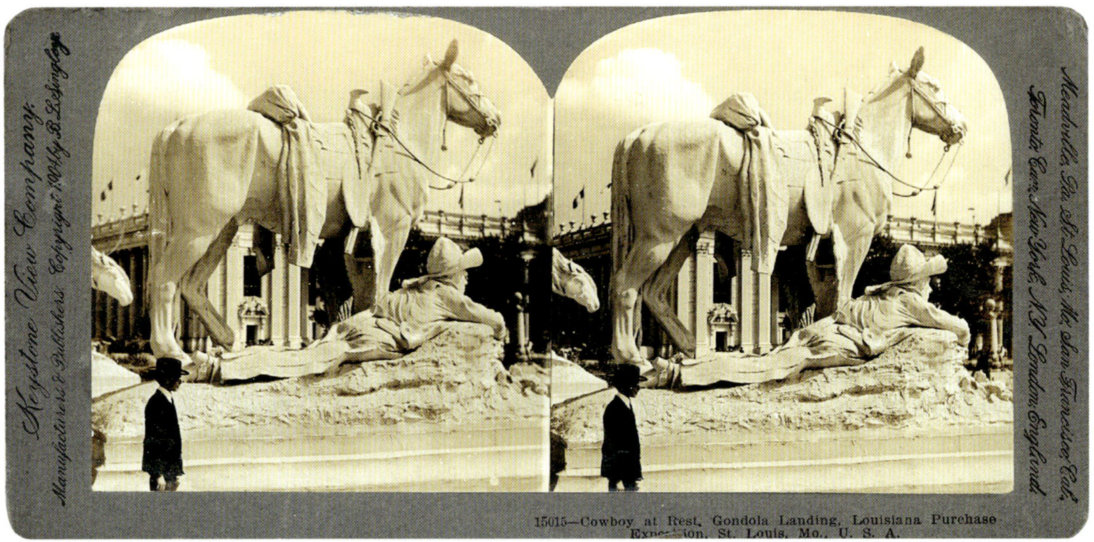

Fig. 125. Solon Hannibal Borglum. *Cowboy at Rest*, Louisiana Purchase Exposition, Saint Louis, 1904. Stereograph by Keystone View Company

given that the Louisiana Purchase Exposition was all about American expansion. Borglum's cowboy, as Andrew J. Walker has suggested, epitomizes a "dignified and resourceful engine of progress,"[47] while Remington's bucking horse with rider reflects a tamed West and a conquerable world beyond, one being vanquished by McKinley-era expansionism. It was no accident, either, that the Rough Riders selected a *Broncho Buster* statuette (fig. 2) to give to Roosevelt as a tribute when they mustered out after the Spanish-American War.[48]

Another artist from the West, Charles M. Russell, visited the Saint Louis Exposition in late 1903, before the official opening in May

went on to visit New York. There he was introduced to many other artists, including Remington, and no doubt saw a cast of *Coming through the Rye* in the display window of Tiffany & Co. During his stay Russell, who had been experimenting with small wax models for years, produced a finished bronze sculpture. That nascent effort, *Smoking Up* (fig. 126), with its revolver-brandishing cowboy on a rearing horse, was one of the freshest and most spirited sculptures Russell ever shaped. In 1905 he sent a cast of the bronze to Roosevelt.

At the time Russell embarked on his wrangler career, in the early 1880s, observers of Montana cowboys generally divided them

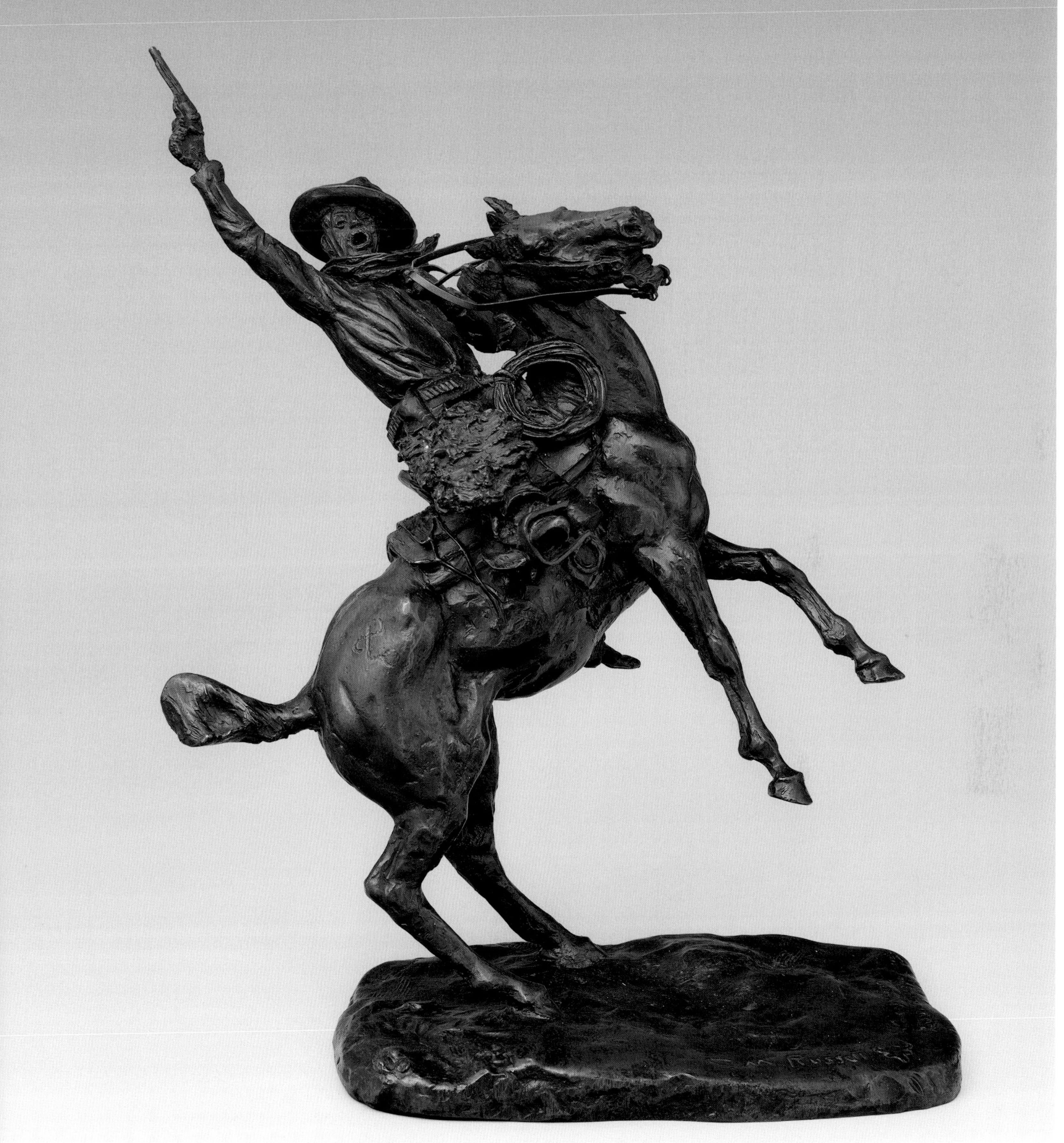

Fig. 126. Charles M. Russell. *Smoking Up*, 1904 (cast 1904). Cat. 58

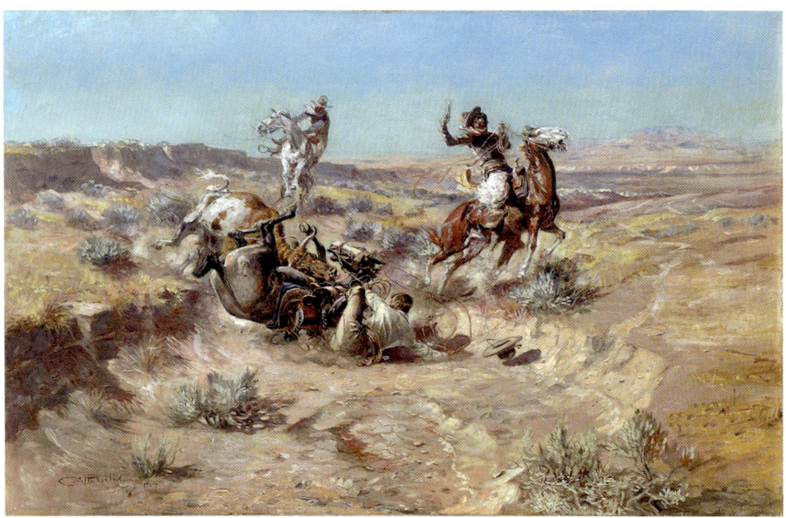

Fig. 127. Charles M. Russell.
The Broken Rope, 1904. Oil on canvas,
24 × 36⅛ in. (61 × 91.8 cm).
The Petrie Collection

Fig. 128. Solon Hannibal Borglum.
Bucky O'Neill, 1906 (cast ca. 1907).
Cat. 10

entertainment of eastern audiences.[50] Given that Russell specifically intended *Smoking Up* for the eastern market, it has generally been assumed that he envisioned it as a liquor-besotted horseman on a bender, inspired by one of the figures in Remington's *Coming through the Rye*. There is, however, another possible interpretation. Like some Russell paintings of this same period—such as *The Broken Rope* of 1904 (fig. 127), which pictures cowboys at work—the bronze could actually mirror the prevailing assessment out West of cowboys as active and hardy, as well as happy, horsemen.[51]

into two classes, the vast majority being "active, hardy, well-built horsemen," but with a few others who were "lawless ruffians."[49] As mentioned above, it was widely felt that the ruffian element was being unfairly singled out for the

Though more restrained in action and pose, Borglum's last cowboy bronze, *Bucky O'Neill* (fig. 128), resembles Russell's first effort. In 1905, following the success of his monuments in Saint Louis, Borglum received significant commissions for two bronze equestrian

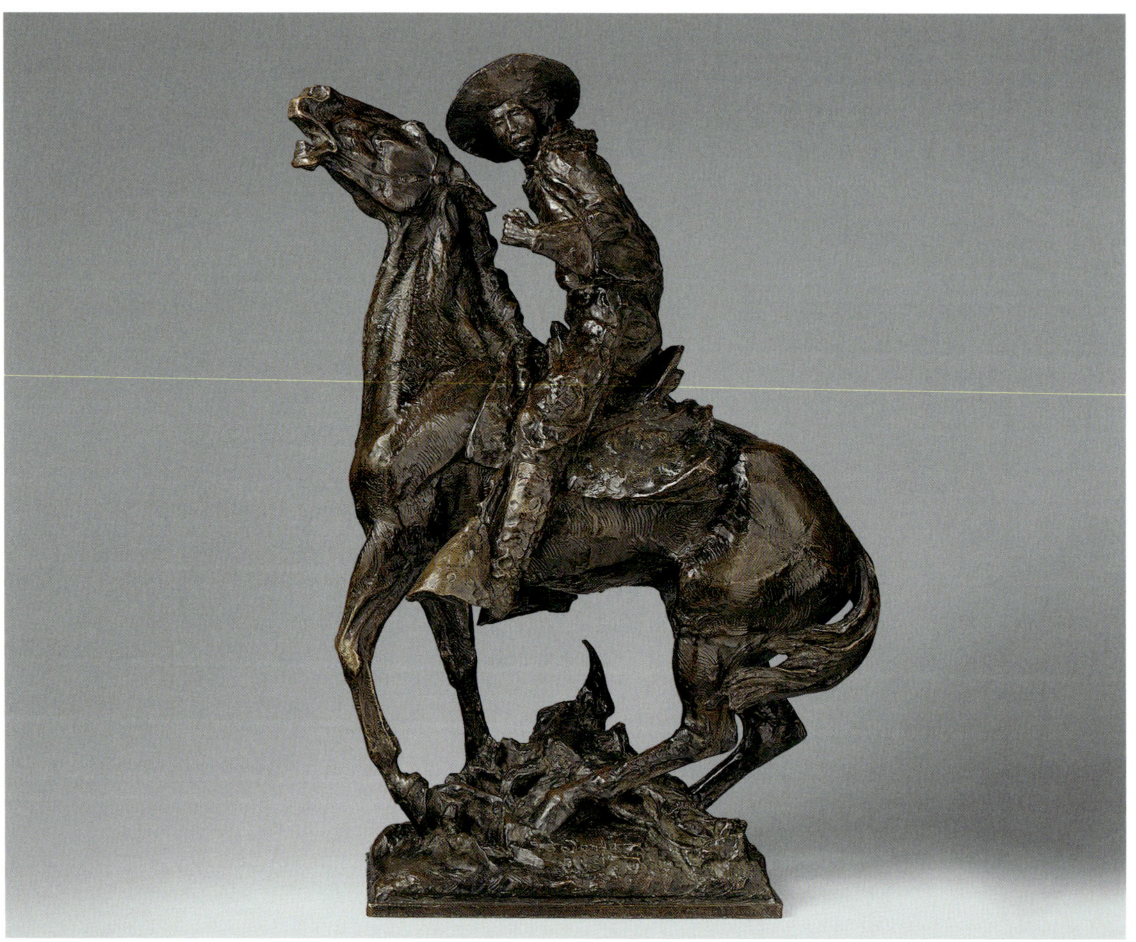

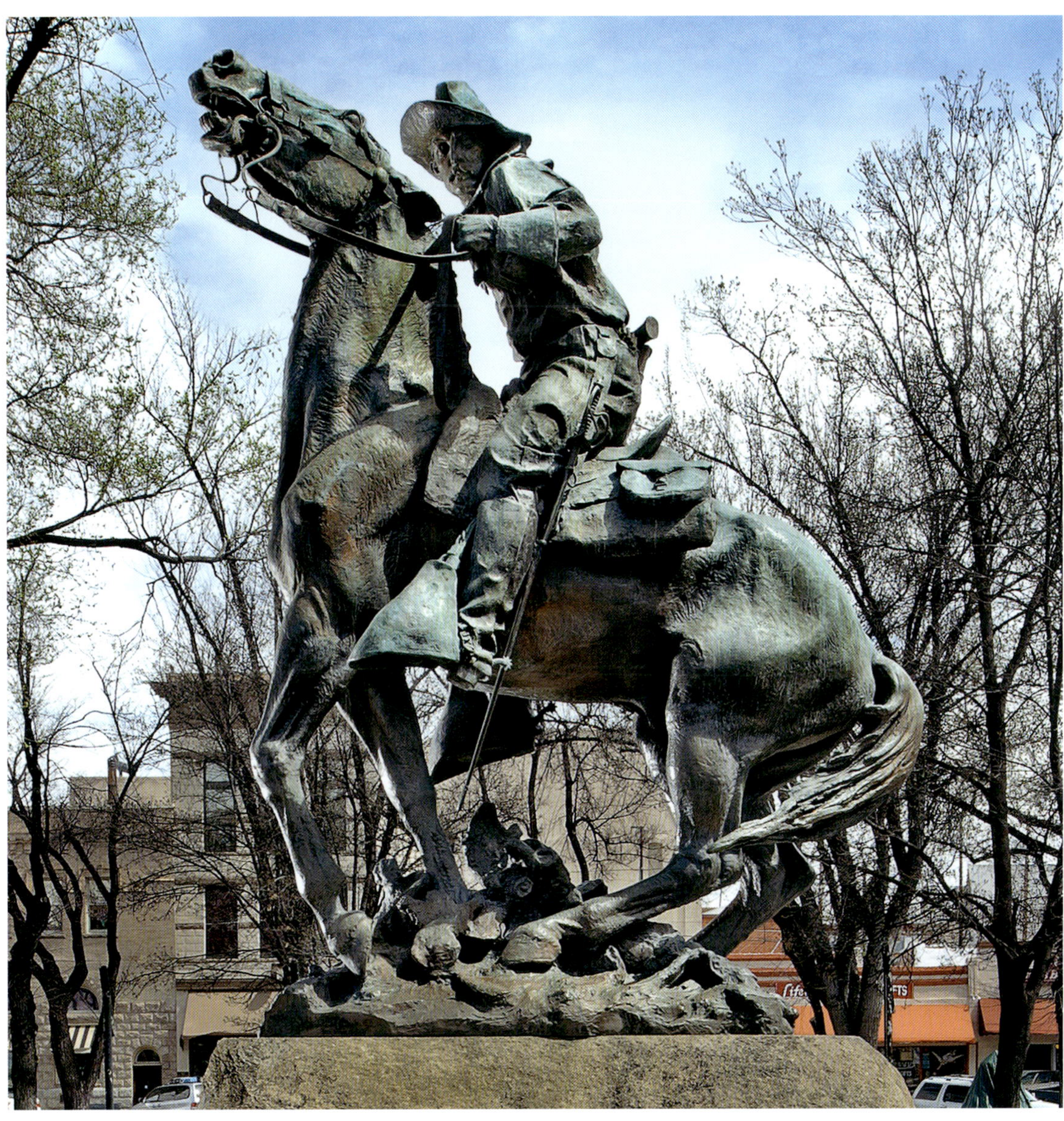

Fig. 129. Solon Hannibal Borglum. *Rough Rider Bucky O'Neill*, 1906–7 (dedicated 1907). Yavapai County (Prescott), Arizona

monuments. One came from the city of Prescott, Arizona, where the citizens wanted to commemorate their legendary mayor and sheriff, William Owen "Bucky" O'Neill.[52] Exhilarated by the hawkish passions that led to the Spanish-American War, O'Neill had organized and eventually led the first Rough Riders into battle in Cuba. Though a journalist and politician, he became captain of a troop composed almost entirely of Arizona cowboys. One of Roosevelt's favorite officers, he was killed while taunting the enemy in order to inspire valor among his soldiers just before the charge up Kettle Hill. Roosevelt described his death as "the most serious loss that I and the regiment could have suffered."[53] Borglum's assignment was to capture the final moment of Roosevelt's hero, "the iron-nerved, iron-willed fighter from Arizona."[54] The monument that resulted (fig. 129) received ecstatic approbation; one critic claimed it "the finest specimen of that class of art in America."[55] Certainly its vigor, latent energy, anatomical accuracy, and expressive intensity far exceeded the staid classicism of the more common equestrian monuments of the day.

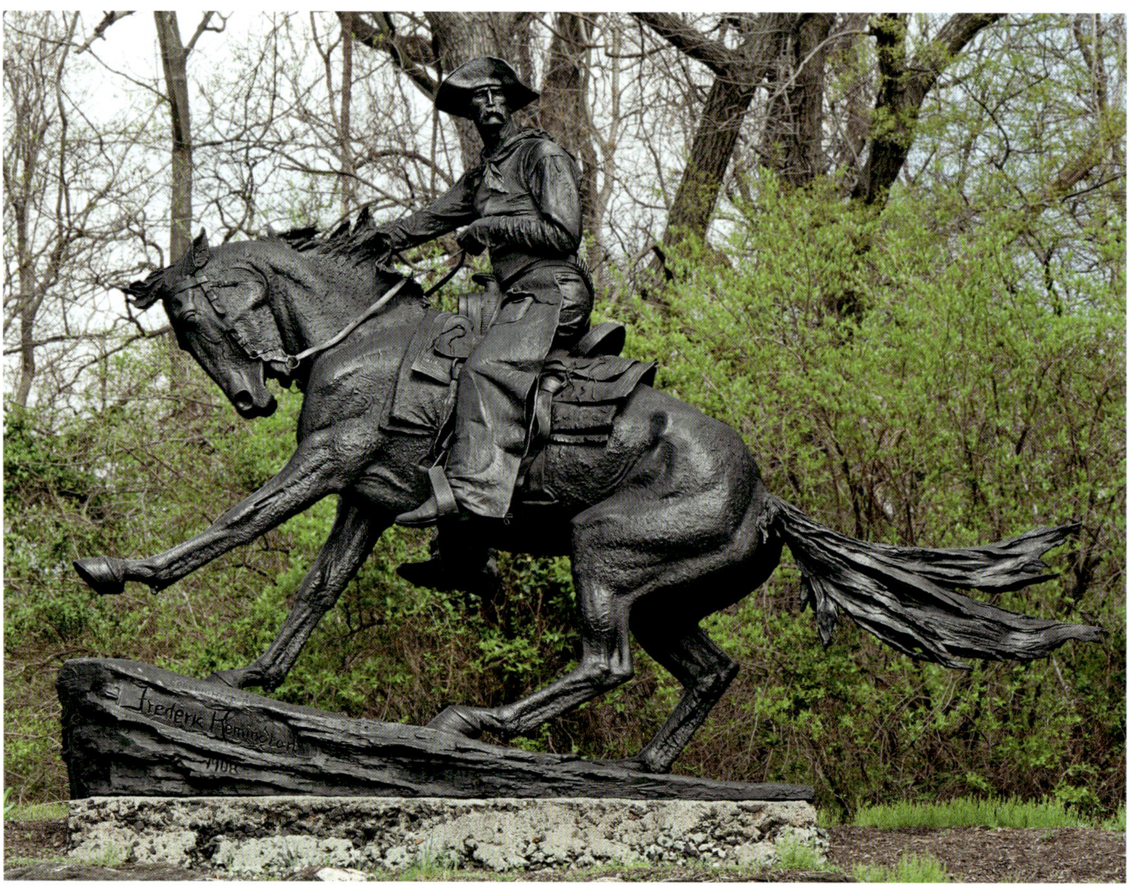

Fig. 130. Frederic Remington. *The Cowboy*, 1905–8 (dedicated 1908). Association for Public Art (formerly Fairmount Park Association), Kelly Drive, Philadelphia

Roosevelt, in writing about O'Neill, praised the Arizonan's tendency to reach for the stars. Borglum captured that characteristic in his bronze, with the skyward thrust of the man and his horse. In a larger context, this posture could be considered a metaphor for the nation's imperial motivations, according to art historian Alexander Nemerov.[56] The war also offered, according to one of the cowboys' prime chroniclers, Philip Ashton Rollins, an emotional and physical outlet for ranchers and cowboys disillusioned by the demise of ranch life at the end of the century.[57] *Bucky O'Neill* helped soften that transition.

After *Bucky O'Neill*, Borglum never again returned to the subject of cowboys, but Remington and Russell were far from through with them. In 1908, the year after Borglum's memorial was dedicated, Remington unveiled his own monumental tribute, *The Cowboy*

(fig. 130), in Philadelphia's Fairmount Park. A troupe of cowboys from the Buffalo Bill Wild West attended the ribbon cutting and this time applauded the accomplishment, despite the fact that Remington had recently been quoted in print saying "Cowboys! There are no cowboys anymore."[58] Russell's next cowboy bronze, though not a monument, was both his largest to date and one of his most sculpturally complex. Known as *A Bronc Twister* (figs. 131, 132), it was modeled in 1911. Theodore B. Starr, who had supported Borglum and the sculptor Henry Merwin Shrady for some time, immediately ordered four casts. Borglum was still showing with Starr at that time, and Russell could have been aware of Borglum's bronco sculpture of 1902, *One in One Thousand* (fig. 133), which is similarly fluid and graceful in capturing the dynamic of the contest between cowboy and bucker.[59]

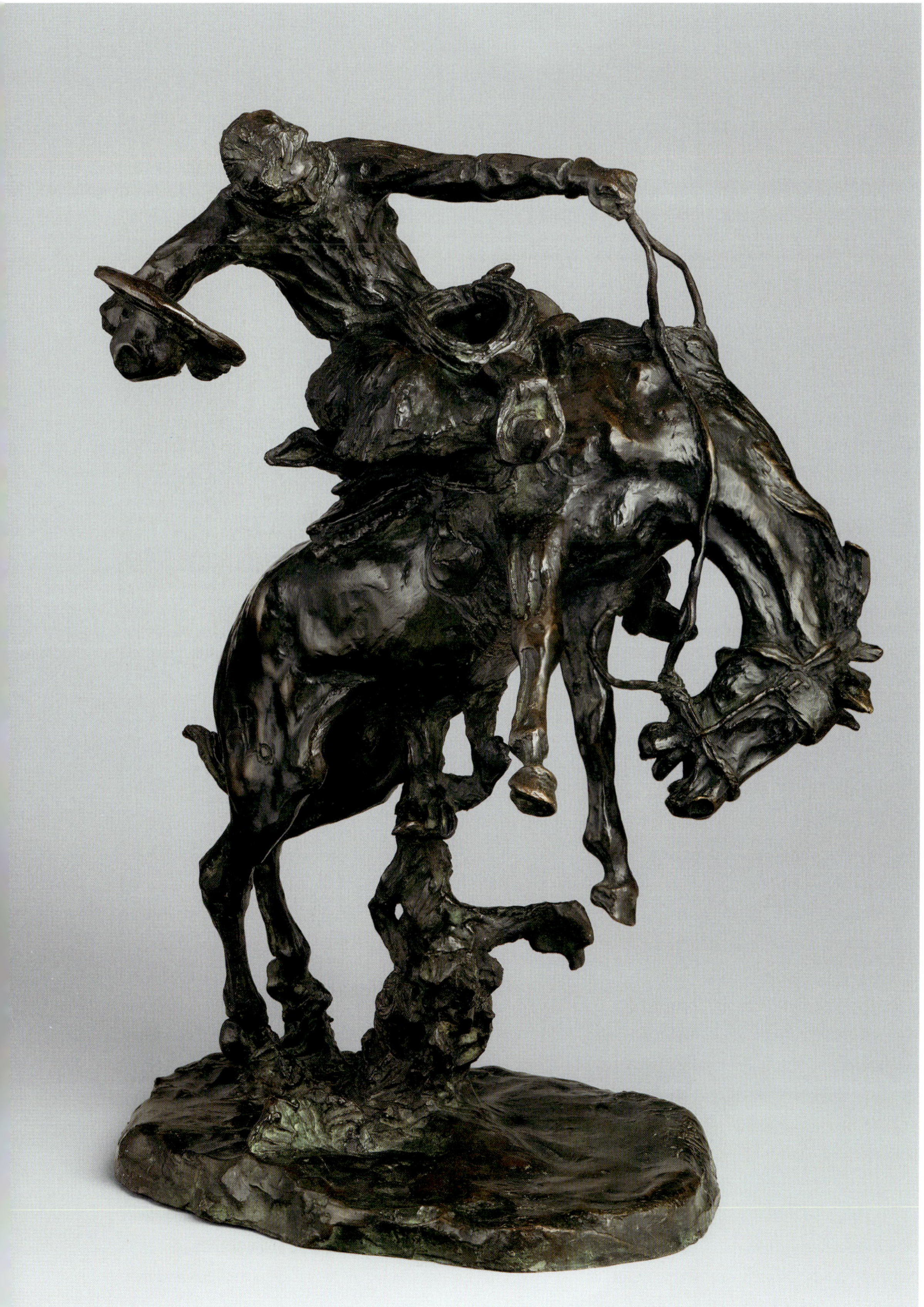

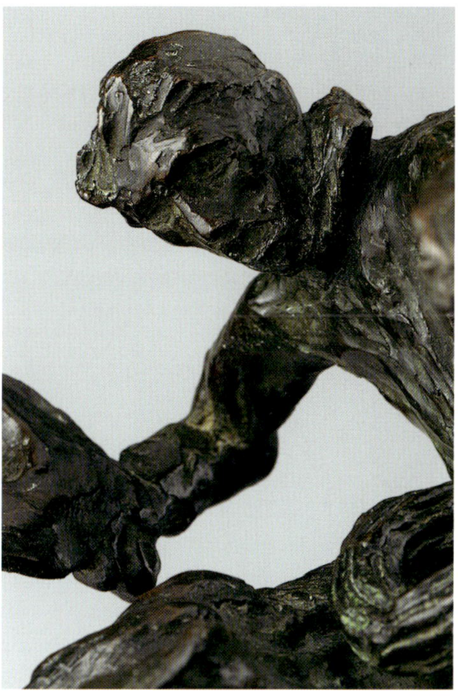

Figs. 131, 132. Charles M. Russell.
A Bronc Twister (The Weaver), 1911
(cast 1911 or 1912). Cat. 61

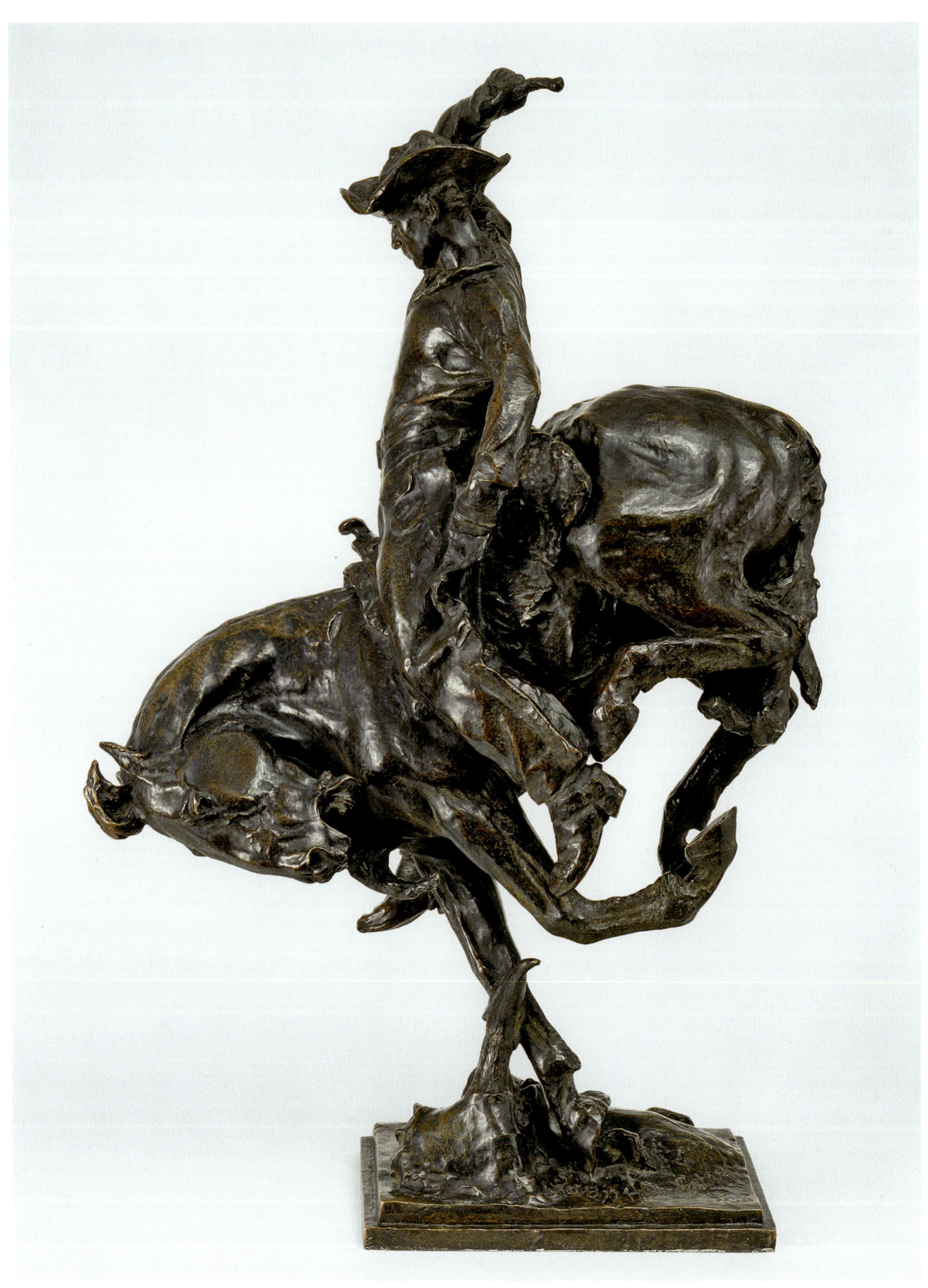

Fig. 133. Solon Hannibal Borglum. *One in One Thousand*, 1902. Bronze, 42 × 15 × 11 in. (106.7 × 38.1 × 27.9 cm). Buffalo Bill Center of the West, Cody, Wyoming

In a sense, Russell's *Bronc Twister* (originally called *The Weaver*) was a statement of
dissent against Remington's *Broncho Buster*.
Though not cast until two years after Remington's death in 1909, it had in fact been inspired
in 1904, during Russell's first visit to New York.
At that time he painted a remarkably true-to-
life watercolor, *A Bad Hoss* (fig. 134), that
was illustrated in *Scribner's* with the subtitle
"A cowboy riding a horse known as a weaver."[60]
It was probably watercolors such as this that
empowered western historian Emerson Hough
in 1908 and Texas photographer Erwin Smith
in 1909 to favor Russell over Remington and
attack the latter as a charlatan. Hough accused
Remington of having spawned a whole class
of eastern artists who knew nothing about
the West, while Smith lambasted *The Broncho
Buster* as ill-informed and incorrectly posed.
Russell, in contrast, was lauded as the only artist who, in works like *A Bad Hoss*, had "truth-
fully caught the cowboy and painted him in
action as he is."[61] Now, with *A Bronc Twister*, it
was Russell's turn to portray the bronco buster
as faithfully in bronze as he had in paint. The
result was a masterpiece in animal motion and a
thoroughly three-dimensional work.

Gutzon Borglum, though rarely known
for his tact and a devious competitor with his
brother Solon, compared Russell's and Remington's bronzes of cowboys rather more objec-
tively. In 1926 he wrote: "In motive they show
the same keen power of observation and ability
to select the instant the action is most complete
and most expressive. . . . Russell had not only
the wit to see the dual situation attached to any
great movement, but he had, and with an ability Remington had never shown, the power to
draw animals, horses, cattlemen, in the mixed-
up, tangled-up situations daily occurring in the
wild unfenced West."[62]

Russell's work, as exemplified by *A Bronc
Twister,* was visually situational, of the moment,
while Remington's was a more temporally

distant, idealized, grand interpretation of
action. This may be why no efforts were ever
made to create a monument of *A Bronc Twister,*
whereas multiple attempts were made after
Remington died to enlarge his *Broncho Buster*
to heroic proportions. In 1910 Remington's
widow, Eva, was bombarded with ideas for a
bronze monument of *The Broncho Buster*. Theodore Roosevelt advocated for some western
city, particularly Cheyenne or Denver, to set up
a large-scale Remington bronco.[63] When such
endeavors fell short, Remington's protégé, Sally
James Farnham, stepped forward after World
War I to reinvigorate the discussion. Sadly, that
effort languished too, and Remington's legacy
as a monumental sculptor has had to be ful-
filled by only *The Cowboy* in Fairmount Park.[64]

One small western spark did ignite to
heroic proportions during this period. Buffalo Bill died in Denver in 1917, and an initia-
tive was set in motion to produce a monument

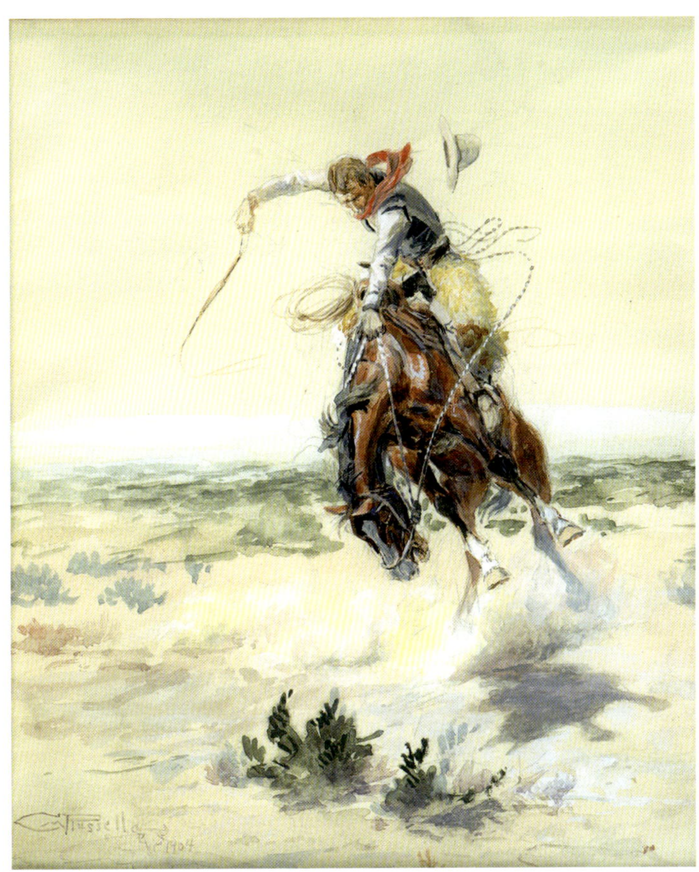

Fig. 134. Charles M. Russell.
A Bad Hoss, 1904. Watercolor on
paper, 12 × 9¾ in. (30.5 × 24.8 cm).
Private collection through J. N.
Bartfield Galleries, New York

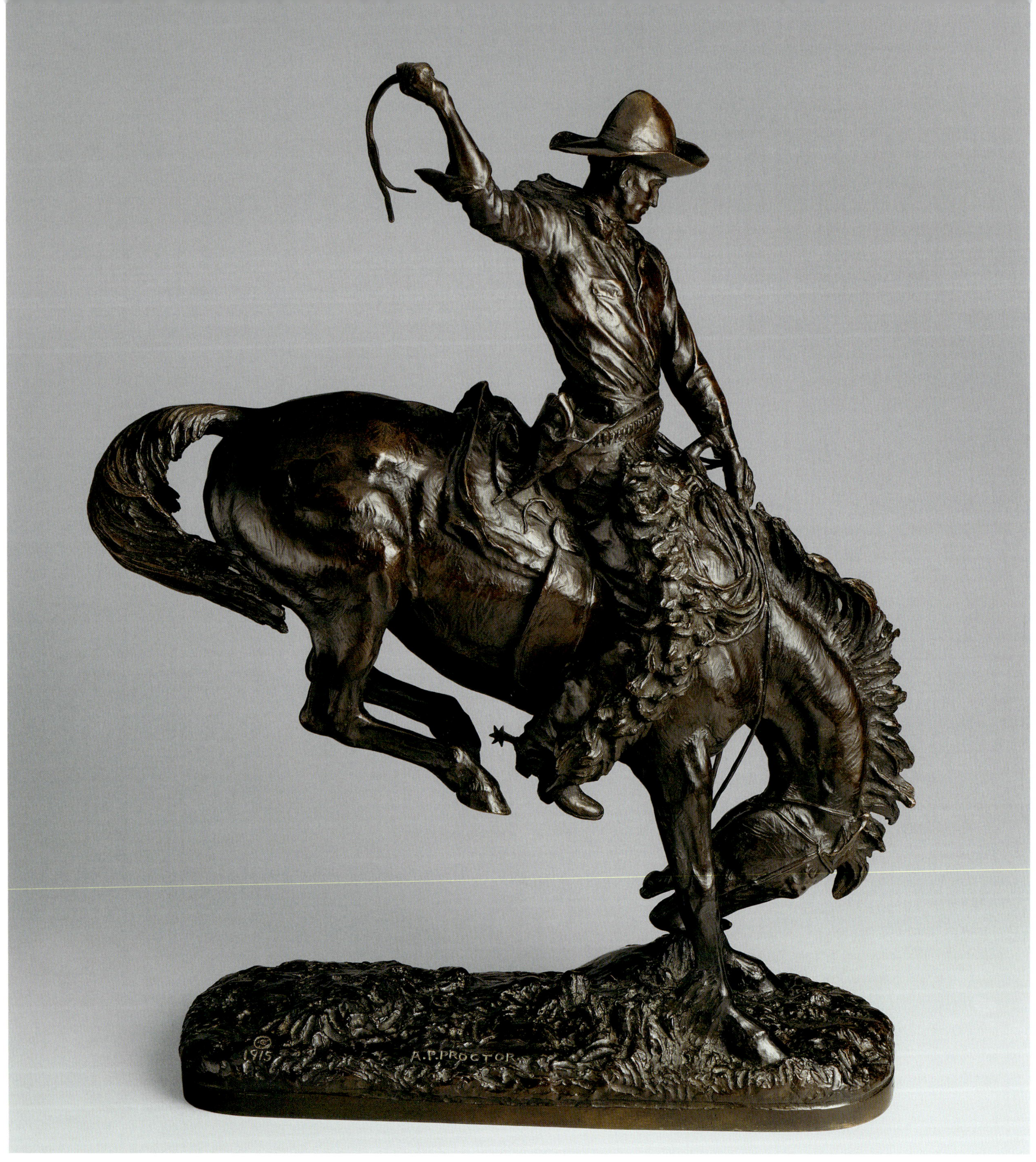

Fig. 135. Alexander Phimister Proctor. *Buckaroo*, 1914 (cast 1915 or after). Cat. 43

at his grave site. Proctor came to the funeral both out of respect for the legendary showman and in hopes of garnering the commission. He found that, despite Roosevelt's initial leadership, money could not be raised at a time when America's involvement in World War I was increasing.[65] Nonetheless, his journey was not in vain, and Proctor left Denver with not one but two commissions for monumental equestrian bronzes—one was an Indian warrior, the other a mounted cowboy.

After his initial brush with cowboy sculpture at the World's Columbian Exposition, Proctor avoided the theme for over twenty years. Unlike Russell and Borglum, he was not associated with the cowboy in the public mind. He had long been known as a sportsman hunter, an identity that served him well as an animal artist. Proctor had altered his course in 1914 by attending Oregon's Pendleton Round-Up. There he was swept up in the thrill of the rodeo and, as fellow artist Ernest Peixotto observed, "He lived in constant touch with the cow-puncher's life."[66] The experience resulted in Proctor's interpretation of a bucking horse and rider, *Buckaroo* (fig. 135), which he sculpted that fall. The finished work was an elegant, idealized Beaux-Arts statuette that, according to a critic for the Portland *Morning Oregonian*, retained "the rare sense of decorative beauty which is characteristic of his more monumental" animal sculptures.[67] Though modeled in the controlled fashion learned at the Académie Julian, *Buckaroo* nonetheless established Proctor as a truly American voice.

Proctor and some of his West Coast supporters tried in vain to have *Buckaroo* erected as a monument in Oregon, but it was Denver that made this dream a reality. At the time of Cody's funeral, Proctor met with Denver's mayor, Robert Speer, who embraced the idea of installing two monumental bronzes in the city's new Civic Center. By 1920 the first work was dedicated as the *Broncho Buster* (fig. 136),

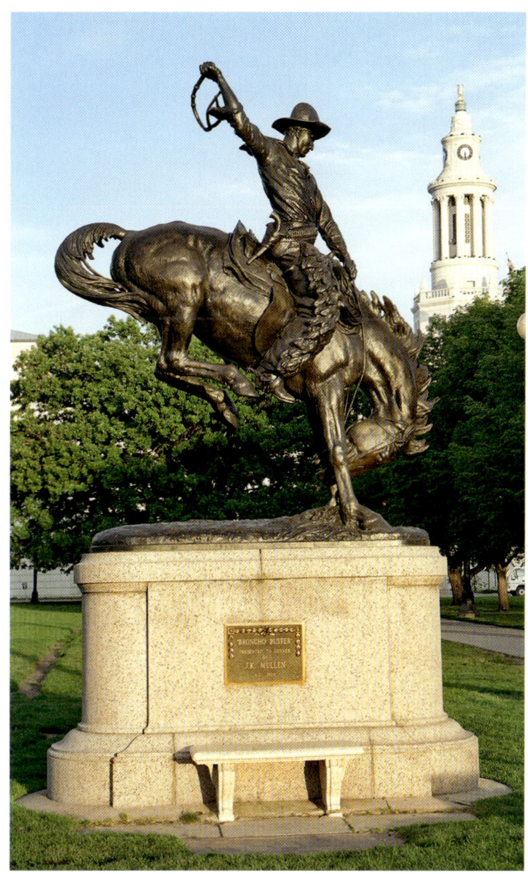

Fig. 136. Alexander Phimister Proctor. *Broncho Buster*, 1917–19 (dedicated 1920). Civic Center Park, Denver

less than twenty years after Proctor's staff *Cowboy* had been dismantled in a nearby Denver park. An equestrian Indian figure, *On the War Trail*, was dedicated in 1922. In the meantime, Solon Hannibal Borglum had been invited by Denver's art doyenne Ann Evans to supply ideas for two similar monuments to be installed across from Proctor's, but money was never raised for them.[68]

When Proctor first produced *Buckaroo* as a tabletop-size bronze in 1915, it was described as a rider "with upraised quirt and tousled chaps upon an outlaw horse."[69] It turned out, however, that the real outlaw was the rider, not the horse. The model, a cowboy named Bill "Slim" Ridings, was arrested shortly after Proctor finished modeling the clay and thrown in jail on charges of horse theft. This must have been more than a little embarrassing for the artist and certainly diminished chances of the piece's being employed as the study for a monument,

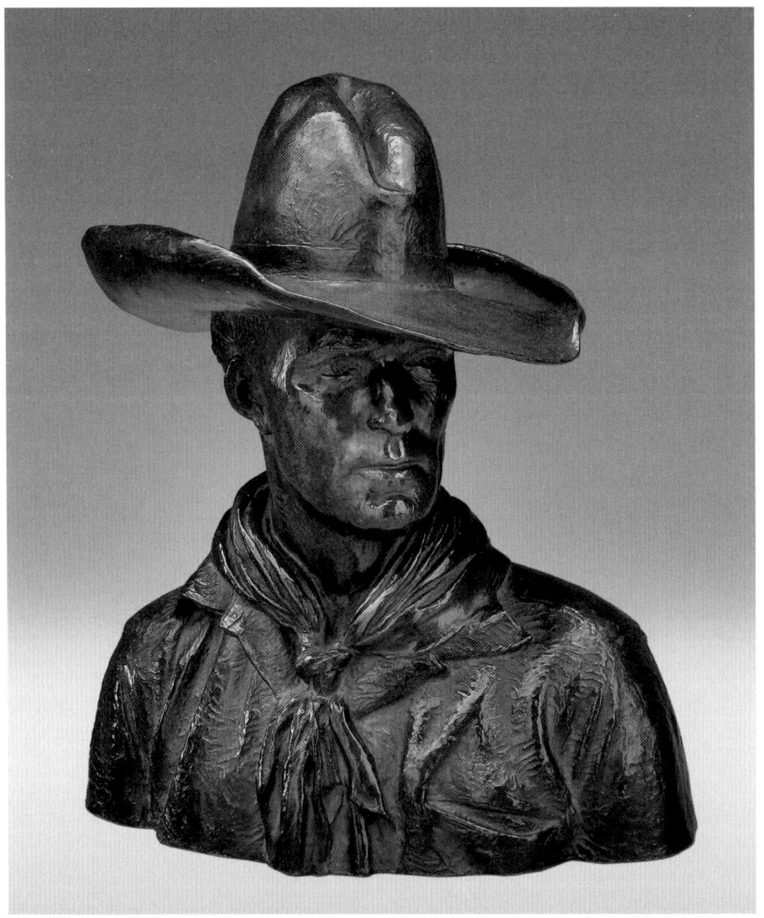

Fig. 137. Alexander Phimister Proctor. *Slim*, 1914 (cast 1915 or after). Cat. 45

Fig. 138. Sally James Farnham. *Cowboy Fun*, 1905. Bronze, 9½ × 15½ × 6¼ in. (24.1 × 39.4 × 15.9 cm). Frederic Remington Art Museum, Ogdensburg, New York

at least in the state of Oregon. When Proctor took the idea to Colorado a few years later, he changed the name of the rider to that of another cowboy, Del Blanchett. *Slim* (figs. 105, 137), Proctor's small portrait bust of Ridings, was modeled at the same time as *Buckaroo* but, perhaps understandably, was cast fewer than five times. So while Remington's and Russell's ruffian cowboys in *Coming through the Rye* and *Smoking Up* were essentially fictionalized bad guys created for eastern audiences, Proctor's *Buckaroo*, a genuine felon, found a home in disguise as a monument for one of the most western of cities.

Although cowboy bronzes were primarily the province of male artists, Remington's protégé Sally James Farnham proved an exception. Farnham, who excelled as a rider, had turned to sculpture in 1901. Like Remington, who was a family friend and her enthusiastic

mentor, she was in her early thirties when she began making sculpture. She and her husband, the well-known jewelry designer George Paulding Farnham, owned a ranch in British Columbia. Drawing on that western experience and remembering Remington's encouragement, she produced *Cowboy Fun* (fig. 138) in 1905, possibly as a gift to him. Later in her rather remarkable career, she returned to cowboy subjects. When, in 1936, she decided to enter *Will Rogers* (fig. 139) in a competition for a Claremore, Oklahoma, monument to the great western sage, she chose a cowboy pose. Farnham portrayed Rogers in a contemplative mood astride his famous roping horse, Dopey. A lariat loops over his shoulder as he allows his horse to graze, a metaphor for the many hunger-relief efforts Rogers supported during the Depression. For Farnham, the translation of human nature into art was paramount to its success,[70] and her interpretation of Rogers captured the spirit and the self-image of the man. Unfortunately, Rogers's widow wanted to preserve the image of Rogers as a statesman and pundit instead. Jo Davidson won the competition, picturing the famed comedian as a humorless, aw-shucks diplomat in a business suit. Rogers, an actor and performer, had starred in three one-reel movies. Perhaps his favorite was *The Roping Fool* (1922), in which he demonstrates three decades' worth of his rope tricks. "I don't think you might consider it Art," he said about

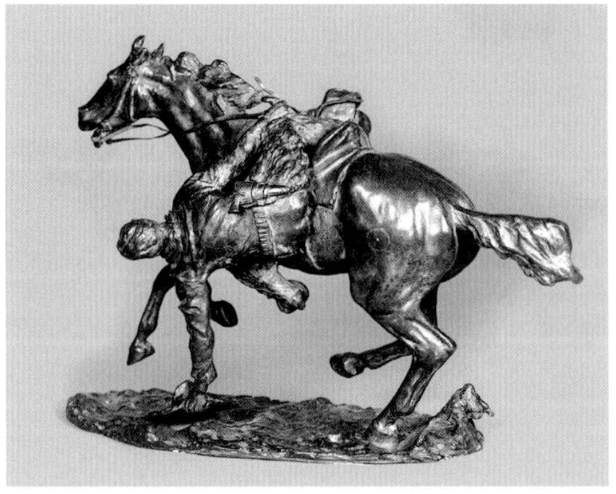

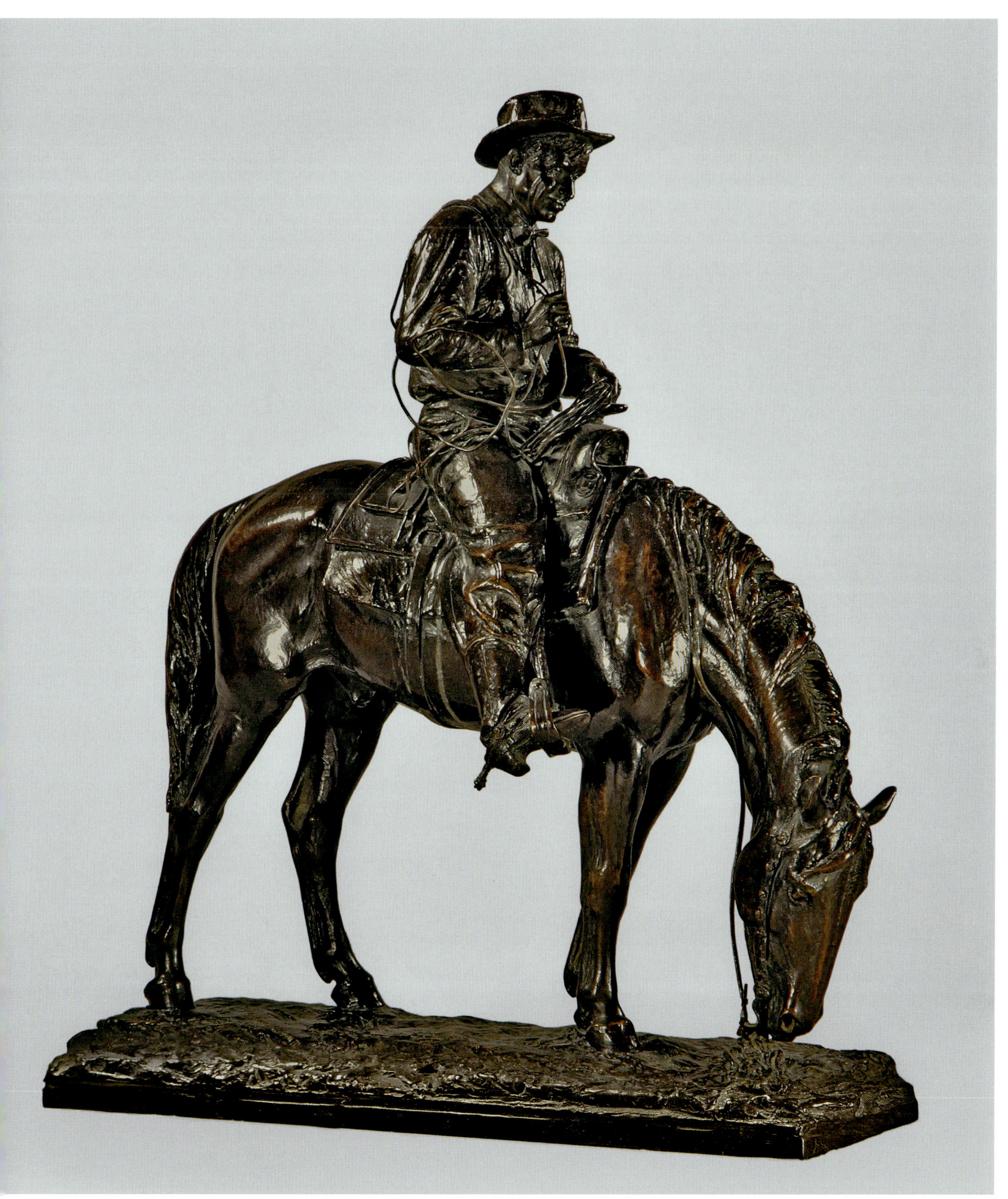

Fig. 139. Sally James Farnham. *Will Rogers*, 1936 (cast 1938). Cat. 20

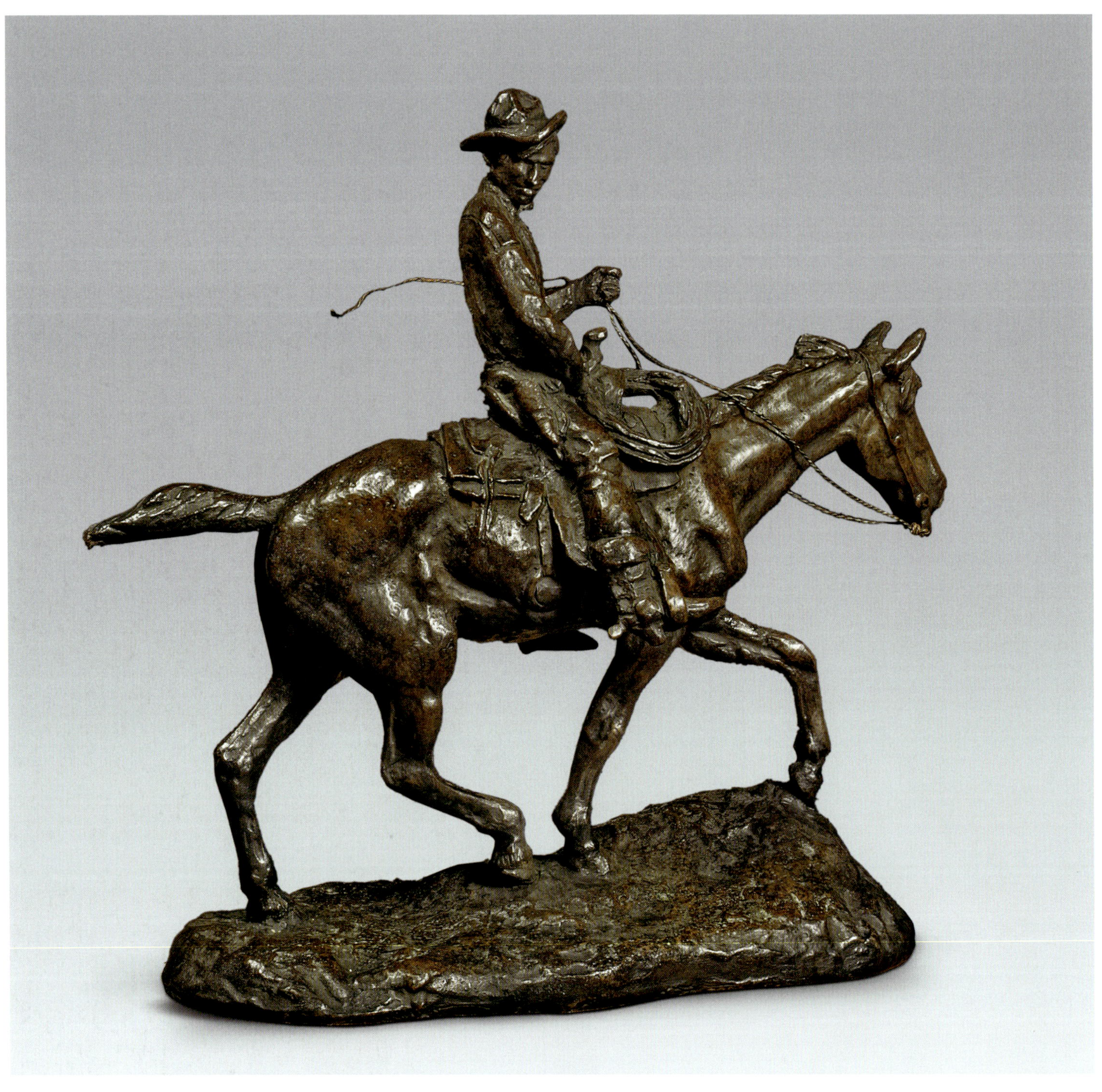

the film, "but there are 30 years of hard practice in it."[71] He, at least, was supremely proud of his cowboy skills.

Russell, who also portrayed Rogers in sculpture (fig. 140), was a favorite of another western actor and filmmaker, William S. Hart (fig. 141). Near the end of the artist's life, Russell enjoyed rubbing shoulders with the Hollywood crowd, but he also delighted in satirizing the actor's craft and the emerging image of the cowboy as moral paragon and savior of fair damsels in distress (fig. 142). Hart was the

archetype of this new protagonist, a formu-
laic character that would initially elevate but
ultimately usher out the cowboy as a viable
American hero.[72] Beginning in 1917 and, rather
oddly, not calling on Russell to do the hon-
ors, Hart commissioned Charles Cristadoro
to produce a series of sculptures of himself
and family members. Cristadoro had studied
sculpture with French-trained Clement Barnhorn in Cincinnati, the same teacher who had
initially inspired Solon Hannibal Borglum.
One of Cristadoro's first pieces was the bronze
Two Gun Bill (fig. 143), which presents the
actor characteristically saving the day, with his
pistols drawn and his snaky eyes alert to any
threat—a stance that followed the script of his
most recent film, *The Gun Fighter*, of 1916. *Two
Gun Bill* was modeled the next year (though
not cast in bronze until 1925).

Hart's character was defending as well
as mythologizing Anglo-Saxon masculinity,
Christian values, and self-advancement within
a western setting. His hunched-over, self-
restrained determination in the bronze and
in scenes from the film (fig. 144) represented
the antithesis of the more histrionic display
of manhood and nationalistic bravado common in previous sculptural interpretations of
the cowboy. The celluloid cowboy was placed
in a role of rescuing women—ironically, just
at a time when the figure of the independent
woman, cowgirls included, was emerging
and didn't need to be saved—and of ensuring that justice reigned. Hart had abandoned
the physical display of the strenuous life that
Roosevelt, Remington, Farnham, Russell, and
even Borglum had extolled. Moreover, there
was no room in Hart's character for Borglum's
poetic, nature-loving cowboy. For Hart, it was
all moralistic self-righteousness. He effectively
romanced audiences for a decade or so, then
disappeared—like his image of a venerated
frontier epoch in his final movie, *Tumbleweeds*
of 1925. One later sculpture helped salvage

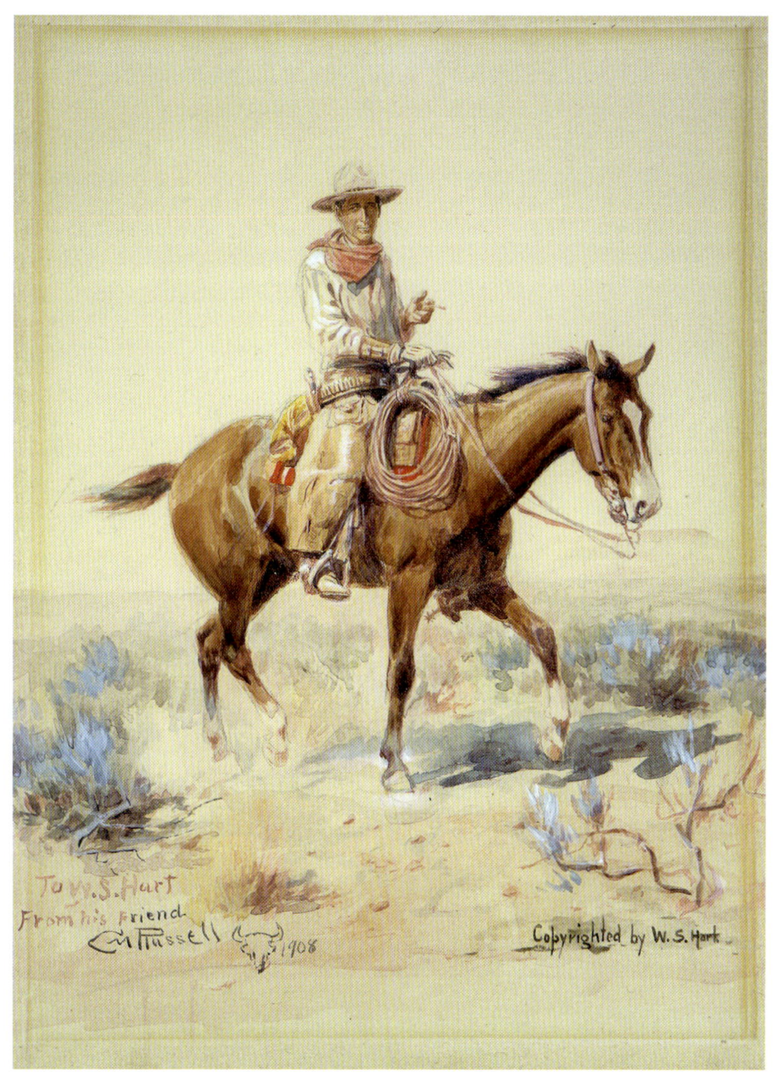

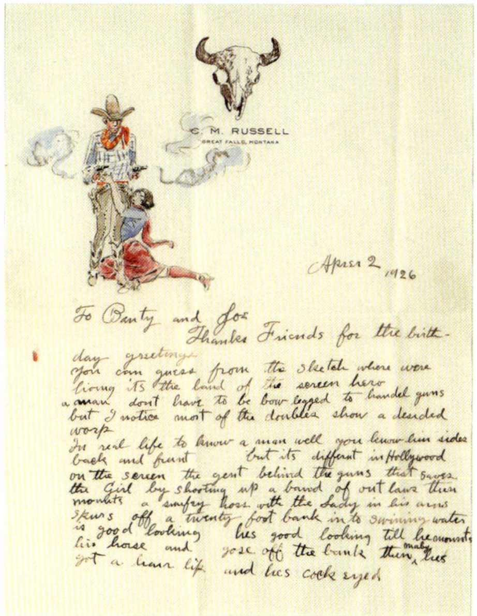

Fig. 141. Charles M. Russell. *William
S. Hart*, 1908. Watercolor on paper,
15½ × 11 in. (39.4 × 27.9 cm). Natural
History Museum of Los Angeles
County, William S. Hart Collection

Fig. 142. Charles M. Russell. *Letter to
Banty and Joe De Yong*, 1926. Ink and
watercolor on paper, 11 × 8 in. (27.9 ×
20.3 cm). National Cowboy
& Western Heritage Museum,
Oklahoma City

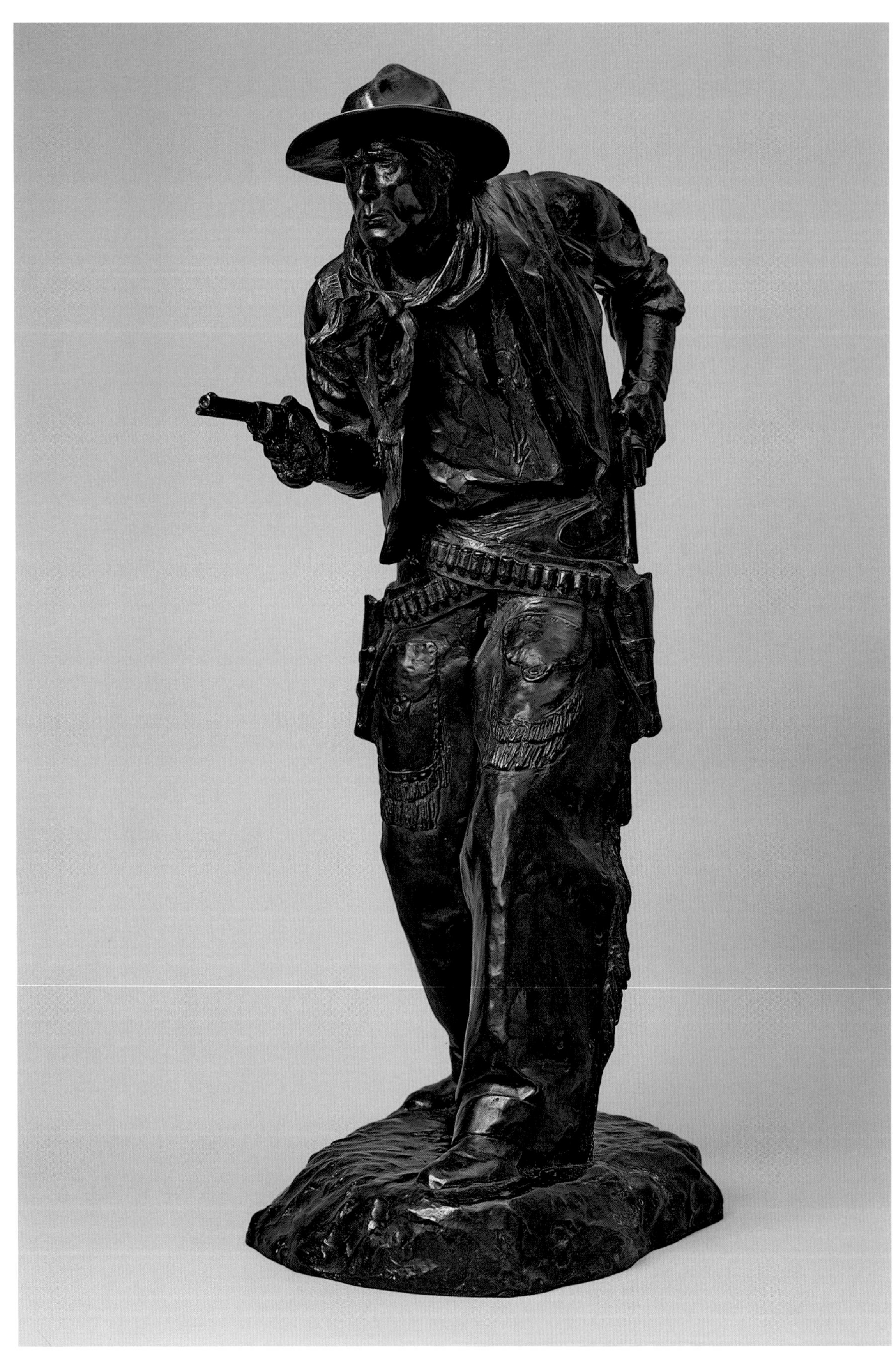

Fig. 143. Charles
Cristadoro. *Two Gun Bill*
(William S. Hart), 1917
(cast 1925 or after). Cat. 15

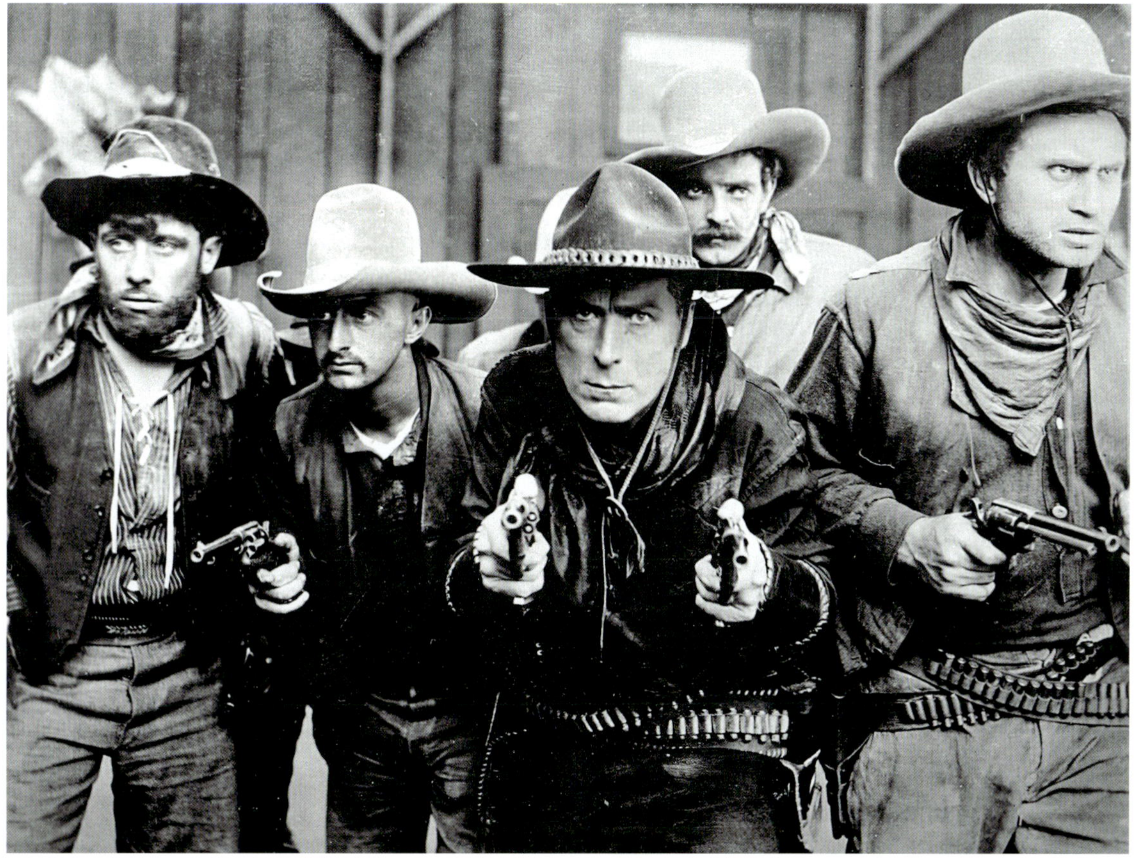

Fig. 144. William S. Hart as Two
Gun Bill, from *The Gun Fighter*,
1916. Seaver Center for Western
History Research, Natural History
Museum of Los Angeles County

Fig. 145. Charles Cristadoro.
The Range Rider of the Yellowstone,
1927. Billings, Montana

Hart's image as a cowboy from the hackneyed
do-gooder of his film career. In 1927 Cristadoro
was commissioned to produce a final portrayal
of the actor, a monument for Billings, Montana,
that was called *The Range Rider of the Yellowstone* (fig. 145). There, reminiscent of Borglum's
Cowboy at Rest, Hart stands dismounted while
his horse grazes, and he stares knowingly,
though rather imperially, over the distant range.
Hart seems to be pondering the expanse of the
West and, firmly afoot, establishes himself as an
empathetic player in its destiny and its legacy.

With Cristadoro's *Range Rider of the Yellowstone*, the image of the cowboy had swung 180
degrees from the earliest genre treatments of
the 1880s. The laconic horseman of the plains
had been a national hero for forty years, but
now, in the mid-1920s, the realists and the historians began to formalize the narrative and
analyze the realities. The cowboy hero in his

various manifestations in American sculpture
had served the artists and the nation's art well
through those decades and would continue to
do so for decades to come.

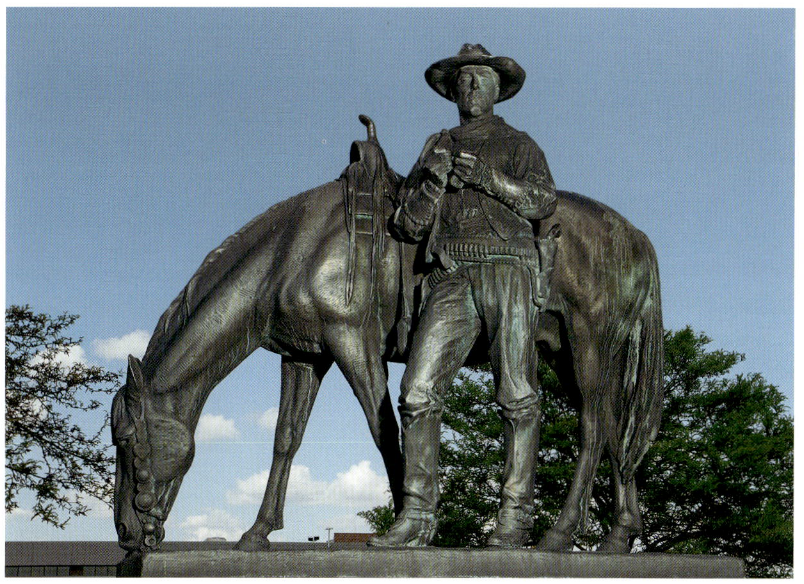

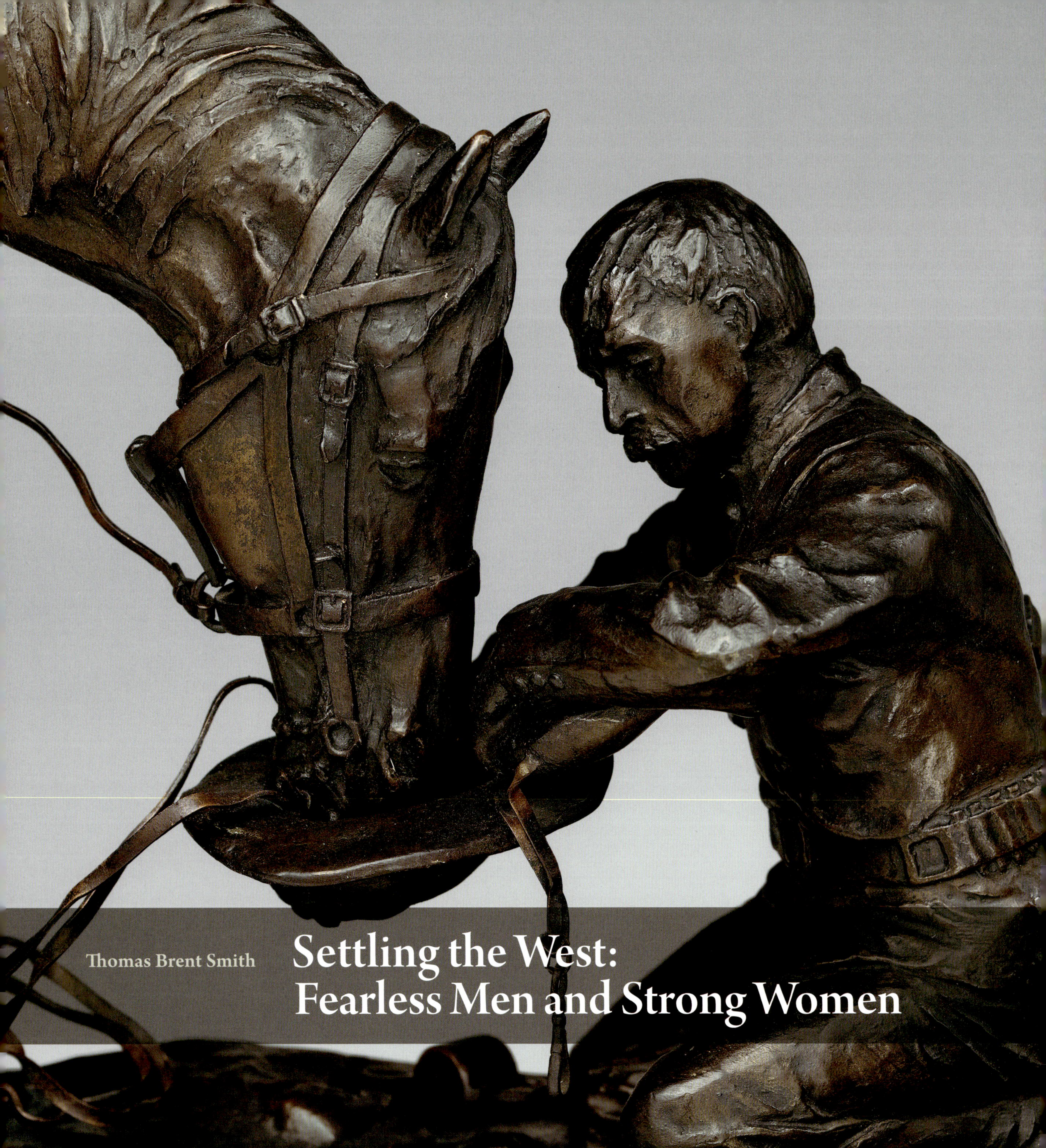
Thomas Brent Smith
Settling the West:
Fearless Men and Strong Women

Walt Whitman, from Leaves of Grass, 1867

In the first decades of the twentieth century, as the last continental territories organized themselves into states, sculptors expanded beyond the familiar subjects of Indians, cowboys, and wildlife. They began modeling cavalrymen, mountain men, prospectors, and pioneer women—paying homage, as Whitman had done, to those who had borne "the brunt of danger" in exploring and then settling the West. Sculptures ranging from tabletop statuettes to larger-than-life monuments (often erected in newly established western parks) idealized these characters, whether based on fact, fiction, or a bit of both.

The final episodes of the decades-long Indian Wars had concluded in the Southwest during the 1880s, but it wasn't until after those campaigns ended that the cavalryman became a popular hero in literature and art. Frederic Remington's illustrations, paintings, and bronzes present a particularly vivid image of military adventures on the frontier. The western novelist Owen Wister observed in 1903 that his friend Remington, "with his piercing and yet imaginative eye has taken the likeness of the modern American soldier and stamped it upon our minds with a blow as clean-cut as is the impression of the American Eagle upon our coins in the Mint."[1] On assignment for *Century Magazine*, Remington traveled to Arizona in May 1888 to report on the African American soldiers of the Tenth Cavalry Regiment, commonly known as the Buffalo Soldiers.[2] They were commanded by Powhatan Henry Clarke, a dashing young lieutenant who told Remington about his experiences as a horse soldier. In 1891 Lieutenant Clarke would receive the Medal of Honor for having rescued a wounded soldier years earlier, during the Indian Wars in Sonora, Mexico. The official citation proclaimed that he had "rushed forward to the rescue of a soldier who was severely wounded and lay, disabled, exposed to the enemy's fire, and carried him to a place of safety."[3]

Clarke's heroic rescue, which he no doubt recounted to Remington, was likely an inspiration for the gallant rider in *The Wounded Bunkie* (figs. 147, 148), modeled by Remington in 1896. Two cavalrymen are retreating at full gallop, presumably from an unseen battle with Indian combatants.[4] That one of the troopers has just been shot in the back is clear from his limp arms and lolling head; only the outstretched arm of his bunkmate, or "bunkie,"[5] keeps him from falling out of his saddle. Remington makes a poignant statement about the bonds among the rough-and-ready men of the cavalry, showing two sides to the protagonist: his fearless heroism and his deep concern for his fellow soldier. *The Wounded Bunkie* is a good example of how the experienced and the imagined mix in Remington's work.[6] The artist's

Fig. 146. Charles Schreyvogel, detail of *The Last Drop*, 1903 (cast 1904). Cat. 70

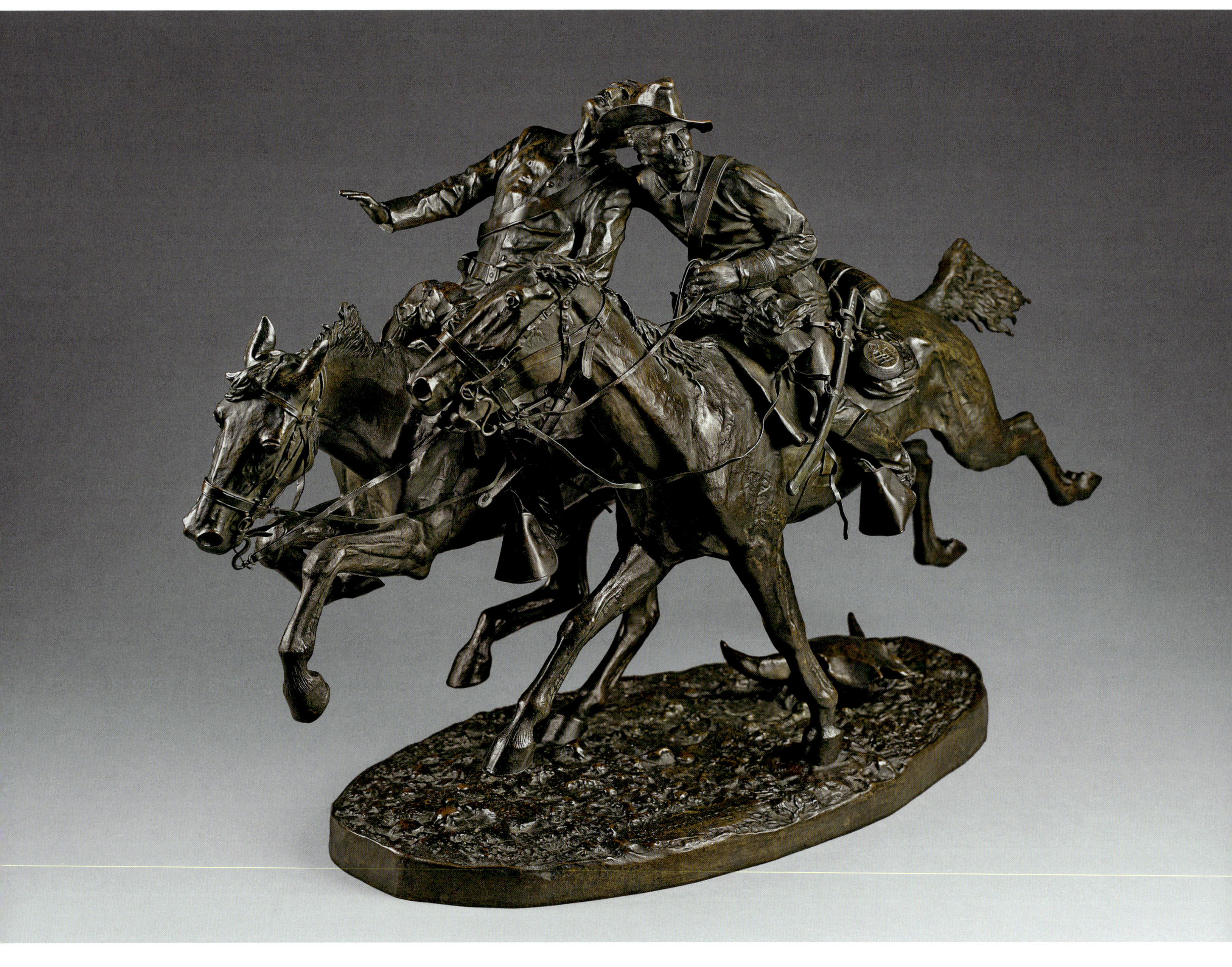

Fig. 147. Frederic Remington. *The Wounded Bunkie*, 1896 (cast 1896). Cat. 52

own experience, in this case, was traveling to Arizona and gathering details from Lieutenant Clarke, but in creating *The Wounded Bunkie*, he constructed a tale with even greater visual drama. Remington invigorated this life-and-death narrative with a dynamic composition in which the bronze statuette is supported by only two of the horses' eight legs. In addition, the forward thrust of the composition broke with the upright, static equestrian poses more familiar to viewers of the period.

Although the dynamism of Remington's composition was new to American sculpture, *The Wounded Bunkie* is partially a

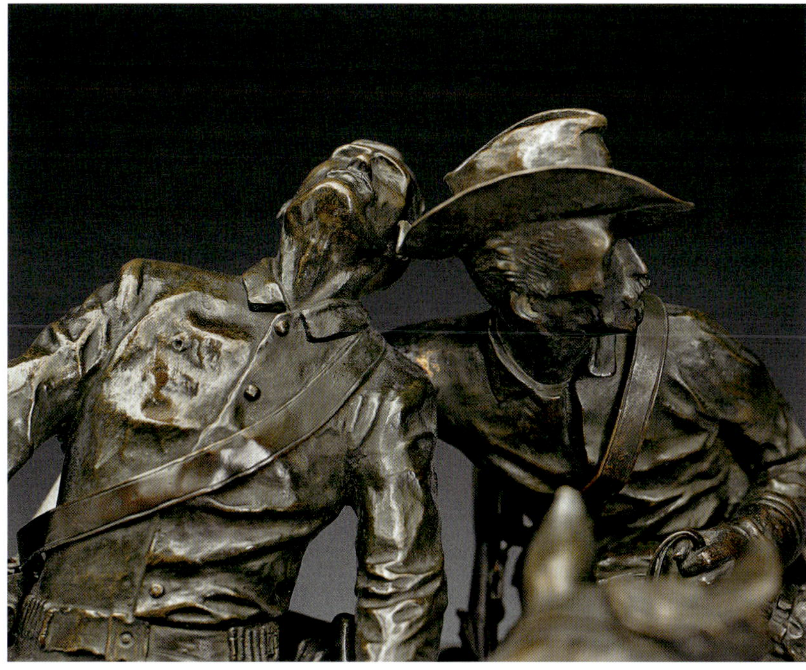

Fig. 148. Frederic Remington,
detail of *The Wounded Bunkie*

Fig. 149. Frederic Remington.
A Dash for the Timber, 1889.
Oil on canvas, 48½ × 84⅛ in.
(123.2 × 213.7 cm). Amon Carter
Museum of American Art, Fort
Worth, Texas

reinterpretation of the artist's earlier works in other media.[7] One such example is *A Dash for the Timber* (fig. 149), a painting of 1889 that depicts a cowboy being assisted in the same fashion. Two years before that, Remington had first depicted a rescue on horseback in the line engraving *A Suspended Equestrienne* (fig. 150). Anticipating the impact of *The Wounded Bunkie*, Remington boasted to Wister, "I . . . am going to knock the eye out of the art world this

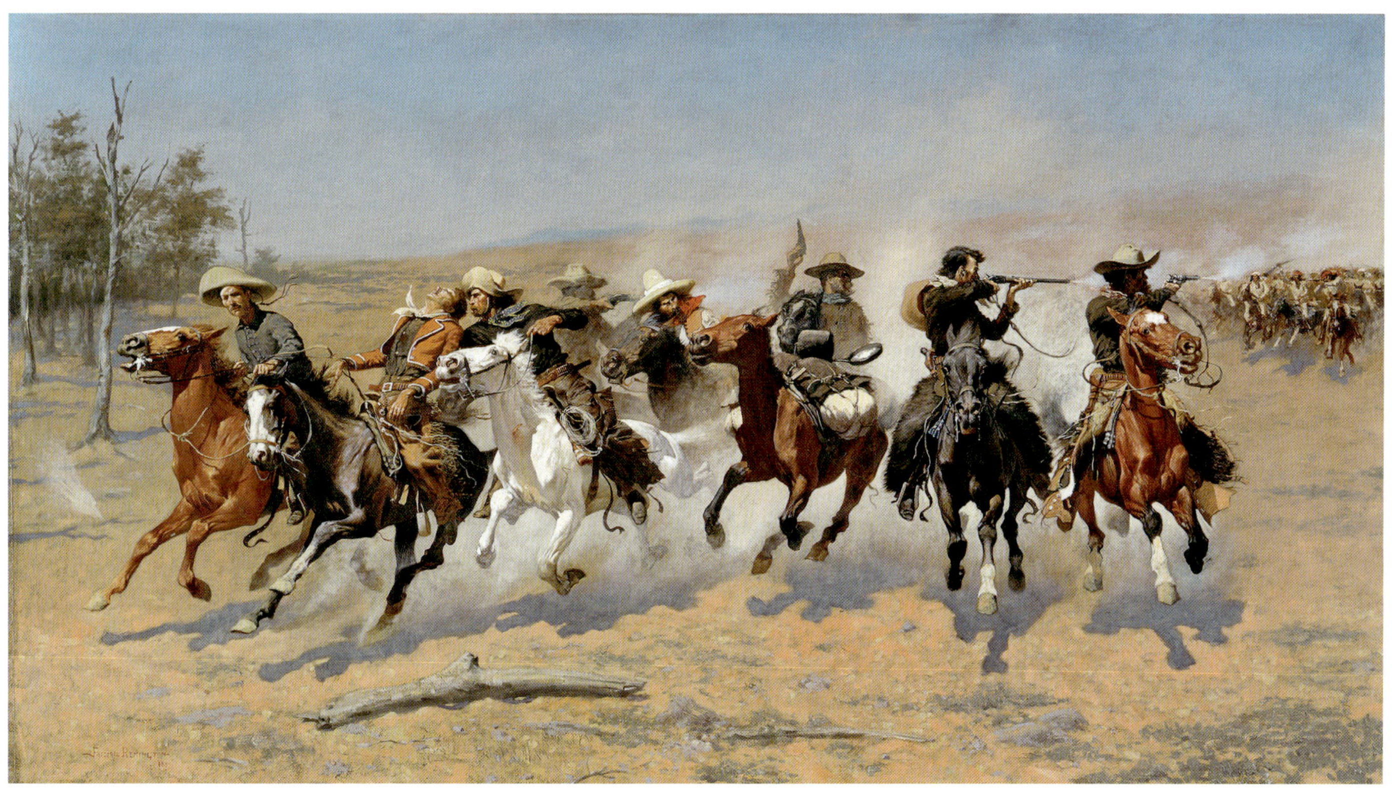

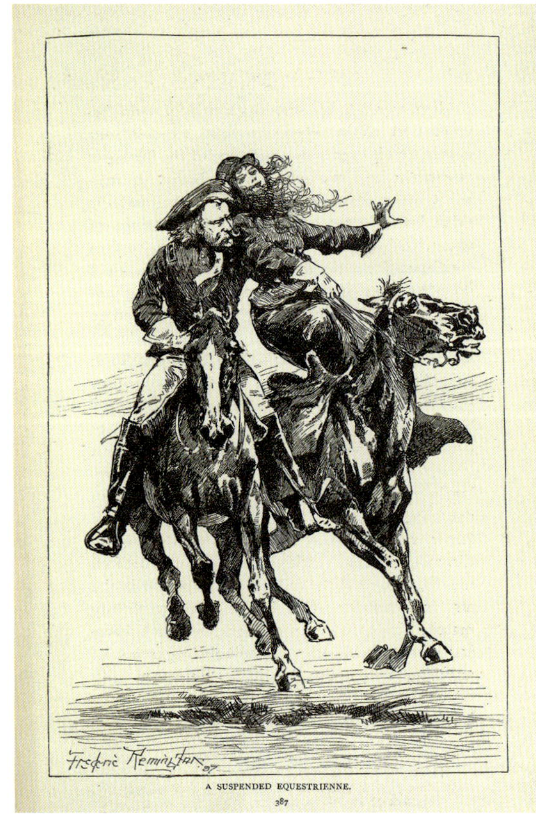

Fig. 150. Frederic Remington. *A Suspended Equestrienne*, 1887. From *Tenting on the Plains; Or, General Custer in Kansas and Texas*, by Elizabeth B. Custer

Opposite:

Fig. 151. Charles Schreyvogel. *My Bunkie*, finished 1899. Cat. 69

coming winter."[8] Indeed, in October 1896 *Town Topics* praised the bronze statuette as "a spirited artistical achievement."[9] Yet despite the fact that Remington's multihorse composition was highly innovative, it would be one of his least commercially successful bronzes. In comparison to Remington's *Broncho Buster* (figs. 2, 114), which was cast over 150 times during the artist's life, there were only 14 lifetime casts of *The Wounded Bunkie*.[10]

Charles Schreyvogel was similarly dedicated to portraying the West, in particular the horse soldiers of the Indian Wars. This relatively unknown New York artist suddenly found himself in the spotlight when, in 1900, he was awarded the prestigious Thomas B. Clarke Prize for the best figure painting by an American at the National Academy of Design's annual exhibition. According to Schreyvogel, the event depicted in this painting, *My Bunkie* (fig. 151), had been described by a trooper he met on a visit to Colorado in 1893.[11] A writer for

Brush and Pencil commented that *My Bunkie* "represents some United States soldiers dashing across the plains, while one of them has caught up a wounded comrade and draws him on his horse. The work recalls that of Frederick [*sic*] Remington, as all such themes must; but it is drawn better, painted better, and has some notion of color, a quality not often claimed for the better known illustrator."[12] Other contemporary reviews praised the painting as well, while also remarking on its likeness to Remington's earlier *Wounded Bunkie*. Though treading on Remington's turf, Schreyvogel was garnering the sort of praise that had eluded Remington.

One of Schreyvogel's first paintings after his newfound success was *The Last Drop* (fig. 152), again with a compassionate cavalryman as the protagonist. Unlike his more typical works, which depict violent conflict on the plains, here Schreyvogel portrays a trooper kneeling before his mount, using his campaign hat to share the last of the water from his canteen. A contemporary critic noted that Schreyvogel "is a sculptor as well as a painter, though he rarely if ever exhibits sculpture and employs that branch of art only as an aid to his painting."[13] As was his custom, he created a clay model to assist him in painting *The Last Drop*. In this case, however, the artist departed from his usual practice, and in 1903 he began casting the model as his second and final bronze, retaining the same title as the painting (figs. 146, 153). The three-dimensionality of the statuette allowed Schreyvogel to detail the soldier's accoutrements even more precisely than in the painting. The terrain represented by the sculpture's base is not only the actual foundation of the sculpture but also a symbol of the land that the cavalryman fights to control. Schreyvogel's depiction of the interconnectedness of the trooper, horse, and water, all of which were essential to conquering the West, resonated with audiences. Because of

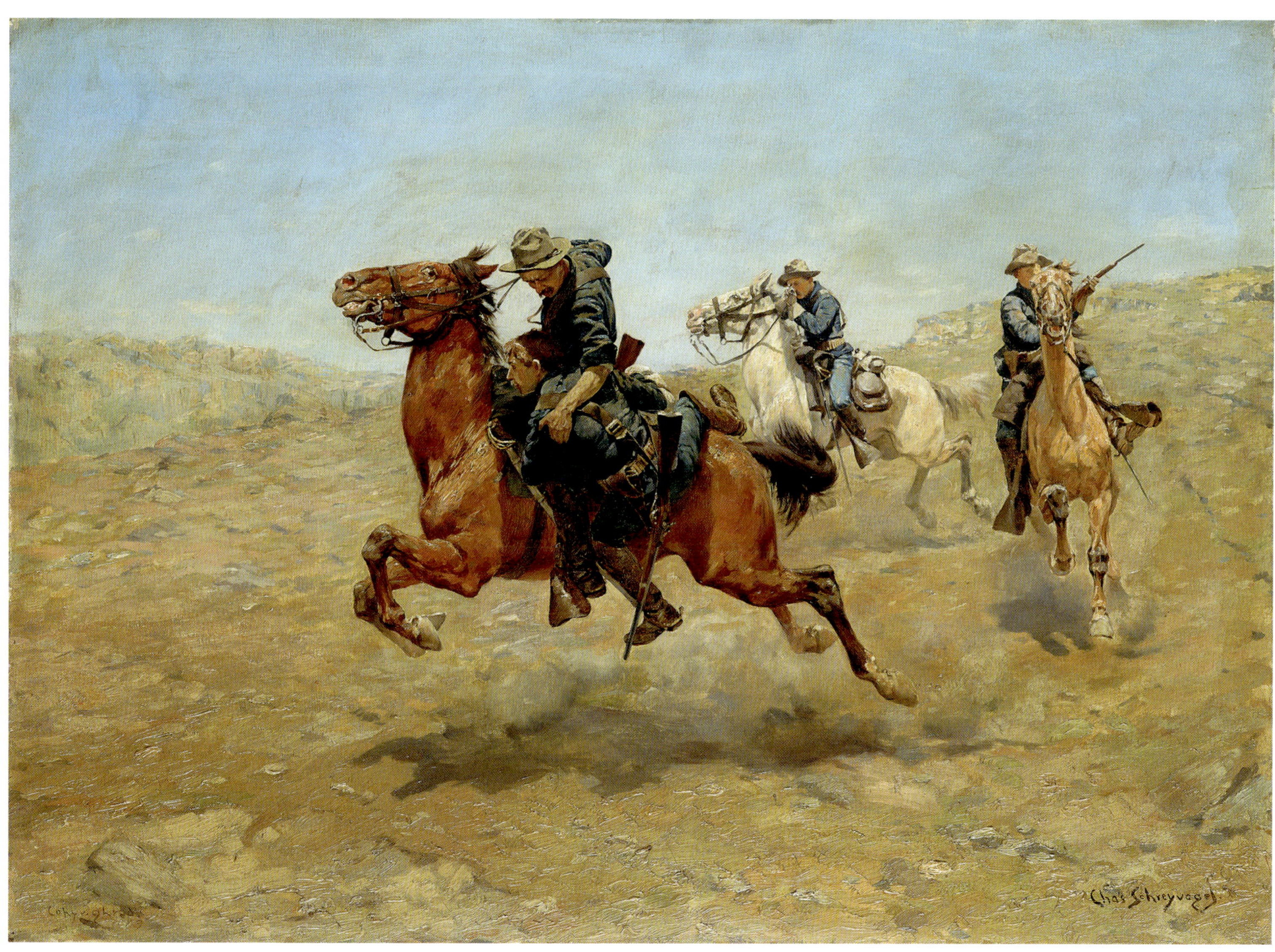

its popularity, more than 150 authorized casts of *The Last Drop* were produced during the artist's lifetime as well as posthumously by his widow—among the most numerous for any bronze statuette with a western theme.[14]

Down the edges, through the passes, up the mountains steep,
Conquering, holding, daring, venturing, as we go, the unknown ways,
Pioneers! O pioneers!

Equal parts trapper and explorer, the Rocky Mountain man played a central role in the North American fur trade, which reached its peak in the 1830s and 1840s, fueled by the European demand for top hats made of beaver pelts. Overhunting and a change in fashion brought a quick conclusion to the trapper era by the end of the 1840s, at which point the mountain men's familiarity with overland trails made them highly valued as army scouts, wagon-train guides, and later, prospectors for gold. The

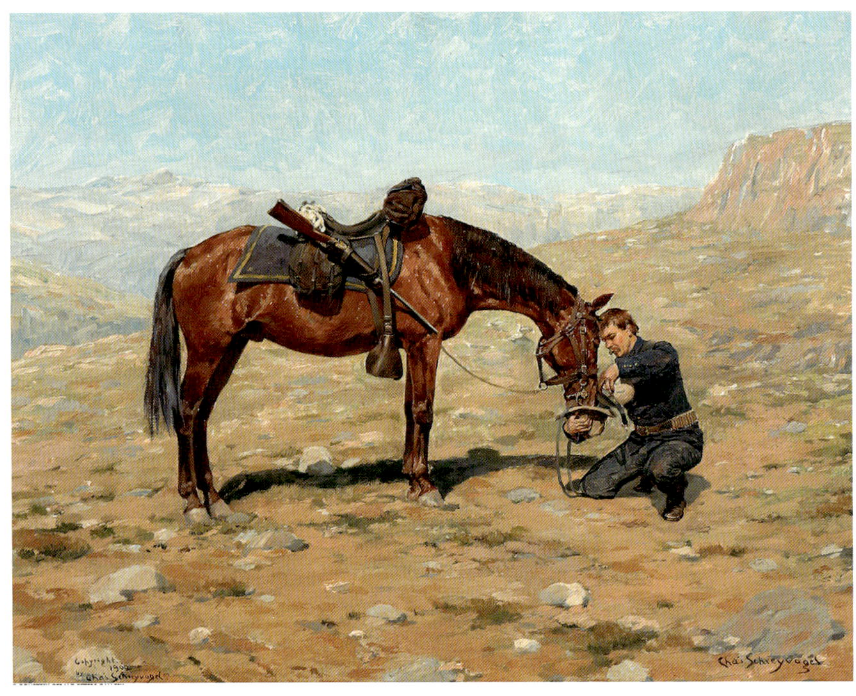

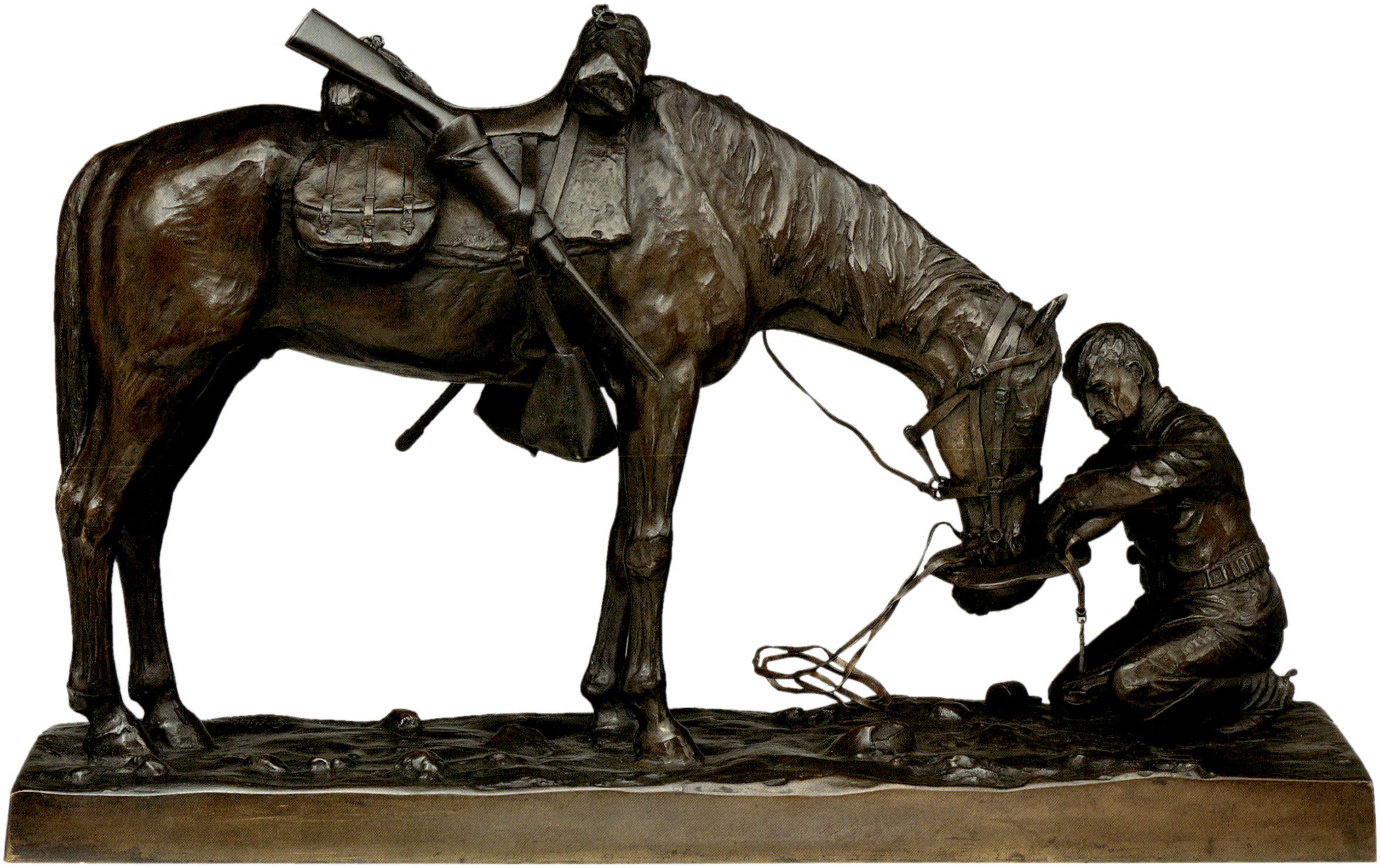

Fig. 152. Charles Schreyvogel. *The Last Drop*, 1899. Oil on canvas, 16 × 20 in. (40.6 × 50.8 cm). Courtesy of the Haub Family Trust

Fig. 153. Charles Schreyvogel. *The Last Drop*, 1903 (cast 1904). Cat. 70

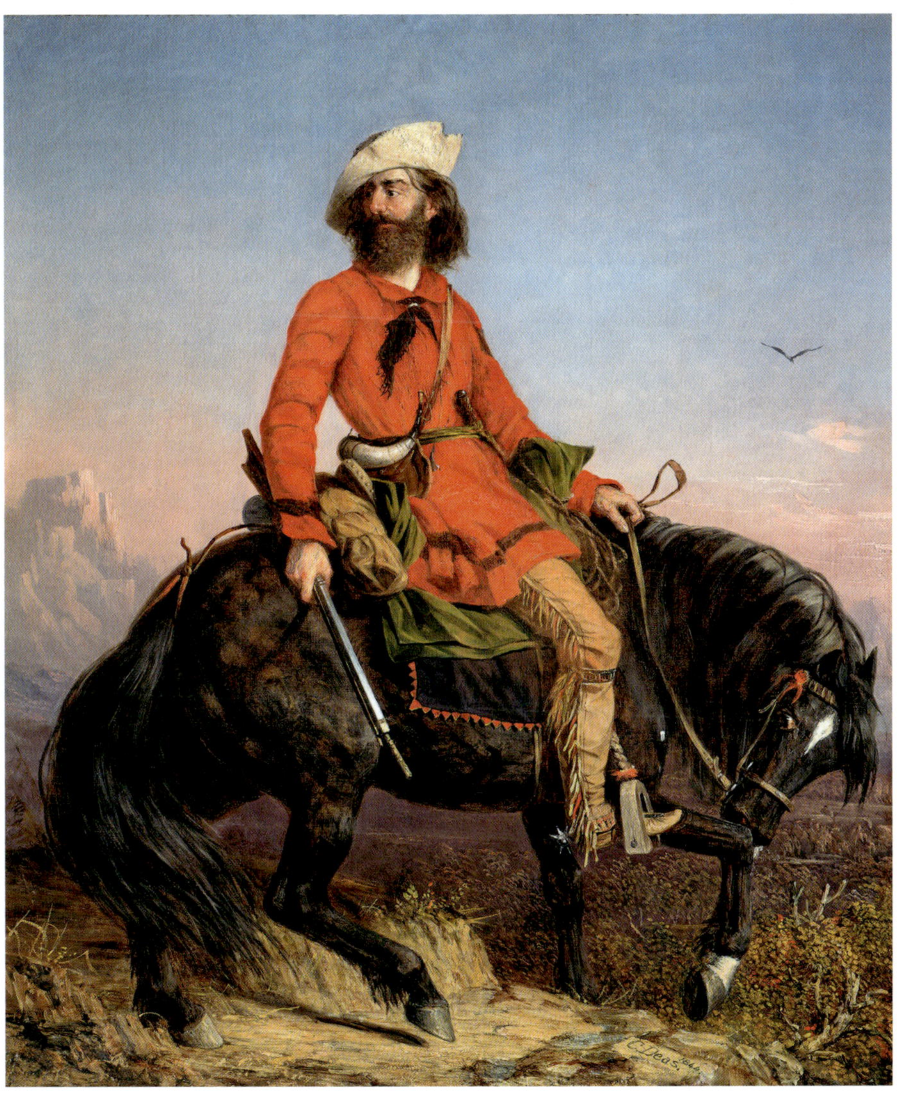

trapper was elevated to heroic stature in paintings by such mid-nineteenth-century artists as George Caleb Bingham, Charles Deas (fig. 154), and Alfred Jacob Miller. Sculptors, however, did not explore this theme until the early twentieth century, well after the mountain man had been supplanted in the public imagination by the cowboy as the quintessential Westerner. Not surprisingly, the best-known examples of trappers in bronze come from artists celebrated for portraying cowboys: Remington and Charles M. Russell. Known as "the Cowboy Artist," Russell later contended that when he set out for Montana as a young man, in 1880, it was with hopes of becoming a mountain man. During his early years in Montana, the aspiring artist spent a couple of years as a sidekick to Jake Hoover, whom Russell described as "a hunter, trapper, prospector and an all-around Mountain man."[15]

Jim Bridger (fig. 155), modeled in clay just months before Russell's death in 1926, is not only an homage to a legendary fur trapper but also an introspective, personal work that likely reflects upon the artist's lineage in the Old West (he was a descendant of the Bent family, whose fort was an important outpost on the old Santa Fe Trail).[16] One of the most celebrated of the mountain men, James "Jim" Bridger was best known for trailblazing while

Fig. 154. Charles Deas (American, 1818–1867). *Long Jakes, "the Rocky Mountain Man,"* 1844. Oil on canvas, 30 × 25 in. (76.2 × 63.5 cm). Denver Art Museum, jointly owned by the Denver Art Museum and American Museum of Western Art—The Anschutz Collection, Denver; purchased in memory of Bob Magness with funds from 1999 Collectors' Choice, Sharon Magness, Mr. and Mrs. William D. Hewitt, Carl and Lisa Williams, Estelle Rae Wolf-Flowe Foundation, and the T. Edward and Tullay Hanley Collection by exchange (1998.241)

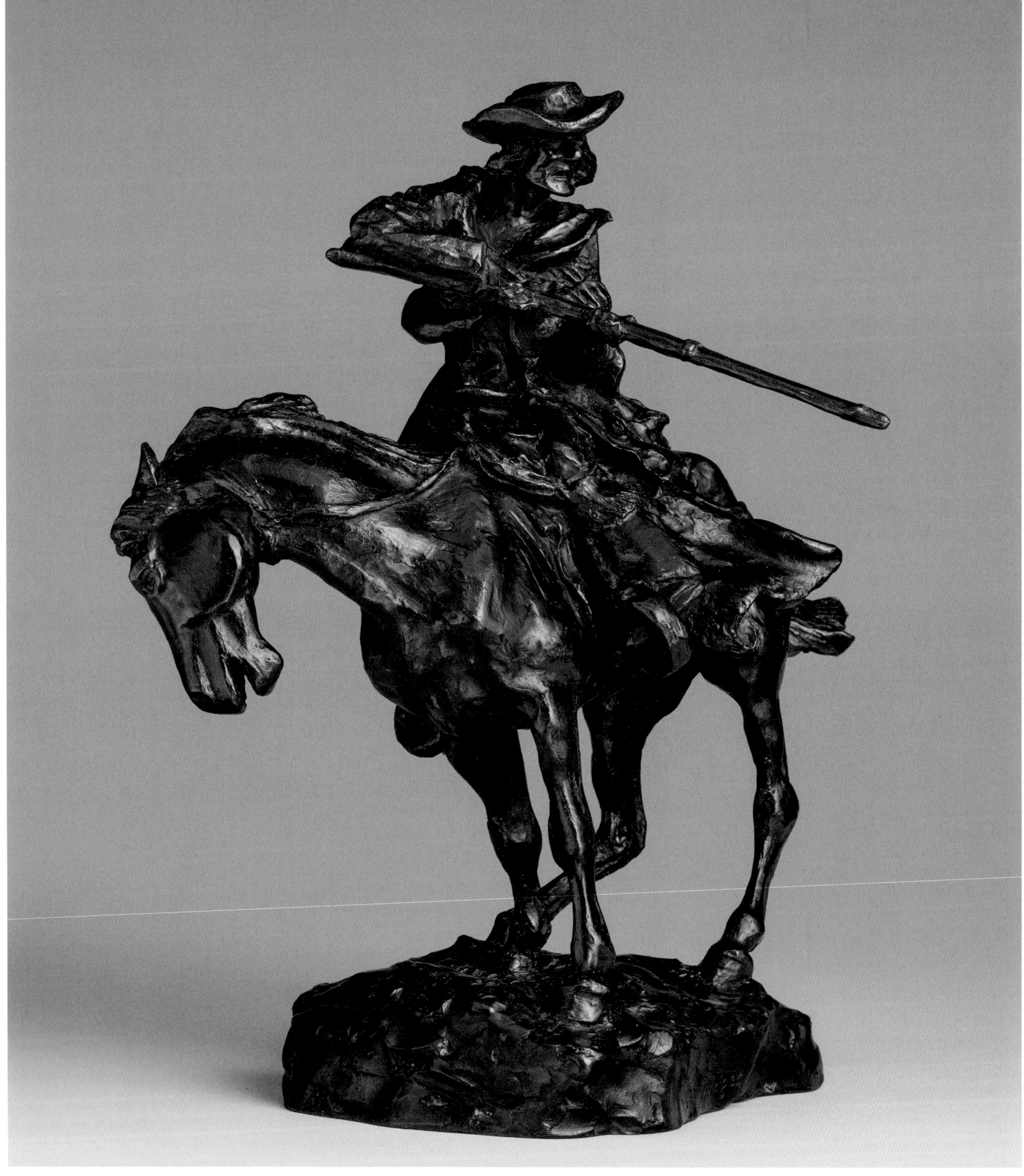

Fig. 155. Charles M. Russell. *Jim Bridger*, 1926 (cast 1927–28). Cat. 68

exploring major water sources in Colorado and Wyoming, as well as for discovering the Great Salt Lake. He also located the South Pass over the Rocky Mountains, which became the principal overland thoroughfare for westward migration.[17] Although inscribed with the title *Jim Bridger*, Russell's bronze statuette is hardly a portrait of a specific individual. In fact, it is difficult to differentiate the artist's depictions of Bridger from those by him of Christopher "Kit" Carson. The mountain men in Russell's oeuvre share the same basic characteristics—they are dressed in buckskins, have long hair and clean-shaven faces, and generally wear similar hats—suggesting that the artist was interested in creating a western type rather than a specific individual.[18] In the 1913 painting *Carson's Men* (fig. 156), the artist depicts three riders in the western landscape, none of whom is intended to be the famous scout Kit Carson, as the title might suggest; rather, they are presented as archetypes of the mountain man. Russell often included a setting sun in his paintings to lament the passing of the Old West, and in *Jim Bridger* he achieved a similarly nostalgic effect by positioning his subject turned in his saddle, looking back on a bygone era.[19]

Remington's admiration for the mountain man is apparent throughout his early illustrations as well as in his major oil paintings, but he attempted only one such subject in bronze. *The Mountain Man* of 1903 (figs. 157, 158) depicts a trapper and his mount descending a treacherous slope. The rider leans back to balance himself while grasping the saddle's tail strap, and the sense of potential danger in their precarious downward journey adds narrative tension. Remington described the bronze as

Fig. 156. Charles M. Russell. *Carson's Men*, 1913. Oil on canvas, 24 × 35½ in. (61 × 90.2 cm). Gilcrease Museum, Tulsa, Oklahoma

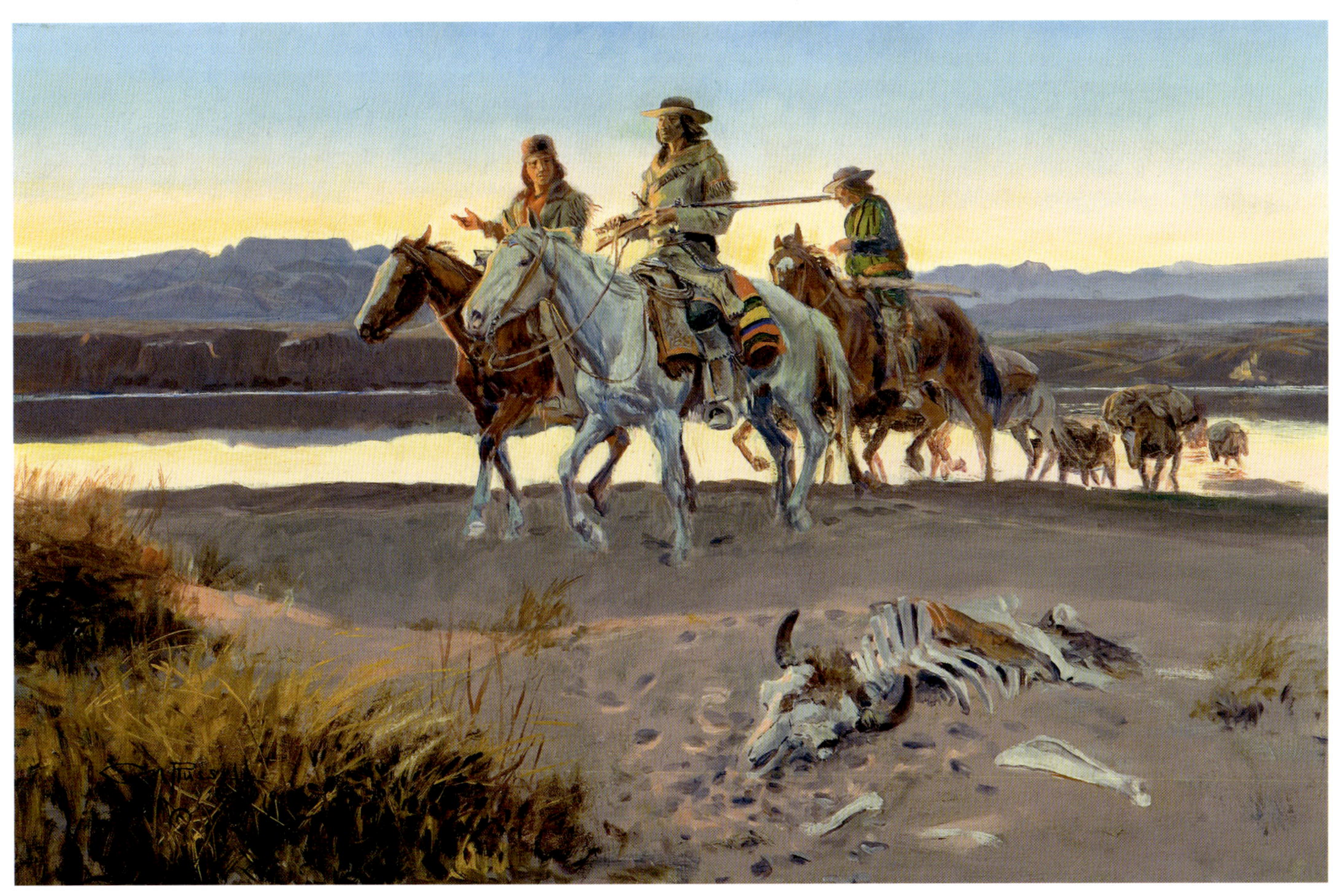

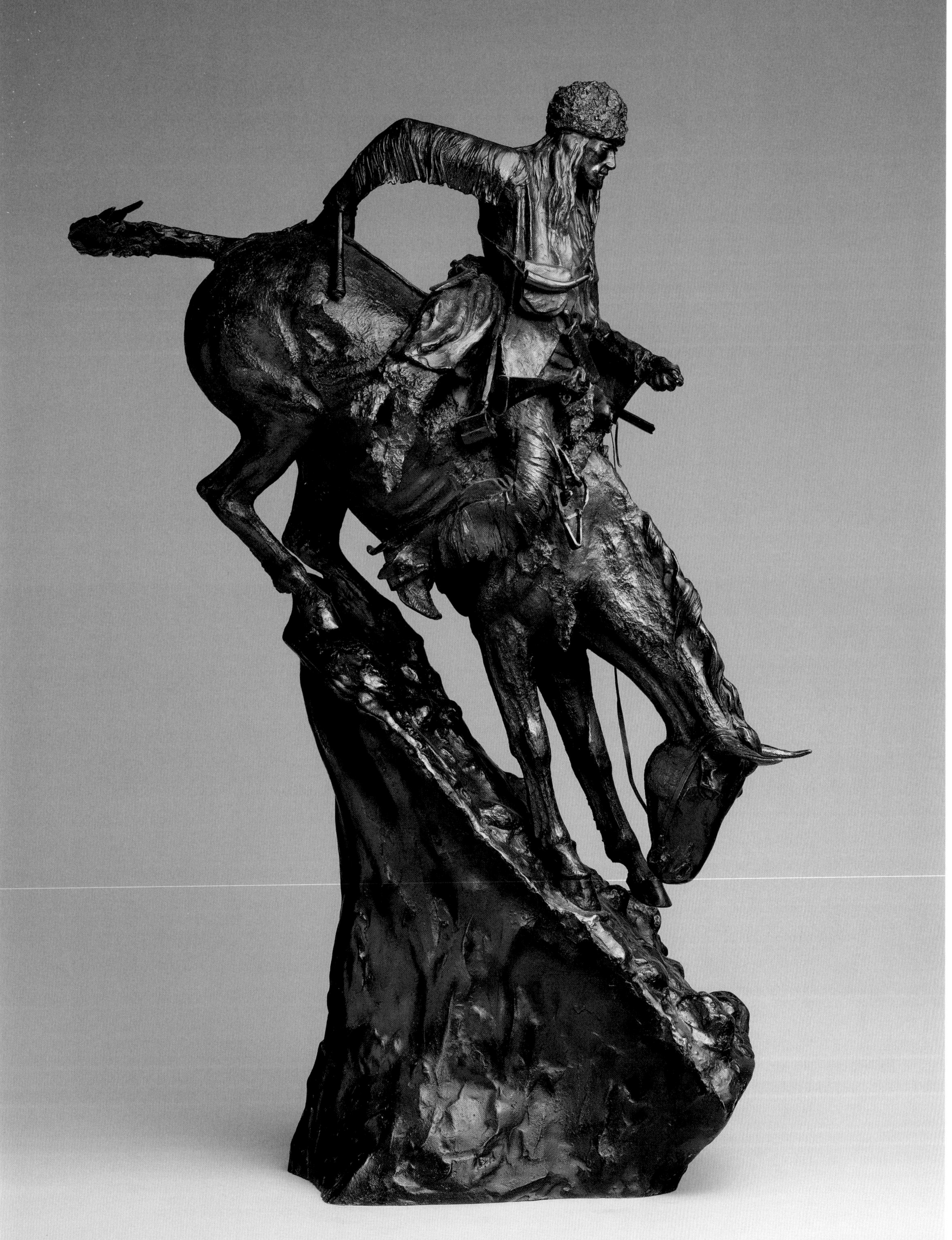

portraying an "old Iriquois [*sic*] trapper who followed the Fur Companies in the Rocky Mountains in the 30 & 40'ties," but the focus is less on the mountain man himself than on the interdependence of horse and rider.[20] The artist's eagerness to challenge the physical limits of sculpture is again evident, this time in the verticality of the composition. Remington repeatedly tried to make his sculptures appear to be structurally free of the base, and here only two of the horse's hooves are attached to it. The steep, rocky base is fully incorporated into the design, playing an essential role in the narrative.[21] *The Mountain Man* garnered the critical acceptance that Remington had sought, and casts were purchased by the Corcoran Gallery of Art in 1905 and The Metropolitan Museum of Art in 1907.

We the rivers stemming, vexing we, and piercing deep the mines within;
We the surface broad surveying, the virgin soil up-heaving,
Pioneers! O pioneers!

Of all the male types associated with settling the American West, the least depicted in sculpture is the prospector. The discovery of gold in California in 1848 attracted some three hundred thousand prospectors to California from North America and abroad by 1854.[22] Approximately half of them weathered the overland trails, and the others arrived by sea. Many of the gold seekers, commonly known as "forty-niners," settled in California and eventually farmed the lush agricultural regions.

The San Francisco sculptor Arthur Putnam observed firsthand how the gold rush had transformed California. Putnam, known primarily for his depictions of the state's wildlife (see fig. 98), modeled *Prospector* in 1903 (fig. 159). The tactile modeling, undulating surface, and exaggerated musculature of *Prospector* appear to have been influenced by the French sculptor Auguste Rodin, whose work had been on view in San Francisco and whom Putnam would meet in Paris in 1906. Rodin and many of his followers were interested in the physical and emotional toll of labor, and Putnam's small model depicting a prospector squatting next to his pickax is as much about the ethos of labor as it is about the gold rush. Prospectors were known for their backbreaking toil; as one forty-niner lamented: "Mining is the hardest work imaginable and an occupation which very much endangers health. A weakly man might about as well go digging his grave as to dig gold."[23] *Prospector* could also be seen as self-reflective: Putnam's biographers noted his own hard work as well as the torment he felt while casting his bronzes. "I've had to sweat blood for every drop of bronze," he wrote to the gallerist William Macbeth.[24]

Opposite:
Fig. 157. Frederic Remington. *The Mountain Man*, 1903 (cast by 1907). Cat. 56

Fig. 158. Frederic Remington, detail of *The Mountain Man*

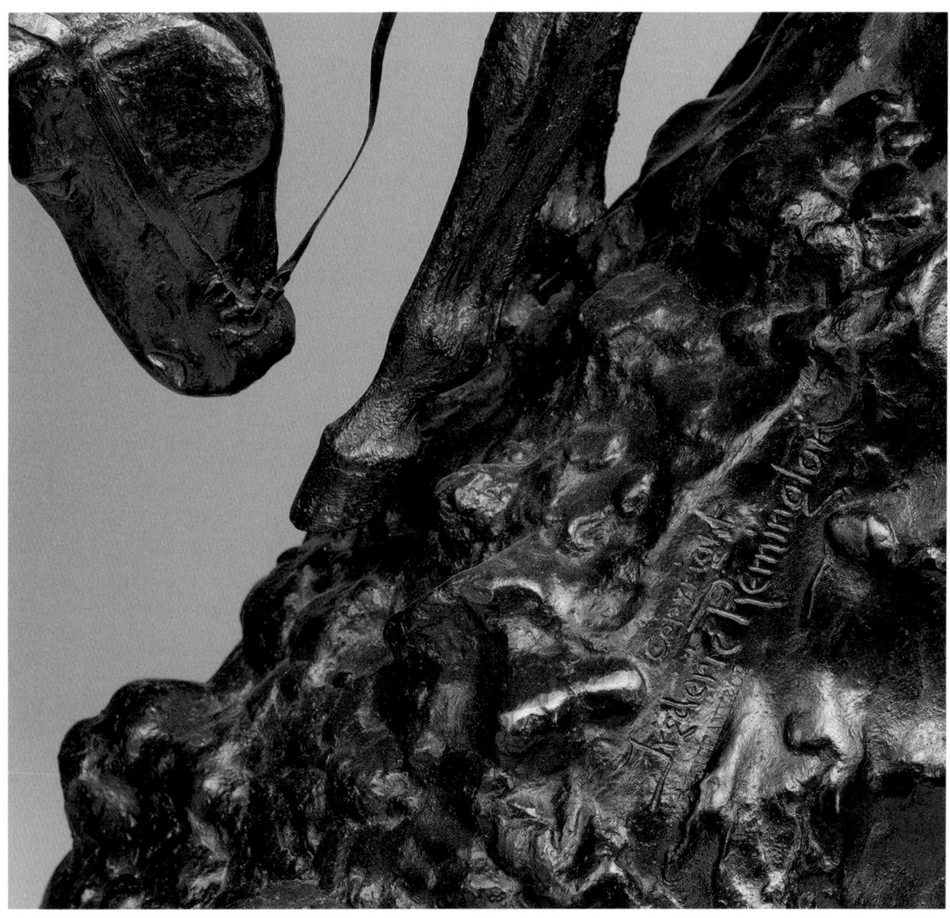

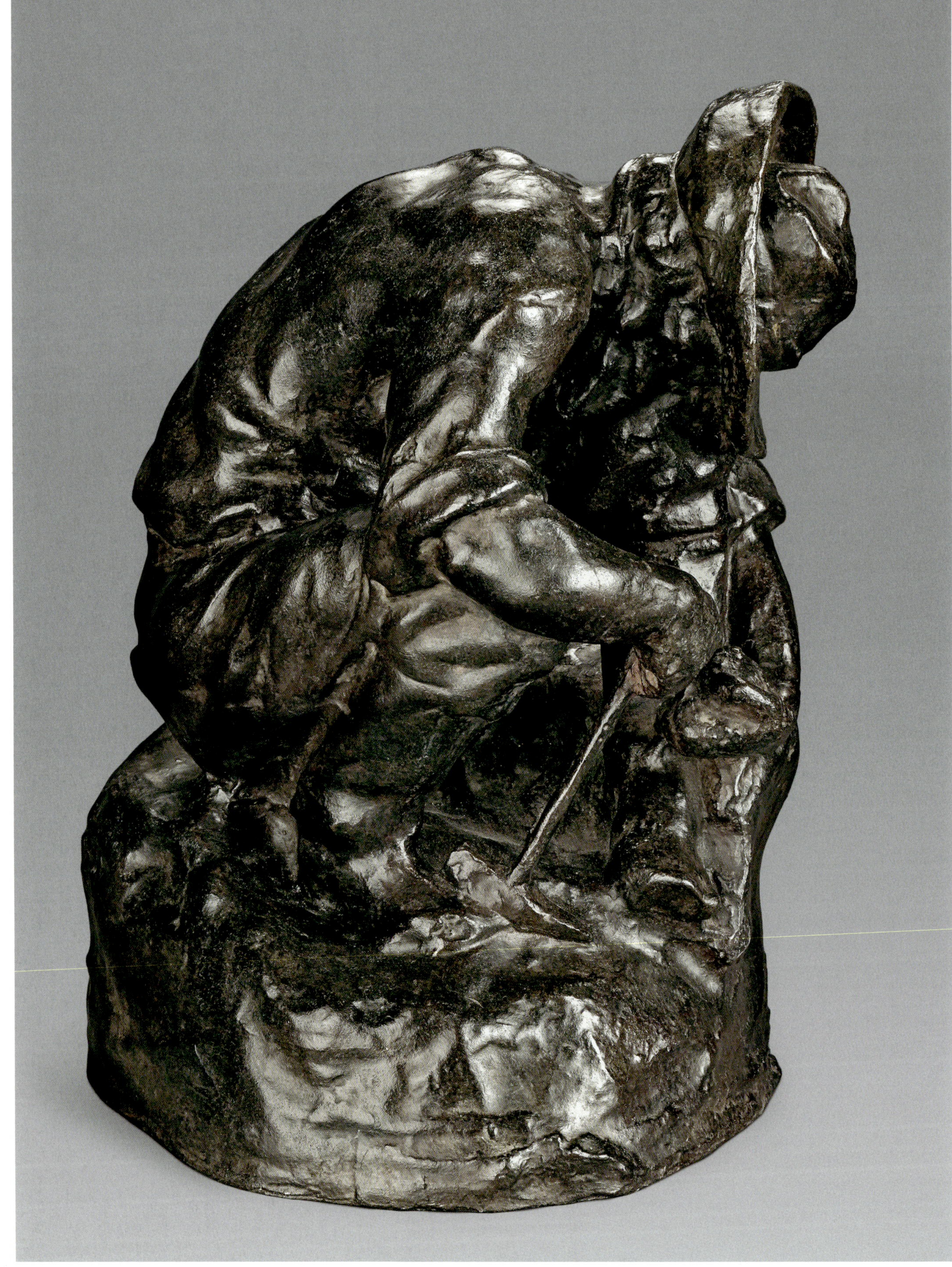

Fig. 159.
Arthur Putnam.
Prospector, 1903
(cast ca. 1921).
Cat. 48

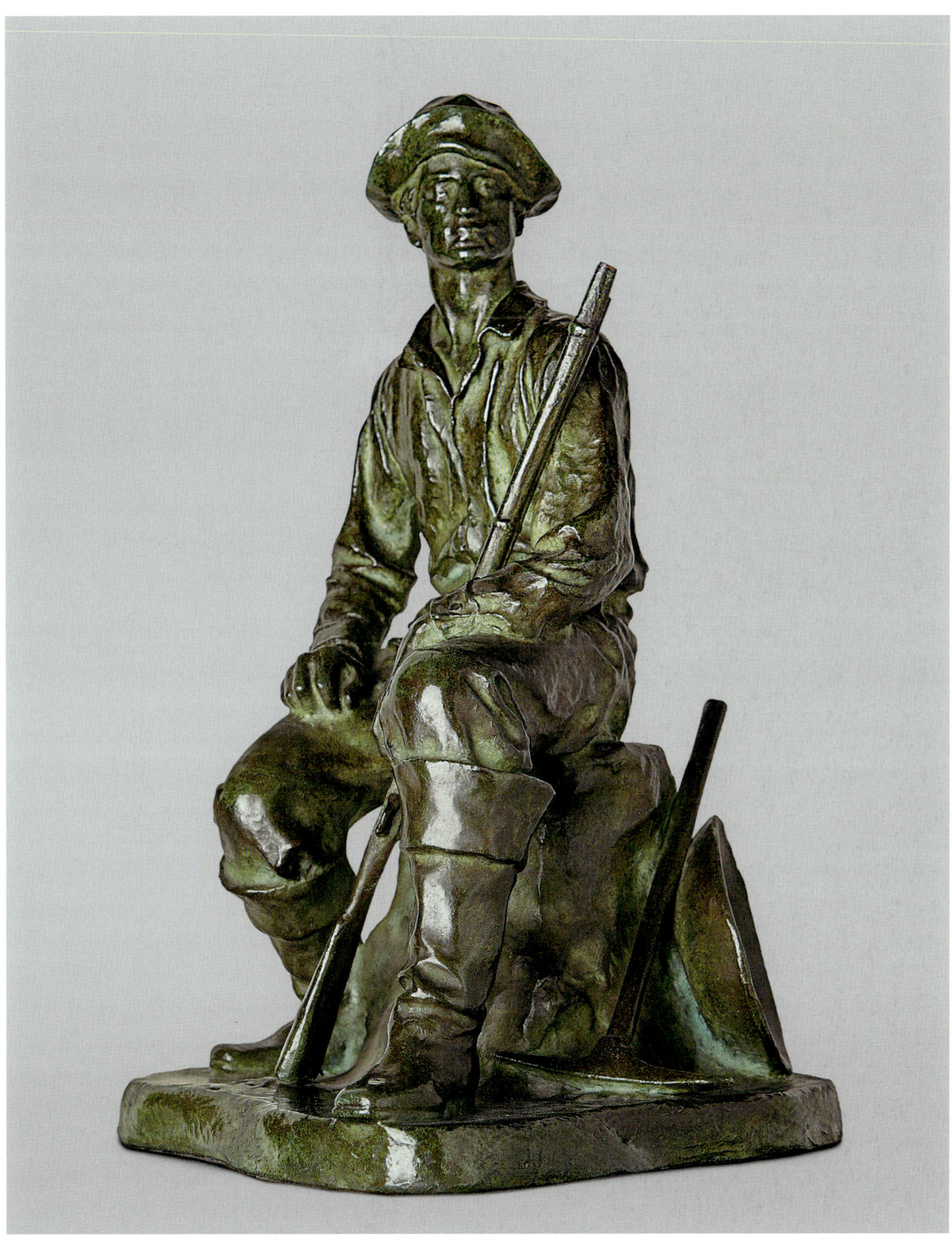

Like Putnam, the Armenian-born artist Haig Patigian was studying in Paris in 1906, and he too would become an important sculptor in San Francisco, known for his portrait busts as well as his architectural and monumental works. Patigian's family had originally immigrated to Fresno, California, where he was raised in the company of those who had pioneered the San Joaquin Valley. His *Pioneer* (fig. 160) is an upright and stoic figure equipped with rifle, pickax, and mining pan.

Fig. 160. Haig Patigian. *Pioneer*, 1926 (cast ca. 1935). Cat. 35

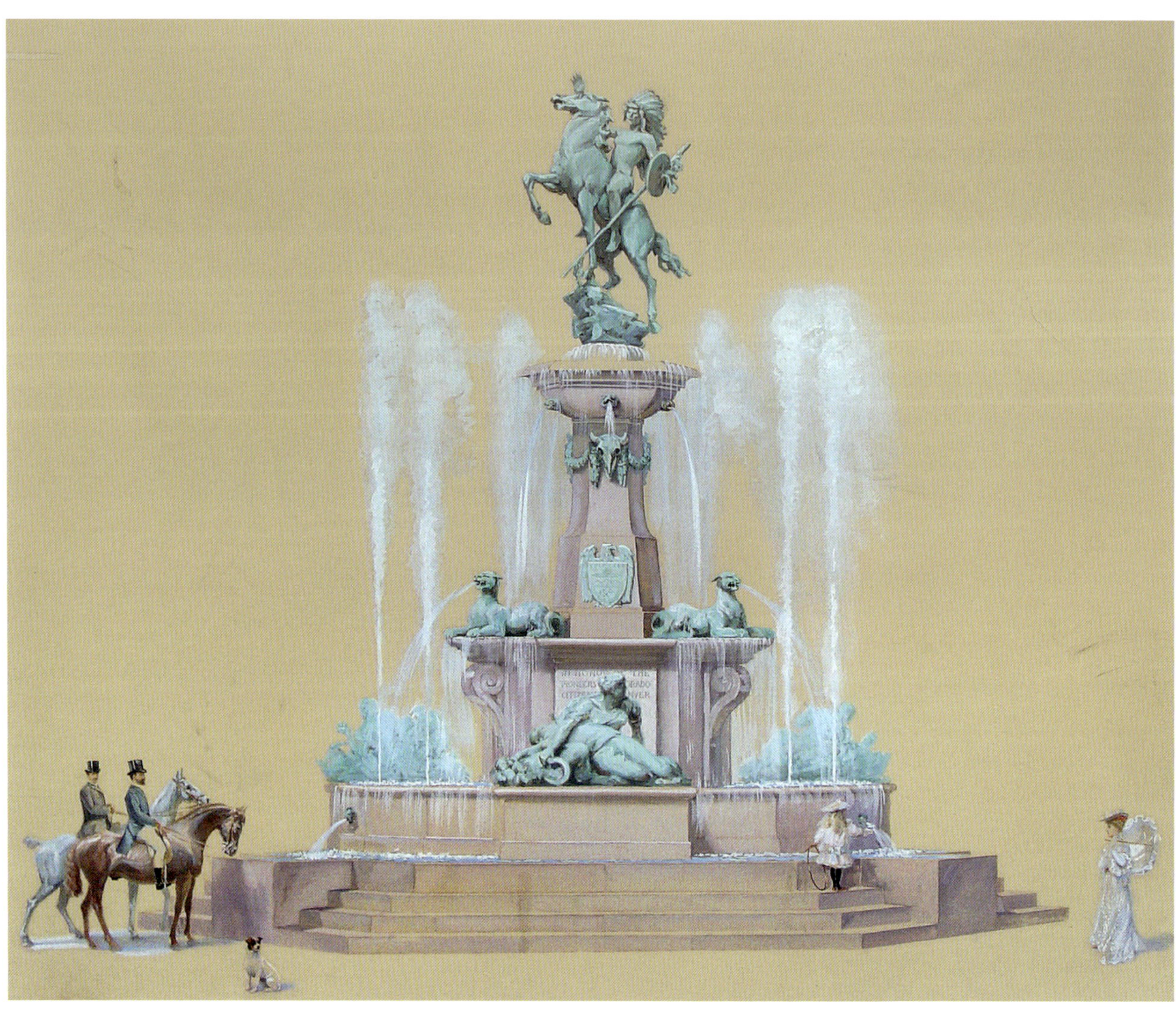

Fig. 161. Frederick William MacMonnies. *Presentation Drawing for "Pioneer Monument,"* 1907. Watercolor on paper, 42 × 46 in. (106.7 × 116.8 cm). Denver Public Library

All the pulses of the world,
Falling in, they beat for us, with the western movement beat;
Holding single or together, steady moving, to the front, all for us,
Pioneers! O pioneers!

As early as 1905, some of Denver's citizens decided to pay tribute to the city's early settlers by erecting a monument in their honor. Starting out with the highest aspirations, they initially offered the commission to Augustus Saint-Gaudens, the nation's most celebrated sculptor of public monuments. He declined, probably because of ill health and because he judged the proposed payment inadequate. Saint-Gaudens did, however, guide John S. Flower, chairman of the Public Improvement Committee, in selecting an artist and determining an appropriate fee. The city fathers chose the French-trained American expatriate Frederick William MacMonnies, whose sculptures featured the animated surfaces and fluid dynamism characteristic of the Beaux-Arts style, as the "logical man" for the commission.[25]

MacMonnies's sole work with a western subject, the monument went through some of the protracted complications typical of public commissions. The artist initially proposed a five-tiered fountain, with a variety of

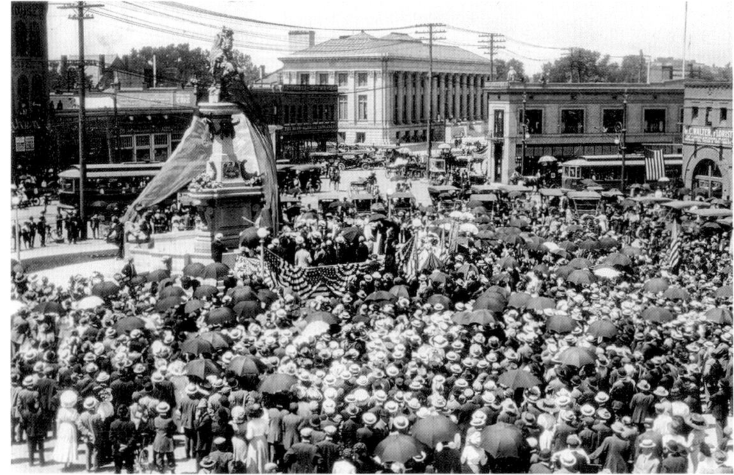

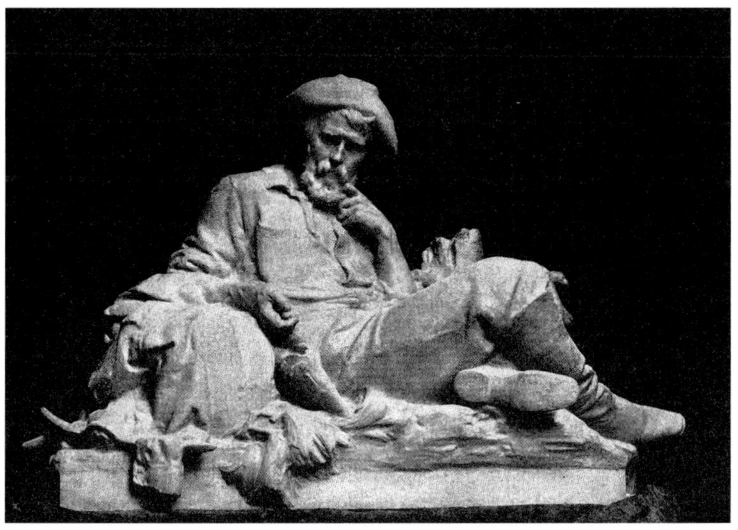

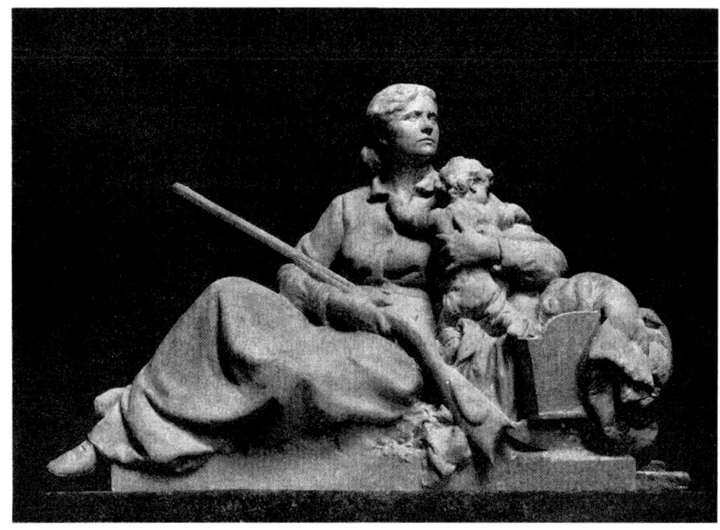

stereotypical pioneers (miners, trappers, cowboys, mothers) on the lower levels (see fig. 161). He originally planned to top the fountain with an Indian chief wearing a war bonnet, raising his hand in peace.[26] However, Denverites objected to the sculptor's plans to "giv[e] their cruel Indian enemy the position of honor."[27] Even though MacMonnies countered that the figure was not "the hero of the occasion" but only a finial, he bowed to popular sentiment and decided to visit the Rockies in order to adjust his image of the West.[28] While in Denver, MacMonnies agreed to replace the Indian with a likeness of Kit Carson—a choice well received because Carson, having been a hunter,

a miner, and a ranchman, was seen at the time as an apt symbol for all settlers.[29]

MacMonnies continued to revise and refine the fountain design for two years, in accord with ongoing advice from his Denver patrons, until the completed monument was unveiled in 1911 (figs. 16, 162). Consisting of a granite shaft decorated with buffalo skulls and oak garlands, it rises to Carson astride his horse, with arm upraised, inviting pioneers to continue westward.[30] The basins contain bronze groups of a prospector (fig. 163), a hunter, and one of the first sculptures of a pioneer mother and child (fig. 164), making this a rare monument with a western theme not to include a

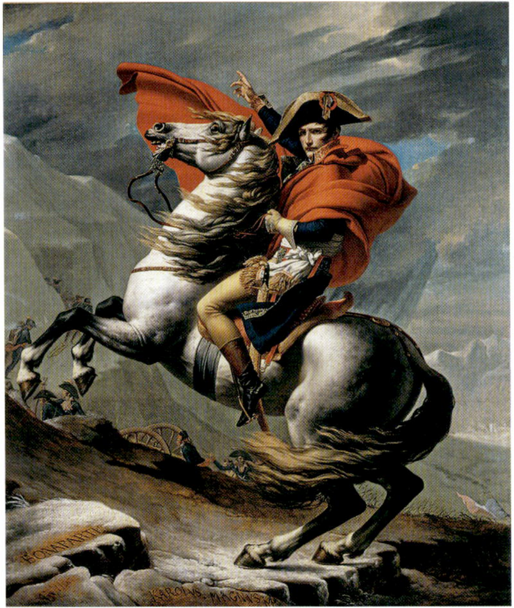

Fig. 165. Jacques-Louis David (French, 1748–1825). *Napoleon at the Saint Bernard Pass*, 1801. Oil on canvas, 9 ft. ¼ in. × 7 ft. 7⅜ in. (275 × 232 cm). Österreichische Galerie Belvedere, Vienna

Fig. 166. Frederick William MacMonnies. *Kit Carson*, ca. 1907–11 (cast by 1915). Cat. 26

cowboy or an American Indian. A review in *Denver Municipal Facts* praised MacMonnies upon the work's completion: "In developing the main motive of the monument, which seeks to express the expansive character of the West and its people, the sculptor has sought to reconcile sculpturesque quality and decorative style with the portrayal of types of character, without the loss of local definition. He has sought dignity by avoiding momentary, story-telling situations, and in the portrayal of character rather than episode, has endeavored to condense all that is most broadly typical of the West."[31]

In time, the public would criticize MacMonnies for incorrectly representing Carson

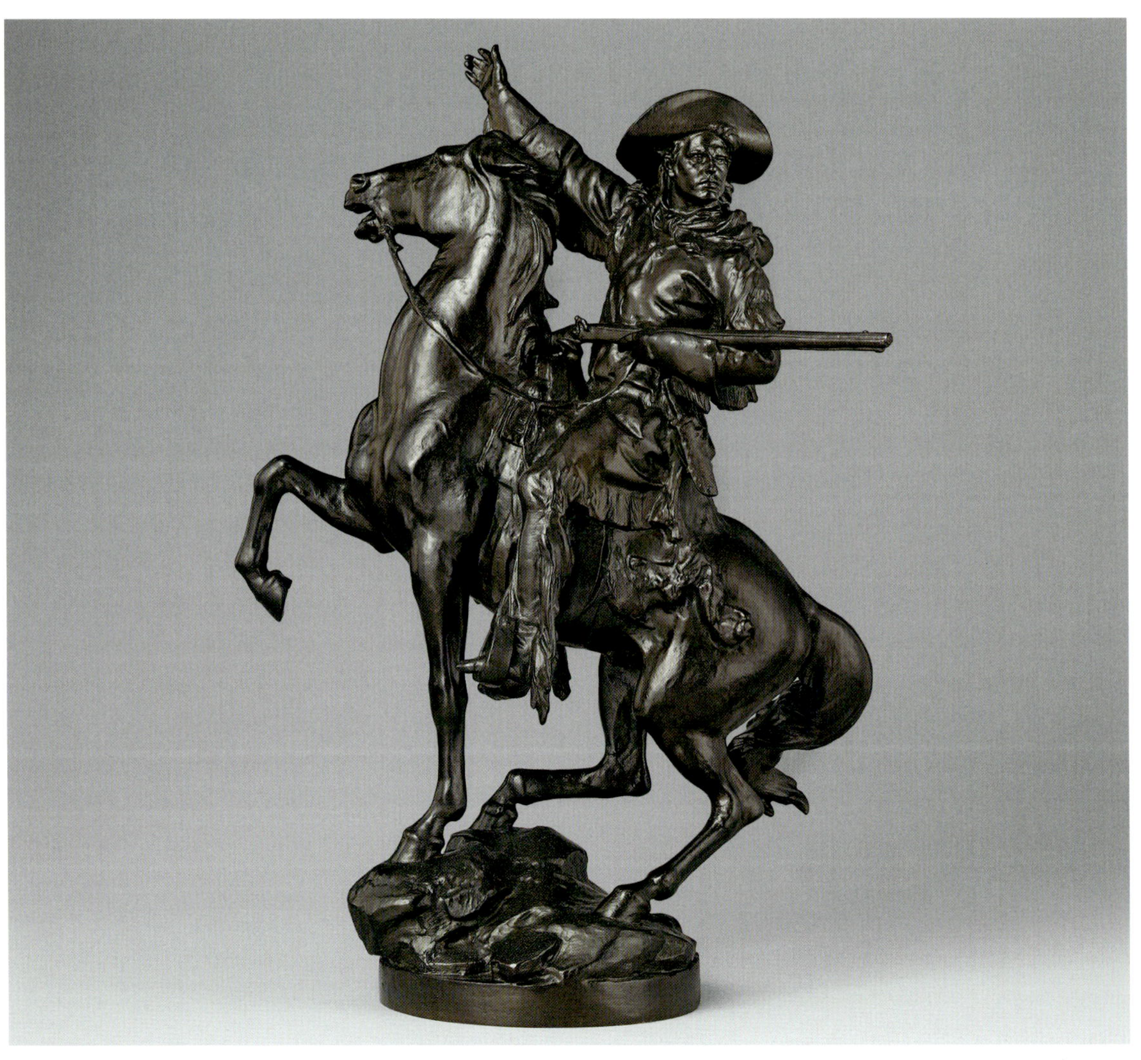

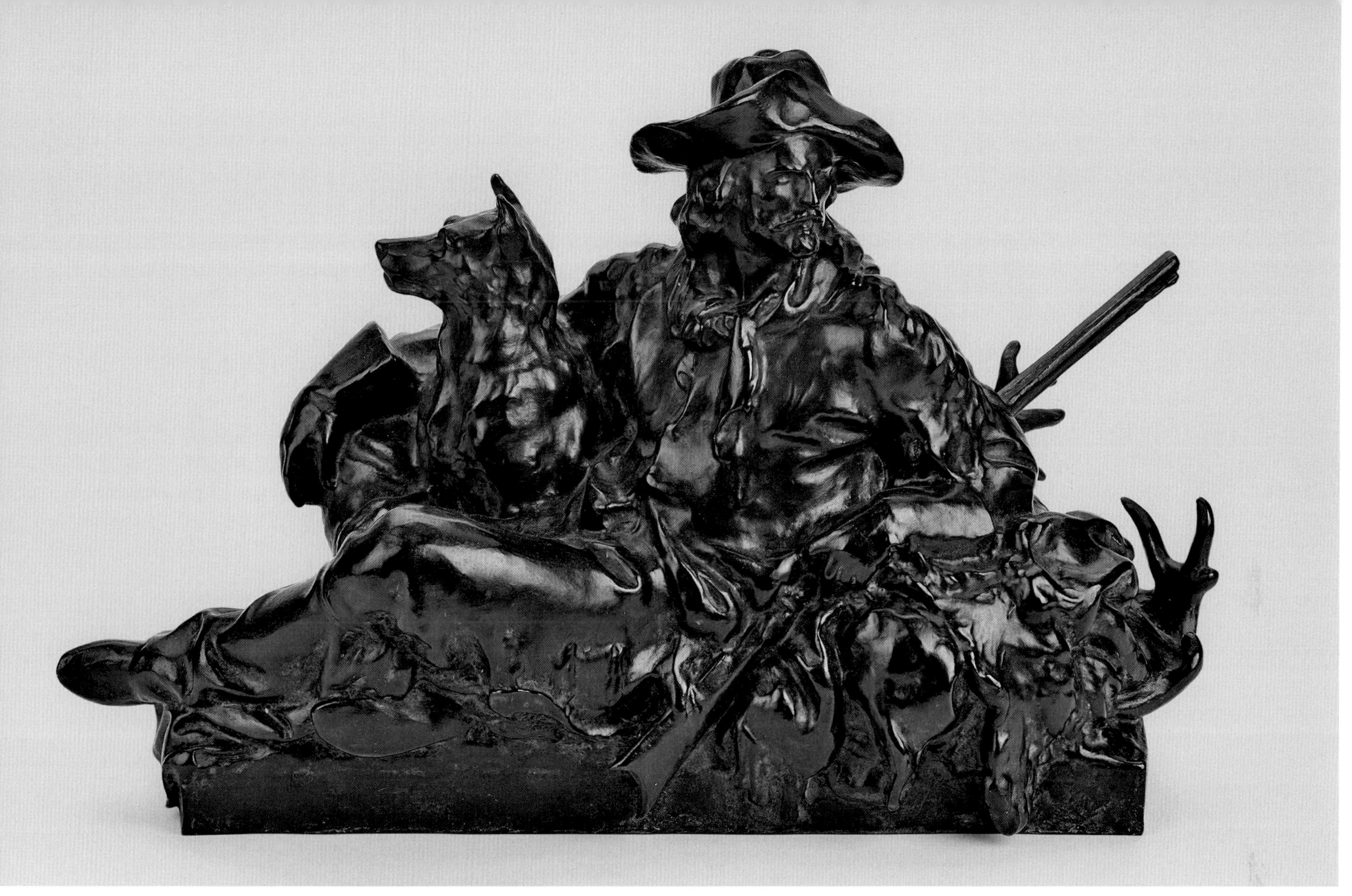

as clean-shaven, wearing gloves, and holding his gun the wrong way. Oliver Wiggins, a scout who had been Carson's companion for twelve years, was quoted as saying, "It don't look any more like him than the man in the moon." He continued, "Who ever heard of sending to France to get a likeness of an old plainsman for a pioneer monument?"[32] The sculpture did indeed have roots in France: longtime expatriate MacMonnies derived both the composition and the iconography of the Carson figure from the grand tradition of nineteenth-century French history painting, looking specifically to Jacques-Louis David's *Napoleon at the Saint Bernard Pass* (fig. 165), of 1801, which depicts Napoleon Bonaparte in the uniform of a general leading his army across the Alps. Mac-Monnies's Carson has, in essence, become Napoleon in western attire, the artist having exchanged the French leader's gold-trimmed bicorne and voluminous cloak for a western slouch hat and fringed buckskins. However, the symbolism of Kit Carson blazing the way for civilization would have been apparent even to those not familiar with the French precedents. MacMonnies exhibited bronze-colored plasters of Kit Carson and of the three pioneer groups at the Paris Salon of 1911. Since the 1890s he had been astute about the benefits, financial and otherwise, of casting small bronzes based on his well-known public sculptures. In this case, MacMonnies leveraged Carson's notoriety by casting statuettes at the Jaboeuf et Rouard and Gruet foundries in Paris and then at Roman Bronze Works in New York (fig. 166). *The Hunter* (fig. 167), although lacking Carson's celebrity, also was cast in a small edition.

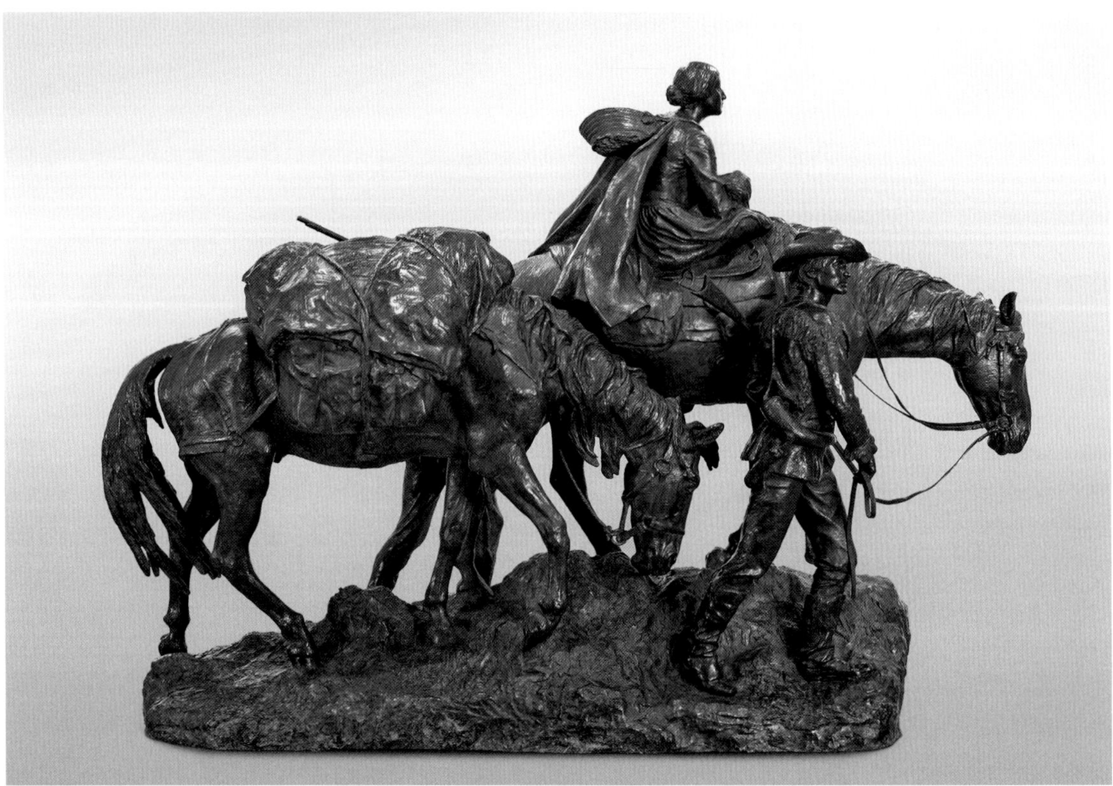

Fig. 168. Alexander Phimister Proctor. *Pioneer Mother*, 1925 (cast 1927). Cat. 46

O you daughters of the west!
O you young and elder daughters! O you mothers and
you wives!
Never must you be divided, in our ranks you move
united,
Pioneers! O pioneers!

Alexander Phimister Proctor, an experienced sculptor of monuments, sought for many years to produce a tribute to pioneer women. He later wrote in his autobiography: "My vision of the statue was a group of weary pioneers traveling westward over the prairie." He continued, "The young mother, the principal figure, rode horseback, carrying a baby in her arms—the hope for the future of the West."[33] It wasn't until 1923, when he met Howard Vanderslice, a wealthy businessman from Kansas City, that Proctor was finally able to realize such an ambitious commission. The two men shared not only roots in pioneer families but also the desire to realize a monument to honor them.[34]

Vanderslice commissioned Proctor to create a sculpture celebrating the pioneer mothers who had crossed the country on western trails; it was to be located in Penn Valley Park in Kansas City, Missouri—Vanderslice's hometown and a starting point on the old Santa Fe Trail.

Proctor intended that his sculpture express the emotional and physical trials of the long journey west. "My pioneers were not beginners," explained the artist. "Their equipment and attitudes showed that they had already had much experience. I wanted to convey the sense of travel across the dreary expanse of plains under burning sun, rain, and storms, braving hunger and thirst, fording rivers, prairie fires, beset by many dangers on the way." He also aimed to acknowledge the active role of women in westward expansion. "It seemed to me," he wrote, "that most people, in thinking of pioneers, thought solely of the men. I considered the heroism of the women equal to, and perhaps greater than, the men's."[35] Although two male figures walk beside the horse that carries the mother and child, there is no doubt that the mother leads. Her forward trajectory and uptilted chin suggest her determination to move the family onward.

After creating a reduced version in his Hollywood studio, which was later cast in bronze (fig. 168), Proctor moved to Rome to complete the full-size monument (fig. 15). After two years in Italy, it was finished, cast, and shipped to Kansas City, where the monument was unveiled in 1927 before a crowd of thirty thousand.[36] Fittingly, like many immigrant pioneers themselves, Proctor's *Pioneer Mother* had crossed the ocean and traveled halfway across the continent to reach its home on the plains.

The month before Proctor's monument was unveiled, twelve sculptors gathered at the Reinhardt Galleries in New York to exhibit their small bronze models for another public tribute to the pioneer woman, this one proposed for Ponca City, Oklahoma. Commissioned by the oil magnate E. W. Marland, the colossal bronze was to occupy a plot on the Cherokee Strip, described as the last parcel of government land to have been opened to homesteaders, in 1893. Marland conceived of the project as a competition and invited accomplished sculptors including Alexander Stirling Calder, James Earle Fraser, Hermon Atkins MacNeil, and others to vie for the commission.[37] Each artist was asked to submit a two-foot model, which would circulate from New York to cities throughout the East, Midwest, and as far west as Denver. In each venue the models were voted on by the public. Over 750,000 people attended the exhibitions and participated in what would become the only commission of the era to be determined by public vote. The winner, by a wide margin, was the model by Bryant Baker, a London-born sculptor.

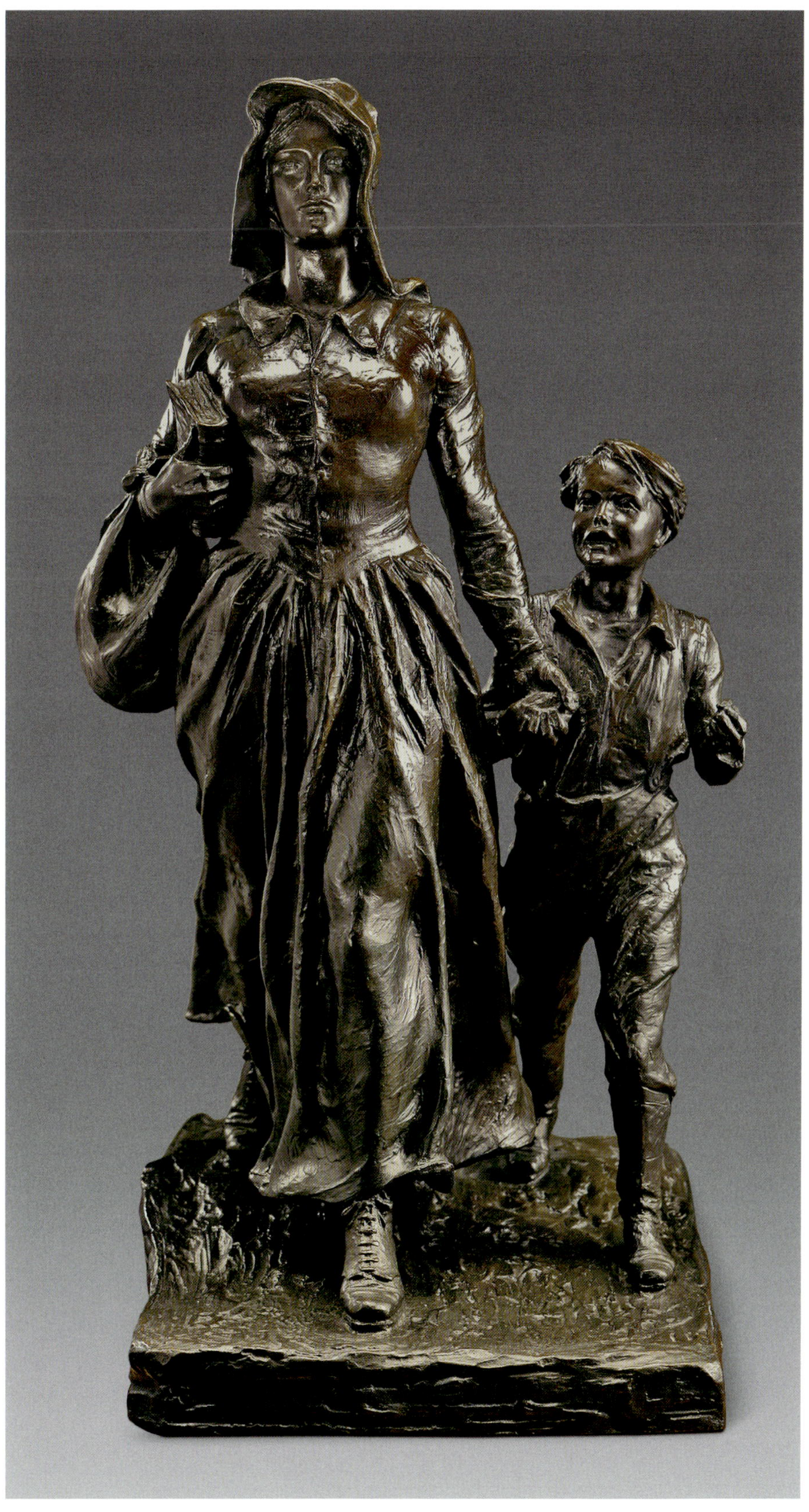

Fig. 169. Bryant Baker. *Pioneer Woman*, 1927. Cat. 1

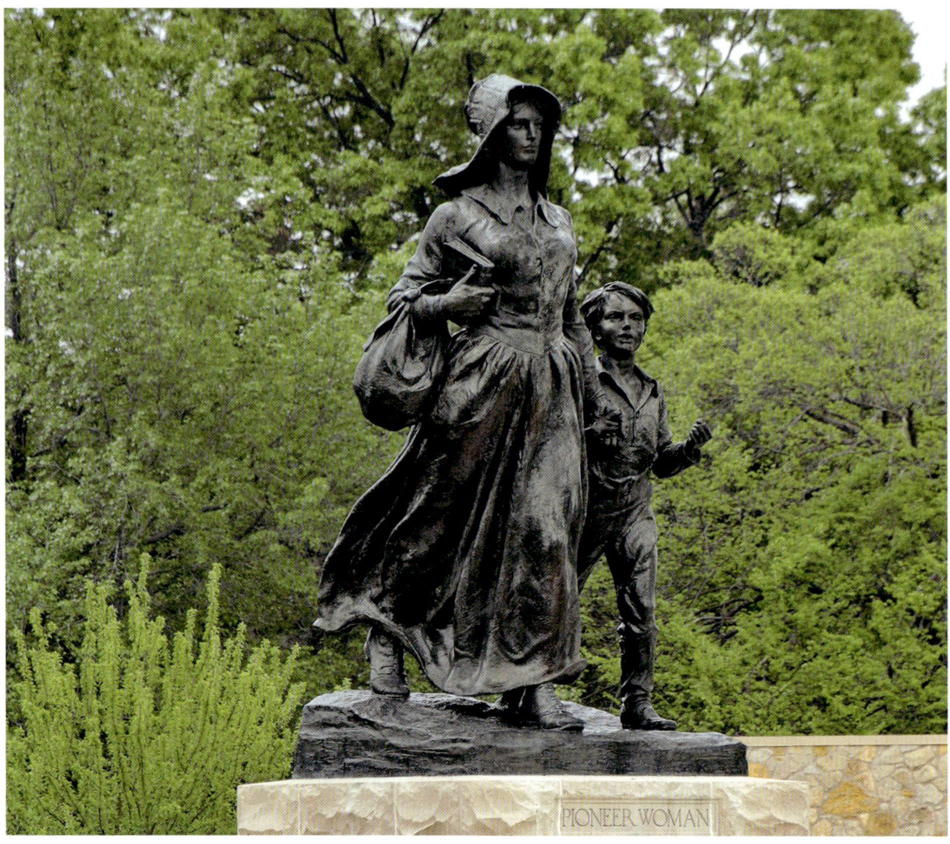

Fig. 170. Bryant Baker. *Pioneer Woman*, 1927–30 (dedicated 1930). Ponca City, Oklahoma

In the statuette (fig. 169), as in the final monument (fig. 170), Baker's young mother strides forward purposefully, her skirt blowing in a prairie breeze. She carries a Bible and a sack in one hand—alluding both to her faith and to her status as provider; the other grasps the hand of her son, who symbolizes the future of the West, "the man of tomorrow," as the artist recalled in 1967.[38] Following a lengthy visit to Ponca City in 1927, Baker refined his model, which was realized as a seventeen-foot bronze monument. Unveiled in April 1930, it was praised by President Herbert Hoover in a nationwide radio address: "It was those [pioneer] women who carried the refinement, the moral character, and spiritual force into the West."[39]

Baker's statuette was arguably the most conservative submission, so it is perhaps understandable that it was the popular choice. The other entries ranged in style from Beaux-Arts naturalism to modernism to Art Deco. The art critic Helen Appleton Read considered the most accomplished sculptor of the group to be Hermon Atkins MacNeil, whose *Pioneer Woman* (fig. 171) carries an ax in one hand, recalling a more primitive past, and her child in the other, again alluding to the future.[40] Read also noted that "the sophisticated in art matters voted heavily for Maurice Sterne," the most aesthetically forward-thinking among the artists.[41] Another art critic, Thomas Craven, wrote a scathing review deploring not only all of the submissions but also Marland's decision to award the commission based on a popular vote, accusing him of "complete ignorance of the fine arts."[42] The Pioneer Woman competition coincided with a transition away from traditional figurative sculpture in America. The nation was changing, and with it would come a more modern aesthetic sensibility.

Although far fewer bronze statuettes of pioneers were made than those of Indians,

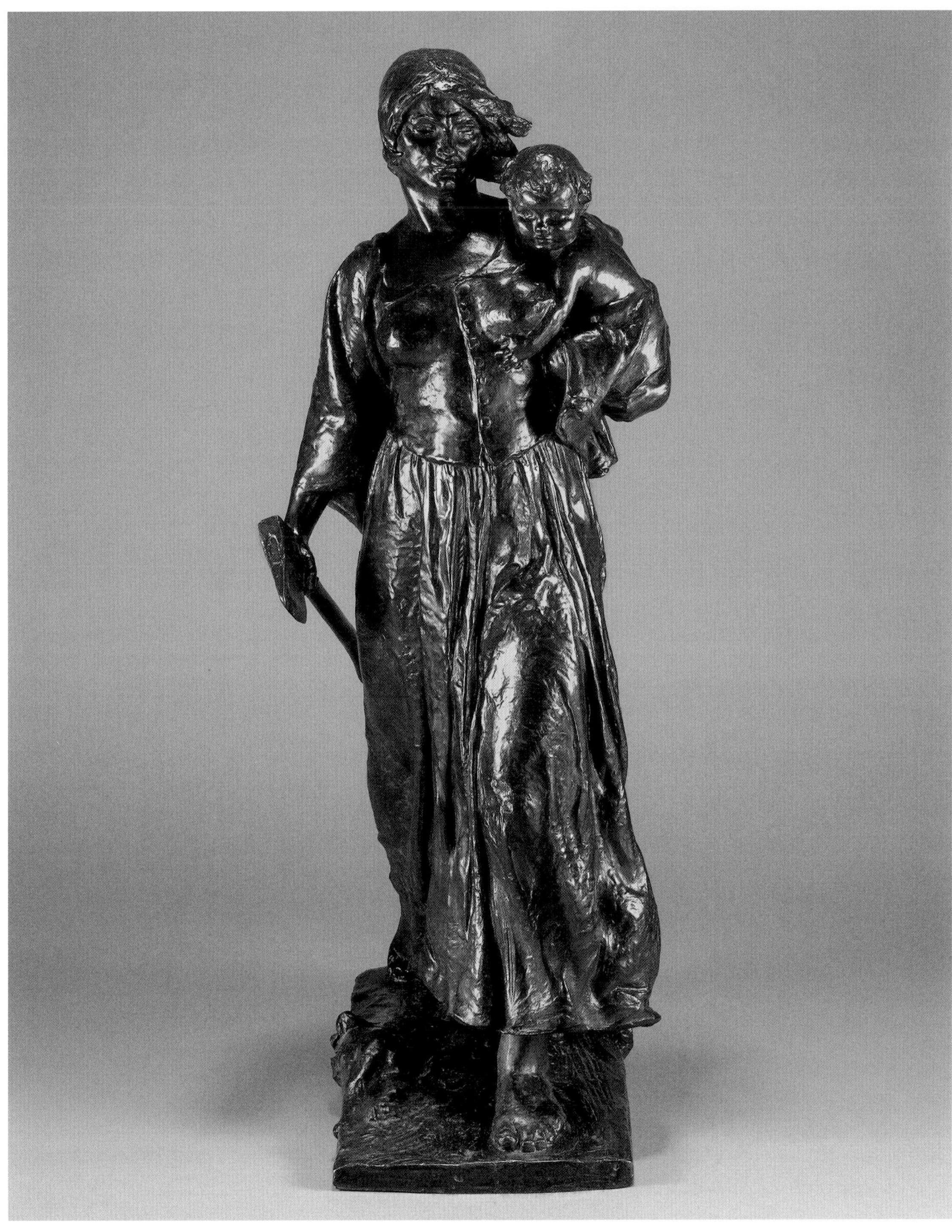

cowboys, and wildlife, they commemorate a group of characters equally central to the history of the American West. Their diversity, their fearlessness, and their strength were succinctly captured by the sculptors and by Whitman:

All the past we leave behind;
We debouch upon a newer, mightier world, varied world;
Fresh and strong the world we seize, world of labor and the march,
Pioneers! O pioneers!

Chronology

1846

The United States government declares war on Mexico, following a dispute over the Texas border and an attack by Mexican troops.

In a border treaty with Great Britain, the United States acquires Oregon Territory, which also includes sections of present-day Washington, Idaho, Wyoming, and Montana.

Brigham Young departs with his followers on a journey from Illinois to Utah, to establish a new Mormon community.

John Mix Stanley accompanies Colonel Stephen Watts Kearny's expedition to New Mexico, then continues to California, Oregon, and Washington, painting landscapes and scenes of American Indian life.

1848

Gold deposits are discovered at Sutter's Mill, California, setting off a gold rush that attracts more than forty thousand prospectors in two years.

At the conclusion of the Mexican-American War, Mexico cedes Texas as well as the land that will become the states of California, Nevada, Utah, and parts of New Mexico, Arizona, Wyoming, and Colorado.

Wisconsin becomes a state.

1849

Henry Kirke Brown casts *Choosing of the Arrow* in his Brooklyn studio and foundry, one of the first successful American endeavors in art bronze casting.

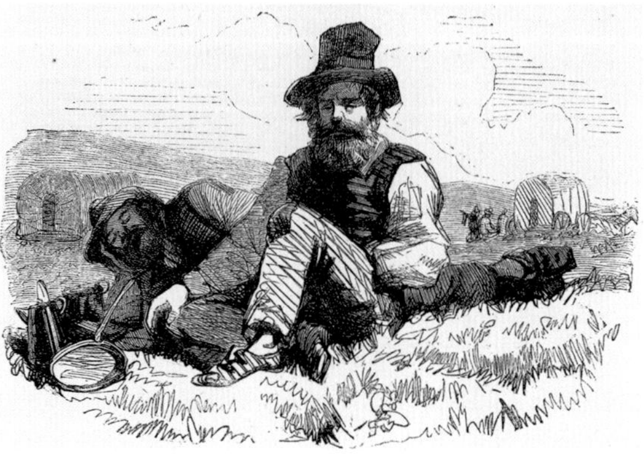

Fig. 172.
"A Pike's Peaker,"
Harper's Weekly,
August 13, 1859

Francis Parkman publishes *The Oregon Trail: Sketches of Prairie and Rocky-Mountain Life.*

1850

California joins the Union as a free state; New Mexico and Utah are admitted as territories.

1851

With the Treaty of Fort Laramie, representatives of the U.S. government divide the Great Plains region into territories for each of the local Indian tribes, promising them protection and annuities in exchange for safe passage for settlers as well as the right to build roads and military outposts on these lands.

The Erie Railroad connects New York and the Great Lakes.

1853

With the Gadsden Purchase, thirty thousand square miles are acquired from Mexico—the last expansion of the contiguous United States; this land will become part of southern Arizona and southern New Mexico.

Washington Territory is formed from the northern portion of Oregon Territory.

1854

The Baltimore & Ohio Railroad is completed, connecting Chicago to the Eastern Seaboard.

Copper is discovered in Arizona.

1858

The Pike's Peak Gold Rush in Cherry Creek, Kansas Territory (present-day Colorado), lures prospectors to the region (fig. 172).

William H. Larimer organizes the Denver City Town Company at the junction of Colorado's Cherry Creek and South Platte River, naming it for James William Denver, former governor of Kansas Territory. Colorado is named a territory in 1861, and the town's name is shortened to Denver when it becomes the territorial capital in 1867.

1859

Frederick W. Lander leads a government-sponsored expedition to the Rocky Mountains; his

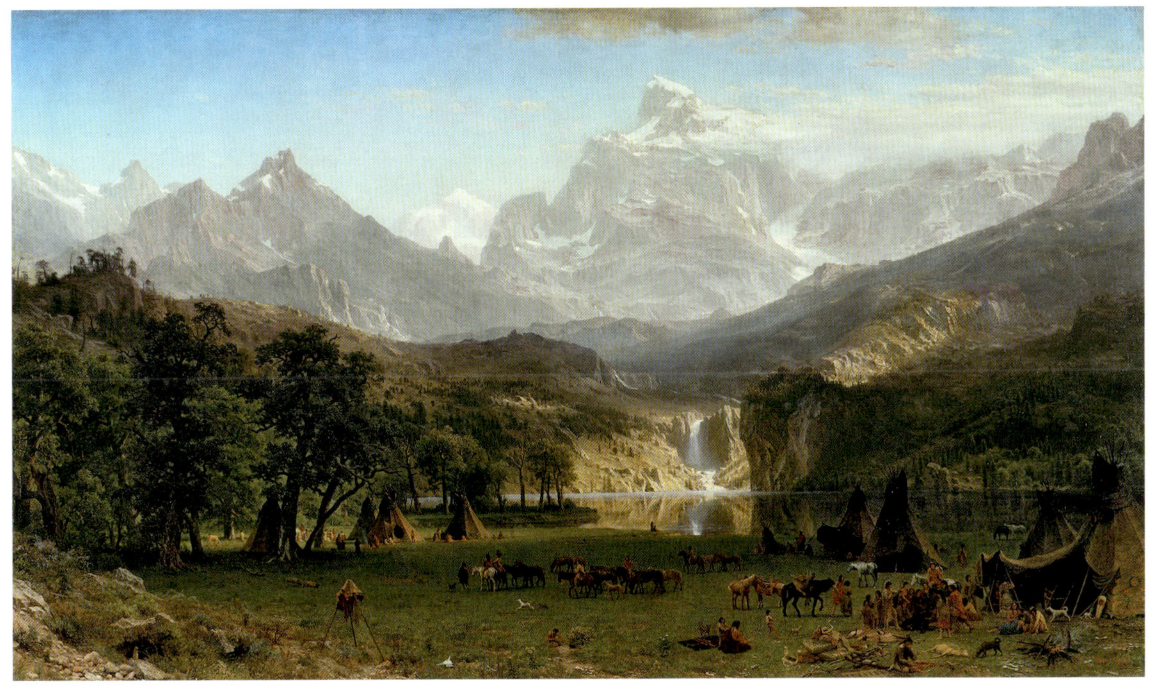

Fig. 173. Albert Bierstadt (American, born Germany, 1830–1902). *The Rocky Mountains, Lander's Peak*, 1863. Oil on canvas, 6 ft. 1½ in. × 10 ft. ¾ in. (186.7 × 306.7 cm). The Metropolitan Museum of Art, Rogers Fund, 1907 (07.123)

Fig. 174. Carleton E. Watkins (American, 1829–1916). *Nevada Fall, 700 Feet, Yosemite*, ca. 1872, printed ca. 1876. Albumen silver print from glass negative, 13¼ × 10½ in. (33.6 × 26.7 cm). The Metropolitan Museum of Art, Gift of Carole and Irwin Lainoff, Ruth P. Lasser and Joseph R. Lasser, Mr. and Mrs. John T. Marvin, Martin E. and Joan Messinger, Richard L. Yett and Sheri and Paul Siegel, 1986 (1986.1189.41)

party includes the artists Albert Bierstadt (fig. 173), Francis Seth Frost, and Henry Hitchings.

Oregon becomes a state.

The discovery of a silver deposit at the Comstock Lode, in present-day Nevada, sets off a silver rush.

1860

Congress commissions Emanuel Leutze to paint *Westward the Course of Empire Takes Its Way* for the U.S. Capitol.

Abraham Lincoln is elected president.

The Pony Express establishes a mail route spanning nineteen hundred miles from Missouri to California.

1861

April 12: The Civil War begins with a Confederate attack on Fort Sumter, South Carolina; seven states have already seceded from the Union.

The first transcontinental telegraph links New York and San Francisco.

1862

The Homestead Act, signed into law by Lincoln, allows private citizens to purchase up to 160 acres of public land for $1.25 per acre; they are entitled to own the land after five years of residence and improvement.

The Pacific Railway Act authorizes the Union Pacific Railroad to build a line from Nebraska to Utah, where it will connect with the Central Pacific Railroad's expansion eastward from Sacramento, California.

The Dakota War, led by Chief Little Crow—in which approximately six hundred settlers and soldiers are killed—is suppressed by the U.S. Army. Thirty-nine Sioux leaders are tried and sentenced; thirty-eight are hanged, in Mankato, Minnesota.

Carleton E. Watkins exhibits in New York his photographs of California's Yosemite Valley, raising awareness of the region's spectacular landscape (fig. 174).

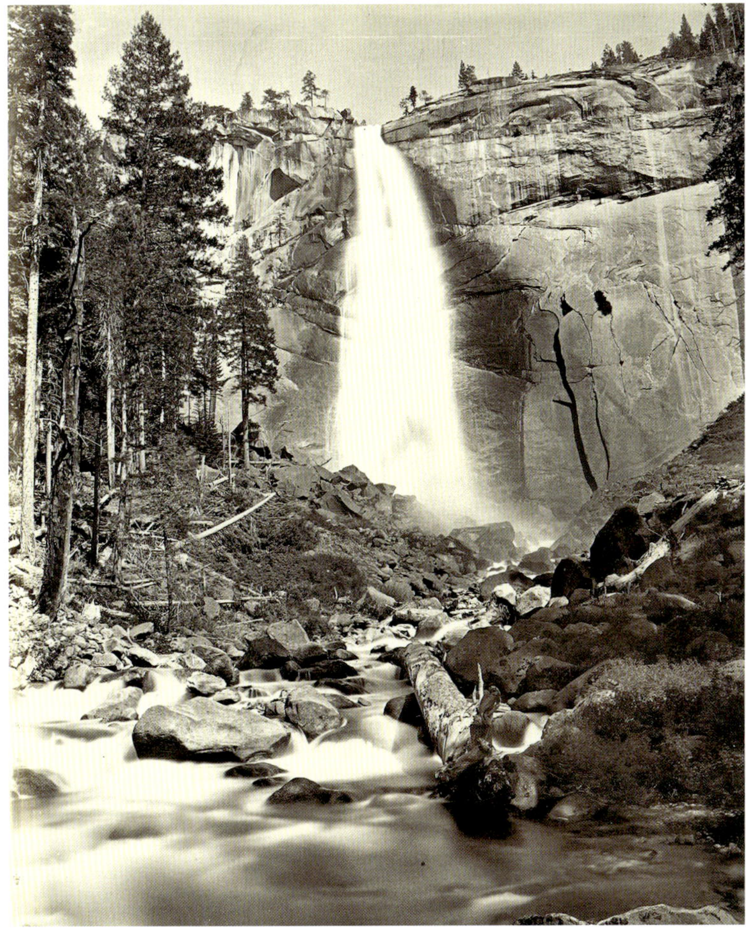

1863

January 1: The Emancipation Proclamation takes effect, freeing slaves in the Confederate states.

1864

Yosemite is designated a California state park and nature preserve; it will be named a national park in 1890.

Nevada becomes a state.

A Cheyenne and Arapaho camp on Sand Creek, Colorado, is attacked by volunteer Union troops, ending in the massacre of at least 150 men, women, and children.

After Christopher "Kit" Carson's troops systematically destroy Navajo crops and livestock, some eight thousand Navajo surrender and are forced to relocate from northeastern Arizona to Bosque Redondo, New Mexico. They are held as prisoners of the U.S. government until a treaty signed in 1868 grants them reservation land.

The Central Park Menagerie (later the Central Park Zoo) is opened to visitors in New York.

1865

April 9: The Civil War ends with Robert E. Lee's surrender to Ulysses S. Grant in Appomattox, Virginia.

April 14: Lincoln is shot by John Wilkes Booth in Washington, D.C., and dies the next day.

1867

Alaska is purchased from Russia for 7.2 million dollars in a deal overseen by Secretary of State William H. Seward.

Nebraska becomes a state.

Congress establishes territories in current-day Oklahoma for the so-called Five Civilized Tribes—Cherokee, Chickasaw, Choctaw, Creek, and Seminole—as well as many American Indian groups from the Northeast.

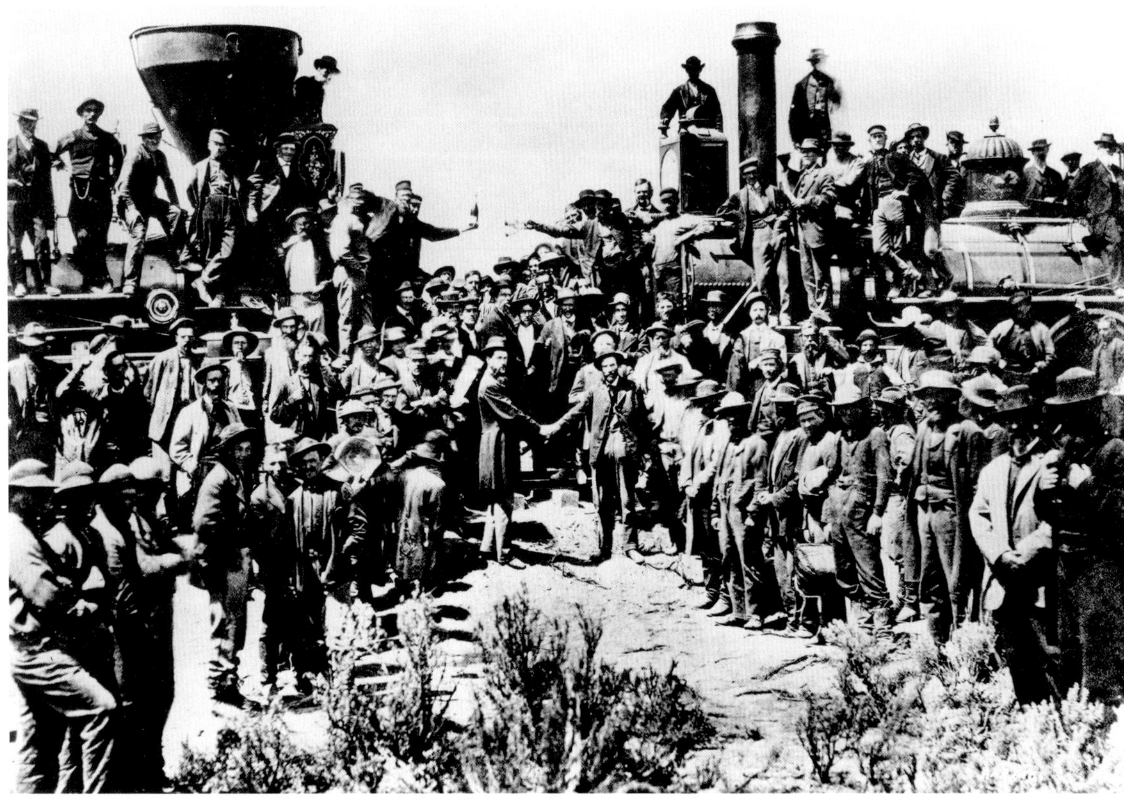

Fig. 175. *Golden Spike Ceremony at Promontory, Utah,* May 10, 1869

Texas cattle farmers begin driving their herds up the Chisholm Trail to Abilene, Kansas, for shipping by rail to Chicago meat-packers.

The Pullman Palace Car Company is founded; first-class cars are developed to transport transcontinental travelers in luxury.

1868

Wyoming Territory is formed from sections of Dakota, Utah, and Idaho Territories.

The Treaty of Fort Laramie establishes the Great Sioux Reservation, composed of land in present-day South Dakota and Nebraska.

1869

May 10: The Golden Spike ceremony in Promontory Summit, Utah Territory, where the Union Pacific line meets the Central Pacific line, marks completion of the first transcontinental railroad (fig. 175).

On an expedition funded by Congress, John Wesley Powell covers more than one thousand miles of the Colorado River and explores the Grand Canyon.

The Wyoming Territorial Legislature gives women the right to vote.

1871

Photographer William Henry Jackson and painter Thomas Moran accompany Ferdinand V. Hayden's expedition on a geological survey of the Rocky Mountains and the Yellowstone region; their subsequent depictions help raise public and official interest in these locations (fig. 177).

Congress passes the Indian Appropriation Act, ending the treaty system that had recognized tribes as independent domestic nations and bringing Indian affairs under congressional control.

The U.S. Army moves the Apache onto reservation land in New Mexico and Arizona.

1872

Yellowstone is designated the first national park.

Clarence King publishes *Mountaineering in the Sierra Nevada,* following his extended travels for the U.S. Geological Exploration of the Fortieth Parallel.

Mark Twain publishes *Roughing It,* an account of his travels throughout the West between 1861 and 1867.

1875–78

In the aftermath of the Indian Wars, seventy-two Southern Plains chiefs and warriors are imprisoned by the U.S. military at Fort Marion, Florida.

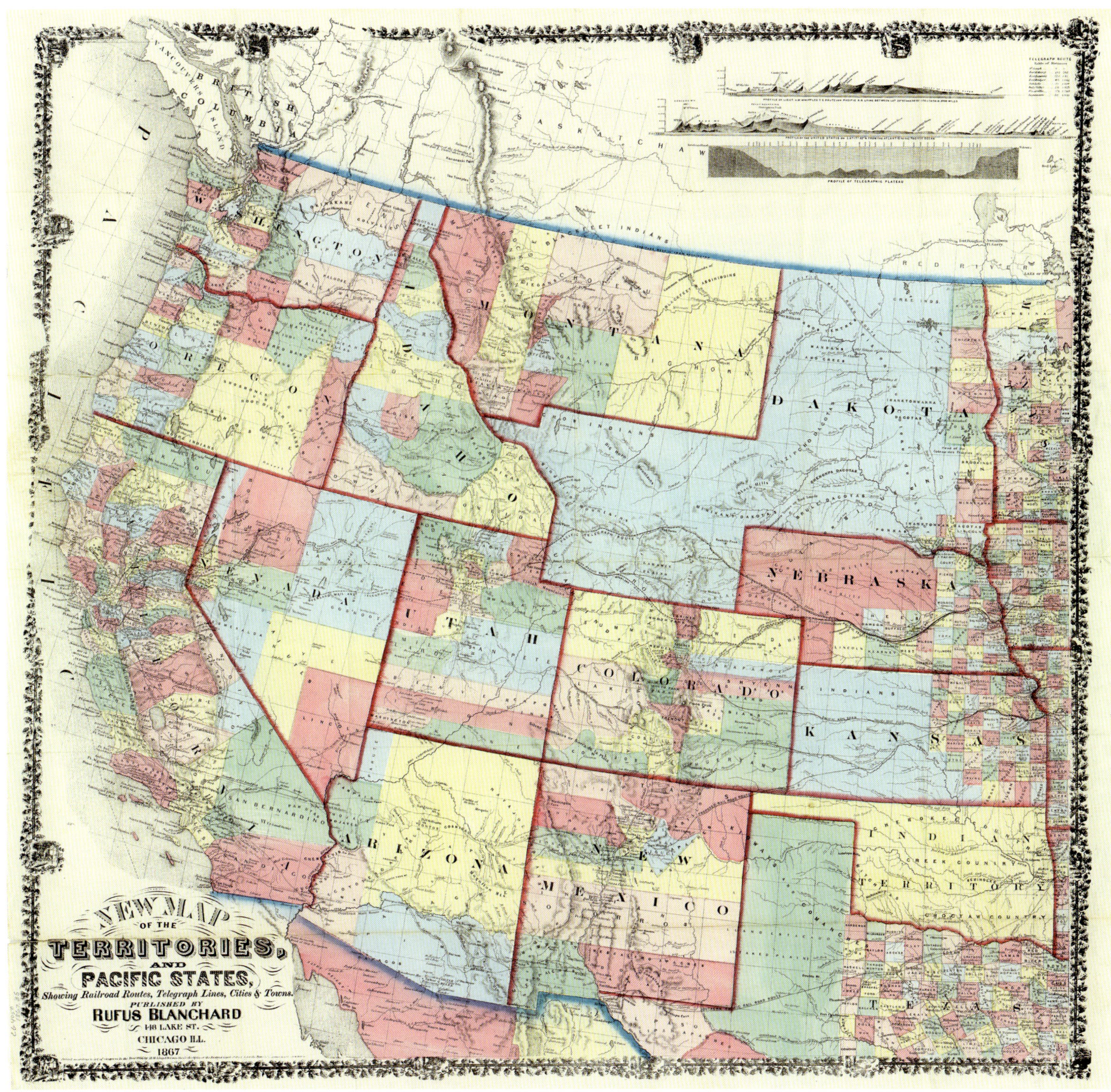

Fig. 176. *New Map of the Territories and Pacific States, Showing Railroad Routes, Telegraph Lines, Cities & Towns.* Rufus Blanchard, 1867. Denver Public Library

1876

Theodore Baur, Edward Kemeys, Randolph Rogers, and Olin Levi Warner exhibit sculptures at the Centennial Exhibition in Philadelphia.

General George Armstrong Custer is defeated by Sioux and Cheyenne warriors (led by chiefs Sitting Bull, Crazy Horse, and Gall) at the Battle of the Little Bighorn in Montana Territory.

Colorado becomes a state.

1877

Nez Percé Indians, led by Chief Joseph, are defeated by U.S. troops after fighting across Washington, Oregon, Idaho, and Montana.

1878

Edward L. Wheeler's *Deadwood Dick on Deck: or, Calamity Jane, the Heroine of Whoop-Up* is published, featuring two of the most celebrated characters in dime novels set in the West.

1879

U.S. troops suppress an uprising of the Ute and relocate them from Colorado to Utah.

1881

A legendary gunfight between frontier lawmen, including Wyatt Earp and Doc Holliday, and an outlaw gang takes place at the O.K. Corral in Tombstone, Arizona.

Helen Hunt Jackson publishes *A Century of Dishonor: A Sketch of the United States Government's Dealings with Some of the Indian Tribes,* a nonfiction account of the mistreatment of American Indians told through tribal histories.

1882

Copper deposits are found in a mine in Butte, Montana, triggering a copper rush.

The Chinese Exclusion Act restricts the number of Chinese immigrants, many of whom worked in western mining and railroad construction.

1883

William F. "Buffalo Bill" Cody organizes Buffalo Bill's Wild West, a traveling show featuring shooting, roping, and riding; performances of rituals and dances by American Indians; reenactments of famous holdups and Indian battles; and displays of western animals.

Railroad standard time is adopted so that U.S. and Canadian train schedules conform to four uniform time zones.

1884

Perhaps the last shipment of robes and hides from the thoroughly depleted bison population travels by rail from western Dakota Territory.

Helen Hunt Jackson publishes *Ramona,* a romantic novel about a young woman of mixed blood and her American Indian husband; it becomes a best seller and stimulates tourism to California, where it takes place.

The Henry-Bonnard Bronze Company, New York, is incorporated. America's premier sandcasting foundry, it produces bronze statuettes for Theodore Baur, John Quincy Adams Ward, and beginning in 1895, Frederic Remington.

1885

Congress passes laws preventing cattle ranchers and railroad companies from fencing off western land for independent business ventures.

Chief Sitting Bull performs with Buffalo Bill's Wild West. Annie Oakley (Phoebe Ann Moses; nicknamed "Little Sure Shot" by Sitting Bull in 1884) joins the show, performing for sixteen of the next seventeen seasons (fig. 178).

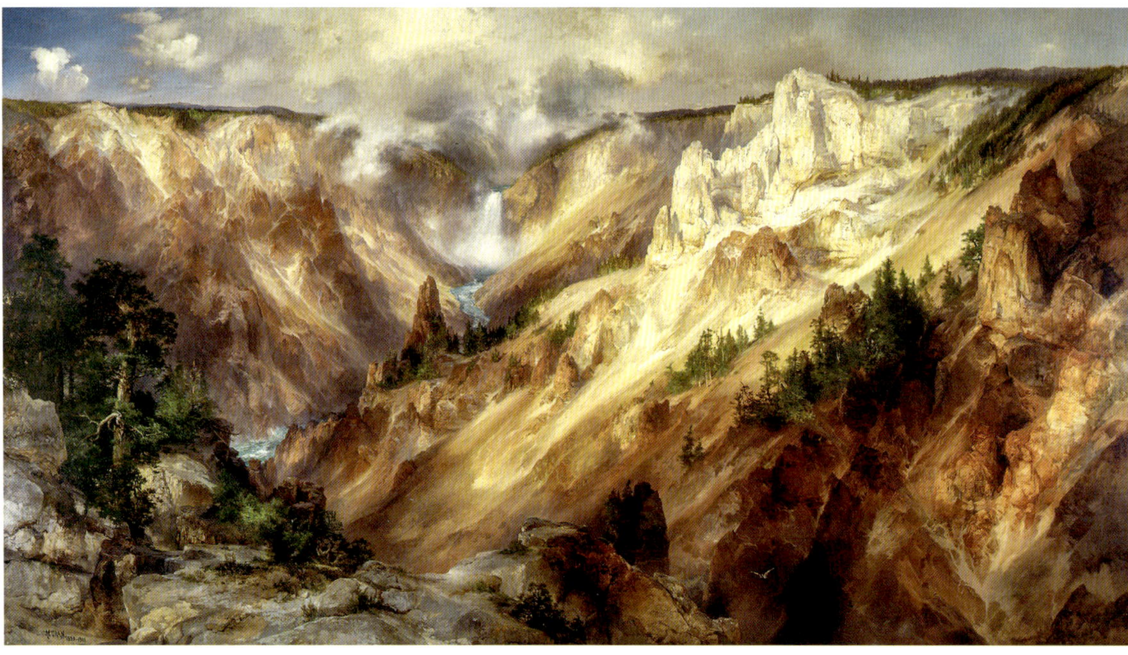

Fig. 177. Thomas Moran (American, born England, 1837–1926). *The Grand Canyon of the Yellowstone,* 1893–1901. Oil on canvas, 8 ft. ½ in. × 14 ft. ⅜ in. (245.1 × 427.8 cm). Smithsonian American Art Museum, Washington, D.C., Gift of George D. Pratt

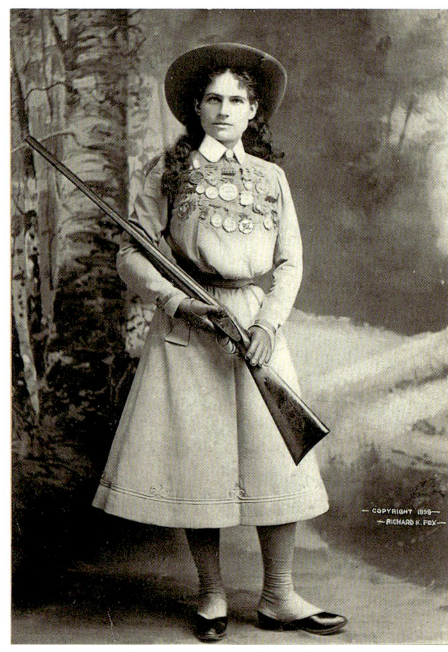

Fig. 178. *Annie Oakley,* 1899. Halftone print, 13⅞ × 9⅛ in. (35.3 × 23.1 cm). Prints and Photographs Division, Library of Congress, Washington, D.C.

1886

After years of resistance to the U.S. government and several escapes from an Arizona reservation, the Chiricahua Apache leader and warrior Geronimo is the last American Indian to surrender formally to the United States. He is exiled to Florida and later to Oklahoma. Meanwhile, nearly five hundred Apache are imprisoned at Fort Marion, Florida.

The Division of Forestry is officially recognized by the Department of Agriculture.

1887

Congress passes the Dawes Severalty Act, granting allotments of Indian reservation land to individual tribe members and making surplus land available to white settlers.

The Boone and Crockett Club, a wildlife conservation organization, is founded by George Bird Grinnell and Theodore Roosevelt.

Buffalo Bill's Wild West travels to London and gives a command performance for Queen Victoria on the occasion of her Golden Jubilee.

1888

Remington illustrates Roosevelt's "Ranch Life in the Far West," a series of articles for *Century Magazine*.

1889

Land in Oklahoma is opened to white settlement, resulting in a land rush.

North Dakota, South Dakota, Montana, and Washington become states.

Roosevelt's multivolume history of the frontier, *The Winning of the West*, begins publication (completed 1896).

Buffalo Bill's Wild West begins a tour through France, Spain, Italy, Austria, and Germany.

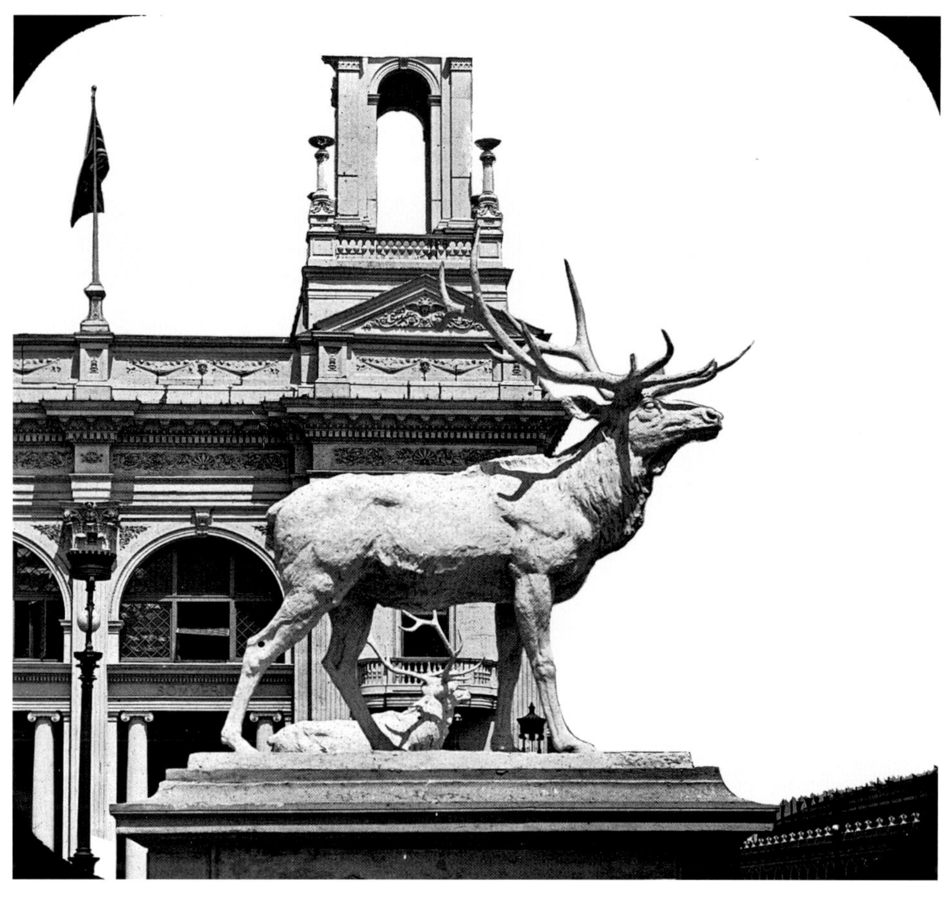

Fig. 179. Alexander Phimister Proctor. *Elk*, World's Columbian Exposition, Chicago, 1893

1890

The U.S. Census declares that the western United States has been populated to the extent that there is no longer an official frontier.

Chief Sitting Bull—a leader of Sioux resistance who also became involved in the Ghost Dance movement to restore traditional Indian culture and lands—is arrested by U.S. Indian Agent James McLaughlin on a reservation in Grand River, South Dakota, and killed in a fight with his captors.

The Seventh U.S. Cavalry Regiment (General Custer's old regiment) massacres an estimated two hundred Sioux at Wounded Knee, South Dakota, including Chief Big Foot, ending the long era of the Indian Wars.

Oklahoma Territory is established. Idaho and Wyoming become states.

Sequoia and Yosemite national parks are established in California.

1891

The Forest Reserve Act allows the president to put aside public land for national parks.

Land in Oklahoma previously ceded to the government by the Sauk, Fox, and Potawatomi is opened to settlement.

1892

More land in Oklahoma, earlier owned by the Cheyenne and Arapaho, is opened to white settlers; Crow land in Montana is similarly opened.

Congress bans the sale of alcohol on Indian land.

Edward MacDowell composes *Suite No. 2 for Orchestra (Indian Suite)*, inspired by traditional American Indian music; it is first performed in New York in 1896.

1893

The World's Columbian Exposition is held in Chicago; more than twenty-seven million visitors attend. Kemeys and Alexander Phimister Proctor create lifesize plaster sculptures of animals to decorate the fairgrounds (fig. 179); Proctor is also commissioned to model large-scale monuments of an Indian and a cowboy. Sculptures with western themes displayed in the Fine Arts Building include those by Gutzon Borglum, Cyrus Edwin Dallin, Kemeys, Proctor, and Warner.

In Chicago, Frederick Jackson Turner presents his address "The Significance of the Frontier in American History," concluding, "And now, four centuries from the discovery of America, at the end

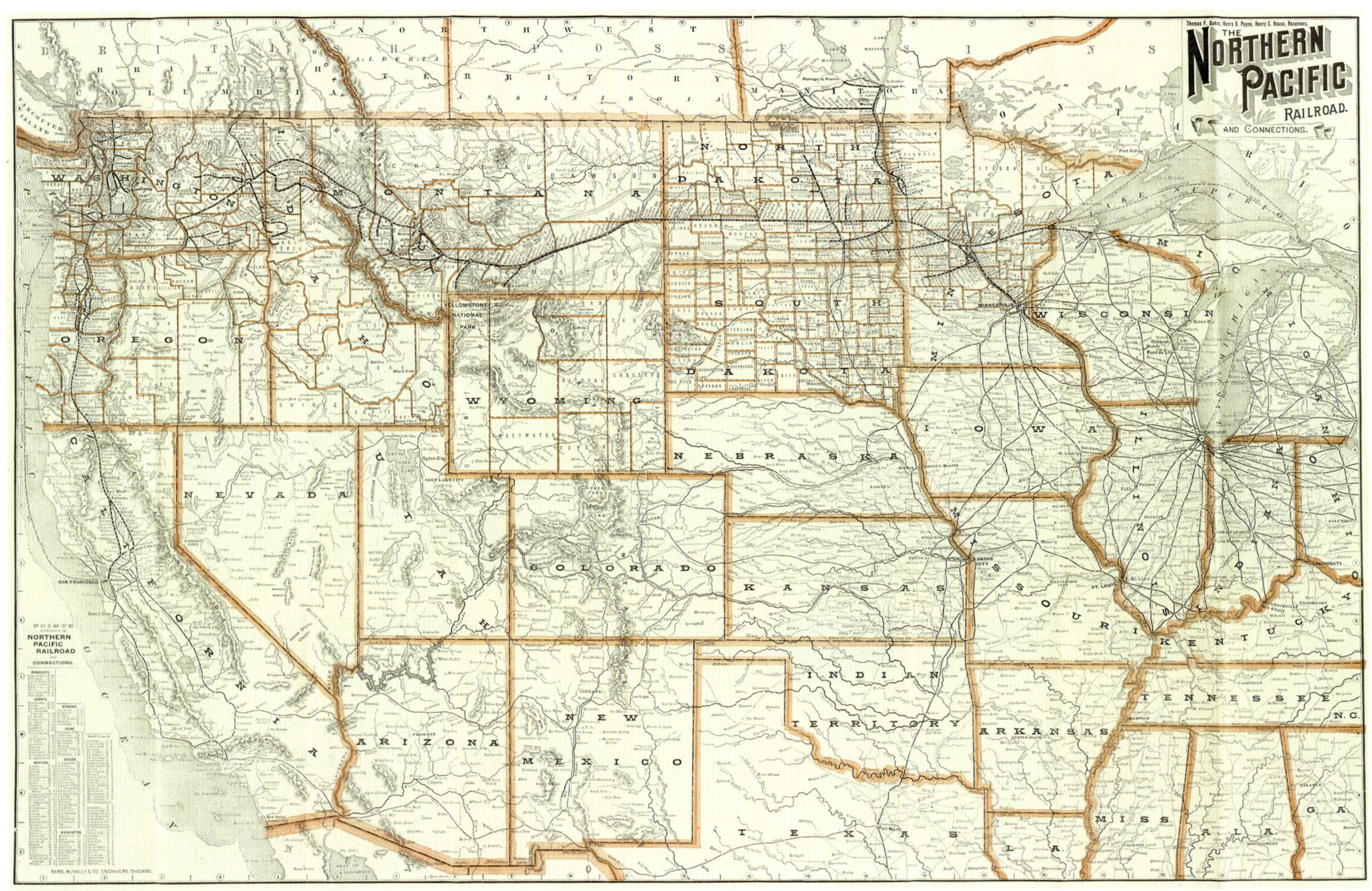

Fig. 180. *The Northern Pacific Railroad and Connections.* Rand McNally and Company, 1893. Denver Public Library

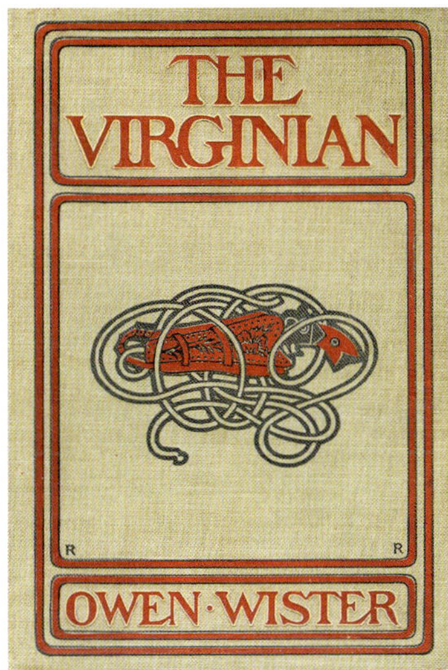

Fig. 181. First edition of *The Virginian*, 1902, by Owen Wister

of a hundred years of life under the Constitution, the frontier has gone, and with its going has closed the first period of American history."

Cherokee land in Kansas and Oklahoma, purchased by the U.S. government in 1891, is opened for settlement.

The Great Northern Railway reaches Seattle, becoming the second northern transcontinental line.

1894

The Yellowstone Game Protection Act to protect wildlife in the park is signed into law by President Grover Cleveland.

Thomas Edison's motion picture studio produces the film shorts *Annie Oakley, Buffalo Dance*, and *Sioux Ghost Dance*, all showing routines from Buffalo Bill's Wild West.

1896

Utah becomes a state.

1898

Spain breaks off diplomatic relations and declares war on the United States; the war lasts eight months. In Cuba, Colonel Roosevelt's leadership of the "Rough Riders"—a cavalry regiment of cowboys and others from the Southwest—increases his popularity and leads to his election as governor of New York.

1899

The New York Zoological Park (later the Bronx Zoo) opens to the public; one of its goals is to preserve native animal species.

1900

The Exposition Universelle takes place in Paris. Sculptures with western themes are exhibited by artists including Solon Hannibal Borglum, Dallin, MacNeil, and Proctor.

Roman Bronze Works in New York, the first American foundry to employ exclusively the lost-wax technique, begins casting bronze statuettes. Remington casts all of his subsequent bronzes with the foundry. Other artists—including Solon Hannibal Borglum, Paul Manship, and Charles M. Russell —cast statuettes there as well.

1901

The Pan-American Exposition opens in Buffalo. Henry Merwin Shrady creates eight monumental versions of his *Bull Moose* and *Buffalo* for the fairgrounds. Other sculptures with western themes are exhibited by Solon Hannibal Borglum, Dallin, Eli Harvey, MacNeil, Proctor, Remington, and Adolph Alexander Weinman.

President William McKinley is assassinated in Buffalo; Vicepresident Roosevelt is sworn in as president.

United States citizenship is granted to the Cherokee, Chickasaw, Choctaw, Creek, and Seminole (the so-called Five Civilized Tribes).

1902

Owen Wister publishes his most famous western novel, *The Virginian* (fig. 181); it introduces the archetype of the strong, silent, justice-seeking cowboy to American literature. The first of four film adaptations is released in 1914, directed by Cecil B. DeMille.

President Roosevelt passes the Newlands Reclamation Act, which authorizes the building of dams in the West.

1903

The Great Train Robbery, a twelve-minute movie directed by Edwin S. Porter, is shot in New Jersey (fig. 182); it is an early milestone in the genre of Westerns.

Jack London publishes *The Call of the Wild*. The novel is set in the Yukon at the time of the Klondike Gold Rush (1896–99), with a sled dog named Buck as its central character. The first printing of ten thousand copies sells out immediately; the book is first adapted to film by D. W. Griffith in 1908.

1904

The Louisiana Purchase Exposition is held in Saint Louis. Solon Hannibal Borglum is commissioned

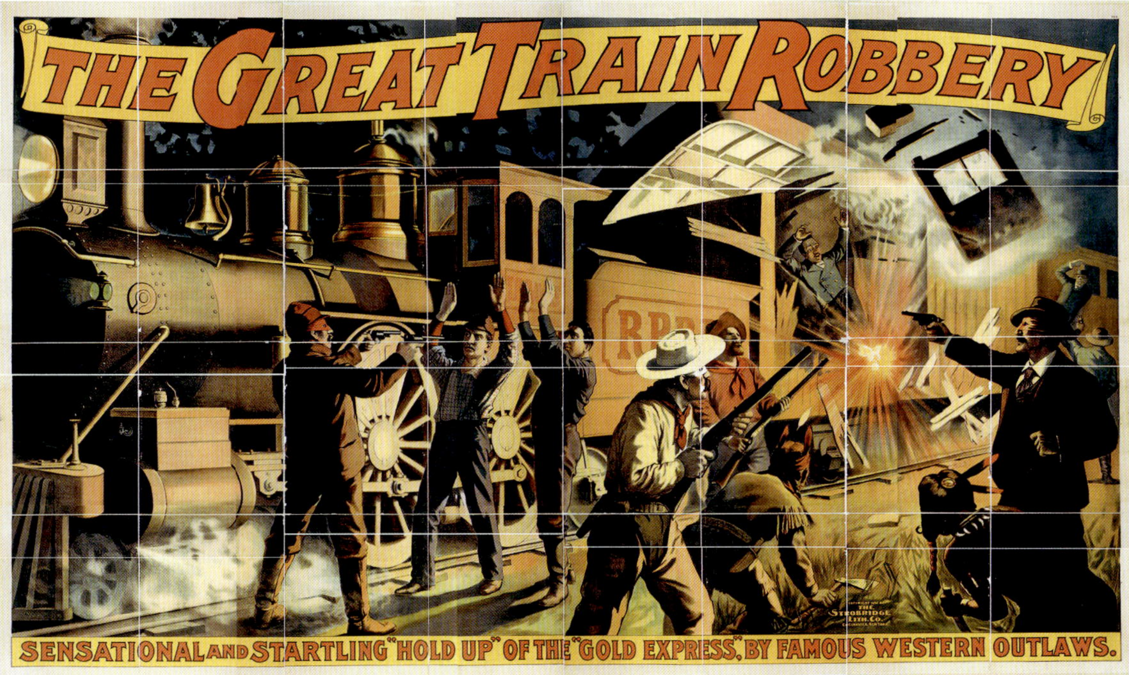

Fig. 182. The Strobridge Lithographing Company. Movie poster for *The Great Train Robbery*, ca. 1903. Color lithograph, 9 ft. 2⅝ in. × 15 ft. 6¼ in. (281 × 473 cm). Prints and Photographs Division, Library of Congress, Washington, D.C.

to create four monumental sculptures of western subjects. Remington's *Coming through the Rye* and Weinman's *Destiny of the Red Man* are shown in enlarged temporary versions. Small groups with western subjects are exhibited by Solon Hannibal Borglum, Dallin, Kemeys, MacNeil, and Proctor.

Roosevelt is elected president after serving out McKinley's term.

Zane Grey publishes *The Spirit of the Border*, a historical novel based on the accounts of frontiersmen and missionaries in the Ohio Valley.

1905

The Lewis and Clark Exposition, a centennial celebration of the Lewis and Clark Expedition, is held in Portland, Oregon.

The National Audubon Society is established to focus on the conservation of America's birds. The American Bison Society is founded in an effort to repopulate herds in western preserves.

1906

April 18: An earthquake and resulting fires level much of San Francisco.

Roosevelt dedicates Devils Tower, Wyoming, as the first national monument.

Representatives for the railroad companies and the National Parks initiate a "See America First" campaign, encouraging visitors to the natural attractions of the American West.

1907

Oklahoma becomes a state.

Fifteen bison from the Bronx Zoo are shipped to a game preserve in Oklahoma (now called the Wichita Mountains Wildlife Refuge) to help repopulate the bison of the western plains.

The first volume of Edward Sheriff Curtis's *North American Indian*, a photographic record of American Indian tribes, is published with financing from J. Pierpont Morgan; the remainder of the twenty volumes will be published at intervals through 1930 (fig. 183).

1908

President Roosevelt declares the Grand Canyon a national monument.

Cowboy songwriter N. Howard "Jack" Thorp publishes *Songs of the Cowboys*, the first collection of traditional cowboy music.

1909

The Alaska-Yukon-Pacific Exposition is held in Seattle; Edwin Willard Deming and Russell exhibit works.

President William Howard Taft sets aside three million acres of public land in the West for conservation.

The U.S. government opens land in Washington, Montana, and Idaho for settlement.

1910

The Mexican Revolution begins; the U.S. government will send troops across the border in 1913 and 1916.

The musicologist and folklorist John A. Lomax publishes the book *Cowboy Songs, and Other Frontier Ballads*, preserving these vernacular compositions for future musicians and scholars.

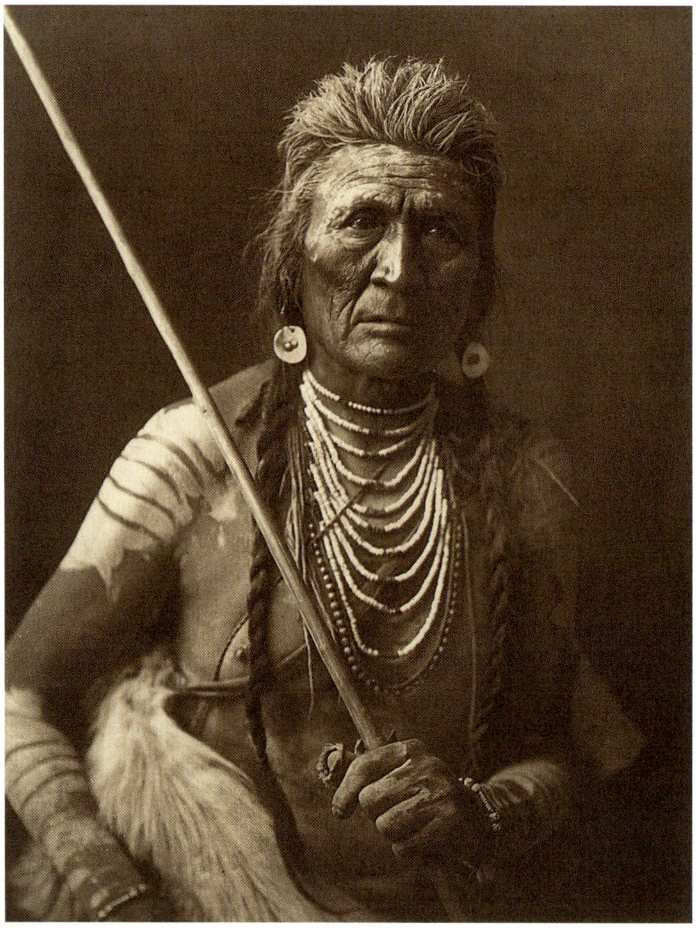

1912

Zane Grey's best-selling novel *Riders of the Purple Sage* is published; set in Utah in 1871, it tells the tale of a young Mormon who breaks away from her community with the assistance of a chivalrous gunslinger.

New Mexico and Arizona become states.

1913

The International Exhibition of Modern Art (the Armory Show) opens in New York; Solon Hannibal Borglum, James Earle Fraser, and Arthur Putnam exhibit sculptures.

Proctor moves his casting enterprise to Gorham Co. Founders, Providence, Rhode Island. This major foundry, with a retail outlet in New York, also casts editions of works by artists including Dallin, Harvey, and Louis McClellan Potter.

Willa Cather publishes *O Pioneers!*, the first novel in a trilogy about frontier life.

1913–14

Striking mine workers in Ludlow, Colorado, are attacked by Colorado Fuel and Iron Company guards and the Colorado National Guard; as many as two hundred lives are lost in the so-called Ludlow Massacre and its aftermath, a ten-day war of retaliation.

1914

July: War breaks out in Europe; the United States maintains neutrality.

The Panama Canal is completed.

1915

The Panama-Pacific International Exposition is held in San Francisco;

Fig. 183. Edward Sheriff Curtis (American, 1868–1952). *Apsaroke, Hidatsa*, from *The North American Indian*, volume 4, 1909. The Metropolitan Museum of Art, Rogers Fund, 1911, transferred from the Library (1976.505.4)

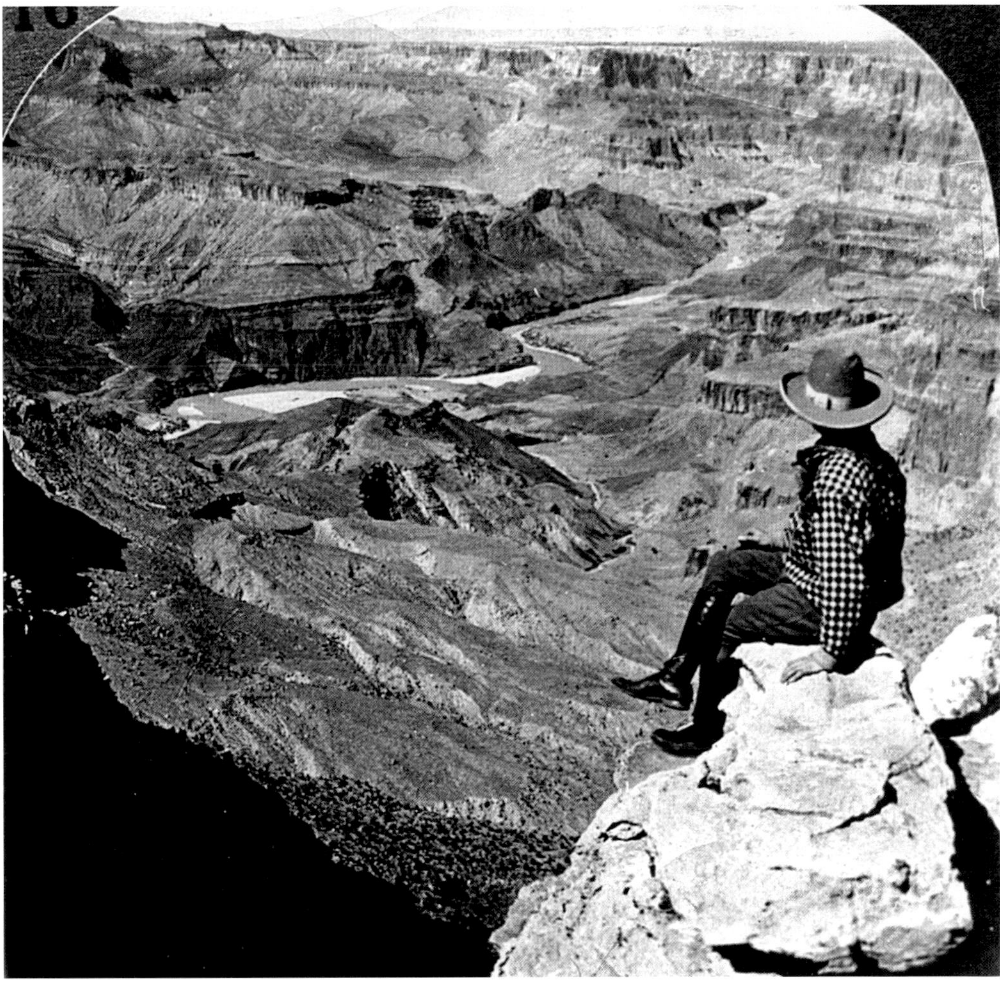

Fig. 184. *The Grand Canyon from Navajo Point, Looking North toward Marble Canyon, Vermillion Cliffs, Painted Desert*, ca. 1920. Detail of photograph by Keystone Stereograph

Fraser's large-scale *End of the Trail* is displayed on the fairgrounds. Sculptures with western themes by Dallin, Deming, Kemeys, Proctor, Putnam, Remington, Warner, and Weinman are also on view.

Rocky Mountain National Park is established in Colorado.

1916

The National Park Service is established.

1917

The United States enters World War I.

Buffalo Bill dies in Denver.

1918

World War I ends.

1919

Grand Canyon National Park is established in Arizona (fig. 184).

1920

Russell travels to Southern California and spends time on the sets of two Westerns, William S. Hart's *Toll Gate* and Tom Mix's *Daredevil*.

Congress passes the Mineral Leasing Act, which authorizes the leasing of federally owned land to commercial mining interests for coal, oil, and gas development.

1923

The Remington Art Memorial (now the Frederic Remington Art Museum) is established in Ogdensburg, New York.

1924

Congress declares all American Indians to be citizens of the United States.

Artists' Biographies

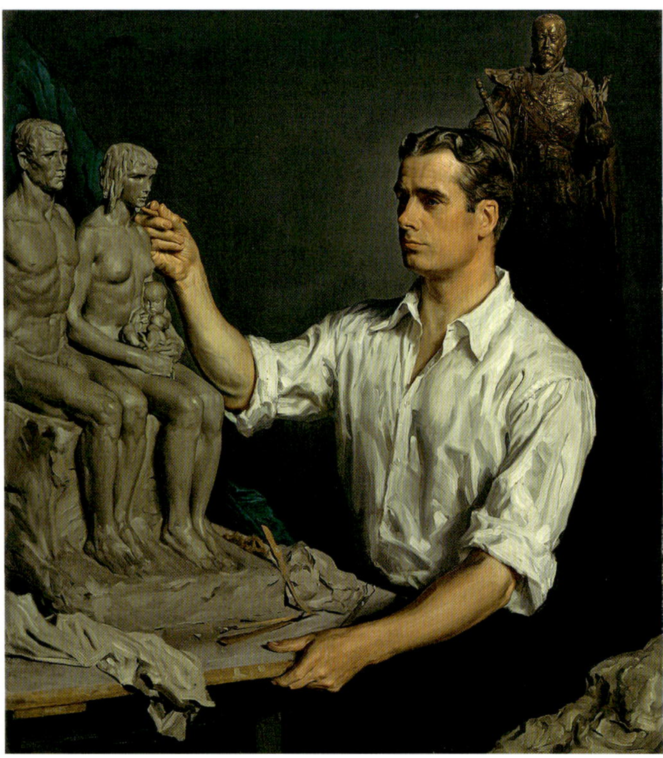

Fig. 185. Sidney Edward Dickinson (American, 1890–1980). *Bryant Baker*, 1925. Oil on canvas, 46 × 40 in. (116.9 × 101.6 cm). National Portrait Gallery, Smithsonian Institution, Washington, D.C., Gift of Bryant Baker

Bryant Baker

(American, born Percy Bryant Baker, London 1881–1970 New York)

Pioneer Woman, 1927. Cat. 1

Born to a long line of craftsmen, Bryant Baker first trained under his father, John Baker, an architectural sculptor who carved elements of Westminster Abbey. Bryant subsequently studied at the City and Guilds Technical Institute in London and graduated from the Royal Academy of Arts in 1913. His early portrait sculpture won the approval of Queen Alexandra and led to several royal commissions. At the outbreak of World War I, Baker attempted to enlist in the British military but was rejected on medical grounds. In 1916 he immigrated to the United States, living in Boston until he moved to Washington, D.C., the next year. He enlisted as a sergeant in the Army Medical Corps, modeling limbs and facial masks. Baker became an American citizen in 1923 and, that same year, received acclaim for a solo exhibition at the Corcoran Gallery of Art in Washington, D.C. He later moved to New York. In 1926, despite having no apparent connection to the American West, he was one of twelve sculptors (including Hermon Atkins MacNeil and James Earle Fraser) invited to submit a design for the Pioneer Woman competition—a campaign to create a monument for Ponca City, Oklahoma, sponsored by the oil magnate E. W. Marland. The models toured across America and were voted on by visitors to each venue. Baker's model won by a resounding margin, and the resulting bronze monument was dedicated in 1930 (fig. 170). Baker received numerous commissions for portrait sculptures of statesmen for public buildings, most notably the U.S. Capitol, the U.S. Supreme Court, and the Georgia State Capitol in Atlanta. Throughout his career, he regularly participated in the annual exhibitions of the Salons in Paris and at the National Academy of Design in New York. Following his death, Ponca City purchased the contents of Baker's New York studio, which it placed on permanent public display in the Bryant Baker Gallery at the Marland Mansion.

REFERENCES

Baker, Bryant. Smithsonian American Art Museum/National Portrait Gallery Library Art and Artists files, Smithsonian Institution, Washington, D.C.

Flambeau, Viktor. "British Sculptor Exhibits in Capital." *Washington Herald*, May 6, 1923, second news section, p. 5.

Parks, Kineton. "An Anglo-American Sculptor: Bryant Baker." *Apollo* 16 (November 1932), pp. 221–30.

Broder, Patricia J. "The Pioneer Woman, Image in Bronze." *American Art Review* 2 (September–October 1975), pp. 127–34.

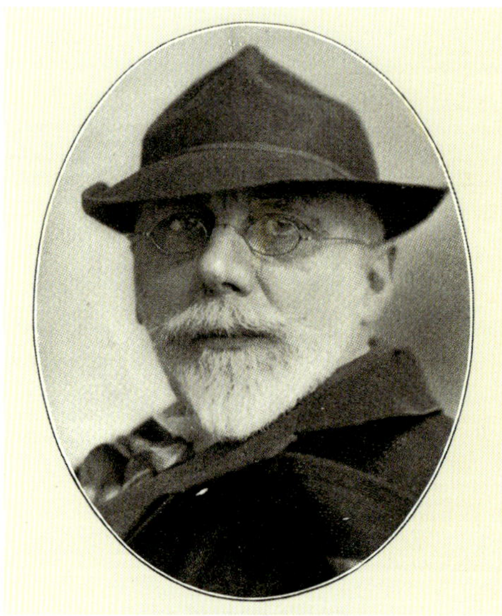

Fig. 186. *Theodore Baur*, ca. 1896. From *Notable New Yorkers of 1896–1899: A Companion Volume to King's Handbook of New York City*

Theodore Baur

(American, Württemberg, Germany 1835–active until 1904 New York)

The Buffalo Hunt, 1876 (cast ca. 1876–86). Cat. 2
Indian Chief, 1885. Cat. 3

A rather enigmatic figure, Baur arrived in New York in 1852 and remained active there until 1904, except for a brief residence in Detroit in about 1891 and trips to Germany in 1896 and 1902. Although the details of his education remain undocumented, he was well established in the art world as a member of the National Academy of Design, founding member of the National Sculpture Society (1893), and regular contributor to exhibitions organized by the Society of American Artists and the Architectural League of New York. Baur participated in several world's fairs, modeling *The Buffalo Hunt* (cat. 2) for the Centennial Exhibition (Philadelphia, 1876); numerous over-lifesize figures and a fantastical sphinx for the World's Columbian Exposition (Chicago, 1893); and a thirty-foot-long frieze for the Building of Mines and Metallurgy at the Louisiana Purchase Exposition (Saint Louis, 1904). Characterized by contemporary critics as a romantic artist, Baur favored narrative and allegorical subjects for both his paintings and his sculpture. His sculptural work ranges from small decorative utilitarian objects, such as doorknobs and bells, to public monuments, including a memorial to Major John André (1880; Tarrytown, New York), *Figure of Patriotism* (dedicated 1882; Augusta, Maine), and a bronze statue of Beethoven and other designs for the Reading Room of the Library of Congress (1896; Washington, D.C.). Baur frequently collaborated with New York decorative firms and architects. A familiar figure in New York's artistic circles, he was a member of the Fellowcraft Club, an art and literary club in Manhattan.

REFERENCES

Montezuma [Montague Marks]. "My Note Book." *Art Amateur* 12 (April 1885), pp. 97–98.

Hartmann, Sadakichi. *A History of American Art.* 2 vols. Boston: L. C. Page and Company, 1901, vol. 2, pp. 64–65.

Caffin, Charles H. *American Masters of Sculpture, Being Brief Appreciations of Some American Sculptors and of Some Phases of Sculpture in America.* New York: Doubleday, Page & Company, 1903, pp. 223–25.

"Sculpture for St. Louis: Baur's Frieze on the Building for Mines at the World's Fair." *New York Times*, June 4, 1903, p. 8.

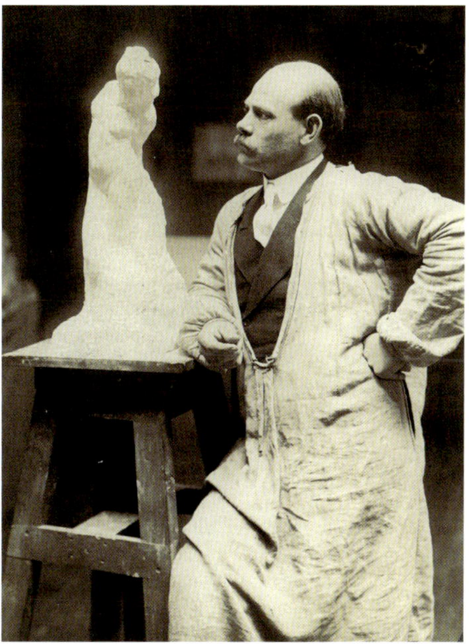

Fig. 187. Jessie Tarbox Beals (American, born Canada, 1870–1942). *Gutzon Borglum Standing Next to Sculpture Model* (detail), ca. 1905–10. Photographic print, 9½ × 7¼ in. (24.1 × 18.4 cm). American Sculpture Photograph Study Collection, Photograph Archives, Smithsonian American Art Museum, Washington, D.C., Gift of Jessie Tarbox Beals

Gutzon Borglum

(American, born John Gutzon de la Mothe Borglum, Bear Lake, Idaho Territory 1867–Chicago 1941)

Fallen Warrior (Death of the Chief), ca. 1891. Cat. 4

Best known as the sculptor of Mount Rushmore (begun 1927; Black Hills, South Dakota), Borglum completed over 180 sculptures and mural paintings during his prolific career. Like his younger brother, Solon, he was steeped in the culture of ranch life at a young age, following their father—a Danish Mormon wood-carver-turned-physician—through Utah, Missouri, Nebraska, and California. In 1884 Gutzon apprenticed for six months with a Los Angeles lithographer before moving to San Francisco to study painting for two years at the San Francisco Art Association. In 1890 he traveled to Paris and studied painting with Jules-Joseph Lefebvre and sculpture with Antonin Mercié at the Académie Julian, while also becoming closely acquainted with Auguste Rodin. Borglum exhibited one of his first sculptures—*Fallen Warrior (Death of the Chief)* (cat. 4)—at the Salon of 1891, earning his election to the Société

Nationale des Beaux-Arts. He subsequently spent a year in Spain before returning to California and settling in Sierra Madre, with Solon, from 1893 to 1896. Gutzon traveled to Europe again in 1896 to paint murals and portraits in England, then returned to the United States permanently in 1901, establishing a studio in New York and, in 1910, a country studio in Stamford, Connecticut. After 1925 he rekindled his connection to the West, setting up an additional studio in San Antonio, Texas. Borglum's reputation as a sculptor was firmly established when he won a gold medal for a group of eighteen works at the Louisiana Purchase Exposition (Saint Louis, 1904). His numerous monumental commissions included twelve stone apostles for the Cathedral Church of Saint John the Divine (1905; New York), a colossal marble head of Abraham Lincoln (1908; U.S. Capitol Rotunda, Washington, D.C.), a bronze equestrian statue of General Philip H. Sheridan (1908; Sheridan Circle, Washington, D.C.), and the *Trail Drivers Memorial* (dedicated 1940; San Antonio, Texas). A founding member of the Association of American Painters and Sculptors, Borglum helped organize the groundbreaking Armory Show (1913). He died abruptly following minor surgery, leaving completion of Mount Rushmore to his son, Lincoln Borglum.

REFERENCES

Borglum, Gutzon, Collection. San Antonio Museum of Art, Texas. Microfilmed for Archives of American Art, Smithsonian Institution, Washington, D.C., microfilm reel 3056.

Borglum, Gutzon, Papers. Manuscript Division, Library of Congress, Washington, D.C.

Mechlin, Leila. "Gutzon Borglum, Painter and Sculptor." *International Studio* 28 (April 1906), pp. xxxv–xliii.

Carter, Robin Borglum. *Gutzon Borglum: His Life and Work.* Austin, Tex.: Eakin Press, 1998.

[Portell, Rosa.] *Out of Rushmore's Shadow: The Artistic Development of Gutzon Borglum (1867–1941).* Exh. cat. Stamford, Conn.: Stamford Museum and Nature Center, 1999.

Taliaferro, John. *Great White Fathers: The Story of the Obsessive Quest to Create Mount Rushmore.* New York: Public Affairs, 2002.

Solon Hannibal Borglum

(American, born Solon Hannibal de la Mothe
Borglum, Ogden, Utah Territory 1868–
1922 Stamford, Connecticut)

Lassoing Wild Horses, 1898
(cast ca. 1900–1902). Cat. 5
On the Border of the White Man's Land, 1899
(cast 1906–7). Cat. 6
Bulls Fighting, 1899–1900 (cast 1906–7). Cat. 7
Blizzard, 1900. Cat. 8
Rough Rider, 1900. Cat. 9
Bucky O'Neill, 1906 (cast ca. 1907). Cat. 10

Solon Hannibal Borglum's lifelong
connection with the West earned him
the sobriquet "Sculptor of the Prairie." The
younger brother of Gutzon Borglum, he
spent his teens working as a ranch hand first
in California and then in Nebraska, where his
family had settled. He showed an aptitude for
sketching and painting animals on the ranch
and, at Gutzon's encouragement, in 1893 he
returned to California to paint. Beginning in
1895, he spent two years at the Art Academy of
Cincinnati. Borglum moved to Paris in 1897 to
attend classes at the Académie Julian, where
he studied with the sculptor Denys Puech;
he later sought out the animalier Emmanuel
Fremiet. Borglum became closely acquainted
with other aspiring American sculptors abroad,
in particular Alexander Phimister Proctor,
whom he met while sketching animals at the
Ménagerie du Jardin des Plantes. Borglum's
memories of the West inspired numerous
small equestrian sculptures that he executed
in Paris, exhibited at the annual Salons, and
sold through the dealer Theodore B. Starr in
New York. He spent the summer of 1899 on
a Sioux reservation in South Dakota, after
which he increasingly incorporated figures
of American Indians into his work. After
winning a silver medal at the Paris Exposition
Universelle (1900), he moved back to the
United States in 1901, establishing a home and
studio in 1906 near Norwalk, Connecticut,
where he became active with the Silvermine
artists' colony. Following World War I,
Borglum founded the School of American
Sculpture in New York and devoted his
attention to teaching. He achieved international
recognition, sending numerous works to
world's fairs in Buffalo (1901), Saint Louis
(1904), and San Francisco (1915). Among his
esteemed public monuments is *Rough Rider
Bucky O'Neill* (1906–7; Prescott, Arizona;
fig. 129), dedicated in 1907.

REFERENCES
Borglum, Solon H., Papers. Manuscript Division,
Library of Congress, Washington, D.C.

Borglum, Solon H., and Borglum Family Papers.
Archives of American Art, Smithsonian Institution,
Washington, D.C., microfilm reels N69–98, 1054.

Goodrich, Arthur. "The Frontier in Sculpture."
World's Work 3 (March 1902), pp. 1857–74.

Sewall, Frank. "A Sculptor of the Prairie: Solon H.
Borglum." *Century Magazine* 68 (June 1904),
pp. 247–51.

Hassrick, Peter H. "Solon Borglum: Poet Sculptor
of the West." In *Shaping the West: American Sculptors
of the 19th Century*, pp. 26–53. Western Passages.
Denver: Petrie Institute of Western American Art,
Denver Art Museum, 2010.

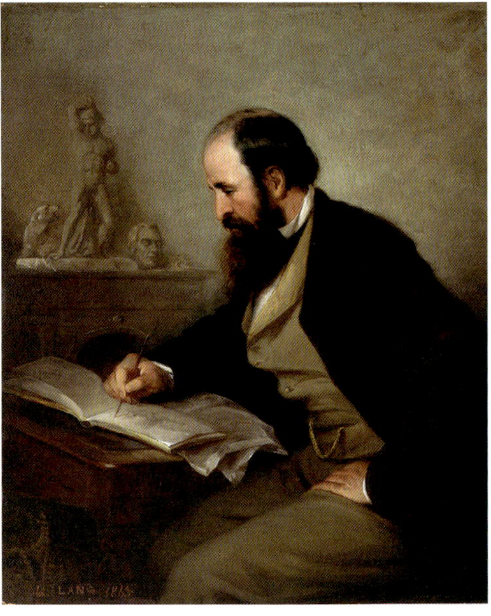

Fig. 189. Louis Lang (German, 1814–1893). *Henry Kirke
Brown*, 1863. Oil on board, 15¾ × 13 in. (40 × 33 cm).
National Portrait Gallery, Smithsonian Institution,
Washington, D.C.

Henry Kirke Brown

(American, Leyden, Massachusetts 1814–1886
Balmville, New York)

Choosing of the Arrow, 1849. Cat. 11
Panther and Cubs, ca. 1850–55. Cats. 12, 13

Brown was one of the first sculptors to
cast bronze successfully in the United
States and among the earliest to represent the
American Indian in sculpture. Raised on a farm
in rural Massachusetts, he studied painting
in Boston in 1832 with the portraitist Chester
Harding. Brown began sculpting between 1836
and 1839 while living in Cincinnati, a thriving

Fig. 188. Gertrude
Käsebier (American,
1852–1934). *Solon
Borglum*, ca. 1902.
Glass-plate negative,
8 × 10 in. (20.3 ×
25.4 cm). Prints
and Photographs
Division, Library
of Congress,
Washington, D.C.,
Gift, Mina Turner,
1964

arts center, supporting himself through seasonal work as a surveyor mapping the rugged Ohio frontier for the Illinois Central Railroad. In the early 1840s he traveled through upstate New York as an itinerant portrait sculptor before moving to Italy in 1842. After living in Florence and Rome for four years, Brown returned to the United States, determined to cultivate broader support for sculpture. He settled in New York and forged close ties to the leading cultural figures William Cullen Bryant and Asher Brown Durand. In his effort to reach a wide popular audience, Brown worked in a realist style, favoring subjects that were regarded as nationally significant and uniquely American. In 1848 he established a studio and rudimentary foundry in Brooklyn, where he produced limited editions of highly refined bronze statuettes for the American Art-Union, including *Choosing of the Arrow* (cat. 11), which was based on his 1848 studies of American Indians on Mackinac Island, Michigan. His pioneering efforts—especially evident in the monuments he cast in collaboration with Ames Manufacturing Company, a firearms factory in Chicopee, Massachusetts (*De Witt Clinton*, 1853, Green-Wood Cemetery, Brooklyn; and *George Washington*, 1856, Union Square, New York)—helped establish the art bronze industry in the United States and paved the way for future generations of American artists to cast sculptures domestically. Brown served on the first National Art Commission (1859; Washington, D.C.) and was instrumental in establishing National Statuary Hall in the U.S. Capitol. His protégé John Quincy Adams Ward shared his abiding interest in American Indian subjects.

REFERENCES

Brown, Henry Kirke, Papers. Archives of American Art, Smithsonian Institution, Washington, D.C., microfilm reels 2770, 2771.

Bush-Brown, Henry Kirke, Papers. Manuscript Division, Library of Congress, Washington, D.C.

Craven, Wayne. "Henry Kirke Brown: His Search for an American Art in the 1840's." *American Art Journal* 4, no. 2 (November 1972), pp. 44–58.

Lemmey, Karen. "Henry Kirke Brown and the Development of American Public Sculpture in New York City, 1846–1876." Ph.D. diss., City University of New York, 2005.

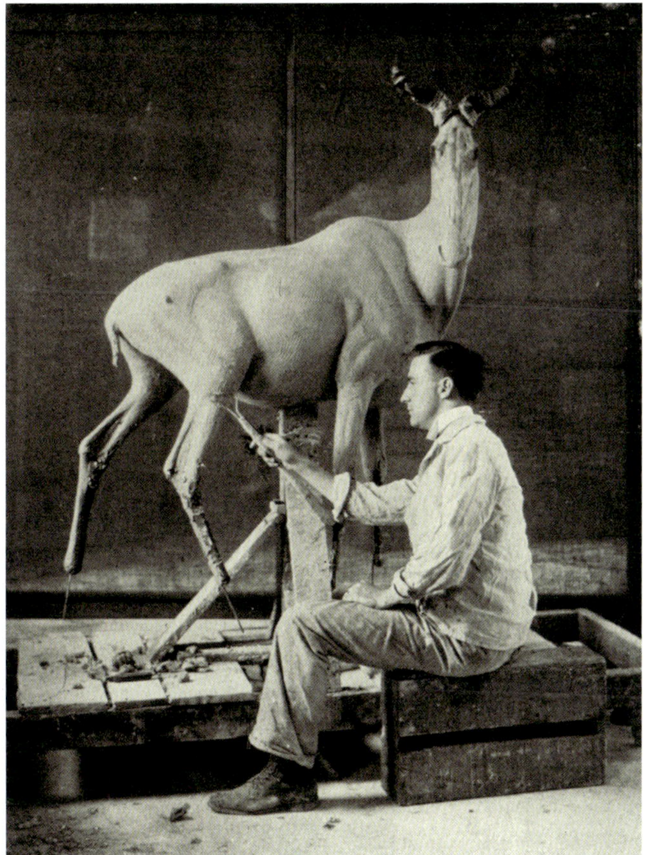

Fig. 190. *James L. Clark at Work in His Studio* (detail), 1910. From Frank Owen Payne, "Noted American Sculptors at Work," *Art and Archaeology*, March 1926

James L. Clark

(American, born James Lippitt Clark, Providence, Rhode Island 1883–1969 New York)

Alaskan Kodiak Bear, 1904. Cat. 14

An accomplished big-game hunter, taxidermist, and sculptor, Clark created numerous animal displays for the American Museum of Natural History (AMNH) in New York across a five-decade career that closed with his retirement in 1949. At age fifteen he began a three-year apprenticeship at the Gorham Co. Founders in Providence, where he observed fundamental modeling and casting techniques while attending weekly evening classes at the Rhode Island School of Design. In 1902, at age eighteen, Clark was hired by the AMNH to sculpt the lifesize animal figures that taxidermists would use to support skins in museum displays. He relied on visits to the Central Park and Bronx zoos to study animals. Under the auspices of the AMNH, he spent three months at the Field Museum in Chicago, learning Carl Akeley's innovative taxidermy methods of preparing figures in lifelike poses and incorporating the skeletons, skins, and horns of captured animals. In 1907 Clark made his first specimen-gathering expedition for the AMNH to Yellowstone National Park and afterward led numerous expeditions not only to the American West but also to Africa and Central Asia, where he and his wife hunted wildlife for museum habitat displays. In addition to this work, in 1910 Clark opened a sculpture and taxidermy studio in the Bronx; there, over the next three decades, he employed as many as twenty craftsmen at a time, producing numerous small bronze sculptures of animals that he sold through New York art galleries. In the 1920s Clark served as vice-president of the Akeley Camera Company, which made movies as well as motion-picture cameras. Elected to the National Sculpture Society in 1932, he was also an active member of the Campfire Club and the Explorers Club, through which he became acquainted with William F. "Buffalo Bill" Cody and other iconic figures of the American West.

REFERENCES

Clark, James L. *Trails of the Hunted*. Boston: Little, Brown, and Company, 1928.

———. *The James L. Clark Studios*. New York: James L. Clark Studios, 1931.

———. *Good Hunting: Fifty Years of Collecting and Preparing Habitat Groups for the American Museum*. Norman: University of Oklahoma Press, 1966.

———. *The Bronzes of James L. Clark*. New York: Hunting World, 1967.

Harris, Adam Duncan. *Wildlife in American Art: Masterworks from the National Museum of Wildlife Art*. Norman: University of Oklahoma Press, 2009, pp. 137–39.

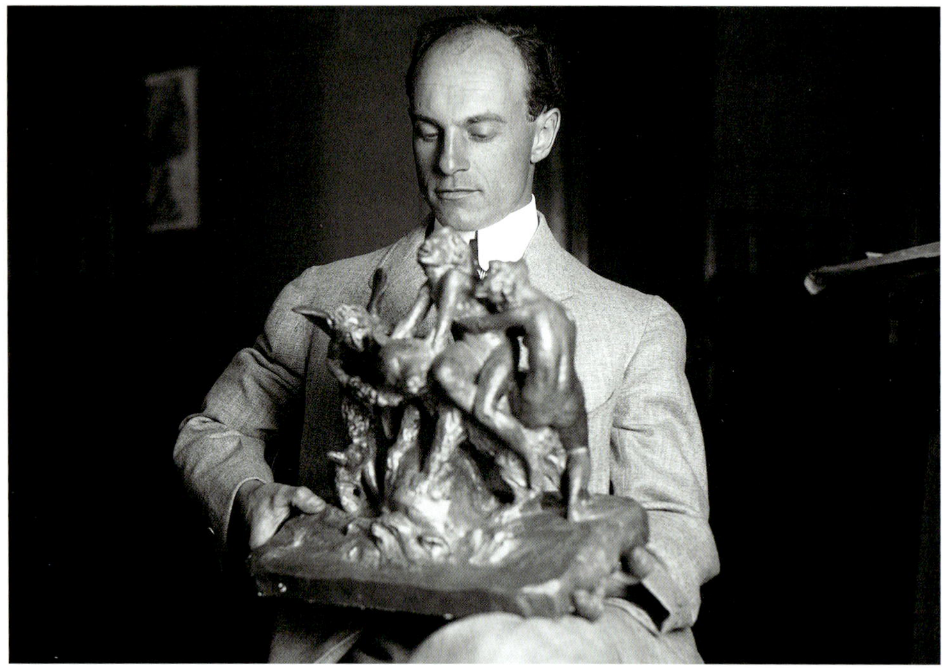

Fig. 191. *Charles Cristadoro Holding One of His Sculptures,* ca. 1912. Glass-plate negative, 5 × 7 in. (12.7 × 17.8 cm). San Diego History Center, California

Charles Cristadoro

(American, born Charles Clarence Cristadoro, New York 1881–1967 San Dimas, California)

Two Gun Bill (William S. Hart), 1917 (cast 1925 or after). Cat. 15

Cristadoro was a California artist with close ties to the Hollywood entertainment industry and an eclectic range of experience, from inventor to puppet maker. He developed an interest in sculpture at age twelve, while working at the World's Columbian Exposition (Chicago, 1893). In about 1903 he enrolled in painting classes at the New York School of Art, studying with Robert Henri and the school's founder, William Merritt Chase. Cristadoro subsequently studied at the Art Academy of Cincinnati, possibly with the sculptor Clement Barnhorn. Cristadoro excelled at direct carving, especially in miniature, cutting figures from ivory billiard balls and bone. In 1908 he moved to San Diego, where he completed two figural relief groups in tinted plaster for the interior of the Spreckels Theatre (ca. 1912). At the Panama-Pacific International Exposition (San Francisco, 1915), he oversaw a sculpture production studio and won a bronze medal for *Tower of Jewels,* a monumental temporary sculpture. In 1928 Cristadoro moved to Los Angeles, where, during the 1930s, he made puppets for the WPA Federal Theatre Project and created animated models and special effects for films, including *King Kong* (1933). On several occasions between 1938 and 1953, he worked for Walt Disney Production's Character Development Department, sculpting models for animation characters, including Pinocchio, Dumbo, and Bambi. Cristadoro's only monumental work was *The Range Rider of the Yellowstone* (1927; Billings, Montana; fig. 145), depicting the actor William S. Hart standing beside his horse. Cristadoro was active in a number of California art organizations, serving on the board of directors of the San Diego Fine Arts Society (1925) and as president of the San Diego Art Guild (1926–27); he also taught at the Art Students League of Los Angeles.

REFERENCES

"A Famous Carver of Miniatures." *Dallas Morning News,* November 7, 1921, p. 7.

Kamerling, Bruce. "Early Sculpture and Sculptors in San Diego." *Journal of San Diego History* 35, no. 3 (Summer 1989), pp. 174–78.

Hughes, Edan Milton. *Artists in California, 1786–1940.* 3rd ed. 2 vols. 1986. Sacramento, Calif.: Crocker Art Museum, 2002, vol. 2, p. 258.

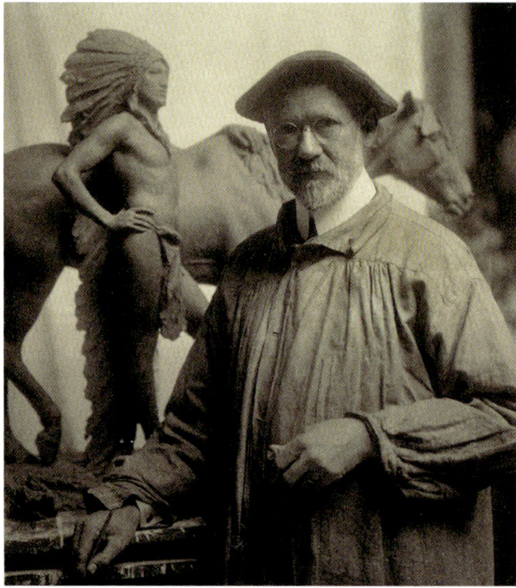

Fig. 192. Alice Austin (American, 1859–1933). *Cyrus Edwin Dallin* (detail), ca. 1914. Platinum print, 7⅞ × 5⅞ in. (20 × 14.9 cm). Museum of Fine Arts, Boston, Gift of Miss Leonora Austin

Cyrus Edwin Dallin

(American, Springville, Utah Territory 1861–1944 Arlington Heights, Massachusetts)

Medicine Man, 1899 (cast ca. 1899). Cat. 16
Appeal to the Great Spirit, 1912 (cast ca. 1922). Cat. 17
Appeal to the Great Spirit, 1913 (cast ca. 1916). Cat. 18

Dallin grew up in close contact with the Ute and Paiute peoples of Utah, yet the sculptures for which he is best remembered portray Indians of the Great Plains. The son of English pioneers, he was raised in a log cabin and worked in his father's silver mine, modeling sculptures with clay taken from there. In 1879 his clay portraits impressed two visitors to a fair in Salt Lake City, who then sponsored his journey to Boston to apprentice for one year with the sculptor Truman Bartlett. Dallin subsequently spent almost two years collaborating on funerary statues with Sidney Morse in Quincy, Massachusetts, before establishing his own studio in Boston. After winning several prizes and commissions, including a gold medal for *Indian Hunter* at the American Art Association's exhibition in New York in 1888, Dallin sought further training in Paris and enrolled later that year at the Académie Julian, studying under sculptor Henri-Michel-Antoine Chapu. In 1889 Dallin declined a coveted invitation to enroll at the

École des Beaux-Arts, choosing instead to settle in Arlington Heights, Massachusetts. His interest in American Indians had been rekindled by a performance of Buffalo Bill's troupe in the Bois de Boulogne, after which he sculpted *The Signal of Peace* (1894; Lincoln Park, Chicago), which won an honorable mention when displayed in plaster at the Salon of 1890 and a first-class medal when shown as a monumental bronze at the World's Columbian Exposition (Chicago, 1893). He returned to Paris in 1896–99 to study with the Art Nouveau sculptor Jean-Auguste Dampt. Dallin won a silver medal at the Exposition Universelle (Paris, 1900) and gold medals at the Louisiana Purchase Exposition (Saint Louis, 1904), the Salon of 1909 (*Appeal to the Great Spirit*), and the Panama-Pacific International Exposition (San Francisco, 1915). In addition to his depictions of Indians—among them, a monumental version of *Appeal to the Great Spirit* in front of the Museum of Fine Arts, Boston (fig. 29)—Dallin sculpted public statues of Paul Revere (begun 1884; North End, Boston) and Isaac Newton (1895; Library of Congress, Washington, D.C.). An accomplished longbow archer, he was a National Archery Champion (1915) and president of the National Archery Society (1919).

REFERENCES
Dallin, Cyrus Edwin, Papers. Dallin family and Robbins Memorial Library, Arlington, Massachusetts. Microfilmed for Archives of American Art, Smithsonian Institution, Washington, D.C., microfilm reels 141, 178–84.

Downes, William Howe. "Cyrus E. Dallin, Sculptor." *Brush and Pencil* 5 (October 1899), pp. 2–18.

———. "Mr. Dallin's Indian Sculptures." *Scribner's Magazine* 57 (June 1915), pp. 779–82.

Ewers, John C. "Cyrus E. Dallin: Master Sculptor of the Plains Indians." *Montana: The Magazine of Western History* 18 (Winter 1968), pp. 34–43.

Francis, Rell G. *Cyrus E. Dallin: Let Justice Be Done.* Springville, Utah: Springville Museum of Art, 1976.

Ahrens, Kent, and Fred Licht. *Cyrus E. Dallin, His Small Bronzes and Plasters.* Exh. cat. Corning, N.Y.: Rockwell Museum, 1995.

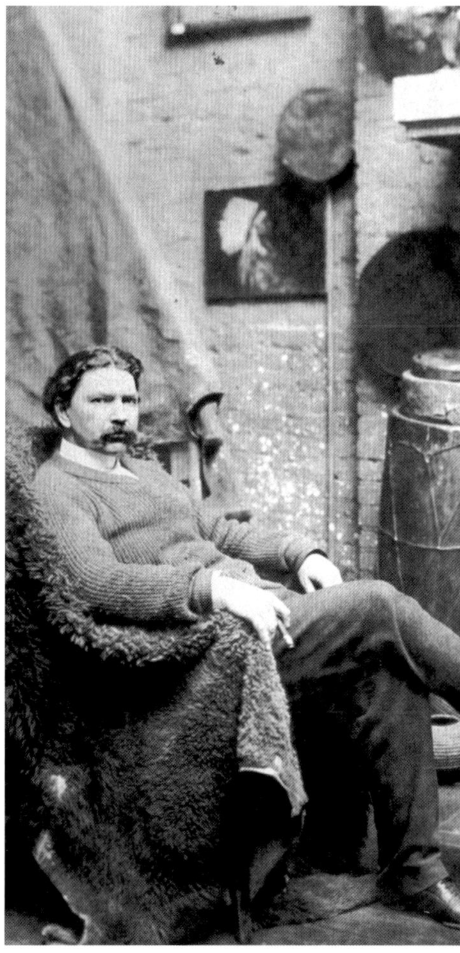

Fig. 193. Jessie Tarbox Beals (American, born Canada, 1870–1942). *Portrait of American Painter and Sculptor Edwin Willard Deming* (detail), ca. 1908–18. Gelatin silver print, 10 × 8 in. (25.4 × 20.3 cm). Schlesinger Library on the History of Women in America, Radcliffe Institute, Harvard University, Cambridge, Massachusetts

Edwin Willard Deming

(American, Ashland, Ohio 1860–1942 New York)

The Fight, ca. 1906. Cat. 19

Best known as a painter and illustrator of Indian subjects, Deming also created close to forty small bronzes, primarily of animals and American Indians. He grew up on the western Illinois frontier, among the neighboring Sac and Fox people, and was hunting big game by his teen years. He made his first artworks as a youth, using house paint and clay dug from the banks of the Mississippi. After briefly studying business law in Chicago in 1880, Deming enrolled at the Art Students League, New York, in January 1883. By October he had moved to Paris to study painting at the Académie Julian. He returned to New York in June 1885 and moved to Macdougal Alley, filling his studio with Indian artifacts and big-game pelts that he collected on regular summer trips west. He made several extended visits in the late 1880s to live among the Apache, Pueblo, Umatilla, Sioux, Crow, and other Indian nations, observing their customs in order to create "a pictorial preservation of the life of the old, unspoiled Indian." Made an honorary member of the Blackfoot in 1898, Deming was given the name Eight Bears, an allusion to his wife and six children, who often accompanied him. In World War I he became a captain in the U.S. Army, serving as a marksman instructor and camouflage painter. After the war he spent seven months traveling through Mesoamerica and South America. He collaborated with his wife, Therese, on several books about their travels, including *Red Folk and Wild Folk* (1902) and *American Animal Life* (1916). Deming's most significant commission was a set of murals depicting the principal Indian nations for the American Museum of Natural History in New York (1914–16). He also sold numerous small paintings of Indian life. His sculptures, most of which were modeled between 1905 and 1910, were exhibited widely in his lifetime, including at the Alaska-Yukon-Pacific Exposition (Seattle, 1909) and the Panama-Pacific International Exposition (San Francisco, 1915).

REFERENCES
Deming, Edwin Willard, Papers, 1880–1931. Manuscripts and Archives Division, New York Public Library.

Deming, Edwin, Papers. Special Collections and University Archives, University of Oregon Libraries, Eugene.

Deming, E[dwin] W[illard]. "The Indian—A Subject for Art." *American Museum Journal* 13 (March 1913), pp. 103–11.

Deming, Therese O., comp.; Henry Collins Walsh, ed. *Edwin Willard Deming.* New York: Riverside Press, 1925.

Frink, Maurice. "Edwin W. Deming: 'That Man, He Paint!'" *American Scene* 12, no. 3 (1971), n.p.

Lamb, Thomas G. *Eight Bears: A Biography of E. W. Deming, 1860–1942.* Oklahoma City: Griffin Books, 1978.

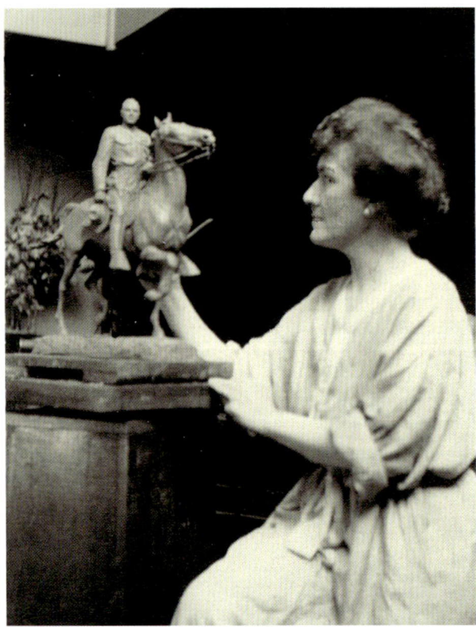

Fig. 194. *Farnham and Her Equestrian Statuette, "Colonel William Hayward, 15th Infantry"* (detail), 1918. Photographic print, 5¾ × 3½ in. (14.5 × 9 cm). John and Erika McMahon

Sally James Farnham

(American, born Sarah Welles James, Ogdensburg, New York 1869–1943 Great Neck, New York)

Will Rogers, 1936 (cast 1938). Cat. 20

Among the first women to compete successfully for national sculpture commissions, Farnham completed dozens of public monuments during her forty-year career. She had no formal training but was exposed to art at a young age while traveling through Europe and Japan with her father, a U.S. Army colonel. Farnham first began modeling in clay in 1901, at age thirty-two, as a diversion suggested by her husband, George Paulding Farnham (a jewelry designer for Tiffany & Co.), during her recovery from a long illness. Demonstrating an aptitude for modeling, she received encouragement and guidance from her close friend Frederic Remington (also a native of Ogdensburg), as well as from other sculptors, including Henry Merwin Shrady. By 1905 Farnham had achieved critical and public success with her monumental *Spirit of Liberty*, *Soldiers Memorial* (Bloomfield, New Jersey). While raising three children and undergoing a divorce (in 1915), Farnham maintained studios in New York and Great Neck, Long Island, where she executed works that ranged

from probing portraits of prominent cultural, political, and society figures to allegorical groups and war memorials. Beginning in the early 1900s, she made several long excursions to the West, especially to the Farnham family ranch in the mountains of British Columbia. In 1923 Farnham traveled to Los Angeles and won a commission for a monument for the nearby San Fernando Mission, for which she created a bronze group depicting the missionary Father Junipero Serra protectively embracing an American Indian boy (dedicated 1925). An avid and accomplished rider, Farnham was particularly skilled at depicting horses, and she paid homage to Remington with several compositions of broncos and cowboys, including *Cowboy Fun* (1905; fig. 138), *Sunfisher* (1925; Buffalo Bill Center of the West, Cody, Wyoming), and *Payday* (1930; Woolaroc Museum, Bartlesville, Oklahoma). Among her most ambitious public sculptures is *Simon Bolívar* (commissioned by the Venezuelan government for Central Park, New York, and dedicated in 1921).

REFERENCES

Barry, Kathleen Eileen. "An American Woman's Sculpture." *New York Herald*, September 24, 1905, p. 8.

McFarland, George F. "Sally James Farnham: The Remington Years." *St. Lawrence County Historical Association Quarterly* 36 (Summer 1991), pp. 3–11, 26–28.

Hassrick, Peter H. *The Art of Being an Artist: Sally James Farnham, American Sculptor*. Ogdensburg, N.Y.: Frederic Remington Art Museum, 2005.

James Earle Fraser

(American, Winona, Minnesota 1876–1953 Westport, Connecticut)

End of the Trail, 1918 (cast 1918). Cat. 21

A versatile and prolific artist, Fraser made sculptures that range from designs for the Indian head and buffalo nickel (minted 1913–38; fig. 12) to a sixty-five-foot-tall statue of George Washington at the 1939 New York World's Fair. Fraser spent much of his youth

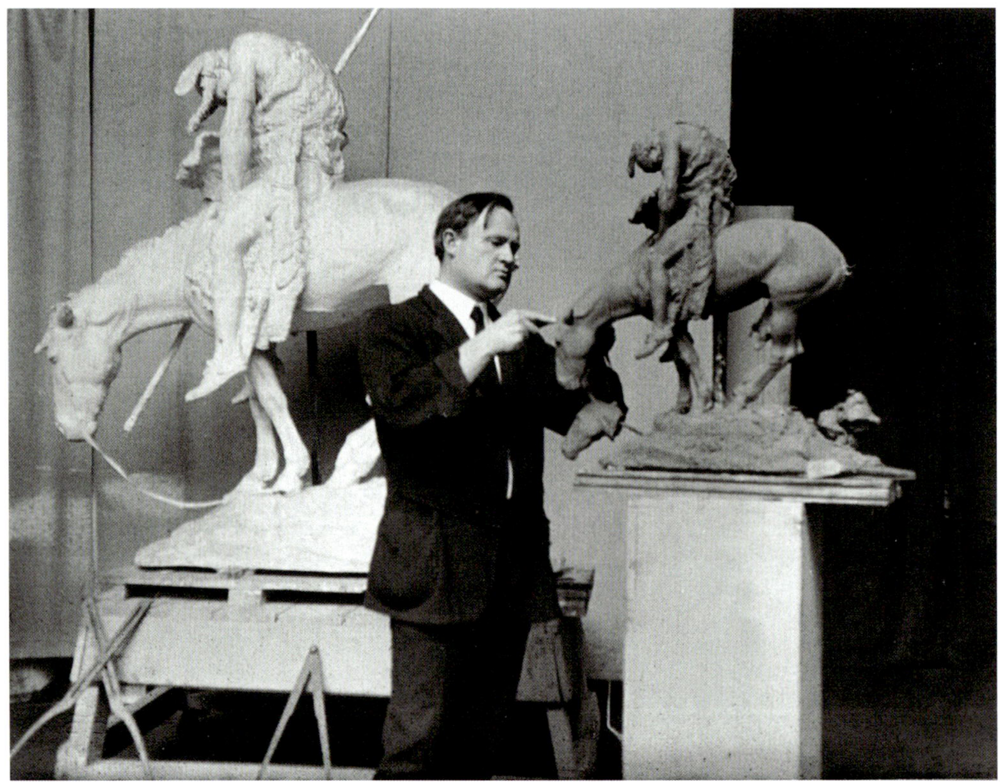

Fig. 195. *James Earle Fraser in His Studio with a Clay Maquette of the "End of the Trail" Sculpture*, ca. 1910. Silver nitrate photograph, 4⅞ × 6¼ in. (12.4 × 15.8 cm). James Earle and Laura Gardin Fraser Papers, Special Collections Research Center, Syracuse University Libraries, New York

on his family's ranch in Dakota Territory and later attended school in Minneapolis. After his family moved to Chicago in about 1890, Fraser apprenticed in the studio of sculptor Richard W. Bock and attended evening classes at the Art Institute of Chicago. Fraser went to Paris in 1896, studying at the Académie Colarossi before entering the École des Beaux-Arts in the atelier of Jean-Alexandre-Joseph Falguière. In Paris, Fraser exhibited at the Salon of 1898 and at the American Art Association, earning praise from Augustus Saint-Gaudens, who eventually made him chief assistant in his Paris and Cornish, New Hampshire, studios. In 1902 Fraser established his own studio in New York on Macdougal Alley, building a national reputation as portraitist, medalist, and sculptor of monuments. His early exposure to the frontier remained a strong influence, leading him to include figures of American Indians in several compositions, such as the large equestrian *Cherokee Indian* (Louisiana Purchase Exposition, Saint Louis, 1904) and the iconic *End of the Trail*, a twice-lifesize sculpture that won a gold medal at the Panama-Pacific International Exposition (San Francisco, 1915; fig. 13). Despite his role as a founding member of the Association of American Painters and Sculptors, which organized the landmark Armory Show (1913), Fraser never diverged from a naturalistic Beaux-Arts style. He is credited with creating more public monuments for Washington, D.C., than any other artist.

REFERENCES
Fraser, James Earle, and Laura Gardin Papers. Special Collections Research Center, Syracuse University Libraries, New York

Fraser, James Earle, and Laura Gardin Papers. Originals privately owned. Microfilmed for Archives of American Art, Smithsonian Institution, Washington, D.C., microfilm reels 2548–49.

Krakel, Dean. *End of the Trail: The Odyssey of a Statue.* Norman: University of Oklahoma Press, 1973.

Freundlich, A[ugust] L. *The Sculpture of James Earle Fraser.* [Parkland, Fla.]: Universal Publishers, 2001.

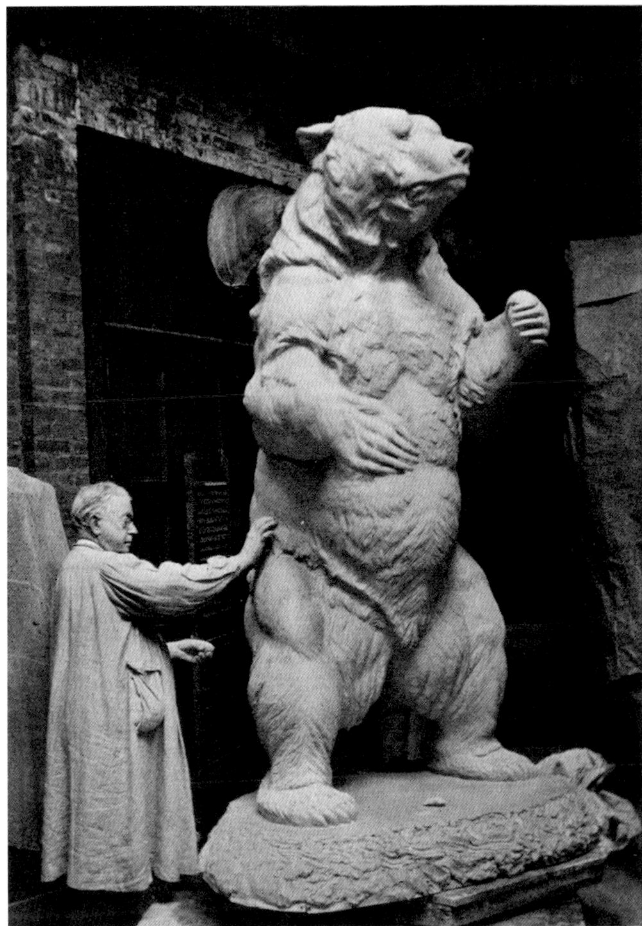

Fig. 196. *Eli Harvey Sculpting Alaskan Brown Bear,* ca. 1923. From *Sculpture by Eli Harvey* (Pawleys Island, S.C.: Brookgreen Gardens, 1937)

Eli Harvey

(American, Ogden, Ohio 1860–1957 Alhambra, California)

Bull Elk, 1904 (cast probably 1905). Cat. 22

Born to a family of Quaker farmers, Harvey sold crayon portraits to pay for his education at the McMicken School of Design (later the Art Academy of Cincinnati), where he enrolled in 1882 and spent seven years studying under Thomas S. Noble and Louis T. Rebisso. In 1889 he moved to Paris and studied drawing and painting first at the Académie Julian—with Jean-Joseph-Benjamin Constant, Jules-Joseph Lefebvre, and Lucien Doucet—and then at the Académie Delecluse. He remained in Paris for twelve years, regularly exhibiting his paintings at the Salon between 1895 and 1900. He became closely acquainted with the painter Jean-Léon Gérôme and the premier animalier Emmanuel Fremiet, from whom Harvey learned to model animals at the Ménagerie du Jardin des Plantes. After 1899 he increasingly focused on animals, which he studied exclusively in captivity and rendered with anatomical exactitude. In 1901 he won a large commission for freestanding and relief marble figures for the Lion House at the New York Zoological Park (completed 1903; Bronx Zoo) and established a studio in Greenwich Village. Harvey is best remembered for two iconic mascots: *Bull Elk* (cat. 22) for the Benevolent and Protective Order of Elks and *Brown Bear* (1923) for Brown University. His work won bronze medals at several world's fairs, including the Pan-American Exposition (Buffalo, 1901), the Louisiana Purchase Exposition (Saint Louis, 1904), and the Panama-Pacific International Exposition (San Francisco, 1915). Harvey's smaller sculptures and two-dimensional works were shown in a solo exhibition in 1912 at the New York showroom of Theodore B. Starr, a commercial dealer and jeweler. After Harvey relocated to California in 1929, his artistic production diminished considerably, but he continued to exhibit his sculptures, including at a large solo exhibition in 1930 at the Los Angeles County Museum of History, Science, and Art.

REFERENCES
McIntyre, R. G. "Eli Harvey—Sculptor." *Arts and Decoration* 3 (December 1912), pp. 58–59, 74.

Lamont, Jessie. "Impressions in the Studio of an Animal Sculptor." *International Studio* 51 (November 1913), pp. cvi–cviii, supp.

Bicker, Dorothy Z., Jane Z. Vail, and Vernon G. Wills, eds. *The Autobiography of Eli Harvey, Quaker Sculptor from Ohio.* 2nd ed. Wilmington, Ohio: Clinton County Historical Society, 1966.

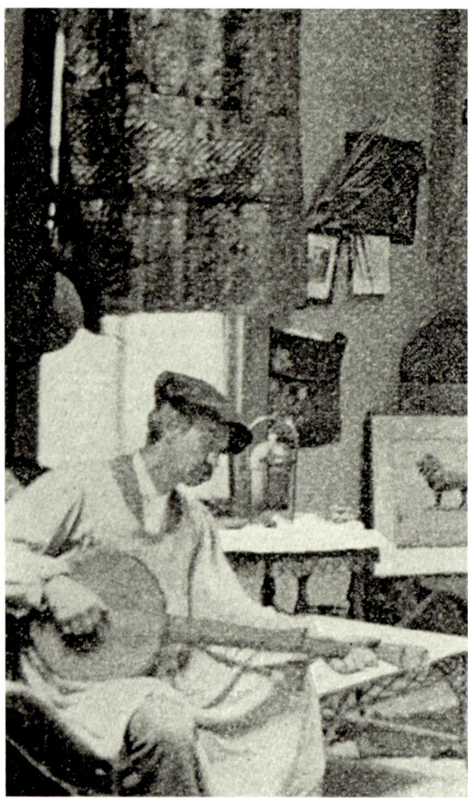

Fig. 197. *Kemeys at Home* (detail), ca. 1895. From Hamlin Garland, "Edward Kemeys: A Sculptor of Frontier Life and Wild Animals," *McClure's Magazine*, July 1895

Edward Kemeys

(American, Savannah, Georgia 1843–1907 Washington, D.C.)

Buffalo and Wolves, 1876 (cast probably 1878 or 1879). Cat. 23
The Soul of Contentment (Black Bear), 1886 (cast ca. 1886–99). Cat. 24
Still Hunt, 1894. Cat. 25

Kemeys, America's first sculptor devoted principally to animal subjects, was self-trained. Raised in New York, he spent several summers in the mid-1850s on a relative's farm on the Illinois prairie, where he developed an abiding interest in wildlife. During the Civil War he served as a captain in the Union Army and, beginning in 1868, worked with laborers building New York's Central Park. Kemeys began sculpting after watching an artist make wax studies of animals in the park's menagerie. He soon shunned the study of captive animals and—with the earnings from his first major commission, *Hudson Bay Wolves Quarreling over the Carcass of a Deer* (1872), a bronze

monument for Philadelphia's Fairmount Park (now in the Philadelphia Zoo)—Kemeys took his first of many trips to the western plains and the Rockies to hunt and study wildlife. He exhibited three sculptures at the Centennial Exhibition (Philadelphia, 1876). The following year he traveled to London, where he held a solo exhibition, and then to Paris, where he exhibited the plaster model of *Buffalo and Wolves* (cat. 23) at the Salon of 1878. Although he admired the work of Antoine-Louis Barye, Kemeys departed from the French *animalier* tradition by focusing on North American mammals. In 1878 he returned to New York and established a studio where he executed numerous outdoor sculptures, including *Still Hunt* (1881–83)—a lifesize depiction in bronze of a panther poised to pounce from a rocky outcropping in Central Park (fig. 76). In 1892 Kemeys moved to Chicago, where he remained for eight years, executing high-relief bronze panels with portraits of Indian chiefs and French explorers for the Marquette Building (1894); figures of grizzly bears, panthers, and bison for the grounds of the World's Columbian Exposition (1893; fig. 79); and a pair of standing bronze lions for the main entrance to the Art Institute of Chicago (1894). The amount of his artistic production began to decline by 1902, when he settled in Washington, D.C., but his work continued to appear at exhibitions, including the Louisiana Purchase Exposition (Saint Louis, 1904). A memorial retrospective of more than 150 works was held at the Corcoran Gallery of Art, Washington, D.C., in 1907.

REFERENCES

Hawthorne, Julian. "American Wild Animals in Art." *Century Magazine* 28, no. 2 (June 1884), pp. 213–19.

Garland, Hamlin. "Edward Kemeys: A Sculptor of Frontier Life and Wild Animals." *McClure's Magazine* 5 (July 1895), pp. 120–31.

Mechlin, Leila. "Edward Kemeys: An Appreciation." *International Studio* 26 (1905), pp. x–xiv.

Richman, Michael. *Edward Kemeys, 1843–1907: America's First Animal Sculptor*. Middleburg, Va.: Kemeys Foundation, 1972.

Wagner, David J. *American Wildlife Art*. Seattle: Marquand Books, 2008, pp. 153–89.

Frederick William MacMonnies

(American, Brooklyn 1863–1937 New York)

Kit Carson, ca. 1907–11 (cast by 1915). Cat. 26
The Hunter (*Pioneer Monument* sketch), ca. 1907–11 (cast 1916). Cat. 27

MacMonnies joined the Manhattan studio of Augustus Saint-Gaudens as a shop hand in 1880. Two years later he was promoted to assistant and also began attending classes at the Cooper Union and the National Academy of Design. At the encouragement of Saint-Gaudens, MacMonnies went to Paris in September 1884 and began preparing for entrance to the École des Beaux-Arts by attending classes at the Académie Colarossi as well as Jean-Léon Gérôme's open drawing sessions at the École. A cholera epidemic in Paris led MacMonnies to spend brief interludes in New York and Munich, where he enrolled at the Royal Academy. In summer 1886 MacMonnies finally enrolled at the École and began a two-year course of study with Jean-Alexandre-Joseph Falguière; he also studied privately with Antonin Mercié. MacMonnies twice won the Prix d'Atelier, the École's highest honor available to foreign students. He rapidly earned international acclaim, winning a Grand Prix at the 1900 Exposition Universelle in Paris and maintaining studios in New York, Paris, and Giverny. Among his best-known monuments are *The Barge of State* (1893; World's Columbian Exposition, Chicago), *Nathan Hale* (1893; City Hall Park, New York), *Bacchante and Infant Faun* (1893–94; The Metropolitan Museum of Art)—a nude dancing female figure that drew great controversy when it was proposed as a gift to the Boston Public Library in 1896—and *Horse Tamers* (1899; Prospect Park, Brooklyn). Like Saint-Gaudens, MacMonnies frequently collaborated with the architectural firm McKim, Mead & White and profited by selling reductions of his monuments at commercial galleries. At the turn of the century, he experimented with painting but returned to sculpture, with renewed success, in 1905. Even though he had no connection to the American West, in 1907 (at the recommendation of Saint-Gaudens) MacMonnies was awarded the commission for Denver's *Pioneer Monument* (1907–11; fig. 16). Although he made a preparatory trip to Denver, MacMonnies

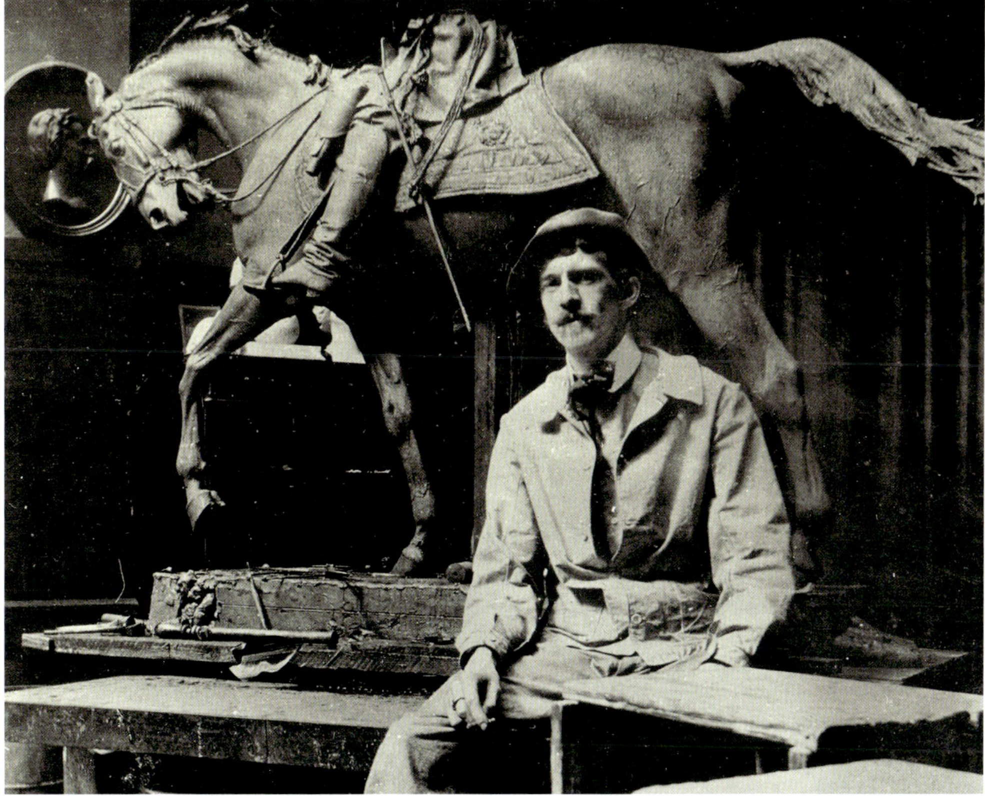

Fig. 198. Peter A. Juley & Son. *Frederick William MacMonnies with Equestrian Statue* (detail), ca. 1900. Gelatin silver print, 8¼ × 8 in. (21 × 20.3 cm). Frederick William MacMonnies Papers, Archives of American Art, Smithsonian Institution, Washington, D.C.

produced the sculptural components of the monument in Paris, exhibiting plaster versions at the Salon of 1911, and he cast the bronzes (cats. 26, 27) at foundries there as well. MacMonnies left Paris at the outbreak of World War I and returned to New York, where he spent the last two decades of his life completing several major monument commissions, including the *Princeton Battle Monument* (1908–22; New Jersey), *Civic Virtue* (1922; originally City Hall Park, New York), and marble figures for the New York Public Library (1935).

REFERENCES

MacMonnies, Frederick William, Papers. Archives of American Art, Smithsonian Institution, Washington, D.C., microfilm reels D245, 3042, 3134, and unmicrofilmed material.

Low, Will H. "Frederick MacMonnies." *Scribner's Magazine* 18 (November 1895), pp. 617–28.

Greer, H. H. "Frederick MacMonnies, Sculptor." *Brush and Pencil* 10 (April 1902), pp. 1–15.

Smart, Mary. *A Flight with Fame: The Life and Art of Frederick MacMonnies (1863–1937)* [catalogue raisonné of sculpture and checklist of paintings by E(thelyn) Adina Gordon]. Madison, Conn.: Sound View Press, 1996.

Gordon, Ethelyn Adina. "The Sculpture of Frederick William MacMonnies: A Critical Catalogue." Ph.D. diss., Institute of Fine Arts, New York University, 1998.

Hermon Atkins MacNeil

(American, Everett, Massachusetts 1866–1947 New York)

The Moqui Prayer for Rain, 1895–96 (cast ca. 1897). Cat. 28
The Sun Vow, 1899 (cast ca. 1906 or after). Cat. 29
A Chief of the Multnomah Tribe, 1903. Cat. 30
Pioneer Woman, 1926. Cat. 31

After graduating from the Massachusetts Normal Art School, Boston, in 1885, MacNeil taught art at Cornell University for three years. In 1889 he left to study sculpture in Paris at the Académie Julian under Henri-Michel-Antoine Chapu. The following year he trained at the École des Beaux-Arts with Jean-Alexandre-Joseph Falguière. In 1891 MacNeil returned to the United States and assisted Philip Martiny on architectural sculptures for the World's Columbian Exposition (Chicago, 1893); he also created statues for the Electricity Building there. MacNeil established a studio in Chicago, where he executed his first major commission—four narrative reliefs on the life of Père Marquette for the Marquette Building (1894). Fascinated by American Indian cultures, MacNeil traveled to the Southwest in 1895 on a sketching expedition that led him to Window Rock, Arizona, where he witnessed various ceremonies, notably the Hopi (Moqui) Snake Dance. The ethnographic studies he made during this trip served as the basis for several sculptures of Indians, a subject that he is principally identified with despite his vast, highly diverse oeuvre. Beginning in 1896, MacNeil spent three years in Rome as a recipient of the Rinehart Scholarship for sculpture, during which time he executed *The Moqui Prayer for Rain* (cat. 28) and *The Sun*

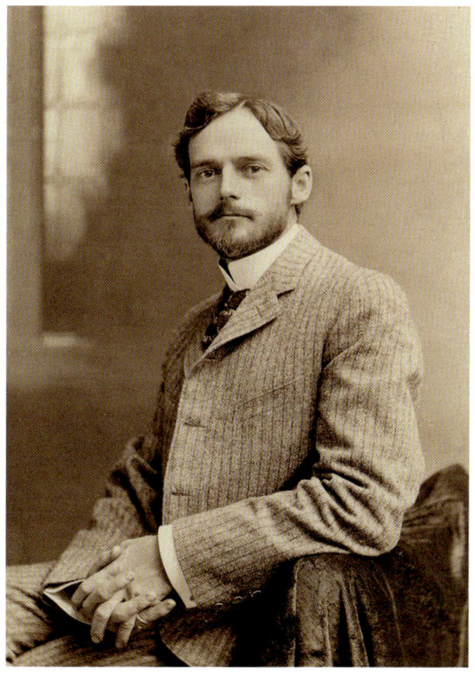

Fig. 199. Rockwood, Photographer. *Studio Portrait of Hermon Atkins MacNeil*, 1905. Photographic print, 5½ × 4 in. (14.5 × 10.5 cm). Artist file, Thomas J. Watson Library, The Metropolitan Museum of Art

Vow (cat. 29). He subsequently spent one year in Paris and then established a studio in New York, where he lived with his wife, the sculptor Carol Brooks MacNeil, and taught at the Art Students League, the Pratt Institute, and the National Academy of Design. For the fairgrounds of the Louisiana Purchase Exposition in Saint Louis (1904), MacNeil created *Physical Liberty*, a representation of an Indian hunting a bison. He earned numerous commissions for public monuments, including *Coming of the White Man* (1904; Washington Park, Portland, Oregon; fig. 54), *Soldiers and Sailors Monument* (1912; Washington Park, Albany, New York), and the east pediment of the U.S. Supreme Court (1935; Washington, D.C.). He also created several important numismatic designs, including the Standing Liberty quarter (minted 1916–30).

REFERENCES

MacNeil, Hermon Atkins, Papers. Archives of American Art, Smithsonian Institution, Washington, D.C., microfilm reels 2726–27.

MacNeil, Hermon Atkins, Papers. Division of Rare Books and Manuscript Collections, Cornell University Library, Ithaca, New York.

Chapin, Harriet Warner. "Hermon Atkins MacNeil." *Pacific Monthly* 15 (April 1906), pp. 409–17.

Holden, Jean Stansbury. "The Sculptors MacNeil: The Varied Work of Mr. Hermon A. MacNeil and Mrs. Carol Brooks MacNeil." *World's Work* 14 (October 1907), pp. 9403–19.

Walker, Andrew J. "The Aesthetics of Extinction: Art and Science in the Indian Sculptures of Hermon Atkins MacNeil." In *Perspectives on American Sculpture before 1925* [Papers from a symposium held at The Metropolitan Museum of Art, New York, October 26, 2001], edited by Thayer Tolles, pp. 96–115. New York: The Metropolitan Museum of Art, 2003.

———. "Hermon Atkins MacNeil and the 1904 World's Fair: A Monumental Program for the American West." In *Shaping the West: American Sculptors of the 19th Century*, pp. 54–67. Western Passages. Denver: Petrie Institute of Western American Art, Denver Art Museum, 2010.

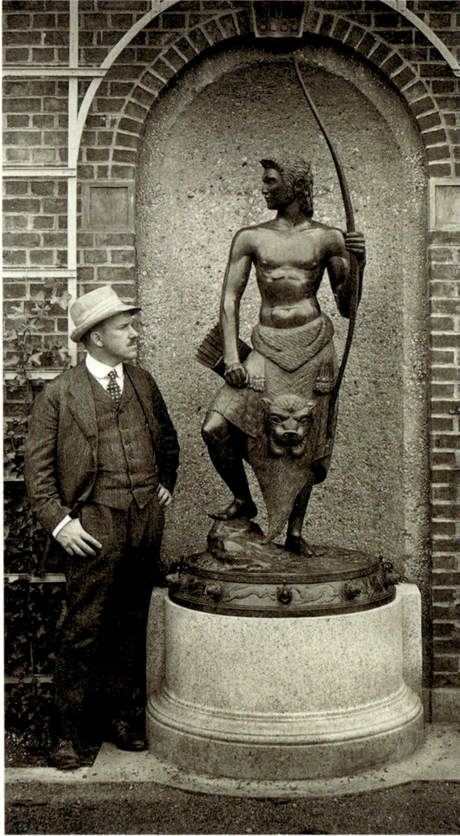

Fig. 200. *Paul Manship with "Spirit of the Chase"* (detail), 1915. Herbert L. Pratt estate, Glen Cove, New York, ca. 1915. Paul Manship Family Papers, Margaret Cassidy and John Paul Manship Collection

Paul Manship

(American, born Paul Howard Manship, Saint Paul, Minnesota 1885–1966 New York)

Indian Hunter, 1914 (cast 1915). Cat. 32
Pronghorn Antelope, 1914 (cast 1915). Cat. 33
Indian Hunter and His Dog, 1926. Cat. 34

Manship attended the Saint Paul School of Art and then worked as a commercial artist before relocating to New York in 1905. He studied under sculptors Jo Davidson and Hermon Atkins MacNeil at the Art Students League and entered the studio of Solon Hannibal Borglum, an influential mentor who taught him animal anatomy. Manship subsequently studied with William Merritt Chase and Charles Grafly at the Pennsylvania Academy of the Fine Arts in Philadelphia. He later worked in New York for the sculptor Isidore Konti, who encouraged him to compete for a fellowship at the American Academy in Rome, which Manship won in 1909. During his three-year fellowship, he traveled around the Mediterranean to study antiquities and later drew on ancient Egyptian, Archaic Greek, Assyrian, and Indo-Greco art to develop a distinctive Art Deco style that combined stylized linear forms with ornamental detail. After returning to New York in 1912, Manship won several awards, including the National Academy of Design's Barnett Prize (1914 and 1917). He won a gold medal at the Panama-Pacific International Exposition (San Francisco, 1915) for his sculptures, which included *Indian Hunter* and *Pronghorn Antelope* (cats. 32, 33). During World War I, Manship volunteered with the Red Cross in Italy and remained in Europe until 1926, when he established a studio in New York. He kept a studio in Paris until 1937. A prolific and highly influential sculptor, Manship enjoyed wide success for small bronzes and medals as well as monuments, including ornamental gates for the Bronx Zoo (1934), large groups for the 1939 New York World's Fair, and his most famous work, *Prometheus Fountain* (1934; Rockefeller Center, New York). In 1943 Manship purchased land for a studio and home near Gloucester, Massachusetts. He held leadership roles in many arts organizations, serving as president of the National Sculpture Society (1939–42) and of the American Academy of Arts and Letters (1948–54).

REFERENCES

Manship, Paul, Papers. Originals privately owned. Microfilmed for Archives of American Art, Smithsonian Institution, Washington, D.C., microfilm reels NY59-15–NY59-17, N714-17.

Manship Estate, Paul, Papers. Archives of American Art, Smithsonian Institution, Washington, D.C., microfilm reel 3829.

Gallatin, A. E. *Paul Manship: A Critical Essay on His Sculpture and an Iconography*. New York: John Lane Company, 1917.

Murtha, Edwin. *Paul Manship*. New York: Macmillan, 1957.

Manship, John. *Paul Manship*. New York: Abbeville Press, 1989.

Rand, Harry. *Paul Manship*. Exh. cat. Washington, D.C.: National Museum of American Art; Smithsonian Institution Press, 1989.

Rather, Susan. *Archaism, Modernism, and the Art of Paul Manship*. Austin: University of Texas Press, 1993.

Haig Patigian

(American, Van, Armenia [now Turkey] 1876–1950 San Francisco)

Pioneer, 1926 (cast ca. 1935). Cat. 35

Despite limited formal training, Patigian created more architectural sculptures for San Francisco than any other artist. After attending the American Mission School in Van, Armenia, where his parents taught, he immigrated in 1891 to Fresno, California, where his father had settled after fleeing Ottoman authorities in 1888. Patigian worked as a laborer in the vineyards and then as a sign painter. By 1899 he moved to San Francisco and worked as an illustrator for the *San Francisco Bulletin* and audited classes at the Mark Hopkins Institute of Art. He began sculpting in about 1904 and completed his first major commission in 1906—a bronze statue of President William McKinley for Arcata, California. In October of that year Patigian traveled to Paris, where he received critiques from the sculptor Alix Marquet. After exhibiting at the Salon of 1907, Patigian established a studio in San Francisco. He traveled to Paris again in 1913, where he received praise from Auguste Rodin, whom he met through their mutual acquaintance Gutzon Borglum. Over the next several decades Patigian executed numerous stone and bronze architectural sculptures and monuments, including *Abraham Lincoln* (1926; Civic Center, San Francisco), a pediment for the U.S. Department of Commerce Building (1931; Washington, D.C.), and *Thomas Starr King* (1931; U.S. Capitol, Washington, D.C.). Patigian modeled busts of several public figures, notably President Herbert Hoover (1928; the White House, Washington, D.C.) and Wimbledon tennis champion Helen Wills (1927; Oakland Museum of California). He created an extensive sculptural ensemble for the Palace of Machines at the Panama-Pacific International Exposition (San Francisco, 1915). In 1920 he completed several allegorical figures representing California history—*Pioneer Man, Pioneer Woman, Indian, Explorer, Missionary*—for the de Young Memorial Museum Building (removed 1950). Patigian served four terms as president of the Bohemian Club, a gentlemen's club in San Francisco.

REFERENCES

Pratt, Harry Noyes. "Haig Patigian, California's Noted Sculptor." *Overland Monthly and Out West Magazine* 81 (August 1923), p. 11.

Gavoor, Rouben. "Haig Patigian—The Sculptor." *Armenian Review* (Spring 1951), pp. 5–9.

Elsner, William H. "Four San Francisco Sculptors." *Bulletin of the California Palace of the Legion of Honor* 25 (May–June 1967), n.p.

Wright, Lois M. "Catalogue of the Life Works of Haig Patigian, San Francisco Sculptor, 1876–1950." Unpublished manuscript, ca. 1967. Original owned by Oakland Museum Library. Microfilmed for Smithsonian American Art Museum/National Portrait Gallery Library, Smithsonian Institution, Washington, D.C., microfilm reel 000040.

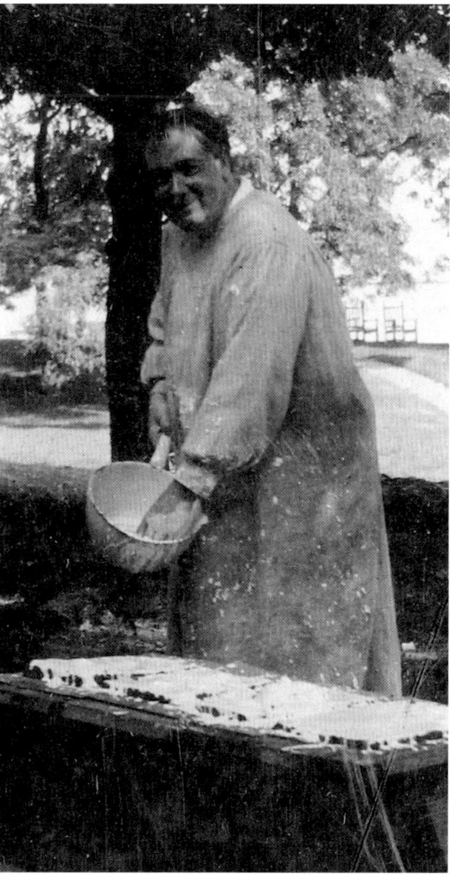

Fig. 202. *Potter Standing under Trees, Filling a Mold* (detail), ca. 1900. Photographic print, 4⅜ × 2¾ in. (11.1 × 7 cm). Louis McClellan Potter Papers, Archives of American Art, Smithsonian Institution, Washington, D.C.

Louis McClellan Potter

(American, Troy, New York 1873–1912 Seattle)

Basket Weavers, 1905. Cat. 36

Painter, etcher, and sculptor, Potter is best remembered for his perceptive ethnographic studies of American Indians, particularly of the Sioux and Tlingit. Having studied painting at the Connecticut League of Art Students in Hartford and earned a B.A. in 1896 from Trinity College, Hartford, Potter

Fig. 201. Arnold Genthe (American, born Germany, 1869–1942). *Haig Patigian* (detail), 1927. Nitrate negative, 3⅞ × 2½ in. (8.8 × 6.3 cm). Arnold Genthe Collection, Prints and Photographs Division, Library of Congress, Washington, D.C.

spent three years in Paris, studying painting with Luc-Olivier Merson and sculpture with Jean-Auguste Dampt. After exhibiting a marble bust at the Société Nationale des Beaux-Arts in 1899, Potter spent a year in Tunis, Tunisia, where he lived in the Arab Quarter and sculpted local subjects. At the behest of the Bey of Tunis, Potter's statuettes of Bedouins represented Tunis at the Exposition Universelle (Paris, 1900) and earned the artist the Order of Renown from the Bey. In 1901 Potter established a studio in New York and that year sent his *Snake Charmer* (unlocated) to the Pan-American Exposition in Buffalo. In 1904 he created a terracotta relief panel, *Sun Worshippers*, for the Louisiana Purchase Exposition in Saint Louis. That same year he traveled to the Pacific Northwest and made studies of the Tlingit of southeast Alaska, which served as the basis for eighteen bronze sculptures—among them *Basket Weavers* (cat. 36)—that were cast at Gorham Co. Founders for commercial sale. His first and only solo exhibition was in 1909 at the Modern Athenian Club in New York. An insightful portraitist, he executed busts of Brigham Young (1908; Brigham Young University), Charles W. Eliot (1910; Harvard University), and Mark Twain (1910; Wadsworth Atheneum, Hartford, Connecticut). Potter also designed utilitarian cast-metal objects, such as doorknobs, book-ends, and andirons. While his earlier works are characterized by sharp realism, his later depictions of Native peoples and his allegorical compositions are imbued with a spiritual sensibility, such as his monumental *The Earth Man* and *The Earth's Unfoldment* (Wadsworth Atheneum) shown in Paris at the Salon des Artistes Français in 1912. Potter died young, following treatment by an alleged doctor of Chinese medicine.

REFERENCES

Potter, Louis McClellan, Papers. Archives of American Art, Smithsonian Institution, Washington, D.C., unmicrofilmed material.

MacDonald, M. Irwin. "Louis Potter: A Sculptor Who Draws His Symbolism from an Intimate Understanding of Primitive Human Nature." *Craftsman* 16 (June 1909), pp. 257–65.

"Louis Potter: Sculptor." *International Studio* 47 (October 1912), pp. lxv–lxvi.

Tolles, Thayer, et al. *American Sculpture in The Metropolitan Museum of Art.* Vol. 2, *A Catalogue of Works by Artists Born between 1865 and 1885.* New York: The Metropolitan Museum of Art, 2001, pp. 568–69.

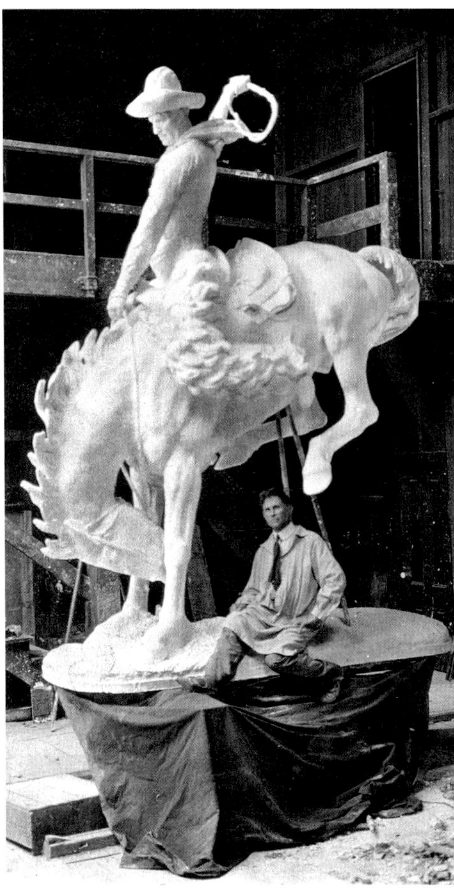

Fig. 203. *Proctor with His Monumental Plaster "Broncho Buster," Los Altos, California*, 1919. Contact print, 4¾ × 3¼ in. (12.1 × 8.3 cm). Alexander Phimister Proctor Collection, MS 242, Buffalo Bill Center of the West, Cody, Wyoming, Gift of Phimister and Sally Church

Alexander Phimister Proctor

(American, Bosanquet, Ontario, Canada 1860–1950 Palo Alto, California)

Stalking Panther, 1891–93 (cast ca. 1905–13). Cat. 37
Indian Warrior, 1898 (cast 1913 or after). Cat. 38
Indian Warrior, 1898 (cast between 1913 and 1918). Cat. 39
Head of Brown Bear (Kodiak), 1908. Cat. 40
Buffalo, 1912 (cast 1913 or after). Cats. 41, 42
Buckaroo, 1914 (cast 1915 or after). Cat. 43
Pursued, 1914. Cat. 44
Slim, 1914 (cast 1915 or after). Cat. 45
Pioneer Mother, 1925 (cast 1927). Cat. 46

An avid hunter and outdoorsman, Proctor drew on his experience in the wilderness and his youth in Denver, where his family had settled in 1871, to sculpt the animal, cowboy, and American Indian subjects for which he is best known. After working briefly in Denver as an engraver, Proctor arrived in New York in 1885 to study painting at the National Academy of Design, transferring a year later to the Art Students League. After turning to sculpture, he spent time in the studio of genre sculptor John Rogers, studied animals at the Central Park Menagerie, dissected specimens, and scrutinized animal casts at the American Museum of Natural History. Proctor's reputation rose swiftly in 1893, when he completed thirty-five lifesize naturalistic sculptures of animals and equestrian representations of an American Indian and a cowboy for the grounds of the World's Columbian Exposition (Chicago; figs. 79, 111, and 179), to which he also sent smaller works, notably *Stalking Panther* (cat. 37). Although now a recognized artist, he moved to Paris in 1893 to seek further training and enrolled at the Académie Julian, interrupting his studies to assist Augustus Saint-Gaudens with sculpting a horse for an equestrian monument to General John Logan (1894–97; Grant Park, Chicago) and later one for the Sherman Monument (1892–1903; Grand Army Plaza, New York). Proctor returned to Paris in 1896 as a recipient of the American Academy in Rome's Rinehart Scholarship. He resumed his studies at the Académie Julian and took courses at the Académie Colarossi with Antoine Injalbert, becoming fully versed in the Beaux-Arts style. He received critical acclaim at the Salon of 1898 and the Exposition Universelle in 1900, winning a gold medal at the latter for a display that included *Indian Warrior* (cats. 38, 39) and *Stalking Panther*. In 1900 Proctor established a studio in New York, and he later worked in Wilton, Connecticut; Palo Alto, California; and Pendleton, Oregon, among other cities, including Rome, where he was artist-in-residence at the American Academy from 1925 to 1927. Proctor won numerous monumental commissions, including four bronze buffalo for the Q Street (Dumbarton) Bridge (1911–14; Washington, D.C.; fig. 96), a pair of equestrian statues for Denver's Civic Center Park (*Broncho*

Buster, 1917–19, fig. 136; and *On the War Trail*, 1918–21), *Pioneer Mother* (1925–27; Penn Valley Park, Kansas City, Missouri; fig. 15), and *Mustangs* (1949; University of Texas, Austin).

REFERENCES

Papers concerning Alexander Phimister Proctor's statue, *The Pioneer Mother*, 1924–1950. Archives of American Art, Smithsonian Institution, Washington, D.C., unmicrofilmed material. These papers concern only the commission for his *Pioneer Mother* in Kansas City (cat. 46).

Proctor, Alexander Phimister, Collection. Harold McCracken Research Library, Buffalo Bill Center of the West, Cody, Wyoming.

Taft, Lorado. "A. Phimister Proctor." *Brush and Pencil* 2 (September 1898), pp. 241–48.

Cortissoz, Royal. "Some Wild Beasts Sculptured by A. Phimister Proctor." *Scribner's Magazine* 48 (November 1909), pp. 637–40.

Brush, Edward Hale. "An Animal Sculptor." *Arts and Decoration* 1 (August 1911), pp. 392–94.

Peixotto, Ernest. "A Sculptor of the West." *Scribner's Magazine* 68 (September 1920), pp. 266–77.

Hassrick, Peter H., et al. *Wildlife and Western Heroes: Alexander Phimister Proctor, Sculptor.* Exh. cat. Fort Worth, Tex.: Amon Carter Museum; London: Third Millennium Publishing, 2003.

Proctor, Alexander Phimister. *Sculptor in Buckskin: The Autobiography of Alexander Phimister Proctor.* Edited by Katharine C. Ebner; foreword by Peter H. Hassrick. Rev. ed. 1971. Norman: University of Oklahoma Press, 2009.

Arthur Putnam

(American, Waveland, Mississippi 1873–1930 Ville d'Avray, France)

Puma and Deer, 1902 (copyright 1912). Cat. 47
Prospector, 1903 (cast ca. 1921). Cat. 48

Putnam is best known for his bronze depictions of cougars, pumas, and other felines of the American West, most of which he modeled in a decade of intense production that ended in 1911. Raised in Nebraska and California, he worked briefly for a photoengraver in Omaha before beginning his limited formal art education, which consisted of one year of drawing classes at the San Francisco Art Students League in 1894, time as a studio assistant with sculptor Rupert Schmid, and one year in the Chicago studio of Edward Kemeys in 1897. He also may have learned techniques from his many artist friends, including Gutzon Borglum. Putnam gained knowledge of animal anatomy by working in a slaughterhouse and as a trapper and rancher. Early in his career, he modeled terracotta ornamentation for San Francisco building facades (many of which were destroyed by the earthquake and fire of 1906). In 1903 he received a commission for five outdoor sculptures for the San Diego ranch of the newspaper publisher E. W. Scripps. This commission, along with support from the family of the philanthropist William H. Crocker, enabled Putnam to travel to Rome late in 1905 and then to Paris, where his work was exhibited at annual Salons and earned praise from Auguste Rodin. In 1906 Putnam returned to San Francisco and sculpted numerous decorations for local banks, hotels, and public buildings. Drawing on his experience working in an iron foundry and his study of lost-wax casting in Europe, in 1909 he established a bronze foundry, Putnam and Storey, in San Francisco in partnership with his brother-in-law, Frederick Storey. His production dramatically declined after 1911, when surgery caused partial paralysis and brain damage. Nonetheless, he was elected to the National Sculpture Society in 1913, and his work continued to appear in exhibitions, including at the Macbeth Gallery, New York; the Armory Show, 1913; and the Panama-Pacific International Exposition (San Francisco, 1915), where he won a gold medal. Putnam earned sustained praise for his sculptures, especially from modernists who favored their smooth surfaces and simplified forms. In 1921 Alma de Bretteville Spreckels bought fifty-five plasters from Putnam that were cast by Alexis Rudier in Paris (one set is at the Fine Arts Museums of San Francisco, and a second is at the San Diego Museum of Art). Putnam moved to France in 1921 to oversee the casting, remaining there until his death.

REFERENCES

Porter, Bruce. "Arthur Putnam's Animal Sculpture." *Sunset* 14 (November 1904), pp. 54–58.

Berry, Rose V. S. "Arthur Putnam—California Sculptor." *American Magazine of Art* 20 (May 1929), pp. 276–82.

Heyneman, Julie Helen. *Arthur Putnam: Sculptor.* San Francisco: Johnck and Seeger, 1932. British edition, *Desert Cactus: The Portrait of a Sculptor.* London: Geoffrey Bles, 1934.

Osborne, Carol M. "Arthur Putnam, Animal Sculptor." *American Art Review* 3 (September–October 1976), pp. 71–81.

Kamerling, Bruce. "Arthur Putnam: Sculptor of the Untamed." *Antiques and Fine Art* 7 (July–August 1990), pp. 122–29.

Nemerov, Alexander. "The Dark Cat: Alexander Putnam and a Fragment of Night." *American Art* 16, no. 1 (Spring 2002), pp. 36–59.

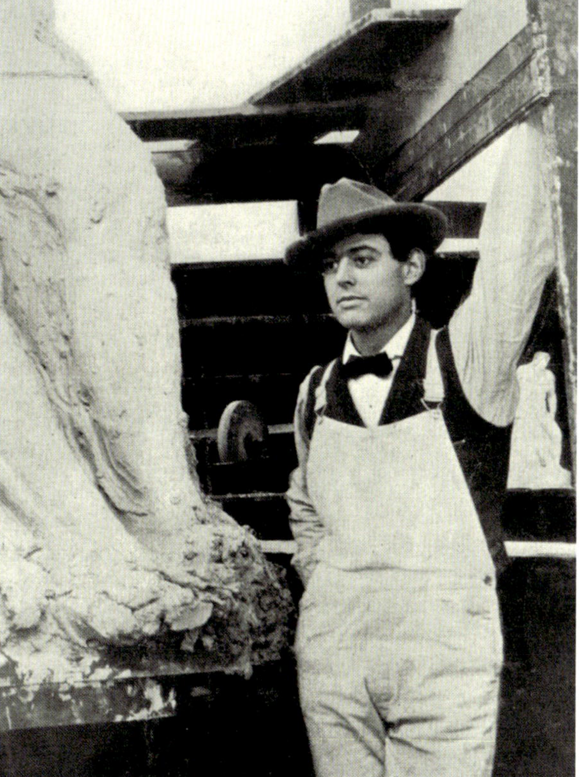

Fig. 204. *Arthur Putnam at Work on "The Indian" for E. W. Scripps*, ca. 1904–5. From Julie Helen Heyneman, *Arthur Putnam: Sculptor* (San Francisco: Johnck and Seeger, 1932)

Frederic Remington

(American, born Frederic Sackrider Remington,
Canton, New York 1861–1909 Ridgefield,
Connecticut)

Turn Him Loose, Bill, ca. 1893. Cat. 49
The Broncho Buster, 1895 (cast by 1898). Cat. 50
The Broncho Buster, 1895 (cast 1906). Cat. 51
The Wounded Bunkie, 1896 (cast 1896). Cat. 52
The Norther, 1900. Cat. 53
The Cheyenne, 1901 (cast by 1903). Cat. 54
Coming through the Rye, 1902 (cast 1907). Cat. 55
The Mountain Man, 1903 (cast by 1907). Cat. 56

Remington created his first sculpture,
The Broncho Buster (cats. 50, 51), in 1895,
when he was already a highly accomplished
illustrator and painter. In the wake of its instant
success, he modeled twenty more sculptural
compositions in the years before his death.
Raised in Ogdensburg, New York, Remington
attended Highland Military Academy

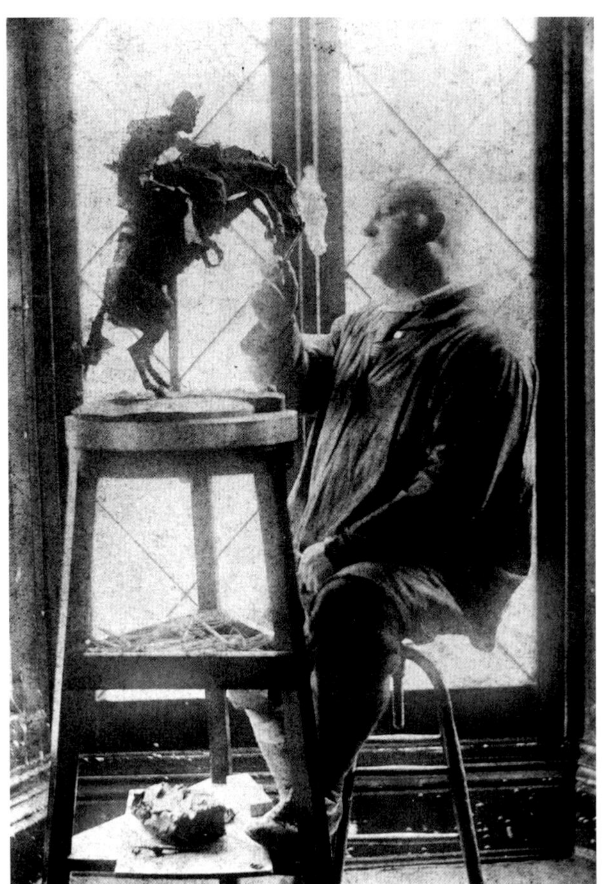

Fig. 205. *Remington Modeling His First Sculpture, "The Broncho Buster,"* 1895.
Photograph on board, 12 × 10 in. (30.5 × 25.4 cm). Frederic Remington Art
Museum, Ogdensburg, New York

(Worcester, Massachusetts) and received
training in art while enrolled at Yale University,
studying drawing with John Niemeyer at the
School of Fine Arts there between 1878 and
1880. He took sketching and painting classes
for three months in 1886 at the Art Students
League in New York. Remington traveled
to Montana Territory in summer 1881 and
thereafter frequently returned to the West, for
a time establishing a studio in Kansas City,
Missouri. His popular images idealizing a
rapidly vanishing Old West appeared in forty-
one periodicals, including *Harper's Weekly* and
Collier's, sometimes alongside his own articles
about the frontier. After briefly establishing a
studio in Brooklyn, he settled in New Rochelle,
New York, in 1890. After 1892 Remington
traveled extensively, accompanying journalist
Poultney Bigelow to North Africa, Europe, and
Russia and working as a war correspondent
in Cuba during the Spanish-American War.

In 1894 he learned the rudiments
of building armatures and clay
modeling from the sculptor Frederick
Wellington Ruckstull. Remington
rendered his finished sculptures
exclusively in bronze, fully exploiting
the medium's ability to capture
complex multifigure arrangements
or the arrested motion of galloping
horses. To a degree unprecedented in
American sculpture, he collaborated
closely with two foundries, first sand
casting at the Henry-Bonnard Bronze
Company and, beginning in 1900,
lost-wax casting with Roman Bronze
Works, achieving a remarkable range
of compositional detail and surface
treatment. He executed only one
permanent bronze monument, *The
Cowboy* (1905–8; Fairmount Park,
Philadelphia; fig. 130), although
his group *Coming through the Rye*
(cat. 55) was enlarged in staff for
temporary display at the Louisiana
Purchase Exposition (Saint Louis,
1904). Shortly after moving to
Connecticut in 1909, Remington
died at age forty-eight, following an
appendectomy.

REFERENCES

Remington, Frederic, Papers. Frederic Remington
Art Museum, Ogdensburg, New York.

Remington, Frederic, Papers. Owen D. Young Library,
Saint Lawrence University, Canton, New York.

Samuels, Peggy, and Harold Samuels, eds. *The
Collected Writings of Frederic Remington*. Garden City,
N.Y.: Doubleday & Company, 1979.

Shapiro, Michael Edward. *Cast and Recast:
The Sculpture of Frederic Remington*. Exh. cat.
Washington, D.C.: National Museum of American
Art; Smithsonian Institution Press, 1981.

Shapiro, Michael Edward, et al. *Frederic Remington:
The Masterworks*. Exh. cat. New York: Harry N.
Abrams; Saint Louis: Saint Louis Art Museum, 1988.

Stewart, Rick. *Frederic Remington: Masterpieces from
the Amon Carter Museum*. Fort Worth, Tex.: Amon
Carter Museum, 1992.

Hassrick, Peter H., and Melissa J. Webster. *Frederic
Remington: A Catalogue Raisonné of Paintings,
Watercolors and Drawings*. Cody, Wyo.: Buffalo Bill
Historical Center, 1996.

Greenbaum, Michael D. *Icons of the West: Frederic
Remington's Sculpture*. 2nd ed. 1996. Ogdensburg,
N.Y.: Frederic Remington Art Museum, 2012.

Randolph Rogers

(American, Waterloo, New York 1825–
1892 Rome)

The Last Arrow, 1879–80 (cast 1880). Cat. 57

The son of a carpenter, Rogers grew up in
Ann Arbor in the years during Michigan's
transformation from territory to state. His first
foray into art was in 1843, making woodcut
advertisements for the local newspaper.
In about 1847 Rogers moved to New York,
seeking work as an engraver; he settled for a
position in a dry-goods store. His employers
took note of the plaster models he produced
in his spare time and sent him to Florence in
1848 to study sculpture with the Neoclassical
master Lorenzo Bartolini at the Accademia di
Belle Arti. In 1851 Rogers established a studio
in Rome, where he remained the rest of his
life. He became a mainstay of the expatriate
art colony and enjoyed a lucrative career as
a sculptor of idealized marble sculptures,
often depicting literary themes or sentimental

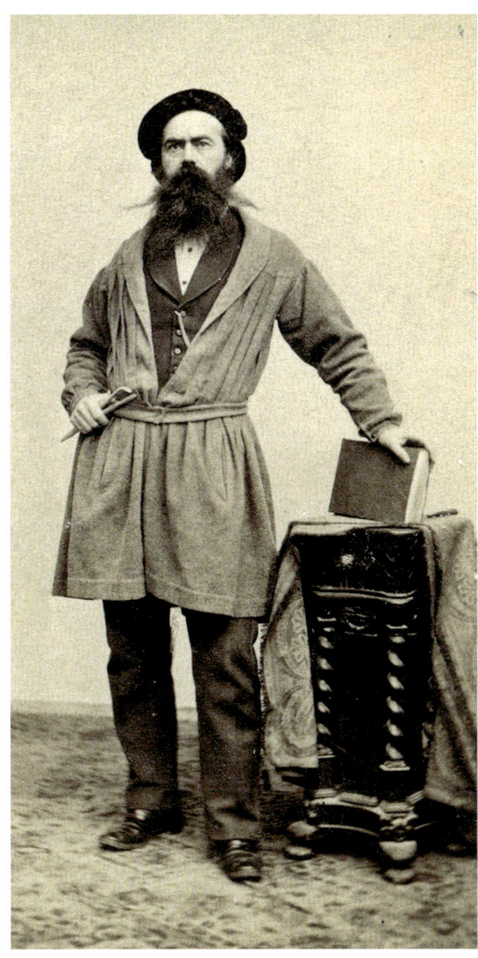

Fig. 206. *Randolph Rogers* (detail), 1861. Carte de visite, 4 × 2½ in. (10.2 × 6.4 cm). The Valentine Richmond History Center, Richmond, Virginia

figures of children, both of which were highly sought after by Americans on the Grand Tour. Several of Rogers's compositions, such as *Nydia* (ca. 1853–54), were in such high demand that his studio assistants executed dozens of marble replicas. Rogers won numerous commissions for monuments in the United States, most notably a set of bronze doors (1863) for the U.S. Capitol. He produced Civil War memorials for Cincinnati (1864–65); Providence, Rhode Island (1871); Detroit (1872); and Worcester, Massachusetts (1874). In Italy, Rogers was elected to Rome's venerable Accademia di San Luca (1873) and knighted Cavaliere dell'Ordine della Corona d'Italia (1884). Like other American sculptors at home and abroad, Rogers recognized the popular appeal of American Indian themes. He sculpted at least four compositions with Indian figures in

his studio in Rome: *Atala and Chactas* (1854), the pendant pair *Indian Fisher Girl* and *Indian Hunter Boy* (ca. 1866), and *The Last Arrow* (cat. 57), which was his last ideal composition and a comparatively rare example of the artist's work in bronze.

REFERENCES

Rogers, Randolph, Papers. Archives of American Art, Smithsonian Institution, Washington, D.C., microfilm reels 501 (originals owned by Michigan Historical Collections, Ann Arbor), 3471.

Rogers, Millard F., Jr. *Randolph Rogers, American Sculptor in Rome.* Amherst: University of Massachusetts Press, 1971.

Fryd, Vivien Green. "Randolph Rogers' *Indian Hunter Boy*: Allegory of Innocence." *University of Wisconsin-Madison Bulletin/Annual Report 1984–85* (1986), pp. 29–37.

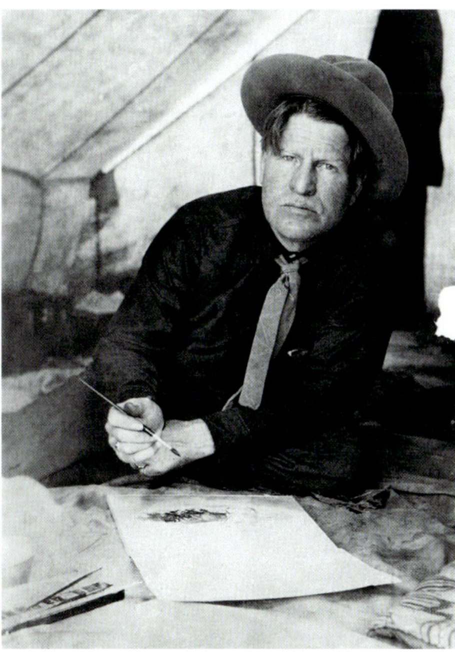

Fig. 207. M. O. Hammond (Canadian, 1876–1934). *Russell Painting an Incident of the Buffalo Roundup*, May 26, 1909. Photographic print, 5⅛ × 3¾ in. (13 × 9.5 cm). Britzman Collection, Gilcrease Museum, Tulsa, Oklahoma

Charles M. Russell

(American, born Charles Marion Russell, Saint Louis 1864–1926 Great Falls, Montana)

Smoking Up, 1904 (cast 1904). Cat. 58
Buffalo Hunt, 1905 (cast 1905). Cat. 59
The Combat, 1908 (cast ca. 1912). Cat. 60
A Bronc Twister (*The Weaver*), 1911 (cast 1911 or 1912). Cat. 61
Buffalo Hunt [*No. 40*], 1919. Cat. 62
An Enemy That Warns, 1921 (cast ca. 1922–28). Cat. 63
Meat for Wild Men, 1924 (cast 1924). Cats. 64, 65
Mountain Mother, 1924 (cast ca. 1924–28). Cat. 66
The Range Father, 1926 (cast ca. 1926–28). Cat. 67
Jim Bridger, 1926 (cast 1927–28). Cat. 68

Born to a Midwestern family descended from pioneers, explorers, and traders—the Bent family had a famous fort on the Santa Fe Trail—Russell was raised in a suburb of Saint Louis. As a child, he displayed an aptitude for drawing and for modeling wax figures. Russell dropped out of school in 1880 to travel to Montana, where he worked briefly on a sheep ranch and then assisted Jake Hoover, a hunter and trapper, for two years. Over the next dozen years, Russell worked for various roundups and as a night wrangler, devoting his daylight hours to sketching, painting, and modeling wax sketches of cowboys, Indians, and wildlife, many of which he gave to friends. By 1885 Russell painted his first major oil, and by 1887 he had earned the moniker "the Cowboy Artist." Russell exhibited at the World's Columbian Exposition (Chicago, 1893), and that same year he received a commission for several paintings with western themes from a hardware merchant in Saint Louis, which prompted him to pursue a full-time career as an artist. He established a studio in Great Falls, Montana, in 1900. In 1903 Russell had his first solo exhibition, at a gallery in Saint Louis; he also participated in the Louisiana Purchase Exposition there in 1904. Russell traveled to New York in 1904, where he completed illustrations for *McClure's*, *Leslie's Illustrated Weekly*, and other magazines. While there, he cast his first bronze statuette—*Smoking Up* (cat. 58)—eventually producing forty-six compositions in bronze over the next two decades, which brought him commercial success. Russell relied heavily on personal experience to create sculptures with strong narratives celebrating the Old West; these included highly animated horses and riders, as well as wild animals in their natural habitats. Russell had solo exhibitions of his paintings and sculpture that he titled "The West That Has Passed" at the Folsom Galleries (New York,

1911) and the Doré Gallery (London, 1914).
In the 1920s and 1930s many of his richly illustrated letters and recollections of life in the
West were collected for publication in books
aimed at popular audiences. Among Russell's
few public commissions was a twenty-five-
foot-long mural for the Montana State House
of Representatives (unveiled 1912).

REFERENCES

Hassrick, Peter H. *Charles M. Russell.* New York:
Harry N. Abrams; Washington, D.C.: National
Museum of American Art, Smithsonian Institution,
1989.

Dippie, Brian W., comp. *Charles M. Russell, Word
Painter: Letters 1887–1926.* Fort Worth, Tex.: Amon
Carter Museum, 1993.

Stewart, Rick. *Charles M. Russell, Sculptor.* Fort
Worth, Tex.: Amon Carter Museum, 1994.

Dippie, Brian W., ed. *Charlie Russell Roundup:
Essays on America's Favorite Cowboy Artist.* Helena:
Montana Historical Society Press, 1999.

Price, B. Byron, et al. *Charles M. Russell: A Catalogue
Raisonné.* Norman: University of Oklahoma Press;
Great Falls, Mont.: Charles M. Russell Center for the
Study of the American West and the C. M. Russell
Museum, 2007.

Troccoli, Joan Carpenter, et al. *The Masterworks
of Charles M. Russell: A Retrospective of Paintings
and Sculpture.* Exh. cat. Norman: University of
Oklahoma Press; Denver: Denver Art Museum,
2009.

Charles Schreyvogel

(American, New York 1861–1912 Hoboken,
New Jersey)

My Bunkie, finished 1899. Cat. 69
The Last Drop, 1903 (cast 1904). Cat. 70
The Last Drop, 1903 (cast 1906). Cat. 71

Best known as a painter and lithographer
of American western scenes, Schreyvogel
executed only a handful of sculptures. Born
in New York to German immigrants, he was
apprenticed at a young age to a diemaker and
then to a lithographer until 1886, while also
attending classes at the Newark Art League
with the portrait painter Henry August
Schwabe. In 1886 Schreyvogel traveled to
Germany and spent three years studying with
Franck Kirchbach and the American painter

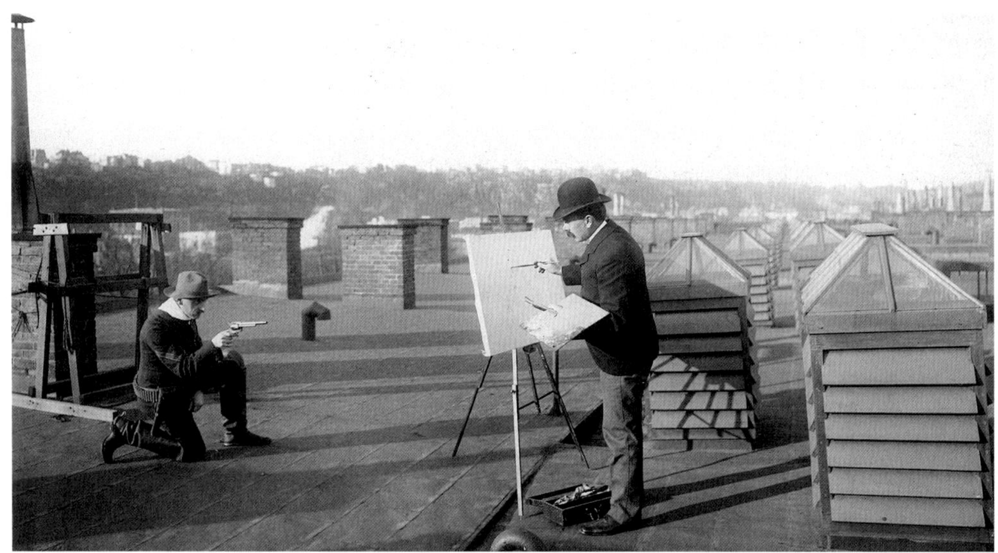

Fig. 208. *Schreyvogel Painting on Roof of His Hoboken, New Jersey, Studio* (detail), ca. 1903. Photographic print, 8 × 9¾ in. (20.3 × 24.8 cm). Charles Schreyvogel Papers, National Cowboy & Western Heritage Museum, Oklahoma City

Carl Marr. He returned to the United States
in 1890 to establish a studio in Hoboken,
New Jersey, where he often set up his easel
and models on the building's rooftop. He
completed oil portraits, ivory miniatures, and
commercial illustrations, receiving at least one
commission through his friend Edwin Willard
Deming. After seeing Buffalo Bill's Wild West
show and befriending William F. "Buffalo Bill"
Cody, Schreyvogel began depicting cowboys,
cavalry, and Indians—the subjects for which
he is best remembered. In 1893 he made his
first visit to the West, spending time on a
Ute reservation in Colorado and among the
Apache of Arizona while collecting artifacts
that would appear in his carefully researched
paintings. He subsequently made summer
trips to the West, especially to the Dakotas and
Montana, until 1905, when he purchased a farm
in New York's Catskill Mountains. Schreyvogel
began experimenting with sculpture in about
1894, modeling small-scale, highly detailed
compositions, including *The Last Drop* (cats.
70, 71). Schreyvogel's first major critical success
came in 1900, when his painting *My Bunkie*
(cat. 69) won the Thomas B. Clarke Prize at
the National Academy of Design; he was
elected associate member of the Academy the
following year. He won medals at the world's
fairs in Buffalo (1901) and Saint Louis (1904).
After Remington's death in 1909, Schreyvogel
was briefly the country's leading artist of
western subjects, until he succumbed to blood
poisoning in 1912.

REFERENCES

Schreyvogel, Charles, Papers. Dickinson Research
Center, National Cowboy & Western Heritage
Museum, Oklahoma City.

Kobbé, Gustav. "A Painter of the Western Frontier."
Cosmopolitan 31 (October 1901), pp. 563–73.

Souvenir Album of Paintings by Chas. Schreyvogel.
Hoboken, N.J.: Chas. F. Kaegebehn, 1907.

Horan, James David. *The Life and Art of Charles
Schreyvogel, Painter-Historian of the Indian-fighting
Army of the American West.* New York: Crown
Publishers, 1969.

Henry Merwin Shrady

(American, New York 1871–1922 New York)

Buffalo, 1899 (cast ca. 1901). Cat. 72
Bull Moose, 1900. Cat. 73

Principally self-trained, Shrady was an
accomplished sculptor of both small-
scale and monumental public sculptures.
The son of a prominent New York physician,
Shrady earned a B.A. at Columbia University
in 1894 and then, while pursuing a law
degree there, suffered an attack of typhoid
fever that abruptly ended his studies. From
1895 to 1900 he served as president of the

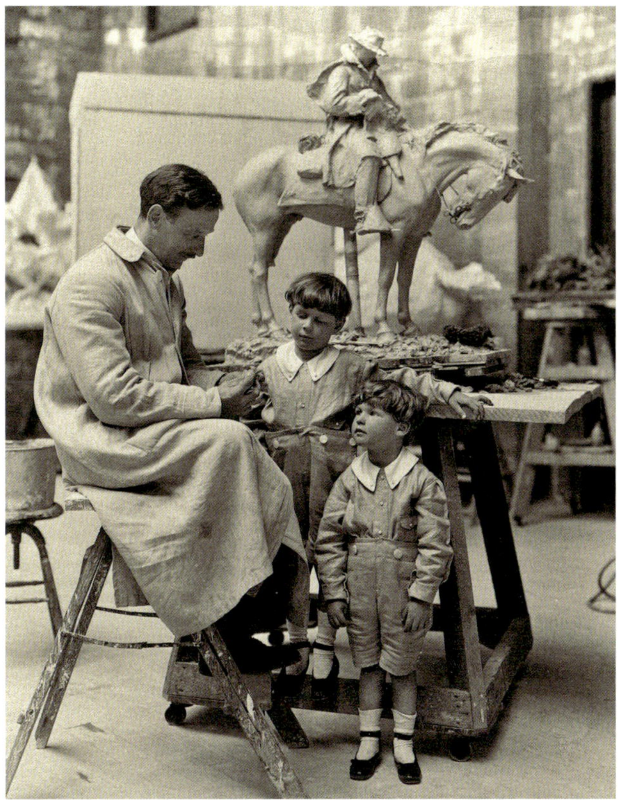

Fig. 209. Ira L. Hill (American, 1877–1947). *Henry Merwin Shrady and His Sons* (detail), ca. 1911. Photographic print, 10 × 8 in. (25.4 × 20.3 cm). Henry Merwin Shrady Papers, Archives of American Art, Smithsonian Institution, Washington, D.C.

the West entirely in New York, relying on the city's zoological collections as well as historical and anatomical publications for study. Shrady's reputation rose suddenly when Karl Bitter, director of sculpture for the 1901 Pan-American Exposition in Buffalo, requested that he create eight monumental versions of *Buffalo* and *Bull Moose* for the fairgrounds. Bitter invited Shrady to use his studio in Weehawken, New Jersey; this was Shrady's first experience working in a professional sculpture studio, and it served as a de facto apprenticeship. Subsequently, he won several major monumental commissions, notably *George Washington at Valley Forge* (1906), an equestrian bronze in Williamsburg, Brooklyn. He devoted the last twenty-some years of his life to the *General Ulysses S. Grant Memorial* (1901–24), a colossal multifigure composition located at the eastern terminus of the National Mall, Washington, D.C.; additional relief elements were completed after his death, based on his sketches.

Continental Match Company, owned by his brother-in-law. During this time he began painting watercolor studies of animals, which he based on observation at the Bronx Zoo and knowledge from undergraduate biology classes. An avid recreational rider, Shrady also experimented with modeling horses. In about 1898 he completed his first sculptural composition, *Artillery Going into Action* (unlocated), a photoengraving of which immediately caught the attention of the New York art dealer and jeweler Theodore B. Starr. He encouraged Shrady to create other statuettes, for which the dealer purchased the copyrights and then sold the casts in his Fifth Avenue gallery. These bronzes, including *Buffalo* and *Bull Moose* (cats. 72, 73), were among the first to be cast in America through the lost-wax process, a technique ideally suited to capturing the textural details of Shrady's work. He produced these statuettes of animals and cavalry scenes closely associated with

REFERENCES

Shrady, Henry Merwin, Papers. Archives of American Art, Smithsonian Institution, Washington, D.C., microfilm reel 647.

Garrett, Charles Hall. "The New American Sculptor." *Munsey's Magazine* 29 (July 1903), pp. 545–52.

Church, Mrs. Benjamin S. "A Great American Sculptor: Henry Merwin Shrady." *Journal of American History* 7, no. 2 (April–June 1913), pp. 1005–14.

Montagna, Dennis R. "Henry Merwin Shrady's Ulysses S. Grant Memorial in Washington, D.C." Ph.D. diss., University of Delaware, 1987.

"Henry Merwin Shrady." In *European Sculpture of the Nineteenth Century*, by Ruth Butler et al., pp. 469–74. The Collections of the National Gallery of Art Systematic Catalogue. Washington, D.C.: National Gallery of Art, 2000.

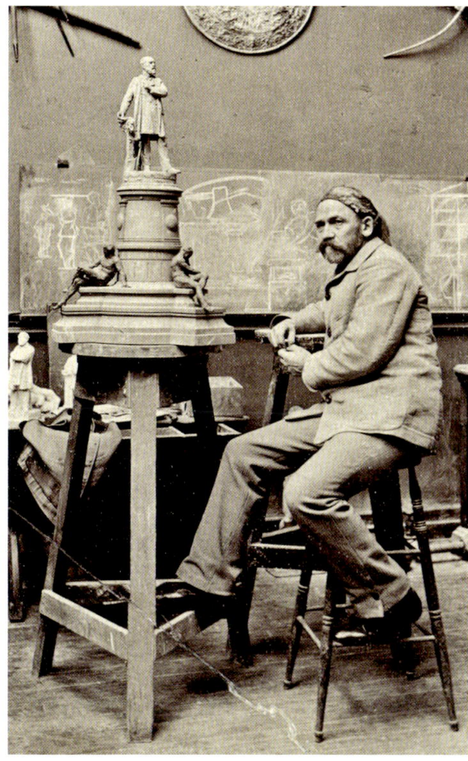

Fig. 210. Pach Brothers. *John Quincy Adams Ward in His Studio* (detail), ca. 1887. Albumen print, 10 × 8 in. (25.4 × 20.3 cm). Archives of American Art, Smithsonian Institution, Washington, D.C.

John Quincy Adams Ward

(American, Urbana, Ohio 1830–1910 New York)

Indian Chief, ca. 1860. Cat. 74
The Indian Hunter, 1860. Cat. 75
The Indian Hunter, 1860 (cast ca. 1885). Cat. 76

During the six highly prolific decades of his career, Ward earned the title "the Dean of American Sculpture." Raised on a farm in Ohio, he moved to Brooklyn in 1849 to apprentice in the studio of Henry Kirke Brown, an influential and lifelong mentor. Promoted to assistant, Ward became fully versed in the techniques of sculpting monuments and casting bronze, and he remained with Brown until 1856. From 1858 to 1860 Ward maintained a studio in Washington, D.C., sculpting portraits of politicians; in 1861 he settled permanently in New York. Two of his earliest compositions— *The Indian Hunter* (cats. 75, 76), depicting a youth hunting with his dog, and *The Freedman* (1863), a statuette of an emancipated slave— were exhibited at the Exposition Universelle (Paris, 1867) and received high praise for their distinctively American subjects. In 1864 Ward traveled to the Dakotas to study American Indians as he prepared a monumental bronze version of *The Indian Hunter* for Central Park (dedicated 1869; fig. 34). It was the first of Ward's dozens of public sculptures, many of which he created in collaboration with the architect Richard Morris Hunt, including *Seventh Regiment Memorial* (1874; Central Park, New York), *George Washington* (1883; Federal Hall, New York), and *James Abram Garfield* (1887; the Mall, Washington, D.C.). Ward made his first trip abroad in 1872, visiting the principal cities of Germany, France, and Italy; he returned to several of them again in 1887. His realist approach remained fundamentally unchanged by his travels, although his later work displays the richly textured surface details so characteristic of the contemporary Beaux-Arts style. An influential leader in his field, he served as president of the National Academy of Design, founder and trustee of The Metropolitan Museum of Art, and founder and first president of the National Sculpture Society.

REFERENCES

Ward, John Quincy Adams, Papers. Albany Institute of History and Art, New York.

Ward, John Quincy Adams, Papers. New-York Historical Society. Microfilmed for Archives of American Art, Smithsonian Institution, Washington, D.C., microfilm reels 509–10.

Sheldon, G. W. "An American Sculptor." *Harper's New Monthly Magazine* 57 (June 1878), pp. 62–68.

Sturgis, Russell. "The Work of J. Q. A. Ward." *Scribner's Magazine* 32 (October 1902), pp. 385–99.

Sharp, Lewis I. *John Quincy Adams Ward: Dean of American Sculpture, with a Catalogue Raisonné.* Newark: University of Delaware Press, 1985.

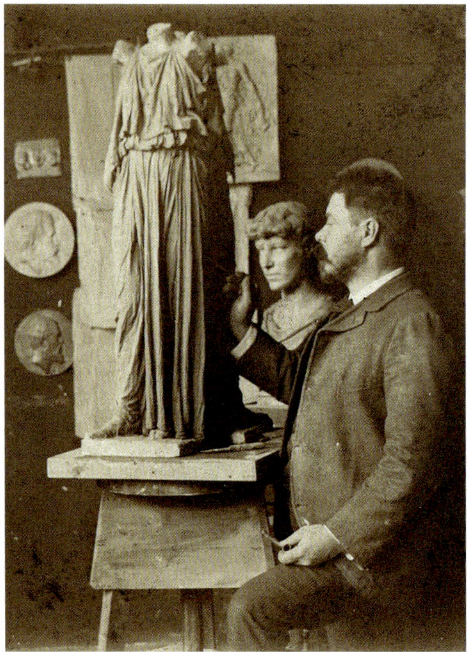

Fig. 211. *Olin Levi Warner in His Studio* (detail), ca. 1880. Photographic print, 5 × 8 in. (12.7 × 20.3 cm). Olin Levi Warner Papers, Archives of American Art, Smithsonian Institution, Washington, D.C.

Olin Levi Warner

(American, West Suffield, Connecticut 1844–1896 New York)

Joseph, Chief of the Nez Percé Indians, 1889 (cast 1906). Cat. 77

Raised in rural New York and Vermont, Warner worked for six years as a railroad telegrapher, earning funds to pursue formal artistic training. He traveled to Paris in May 1869 and studied at the Petite École and in the atelier of François Jouffroy to prepare for entrance to the prestigious École des Beaux-Arts; he was accepted in October 1870. His studies were cut short by the fall of the French Second Empire, although he remained in Paris. In 1872 he received further training in the studio of Jean-Baptiste Carpeaux, mastering a rigorous Beaux-Arts style, then moved to New York later that year. He struggled to attract clients until 1876, when he received recognition at the Philadelphia Centennial Exhibition and became closely acquainted with influential New York critics and dealers. Based in New York, Warner completed several noted public commissions in the 1880s, including seated statues of Governor William A. Buckingham (1883;

State Capitol, Hartford, Connecticut) and William Lloyd Garrison (1885; Commonwealth Avenue, Boston). He made extended trips to Portland, Oregon, in the 1880s and 1890s to visit his patron Charles Erskine Scott Wood, through whom he received a commission for Portland's Skidmore Fountain (1888). While in the Pacific Northwest, he modeled from life profile portraits of several Columbia River Indians (see cat. 77). He was best known for rendering intimate portraits such as these, although he also executed a few ideal compositions, such as *Twilight* (1877–78) and *Diana* (ca. 1885–87; both The Metropolitan Museum of Art). In New York, Warner taught at the Cooper Union, the Art Schools of the Metropolitan Museum, and the National Academy of Design. In the mid-1890s he served as a consultant on the decorative program for the Library of Congress, for which he also sculpted two sets of monumental bronze doors, his most significant public commission. Because Warner died young and completed so few public commissions, he remains little known today; nevertheless, he was celebrated in his time.

REFERENCES

Warner, Olin Levi, and Warner Family Papers. Archives of American Art, Smithsonian Institution, Washington, D.C., microfilm reels 270, 414, 3746–47.

Wood, C. E. S. "Famous Indians: Portraits of Some Indian Chiefs." *Century Magazine* 46 (July 1893), pp. 436–45.

Brownell, W[illiam] C[rary]. "The Sculpture of Olin Warner." *Scribner's Magazine* 20 (October 1896), pp. 428–41.

Gurney, George. "Olin Levi Warner (1844–1896): A Catalogue Raisonné of His Sculpture and Graphic Works." Ph.D. diss., University of Delaware, 1978.

Adolph Alexander Weinman

(American, Karlsruhe, Germany 1870–1952 New York)

Chief Blackbird, Ogallala Sioux, 1903. Cat. 78
Chief Blackbird, the Ogalla Sioux, 1903. Cat. 79

At age ten Weinman immigrated with his family to New York, where he was apprenticed to a wood and ivory carver. Beginning in 1888 he spent three years studying

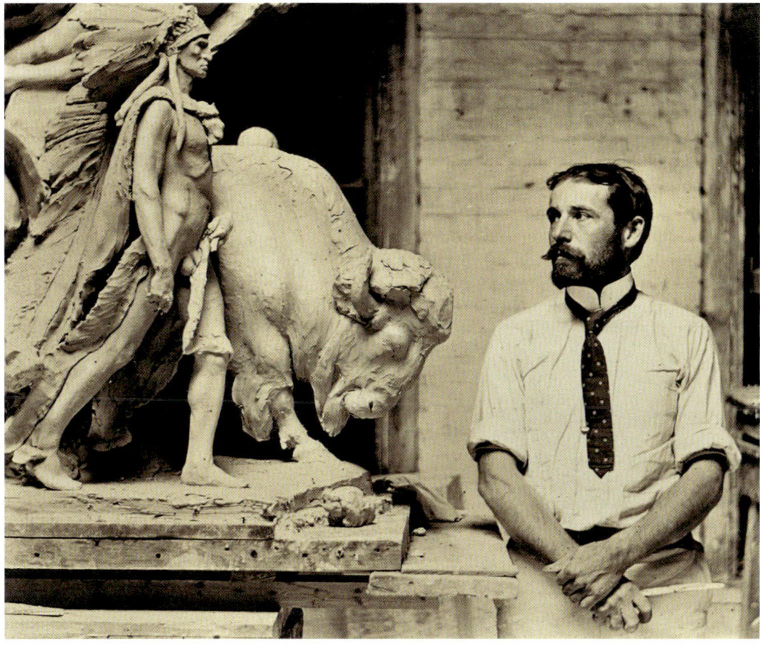

Fig. 212. *Adolph Alexander Weinman with "Destiny of the Red Man"* (detail), ca. 1905. Photographic print, 5 × 7 in. (12.7 × 17.8 cm). Adolph A. Weinman Papers, Archives of American Art, Smithsonian Institution, Washington, D.C.

at the Cooper Union; between 1896 and 1900 he also attended evening classes at the Art Students League. This academic training was complemented by the experience he gained between 1890 and 1904 working as an assistant in the studios of the prominent American sculptors Daniel Chester French, Philip Martiny, Charles Henry Niehaus, Augustus Saint-Gaudens, and Olin Levi Warner, from whom he absorbed the Beaux-Arts style. In 1904 Weinman established his own studio in New York and won a silver medal at the Louisiana Purchase Exposition (Saint Louis) for his monumental *Destiny of the Red Man* (fig. 10), which he based, in part, on studies of Oglala Sioux performers he met in New York. He won further recognition at the Panama-Pacific International Exposition (San Francisco, 1915), to which he sent twenty-nine sculptures. Weinman executed numerous architectural sculptures for the renowned firm McKim, Mead & White, completing keystones in 1909 for the firm's Fifth Avenue facade of The Metropolitan Museum of Art and elements of its Pennsylvania Station. He also won commissions for pediments for the state capitols of Wisconsin (1912; Madison) and Missouri (1927; Jefferson City) and for the National Archives (1933–35; Washington, D.C.). Weinman served on the National Commission of Fine Arts from 1928 to 1932 and was president of the National Sculpture Society from 1928 to 1931. In addition to his monumental work, he was highly regarded for his numismatic and medallic designs, which included the U.S. Mercury dime and the Walking Liberty half-dollar (both 1916).

REFERENCES

Weinman, Adolph A., Papers. Archives of American Art, Smithsonian Institution, Washington, D.C., microfilm reels 283, 414, and unmicrofilmed material.

Lockman, DeWitt McClellan. Interview with Adolph Alexander Weinman, April 28, 1926. Transcript, Manuscripts Department, New-York Historical Society. Microfilmed for DeWitt McClellan Lockman Papers. Archives of American Art, Smithsonian Institution, Washington, D.C., microfilm reel 504, frames 1046–61.

"Adolph Alexander Weinman." *Bulletin of the Pan American Union* 45 (December 1917), pp. 775–87.

"Adolph A. Weinman's Sculptures in Bronze." *Metal Arts* 2 (September 1929), pp. 423–27, 436.

Weinman, Robert A. "Adolph A. Weinman, 1870–1952, Eleventh President, National Sculpture Society." *National Sculpture Review* 14 (Winter 1965–66), pp. 22, 28.

Tolles, Thayer, et al. *American Sculpture in The Metropolitan Museum of Art*. Vol. 2, *A Catalogue of Works by Artists Born between 1865 and 1885*. New York: The Metropolitan Museum of Art, 2001, pp. 534–37.

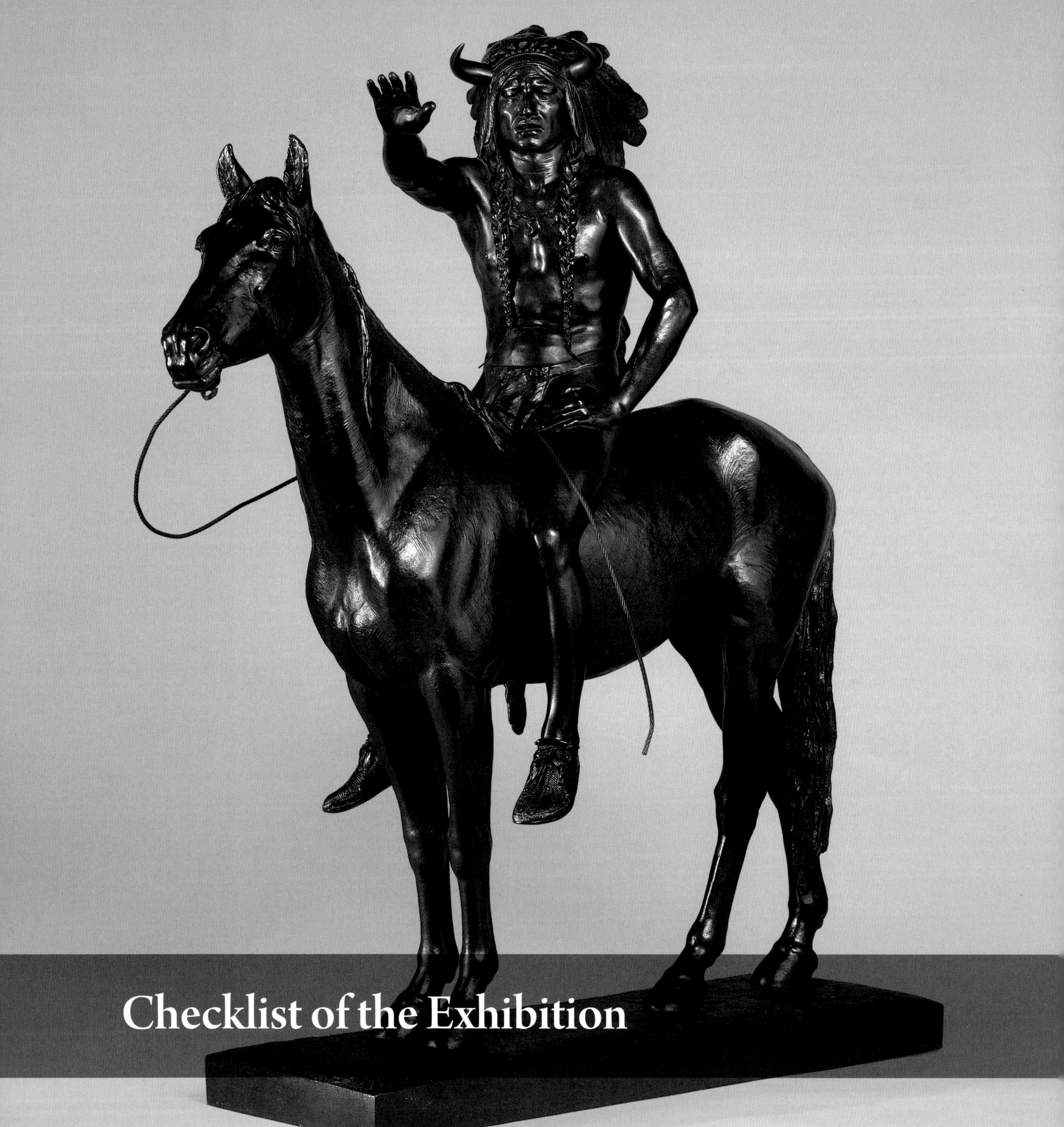

Checklist of the Exhibition

Unless otherwise indicated, all works are in bronze.

The date directly after the title of a sculpture indicates the year it was modeled. If a date follows in parentheses, it refers to the casting date of the bronze included in the exhibition.

If a work was on view in only one venue of the exhibition—The Metropolitan Museum of Art, New York, or the Denver Art Museum—that location is noted.

Fig. 213. Cyrus Edwin Dallin. *Medicine Man*, 1899 (cast ca. 1899). Cat. 16

Cat. 1
Bryant Baker
American (born England), 1881–1970
Pioneer Woman, 1927
32 × 15 × 16¼ in.
(81.3 × 38.1 × 41.3 cm)
Woolaroc Museum, Bartlesville, Oklahoma (SCT-30)
Fig. 169

Cat. 2
Theodore Baur
American (born Germany), 1835–active until 1904
The Buffalo Hunt, 1876 (cast ca. 1876–86)
Silvered electrotype
21¾ × 29 × 16 in.
(55.2 × 73.7 × 40.6 cm)
Gerald and Kathleen Peters
Fig. 35

Cat. 3
Theodore Baur
American (born Germany), 1835–active until 1904
Indian Chief, 1885
28½ × 17½ × 12½ in.
(72.4 × 44.5 × 31.8 cm)
Denver Art Museum, Museum Purchase (1966.135)
Fig. 39

Cat. 4
Gutzon Borglum
American, 1867–1941
Fallen Warrior (Death of the Chief), ca. 1891
10⅞ × 14⅞ × 8⅜ in.
(27.6 × 37.8 × 21.3 cm)
Gilcrease Museum, Tulsa, Oklahoma (0876.125)
Fig. 41

Cat. 5
Solon Hannibal Borglum
American, 1868–1922
Lassoing Wild Horses, 1898 (cast ca. 1900–1902)
31¾ × 19¾ × 33¼ in.
(80.6 × 50.2 × 84.5 cm)
National Cowboy & Western Heritage Museum, Oklahoma City, Museum Purchase (1972.20)
Fig. 116

Cat. 6
Solon Hannibal Borglum
American, 1868–1922
On the Border of the White Man's Land, 1899 (cast 1906–7)
18½ × 27 × 10¼ in.
(47 × 68.6 × 26 cm)
The Metropolitan Museum of Art, Rogers Fund, 1907 (07.104)
Fig. 43

Cat. 7
Solon Hannibal Borglum
American, 1868–1922
Bulls Fighting, 1899–1900 (cast 1906–7)
4¼ × 20½ × 2⅜ in.
(10.8 × 52.1 × 6 cm)
The Metropolitan Museum of Art, Rogers Fund, 1907 (07.105)
Fig. 86

Cat. 8
Solon Hannibal Borglum
American, 1868–1922
Blizzard, 1900
5¾ × 10⅛ × 6¾ in.
(14.6 × 25.7 × 17.1 cm)
Detroit Institute of Arts, Gift of Ralph Harman Booth (16.9)
Fig. 119

Cat. 9
Solon Hannibal Borglum
American, 1868–1922
Rough Rider, 1900
19¼ × 8 × 6½ in.
(48.9 × 20.3 × 16.5 cm)
Detroit Institute of Arts, Gift of Ralph Harman Booth (16.10)
Fig. 118

Cat. 10
Solon Hannibal Borglum
American, 1868–1922
Bucky O'Neill, 1906 (cast ca. 1907)
41 × 15½ × 29 in.
(104.1 × 39.4 × 73.7 cm)
Buffalo Bill Center of the West, Cody, Wyoming, Gertrude Vanderbilt Whitney Trust Fund Purchase (5.60)
Fig. 128

Cat. 11
Henry Kirke Brown
American, 1814–1886
Choosing of the Arrow, 1849
22 × 11⅜ × 5⅝ in.
(55.9 × 28.9 × 14.3 cm)
The Metropolitan Museum of Art, Purchase, Mia R. Taradash and Dorothy Schwartz Gifts, and Morris K. Jesup and Rogers Funds, 2005 (2005.405a–d)
Fig. 31

Cat. 12
Henry Kirke Brown
American, 1814–1886
Panther and Cubs, ca. 1850–55
9⅞ × 18⅝ × 7¾ in.
(25.1 × 47.3 × 19.7 cm)
The Metropolitan Museum of Art, Purchase, Gifts in memory of James R. Graham, 1992 (1992.372)
Fig. 72
New York only

Cat. 13
Henry Kirke Brown
American, 1814–1886
Panther and Cubs, ca. 1850–55
10 × 19 × 7½ in.
(25.4 × 48.3 × 19.1 cm)
John Russell Kaufman, William Tyler Kaufman, and Meredith Anne Kaufman
Denver only

Cat. 14
James L. Clark
American, 1883–1969
Alaskan Kodiak Bear, 1904
7 × 11 × 4 in. (17.8 × 27.9 × 10.2 cm)
American Museum of Natural History, New York, Department of Library Services, Gift of James Lippitt Clark, 1965 (#397)
Fig. 93

Cat. 15
Charles Cristadoro
American, 1881–1967
Two Gun Bill (William S. Hart), 1917 (cast 1925 or after)
37⅞ × 12 × 19 in.
(96.2 × 30.5 × 48.3 cm)
Autry National Center of the American West, Los Angeles (88.379.1)
Fig. 143

Cat. 16
Cyrus Edwin Dallin
American, 1861–1944
Medicine Man, 1899
(cast ca. 1899)
31⅛ × 29⅛ × 8⅞ in.
(79.1 × 74 × 22.5 cm)
Amon Carter Museum of
American Art, Fort Worth,
Texas (2005.1)
Fig. 213

Cat. 17
Cyrus Edwin Dallin
American, 1861–1944
Appeal to the Great Spirit, 1912
(cast ca. 1922)
39¾ × 26¼ × 37 in.
(101 × 66.7 × 94 cm)
Hood Museum of Art, Dart-
mouth College, Hanover, New
Hampshire, Purchased through a
gift from the Honorable Leslie P.
Snow, Class of 1886 (S.928.15)
Fig. 214

Cat. 18
Cyrus Edwin Dallin
American, 1861–1944
Appeal to the Great Spirit, 1913
(cast ca. 1916)
21½ × 14½ × 22 in.
(54.6 × 36.8 × 55.9 cm)
Private collection, courtesy
Gerald Peters Gallery, New York
Fig. 30

Cat. 19
Edwin Willard Deming
American, 1860–1942
The Fight, ca. 1906
8 × 3¼ × 5½ in.
(20.3 × 8.3 × 14 cm)
The Metropolitan Museum
of Art, Rogers Fund, 1907 (07.42)
Fig. 215

Cat. 20
Sally James Farnham
American, 1869–1943
Will Rogers, 1936 (cast 1938)
22 × 9 × 19 in.
(55.9 × 22.9 × 48.3 cm)
Private collection, in memory
of Priscilla Farnham
Fig. 139

Cat. 21
James Earle Fraser
American, 1876–1953
End of the Trail, 1918
(cast 1918)
33 × 26 × 8¾ in.
(83.8 × 66 × 22.2 cm)
The Metropolitan Museum
of Art, Purchase, Friends of the
American Wing Fund, Mr. and
Mrs. S. Parker Gilbert Gift, Morris
K. Jesup and 2004 Benefit Funds,
2010 (2010.73)
Fig. 61

Cat. 22
Eli Harvey
American, 1860–1957
Bull Elk, 1904
(cast probably 1905)
33¼ × 23¼ × 9½ in.
(84.5 × 59.1 × 24.1 cm)
The Metropolitan Museum
of Art, Morris K. Jesup Fund,
2011 (2011.202)
Fig. 91

Cat. 23
Edward Kemeys
American, 1843–1907
Buffalo and Wolves, 1876
(cast probably 1878 or 1879)
20 × 30⅜ × 19½ in.
(50.8 × 77 × 49.5 cm)
Smithsonian American Art
Museum, Washington, D.C., Gift
of J. Willis Johnson (1984.141.2)
Fig. 73

Cat. 24
Edward Kemeys
American, 1843–1907
*The Soul of Contentment
(Black Bear)*, 1886
(cast ca. 1886–99)
10½ × 14 × 10 in.
(26.7 × 35.6 × 25.4 cm)
The Art Institute of Chicago,
Gift of Margaret S. Watson
(1899.45)
Fig. 81

Cat. 25
Edward Kemeys
American, 1843–1907
Still Hunt, 1894
22⅛ × 28 in. (56.2 × 71.1 cm)

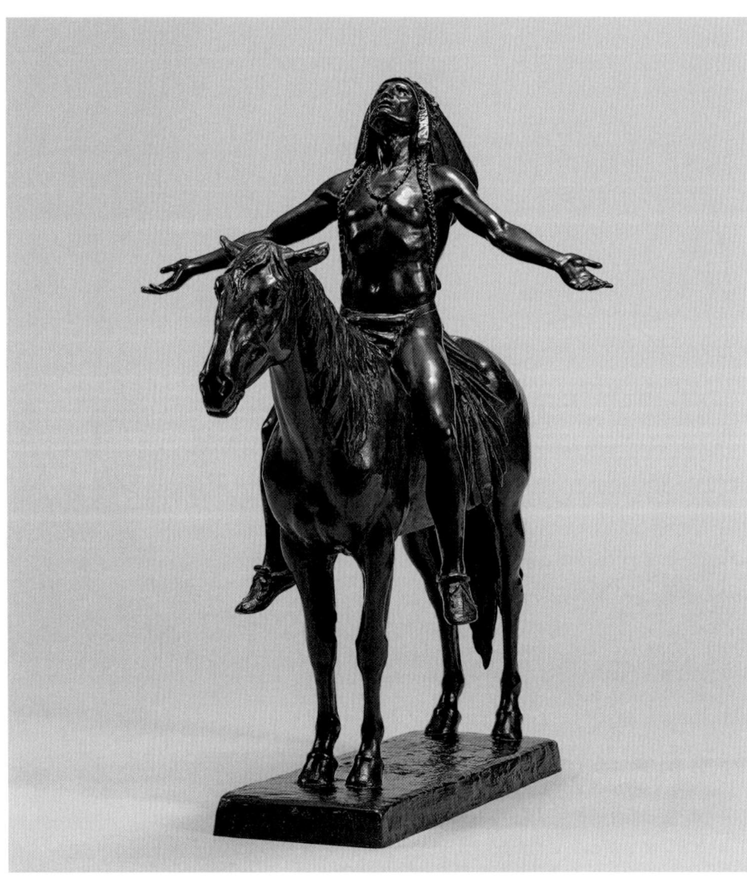

Fig. 214. Cyrus Edwin Dallin. *Appeal to the Great Spirit*, 1912 (cast ca. 1922). Cat. 17

The Metropolitan Museum
of Art, Rogers Fund, 1972
(1972.54)
Fig. 77

Cat. 26
Frederick William MacMonnies
American, 1863–1937
Kit Carson, ca. 1907–11
(cast by 1915)
25⅛ × 16¾ × 10⅜ in.
(63.8 × 42.5 × 26.4 cm)
Sagamore Hill National Historic
Site, Oyster Bay, New York
(SAHI-919)
Fig. 166

Cat. 27
Frederick William MacMonnies
American, 1863–1937
The Hunter (*Pioneer Monument*
sketch), ca. 1907–11 (cast 1916)
14½ × 21 × 7⅞ in.
(36.8 × 53.3 × 20 cm)

Gilcrease Museum, Tulsa,
Oklahoma (0826.96)
Fig. 167

Cat. 28
Hermon Atkins MacNeil
American, 1866–1947
The Moqui Prayer for Rain,
1895–96 (cast ca. 1897)
22¼ × 11 × 25¼ in.
(56.5 × 27.9 × 64.1 cm)
Daniel and Mathew Wolf, in
memory of Diane R. Wolf
Fig. 46

Cat. 29
Hermon Atkins MacNeil
American, 1866–1947
The Sun Vow, 1899
(cast ca. 1906 or after)
33⅜ × 14⅞ × 22⅛ in.
(84.8 × 37.8 × 56.2 cm)
Gilcrease Museum, Tulsa,
Oklahoma (0826.103)
Fig. 50

Cat. 30
Hermon Atkins MacNeil
American, 1866–1947
A Chief of the Multnomah Tribe, 1903
37½ × 9 × 11 in.
(95.3 × 22.9 × 27.9 cm)
Private collection, courtesy
Gerald Peters Gallery, New York
Fig. 53

Cat. 31
Hermon Atkins MacNeil
American, 1866–1947
Pioneer Woman, 1926
35 × 12 × 15 in.
(88.9 × 30.5 × 38.1 cm)
Saint Louis Art Museum,
Gift of Furniture Brands
(78:2007)
Fig. 171
Denver only

Cat. 32
Paul Manship
American, 1885–1966
Indian Hunter, 1914
(cast 1915)

13 × 10⅛ × 8 in.
(33 × 25.7 × 20.3 cm)
Amon Carter Museum of
American Art, Fort Worth, Texas,
Purchase with funds from the
Ruth Carter Stevenson Acquisitions Endowment (1997.3.A)
Fig. 66

Cat. 33
Paul Manship
American, 1885–1966
Pronghorn Antelope, 1914
(cast 1915)
12 × 10⅛ × 8¼ in.
(30.5 × 25.7 × 21 cm)
Amon Carter Museum of
American Art, Fort Worth, Texas,
Purchase with funds from the
Ruth Carter Stevenson Acquisitions Endowment (1997.3.B)
Fig. 67

Cat. 34
Paul Manship
American, 1885–1966
Indian Hunter and His Dog, 1926
21½ × 23½ × 8⅛ in.

(54.6 × 59.7 × 20.6 cm)
The Metropolitan Museum
of Art, Gift of Thomas Cochran,
1929 (29.162)
Fig. 69

Cat. 35
Haig Patigian
American (born Armenia),
1876–1950
Pioneer, 1926 (cast ca. 1935)
13 × 8 × 8 in.
(33 × 20.3 × 20.3 cm)
Private collection
Fig. 160

Cat. 36
Louis McClellan Potter
American, 1873–1912
Basket Weavers, 1905
15 × 14 × 15¾ in.
(38.1 × 35.6 × 40 cm)
Gilcrease Museum, Tulsa,
Oklahoma (0837.144)
Fig. 51

Cat. 37
Alexander Phimister Proctor
American (born Canada),
1860–1950
Stalking Panther, 1891–93
(cast ca. 1905–13)
10¼ × 31 × 4½ in.
(26 × 78.7 × 11.4 cm)
Corcoran Gallery of Art,
Washington, D.C., Bequest of
James Parmelee (41.79)
Fig. 83

Cat. 38
Alexander Phimister Proctor
American (born Canada),
1860–1950
Indian Warrior, 1898
(cast 1913 or after)
39¼ × 29½ × 9¼ in.
(99.7 × 74.9 × 23.5 cm)
Daniel and Mathew Wolf, in
memory of Diane R. Wolf
Fig. 57
New York only

Cat. 39
Alexander Phimister Proctor
American (born Canada),
1860–1950
Indian Warrior, 1898
(cast between 1913 and 1918)

40 × 30¼ × 16 in.
(101.6 × 76.8 × 40.6 cm)
Corcoran Gallery of Art,
Washington, D.C., Museum
purchase (18.1)
Denver only

Cat. 40
Alexander Phimister Proctor
American (born Canada),
1860–1950
Head of Brown Bear (Kodiak),
1908
6⅛ × 6⅜ × 4¼ in.
(15.6 × 16.2 × 10.8 cm)
Private collection
Fig. 216

Cat. 41
Alexander Phimister Proctor
American (born Canada),
1860–1950
Buffalo, 1912 (cast 1913 or after)
13½ × 19 × 9¾ in.
(34.3 × 48.3 × 24.8 cm)
The Metropolitan Museum
of Art, Bequest of George D.
Pratt, 1935 (48.149.29)
Fig. 97
New York only

Cat. 42
Alexander Phimister Proctor
American (born Canada),
1860–1950
Buffalo, 1912 (cast 1913 or after)
13¼ × 18 × 9½ in.
(33.7 × 45.7 × 24.1 cm)
Denver Art Museum, Funds
from the Harry I. and Edythe
Smookler Memorial Endowment,
Estelle Wolf, and the Flowe
Foundation (2011.276)
Denver only

Cat. 43
Alexander Phimister Proctor
American (born Canada),
1860–1950
Buckaroo, 1914
(cast 1915 or after)
26¼ × 21⅜ × 8¼ in.
(66.7 × 54.3 × 21 cm)
Denver Art Museum, Funds
from William Sr. and Dorothy
Harmsen Collection by exchange
(2005.12)
Fig. 135

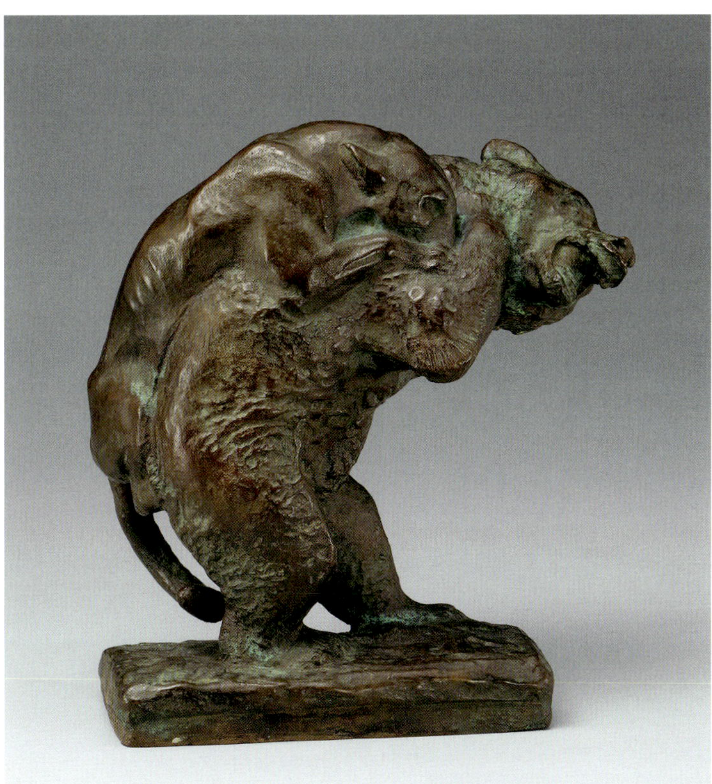
Fig. 215. Edwin Willard Deming. *The Fight*, ca. 1906. Cat. 19

Cat. 44
Alexander Phimister Proctor
American (born Canada),
1860–1950
Pursued, 1914
17¾ × 24⅛ × 6½ in.
(45.1 × 61.3 × 16.5 cm)
Charles and Barbara Griffith
Fig. 58

Cat. 45
Alexander Phimister Proctor
American (born Canada),
1860–1950
Slim, 1914 (cast 1915 or after)
11⅞ × 10¼ × 5¾ in.
(30.2 × 26 × 14.6 cm)
Oregon Historical Society, Port-
land, Bequest of Mrs. Hamilton
Corbett, 1982 (82-130)
Fig. 137

Cat. 46
Alexander Phimister Proctor
American (born Canada),
1860–1950
Pioneer Mother, 1925 (cast 1927)
56 × 28½ × 82 in.
(142.2 × 72.4 × 208.3 cm)
Santa Barbara Museum of Art,
Gift of the A. E. Clegg Family
(1991.89.11)
Fig. 168
Denver only

Cat. 47
Arthur Putnam
American, 1873–1930
Puma and Deer, 1902
(copyright 1912)
11¼ × 10¼ × 15¼ in.
(28.6 × 26 × 38.7 cm)
Los Angeles County Museum
of Art, Purchased with funds
provided by the Clifton Webb
Bequest, the Felicia Meyer Marsh
Bequest, the Blanche and George
Jones Fund, Inc., and Mrs.
Stevenson Scott (84.4)
Fig. 98

Cat. 48
Arthur Putnam
American, 1873–1930
Prospector, 1903 (cast ca. 1921)
11 × 8½ × 8½ in.
(27.9 × 21.6 × 21.6 cm)
Fine Arts Museums of

San Francisco, Gift of Alma de
Bretteville Spreckels (1924.119.1)
Fig. 159

Cat. 49
Frederic Remington
American, 1861–1909
Turn Him Loose, Bill, ca. 1893
Oil on canvas on Masonite
25 × 33 in. (63.5 × 83.8 cm)
American Museum of Western
Art—The Anschutz Collection,
Denver (#0258)
Fig. 217

Cat. 50
Frederic Remington
American, 1861–1909
The Broncho Buster, 1895
(cast by 1898)
23¾ × 21⅛ × 11⅞ in.
(60.3 × 53.7 × 30.2 cm)
Sagamore Hill National Historic
Site, Oyster Bay, New York
(SAHI-918)
Fig. 2

Cat. 51
Frederic Remington
American, 1861–1909
The Broncho Buster, 1895
(cast 1906)
22⅝ × 22¾ × 15¼ in.
(57.5 × 57.8 × 38.7 cm)
The Museum of Fine Arts,
Houston, The Hogg Brothers
Collection, gift of Miss Ima Hogg
(43.73)
Fig. 114

Cat. 52
Frederic Remington
American, 1861–1909
The Wounded Bunkie, 1896
(cast 1896)
20¾ × 11 × 31 in.
(52.7 × 27.9 × 78.7 cm)
Birmingham Museum of Art,
Gift of Dr. and Mrs. Harold E.
Simon (1973.148)
Fig. 147

Cat. 53
Frederic Remington
American, 1861–1909
The Norther, 1900
22 × 20½ × 8 in.
(55.9 × 52.1 × 20.3 cm)

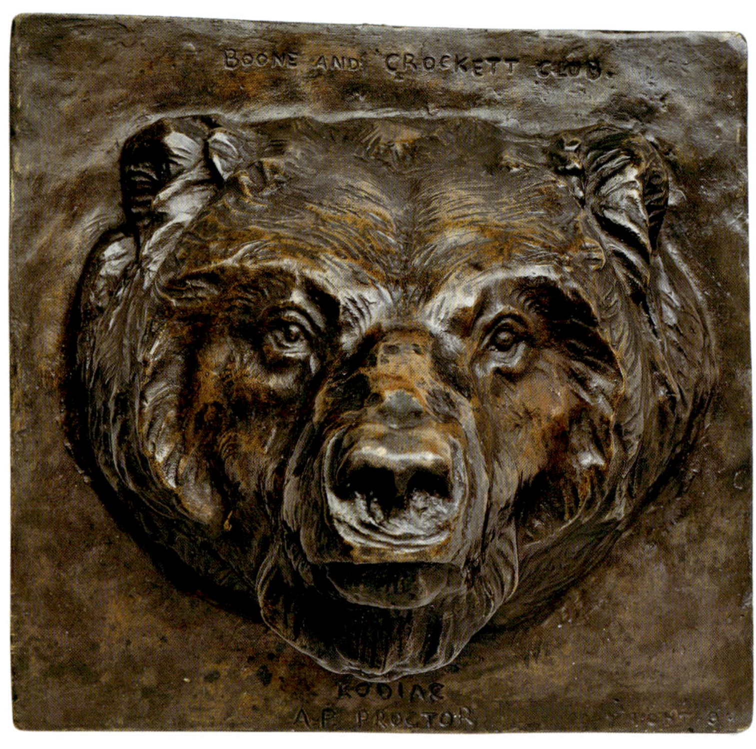

Fig. 216. Alexander Phimister Proctor. *Head of Brown Bear (Kodiak)*, 1908. Cat. 40

The Rees-Jones Collection
Fig. 120

Cat. 54
Frederic Remington
American, 1861–1909
The Cheyenne, 1901
(cast by 1903)
20⅞ × 24⅜ × 7½ in.
(53 × 61.9 × 19.1 cm)
Denver Art Museum, Funds from
William D. Hewit Charitable
Annuity Trust (1981.14)
Fig. 44

Cat. 55
Frederic Remington
American, 1861–1909
Coming through the Rye, 1902
(cast 1907)
29 × 31 × 27¼ in.
(73.7 × 78.7 × 69.2 cm)
Buffalo Bill Center of the West,
Cody, Wyoming, Gift of Barbara S.
Leggett (5.66)
Fig. 123
Denver only

Cat. 56
Frederic Remington
American, 1861–1909
The Mountain Man, 1903
(cast by 1907)
27¾ × 12 × 10 in.
(70.5 × 30.5 × 25.4 cm)
The Metropolitan Museum
of Art, Rogers Fund, 1907 (07.79)
Fig. 157

Cat. 57
Randolph Rogers
American, 1825–1892
The Last Arrow, 1879–80 (cast 1880)
44 × 34½ × 16 in.
(111.8 × 87.6 × 40.6 cm)
The Metropolitan Museum
of Art, Bequest of Henry H. Cook,
1905 (05.13.1)
Fig. 38

Cat. 58
Charles M. Russell
American, 1864–1926
Smoking Up, 1904 (cast 1904)
13 × 7½ × 5 in.
(33 × 19.1 × 12.7 cm)
The Petrie Collection
Fig. 126

Cat. 59
Charles M. Russell
American, 1864–1926
Buffalo Hunt, 1905 (cast 1905)
10 × 19 × 12¾ in.
(25.4 × 48.3 × 32.4 cm)
Amon Carter Museum of
American Art, Fort Worth,
Texas (1961.121)
Fig. 11

Cat. 60
Charles M. Russell
American, 1864–1926
The Combat, 1908
(cast ca. 1912)
6½ × 9 × 5 in.
(16.5 × 22.9 × 12.7 cm)
Amon Carter Museum of
American Art, Fort Worth,
Texas (1961.82)
Fig. 99

Cat. 61
Charles M. Russell
American, 1864–1926
A Bronc Twister (The Weaver), 1911

(cast 1911 or 1912)
18⅛ × 15 × 9½ in.
(46 × 38.1 × 24.1 cm)
The Petrie Collection
Fig. 131

Cat. 62
Charles M. Russell
American, 1864–1926
Buffalo Hunt [No. 40], 1919
Oil on canvas
29½ × 47½ in.
(74.9 × 120.7 cm)
The Petrie Collection
Fig. 64

Cat. 63
Charles M. Russell
American, 1864–1926
An Enemy That Warns, 1921
(cast ca. 1922–28)
5⅛ × 8 × 6 in.
(13 × 20.3 × 15.2 cm)
Amon Carter Museum of
American Art, Fort Worth,
Texas (1961.89)
Fig. 102

Cat. 64
Charles M. Russell
American, 1864–1926
Meat for Wild Men, 1924
(cast 1924)
11½ × 38 × 20 in.
(29.2 × 96.5 × 50.8 cm)
The Rees-Jones Collection
Fig. 63
New York only

Cat. 65
Charles M. Russell
American, 1864–1926
Meat for Wild Men, 1924
(cast 1924)
11½ × 37⅝ × 20⅝ in.
(29.2 × 95.6 × 52.4 cm)
The Petrie Collection
Denver only

Cat. 66
Charles M. Russell
American, 1864–1926
Mountain Mother, 1924
(cast ca. 1924–28)
6¾ × 5⅜ × 14¼ in.

(17.1 × 13.7 × 36.2 cm)
The Petrie Collection
Fig. 104

Cat. 67
Charles M. Russell
American, 1864–1926
The Range Father, 1926
(cast ca. 1926–28)
5¼ × 15 × 5 in.
(13.3 × 38.1 × 12.7 cm)
The Rees-Jones Collection
Fig. 103

Cat. 68
Charles M. Russell
American, 1864–1926
Jim Bridger, 1926 (cast 1927–28)
14¼ × 10 × 13½ in.
(36.2 × 25.4 × 34.3 cm)
The Petrie Collection
Fig. 155

Cat. 69
Charles Schreyvogel
American, 1861–1912
My Bunkie, finished 1899
Oil on canvas
25³⁄₁₆ × 34 in. (64 × 86.4 cm)
The Metropolitan Museum
of Art, Gift of friends of the artist,
by subscription, 1912 (12.227)
Fig. 151

Cat. 70
Charles Schreyvogel
American, 1861–1912
The Last Drop, 1903
(cast 1904)
11¾ × 18¾ × 5 in.
(29.8 × 47.6 × 12.7 cm)
Gerald and Kathleen Peters
Fig. 153
New York only

Cat. 71
Charles Schreyvogel
American, 1861–1912
The Last Drop, 1903
(cast 1906)
11¾ × 18¾ × 5 in.
(29.8 × 47.6 × 12.7 cm)
Pete and Lindsey Leavell
Denver only

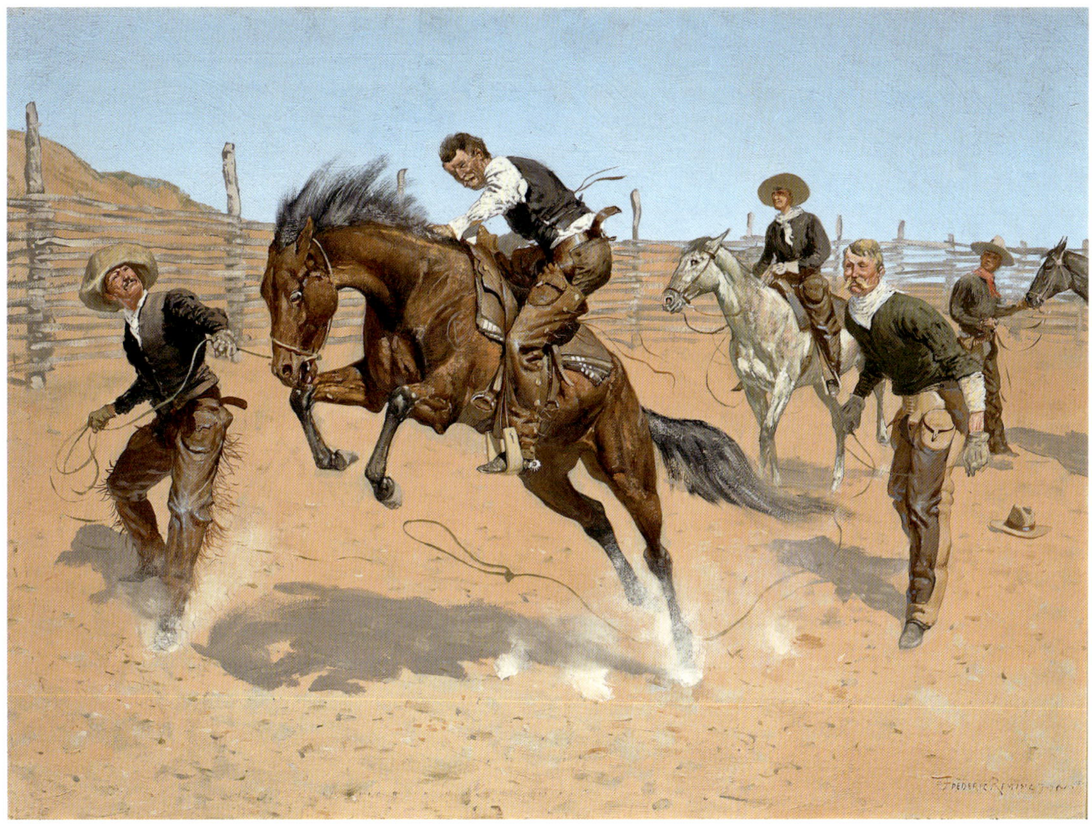

Fig. 217. Frederic Remington. *Turn Him Loose, Bill*, ca. 1893. Cat. 49

Cat. 72
Henry Merwin Shrady
American, 1871–1922
Buffalo, 1899 (cast ca. 1901)
14 × 13½ × 10 in.
(35.6 × 34.3 × 25.4 cm)
Amon Carter Museum of American
Art, Fort Worth, Texas (1999.21)
Fig. 89

Cat. 73
Henry Merwin Shrady
American, 1871–1922
Bull Moose, 1900
19¾ × 15⅜ × 8⅛ in.
(50.2 × 39.1 × 20.6 cm)
The Metropolitan Museum of Art,
Bequest of George D. Pratt, 1935
(48.149.25)
Fig. 90

Cat. 74
John Quincy Adams Ward
American, 1830–1910
Indian Chief, ca. 1860
20 × 8½ × 6¾ in.
(50.8 × 21.6 × 17.1 cm)
Denver Art Museum, Gift
from Estelle Rae Wolf and the
Harry I. and Edyth Smookler
Memorial Endowment Fund in
honor of Lewis I. Sharp (2001.634)
Fig. 218
Denver only

Cat. 75
John Quincy Adams Ward
American, 1830–1910
The Indian Hunter, 1860
16¼ × 9¼ × 14¼ in.
(41.3 × 23.5 × 36.2 cm)
Daniel and Mathew Wolf, in
memory of Diane R. Wolf
Fig. 33
New York only

Cat. 76
John Quincy Adams Ward
American, 1830–1910
The Indian Hunter, 1860
(cast ca. 1885)
16¼ × 15½ × 10¼ in.
(41.3 × 39.4 × 26 cm)
Denver Art Museum, Funds
from 2009 Collectors' Choice in
honor of Lewis I. Sharp and the
Mabel Y. Hughes Charitable Trust
(2009.796)
Denver only

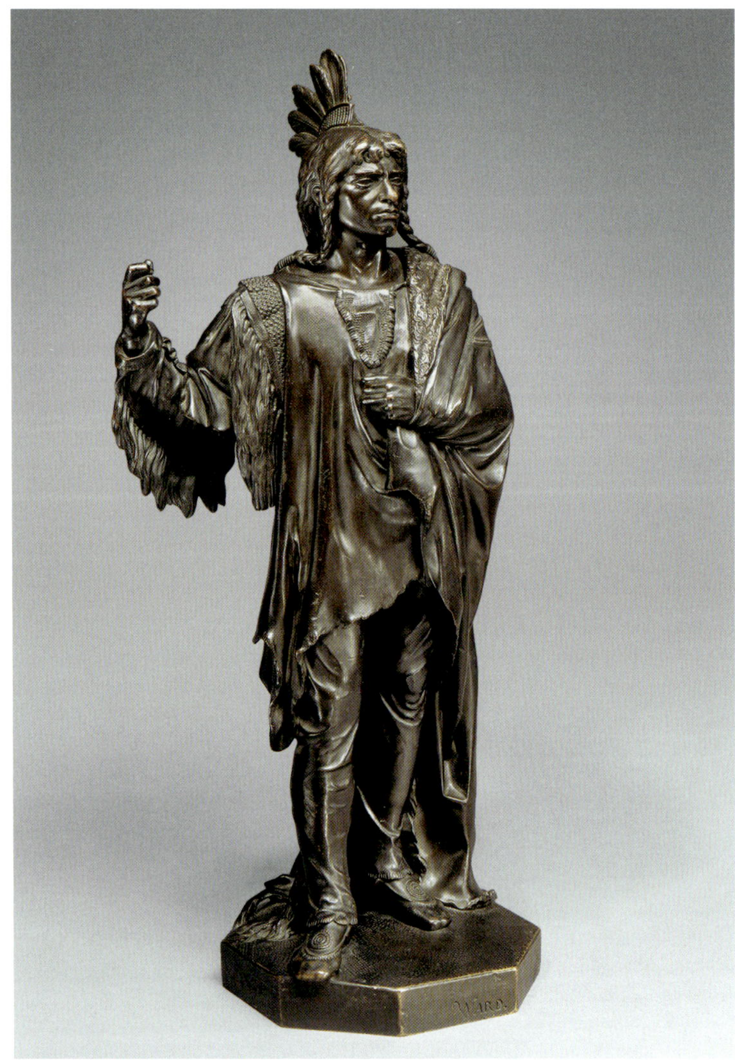

Fig. 218. John Quincy Adams Ward. *Indian Chief*, ca. 1860. Cat. 74

Cat. 77
Olin Levi Warner
American, 1844–1896
*Joseph, Chief of the Nez Percé
Indians*, 1889 (cast 1906)
Diam. 17½ in. (44.5 cm)
The Metropolitan Museum
of Art, Gift of Mr. and Mrs.
Frederick S. Wait, 1906 (06.313)
Fig. 40

Cat. 78
Adolph Alexander Weinman
American (born Germany),
1870–1952
Chief Blackbird, Ogallala Sioux,
1903
16⅜ × 16¼ × 12½ in.

(41.6 × 41.3 × 31.8 cm)
Denver Art Museum, William Sr.
and Dorothy Harmsen Collection,
by exchange (2013.35)
Denver only

Cat. 79
Adolph Alexander Weinman
American (born Germany),
1870–1952
Chief Blackbird, the Ogalla Sioux,
1903
16⅜ × 12½ × 11½ in.
(41.6 × 31.8 × 29.2 cm)
Brooklyn Museum, Gift of
George D. Pratt (15.512)
Fig. 55
New York only

Notes

Preface and Acknowledgments

1. Perriton Maxwell, "Frederic Remington: Most Typical of American Artists," *Pearson's Magazine* 18 (October 1907), p. 407.
2. Giles Edgerton [Mary Fanton Roberts], "Bronze Sculpture in America; Its Value to the Art History of the Nation," *Craftsman* 8, no. 6 (March 1908), pp. 627–28.

Brian W. Dippie, "Western Dreams and Buckskin Fantasies"

Epigraph: Albert-Alexandre de Pourtalès, *On the Western Tour with Washington Irving: The Journal and Letters of Count de Pourtalès*, edited and annotated by George F. Spaulding, translated by Seymour Feiler (Norman: University of Oklahoma Press, 1968), p. 21.

1. Theodore Roosevelt, *The Rough Riders and Men of Action,* The Works of Theodore Roosevelt, National Edition 11 (New York: Charles Scribner's Sons, 1926), pp. 175–76. Roosevelt maintained that he was "glad that our regiment had been organized in the city where the Alamo commemorates the death fight of Crockett, Bowie, and their famous band of frontier heroes." Theodore Roosevelt, "The Rough Riders: To Cuba," *Scribner's Magazine* 25 (February 1899), p. 136.
2. "Ranch Life in the Far West," *Century Magazine* 35 (February 1888), p. 502.
3. Ibid., p. 505.
4. Theodore Roosevelt to Madison Grant, March 3, 1894, in *The Letters of Theodore Roosevelt*, edited by Elting E. Morison, 8 vols. (Cambridge, Mass.: Harvard University Press, 1951–54), vol. 1, p. 367. Grant, a sportsman-conservationist like Roosevelt, would gain notoriety as the author of *The Passing of the Great Race or, The Racial Basis of European History* (New York: C. Scribner, 1916).
5. Roosevelt to Frederic Remington, December 28, 1897, *Letters of Theodore Roosevelt*, vol. 1, pp. 749–50.
6. See William H. Goetzmann and William N. Goetzmann, *The West of the Imagination*, 2nd ed. (1986; Norman: University of Oklahoma Press, 2009); and Brian W. Dippie, *West-Fever* (Los Angeles: Autry Museum of Western Heritage; Seattle: University of Washington Press, 1998).
7. George Catlin, "From Our Correspondent," *Commercial Advertiser* (New York), June 21, 1833; reprinted in Geo[rge] Catlin, *Letters and Notes on the Manners, Customs, and Condition of the North American Indians*, 2 vols. (New York: Wiley and Putnam, 1841), vol. 1, p. 62.
8. Matthew C. Field, *Matt Field on the Santa Fe Trail*, collected by Clyde and Mae Reed Porter, edited by John E. Sunder (Norman: University of Oklahoma Press, 1960), p. 18.
9. Count de Pourtalès to his mother, September 14, 1832, in de Pourtalès, *On the Western Tour with Washington Irving*, p. 21.
10. Field, *Matt Field on the Santa Fe Trail*, p. 19.
11. See Peter Pagnamenta, *Prairie Fever: British Aristocrats in the American West, 1830–1890* (New York: W. W. Norton & Company, 2012).
12. Field, *Matt Field on the Santa Fe Trail*, pp. 41–42. The tourist was Almon Gunnison, *Rambles Overland: A Trip across the Continent* (Boston: Universalist Publishing House, 1884), p. 19.
13. George Catlin, "Mouth of Yellow Stone, July 15, 1832," *Commercial Advertiser* (New York), October 20, 1832.
14. Field, *Matt Field on the Santa Fe Trail*, p. 30.
15. Catlin, "Mouth of Yellow Stone."
16. Matt Field, *Daily Picayune* (New Orleans), February 4, 1844, reporting an incident on July 3, 1843, reprinted in Matthew C. Field, *Prairie and Mountain Sketches*, collected by Clyde and Mae Reed Porter, edited by Kate L. Gregg and John Francis McDermott (Norman: University of Oklahoma Press, 1957), p. 64.
17. John C. Frémont (1842), quoted in Charles Burdett, *The Life of Kit Carson, the Great Western Hunter and Guide* (Philadelphia: Porter and Coates, 1865), p. 161.
18. See Rick Stewart, Joseph D. Ketner II, and Angela L. Miller, *Carl Wimar: Chronicler of the Missouri River Frontier*, exh. cat. (Fort Worth, Tex.: Amon Carter Museum, 1991).
19. See Nancy K. Anderson and Linda S. Ferber, *Albert Bierstadt: Art and Enterprise*, exh. cat. (New York: Hudson Hills Press; Brooklyn: Brooklyn Museum, 1990).
20. Peter H. Hassrick in Linda Bantel et al., *Forging an American Identity: The Art of William Ranney with a Catalogue of His Works*, exh. cat. (Cody, Wyo.: Buffalo Bill Historical Center, 2006), p. 61, no. 45.
21. See Brian W. Dippie, *The Vanishing American: White Attitudes and U.S. Indian Policy* (1982; Lawrence: University Press of Kansas, 1991). For cultural context, the older studies are most informative: John C. McCloskey, "The Campaign of Periodicals after the War of 1812 for National American Literature," *PMLA* 50 (March 1935), pp. 262–73; Benjamin T. Spencer, *The Quest for Nationality: An American Literary Campaign* (Syracuse: Syracuse University Press, 1957); Lillian B. Miller, *Patrons and Patriotism: The Encouragement of the Fine Arts in the United States, 1790–1860* (Chicago: University of Chicago Press, 1966); Neil Harris, *The Artist in American Society: The Formative Years, 1790–1860* (1966; New York: Clarion, 1970); J. Meredith Neil, *Toward a National Taste: America's Quest for Aesthetic Independence* (Honolulu: University Press of Hawai'i, 1975); and see Brian W. Dippie, *Catlin and His Contemporaries: The Politics of Patronage* (Lincoln: University of Nebraska Press, 1990), chap. 1.
22. [Francis Parkman], "James Fenimore Cooper," *North American Review* 74 (January 1852), p. 151; and see Brian W. Dippie, "'Flying Buffaloes': Artists and the Buffalo Hunt," *Montana: The Magazine of Western History* 51, no. 2 (Summer 2001), pp. 2–19; and Dean

Krakel, *End of the Trail: The Odyssey of a Statue* (Norman: University of Oklahoma Press, 1973), chap. 1.

23. Alexander Phimister Proctor, *Sculptor in Buckskin: The Autobiography of Alexander Phimister Proctor*, edited by Katharine C. Ebner, foreword by Peter H. Hassrick, rev. ed. (1971; Norman: University of Oklahoma Press, 2009), p. 191; and see Peter H. Hassrick et al., *Wildlife and Western Heroes: Alexander Phimister Proctor, Sculptor*, exh. cat. (Fort Worth, Tex.: Amon Carter Museum; London: Third Millennium Publishing, 2003), pp. 86–90, 210–13.

24. Wakeman Bryarly, journal entry for June 29, 1849, in *Trail to California: The Overland Journal of Vincent Geiger and Wakeman Bryarly*, edited by David Morris Potter (1945; New Haven: Yale University Press, 1962), p. 126. See *Century Magazine* 41 (November 1890), p. 112, for the Remington drawing; and see Harold McCracken, *The Frederic Remington Book: A Pictorial History of the West* (Garden City, N.Y.: Doubleday & Company, 1966), chaps. 2–3, for Remington's trapper types.

25. Frederic Remington to Poultney Bigelow, January 29, [1893], in *Frederic Remington — Selected Letters*, [edited and annotated] by Allen P. Splete and Marilyn D. Splete (New York: Abbeville Press, 1988), p. 157, for "men with the bark on," which became the title of a collection of Remington essays and stories in 1900. See Peggy and Harold Samuels, *Remington: The Complete Prints* (New York: Crown Publishers, 1990), pp. 68–71, for the eight prints in *A Bunch of Buckskins*.

26. William Henry Milburn, *The Rifle, Axe, and Saddle-bags, and Other Lectures* (New York: Derby & Jackson, 1857), p. 81.

27. F[rank] I. Whitney, ed., *Valley, Plain and Peak: Scenes on the Line of the Great Northern Railway* (1894; Saint Paul: Office of General Passenger and Ticket Agent, 1898), pp. 5, 32; and see Susan Danly et al., *The Railroad in American Art: Representations of Technological Change* (Cambridge, Mass.: MIT Press, 1988), notably the essays by Danly and Kenneth W. Maddox.

28. See Don Russell, *The Lives and Legends of Buffalo Bill* (Norman: University of Oklahoma Press, 1960), the still-standard biography, with a useful bibliography of Buffalo Bill dime novels; and Louis S. Warren, *Buffalo Bill's America: William Cody and the Wild West Show* (New York: Alfred A. Knopf, 2005).

29. Bernard De Voto, *The Year of Decision, 1846* (Boston: Little, Brown & Company, 1943).

30. Thomas Hart Benton, March 1, 1825, *Register of Debates in Congress*, 18th Cong., 2nd sess., p. 712; and see Walter Nugent, *Habits of Empire: A History of American Expansion* (New York: Alfred A. Knopf, 2008).

31. Herman Melville, *Clarel: A Poem and Pilgrimage in the Holy Land* (New York: G. P. Putnam's Sons, 1876), pt. 4, canto 21.

32. See Sandra K. Sagala, *Buffalo Bill on Stage* (Albuquerque: University of New Mexico Press, 2008); Paul L. Hedren, *First Scalp for Custer: The Skirmish at Warbonnet Creek, Nebraska, July 17, 1876*, rev. ed. (1980; Lincoln: Nebraska State Historical Society, 2005); and Sam A. Maddra, *Hostiles?: The Lakota Ghost Dance and Buffalo Bill's Wild West* (Norman: University of Oklahoma Press, 2006), for a revisionist interpretation of these events and their aftermath.

33. [John M. Burke], *Buffalo Bill's Wild West* (Nottingham: Stafford & Co. [Cody and Salsbury], [1892]), p. 62.

34. Frederick Jackson Turner, "The Significance of the Frontier in American History," in *Annual Report of the American Historical Association for the Year 1893* (Washington, D.C.: Government Printing Office, 1894), pp. 227, 199. See William Cronon, *Nature's Metropolis: Chicago and the Great West* (New York: W. W. Norton & Company, 1991), chap. 1, for a pertinent critique of Turner.

35. Turner, "Significance of the Frontier in American History," pp. 226–27. See David M. Wrobel, *The End of American Exceptionalism: Frontier Anxiety from the Old West to the New Deal* (Lawrence: University Press of Kansas, 1993); and Patricia Kelly Hall and Steven Ruggles, "'Restless in the Midst of Their Prosperity': New Evidence on the Internal Migration of Americans, 1850–2000," *Journal of American History* 91 (December 2004), pp. 829–46, for an interesting challenge to some of the many critiques of Turner's thesis.

36. John M. Burke, *"Buffalo Bill," from Prairie to Palace: An Authentic History of the Wild West* (Chicago and New York: Rand, McNally & Company, 1893), quoted in Joy S. Kasson, *Buffalo Bill's Wild West: Celebrity, Memory, and Popular History* (New York: Hill and Wang, 2000), p. 98.

37. D. M. Kelsey, *Our Pioneer Heroes and Their Daring Deeds* (Chicago: Thompson & Thomas, 1900), p. iii.

38. The description of Boone is from Milburn, *Rifle, Axe, and Saddle-bags*, p. 29; Paul Fees, "The Flamboyant Fraternity," *Gilcrease Magazine of American History and Art* 6 (January 1984), pp. 1–8; and see J. H. Beadle, *Western Wilds, and the Men Who Redeem Them: An Authentic Narrative . . .* (Cincinnati: Jones Brothers & Co., [1877]); Frank Triplett, *Conquering the Wilderness; or, New Pictorial History of the Life and Times of the Pioneer Heroes and Heroines of America . . .* (New York: N. D. Thompson & Company, 1883); and J[ames] W. Buel, *Heroes of the Plains; or, Lives and Wonderful Adventures of Wild Bill, Buffalo Bill . . . and Other Celebrated Indian Fighters* (Saint Louis: Moffat Publishing Co., 1881). For an example of the veneration America's frontier heroes continued to enjoy in the 1920s, see Albert Britt, *The Boys' Own Book of Frontiersmen* (New York: Macmillan Company, 1924), p. xiv, which makes the same claim as Kelsey and, for that matter, Roosevelt: "The American frontier was as wide as the continent and as varied. Yet there is a similarity that runs through it all and the riflemen of Kentucky were blood brothers to the men who tamed the mountains."

39. Theodore Roosevelt to Frederic Remington, September 19, 1898, in *Frederic Remington — Selected Letters*, p. 231.

40. Theodore Roosevelt, "Frontier Types," *Century Magazine* 36 (October 1888), p. 831.

41. Theodore Roosevelt and George Bird Grinnell, eds., *American Big-Game Hunting: The Book of the Boone and Crockett Club* (New York: Forest and Stream Publishing Co., 1893), p. 337.

42. *The Artistic Guide to Chicago and the World's Columbian Exposition* (Chicago: Columbian Art Company, 1892), p. 331.

43. Roosevelt and Grinnell, eds., *American Big-Game Hunting*, pp. 319–20. See Daniel Justin Herman, *Hunting and the American Imagination* (Washington, D.C.: Smithsonian Institution Press, 2001); John F. Reiger, *American Sportsmen and the Origins of Conservation*, rev. ed. (1975; Norman: University of Oklahoma Press, 1986); and Douglas Brinkley, *The Wilderness Warrior: Theodore Roosevelt and the Crusade for America* (New York: HarperCollins, 2009).

44. Advertisement, Kohl & Middleton Dime Museum, *Chicago Tribune*, January 26, 1896, for the knife-toting Calamity Jane. And see James D. McLaird, *Calamity Jane: The Woman and the Legend* (Norman: University of Oklahoma Press, 2005). As the Dime Museum's featured attraction, Calamity merited sensational copy: "PIONEER NEW WOMAN / Calamity Jane / The Most Famous of all American Women. The Fearless Intrepid SCOUT, TRAPPER, AND INDIAN SLAYER." In dress or buckskins, she was no conventional pioneer mother.

45. "Remington Collection Contains Many Objects of Rare Interest," *Journal* (Ogdensburg), undated clipping [May 1915], Frederic Remington Art Museum, Ogdensburg, N.Y., Box 18.

46. G[eorge] A[rmstrong] Custer, *My Life on the Plains; or, Personal Experiences with Indians* (New York: Sheldon & Company, 1874), pp. 33–34. Custer's tribute to Wild Bill originally appeared in *The Galaxy* in 1872.

47. See James D. McLaird, *Wild Bill Hickok & Calamity Jane: Deadwood Legends* (Pierre: South Dakota State Historical Society Press, 2008); Robert M. Utley, *Cavalier in Buckskin: George Armstrong Custer and the Western Military Frontier* (Norman:

University of Oklahoma Press, 1988); and Douglas C. McChristian, "Plainsman—or Showman?: George A. Custer's Buckskins," *Military Collector and Historian* 52 (Spring 2000), pp. 2–13.

48. John S. C. Abbott, *Boone, the Backwoodsman* (London: Ward, Lock, and Co., [1885]), p. iii; Burdett, *Life of Kit Carson*, p. 381.

49. See Brian W. Dippie, "Its Equal I Have Never Seen: Custer Explores the Black Hills in 1874," *Columbia: The Magazine of Northwest History* 19 (Summer 2005), pp. 18–27; and *Custer's Last Stand: The Anatomy of an American Myth* (1976; Lincoln: University of Nebraska Press, 1994). Buffalo Bill's publicist, John M. Burke, had fun preparing program filler rattling off the names of legendary frontiersmen in a battle for supremacy: "A Position Difficult to Attain.—A 'Plains Celebrity.'—A Title Imperishable," in *Buffalo Bill's Wild West* [1892], p. 38.

50. *The Progress of Civilization: Thrilling Incidents in Actual Border Life in the Wild West; The Great Drama Enacted by Frontier Heroes* (Philadelphia: Morrell Brothers [for Wild West and Great Forepaugh Show], [1888]), p. [7].

51. Jack Robertson, quoted in Matt Field's diary for August 10, 1843, in Field, *Prairie and Mountain Sketches*, p. 143.

52. C. M. Russell, "A Slice of My Early Life [1917]," in *Charlie Russell Roundup: Essays on America's Favorite Cowboy Artist*, edited by Brian W. Dippie (Helena: Montana Historical Society Press, 1999), p. 315; and see John Taliaferro, *Charles M. Russell: The Life and Legend of America's Cowboy Artist* (Boston: Little, Brown and Company, 1996), chap. 3, pp. 29–45, 276–77. Russell's titles for paintings included *When the Land Belonged to God* (1914; Montana Historical Society, Helena), showing buffalo, and *The World Was All before Them* or *The Romance Makers* (1918; Snite Museum of Art, University of Notre Dame, Notre Dame, Indiana), showing mountain men.

53. *The Passing of the Great West: Selected Papers of George Bird Grinnell*, edited by John F. Reiger (New York: Winchester Press, 1972), p. 44. See Wakeman Bryarly, journal entry for June 29, 1849, in *Trail to California*, p. 125, for a strikingly similar response to an encounter with some trappers and their Native wives on the South Platte: "We found here some trappers who have been laying at this place for two weeks for the purpose of trading with the emigrants. . . . Their mode of getting through life is I think rather captivating than not. They seem not to have a care, & are free from the petty annoyances & scandal of civilization. Money is no object, nothing to sell for it & nothing to buy with it. Game of all sorts in abundance, & when it is driven from one point they follow it."

54. Helen Cody Wetmore, *Last of the Great Scouts: The Life Story of Col. William F. Cody "Buffalo Bill"* (Chicago: Duluth Press Publishing Company, 1899), p. 290. Remington contributed two illustrations to this edition.

55. Helen Cody Wetmore and Zane Grey, *Last of the Great Scouts (Buffalo Bill)* (New York: Grosset & Dunlap, 1918), p. 333.

Carol Clark, "Indians on the Mantel and in the Park"

1. The men are identified in the photograph's caption in *Catalogue of Plaster Reproductions* (Boston: P. P. Caproni and Brother, 1922), p. [3]. Other images of Chief Bald Eagle and the troupe are in the Leslie Jones Collection, Print Department, Boston Public Library. I am grateful to Karen Shafts for her guidance through the collection. "Wild West and Cow Fight Are Features: Dingling Brothers' Show Is Three in One," *Boston Daily Globe*, March 25, 1922, p. 2; http://search.proquest.com/docview/504328761?accountid=8294 (accessed September 24, 2012). The article does not identify the Indian performers by name.

2. See John C. Ewers, "The Emergence of the Plains Indian as the Symbol of the North American Indian," *Annual Report of the Smithsonian Institution for the Year 1964* (Washington, D.C.: Government Printing Office, 1965), pp. 531–62.

3. M. J. Curl quotes Dallin in "Boston Artists and Sculptors in Intimate Talks I: Cyrus E. Dallin," *Boston Herald*, December 12, 1920, magazine section, p. 3. I use the generic designation "Indians" or "Natives" interchangeably to refer to indigenous peoples whose tribal affiliation I do not know. I use the term Show Indians as L. G. Moses and others do, to refer to men who worked as professional performers of Indian identity (L. G. Moses, *Wild West Shows and the Images of American Indians, 1883–1933* [Albuquerque: University of New Mexico Press, 1996], p. xiii). Indian performers proudly called themselves *oskate wicasa* or "show man," a term that news reporters and the Bureau of Indian Affairs used by the early 1890s. With thanks to Kiara Vigil for guiding me to the source of this information at http://segonku.unl.edu/~jheppler/showindian/analysis/show-indians/.

4. Alvan F. Sanborn, "Mr. Dallin in Paris," *Boston Evening Transcript*, April 17, 1909, pt. 3, p. 3.

5. *Catalogue of Plaster Reproductions* [Caproni, 1922], cover.

6. The sizes of the Gorham casts are 8–9 inches (285 casts), 21¾ inches (109 casts), and 37½ inches (9 casts). See entry by Paula M. Kozol in Kathryn Greenthal, Paula M. Kozol, and Jan Seidler Ramirez, *American Figurative Sculpture in the Museum of Fine Arts, Boston* (Boston: Museum of Fine Arts, 1986), pp. 276–78; and letter from Douglas Ward, Manager, Special Projects, Gorham Bronze/Textron, to Kathryn Greenthal, Museum of Fine Arts, Boston, May 25, 1982 (Art of the Americas curatorial files, Museum of Fine Arts, Boston). My thanks to Maureen Melton and Paul McAlpine for assistance with museum records.

7. Fraser remembered Saint-Gaudens's response in James Earle Fraser, "Autobiography," typescript, Augustus Saint-Gaudens Papers, Rauner Special Collections Library, Dartmouth College, cited in Thayer Tolles, "Circling the Borders: Augustus Saint-Gaudens and the American West," in *Shaping the West: American Sculptors of the 19th Century*, Western Passages (Denver: Petrie Institute of Western American Art, Denver Art Museum, 2010), p. 22.

8. William H. Truettner, "Museums and Historical Amnesia," in *Museums and Difference*, edited by Daniel J. Sherman (Bloomington: Indiana University Press, 2008), p. 369.

9. Two scholars have especially inspired my approach to the sculpted image of the Indian: William H. Truettner, particularly his *Painting Indians and Building Empires in North America, 1710–1840* (Berkeley and Los Angeles: University of California Press, 2010); and Alan Trachtenberg, *Shades of Hiawatha: Staging Indians, Making Americans, 1880–1930* (New York: Hill and Wang, 2004). I am further indebted to Bill Truettner for his wide-ranging scholarship on the art of the American West and for his generosity in reading my work and talking with me about ideas for this essay.

10. *Bulletin of the American Art-Union* 2, no. 1 (April 1849), p. 10. For Brown's travels and the commission from the American Art-Union, I rely on Karen Lemmey, "Henry Kirke Brown and the Development of American Public Sculpture in New York City, 1846–1876" (Ph.D. diss., City University of New York, 2005); and on Wayne Craven, "Henry Kirke Brown in Italy, 1842–1846," *American Art Journal* 1, no. 1 (Spring 1969), pp. 65–77, and Craven, "Henry Kirke Brown: His Search for an American Art in the 1840's," *American Art Journal* 4, no. 2 (November 1972), pp. 44–58.

11. Lemmey, "Henry Kirke Brown," pp. 66–80.

12. West, quoted in John Galt, *The Life, Studies, and Works of Benjamin West* (London: T. Cadell and W. Davies, 1820), p. 101. William H. Truettner extends the scholarship on Benjamin West, Mohawks, and the Apollo Belvedere in Truettner, *Painting Indians and Building Empires*, pp. 7ff.

13. Although none of the watercolors Brown painted in Michigan show such hair treatment, the presence of a related topknot on one of Brown's two

small, naturalistic busts of phenotypically Native men modeled while he was at Lake Michigan (casts in, among other collections, the Amon Carter Museum of American Art) suggests that he may have seen such hair arrangements. Yet the particular way the hair is braided and positioned on *Choosing of the Arrow* (fig. 31) also recalls the hairstyle of the Apollo Belvedere. With thanks to Karen Lemmey for discussions about this sculpture; I am also grateful to Gaylord Torrence for his assistance with this analysis, especially for showing me that Indian men on the Great Plains wore topknots of similar forms and for enlisting the help of Robert Cohen, who drew our attention to the Apollo Belvedere's topknot.

14. Letter from Henry Kirke Brown to Lydia Brown, Macanaw [*sic*, Mackinac], September 13, 1848, Henry Kirke Bush-Brown Papers, Manuscript Division, Library of Congress, Washington, D.C., vol. 2, p. 548/72, cited by Lemmey, "Henry Kirke Brown," p. 74.

15. *Providence Journal*, November 13, 1849, in clippings, American Art-Union Records, 1838–1863, cited by Lillian B. Miller, *Patrons and Patriotism: The Encouragement of the Fine Arts in the United States, 1790–1860* (Chicago: University of Chicago Press, 1966), p. 223.

16. "Nudity in Art," *Home Journal* 2, no. 204 (January 5, 1850), p. 2. The casts at the Amon Carter Museum of American Art and The Metropolitan Museum of Art retain what might be early fig leaves. My thanks to Rebecca Lawton for enabling my examination of the Carter Museum's collection of bronzes.

17. "Art: Mr. Ward's 'Indian Hunter,'" *Round Table* 8 (October 28, 1865), p. 124; http://search.proquest.com/docview/127984090?accountid=8294 (accessed November 24, 2012). A photograph taken of Ward's studio about 1885 shows the cast of the Borghese Gladiator. See Lewis I. Sharp, *John Quincy Adams Ward: Dean of American Sculpture, with a Catalogue Raisonné* (Newark: University of Delaware Press, 1985), p. 147. Ward's

sculpture also relies on a marble by the English artist John Gibson, *The Hunter and His Dog* (1847; Usher Gallery, Lincoln, England). Ward might not have seen Gibson's then-renowned work in person, but it was prominently reproduced in line engravings. One contemporary writer assumed that Ward knew Gibson's work; see "The Indian Hunter in Central Park," *Fine Arts* 1, no. 8 (October 1872), pp. 130–32. My thanks to Roberto C. Ferrari, who shared his thoughts about this connection.

18. "Mr. Ward's Statue of the Fugitive Negro, at the Academy of Design," *New York Times*, May 3, 1863, p. 5.

19. "Fine Arts: Mr. Ward's Indian Hunter," *Nation* 1, no. 16 (October 19, 1865), p. 507. The *Nation*'s critic saw the full-scale plaster on view at Snedecor's New York gallery and anticipated its final form in marble or bronze. A group of citizens purchased the bronze from Ward for installation in Central Park. I am grateful to Janis Conner and Joel Rosenkranz for discussions about Ward's *Indian Hunter* as well as for sharing their research on other works discussed in this essay.

20. Lorado Taft, *The History of American Sculpture* (New York: Macmillan Company, 1903), p. 220.

21. Patricia Janis Broder states, without citing evidence, that "Bauer [alternate spelling] based the Indian on sketches and studies made at museum exhibitions and the buffalo on specimens in the New York Zoo." *Bronzes of the American West* (New York: Harry N. Abrams, [1974]), p. 258. For a brief mention of bison in the Central Park Menagerie by 1876, see Joan Scheier, *The Central Park Zoo* (Charleston, S.C.: Arcadia, 2002), p. 24. Division of Anthropology, American Museum of Natural History, "North American Ethnographic Collection at AMNH," http://research.amnh.org/anthropology/database/nae_sub, references materials at the original site of that museum.

22. Walter Smith, *The Masterpieces of the Centennial International Exhibition Illustrated*, vol. 2, *Industrial Art* (Philadelphia: Gebbie & Barrie, [1876–78]),

p. 46. My thanks to Alice Levi Duncan for sharing her research on Baur's *Buffalo Hunt* and on other works I discuss in this essay.

23. Ibid. On industrial expansion and the near extinction of the bison in the 1870s and early 1880s, see Andrew C. Isenberg, *The Destruction of the Bison: An Environmental History, 1750–1920* (Cambridge and New York: Cambridge University Press, 2000), pp. 130–43.

24. Rogers modeled and cast *The Last Arrow* in Rome. Lauretta Dimmick makes the connection to the Dying Gaul in "Randolph Rogers, *The Last Arrow*," in Thayer Tolles et al., *American Sculpture in The Metropolitan Museum of Art*, vol. 1, *A Catalogue of Works by Artists Born before 1865* (New York: The Metropolitan Museum of Art, 1999), p. 120.

25. The early plaster is illustrated in Millard F. Rogers, Jr., *Randolph Rogers, American Sculptor in Rome* (Amherst: University of Massachusetts Press, 1971), p. 146, fig. 81.

26. Montezuma [Montague Marks], "My Note Book," *Art Amateur: A Monthly Journal Devoted to Art in the Household* 12, no. 5 (April 1885), p. 97.

27. In "My Note Book," Montezuma [Montague Marks] wrote that Baur modeled "the rough study from 'Sitting Bull,' but has not attempted a portrait of that worthy." I have not found documentation of when the sculpture was first identified as Crazy Horse, but it may not have been until the mid-twentieth century (Curatorial Records, Denver Art Museum). My thanks to Alice Levi Duncan and Alexandra Polemis for sharing their research on this sculpture.

28. Wood also commissioned seven other Indian portrait medallions from Warner. On all eight, see George Gurney, "Olin Levi Warner (1844–1896): A Catalogue Raisonné of His Sculpture and Graphic Works" (Ph.D. diss., University of Delaware, 1978), vol. 2, pp. 684–91; and Thayer Tolles, Olin Levi Warner entries in Tolles et al., *American Sculpture in The Metropolitan Museum of Art*, vol. 1, pp. 226–36, nos. 95–102.

29. "Chief Joseph," *Harper's Weekly* 34, no. 1756 (August 16, 1890), p. 644.

30. This was the second annual exhibition of the Société Nationale des Beaux-Arts, which welcomed more modern and more non-French works than the established Salon of the Société Nationale des Artistes Français. Lois Marie Fink, *American Art at the Nineteenth-Century Paris Salons* (Washington, D.C.: National Museum of American Art, Smithsonian Institution; Cambridge and New York: Cambridge University Press, 1990), pp. 120–25.

31. See John E. Carter, "Making Pictures for a News-Hungry Nation," in *Eyewitness at Wounded Knee*, by Richard E. Jenson et al. (Lincoln: University of Nebraska Press, 1991), pp. 37–60. My thanks to Marni Sandweiss for alerting me to this important source.

32. Albert Rothery, "Remarkable Success of an Omaha Sculptor," *Omaha World Herald* 35, no. 15 (October 15, 1899), p. 19 (clipping in Solon H. Borglum Papers, Manuscript Division, Library of Congress, Washington, D.C.). A detail of the sculpture—an eagle feather tied to the horse's tail—corresponds with this story. See Peter H. Hassrick, "Solon Borglum: Poet Sculptor of the West," in *Shaping the West*, pp. 26–53. I am grateful to Peter Hassrick for sharing his further research into the story, which is hard to corroborate.

33. Arthur Goodrich, "The Frontier in Sculpture," *World's Work* 3 (March 1902), p. 1872. Borglum enclosed this article in a letter to Frank Edwin Elwell, curator of Ancient and Modern Statuary at The Metropolitan Museum of Art, July 11, 1902 (Frank Edwin Elwell papers, Thomas J. Watson Library, The Metropolitan Museum of Art). Reviews of 1907 and 1908, collected in the Solon H. Borglum Papers, Library of Congress, cite this story for the sculpture.

34. Paul K. M. Thomas, "How and Where Borglum, Once a Son of Cincinnati, Gives to Marble Life," *Cincinnati Times-Star*, December 6, 1908 (clipping in Solon H. Borglum Papers, Library of Congress).

35. Rothery, "Remarkable Success of an Omaha Sculptor," p. 19.

36. Brian W. Dippie, *The Vanishing American: White Attitudes and U.S. Indian Policy* (Middletown, Conn.: Wesleyan University Press, 1982).

37. Letter from Remington to Owen Wister, [late April 1900], Owen Wister Papers, Manuscript Division, Library of Congress, Washington, D.C., reprinted in *Frederic Remington—Selected Letters*, [edited and annotated] by Allen P. Splete and Marilyn D. Splete (New York: Abbeville Press, 1988), p. 296.

38. In "Artist Wanderings among the Cheyennes," *Century Illustrated Monthly Magazine* 38, no. 4 (August 1889), pp. 483–545, Remington recounts this event and others during his four-day visit to Fort Reno in July 1888. The novel is *The Way of an Indian* (New York: Fox, Duffield & Company, 1906), which Remington completed in the summer of 1901, as noted in Peter H. Hassrick, "Frederic Remington, *The Cheyenne*," in *Twelve American Masterpieces*, dealer cat. (New York: Spanierman Gallery, 1998), p. 83 n. 10.

39. Frederic Remington, "How Stilwell Sold Out," *Collier's Weekly*, December 16, 1899, reprinted in Peggy and Harold Samuels, eds., *The Collected Writings of Frederic Remington* (Garden City, N.Y.: Doubleday & Company, 1979), p. 397, quoted by Brian W. Dippie in *Seeing America: Painting and Sculpture from the Collection of the Memorial Art Gallery of the University of Rochester*, by Marjorie B. Searl et al. (Rochester, N.Y.: Memorial Gallery of the University of Rochester, 2006), p. 126.

40. Hamlin Garland, "Among the Moki Indians," *Harper's Weekly* 40 (August 15, 1896), pp. 801–7. MacNeil later recalled this trip in "Autobiographical Sketch," June 1943, typescript, pp. 10–13 (Hermon Atkins MacNeil Papers, Division of Rare and Manuscript Collections, Cornell University Library). On representation of the Hopi Snake Dance, see Leah Dilworth, *Imagining Indians in the Southwest: Persistent Visions of a Primitive Past* (Washington, D.C.: Smithsonian Institution Press, 1996), pp. 21–75.

41. Dilworth includes these late nineteenth-century titles in *Imagining Indians*, p. 21.

42. MacNeil recounts Ayer's visit in "Autobiographical Sketch," pp. 15–16. Ayer ordered ten bronze casts, two of which he kept and the others he sold. See Andrew J. Walker, "The Aesthetics of Extinction: Art and Science in the Indian Sculptures of Hermon Atkins MacNeil," in *Perspectives on American Sculpture before 1925* [Papers from a symposium held at The Metropolitan Museum of Art, New York, October 26, 2001], edited by Thayer Tolles (New York: The Metropolitan Museum of Art, 2003), p. 106.

43. MacNeil to Winifred E. Howe, General Assistant, Educational Work, The Metropolitan Museum of Art, February 14, 1920 (Archives, MMA).

44. MacNeil to "Miss B [illeg.]," May 3, 1937, Pine Bluff, North Carolina (photocopy of letter in MacNeil file, Conner•Rosenkranz, New York).

45. In this way *The Sun Vow* was in keeping with the allegorical idealism expressed at the world's fairs where MacNeil exhibited the statuette: the Exposition Universelle (Paris, 1900), the Pan-American Exposition (Buffalo, 1901), and the Louisiana Purchase Exposition (Saint Louis, 1904). See Andrew Walker's discussion of *The Sun Vow* and of MacNeil's transformation of the Moqui runner into the more universalized monumental figure *Physical Liberty* for the 1904 fair: Andrew [J.] Walker, "Hermon Atkins MacNeil and the 1904 World's Fair: A Monumental Program for the American West," in *Shaping the West*, pp. 54–67. See, too, discussion of *Moqui Runner* and *The Sun Vow* in Judith A. Barter and Andrew J. Walker, *Window on the West: Chicago and the Art of the New Frontier, 1890–1940*, exh. cat. (Chicago: Art Institute of Chicago, 2003), pp. 41–43; and Walker, "The Aesthetics of Extinction," pp. 96–115.

46. MacNeil to "Miss B [illeg.]," May 3, 1937, Pine Bluff, North Carolina.

47. Jean Stansbury Holden, "The Sculptors MacNeil: The Varied Work of Mr. Hermon A. MacNeil and Mrs. Carol Brooks MacNeil," *World's Work* 14 (October 1907), p. 9415.

48. Ledger 2, p. 100, Roman Bronze Works Archive, Amon Carter Museum of American Art Archives, Fort Worth, Texas.

49. I am indebted to Karen Lemmey for alerting me to this photograph in the Louis McClellan Potter Papers, Archives of American Art, Smithsonian Institution, Washington, D.C.

50. Items for sale come from the shop's sign in a ca. 1900 photograph, frontispiece of India M. Spartz, ed., *Guide to the Winter and Pond Collection: Southeast and Alaska-Yukon Related Views, 1893–1943, Located in the Alaska State Library and Archives, Historical Library Section, Juneau, Alaska* (Juneau: Alaska Department of Education, Division of Libraries and Archives, 1989). The women are identified as Mrs. Jim Jacobs (center) and Mrs. Billy Williams (right) in a database of the James Wickersham collection, "Alaska's Gold Lode: A Database of Alaskan Primary Sources," http://education.alaska.gov/temp_lam_pages/library/gold/simpledetail.cfm?DetailID=1335 (accessed October 26, 2012). Information about the objects on display comes from catalogue information about the print in the Seattle Historical Society Collection, http://content.lib.washington.edu/cdm4/item_viewer.php?CISOROOT=/loc&CISOPTR=125 (accessed October 26, 2012).

51. See, for example, ethnographer G. T. Emmons, "The Basketry of the Tlingit," *Memoirs of the American Museum of Natural History* 3, no. 2 (July 1903), pp. 229–77; and collector George Wharton James, *Indian Basketry* (New York: H. Malkan, 1901). My discussion is indebted to Dilworth, *Imagining Indians*, especially chap. 3; and to Elizabeth Hutchinson, *The Indian Craze: Primitivism, Modernism, and Transculturation in American Art, 1890–1915* (Durham, N.C.: Duke University Press, 2009), especially chap. 1. Also unlike the Winter and Pond photograph is that at least one of Potter's statuettes depicts a technique described by ethnographers: a Tlingit basket weaver freed her hands by holding a root strand taut between her teeth. This cast, illustrated in "Louis Potter's Bronze Groups of Alaskan Indians," *International Studio* 32, no. 125 (May 1907), p. xvii, clearly shows one woman using this weaving technique, which Emmons describes in "Basketry of the Tlingit," p. 236.

52. Notes, signed F. D. [Faith Dennis, Assistant Curator, Department of Renaissance and Modern Art, The Metropolitan Museum of Art], of a telephone interview with MacNeil, June 8, 1939 (MacNeil files, The American Wing, MMA). Cited by Donna J. Hassler, in Thayer Tolles et al., *American Sculpture in The Metropolitan Museum of Art*, vol. 2, *A Catalogue of Works by Artists Born between 1865 and 1885* (New York: The Metropolitan Museum of Art, 2001), p. 481.

53. "Notes," *Craftsman* 16, no. 6 (September 1909), p. 710.

54. The sculpture, made of staff (plaster mixed with straw, a medium favored for temporary monuments), was destroyed after the exposition. Weinman cast his smaller study for the group in 1946 for R. W. Norton, Jr. (R. W. Norton Art Gallery, Shreveport, Louisiana).

55. Weinman identified his historical sources and recounted his modeling of Sioux and Iroquois performers in a letter to R. W. Norton, Jr., May 3, 1947 (collection of the R. W. Norton Art Foundation; my thanks to Jerry Bloomer for providing me a copy of this letter). Cummins's appearance in New York is covered in "Indians at the Garden," *New York Times*, September 18, 1903, p. 7. Weinman's sculpture is inscribed *Chief Blackbird, Ogallala Sioux* (cat. 78) and *Chief Blackbird, the Ogalla Sioux* (cat. 79); "Oglala" is the currently preferred spelling.

56. Blackbird is listed in Thomas R. Buecker and R. Eli Paul, eds., *The Crazy Horse Surrender Ledger* (Lincoln: Nebraska State Historical Society, 1994), p. 158. See Catalogue Notes and Provenance for Blackbird's shirt, sold at Sotheby's, New York (*American Indian Art*, May 18, 2011, sale N08752, lot 16); http://www.sothebys.com/en/auctions/ecatalogue/2011

/american-indian-art-n08752/lot.16.html (accessed November 12, 2012).

57. Weinman to R. W. Norton, Jr., May 3, 1947.

58. The comment was published in the *Chicago Evening Post*, June 24, 1899. For this and other information about *Indian Warrior*, I rely on Peter H. Hassrick et al., *Wildlife and Western Heroes: Alexander Phimister Proctor, Sculptor*, exh. cat. (Fort Worth, Tex.: Amon Carter Museum; London: Third Millennium Publishing, 2003), pp. 123–25. Hassrick lists the early exhibitions and gives location and acquisition dates, when known, of the two cast sizes. For example, a large cast entered the National Gallery of Canada, Ottawa, in 1909 and the Portland Art Museum, Oregon, in 1911; the Brooklyn Museum acquired a small cast in 1912. Several of these early acquisitions came from private collections.

59. Hassrick et al., *Wildlife and Western Heroes*, pp. 177–81; and Peter H. Hassrick, "Sculptor Alexander Phimister Proctor in Montana," *Montana: The Magazine of Western History* 53, no. 3 (Autumn 2003), pp. 54–59.

60. George Bird Grinnell, *The Fighting Cheyennes* (New York: Charles Scribner's Sons, 1915), p. v.

61. "Description of Drawings and Plans," in *The National American Indian Memorial at Fort Wadsworth, Harbor of New York* (brochure printed for the ground-breaking ceremony, 1913), n.p. My thanks to Ellen Sieber for providing me a copy of the brochure from the Wanamaker collection of the Mathers Museum of World Cultures, Indiana University.

62. I rely on Alan Trachtenberg's excellent discussion of the Memorial project and its meanings in *Shades of Hiawatha*, pp. 256–66.

63. Letter from Fraser to James Truslow Adams (Fraser files, The American Wing, MMA), published in "Noted Sculptor Tells of Pioneer Boyhood Spent in Mitchell," *Middle Border Bulletin* (Mitchell, South Dakota) 3, no. 3 (Winter 1944), pp. 1, 3.

64. Transcript of an interview with Julie Haggeman, "Spotlight on Youth," Bridgeport, Conn., August 8, 1947,

pp. 6–7. James Earle and Laura Gardin Fraser Papers, Archives of American Art, Smithsonian Institution, Washington, D.C., microfilm reel 2548, frames 0563–0564.

65. Stella G. S. Perry, *The Sculpture & Murals of the Panama-Pacific International Exposition: The Official Handbook* (San Francisco: Wahlgreen Co., 1915), p. 56.

66. Typescript copy of a note from Borglum to Alexander Stirling Calder, ca. 1914 (Solon H. Borglum Papers, Library of Congress), quoted in Hassrick, "Solon Borglum, Poet Sculptor of the West," p. 51. Perry, *Sculpture & Murals of the Panama-Pacific International Exposition*, p. 57.

67. Fraser received a gold medal for outstanding sculptural work at the exposition (certificate in the collection of the National Cowboy & Western Heritage Museum, Oklahoma City).

68. "A Sculptor of People and Ideals: Illustrated with the Work of James Earle Fraser," *Touchstone* 7, no. 2 (May 1920), p. 93.

69. *Official Guide to the Panama-Pacific International Exposition . . .* (San Francisco: Wahlgreen Co., 1915), p. 75.

70. See Brian W. Dippie, "'Flying Buffaloes': Artists and the Buffalo Hunt," *Montana: The Magazine of Western History* 51, no. 2 (Summer 2001), pp. 2–19; and Anne Morand, "Creative Sources of a Young Artist Painting the Old West," in *The Masterworks of Charles M. Russell: A Retrospective of Paintings and Sculpture*, by Joan Carpenter Troccoli et al., exh. cat. (Norman: University of Oklahoma Press; Denver: Denver Art Museum, 2009), pp. 129–51.

71. I rely on Rick Stewart, *Charles M. Russell, Sculptor* (Fort Worth, Tex.: Amon Carter Museum, 1994).

72. Catlin, quoted in Stewart, *Charles M. Russell, Sculptor*, p. 286.

73. Susan Rather, *Archaism, Modernism, and the Art of Paul Manship* (Austin: University of Texas Press, 1993), pp. 104–5.

74. William T. Hornaday, *Our Vanishing Wild Life: Its Extermination and Preservation* (New York: New York Zoological Society, 1913), p. 159. The

1897 plan proposed for the New York Zoological Park included space for the pronghorn antelope, but the animal did not thrive in captivity. See William Bridges, *Gathering of Animals: An Unconventional History of the New York Zoological Society* (New York: Harper and Row, 1974), pp. 70ff. I am indebted to Carlyle Eubank for connecting the two endangered species. Helen L. Horowitz argued for an ideological relationship between the early history of zoos and contemporary racism in "Animal and Man in the New York Zoological Park," *New York History* 56, no. 4 (October 1975), p. 434.

75. Alexander Phimister Proctor, *Sculptor in Buckskin: The Autobiography of Alexander Phimister Proctor*, edited by Katharine C. Ebner, foreword by Peter H. Hassrick, rev. ed. (1971; Norman: University of Oklahoma Press, 2009), p. 151. George D. Pratt bequeathed his statuettes to The Metropolitan Museum of Art. See Joan M. Marter entries in Tolles et al., *American Sculpture in The Metropolitan Museum of Art*, vol. 2, p. 751.

76. An undated photograph shows the pair on the grounds of The Braes, Pratt's estate in Glen Cove, New York. Manship is quoted by Charles H. Morgan, director of the Mead Art Museum, in notes for a presentation at the Century Association, New York, December 9, 1958 (Mead Art Museum, Amherst College, curatorial files).

Thayer Tolles, "Preserved in Bronze: The West's Vanishing Wildlife"

1. Theodore Roosevelt, "Ranch-Life and Game-Shooting in the West: I. The Ranch," *Outing* 7 (March 1886), p. 611. On Roosevelt's leading role in the Conservation Movement, see Douglas Brinkley, *The Wilderness Warrior: Theodore Roosevelt and the Crusade for America* (New York: HarperCollins, 2009).

2. A photograph of *Indian and Panther* is illustrated in Patricia Janis Broder, *Bronzes of the American West* (New

York: Harry N. Abrams, [1974]), p. 32. Brown described the narrative of the group in a letter to his patron Ezra Prentice, January 21, 1850, Henry Kirke Brown Papers, Archives of American Art, Smithsonian Institution, Washington, D.C., microfilm reel 2770, frame number obscured; partially published in Broder, *Bronzes of the American West*, p. 32.

3. Kemeys, quoted in Hamlin Garland, "Edward Kemeys: A Sculptor of Frontier Life and Wild Animals," *McClure's Magazine* 5 (July 1895), p. 126.

4. *Explication des ouvrages de peinture, sculpture . . .*, Société des Artistes Français, Salon de 1878 (Paris: Imprimerie National, 1878), p. 383, no. 4358, as "Combat d'un bison contre des loups: —groupe, plâtre." When shown at the annual exhibition of the National Academy of Design in 1879, it was lauded as "the most virile piece of sculpture in the exhibition." "The Academy Sculptors," *Evening Post* (New York), April 26, 1879, p. 1.

5. See Bruce Hampton, "Shark of the Plains: Early Western Encounters with Wolves," *Montana: The Magazine of Western History* 46 (Spring 1996), pp. 2–13.

6. Quoted in James Willard Schultz, *Blackfeet and Buffalo: Memories of Life among the Indians* (Norman: University of Oklahoma Press, 1962), pp. 166–67, as quoted in Hampton, "Shark of the Plains," pp. 12–13.

7. Barye's sculpture was eagerly collected on the East Coast, notably by the Baltimoreans George A. Lucas and William T. Walters, who assembled extensive collections of his bronzes in the 1870s and 1880s and made them accessible to the public in Baltimore and Washington, D.C., beginning in 1874. William R. Johnston, "Barye's American Patrons," in *Untamed: The Art of Antoine-Louis Barye*, by William R. Johnston and Simon Kelly, exh. cat. (Baltimore: Walters Art Museum, 2006), esp. pp. 52–55. These bronzes are now housed at the Baltimore Art Museum (166 bronzes), the Walters Art Museum (175), and the Corcoran Gallery of Art (120). Barye mania during the 1880s

continued with the publication of American notices on his work. See especially William T. Walters, *Antoine-Louis Barye from the French of Various Critics* (Baltimore, 1885), with an introduction dedicated "To the Young Artists of America"; and Theodore Child, "Antoine-Louis Barye," *Harper's New Monthly Magazine* 71 (September 1885), pp. 585–603.

8. Kemeys exhibited reductions of *Still Hunt* in New York at Tiffany & Co. and in an exhibition of taxidermy and wildlife sculpture in 1885, as well as in Washington, D.C., at the Smithsonian Institution's United States National Museum, where he placed twenty-four plaster models in 1883. See David J. Wagner, *American Wildlife Art* (Seattle: Marquand Books, 2008), p. 170. Kemeys's wolf head with half-moon device, which appears on many of his bronzes, was described by his friend Perk Van Lith as "his trade-mark, or, better said, 'remark,' for . . . it was by the modeling of a wolf's head that he discovered his true vocation." See "The Kemeys' at Home," *Collector* 7 (November 1, 1895), p. 7.

9. See *The Kemeys Collection: Sketches and Portraits in Clay by Edward Kemeys, Reproduced in Bronze by the Winslow Bros. Co. Chicago, 1894* (Chicago, 1894).

10. See ibid. See also Adam Duncan Harris, *Wildlife in American Art: Masterworks from the National Museum of Wildlife Art* (Norman: University of Oklahoma Press, 2009), pp. 92–93.

11. Julian Hawthorne, "American Wild Animals in Art," *Century Magazine* 28, no. 2 (June 1884), p. 215.

12. See *Official Catalogue, World's Columbian Exposition, 1893. Part X. Department K., Fine Arts* (Chicago, 1893), p. 12, no. 73, as *American Black Bear*. See also Carolyn Kinder Carr et al., *Revisiting the White City: American Art at the 1893 World's Fair*, exh. cat. (Washington, D.C.: National Museum of American Art and National Portrait Gallery, 1993), p. 367. The bronze sculpture was priced at two hundred dollars. The role of animal sculpture, particularly by Kemeys and Proctor,

at the World's Columbian Exposition is expertly analyzed in Wagner, *American Wildlife Art*, pp. 173–85.

13. Proctor summarized his student routine as follows: "My usual practice was to go to the menagerie very early, work at the league later in the morning, and model in the afternoon. I also went to the Metropolitan Museum of Art as often as I could." Alexander Phimister Proctor, *Sculptor in Buckskin: The Autobiography of Alexander Phimister Proctor*, edited by Katharine C. Ebner, foreword by Peter H. Hassrick, rev. ed. (1971; Norman: University of Oklahoma Press, 2009), p. 99.

14. See *Catalogue of the Works of Antoine-Louis Barye Exhibited at the American Art Galleries . . . under the Auspices of the Barye Monument Association . . . for the Benefit of the Barye Monument Fund* (New York, 1889).

15. See Peter H. Hassrick et al., *Wildlife and Western Heroes: Alexander Phimister Proctor, Sculptor*, exh. cat. (Fort Worth, Tex.: Amon Carter Museum; London: Third Millennium Publishing, 2003), pp. 88–89.

16. In 1894 President Grover Cleveland signed into law the Yellowstone Game Protection Act to protect birds and animals in the park—the first federal legislation to protect bison and to make poaching and other attacks on wildlife illegal. For further discussion of wildlife protection in Yellowstone, see Michael Punke, *Last Stand: George Bird Grinnell, the Battle to Save the Buffalo, and the Birth of the New West* (Washington, D.C.: Smithsonian Books, 2007).

17. See John F. Reiger, *American Sportsmen and the Origins of Conservation*, 3rd ed. (1975; Corvallis: Oregon State University Press, 2001), pp. 45ff. *American Sportsman* was absorbed by *Forest and Stream* in 1877.

18. On the Boone and Crockett Club, see Reiger, *American Sportsmen and the Origins of Conservation*, pp. 146–74; and Brinkley, *Wilderness Warrior*, pp. 201ff.

19. See Lisa Mighetto, *Wild Animals and American Environmental Ethics* (Tucson: University of Arizona Press, 1991), pp. 9–26.

20. See E. D. Palmer, "The Kansas Exhibit of Mounted Specimens of the

Animals of the State," *Scientific American* 69 (July 15, 1893), p. 42.

21. Proctor's description of the members' activities and of the cabin's interior appears in Proctor, *Sculptor in Buckskin*, p. 111. The sculptor remained an active member of the club until the 1940s. In 1908 he completed a frontal high-relief *Head of Brown Bear (Kodiak)* (cat. 40) that was made specifically for the Boone and Crockett Club. Proctor distributed plaster casts of it to attendees at that year's annual dinner, and members subsequently purchased bronze replicas. Hassrick et al., *Wildlife and Western Heroes*, p. 152.

22. Garland, "Edward Kemeys," p. 128.

23. See especially Hassrick et al., *Wildlife and Western Heroes*, pp. 102–5. Proctor reveled in recounting the story of how, at age eighteen, he shot his first grizzly and an elk on the same day; see Proctor, *Sculptor in Buckskin*, pp. 38–40.

24. Proctor, *Sculptor in Buckskin*, pp. 87–88.

25. Lorado Taft, "A. Phimister Proctor," *Brush and Pencil* 2 (September 1898), p. 247.

26. Proctor, *Sculptor in Buckskin*, p. 120.

27. Proctor recalled Roosevelt's description of the presentation, ibid., pp. 89–90. A drawing of *Stalking Panther* was chosen as the frontispiece for Roosevelt's book *The Strenuous Life* (1900).

28. Solon H. Borglum, "Our Vanishing Types," *Youth's Companion* 84 (November 24, 1910), p. 654. For a contextual discussion of the horse in the American West, see Pekka Hämäläinen, "The Rise and Fall of Plains Indian Horse Cultures," *Journal of American History* 90 (December 2003), pp. 833–62. Thanks to Peter H. Hassrick for generously sharing his insights on Proctor and Borglum.

29. Illustrated in Arthur Goodrich, "The Frontier in Sculpture," *World's Work* 3 (March 1902), pp. 1865–66, 1868. A marble carving of *Our Slave* (1901) is in the Joslyn Art Museum, Omaha.

30. Borglum, "Our Vanishing Types," p. 654. See also Peter H. Hassrick,

"Solon Borglum: Poet Sculptor of the West," in *Shaping the West: American Sculptors of the 19th Century*, Western Passages (Denver: Petrie Institute of Western American Art, Denver Art Museum, 2010), p. 37.

31. Brian W. Dippie, "'Flying Buffaloes': Artists and the Buffalo Hunt," *Montana: The Magazine of Western History* 51, no. 2 (Summer 2001), p. 17.

32. Remington to Shrady, May 6, [1908], courtesy J. N. Bartfield Galleries, New York.

33. Charles Hall Garrett, "The New American Sculptor," *Munsey's Magazine* 29 (July 1903), p. 548. The business arrangement is outlined in Starr to Shrady, February 8, 1901, Henry Merwin Shrady Papers, Archives of American Art, Smithsonian Institution, Washington, D.C., microfilm reel 647, frame 553.

34. Contemporary literature on the extermination of the bison is, not surprisingly, vast, but the overhunted North American moose, too, was the subject of cautionary publications. See, for instance, Madison Grant, "The Vanishing Moose, and Their Extermination in the Adirondacks," *Century Illustrated Magazine* 47 (January 1894), pp. 345–56.

35. Proctor, quoted in Bertha H. Smith, "The Wild Animal in Art," *Outlook* 81 (September 23, 1905), p. 214. Proctor was featured in the article "When Leo Poses: Wild Animals at the Zoo Are Patient Models," *New York Herald*, May 25, 1902, section 5, p. 16, a charming survey of the daily routine of animal artists at the Central Park Menagerie.

36. Madison Grant, "History of the Zoological Society," *Zoological Society Bulletin*, no. 37 (January 1910), pp. 590–91, quoted in Helen L. Horowitz, "Animal and Man in the New York Zoological Park," *New York History* 56, no. 4 (October 1975), p. 428. For further discussion of the Boone and Crockett Club's involvement at the zoo, see also pp. 427, 438–43.

37. William Bridges, *Gathering of Animals: An Unconventional History of the New York Zoological Society* (New York: Harper and Row, 1974), pp. 143–44.

38. Harvey, quoted in Dorothy Z. Bicker, Jane Z. Vail, and Vernon G. Wills, eds., *The Autobiography of Eli Harvey, Quaker Sculptor from Ohio*, 2nd ed. (Wilmington, Ohio: Clinton County Historical Society, 1966), p. 58.

39. Harvey, quoted ibid., p. 55.

40. "Largest Bull Moose Killed in Canada by a Sculptor," *World* (New York), May 26, 1902, in scrapbook #1, p. 9, Alexander Phimister Proctor Collection, Harold McCracken Research Library, Buffalo Bill Center of the West, Cody, Wyoming. Proctor maintained an affiliation with the American Museum of Natural History, later exhibiting representations of lions in a show there in 1914. See Hassrick et al., *Wildlife and Western Heroes*, p. 71.

41. Harvey, quoted in Bicker, Vail, and Wills, eds., *Autobiography of Eli Harvey*, p. 76.

42. James L. Clark, *Trails of the Hunted* (Boston: Little, Brown, and Company, 1928), p. 221.

43. For a history of the creation of habitat dioramas at the museum, including the Hall of North American Mammals, see Stephen Christopher Quinn, *Windows on Nature: The Great Habitat Dioramas of the American Museum of Natural History* (New York: Harry N. Abrams; American Museum of Natural History, 2006). The Hall of North American Mammals recently underwent a comprehensive renovation, reopening in 2012.

44. James L. Clark, *Good Hunting: Fifty Years of Collecting and Preparing Habitat Groups for the American Museum* (Norman: University of Oklahoma Press, 1966), p. 150.

45. Ibid., p. 10.

46. "Bears of New York City," *Forest and Stream* 65 (September 2, 1905), p. 188.

47. Clark, *Trails of the Hunted*, pp. 203–4.

48. Andrew C. Isenberg, *The Destruction of the Bison: An Environmental History, 1750–1920* (Cambridge and New York: Cambridge University Press, 2000), p. 169. In 1907 fifteen bison from the Bronx Zoo were shipped to the Wichita Forest Reserve, Oklahoma. Horowitz, "Animal and Man in the New York Zoological Park," p. 442.

49. The original Buffalo Mantel was removed during remodeling of the White House between 1949 and 1952; it is now in the Harry S. Truman Library and Museum, Independence, Missouri. A replica was carved and installed as part of renovations during the Kennedy administration. Hassrick et al., *Wildlife and Western Heroes*, pp. 160–61. On Theodore Roosevelt's advocacy for using native animals in architectural decoration, see Roosevelt, letter to American Institute of Architects, read December 7, 1916, *Proceedings of the Fiftieth Annual Convention of the American Institute of Architects* (Washington, D.C.: American Institute of Architects, 1917), p. 45.

50. Pratt's casts are in The Metropolitan Museum of Art (cat. 41); the Brooklyn Museum; the Art Institute of Chicago; the Cleveland Museum of Art; and the Toledo Museum of Art. Hassrick et al., *Wildlife and Western Heroes*, p. 169. Pratt also gave the Brooklyn Museum nine other Proctor bronzes between 1912 and 1914, and he bequeathed *Buckaroo* (1914; cast 1915) to the Metropolitan in 1935.

51. Putnam, quoted in Julie Helen Heyneman, *Arthur Putnam: Sculptor* (San Francisco: Johnck and Seeger, 1932), p. 41, as quoted in Harris, *Wildlife in American Art*, p. 111.

52. On Putnam, his fascination with pumas, and their association with night and death, see Alexander Nemerov, "The Dark Cat: Arthur Putnam and a Fragment of Night," *American Art* 16, no. 1 (Spring 2002), pp. 36–59. For a contemporary assessment of the puma, "an animal of many names, of which puma, cougar, panther, painter and mountain lion are some of the best known," see "The Pumas," *Forest and Stream* 58 (January 4, 1902), p. 6.

53. For the casting history of *Puma and Deer* bronzes, see Ilene Susan Fort and Michael Quick, *American Art: A Catalogue of the Los Angeles County Museum of Art Collection* (Los Angeles: Los Angeles County Museum of Art, 1991), p. 402. Putnam produced bronzes in his own foundry in San Francisco, at Rudier in Paris, and at Roman Bronze Works in New York. This particular cast (cat. 47) does not have a foundry mark.

54. Rick Stewart, *Charles M. Russell, Sculptor* (Fort Worth, Tex.: Amon Carter Museum, 1994), pp. 53–54.

55. Ibid., p. 47.

56. Nancy C. Russell, "Jake Hoover," unpublished biographical manuscript, undated, Helen E. and Homer E. Britzman Collection, Taylor Museum for Southwestern Studies of the Colorado Springs Fine Arts Center, quoted in Stewart, *Charles M. Russell, Sculptor*, p. 16.

57. C. M. Russell, "A Slice of My Early Life [1917]," in *Charlie Russell Roundup: Essays on America's Favorite Cowboy Artist*, edited by Brian W. Dippie (Helena: Montana Historical Society Press, 1999), p. 315.

58. Stewart, *Charles M. Russell, Sculptor*, p. 186.

59. Ibid., pp. 61–62.

60. William T. Hornaday, *The American Natural History*, 2 vols. (1904; New York: Charles Scribner's Sons, 1914), vol. 1, p. 53, quoted in Valerie M. Fogelman, "American Attitudes towards Wolves: A History of Misperception," *Environmental Review: ER* 13 (Spring 1989), p. 70. Russell owned a copy of *The American Natural History*. See Stewart, *Charles M. Russell, Sculptor*, p. 63.

61. Nancy C. Russell, quoted in *The First Memorial Exhibition of the Works of Charles Marion Russell, "Painter of the West"* (Santa Barbara: Art League of Santa Barbara, 1927), n.p., quoted in Stewart, *Charles M. Russell, Sculptor*, p. 230.

62. Stewart, *Charles M. Russell, Sculptor*, p. 274.

63. Royal Cortissoz, "The Field of Art. Some Wild Beasts Sculptured by A. Phimister Proctor," *Scribner's Magazine* 48 (November 1909), p. 637.

Peter H. Hassrick, "Cowboys in Bronze"

1. Typescript copy of a letter from William Holbrook Beard to his wife, Carrie Le Clear Beard, dated July 9, 1866, Robert Taft Papers, Kansas State Historical Society, Topeka.

2. Whittredge, from *The Autobiography of Worthington Whittredge, 1820–1910*, edited and annotated by John I. H. Baur (1942; New York: Arno Press, 1969), p. 45.

3. Ibid., p. 48.

4. Bayard Taylor, *Colorado: A Summer Trip* (New York: G. P. Putnam and Son, 1867), p. 6.

5. Lonn Taylor and Ingrid Maar, *The American Cowboy*, exh. cat. (Washington, D.C.: Library of Congress, 1983), p. 18.

6. For a complete account of the Wild West programs over the next decade and more, see Sarah Jane Blackstone, "Buffalo Bill's Wild West: A Study of the History, Structure, Personnel, Imagery and Effect" (Ph.D. diss., Northwestern University, Evanston, Ill., 1983), pp. 293–305.

7. *Buffalo Bill's Wild West*, programs for 1883 and 1885 from the Harold McCracken Research Library, Buffalo Bill Center of the West, Cody, Wyoming. Cody's promotional agent, John M. Burke, talked about the dual image of the cowboy in these early years. See his essay "What Is a Cowboy?" in *Buffalo Bill: From Prairie to Palace* (Chicago: Rand, McNally and Company, Publishers, 1893), pp. 36–43. Buffalo Bill discusses his own brief life as a cowboy early in his western experiences in [William F. Cody], *The Life of Hon. William F. Cody Known as Buffalo Bill . . .* (Hartford, Conn.: Frank E. Bliss, 1879), pp. 362–63. Although the "American Cowboy" poster (fig. 106) was not copyrighted until 1896, it portrays Buck Taylor, whose heyday with the Wild West was 1884 through 1890, when he left to start his own show.

8. Bill Nye, "The Real and the Ideal Cowboy Contrasted to the Latter's Disadvantage," *World* (New York), October 3, 1887.

9. Letter from an unidentified representative of the Union Stock Yard and Transit Company of Chicago to John D. Gillett, dated August 24, 1888, in the collection of the Chicago History Museum Research Center, Chicago.

10. Theodore Roosevelt, "Ranch Life in the Far West," *Century Magazine* 35 (February 1888), pp. 495–510. The articles continued through October that year and were published as a book, *Ranch Life and the Hunting-Trail* (New York: Century Co., 1888).

11. As early as 1885, Roosevelt was promoting the virtues of the cowboy. See Theodore Roosevelt, *Hunting Trips of a Ranchman: Hunting Trips on the Prairie and in the Mountains* (New York: Review of Reviews Company, 1885), pp. 10–13. Also, later, see Theodore Roosevelt, "Frontier Types," *Century Magazine* 36 (October 1888), pp. 835–36.

12. Remington diaries for summer 1886 in the Robert Taft Papers, Kansas State Historical Society, Topeka. Others at the time joined in this assessment, including Joseph Nimmo, Jr., "The American Cow-boy," *Harper's New Monthly Magazine* 73 (November 1886), pp. 880, 884. During his travels in Arizona the year before, Remington must have encountered many cowboys as well; about half of his paintings from that trip are of cowboys. See Peter H. Hassrick and Melissa J. Webster, *Frederic Remington: A Catalogue Raisonné of Paintings, Watercolors and Drawings* (Cody, Wyo.: Buffalo Bill Historical Center, 1996), pp. 69–72.

13. See Rufus Fairchild Zogbaum's account of his time with the cowboys, "A Day's 'Drive' with Montana Cowboys," *Harper's New Monthly Magazine* 71 (July 1885), pp. 188–93.

14. "About the Studios: Work of the Young Phimister Proctor," *Daily Inter Ocean* (Chicago), May 19, 1893.

15. "Objected to the Pose," *Daily Inter Ocean* (Chicago), May 26, 1893.

16. See Peter H. Hassrick et al., *Wildlife and Western Heroes: Alexander Phimister Proctor, Sculptor*, exh. cat. (Fort Worth, Tex.: Amon Carter Museum; London: Third Millennium Publishing, 2003), p. 191.

17. Owen Wister, "The Evolution of the Cow-Puncher," *Harper's Monthly* 91 (September 1895), pp. 602–16; and William Trowbridge Larned, "The Passing of the Cow-Puncher," *Lippincott's Monthly Magazine* 56 (August 1895), pp. 267–70.

18. Roosevelt, "Frontier Types," p. 843.

19. See Larned, "Passing of the Cow-Puncher," p. 268, where he says, "The personality of horse and rider is in a measure merged; the one without the other is only a part of the whole." On this point, see also Philip Ashton Rollins, *The Cowboy: His Characteristics, His Equipment, and His Part in the Development of the West* (New York: Charles Scribner's Sons, 1922), p. 31.

20. Letter from Remington to Owen Wister, dated January 6, 1895, in the Owen Wister Papers, Manuscript Division, Library of Congress, Washington, D.C.

21. Arthur Hoeber, "From Ink to Clay," *Harper's Weekly* 39 (October 19, 1895), p. 993; William A. Coffin, "Remington's 'Broncho Buster,'" *Century Magazine* 52 (June 1896), p. 319; C. M. Fairbanks, "Artist Remington at Home and Afield," *Metropolitan Magazine* 4 (July 1896), p. 448.

22. *Denver Field and Farm*, no. 502 (August 17, 1896), p. 115.

23. Theodore Roosevelt, "In Cowboy-Land," *Century Magazine* 47 (June 1898), p. 276.

24. Lorado Taft, *The History of American Sculpture* (New York: MacMillan Company, 1903), p. 488. Many modern scholars differ with that assessment, including Emily Neff, *Frederic Remington: The Hogg Brothers Collection of the Museum of Fine Arts Houston* (Princeton, N.J.: Princeton University Press, 2000), p. 59.

25. "Sculptor of Plains Visits Life Friend," *San Jose Daily Mercury*, July 11, 1907. This point has been disputed. In "How and Where Borglum Gives to Marble Life," *Cincinnati Times-Star*, December 5, 1907, Paul K. M. Thomas contends that Borglum had made up his mind to be a sculptor before leaving Cincinnati.

26. Louise Eberle, "In Recognition of an American Sculptor," *Scribner's Monthly* 72 (September 1922), p. 379.

27. W. G. Bowdoin, "S. Borglum and His Work," *Art Interchange* 46 (January 1901), p. 2. Other critics observed this difference too, referring to Remington's interpretations as too "theatrical" rather than genuine. See "Some American Bronzes," *Art Collector* 9 (March 1889), p. 43.

28. Letter from Gutzon Borglum to James B. Rankin (an early biographer of Charles M. Russell), dated November 20, 1936, in the Rankin Papers, Montana Historical Society, Helena.

29. Ilene Susan Fort, *The Figure in American Sculpture: A Question of Modernity*, exh. cat. (Seattle: University of Washington Press, 1995), p. 30.

30. See, for example, Charles H. Caffin, "Solon Borglum," in *Catalogue of an Exhibition of Bronzes, Marbles and Other Sculpture* (New York: Frederick Keppel & Co., 1903), p. 6. Examples of those who felt differently about Rodin's sway include Selene Ayer Armstrong. In "Solon H. Borglum, Sculptor of American Life: An Artist Who Knows the Value of 'Our Incomparable Materials,'" *Craftsman* 12 (July 1907), p. 382, she denied even the "trace" of "the despotic influence of Rodin's genius." More recently, James Mackay (*The Animaliers: A Collector's Guide to the Animal Sculptors of the 19th and 20th Centuries* [New York: E. P. Dutton & Co., 1973], p. 110) has contended that Borglum was more "spontaneous and instinctive" than Rodin and aimed, without introspection, "to interpret in a vigorous ensemble the vivid impression of an objective fact."

31. For a further discussion of this, see Beatrice Gilman Proske, *Brookgreen Gardens, Sculpture* (Brookgreen, S.C.: Brookgreen Gardens, 1943), p. 76.

32. See A. Mervyn Davies, *Solon H. Borglum: "A Man Who Stands Alone"* (Chester, Conn.: Pequot Press, 1974), p. 86.

33. See Michael D. Greenbaum, *Icons of the West: Frederic Remington's Sculpture* (Ogdensburg, N.Y.: Frederic Remington Art Museum, 1996), p. 85.

34. See Michael Edward Shapiro et al., *Frederic Remington: The Masterworks*, exh. cat. (New York: Harry N. Abrams; Saint Louis: Saint Louis Art Museum, 1988), pp. 195–96.

35. *The Frozen Sheep-Herder* appeared in *Harper's Weekly* 44 (March 10, 1900), pp. 224–25, and *Drifting before the Storm* appeared in *Collier's Weekly* 53 (July 9, 1904), pp. 14–15.

36. Owen Wister, *The Virginian* (New York: MacMillan Publishers, 1902), p. viii.

37. *Trailing Texas Cattle* was illustrated in *Collier's Weekly* 53 (November 12, 1904), pp. 16–17.

38. Roosevelt, "Frontier Types," p. 836.

39. Ibid., p. 838.

40. *Daily Enterprise* (Livingston, Montana), July 3, 1883; *Laramie Weekly Sentinel*, March 20, 1886.

41. "The 'Cow-Boys' of Arizona," *Harper's Weekly* 26 (February 25, 1882), p. 120.

42. Charles A. Siringo, *A Texas Cow Boy or, Fifteen Years on the Hurricane Deck of a Spanish Pony* (Chicago: Siringo & Dobson, Publishers, 1886), p. 177.

43. See James K. Ballinger, *Frederic Remington* (New York: Harry N. Abrams, 1989), p. 104, for a discussion of this shortcoming.

44. Solon H. Borglum, "Our Vanishing Types," *Youth's Companion* 84 (November 24, 1910), p. 654.

45. Borglum, quoted in Arthur Goodrich, "The Frontier in Sculpture," *World's Work* 3 (March 1902), p. 1864.

46. For a reference to Borglum's connection to Emerson, see Armstrong, "Solon Borglum," p. 382.

47. Andrew [J.] Walker, "Hermon Atkins MacNeil and the 1904 World's Fair: A Monumental Program for the American West," in *Shaping the West: American Sculptors of the 19th Century, Western Passages* (Denver: Petrie Institute of Western American Art, Denver Art Museum, 2010), p. 63.

48. See Theodore Roosevelt, *The Rough Riders* (New York: G. P. Putnam's Sons, 1900), p. 242.

49. Henry J. Winser, *The Great Northwest* (New York: G. P. Putnam's Sons, 1883), p. 173.

50. See Theodore Gerrish, *Life in the World's Wonderland* (Biddeford, Maine: Biddeford Journal Press, 1887), pp. 212–13. Gerrish contends, as Borglum would later, that "the cowboy is the most thoroughly misunderstood man . . . on the face of the earth." In reality he "is noble-hearted, . . . honorable, . . . brave to rashness and generous to a fault." But in the East,

cowboys are "pictured as outcasts of civilization."

51. I am grateful to Russell collector Tom Petrie for sharing this perspective with me.

52. Although the statue is titled *Bucky O'Neill*, his name is generally spelled Buckey.

53. Roosevelt, *Rough Riders*, p. 135.

54. Ibid., p. 77.

55. John N. McGroarty, "A Visitor's Opinion of the Monument," from a contemporary clipping in the Solon H. Borglum and Borglum Family Papers, Archives of American Art, Smithsonian Institution, Washington, D.C. For a similar assessment, see Gutzon Borglum, "Solon H. Borglum," *American Art Magazine* 13 (November 1922), p. 473.

56. Alexander Nemerov, *Frederic Remington and Turn-of-the-Century America* (New Haven and London: Yale University Press, 1995), p. 70.

57. Philip Ashton Rollins, *The Cowboy* (New York: Charles Scribner's Sons, 1922), p. 33.

58. Remington, quoted in Perriton Maxwell, "Frederic Remington: Most Typical of American Artists," *Pearson's Magazine* 18 (October 1907), p. 394.

59. For a discussion of Russell's sales to Starr, see Rick Stewart, *Charles M. Russell, Sculptor* (Fort Worth, Tex.: Amon Carter Museum, 1994), p. 179; and for Borglum's dissatisfaction with Starr, see Peter H. Hassrick, "Solon Borglum: Poet Sculptor of the West," in *Shaping the West*, p. 52.

60. *A Bad Hoss* appeared in a four-part Russell color portfolio accompanied by drawings by his New York studio mate, Will Crawford, in *Scribner's Magazine* 37 (February 1905), p. 159. There are other, similar works from this period, such as *The Bucker* of 1904, a watercolor in the Sid Richardson Museum, Fort Worth, Texas.

61. See Emerson Hough, "Wild West Faking," *Collier's* 42 (December 19, 1908), p. 18; and Smith, quoted in Harry Peyton Steger, "Photographing the Cowboy as He Disappears," *World's Work* 17 (January 1909), p. 11123.

62. Gutzon Borglum, "The End of the Trail," *New York Herald Tribune*, December 5, 1926.

63. Buffalo Bill made one effort; see the letter from W. F. Cody to Eva Remington, August 21, 1910, in the archives of the Frederic Remington Art Museum, Ogdensburg, New York. For discussions of the other efforts, see Atwood Manley and Margaret Manley Mangum, *Frederic Remington and the North Country* (New York: E. P. Dutton, 1988), pp. 219–24. For Roosevelt's efforts, see the Frederic Remington Monument Fund brochure in the archives of the Frederic Remington Art Museum. Articles in western newspapers of the time sometimes confuse whether the monument would be *The Broncho Buster* or a bronze monument of Remington himself. See "Men of the Hour," *Denver Field and Farm*, no. 1239 (September 10, 1910), and "Statue to Remington, T. R.'s Plea," *Denver Post*, August 10, 1910.

64. George F. McFarland, "Sally James Farnham: The Remington Years," *St. Lawrence County Historical Association Quarterly* 36 (Summer 1991), p. 28.

65. See Jeremy Johnston, "The Great Equestrian Statue Race: Theodore Roosevelt and the Efforts to Memorialize Buffalo Bill," *Points West* (Spring 2007), pp. 8–12.

66. Ernest Peixotto, "A Sculptor of the West," *Scribner's Magazine* 68 (September 1920), p. 275.

67. Lillian Tingle, "Sculptor Is Guest," *Morning Oregonian* (Portland), July 13, 1915.

68. Ann Evans issued the invitation in a letter to Solon's sister-in-law, Lucy Borglum, dated April 16, 1921. At the bottom of the letter, Borglum lists five sculptures — *Snow Drift*, *Blizzard* (cat. 8), *Cowboy at Rest* (fig. 125), *Reveries of a Pioneer*, and *One in One Thousand* (fig. 133) — as his suggestions. The letter is in the Solon H. Borglum Papers, Manuscript Division, Library of Congress, Washington, D.C.

69. "Cowboys Live in Clay under Skillful Hands of A. Phimister Proctor," *Evening Telegram* (Portland), July 24, 1915.

70. For a summary of Farnham's art philosophy, see Peter H. Hassrick, *The Art of Being an Artist: Sally James Farnham, American Sculptor* (Ogdensburg, N.Y.: Frederic Remington Art Museum, 2005). Taken from a typescript of remarks by Farnham made before the Art Association of University Women, ca. 1936, in the Farnham Papers, Tinsley Collection, Natural Dam, Arkansas.

71. Rogers, quoted in Donald Day, *Will Rogers: A Biography* (New York: David McKay Company, 1962), p. 115.

72. For a description of the character expectations that were imposed on Hart, see his producer's guidelines in Thomas H. Ince, "The Undergraduate and the Scenario," *Bookman: A Review of Books and Life* 47 (June 1918), p. 4. A fully informed discussion of Hart's evolving character is in Andrew Brodie Smith, *Shooting Cowboys and Indians* (Boulder: University Press of Colorado, 2003), pp. 157–85.

Thomas Brent Smith, "Settling the West: Fearless Men and Strong Women"

All epigraphs are from Walt Whitman, "Pioneers! O Pioneers!" in *Leaves of Grass* (New York: W. E. Chapin & Co., Printers, 1867), pp. 25–30.

1. Owen Wister, "Introduction," in *Done in the Open: Drawings by Frederic Remington* (New York: P. F. Collier & Sons, 1903).

2. Frederic Remington, "A Scout with the Buffalo-Soldiers," *Century Magazine* 37 (April 1889), pp. 899–911.

3. "Clarke, Powhatan H.," in U.S. Senate Committee on Veterans' Affairs Report, *Medal of Honor Recipients: 1863–1978* (Washington, D.C.: Government Printing Office, 1979); citations available at U.S. Army Center of Military History, *Medal of Honor*, http://www.history.army.mil/moh.html (accessed January 30, 2013).

4. Michael Edward Shapiro, *Cast and Recast: The Sculpture of Frederic Remington*, exh. cat. (Washington, D.C.:

National Museum of American Art; Smithsonian Institution Press, 1981), p. 43.

5. For more on the etymology of "Bunkie," see Charles Mason Fairbanks, "The Wounded Bunkie," *Harper's Weekly* 40 (November 28, 1896), p. 1177.

6. For the experienced versus the imagined in Remington's art, see Brian W. Dippie, "Frederic Remington's West: Where History Meets Myth," in *Myth of the West*, by Chris Bruce et al., exh. cat. (Seattle: Henry Art Gallery, University of Washington, 1990), pp. 111–19, 186–87.

7. Remington's reworking of themes and compositions from his own oeuvre has been discussed in Michael Edward Shapiro et al., *Frederic Remington: The Masterworks*, exh. cat. (New York: Harry N. Abrams; Saint Louis: Saint Louis Art Museum, 1988), pp. 199, 218, 219; Margaret C. Conrads, *American Paintings and Sculpture at the Sterling and Francine Clark Art Institute* (New York: Hudson Hills Press, 1990), p. 143; and Michael D. Greenbaum, *Icons of the West: Frederic Remington's Sculpture*, 2nd ed. (1996; Ogdensburg, N.Y.: Frederic Remington Art Museum, 2012), p. 66, among other sources.

8. Remington to Owen Wister, [June 1896], Owen Wister Papers, Manuscript Division, Library of Congress, Washington, D.C. Remington expressed a similar sentiment in an undated letter to Edward Wales (EW A44, courtesy the Winterthur Library: Winterthur Archives, Winterthur Museum, Gardens and Library, Wilmington, Delaware), cited in Peggy and Harold Samuels, *Frederic Remington: A Biography* (Garden City, N.Y.: Doubleday & Co., 1982), p. 241.

9. The Guilder [pseud.], "Frederic Remington as a Sculptor, and Some Older Masters," *Town Topics: The Journal of Society* 36 (October 22, 1896), p. 15.

10. In a letter to F. Edwin Elwell, Remington notes the total number of replicas of *The Wounded Bunkie* as fourteen. In the same letter, Remington refers to the number of extant statuettes of *The Broncho Buster* as "unlimited."

Remington to Elwell, July 16, 1902, Frank Edwin Elwell papers, Thomas J. Watson Library, The Metropolitan Museum of Art. According to Greenbaum's *Icons of the West*, which provides a list of known Remington casts, there are twelve recorded casts of *The Wounded Bunkie* (p. 205). For the small version of *The Broncho Buster*, there are sixty-four known sand casts produced by the Henry-Bonnard Bronze Company and ninety lost-wax versions cast by Roman Bronze Works (pp. 171–83), totaling 154 lifetime casts.

11. Gustav Kobbé, "A Painter of Life on the Frontier," *New York Herald*, December 23, 1900, sec. 5, p. 8.

12. "New York Art News," *Brush and Pencil* 5 (February 1900), p. 218.

13. James David Horan, *The Life and Art of Charles Schreyvogel, Painter-Historian of the Indian-fighting Army of the American West* (New York: Crown Publishers, 1969), p. 27.

14. The Roman Bronze Works ledger entries for Schreyvogel document twenty casts of *The Last Drop* made prior to the artist's death in January 1912. Posthumous casts of *The Last Drop* were made principally at Roman Bronze Works. Casts were also produced at Cellini Bronze Works.

15. Russell, quoted in John Taliaferro, *Charles M. Russell: The Life and Legend of America's Cowboy Artist* (Boston: Little, Brown and Company, 1996), p. 38.

16. Russell's family heritage is outlined in Taliaferro, *Charles M. Russell*, pp. 14–16; and Emily Ballew Neff, "Who Are Carson's Men?" in *The Masterworks of Charles M. Russell: A Retrospective of Paintings and Sculpture*, by Joan Carpenter Troccoli et al., exh. cat. (Norman: University of Oklahoma Press; Denver: Denver Art Museum, 2009), pp. 216, 217; see also Rick Stewart, *Charles M. Russell, Sculptor* (Fort Worth, Tex.: Amon Carter Museum, 1994), p. 326.

17. Stewart, *Charles M. Russell, Sculptor*, p. 326.

18. See Neff, "Who Are Carson's Men?" pp. 209–19, for a discussion of Russell's portrayals of mountain men.

19. For more on Russell's signature backward-facing pose, see Brian W. Dippie, *Looking at Russell*, The Anne Burnett Tandy Lectures in American Civilization 7 (Fort Worth, Tex.: Amon Carter Museum, 1987), pp. 25–31.

20. Remington's letter to Frederick McGuire, January 29, 1905, is quoted in Shapiro, *Cast and Recast*, p. 51.

21. As noted by Shapiro, ibid.; and in Shapiro et al., *Frederic Remington*, p. 231.

22. Malcolm J. Rohrbough, *Days of Gold: The California Gold Rush and the American Nation* (Berkeley and Los Angeles: University of California Press, 1997), p. 1.

23. Ibid., p. 138.

24. The biographers who discuss Putnam's work ethic include Carol M. Osborne in "Arthur Putnam, Animal Sculptor," *American Art Review* 3 (September–October 1976), p. 78; and Rose V. S. Berry in "Arthur Putnam—California Sculptor," *American Magazine of Art* 20 (May 1929), p. 280. Putnam's quotation is from a letter written by the artist to William Macbeth, dated October 14, 1909, reproduced in Osborne, "Arthur Putnam, Animal Sculptor," p. 78. The letter is located in the Macbeth Gallery Records, 1838–1968, Correspondence, Box 67, "Putnam, Arthur and Grace Storey Putnam" (NMc10/2622), 1908–1923, Archives of American Art, Smithsonian Institution, Washington, D.C., unmicrofilmed material.

25. For more information on the conception and commission of the *Pioneer Monument*, see Mary Smart, *A Flight with Fame: The Life and Art of Frederick MacMonnies (1863–1937)* (Madison, Conn.: Sound View Press, 1996), p. 219; Marlene Chambers, "Staking a Claim," in *Elevating Western American Art: Developing an Institute in the Cultural Capital of the Rockies*, edited by Thomas Brent Smith (Denver: Petrie Institute of Western American Art, Denver Art Museum, 2012), pp. 19, 20; and Thayer Tolles, "Circling the Borders: Augustus Saint-Gaudens and the American West," in *Shaping the West: American Sculptors of the 19th Century*, Western Passages (Denver: Petrie Institute of Western American Art, Denver Art Museum, 2010), pp. 20, 21.

26. See Smart, *Flight with Fame*, p. 219; Chambers, "Staking a Claim," pp. 19, 20.

27. Smart, *Flight with Fame*, p. 219.

28. Letter, MacMonnies to Flower, May 17, 1907, cited in "Indian Must Remain or No Monument to the Pioneers," *Rocky Mountain News*, June 2, 1907, p. 222. For the public reception of MacMonnies's fountain design, see "The Story of Denver's Great Memorial to the Pioneers," *Denver Municipal Facts* 3, no. 26 (June 24, 1911), pp. 5, 11–12; Smart, *Flight with Fame*, p. 220; "Indian Must Remain or No Monument to the Pioneers"; "Sons of Colorado Praise *News'* Victory: Society Indorses [*sic*] Decision to Remove Indian from Pioneer Monument," *Rocky Mountain News*, November 28, 1907.

29. Charles M. Harvey, "Kit Carson, Last of the Trail-Makers: Apropos of the Denver Memorial," *Century Illustrated Monthly Magazine* 80 (October 1910), pp. 871–76.

30. "Story of Denver's Great Memorial to the Pioneers," pp. 11–12; Charles M. Harvey, "The MacMonnies Pioneer Monument for Denver: An Embodiment of the Western Spirit," *Century Illustrated Monthly Magazine* 80 (October 1910), pp. 876–79.

31. "Story of Denver's Great Memorial to the Pioneers," p. 12.

32. Undated, untitled news clipping in Box 2, Folders 56 and 57, Mary Smart's Research Files, Frederick William MacMonnies Papers, Archives of American Art, Smithsonian Institution, Washington, D.C., unmicrofilmed material.

33. Alexander Phimister Proctor, *Sculptor in Buckskin: The Autobiography of Alexander Phimister Proctor*, edited by Katharine C. Ebner, foreword by Peter H. Hassrick, rev. ed. (1971; Norman: University of Oklahoma Press, 2009), p. 191.

34. For more information about the circumstances of Proctor's commission by Vanderslice, see ibid., pp. 191–93.

35. Ibid., p. 191.

36. "30,000 Trek to Pioneer Statue," *Kansas City Journal*, November 14, 1927.

37. The other artists were Jo Davidson, John Gregory, Frank Lynn Jenkins, Mario J. Korbel, Arthur Lee, Maurice Sterne, Wheeler Williams, and Mahonri Mackintosh Young. For more about Marland's commission, see Patricia J. Broder, "The Pioneer Woman, Image in Bronze," *American Art Review* 2 (September–October 1975), pp. 127–34.

38. Ibid., p. 131.

39. Herbert Hoover, "Remarks on the Unveiling of the Statue of the Pioneer Woman [April 22, 1930]," cited in *Public Papers of the Presidents of the United States: Herbert Hoover, 1874–1964* (Washington, D.C.: Office of the Federal Register, National Archives and Records Services, General Services Administration; Government Printing Office, 1974–77), vol. 2, p. 152.

40. Helen Appleton Read, "The Pioneer Woman," *Arts* 11 (April 1927), p. 180.

41. Ibid., p. 182.

42. Thomas Craven, "Contemporary American Sculpture," *American Mercury* 13 (March 1928), p. 366.

Selected Bibliography

Barter, Judith A., and Andrew J. Walker. *Window on the West: Chicago and the Art of the New Frontier, 1890–1940.* Exh. cat. Chicago: Art Institute of Chicago, 2003.

Billington, Ray Allen, and Martin Ridge. *Westward Expansion: A History of the American Frontier.* 6th ed. 1949. Albuquerque: University of New Mexico Press, 2001.

Bird, S. Elizabeth, ed. *Dressing in Feathers: The Construction of the Indian in American Popular Culture.* Boulder, Colo.: Westview Press, 1996.

Blackstone, Sarah J. *Buckskins, Bullets, and Business: A History of Buffalo Bill's Wild West.* New York: Greenwood Press, 1986.

Brinkley, Douglas. *The Wilderness Warrior: Theodore Roosevelt and the Crusade for America.* New York: HarperCollins, 2009.

Broder, Patricia Janis. *Bronzes of the American West.* New York: Harry N. Abrams, [1974].

Burns, Emily C. "Innocence Abroad: The Construction and Marketing of an American Artistic Identity in Paris, 1880–1910." Ph.D. diss., Washington University in St. Louis, 2012.

Conn, Steven. *History's Shadow: Native Americans and Historical Consciousness in the Nineteenth Century.* Chicago: University of Chicago Press, 2004.

Craven, Wayne. *Sculpture in America.* Rev. ed. 1968. Newark: University of Delaware Press; New York and London: Cornwall Books, 1984.

Cronon, William. *Nature's Metropolis: Chicago and the Great West.* New York: W. W. Norton & Company, 1991.

Deloria, Philip J. *Indians in Unexpected Places.* Lawrence: University Press of Kansas, 2004.

———. *Playing Indian.* New Haven and London: Yale University Press, 1998.

Dippie, Brian W. *The Vanishing American: White Attitudes and U.S. Indian Policy.* Middletown, Conn.: Wesleyan University Press, 1982.

———. *West-Fever.* Los Angeles: Autry Museum of Western Heritage; Seattle: University of Washington Press, 1998.

Flores, Dan L. *Visions of the Big Sky: Painting and Photographing the Northern Rocky Mountain West.* Norman: University of Oklahoma Press, 2010.

Goetzmann, William H., and William N. Goetzmann. *The West of the Imagination.* 2nd ed. 1986. Norman: University of Oklahoma Press, 2009.

Goodyear, Frank H., III, et al. *Faces of the Frontier: Photographic Portraits from the American West, 1845–1924.* Norman: University of Oklahoma Press; Washington, D.C.: National Portrait Gallery, Smithsonian Institution, 2009.

Handley, William R., and Nathaniel Lewis. *True West: Authenticity and the American West.* Lincoln: University of Nebraska Press, 2004.

Harris, Adam Duncan. *Wildlife in American Art: Masterworks from the National Museum of Wildlife Art.* Norman: University of Oklahoma Press, 2009.

Hassrick, Peter H. *Remington, Russell and the Language of Western Art.* Exh. cat. Washington, D.C.: Trust for Museum Exhibitions, 2000.

———. *The Way West: Art of Frontier America.* New York: Harry N. Abrams, 1977.

Hassrick, Peter H., et al. *The American West: Out of Myth, into Reality.* Exh. cat. Washington, D.C.: Trust for Museum Exhibitions; Jackson: Mississippi Museum of Art, 2000.

———. *Redrawing Boundaries: Perspectives on Western American Art.* Denver: Institute of Western American Art, Denver Art Museum, 2007.

Holliday, J. S., [and William Swain]. *The World Rushed In: The California Gold Rush Experience, An Eyewitnesss Account of a Nation Heading West.* 1981. Norman: University of Oklahoma Press, 2002.

Huhndorf, Shari M. *Going Native: Indians in the American Cultural Imagination.* Ithaca, N.Y.: Cornell University Press, 2001.

Hutchinson, Elizabeth. *The Indian Craze: Primitivism, Modernism, and Transculturation in American Art, 1890–1915.* Durham, N.C.: Duke University Press, 2009.

Isenberg, Andrew C. *The Destruction of the Bison: An Environmental History, 1750–1920.* Cambridge and New York: Cambridge University Press, 2000.

Johnson, Michael L. *Hunger for the Wild: America's Obsession with the Untamed West.* Lawrence: University Press of Kansas, 2007.

Kasson, Joy S. *Buffalo Bill's Wild West: Celebrity, Memory, and Popular History.* New York: Hill and Wang, 2000.

Kort, Pamela, and Max Hollein, eds. *I Like America: Fictions of the Wild West.* Exh. cat. Munich: Prestel; Frankfurt: Schirn Kunsthalle, 2006.

Lamar, Howard R., ed. *The New Encyclopedia of the American West.* Rev. and enl. ed. 1977. New Haven and London: Yale University Press, 1998.

Limerick, Patricia Nelson. *The Legacy of Conquest: The Unbroken Past of the American West.* New York and London: W. W. Norton & Co., 1987.

Mighetto, Lisa. *Wild Animals and American Environmental Ethics.* Tucson: University of Arizona Press, 1991.

Milner, Clyde A., II, Carol A. O'Connor, and Martha A. Sandweiss, eds. *The Oxford History of the American*

West. New York and Oxford: Oxford University Press, 1994.

Moses, L. G. *Wild West Shows and the Images of American Indians, 1883–1933.* Albuquerque: University of New Mexico Press, 1996.

Peavy, Linda, and Ursula Smith. *Pioneer Women: The Lives of Women of the Frontier.* Norman: University of Oklahoma Press, 1998.

Prown, Jules David, et al. *Discovered Lands, Invented Pasts: Transforming Visions of the American West.* Exh. cat. New Haven and London: Yale University Press, Yale University Art Gallery, 1992.

Reddin, Paul. *Wild West Shows.* Urbana: University of Illinois Press, 1999.

Reiger, John F. *American Sportsmen and the Origins of Conservation.* 3rd ed. 1975. Corvallis: Oregon State University Press, 2001.

Roosevelt, Theodore. *An Autobiography.* New York: Macmillan Company, 1913.

———. *Ranch Life and the Hunting-Trail.* New York: Century Co., 1888.

Samuels, Peggy, and Harold Samuels. *The Illustrated Biographical Encyclopedia of Artists of the American West.* Garden City, N.Y.: Doubleday, 1976.

Sandweiss, Martha A. *Print the Legend: Photography and the American West.* New Haven and London: Yale University Press, 2002.

Saunders, Richard H. *Collecting the West: The C. R. Smith Collection of Western American Art.* Austin: Archer M. Huntington Art Gallery, College of Fine Arts, The University of Texas at Austin; University of Texas Press, 1988.

Shaping the West: American Sculptors of the 19th Century. Western Passages. Denver: Petrie Institute of Western American Art, Denver Art Museum, 2010.

Shapiro, Michael Edward. *Bronze Casting and American Sculpture, 1850–1900.* Newark: University of Delaware Press; London and Toronto: Associated University Presses, 1985.

Sides, Hampton. *Blood and Thunder: An Epic of the American West.* New York: Doubleday, 2006.

Slotkin, Richard. *Gunfighter Nation: The Myth of the Frontier in Twentieth-Century America.* New York: Atheneum, 1992.

———. *Regeneration through Violence: The Mythology of the American Frontier, 1600–1860.* Middletown, Conn.: Wesleyan University Press, 1973.

Smith, Thomas Brent, ed. *Elevating Western American Art: Developing an Institute in the Cultural Capital of the Rockies.* Denver: Petrie Institute of Western American Art, Denver Art Museum, 2012.

Stewart, Rick. *A Century of Western Art: Selections from the Amon Carter Museum.* Fort Worth, Tex.: Amon Carter Museum, 1998.

Taft, Lorado. *The History of American Sculpture.* New York: Macmillan Company, 1903.

Tolles, Thayer, et al. *American Sculpture in The Metropolitan Museum of Art.* 2 vols. New York: The Metropolitan Museum of Art, 1999–2001.

Trachtenberg, Alan. *Shades of Hiawatha: Staging Indians, Making Americans, 1880–1930.* New York: Hill and Wang, 2004.

Troccoli, Joan Carpenter, et al. *Painters and the American West: The Anschutz Collection.* Exh. cat. Denver: Denver Art Museum, 2000.

———. *Painters and the American West, Volume 2.* Norman: University of Oklahoma Press, forthcoming.

Truettner, William H. *Painting Indians and Building Empires in North America,* *1710–1840.* Berkeley and Los Angeles: University of California Press, 2010.

Truettner, William H., et al. *The West as America: Reinterpreting Images of the Frontier, 1820–1920.* Exh. cat. Washington, D.C.: National Museum of American Art; Smithsonian Institution Press, 1991.

Turner, Frederick Jackson. *The Frontier in American History.* New York: H. Holt and Co., 1920.

———. "The Significance of the Frontier in American History." Read July 12, 1893, American Historical Association, Chicago. Published in *Proceedings of the State Historical Society of Wisconsin at Its Forty-first Annual Meeting, Held December 14, 1893,* pp. 79–112. Madison, Wis., 1894.

Tyler, Ron. *Visions of America: Pioneer Artists in a New Land.* New York: Thames and Hudson, 1983.

Wagner, David J. *American Wildlife Art.* Seattle: Marquand Books, 2008.

Warren, Louis S. *Buffalo Bill's America: William Cody and the Wild West Show.* New York: Alfred A. Knopf, 2005.

West, Elliott. *The Essential West: Collected Essays.* Norman: University of Oklahoma Press, 2012.

White, G. Edward. *The Eastern Establishment and the Western Experience: The West of Frederic Remington, Theodore Roosevelt, and Owen Wister.* Reprint ed. 1968. Austin: University of Texas Press, 1989.

White, Richard, Patricia Nelson Limerick, and James R. Grossman. *The Frontier in American Culture.* Exh. cat. Chicago: Newberry Library; Berkeley and Los Angeles: University of California Press, 1994.

Worster, Donald. *Under Western Skies: Nature and History in the American West.* New York and Oxford: Oxford University Press, 1992.

Index

Page numbers in *italics* refer to
illustrations. Catalogue numbers refer to
the Checklist of the Exhibition.

Photography Credits

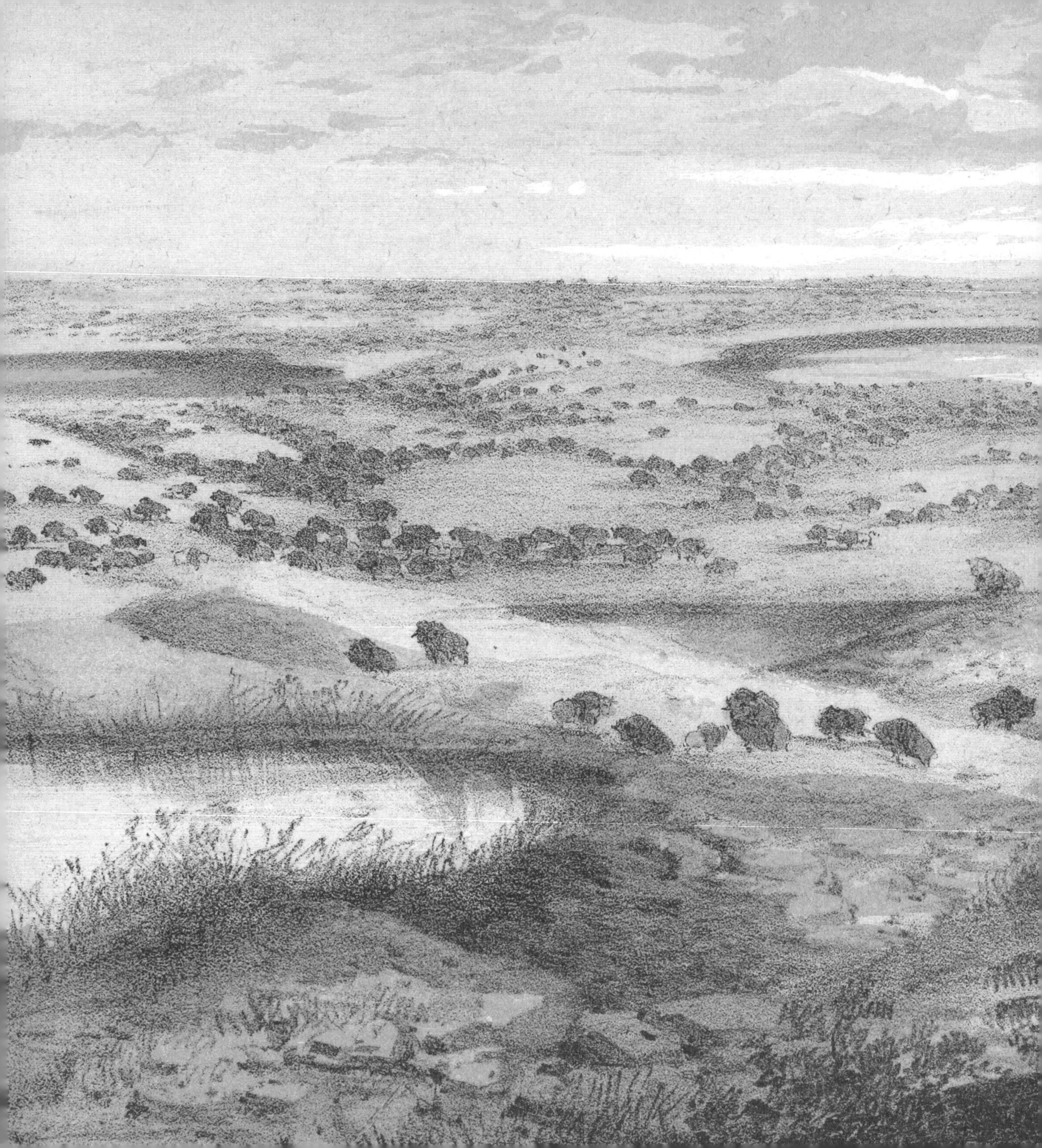